The middle decades of the twentieth century witnessed the great dramas of the end of Western Imperial rule in Africa and Asia. A series of nationalist onslaughts was launched against the British Empire and these greatly reshaped the modern world. Professor Anthony Low has for many years studied the end of the British Empire and its aftermath. This volume brings together for the first time many of his major essays on the subject, particularly those on India and Africa.

Professor Low emphasizes that the end of the British Empire was only part of the story of decolonisation. Other empires were also brought to an end. In the course of this process, and long through the aftermath, Asian and African societies set about creating new socio-political orders for their countries. Moreover, as the author demonstrates, twentieth-century transformations in the relations between ex-colonial countries and their ex-imperial rulers were by no means confined to Asia and Africa. They extended to the Commonwealth at large.

This is the first volume to explore the political ramifications of the entire twentieth-century process of decolonisation in so comprehensive a manner. It will be read by students and specialists of the Empire and Commonwealth, twentieth-century political history and Asian, African and Australian studies.

Eclipse of empire

ECLIPSE OF EMPIRE

D. A. LOW
Smuts Professor of the
History of the British Commonwealth, and
President, Clare Hall, Cambridge

CAMBRIDGE
UNIVERSITY PRESS

Published by the Press Syndicate of the University of Cambridge
The Pitt Building, Trumpington Street, Cambridge CB2 1RP
40 West 20th Street, New York, NY 10011-4211, USA
10 Stamford Road, Oakleigh, Melbourne 3166, Australia

First published 1991
Reprinted 1992
First paperback edition 1993

Printed in Great Britain
by the Athenaeum Press Ltd, Newcastle upon Tyne

British Library cataloguing in publication data

Low, D. A.
Eclipse of empire.
1. Commonwealth, 1900–
I. Title
909′.0971241082

Library of Congress cataloguing in publication data

Low, D. A. (Donald Anthony). 1927–
Eclipse of empire / D. A. Low.
p.   cm.
Includes bibliographical references.
ISBN 0 521 38329 3
1. Great Britain – Colonies – History.
2. Commonwealth of Nations – History
3. Decolonization – History.
I. Title
DA16.L8684   1990
325′.341 – dc20   89–22286   CIP

ISBN 0 521 38329 3 hardback
ISBN 0 521 45754 8 paperback

For
Belle
– who was always there

Contents

Maps

Preface

In the middle and later decades of the twentieth century the great western colonial empires in Asia and Africa finally came to an end. That constituted one of the major developments in the history of the world in the twentieth century, and in quite countless ways has reshaped the world in which we live. It played a major part in establishing a quite new international system. It led to the creation of a large number of new orders in which the greater part of humanity now lives. Whereas during the first half of the twentieth century half a dozen or so western empires had dominated large parts of the globe, these now came to be replaced by 100 or so newly independent states, each with many of its own distinctive characteristics. That is a huge change in circumstance.

This volume brings together a number of previously dispersed attempts to grapple with some of the large number of issues which arise. The rise and fall of empires has long provoked a great deal of interest, and a number of far-flung comparisons could readily be offered. But for the most part the chapters which follow do not deal with these. There is nothing about the end of the Roman, the Carolingian, the Inca, the Ming, the Spanish, the Ottoman or the Soviet empires. The concern is principally, though not exclusively, with the passing of the British Empire in South Asia and in Africa. It is still probably too soon to try to encompass the whole of this story in a single volume, and certainly no attempt is made here to provide a sustained, textbook account of the demise of the British Empire, least of all as seen principally through the eyes of its British metropolitan participants. Some of the necessary outline will be found, however, for South Asia in chapter 3, and for Africa in chapter 9.

By contrast with a number of already published surveys, some fairly regular attempts are made in a number of the chapters that follow to set the story of the eclipse of the British Empire in the twentieth century in a wider, more comparative, contemporary context. Moreover, the focus of this collection is not delimited by the transfer of power. It is as much concerned with the aftermath of the end-of-empire as with the run up to that. Thus, whilst eight chapters are concerned with the processes of decolonisation as such, eight relate to various aspects of the sequel, and several bridge the conventional divide between these. Although the focus is mainly upon political matters, it is hoped that enough attention is paid to other aspects so as to provide a sufficiently illuminating perspective upon the large variety of angles of vision, lines of thought, and differing approaches which are worth pursuing.

For the most part the chapters that follow will speak for themselves. Perhaps, however, a selection of the points which they make may be emphasised here.

There are considerable limitations, as it seems to me, in accounts of end-of-empire which take as their continuing theme the evolution of the colonial policy and decisions of any one colonial power. These were certainly of great importance (and I have written my own essay along these lines in a chapter on 'Sequence in the Demission of Power'. in my *Lion Rampant. Essays in the Study of British Imperialism* (London, 1974). But colonial powers were rarely their own masters (not least in their own colonial territories) as such accounts tend to assume, and a really illuminating account needs to take note of the marked differences in the nature and sequence of the policies and reactions of the different colonial powers.

The idea that the end-of-empire is principally to be explained by the colonial power's progressive loss of colonial collaborators also seems to me questionable. Collaborators were never more than one of the supports of imperial authority. They rarely defected extensively (there would have been far more collapses of regimes if they had). All manner of other factors were at least as important.

I have qualms, too, with those accounts of the processes of decolonisation which simply provide a checklist of varying explanations without attempting to relate these to one another. Decolonisation (so it will be argued here) all but invariably required first the growth of nationalist sentiments and nationalist forces within a colonial territory itself. But this growth alone was never the whole story. Whilst in reality international aspects were rarely of great significance, what was then of prime importance were the particularities of the imperial response, which to a major degree determined the nature of the confrontation which then ensued – though hardly ever the eventual outcome.

It should then be noted that whilst nationalist forces in Asia were for the most part mobilised centrally, ordinarily this was far from being the case in Africa. Yet one should not conclude from this that Africa's nationalisms presented a much lesser challenge. For that would be to overlook the often crucial fact that disaggregated forces could be at least as potent a threat to imperial control as aggregated ones.

Half a dozen chapters in this collection consider a selection of those issues which remained for the various ex-colonial countries to confront after independence. None of these countries was a *tabula rasa*. They all carried significant parts of their colonial pasts with them. Yet, of course, they then worked out their own variations and departures from these extensively.

The last two chapters then serve to signify (they cannot do more than this) that in the later years of the twentieth century these issues confronted not only the South Asian and African countries which were once incorporated in the British Empire, but also Britain itself, the Commonwealth (which rather hamhandedly Britain sought to turn into a buttress for its now changed position in the world), and not least countries of the 'older' Commonwealth, such as Australia. It is worth emphasising that the ramifications of the empire's eclipse in every part of the once British Empire have been far more extensive than is generally appreciated.

And one last word here. There is a tendency in some quarters in Britain to view the end-of-empire almost wholly as a concomitant of the decline of Britain's former position as a great power. That not only smacks of nostalgic myopia. It can be very false to the profound sense of positive achievement, not simply of so many citizens of the former colonial territories themselves, but of a great many British actors too – from Edwin Montagu, the later Arthur Balfour, Ramsey Macdonald, Lord Lothian, Clement Attlee, Stafford Cripps, Oliver Stanley, Mountbatten, through to Creech-Jones, Malcolm Macdonald, Andrew Cohen, Hugh Foot, Iain Macleod, Ernest Vasey and so many other individuals too. For my own part I can think in this connection of a number of my contemporaries – Lalage Bown, Michael Crowder, Terry Ranger, Cherry Gertzel, Colin Leys, Tommy Gee, Cran Pratt, Nigel Oram, Mike Faber, Aidan Southall, Michael McWilliam to name just a few (if they will forgive me for so doing). I am aware that there is an old division here that goes back for a century and more. At the very least it should be allowed that this much more positive sense of direction lasted right through to the end of empire and beyond.

The first chapter serves as an introduction to the whole collection. It reproduces my inaugural lecture as Smuts Professor of the History of the British Commonwealth in the University of Cambridge, delivered in 1984, which the Cambridge University Press published in a small booklet in 1985. I toyed with the idea of stripping this of its personal references and its lecture format. That, however, would have entailed a much larger revision than soon began to seem warranted. Apart, therefore, from some corrections and the insertion (in square brackets) of a paragraph in support of a central argument which is based upon material that has only become available since 1984, the text as delivered is here produced unchanged.

Since it announces many of the themes that are later pursued there are inevitably some repetitions in subsequent chapters. It is to be hoped that these will not be too obtrusive.

The second chapter, on the twentieth century revolutions in Monsoon Asia, began life as part of the Conference Lecture on the occasion of the 1st National Conference of the Asian Studies Association of Australia in Melbourne in 1976. The present version has been put together from various passages in my chapter on 'The Asian Mirror to Tropical Africa's Independence' in *The Transfer of Power in Africa. Decolonisation, 1940–1960*, ed. Prosser Gifford and Wm. Roger Louis (Yale University Press, 1982); from my 'Sequence, Crux and Means: Some Asian Nationalisms Compared', in *Asia – The Winning of Independence*, ed. Robin Jeffrey (Macmillan 1981); and more especially from 'The Asian Revolutions of the Mid Twentieth Century', in *Transfer and Transformation: Political Institutions in the New Commonwealth. Essays in Honour of W.H. Morris-Jones*, ed. Peter Lyon and James Manor (Leicester University Press, 1983). I am grateful to all three publishers for the opportunity to rework these here.

The third chapter appeared originally as the introduction to *Congress and the Raj. Facets of the Indian Struggle 1917–47*, which I edited and which Heinemann Educational Books and Arnold Heinemann Delhi published in 1977. As it seems to continue to have value as a very general statement it seemed worth reproducing, and I am grateful to both publishers for permission to do so. The fourth chapter on 'the Forgotten Bania' was presented as a paper at a conference on the centenary of the Indian National Congress in 1985 which was jointly sponsored by the Centre of Indian Studies of the University of Oxford and the Centre of South Asian Studies of the University of Cambridge. It is reproduced by permission of the Oxford University Press Delhi who in 1988 published it in the conference volume which I edited called *The Indian National Congress. Centenary Hindsights*. It emphasises a further theme which is somewhat underplayed in chapter three.

Chapter 5 – 'Counterpart experiences: India/Indonesia 1920s–1950s' – began as a contribution to the first of a series of four conferences on comparative modern Indian and Indonesian history which were jointly conducted in the mid 1980s by historians from the Centre for the History of European Expansion at Leiden University, the Delhi School of Economics, Gadjah Mada University, Yogyakarta, and the Centre of South Asian Studies in the University of Cambridge. It is reproduced by permission of the editors of *Itinerario* where it first appeared in their Special Issue on 'India and Indonesia the 1920s to the 1950s; The Origins of Planning', 10 no. 1 (1986), 117–43. Chapter 6, 'Emergencies and Elections in India', was delivered as my Kingsley Martin Memorial Lecture in the University of Cambridge in 1980. It appears here by permission of Macmillans who in

1986 published it in *Studies in British Imperial History. Essays in Honour of A.P. Thornton*, ed. Gordon Martel. Once again I trust it is none the worse for appearing here in its original lecture form.

With chapter 7 this collection turns to Africa. That chapter first appeared as the Introduction to *History of East Africa*, volume III, ed. D.A. Low and Alison Smith (Clarendon Press, 1976), which is now out of print. I am especially grateful to my co-author, Dr John Lonsdale, for his readiness to see it reproduced here, and to Oxford University Press for their permission to do so. Chapter 8 is the oldest of the items reprinted here. It was written *in medias res* in 1960 and was originally published as 'The Colonial Demise in Africa' in *Australian Outlook*, 14 no. 2 (1960), 257–68. Since I have not encountered a comparable compilation elsewhere on the torrent of events in Africa in 1960 I hope its reproduction here will be of some value. After all these years I have changed a tense here and a phrase there. I am grateful to the present editor of *Australian Outlook* for agreeing to its reprinting.

Chapter 9 surveys the demise of the British Empire in Africa over a rather longer time-span. It reproduces the chapter I wrote for *Decolonisation and African Independence: The Transfers of Power 1960–1980*, ed. Prosser Gifford and Wm. Roger Louis (Yale University Press, 1988), and I am much indebted to the publishers for enabling me to include it here. Chapter 10, on 'History and independent Africa's political trauma', is new. It derives from lectures and seminars I have given at the Royal College of Defence Studies, to the Defence Studies Group in Cambridge, and at the Institute of Development Studies at the University of Sussex. Chapter 11, on 'Political superstructures in post-colonial states', is based in part upon my chapter on 'Congress and India's Body Politic', in *The Indian National Congress and the Political Economy of India 1885–1985*, ed. Mike Sheppardson and Colin Simmons (Avebury, 1988), and more particularly on the chapter I wrote for *Uganda Now. Between Decay and Development*, ed. Holgar Bernt Hansen and Michael Twaddle, which James Currey published in 1988. I am grateful to both publishers for their agreement to draw extensively upon them here.

Chapter 12 began as a public lecture on 'Little Britain and Large Commonwealth' on the occasion of the opening of the Centre of Commonwealth Studies at the University of Stirling in 1985. In that form it was published in *The Round Table*, 298 (1986), 109–21. I am grateful to the editor for permission to adapt it here, and to Dr John McCracken, the Director of the Stirling Centre, for his kind invitation to speak on that occasion.

The final chapter, called 'Australia in the eastern hemisphere', started as Presidential Addresses to the Biennual Conference of the Asian Studies Association of Australia at Monash University in May 1982, and to the British Australian Studies Association at the University of Warwick in

1986. As will be clear, it has been substantially enlarged since then.

As other people have found, my debts to others are a great deal more numerous than I can at all readily specify. I am especially indebted to those in the Australian National University and in the University of Cambridge who over the last two decades have provided me with so much stimulus. I hope all those many others who have been good enough to provide their ever generous assistance will accept my warm thanks as well.

D. A. Low
Clare Hall, Cambridge

1

The contraction of England; an inaugural lecture 1984

There should be no need for another Smuts Inaugural. Eric Stokes should be with us still. His early death robbed us of a star in our firmament. His sparkling *English Utilitarians and India*,[1] *The Zambesian Past*,[2] and following his return to Cambridge, to India and to Kipling,[3] *The Peasant and the Raj*[4] have been lodestars to very many of us. On so many personal grounds it is hard to accept he is gone. The first Smuts Professor graces our company still. Nicholas Mansergh's superb edition of the British documents on *The Transfer of Power*[5] in India is currently crowding the footnotes. He and I share debts to Keith Hancock; still the doyen of our limb of the profession; and in the fulness of his days Smuts' biographer.[6]

But, as my title implies, it is to another luminary to whom I refer. For precisely a century lay between the publication of John Richard Seeley's Cambridge lectures on *The Expansion of England*[7] and my assumption of the Smuts Chair; and my purpose here is to ruminate upon what has happened in the interval. Seeley, so we were lately told, was the first truly notable Regius Professor of Modern History in the University of Cambridge.[8] The History Faculty named its Library after him, and on 24 April 1945 successfully recommended to the University that it should teach a course on

---

[1] Oxford, 1959.   [2] Edited with R. Brown, Manchester, 1966.
[3] '"The Voice of the Hooligan": Kipling and the Commonwealth Experience', Inaugural Lecture, reprinted in *Historial Perspectives: Studies in English Thought and Society in honour of J.H. Plumb*, ed. Neil McKendrick, London, 1974.
[4] Cambridge, 1978.
[5] 12 volumes, Her Majesty's Stationery Office, London, 1970–83.
[6] W.K. Hancock, *Smuts: The Sanguine Years 1820–1919*, Cambridge, 1962, and *Smuts: The Fields of Force 1919–1950*, Cambridge, 1968.
[7] London, 1883.
[8] G.R. Elton, *The History of England*, Inaugural Lecture, Cambridge, 1984, p. 2.

The Expansion of Europe,[9] that it has done ever since, which is essentially still based on Seeley's perspectives.

It is astonishing to recall that as Seeley lectured, Britain's African empire had scarcely begun. In the ensuing century, precipitated by that, there has been much disputation over economic imperialism. It was given a stir from this University by Gallagher and Robinson with their 'Imperialism of Free Trade'.[10] More recently studies of 'the periphery',[11] and of the relationship between Britain's own economic history and its imperial thrusts rather more precisely,[12] have opened vistas that were never seen down the blind alleys into which Hobson and Lenin led us. But I shall not dwell on these. Nor on that other preoccupation since Seeley's day – the constitutional history of the Empire and Commonwealth; though I confess to one rather special interest in it. For its discussion ordinarily overlooks the fact that Buckingham Palace is as much part of the Westminster system as 10 Downing Street, Whitehall and the Houses of Parliament. Even in the past year the point has been at issue in Queensland, Malaysia, Grenada, Kashmir, Andhra Pradesh, the Solomon Islands, and not so long since in Fiji and Australia too.[13] Early in 1983 some thought it could have been in issue here also.[14]

Let me turn instead to some other matters relating to the expansion of England. From Cambridge we have in recent decades been inducted into 'the official mind'.[15] We have been introduced to the colonial collaborator. 'The choice of indigenous collaborators', so Robinson put it, 'more than anything else, determined the organization and character of colonial rule.'[16] We know about colonial resisters as well.[17] But we must be careful not to let these engross the whole scene. So let me begin by offering some comments on three other considerations: force, legitimacy and assuagement.[18]

---

[9] 'Report of the Faculty Board of History on the Addition of a Paper on The Expansion of Europe to the Schedules of Subjects for the Historical Tripos', 24 April 1945, *Cambridge University Reporter*, 15 May 1945, pp. 729–30.

[10] *Economic History Review*, 2nd ser. 6 no. 1 (1953), 1–15.

[11] D.K. Fieldhouse, *Economics and Empire 1830–1914*, London, 1973.

[12] P.J. Cain and A.G. Hopkins, 'The Political Economy of British Expansion Overseas, 1740–1914', *Economic History Review*, 2nd ser. 33 no. 4 (1980), 463–90.

[13] See now D.A. Low (ed.), *Constitutional Heads and Political Crises, Commonwealth Episodes, 1945–85*, London, 1988; and David Butler and D.A. Low (eds.), *Sovereigns and Surrogates. Constitutional Heads of State in the Commonwealth*, London, 1990.

[14] Correspondence in *The Times* before the 1983 election.

[15] R. Robinson and J. Gallagher with A. Denny, *Africa and the Victorians*, London, 1961.

[16] R. Robinson, 'Non-European Foundations of European Imperialism: Sketch for a Theory of Collaboration', in *Studies in the Theory of Imperialism*, ed. R. Owen and B. Sutcliffe, London, 1972, p. 139.

[17] Especially since T.O. Ranger, *Revolt in Southern Rhodesia 1896–7: A Study in African Resistance*, London, 1967.

[18] I hope that what follows is a development upon my *Lion Rampant*, London, 1973, chs. 1 and 3.

It is time to repeat that empire was fundamentally based upon force. Frontier war in Australia was extraordinarily sophisticated. Aborigines learnt the range of shot and ball, and made tracks to keep out of it. They knew as well how long muskets took to load, and timed their attacks accordingly. Upon the sparse edges of settlement they killed perhaps 2,000 whites. But they were of course overwhelmed themselves, shot down, perhaps 20,000 all told, 25 at Pinjarra in 1834, 28 at Myall Creek in 1838 (for which seven whites were hanged), 59 near Burketown in 1868, and on countless other station battlefields both before and after.[19] 'No doubt the policy of trying to make omelettes without breaking eggs', Lugard was to write from Northern Nigeria, 'has the cordial support of Exeter Hall. . . . It was not the way our Raj was established in India or elsewhere.'[20] It was not indeed. Were there not all those minor imperial wars; big wars to those that lost them? Mahratta wars, Sikh wars, Burmese wars, Kaffir wars, Maori wars, Ashanti wars, Zulu wars, Sudanese wars, Matabele wars. In western Kenya there was a 'punitive expedition' for almost every one of the first twenty-five years of British rule, and upwards of fifty episodes all told.[21] Force did not always of course have to be applied directly: 'Rhodes mowed down a mealie field with machine guns before the paramount of eastern Pondoland and his councillors and explained that their fate would be similar if they did not respond.'[22] They did of course.

It is no use, however, confining this point to the beginnings of empire. Time was when I was a Second Lieutenant in the 16th/5th Lancers whose chief regimental memory even today is that in 1846 they charged the Sikhs at the Battle of Aliwal.[23] They were also, however, the regiment of Lord Allenby which as British High Commissioner he paraded before the prime minister's house in Cairo in 1924 when he thrust at Zaghlul Pasha a draconian ultimatum.[24] By that time in India twenty-eight battalions of British troops, as compared to only twenty-two Indian ones, were invariably committed to internal security duties,[25] and when later the British

[19] E.g. Henry Reynolds, *The Other Side of the Frontier*, Townsville, 1981; C.D. Rowley, *The Destruction of Aboriginal Society*, Harmondsworth, 1970; Clive Turnbull, *Black War*, Melbourne, 1948; Noel Loos, *Invasion and Resistance*, Canberra, 1982.
[20] Lugard to Burdon, 17 April 1902, Nigerian Archives Kaduna S.N.P. 7/3/40, quoted in R.A. Adeleye, *Power and Diplomacy in Northern Nigeria 1804–1906*, London, 1971, p. 257.
[21] J.M. Lonsdale, 'The Politics of Conquest: The British in Western Kenya 1894–1908', *Historical Journal*, 20 no. 4 (1977), 841–70.
[22] Monica Wilson, *Reaction to Conquest*, 2nd edn., London, 1961, p. 412.
[23] Strictly it was the 16th Lancers that charged at Aliwal. The regiment's annual day is still Aliwal Day.
[24] Henry Graham, *History of the Sixteenth, the Queen's Light Dragoons (Lancers) 1912 to 1925*, Devizes, 1926, p. 132; Viscount Wavell, *Allenby in Egypt*, London, 1943, pp. 109–17.
[25] National Archives of India, H. Poll. 79/30.

were faced by the great 'Quit India' movement of 1942 they speedily mobilised no less than 57½ battalions against it.[26]

Force then; but legitimacy too. For in establishing and maintaining their empire it was vital for the British not simply to secure collaborators but to work with (and not against) the grain of local notions of political legitimacy. A former prime minister of Pakistan neatly put the central point thus; 'Whoever could conquer a country was accepted as its legitimate ruler . . . The British had no more and no less right to rob or rule India than all the other rulers who had held the country by force before them.'[27] Lytton's Great Assemblage in Delhi in 1877 at which Queen Victoria was proclaimed Empress of India in ultimate succession to the Mughals,[28] or Rhodes' funeral in the Matopo hills in 1902 at the hands of the Ndebele he had defeated,[29] dramatised such transitions powerfully. It was much the same where the British retained the pre-existing native states. Here, Sir John Kirk, of East African fame, engagingly put it, 'we are the "longest sword" and have become the electors and patrons of the throne';[30] while in those 'stateless society' situations the anthropologists have elucidated for us, it was usually easy for a European district officer to move into the indigenously accepted position of 'Big Man'.[31] Woe betide, however, those who contravened the mores here, as the British discovered with their greased cartridges in 1857, or with their abortive plans for a Malayan Union in 1945.[32]

Then beyond this let me offer a new thought: assuagement. I once traced the collaboration between the British and the native chiefs of Buganda, the largest kingdom in southern Uganda, through three successive phases.[33] The British position there by no means turned only, however, on that collaboration. It depended on British assuagement of the concerns of

---

[26] 'Summary of events . . . during which Communications with Bihar were dislocated', National Archives of India, H. Poll (I) 3/30/42 Pt II; 'Statement made by . . . the Home Member to the National Defence Council . . .', 8 Sept. 1942, H. Poll. (I), 3/26–42 (2).

[27] Firoz Khan Noon, *From Memory*, Lahore, 1966, p. 81.

[28] Professor Bernard Cohn is working on this; see his contribution to *The Invention of Tradition*, ed. E. Hobsbawm and T. Ranger, Cambridge, 1983; and B.S. Cohn, *An Anthropologist among the Historians and Other Essays*, Delhi, 1987.

[29] S.G. Millen, *Rhodes*, London, 1936, ch. 38. There is an interesting comment on the desolation of the Matopo hills in E.L. Woodward, *Short Journey*, London, 1942, pp. 191–3.

[30] Kirk to Anderson, 22 Nov. 1892, Foreign Office Confidential Print, 6362, 214.

[31] E.g. the 'bog barons' in the southern Sudan or kiaps in Papua New Guinea. On the former, see Robert O. Collins, *Shadows in the Grass, Britain in the Southern Sudan, 1918–1956*, New Haven, 1983. On the latter see, e.g., Marshall D. Sahlins, 'Poor Man, Rich Man, Big Man, Chief: Political Types in Melanesia and Polynesia', *Comparative Studies in Society and History*, 5 (1963), 285; J.K. McCarthy, *Patrol into Yesterday: My New Guinea Years*, Melbourne, 1963.

[32] A.J. Stockwell, *British Policy and Malay Politics during the Malayan Union Experiment 1942–1948*, Kuala Lumpur, 1979.

[33] D.A. Low, *Buganda in Modern History*, London, 1971, ch. 3.

Buganda's prosperous peasantry as well. In the 1920s their discontents with the landlord chiefs with whom the British were principally collaborating pushed the British into promulgating a rural rent restriction act,[34] Two decades later further peasant discontent with these earlier chiefs' successors, and with the way peasant cash crops were then being handled, led to the murder of a chief minister and to riots in 1945 and 1949. Assuagement then followed again with the democratisation of the local council, and a plethora of reforms in Uganda's cotton and coffee industries, all of which clearly prevented the further major crisis which followed from reaching flashpoint.[35] The grossest failure to effect assuagement led meanwhile in Kenya to the Mau Mau revolt.[36] The circumstances of a settler colony were no doubt peculiar, but no Indian administrator would have allowed that to happen. In India, the British had their collaborators too: princes, landlords, rural magnates, service communities.[37] But from the mid nineteenth century onwards, their unending stream of rent restriction, tenant security, and moneylenders' limitation acts composed a sustained effort to assuage what they saw as the principal basis of British power, the acquiescence of the better off peasantry.[38] As Gandhi and his followers learnt, at Champaran and Bardoli, the British in India were remarkably quick to assuage peasant discontents when these erupted.[39] In 1907 one viceroy vetoed a crucial Colonisation Bill of the lieutenant governor of the Punjab when the colonists revolted against it.[40] In 1935 another opined that: 'The greatest risk in this country . . . lies in the grievances of the peasantry. The longer they remain unredressed the greater the scope of subversive propaganda.'[41] And in the intervening years one can see in Sir Harcourt Butler's storm-tossed fashioning of the Oudh Rent Bill in 1921, and still more, in Sir Malcolm Hailey's extensive extra-legal reductions of land revenue and rents in 1931, two of Britain's most notable Indian governors wrestling with how to balance the calls of their landlord collaborators with the need to assuage

[34] R.C. Pratt, 'The Politics of Indirect Rule: Uganda, 1900–1955', in D.A. Low and R.C. Pratt (eds.), *Buganda and British Overrule 1900–1955*, London, 1960, pp. 236–9.
[35] Chapters by Gertzel (pp. 67–72) and Lury (pp. 225–33) in *History of East Africa*, ed. D.A. Low and Alison Smith, vol. III, Oxford, 1976.
[36] There is a substantial literature, but nothing has yet replaced Carl G. Rosberg and John Nottingham, *The Myth of Mau Mau*, New York, 1966. See, however, D.W. Throup, *Economic and Social Origins of Man 1945–53*, London 1987.
[37] E.g. R.E. Frykenberg, *Guntur District 1788–1848: A History of Local Influence and Central Authority in South India*, Oxford, 1965.
[38] Dietmar Rothermund, *Government, Landlord and Peasant in India: Agrarian Relations under British Rule 1865–1935*, Wiesbaden, 1978.
[39] Judith M. Brown, *Gandhi's Rise to Power*, Cambridge, 1972, pp. 52–83; D.N. Dhanagare, *Peasant Movements in India 1920–1950*, Delhi, 1983, ch. 4.
[40] N.G. Barrier, 'The Punjab Disturbances of 1907: The Response of the British Government of India to Agrarian Unrest,' *Modern Asian Studies*, 1 no. 4 (1967), 353–83.
[41] Willingdon to Hoare, 5 Sept. 1935, National Archives of India, EHL, L & O 43/14/35.

their tenant subordinates.[42] Plebeian assuagement, I am saying, was at least as important a requirement for effectual imperial rule as the successful enlistment of patrician collaborators.

But it is not about the expansion or maintenance of the British Empire that I am billed to speak, but about its contraction. From all I have said it will perhaps be appreciated, however, that I do not go along with the thesis that this chiefly occurred because the British ran out of collaborators. It is no less important to trace their growing reluctance to shoot to kill; the decline in the legitimacy locally accorded them; and their increasing inability to assuage their subjects' rising demands. Let me allude, however, to two more fundamental propositions. Empire came to Britain – if I may be bold – because, as Seeley said, we had a comparative advantage as an island seapower. It was then enlarged and sustained because we secured the further comparative advantage of being the world's first industrial nation. These advantages first shrank and then disappeared. There is no need to rehearse the details of the shift in world power, principally to America and Russia as Seeley foresaw, that have occurred since he lectured, nor the further developments in Japan and the eastern hemisphere that led in 1983 to the United States trading for the first time more with the Pacific countries than with Europe. (We are now at the point where with South-east Asia as the world's fastest growing region economically, the well informed need to read the *Far Eastern Economic Review* as much as they read *The Economist*.) In an intriguing sense England is still expanding there. Twenty years ago Singapore's primary schools taught mostly in Chinese. Now they teach mainly in English. Since it is a good working rule that what Singapore does today many others will do the day after tomorrow, is it not bizarre that the none-too-easy language of a small island off the north-west coast of Europe should already be much more widely used as the lingua franca of the eastern hemisphere where the most of humanity lives than it is of its own western hemisphere? All the same, we must not exaggerate. In my Cambridgeshire village a stone was recently erected marking the traverse of the Greenwich meridian, but even in Toft we no longer think of ourselves as the centre of the world.

The fundamental fact is that we of the west are the global minority and a shrinking minority at that. We are apt to forget that there are as many Vietnamese in the world as there are British, that for every one of us there is one Filipino, one and half times as many Nigerians, three times as many Indonesians, fourteen times as many Indians, and nearly twenty times as many Chinese. Back in 1800 around 20 per cent of the world's population lived in western Europe; nowadays only 8 per cent do (and by next century

---

42 P.D. Reeves *Landlords and Governments in Uttar Pradesh. Studies in their relations until Zammindari abolition*, Delhi, 1990.

under 5 per cent will).[43] The loss of empire accordingly does not seem to me to have been principally due to a treacherous loss of national nerve, or any other such self-flagellating notion. It was *au fond* the entirely to be expected contraction of the all-too-overstretched dominion of a none-too-large and very distant island brought about, as Charles Wilson once said of another such eventuality, by the nemesis of normalcy.[44] In the late twentieth century a Japanese empire might have been rather more plausible than a continuing British one. I begin therefore by taking my stance with Canute, and not with his cajoling courtiers.

It has after all long been clear that no British government could exercise dominion even over its own kith and kin overseas. I shall not repeat the oft told tale which stretched from the American Revolution, through Durham and Elgin in Canada, to the making of the white Dominions, and their lack of support for Imperial Federation, to the Balfour Report and the Statute of Westminster. The later story is studded with the names of Hughes, Scullin, Mackenzie King, de Valera, Hertzog and Smuts himself.[45] Commonwealth constitutional historians lately took pleasure in the crucial operational importance in the Rhodesian case of the distinction they had always drawn between Responsible Government – which Rhodesia had possessed since 1923 – and Dominion Status – which neither Rhodesia nor the Central African Federation ever had. But even in that case it was not the British who precipitated the downfall, but the much maligned freedom fighters of the ex-Portuguese territories and Zimbabwe itself.[46]

If I were to review the story here I know best, the Australian one, it would no doubt begin with the currency lads, the early Wentworth, and the Irish, and go on to Henry Lawson and the Sydney *Bulletin*.[47] It would certainly include the making of the Australian federation.[48] It would be shot through with ambiguity. 'Even the native born Australians are Britons', Henry Parkes roundly declared in 1890, 'as much as the men born within the cities of London and Glasgow';[49] and on three occasions Australia went to war as soon as Britain did. The crisis came in 1942 when, contrary to every

[43] Sir Bruce Williams, 'The Impact of Technological Change on World Population, Wealth and Employment', Association of Commonwealth Universities, *Technological Innovation: University Roles*, London, 1984, pp. 41–7.
[44] On this, see P.J. Cain and A.F. Hopkins, 'Gentlemanly Capitalism and British Expansion Overseas', *Economic History Review*, 2nd ser. vol. 39 no. 4 (1986), pp. 501–25, and vol. 40 (1987), pp. 1–26.
[45] The latest study is R.F. Holland, *Britain and the Commonwealth Alliance 1918–39*, London, 1981.
[46] John Marcum, *The Angolan Revolution*, 2 vols., Boston 1969, 1978; Parliament of the Commonwealth of Australia, Report of the Joint Committee on Foreign Affairs and Defence, *Zimbabwe*, Canberra 1980, is a most helpful compendium.
[47] Principally by reference to C.M.H. Clark, *A History of Australia*, 5 vols., Melbourne, 1962–81.
[48] J.A. La Nauze, *The Making of the Australian Constitution*, Melbourne, 1972.
[49] A.W. Martin, *Henry Parkes*, Melbourne, 1980, p. 391.

assurance, Britain failed to hold the Singapore base and protect Australia from the Japanese advance. Indeed, but for the check the American fleet inflicted on the Japanese at the Battle of the Coral Sea – Australia's equivalent of the Battle of Britain – Australia stood wide open to Japanese attack. With that Australia's American alliance superseded its British one. In 1951 the ANZUS Treaty was signed. Australian troops fought in Vietnam as no British did, and whilst little love is lost in Australia for the United States, one more poll recently showed solid support for the ANZUS Treaty once again.[50] As late as the 1960s Australia had a prime minister in Menzies who broke down when he told the House of Representatives of George V's death and always spoke unctuously of Elizabeth II.[51] But whereas in 1939 over 40 per cent of Australia's trade was with the United Kingdom, it is now less than 4 per cent;[52] God Save the Queen is nowadays only played when royalty are present; and whatever its origins Australia is now principally to be characterised as one of the two white countries in the up-and-coming eastern hemisphere. Menzies regularly visited London. No Australian prime minister would now do so; what would be the point? The Canadian story is not essentially different. It was capped by the 'patriation' decision in 1981 which finally gave the oldest Dominion the right to amend its constitution without reference to London which every other ex-British territory had had at its inception.[53] Ways have been steadily parting.

Chiefly owing to the greatly missed Jack Gallagher we have lately been reminded of the revivals of British imperial ambitions especially in the Middle East at the end of both world wars.[54] These never, however, came to very much, and instead the central story in the twentieth century has been about the contraction of the British Empire in both Asia and Africa. Let me now turn to this. In Cambridge there has been much pricking of hagiographic bubbles on this point.[55] Those who criticise Cambridge historians for emphasising the self-seeking that accompanied nationalism face difficulties in explaining the prevalence of such antics post-independence. But a balance here needs to be struck, for while many are aware that latter-day imperialist intrusions often stimulated nationalism, while nationalist movements were rarely linear, it is impossible to accept the primacy accorded to domestic constraints and international pressures; while to pass off every nationalist as a freedom fighter and then deny that either had very much influence can be positively obfuscating. One thing is agreed. There is no

50 T.B. Millar, *Australia in Peace and War*, Canberra, 1978.
51 Manning Clark, *A Short History of Australia*, Sydney, 1963, p. 242.
52 On all this see A.F. Madden and W.H. Morris-Jones, *Australia and Britain*, London, 1980; also E. Gough Whitlam, *A Pacific Community*, Boston, 1981.
53 Sheilagh M. Dunn, *The Year in Review 1981: Intergovernmental Relations in Canada*, Kingston, 1982, ch. 2.
54 John Gallagher, *The Decline, Revival and Fall of the British Empire*, Cambridge, 1982.
55 The principal statement was in John Gallagher, Gordon Johnson and Anil Seal, *Locality, Province and Nation: Essays on Indian Politics 1870–1940*, Cambridge, 1973.

teleology to empire's end. The Whigs are dished. But that in no way disposes of the central importance of nationalism and nationalist agitation to empire's end.

The first need here is to take a wider perspective. By the turn of this century nationalism was already in vogue amongst westernised elites in most of Asia.[56] There had already been the Philippines Revolution against the Spanish. Much excitement was then provided by Japan's defeat of Russia in 1905, the Chinese Revolution of 1911, and the Russian Revolution of 1917. In India and Indonesia the first Asian mass movements – of Muslims – meanwhile erupted to inspire others,[57] and out of the First World War there came as well the May Fourth Movement in China, Zaghlul Pasha's nationalist upheaval in Egypt, Gandhi's first national satyagrahas in India, the Young Men's Buddhist Association in Burma, the Ceylon National Congress. In the years that followed there were several major urban strikes and rural revolts in which Asia's first communists were involved. Though these were mostly crushed, secular nationalism nevertheless gathered apace. Great uncertainty followed the Japanese conquests in 1942. But upon the Japanese defeat, the 'new emerging forces', as Sukarno was to call them, were dramatically installed in the three brief years 1946–49 in all of South Asia, the Philippines, Indonesia and China. Given this context we should be wary of overparticularistic explanations of Indian nationalism, especially of an institutional or narrowly economic kind. It is more to the point to see it as one manifestation of a three-quarters-of-a-century-long general crisis in so much of Monsoon Asia that via several abortive leftist revolts in the late 1940s/early 1950s and two successful ones, later moved through the attempted 'renovations' of the late 1950s/early 1960s into the 'second starts' of the late 1960s/early 1970s, only to level out within the last decade or so as conservative regimes have everywhere become entrenched, even in China.[58]

A great deal of recent writing on the earlier period here stems from the opening of the British archives, and that for the unwary has sprung a trap. One needs no persuading that in the expansion of empire Britain's 'official mind' made much of the running.[59] To no such degree did it hold the initiative when it came to the contraction of empire. Whilst the British were often exceedingly skilful in surmounting actual nationalist agitations, they were deeply vulnerable – as was already plain in Egypt as early as 1919[60] –

---

[56] *Asia: The Winning of Independence*, ed. Robin Jeffrey, London, 1981, contains useful summaries, and bibliographies, for this and the ensuing paragraphs.

[57] Francis Robinson, *Separation among Indian Muslims*, Cambridge, 1974, chs. 7–9; Gail Minault, *The Khilafat Movement*, Delhi, 1982; Deliar Noer, *The Modernist Muslim Movement in Indonesia 1900–1942*, Kuala Lumpur, 1973, ch. 3; Sartono Kartodirdjo, *Protest Movements in Rural Java*, Kuala Lumpur, 1973, ch. 5.

[58] Ch. 2 below.   [59] Robinson and Gallagher, *Africa and the Victorians*.

[60] The latest study is John Darwin, *Britain, Egypt and the Middle East: Imperial Policy in the aftermath of War 1918–1922*, London, 1981. See also Wavell, *Allenby in Egypt*.

to any threat of a nationalist storm. This becomes strikingly clear when one looks at Britain's successive declarations of intent in India from the First World War onwards. Each was made in a vain attempt to head off an impending nationalist agitation, or, after their regular mid-term breaks, check its revival. In relation to the three great waves of Indian nationalist agitation – after the First World War; in the early 1930s; during the Second World War – this was as true for the Montagu Declaration of 1917, the Irwin Declaration of 1929, the August offer of 1940, as it was of the Macdonald statement of 1931 or the Cripps Offer of 1942. Each, moreover, was of first importance, as the British never retracted once these had been made: the Cripps Offer clearly presaged the early post-war departure. Contrary examples underline the case. No further such statements were made as the great agitations collapsed. In 1924 there was a good deal of talk about further constitutional advance that centred about the Muddiman Committee; but in 1924 there was no major nationalist agitation, actual or pending, so there was no constitutional advance.[61]

[When it came to Africa the point was very clearly perceived. Rarely was there a consideration of the processes of decolonisation as deliberate as that by the Official Committee in Britain on Commonwealth Membership of 1954, which was presided over by the highly influential secretary of the cabinet, Sir Norman Brook. 'The processes', it roundly told Churchill's last government, 'cannot now be halted or reversed, and it is only to a limited extent that its pace can be controlled by the United Kingdom government. Sometimes it may be possible to secure acceptance of a reasonable and beneficial delay in order to ensure a more orderly transition. But, in the main, the pace of constitutional change will be determined by the strength of nationalist feeling and the development of political consciousness within the territory concerned'.]

But if in the contraction of empire the 'official mind' was no olympian free agent but rather a reactor to nationalism, precisely how, and why, did it react? Here we need to take the important step of discarding the all too prevalent notion that the Indian struggle was in some way its own model. Clear choices stood on offer, and precise choices were made.

In the climactic years, 1946 to 1949, when the victorious Americans granted independence to the Philippines, and the British to four South Asian countries, the far more grievously war-stricken French and Dutch sought to re-establish their dominion over Indochina and Indonesia.[62] The distinction here can be pinpointed. Burma and Indonesia were both conquered by the Japanese. Both had nationalists who resisted the imperial

[61] Ch. 3 below.
[62] E.g. David J. Steinberg, *Philippine Collaboration in World War II*, Ann Arbor, 1967; Anthony Reid, *The Indonesian National Revolution, 1945–50*, Melbourne, 1974; Ellen J. Hammer, *The Struggle for Indochina 1940–1955*, Stanford, 1966.

return. But while the Dutch determined to stay and fight in Indonesia, the British swiftly decreed their departure from Burma.[63] (In view of its importance to the sterling area, it was in these circumstances well nigh miraculous that Britain regained control of Malaya in 1945; but that story only underlines that in the absence of a thrusting nationalism, imperial rule could persist.[64])

The most revealing contrasts had occurred in the 1930s. During those years whilst the Americans were welcoming Filipino nationalists to meetings in Washington to fix a timetable for their independence,[65] the Dutch were moving to incarcerate Indonesia's nationalists for life[66] (in accord with Governor-General de Jonge's blunt dictum that 'we have ruled here for 300 years with the whip and the club and we shall still be doing it in another 300 years'[67]), while the French were busily executing around 700 of Indochina's nationalists and communists in the course of their aptly called White Terror.[68] It was precisely in this context that the British starkly exposed their peculiar ambivalence. In 1929 they promised India Dominion Status – but only in the unforeseeable future. They then invented a new procedure for resisting nationalist agitations whose characteristic ambiguity was neatly captured when it was tellingly dubbed 'civil martial law' – no trials, no killings, no banishments; rather, short term, but indefinite, imprisonments without trial. The British held round table conferences, in London, too, but not to fix any date for independence; chiefly to put this off to the kalends.[69]

The essentials here were that whilst the Americans were bent upon going and were concerned only – as they have always been – to leave a right-of-centre regime behind when they did, and whereas the French were determined to stay, believing that the best that they could do to their colonials was to make cultivated Frenchmen of them, the British were desperately striving to reconcile two ultimate incompatibles. Since their empire was always a far larger component of their vision of themselves as a

[63] Yong Mun Cheong, *H.J. van Mook and Indonesian Independence*, The Hague, 1982; Hugh Tinker, *Burma: The Struggle for Independence 1944–48*, 2 vols., London, 1983–4.

[64] This issue does not seem to have been explored directly, but see Stockwell, *British Policy and Malay Politics*; Cheah Boon Kheng, *Red Star over Malaya*, Singapore, 1983; and W.R. Roff, *The Origins of Malayan Nationalism*, New Haven, 1967.

[65] The fullest account is in B.R. Churchill, *The Philippines' Independence Missions to the United States*, Manila, 1983. But see also T. Friend, *Between Two Empires: The Ordeal of the Philippines 1929–1946*, New Haven, 1965.

[66] John Ingleson, *Road to Exile: The Indonesian Nationalist Movement, 1927–1936*, Singapore, 1979.

[67] Quoted in S. Sjahrir, *Out of Exile*, New York, 1949, p. 112.

[68] Joseph Buttinger, *The Smaller Dragon: A Political History of Vietnam*, New York, 1958, pp. 436–7.

[69] R.J. Moore, *The Crisis of Indian Unity 1917–1940*, Oxford, 1974; D.A. Low, '"Civil Martial Law": The Government of India and the Civil Disobedience Movements, 1930–34' in *Congress and the Raj*, ed. D.A. Low, London, 1974, pp. 165–98.

great world power than it was for the Americans, their yearnings were always to stay. At the same time they found it exceedingly difficult to deny their longstanding commitments to the ideals of self-government, and thus found themselves saying, as Baldwin inelegantly did of India in 1934, 'we have taught her the lesson and she wants us to pay the bill'.[70] It is this exceptional juxtaposition that calls for scholarly attention, not just the fashioning of global strategy.

It is then well to notice the degree to which the particular quality of imperialist reaction largely determined the character of the nationalist confrontation and the extent of nationalist mobilisation. In the Indian case Britain's two-headedness largely explains the phenomenon of Gandhi. His politics directly mirrored Britain's ambivalence. He knew it was necessary to agitate against them; they would never move without this. But non-violence could keep their worst instincts at bay, and allow their better one's to prevail. Gandhi would have been unnecessary in the Philippines, impossible in Vietnam; he precisely fitted nationalist needs against the British in India.[71]

The general point goes wider still. Against the French in Indochina the Vietnamese nationalists needed to develop new ideologies, cadre-led mass movements, and a skilled guerrilla army.[72] Against the Americans the Filipinos had no such requirement.[73] Against the uncertain British, India's nationalists needed less popular support than the Vietnamese, more than the Filipinos. So aside from securing support from India's merchant communities, the Indian National Congress 'went rural', but essentially only in association with India's richer peasants, since against the ambivalent British it was rarely necessary to mobilise any more deeply.[74]

All of this then inspired Africa's embryonic nationalists, and honed Britain's official mind on Africa too. It is sometimes forgotten that on their way to the Colonial Office in the late 1940s Creech Jones, Sydney Caine, and Andrew Cohen read their *Times* on Asia. In a quite novel way they set to work to prepare Africa for self-government. It was to be done, over the two coming decades, by democratising local government first, and so inducing Africans into democratic processes. Indian mistakes were to be avoided: nationalist leaders were to be enlisted in the cause, but were to be forced to compete with local worthies. All round development was thereupon to

---

[70] Quoted in K. Middlemas and J. Barnes, *Baldwin*, London, 1969, p. 713.
[71] E.g. J.M. Brown, *Gandhi and Civil Disobedience: The Mahatma in Indian Politics 1928–1934*, Cambridge, 1977.
[72] E.g. David G. Marr, *Vietnamese Tradition on Trial 1920–1945*, Berkeley, 1981.
[73] On the contrary, the Americans suppressed anti-elitist populist movements; David R. Sturtevant, *Popular Uprisings in the Philippines 1840–1940*, Ithaca, 1976.
[74] Ch. 3 below.

proceed apace.[75] But in the ending of empire the official mind, as I have said, was never its own master. Development unleashed a second colonial occupation that soon stoked many a nationalist fire,[76] while elected councils fatally undermined the unreplaced authority of chiefs; and in the upshot the planning of the late 1940s principally served to multiply the expedients by which nationalist storms might be tempered – particularly by the device of multiplex constitutional advances in place of the former progression from Representative Government to Dominion Status.[77]

For the winds of change then blew, with a gale force no one had expected. Respecting neither the division the French and the Belgians drew between their Africa and British Africa, nor the distinction the British made between 'black' Africa and 'multi-racial' (i.e. white-dominated) Africa, it was a much more febrile phenomenon than ordinarily appeared in Asia, needing less organisation, but being always more difficult for its leaders to control.[78] The suggestion that it principally derived from widening urban and peasant discontents at the protracted economic stringencies of the depression, the Second World War, and its aftermath[79] – that were then thrice turned widdershins by inflation, the Korean War boom and its collapse – presently holds the field. In little more than a decade all those imperial clamps already loosened in Asia were in tropical Africa completely shaken apart. Kwame Nkrumah accurately divined the need to formulate both 'Positive Action' and 'Tactical Action'. It was symptomatic of the sequitur from Asia to Africa that he never needed to employ the former as much as the Congress had in India.[80] To begin with the British were quite prepared to arrest those who threatened their plans; but it was not long before they released Nkrumah, allowed the Kabaka to return to Buganda, and set Kaunda, Banda and even Kenyatta free. They were remarkably consistent, it should be said, in their use of *force majeure*; either against communists and alleged crypto-communists, as in Malaya[81] and British Guiana, or against movements which (à la the IRA) set out to kill, such as Mau Mau, EOKA, and

[75] The literature on this is beginning to grow, e.g. R.D. Pearce, *The Turning Point in Africa 1938–1948*, London, 1982; R. Robinson, 'Sir Andrew Cohen: Proconsul of African Nationalism', in *African Proconsuls*, ed I. H. Gann and P. Duignan, New York, 1978, especially pp. 358–9; and R. Robinson, 'Andrew Cohen and the transfer of power in Tropical Africa 1940–51', in *Decolonization and After*, ed. W.G. Morris-Jones and G. Fischer, London, 1980, ch. 2.

[76] Ch. 7 below.

[77] The change can be sensed in Martin Wright, *British Colonial Constitutions 1947*, Oxford, 1952.

[78] Prosser Gifford and Wm R. Louis (eds.), *The Transfer of Power in Asia: Decolonization 1940–1960*, New Haven, 1982. For one set of details, see e.g. G.A. Maguire, *Towards 'Uhuru' in Tanzania*, Cambridge, 1969.

[79] A.G. Hopkins, *An Economic History of West Africa*, London, 1973, ch. 7.

[80] Kwame Nkrumah, *I Speak of Freedom*, London, 1961, remains the primary text on this topic.

[81] E.g. Anthony Short, *The Communist Insurrection in Malaysia, 1948–60*, London, 1975.

the NLF in Aden.[82] But as the Devlin report on the Nyasaland riots in 1959 eloquently confirmed, there were strict limits to the coercion the British public would countenance[83] (and France's contemporary Algerian experience scarcely suggests it was wrong).

The apotheosis came in 1960, 'Africa Year', which saw the transition from less to more than half Africa becoming independent. 'It has been said', Iain Macleod subsequently wrote, 'that after I became Colonial Secretary [in 1959] there was a deliberate speeding up of the movement towards independence. I agree. There was. And in my view any other policy would have led to terrible bloodshed in Africa.'[84] Every projection as to timing was ratcheted away, and in circumstances where the issue was not whether the British were going but who would hold power when they did, all attention was then concentrated upon determining the pairs of hands to which its symbols should be passed. Those who had not had their minds bent in Asia[85] – the Portuguese and the white Rhodesians – sought for another fifteen years to resist the denouement, but they were eventually violently overwhelmed even so.[86] In the end the official mind did come into its own, with the footnotes, the mini-states in Southern Africa, the West Indies, and the Indian and Pacific Oceans, for which no independence had been planned, but which were frequently marched into independence faster than even their nationalists wanted.[87] Without the proximity and paranoid ruthlessness the Soviets and white South Africans alone possessed, it had all become (as the Americans learnt so searingly in Vietnam) much too hot to handle.

But I have not done. For the contraction of England did not just entail the saga of independence. It left behind upwards of fifty new polities, and as Commonwealth historians we have an obligation to study the characteristics of at least some of them. Everywhere there were innumerable British-type institutions – their universities for a start.[88] But even where their populations were ethnically close to Britain's, distinctive styles invariably developed. Let me give two examples from Australia. The fact that Australia, unlike Britain, has a written constitution means that its body politic often operates in a strikingly different manner. A major controversy over the building of hydro-electric dams in south-west Tasmania in 1983

---

82 E.g. *Myth of Mau Mau*; R.J. Gavin, *Aden under British Rule 1839–1967*, London, 1975, ch. 12.

83 *Report of the Nyasaland Commission of Enquiry* (July 1959), Cmnd 814.

84 *Spectator*, 31 Jan. 1964.

85 There is a plausible argument that the Belgian scuttle from the Congo was prompted in part by the Asian experience of their Dutch and French neighbours.

86 Marcum, *Angolan Revolution*; Parliament of Australia, *Zimbabwe*.

87 E.g. Francis Saemala, 'Solomon Islands: Uniting the Diversity', in R. Crocombe and A. Ali (eds.), *Politics in Melanesia*, Suva, 1982.

88 E. Ashby and M. Anderson, *Universities: British, Indian, African*, London 1966, tells an important part of the story.

was abruptly settled when by 4 votes to 3 the High Court pronounced that because the area was subject to an international Heritage agreement, the federal government had authority to halt these under its foreign affairs power! For eighty years now industrial relations in Australia have turned upon a legally enacted conciliation and arbitration system. Instead of forlornly leaving it to unions and bosses to settle when they will close with each other in their hotel lounges, as Britain so damagingly does, this arraigns them smartly into compulsory hearings, compulsory conferences, and compulsory arbitration.[89]

But what of the political characteristics of the other independent states which have emerged as England has contracted? The prototype here has perhaps been India. It pivots upon Delhi, a capital for six centuries past. It has so far been held together by the remarkable mediating capacity of that extraordinary coalition, the Indian National Congress. Its political economy is firmly structured, as my earlier remarks suggested, upon the persisting alliance between urban commercial communities and richer peasants against which ardent leftists have invariably broken their heads in vain.[90] Aided by one particular device (to which I shall come) it has maintained its democratic regime.

Pakistan ostensibly had a similar heritage. But in fact it could hardly have been more different. Whilst it once had a Bengali majority and until as late as 1947 a Congress government in its Frontier Province, centre stage was seized by the Punjabi Muslims, who then became Pakistan's 'Prussians'. They never supported the Congress, nor, except at the twelfth hour, the Muslim League either. Before 1839 their forebears had belonged to Ranjit Singh's militarised state. In the twenty-year turmoil following his death, every leading Punjab family struggled to survive in a way they never forgot. In the aftermath of their calculated decisions in 1857 to support the British, many of them became remilitarised into the backbone of Britain's Indian army. Exceptionally both landlords and well-to-do peasants had here their tenures secured; canal colonies enlarged their irrigated lands from 3 to 13 million acres; and rural strife became unusually muted. During the interwar years the predominantly Muslim, landlord led, Unionist Party thereafter provided the Punjab with much the strongest provincial government in India, and Partition then rid its Muslims of their Sikh and Hindu associates. When therefore after Independence the inchoate miscellany of Pakistan-wide politicians took to damaging bickering, the well-entrenched Punjabi elite, in direct line with their heritage, hoisted a Punjabi-led military dictatorship, broke with the threatening majority of Bangladeshis,

[89] There is no better introduction than Blanche d'Alpuget, *Robert J. Hawke*, Melbourne, 1982.

[90] W.H. Morris-Jones, *The Government of Politics of India*, London, 1964; Francine R. Frankel, *India's Political Economy 1947–1977*, Princeton, 1978.

suppressed the separatist Baluchis and Pathans, and executed Bhutto the Sindhi.[91]

Kenya has its 'Prussians' too, the Kikuyu, though they have been subtle enough to enlist some non-Kikuyu in their support as their elevation of the Kalenjin President Moi exemplifies. Comparable patterns are to be found elsewhere. In three very different countries, Malaysia, Sri Lanka and Zimbabwe, core majorities with an inherited sense of being disadvantaged have determined to lord it over their rivals: *bumiputras* against Chinese in Malaysia, Sinhalese vis-à-vis Tamils in Sri Lanka, Shona against Ndebele in Zimbabwe.[92] Fiji in the early 1980s provided the astonishing case. For in Fiji there are more Indians than Fijians. Yet thanks to British colonial policy Fijians dominate the police, the bureaucracy, the army, and the land, while their Prime Minister Ratu Mara expertly enticed Fiji's Gujaratis and Indian Muslims into his Alliance government so as to leave Fiji's mainly north Indian Hindus in a political minority.[93] A South Pacific Northern Ireland has so far not eventuated. But following the 1987 military coup it came to look all too like one.

There have been some very different stuctures too. Tanzania, for example, has always seemed to me to turn a good deal on not having 'Prussians', but rather upon President Nyerere occupying the interstitial position between the larger, inherently competing, groups in his country, somewhat as Mohammed did at Medina, or (as Evans-Pritchard taught us) the Grand Sanusi in Cyrenaica.[94] Papua New Guinea is different again. There are no 'Prussians' there either, but rather several powerful regional aggregations of whose leaders Michael Somare has been only one. Its polity turns accordingly on its prime minister being no more than *primus inter pares*. When Somare became more *primus* than *inter pares*, he fell.[95] Although he came back once again, the Papua New Guinea cabinet always needs to contain a representative from each region, or maintain particular contacts with it.

---

91 I owe this picture to conversations with three of my research students: P.H.M. van den Dungen, *The Punjab Tradition*, London 1972; A.J. Major, 'Return to Empire: The Sikhs and the British in the Punjab, 1839–1872', Australian National University, PhD, 1981; Imran Ali, *The Punjab under Imperialism 1885–1947*, Princeton, 1988, and 'Relations between the Muslim League and the Punjab National Unionist Party, 1935–47', *South Asia*, 6 (1976), 51–65. From the abundance of other literature, see especially David Page, *Prelude to Partition*, Delhi, 1982, ch. 3, and Khalid B. Sayeed, *Politics in Pakistan*, New York, 1980.

92 E.g. R.S. Milne, *Government and Politics in Malaysia*, Boston, 1967; James Manor (ed.), *Sri Lanka in Change and Crisis*, London, 1984.

93 Timothy J. Macnaught, *The Fijian Colonial Experience*, Canberra, 1982; Brij V. Lal, 'The Fijian General Election of 1982', *Journal of Pacific History*, 18 nos. 1–2 (1983), 134–57.

94 W.M. Watt, *Muhammad, Prophet and Statesman*, London, 1961; E.E. Evans-Pritchard, *The Sanusi of Cyrenaica*, Oxford, 1949.

95 R.J. May (ed.), *Micronationalist Movements in Papua New Guinea*, Canberra, 1982; J.A. Ballard, *Policy-Making in a New State: Papua New Guinea 1972–77*, St Lucia, 1981.

There have been two surprises in post-independence states. They have not – as was widely expected – endlessly fragmented. Pre-independent federations generally did.[96] There were several partitions at or about independence,[97] and we were regularly warned that India was about to break up further.[98] Yet, despite separatist movements in almost every case – Pukhtunistan, the Southern Sudan, North Solomons, Turkish Cyprus – with the single exception of Bangladesh – uniquely separated from its other half by a large land mass – no further separations have occurred post-independence. The test case was Biafra, with as good a case for separation as any. But it never won international recognition because far too many other new states feared that their own problems would be sorely aggravated if it did.[99]

There have at the same time been far more internal breakdowns than anyone expected. The Colonial Office's characteristic preoccupations with minorities, problems of size, and the independence succession, blinded them – except in the later illuminating case of Malaysia[100] – to the greater necessity before independence for kneading internal political forces into effectively composite wholes. In the event, as we all know, their former charges especially in Africa have seen a plethora of one party states, military regimes and *coups* – over thirty by now in Africa all told.[101] Some Africanists argue that this instability was inevitable,[102] that little else could be expected of those brought up under colonial autocracy; that poor countries cannot afford democratic regimes. They lead by the nose. India, Jamaica, Mauritius, Sri Lanka give them the lie. So do the ten impoverished states of the south-west Pacific which, beginning with Western Samoa and ending with Vanuatu, became independent between 1962 and 1980. Not only have none of these, until Fiji in 1987, had *coups*, military take-overs or one-party regimes. They have now had more than a dozen peaceful constitutional changes of government, including four resumptions of office.[103] Institutional considerations may have been important here. India has had more breakdowns of democratic government at state level than Africa has at national level. Its provision for President's rule gives it a

---

96 The West Indies, Central Africa, and French West and Equatorial Africa.
97 Including Singapore's break with Malaysia.
98 E.g. Selig Harrison, *India: The Most Dangerous Decades*, Princeton, 1960.
99 J. de St. Jorre, *The Nigerian Civil War*, London, 1972.
100 J.A.C. Mackie, *Konfrontasi: The Indonesia–Malaysia dispute 1963–1966*, Kuala Lumpur, 1974, chs. 3–4.
101 The latest survey seems to be Ali A. Mazrui and Michael Tidy, *Nationalism and New States in Africa*, London, 1984. See also John Dunn (ed.), *West African States: Failure and Promise*, Cambridge, 1978; and Dennis Austin, *Politics in Africa*, London, 1984. The number of coups later continued to increase. See ch. 10 below.
102 E.g. J. O'Connell, 'The Inevitability of Instability', *Journal of Modern African Studies*, 5 no. 2 (1967), 181–91.
103 Greg Fry, 'Successions of Government in the Post-Colonial States of the South Pacific: New Support for Constitutionalism?', *Politics*, 18 no. 1 (May 1983), 48–60.

remarkable mechanism for handling breakdowns which Africa lacks.[104] The South Pacific constitution makers were, it seems, generally much more careful than the African ones to detail how precisely parliaments should choose and dismiss prime ministers.[105] But there have been larger matters too. A number of African countries – Sudan, Ghana, Nigeria, Uganda, Zimbabwe are all examples – had deep internal conflicts that, to a greater degree than in the Pacific, preceded independence, and were by no means settled by it. Further, where (as so often in Africa) government controlled export trades comprised a country's most lucrative resource, unbridled competition for government dominance proved exceedingly difficult to check.[106] But it is worth pursuing the South Pacific comparison; for with the single exception of Vanuata, none of them had a party at Independence which commanded a majority. That meant that coalition politics, and the consequential need for compromise, meshed with the strong ideological commitment to consensus – 'the Pacific Way'. By contrast, at Independence most African countries did have numerically triumphant nationalist parties whose leaders were prone as a consequence not only to see themselves as god-given, but all opposition as inherently illegitimate.[107] The insidious spread thereafter in Africa of the fatal doctrine of winner-takes-all had its incalculably debilitating consequences: the innocent were slaughtered, the talented killed or exiled, famines aggravated, farmers alienated, refugees propelled, universities ravaged, bureaucracies cauterised.[108] Ghana was evidently in great trouble here even before Independence. Nkrumah and his Ashanti opponents intemperately denied each others legitimacy, and Ghana irredeemably broke on their mutual intransigence.[109] Even the mild-mannered Nyerere (let alone the aggressive Mboya) made a fateful contrast here in his obduracy towards opponents to a Michael Somare or a Michael Manley.[110]

Of these African countries I know Uganda best. There the Baganda at its core might have become its 'Prussians'. They had earlier, however, been used as sub-imperialists by the British, and, greatly resented everywhere else, had then withdrawn to their core. In 1953 their Cambridge-educated Kabaka saw their dilemma clearly and sought the separated independence

104 Ch. 6 below.   105 Fry, 'Successions of Government'.
106 E.g. Keith Hart, *The Political Economy of West African Agriculture*, Cambridge, 1982; Robert H. Bates, *Markets and States in Tropical Africa*, Berkeley, 1981.
107 Fry, 'Successions of Government'.
108 E.g. Mazrui and Tidy, *Nationalism and New States*.
109 Dennis Austin, *Politics in Ghana 1946–60*, London, 1964; Richard Rathbone, 'Parties socio-economic bases and regional differentiation in the rate of change in Ghana', in Peter Lyon and James Manor, *Transfer and Transformation: Political Institutions in the New Commonwealth*, Leicester, 1983, ch. 7.
110 Cranford Pratt, *The Critical Phase in Tanzania 1945–1968: Nyerere and the Emergence of a Socialist Strategy*, Cambridge, 1976; David Goldsworthy, *Tom Mboya. The Man Kenya wanted to Forget*, Nairobi, 1982. Compare J.A. Ballard, 'Policy Making as Trauma', in *Policy-making in a New State*, pp. 96–132.

of his kingdom. As that would have been rather like excising England from the United Kingdom, the British deported him when he pressed his case. That, however, only rallied his people about him, which in turn led to the rallying of Uganda's non-Baganda majority around Milton Obote. Upon independence in 1962 the Prussian model was thus foreclosed, and no interstitial space existed either. Instead, a deal was struck by which Obote as prime minister accepted the Kabaka as president of Uganda. But this soon collapsed, and in 1966 Obote ordered Colonel Amin to assault the Kabaka's palace. That only ensured, however, that at the core of his country Obote was now denied all legitimacy; and as he vainly struggled with his lot Amin in 1971 tossed him aside. But Amin thereupon simply faced the old dilemmas now compounded, and so turned to terror as the only buttress for his authority. In the end terror devoured his regime from within, so that in 1979 it fell easy prey to a Tanzanian invasion. With that three successive non-royal Baganda interim executive presidents were suddenly provided, now that the Kabaka was dead, with a unique opportunity to secure a position for the Baganda akin to that of Kenya's Kikuyu. This they completely mishandled. As a consequence Obote pushed his way back into power, which in turn drove some Baganda to armed revolt, so that the last state was soon in some ways worse than the first. For thirty years now it has been abundantly clear that Uganda would never be steadied until either the Baganda came to the top or their countrymen assured them a place commensurate with their strength.[111]

That brings me to my penultimate point – which is that since Seeley wrote, not only has England markedly contracted, 'England' as part of the historiography of its former colonial territories has steadily contracted too. There is an apt commentary upon this in the history of Australian painting. Initially landscape and vegetation were painted as if in a mildly exotic England. Then in the 1890s the Heidelberg School of Roberts, McCubbin and Streeten marvellously captured the Australian light. In our own day from Fred Williams' magical Australian landscapes every trace of England has gone.[112] Time was, and not so long since, when all Australian histories began with the convicts' landing at Sydney Cove on 26 January 1788. The Australian historians' remarkable co-operative ten-volume celebration of that event (which in a novel way will have three 'slice' volumes for Australia in 1838, 1888 and 1938 respectively) will open, however, with a volume on Aboriginal Australia, as will the new Oxford History of Australia.[113] We

---

111 There is now a large literature on Uganda's tragedies. My earlier comments are in *Buganda in Modern History*, and 'Uganda Unhinged', *International Affairs*, April 1973, pp. 219–28. See ch. 11 below.

112 There is, of course, a large literature, e.g. Bernard Smith, *Australian Painting 1788–1970*, Melbourne, 1971.

113 F. Crowley, A.D. Gilbert, K.S. Inglis, P. Spearrit (general editors), *Australians. A Historical Library*, 11 vols. Broadway, New South Wales, 1987–8.

now have three radiocarbon dates for early man in Australia at 40,000 years. The latest pollen analysis suggests that it could have been 130,000 years, for at that stage fire-resisting eucalypts displaced fire-prone casuarinas.[114] And therein lies a central point. For aboriginal man's firestick farming – producing better feed for more huntable marsupials – fashioned the floral environment that in the nineteenth century so assisted the white man's sheep and cattle conquests.[115] Even in my own day much African historiography also began, still more ludicrously, with the first Europeans – though without Africa's earlier agricultural revolution its modern history might have been little more than Australia's writ large. These errors have now been rectified.[116] Let me therefore step a little closer. Australian historians used to write about Australian Britons.[117] They are now concerned with Australian colonists.[118] South African historians used to focus on Briton, Boer and Bantu.[119] They now give their minds to 'the shaping of South African society'[120] and the classic case of the growth of an industrial capitalist state.[121] Similarly Dr Christopher Bayly has recently written of eighteenth and nineteenth century India with the British firmly in their place – less the progenitors, more the offspring of its history.[122] Twenty years ago Professor J.F. Ade Ajayi hammered the point that 'in any long-term historical view of African history, European rule becomes just another episode'.[123] With each succeeding year that looks less the exaggeration some thought at the time. And so to my final point.

The rubric for the Smuts Chair says that the Professor should concern himself with Commonwealth studies generally. Let me simply say that the field now encompasses forty-nine independent states, one in north America, one in central America, one in south America, one in western Europe; two in the Mediterranean; three in each of East Africa, Central Africa, South Africa, South Asia, South-east Asia, and the Indian Ocean; four in West Africa; ten in the Caribbean; eleven in the south-west Pacific.

114 E.g. D.J. Mulvaney, *The Prehistory of Australia*, rev. edn, Harmondsworth, 1975; J.P. White and J.F. O'Connell, *A Prehistory of Australians, New Guinea and Sahul*, Sydney, 1982.
115 Geoffrey Bolton, *Spoils and Spoilers: Australians and their Environment*, Sydney, 1981.
116 E.g. by the serial publication of the *The Cambridge History of Africa*.
117 E.g. Brian Fitzpatrick, *The British Empire in Australia*, Melbourne, 1940.
118 K.S. Inglis, *The Australian Colonists*, Melbourne, 1974.
119 W.M. Macmillan, *Bantu, Boer and Briton: The Making of the South African Native Problem*, London, 1929.
120 R. Elphick and H. Giliomee, *The Shaping of South African Society 1652–1820*, London, 1979.
121 E.g. R.H. Davies, *Capital, State and White Labour in South Africa 1900–1960*, Brighton, 1979; Shula Marks and R. Rathbone, *Industrialization and Social Change in South Africa*, London, 1982.
122 C.A. Bayly, *Rulers, Townsmen and Bazaars: North Indian Society in the Age of British Expansion, 1770–1870*, Cambridge, 1983.
123 J.F. Ade Ajayi, 'The Continuity of African Institutions under Colonialism', in T.O. Ranger (ed.), *Emergent Themes of African History*, London, 1968, p. 194.

Outside the royal family (who actually know where Tuvalu is) this development is scarcely understood in this country. 'It was a noble ideal – the Commonwealth', Lord Beloff typically remarked back in 1972, 'a pity it failed.'[124] Its failure to provide the expected support for Britain's *amour propre*, and, to the contrary, its hounding of British policies towards South Africa and Rhodesia were no doubt difficult to take (though it brilliantly saved Britain in 1979 from the ignominy of recognising a government in Rhodesia that scarcely any one else would have done).[125] The difficulty seems to lie in perceiving with the necessary clarity that the Commonwealth is no longer a British institution, but, as Smuts perciplently envisaged it back in 1921, 'a society of free and equal sister states'.[126] I have a photograph taken in a Canberra garden in 1981 of five principal figures in the Commonwealth at that time: Lee Kuan Yew, Kenneth Kaunda, Pierre Trudeau, Malcolm Fraser, Indira Gandhi. Margaret Thatcher was close to hand, but simply as Britain's Prime Minister, she was not as yet in that league.

Back in 1946 there was little prospect that very much would survive. It is a principal result of all I have been discussing that despite a dozen or so withdrawals nearly fifty independent states have decided to maintain the free association in the Commonwealth the Balfour report projected. They cover many cultures. Some are vast, some are rich, some are tiny, some are poor, and some could soon be rich. They encompass a quarter of the world's population, and a third of its states, and extend into most reaches of the globe. Apart from the public fiestas of Commonwealth Games, and cricket, a growing number of workaday linkages are being constructed between them. Their heads of government clearly value their periodic meetings as providing them with unique opportunities to encounter several dozen of their kind and test the temperatures right around the globe. If for some reason Britain were now to quit the Commonwealth there is no good reason why it should cease to exist. As it is, it provides the readiest means available to use for orienting ourselves sensibly to the most of our fellow humans. It is thus well that some of us should be professionally engaged in its study.

[124] M. Beloff, 'The Commonwealth as History', *Journal of Imperial and Commonwealth History*, 1 no. 1 (1972), 111.
[125] The best account of the recent reshaping of the Commonwealth is by its first secretary-general, Arnold Smith with Clyde Sanger, *Stitches in Time*, London, 1981. But see also Denis Judd and Peter Slinn, *The Evolution of the Modern Commonwealth 1902–1980*, London, 1982, pts 5–7.
[126] Hancock, *Smuts: The Field of Force*, p. 46.

2

The twentieth-century revolutions in Monsoon Asia

The great arc of Asia, from India through South-east Asia to China, has seen during the greater part of the twentieth century the working out of something akin to a 'general crisis' of immense proportions. The term 'general crisis' was made familiar as a description of a series of occurrences in western Europe in the seventeenth century, where (so it was argued) there was a far-flung rising of 'the country' against 'the court'. The greater part of Monsoon Asia has passed through a not dissimilar 'general crisis' in the twentieth century, born of a conjuncture between an intensifying revulsion towards continuing imperialist domination and a deepening exasperation with the inefficient, inequitable structures of society with which it was seen to be lumbered.

There is a widespread assumption that the histories of the various countries of this region are quite adequately understood in their own terms. Certainly there has been little inclination to look beyond their own borders. Whilst each country has had its own superabundance of particularities, an over-rigorous concentration upon these does seem, however, to have been at the expense of allowing for the highly significant similarities that in a range of very important respects many of them have at the same time experienced. The briefest of glances at the twentieth-century history of the greater part of the countries of Monsoon Asia will immediately reveal that they have passed through a number of comparable political upheavals, sometimes palpably during the same few years. A wider perspective suggests that these commonalities were a great deal more substantial than has hitherto been appreciated, and that a great many of the revolutionary developments in these countries during the twentieth century – using the term 'revolution' in its very broadest sense – constituted parts of the working out of a much broader and more protracted 'general crisis' than too close a concentration upon one country alone may enable one to see. Closer investigation indicates, indeed, that the plethora of revolutionary upheavals – using the term, to repeat, in its very broadest sense – through which the greater part of Monsoon Asia has passed in the twentieth century were much more extensively impelled by two similar and related purposes than is ordinarily appreciated. In the first place there was the pervasive determination to be rid of imperial and more particularly western political domination and create 'modern', Asian-controlled nation-states in its place, and in the second a widespread urge to create a new, less exploitative, more productive social order. These purposes were not identical with those which (so it was suggested) imbued the 'general crisis' in seventeenth-century western Europe, but they bear a strong family resemblance to them.[1]

One can be fairly precise as to when Monsoon Asia's 'general crisis' began. It was clearly beginning to find expression as the twentieth century opened. There was no similar sequence of upheavals in nineteenth-century Asia. There was the major revolt against the British in north central India in 1857–8, and the Taiping rebellion in China in the following decade. But even when a number of other episodes are taken into account these did not comprise as great a series of related upheavals as have scored Monsoon Asia's twentieth-century history. One can even hazard a guess as to when this 'general crisis' had run its course. It will be argued below at all events that the main political occurrences in Monsoon Asia in the late 1980s did not carry the same undertones of earlier upheavals and, indeed, struck a really very different note.

The 'general crisis' did not extend to all of Monsoon Asia. For a start, the revolutionary episodes which characterised it did not occur in Japan, Thailand or, for the most part, Malaysia; here, in particular, indigenous monarchies quite unusually survived, upheld in each case by respectful governing elites. Nor did it touch very much the first cohort of Asia's newly industrialising countries; Japan again, South Korea, Taiwan, Singapore, Hong Kong.

But whilst the commonalities to be suggested were assuredly matched, if indeed they were not surpassed, by occurrences that were quite distinctive to each of the countries concerned, the dynamics inherent in the major political developments over the greater part of the twentieth century in both the largest (China, India) and several of the smaller countries of the region (Indonesia, Vietnam, the Philippines, Sri Lanka, for a start) were nevertheless much more strikingly in line with each other than has been generally noticed. Indeed, as one contemplates the politically turbulent decades in these countries from around 1900 to around 1945 and then for three or four

---

[1] See the useful collection of articles by Trevor Aston (ed.), *Crisis in Europe 1560–1660*, London, 1965, esp. H.R. Trevor-Roper, 'The General Crisis of the Seventeenth Century', ch. 3.

decades thereafter one can go further. For they would appear to have passed through three successive stages. For shorthand purposes these may be called respectively, the Gropings, the Great Achievements, and the Rectifications. The first were very protracted and seem to have moved through half a dozen phases, each characterised by considerably more similarities between events in adjacent countries than each ordinarily appreciates. The second came, for the most part, quite suddenly, but then often saw a number of significant differences in the experiences of different countries. The third stretched over most of the four decades after 1950, and once again saw great likenesses between events in different places. Each warrants review in turn.[2]

THE GROPINGS

First the Gropings. These stretched out over most of the first half of the twentieth century in varying forms in almost all the countries under discussion here. For the most part they were concerned with the first of the two objectives mentioned above – the eradication of imperialist political domination – but they were varyingly concerned as well with the second – the search for a new social order. Both of the first two sets of Gropings largely petered out. The next two were mainly aborted. A fifth began by looking very much more promising, but was then bewilderingly overtaken by the Second World War.

As the twentieth century opened, western imperial rule could be found in most parts of South and South-east Asia. The British ruled in Malaya, Singapore, North Borneo, and all of South Asia; the Dutch in Indonesia; the French in Indochina; the Americans in the Philippines; while several European powers held 'concessions' in China, where the imperial Manchu dynasty still held sway.

Already, however, a first set of Gropings towards a new era were being undertaken by the first of the western-educated Asian elites in almost all of the countries with which we are concerned. In the Philippines a substantial nationalist revolution against Spanish imperial rule had erupted back in 1896. At the outset this had some strong non-elite involvement, exemplified by the urban-based Katipunan. But that was soon overborne by the revolution's elite military leader, Aguinaldo, who captured and executed the Katipunan leader, Andreas Bonafacio, and then seized the opportunity of the defeat of the Spaniards by the Americans in the Spanish-American war of 1896–8 to declare the independence of the Philippines at Malolos. That, however, did not survive the formal international acquisition of the Philippines by the United States following its defeat of Spain in that war and

---

[2] Select bibliographies on the countries principally concerned are appended at the end of this chapter.

the ensuing conquest of the Philippines by the Americans by 1902. None the less, during the first decade of the new century two major Filipino elite figures, Osmena and Quezon, clearly marked out their position as the Philippines' principal nationalist leaders for the future (and continued to hold on to this over the next four decades).

Elsewhere there were already other new-style, elitist nationalist figures as well. One thinks of Phan Boi Chau and his contemporaries in Vietnam; of Tjoakraminoto and Wahidin Sudironusodo (and the young woman Kartini) in Indonesia; of Naoroji, Tilak, Gokhale, Banerji, Aurobindo and their like in India; of U Ba Pe in Burma; and Sun Yat-Sen in China. Their efforts were given a considerable boost by the dramatic defeat of the European power, Russia, in the Russo-Japanese war of 1904–5. Most of them were 'western educated', good at making speeches, passing resolutions, fashioning the fundamental tenets of Asia's rising nationalisms; but they did not often give themselves to cadre organisation or to open agitation. Some of their younger associates and contemporaries were more active. Some of them indeed – especially in the first decade of the new century, particularly against the British in India and the French in Vietnam – took to the selective use of violence, in the hope of thereby scaring their imperial rulers into retreat.

None of this, however, was to much avail. The early propagandists made next to no headway. The plots of the bomb-throwers all turned out disastrously. Only the Chinese Revolution of 1911 led by Sun Yat-Sen against the long-discredited Manchu dynasty appeared to promise anything really new. For a brief moment Sun Yat-Sen seemed indeed to be the most successful Groper of all. Yet within a few weeks of his triumph he was easily brushed aside by one of China's forceful warlords, and thus ceased, for a while at least, to be the model which he might have been. All in all this first set of Gropings was generally therefore quite unsuccessful. Farsighted reformers necessarily had to consider other possibilities.

These, as it happened, came their way in the latter part of the second decade of the twentieth century when the whole situation became transformed, first by the First World War and then by the Russian Revolution of 1917. As a consequence three further sets of Gropings were now generated.

The chief of these was part and parcel of an all but world-wide phenomenon around the end of the First World War. For following the collapse of the Russian and Austro-Hungarian empires at the end of that war there came into being, often with strong American backing, a number of new nations in Europe, several of whom were immediately faced by social revolutions that could well have been of the Russian kind. Simultaneously the collapse of the Ottoman empire led to the emergence of several new nations in the Middle East as well, while even in the triumphant British

Empire the so-called 'White' Dominions – and even rebellious Ireland – were clearly moving to secure a much greater degree of autonomy too.

It was amidst this much wider concatenation of events that a new temper came to be loosed abroad in Monsoon Asia too. In the years immediately before and after the end of the First World War this became variously exemplified in the May Fourth Movement in China; in the Home Rule Leagues and Gandhi's first nationalist *satyagrahas* in India; in the agitations of U Ottoma and the General Council of Buddhist Associations in Burma; in the creation of the Ceylon National Congress; in the despatch of the first Philippines' Independence Mission in 1919 to the United States; and in some substantial developments in Sarekat Islam in Indonesia.

Sarekat Islam (Islamic Union) was particularly significant. For while these other movements drew much wider support, and were often much more committed to vigorous activity than the pre-war movements, they nevertheless still tended to be markedly elitist in character. Sarekat Islam became a notable exception. Founded in 1912 it spread during the war years well beyond the activist elite to win widespread support amongst Indonesia's very numerous Muslim peasantry. In many respects Sarekat Islam represented the Indonesian version of the much broader religio-political upheavals that were so widely characteristic of the (otherwise largely separate) Islamic world at this time, which reached their climax upon the defeat and dismemberment of the Ottoman empire that for so many centuries had constituted its central core. For that not only had a considerable impact in Indonesia (and in Malaya). It very directly powered the Muslim Khilafat movement in India (that was designed to protect the residual position of the Sultan of Turkey, the Caliph of Islam, against the depredations of the European powers) with which Gandhi's first Non-Co-operation movement of 1921–22 against the British in India became so closely associated.

It seems indeed that it was these Muslim movements rather than any nationalist movement as such which in a crucial way first generated mass public support for political movements in Asia in the twentieth century.[3] Whilst both the Khilafat and Non-Co-operation movements and Sarekat Islam soon lost their way – the Turks themselves abolished the Caliphate, and the Indonesian Communists (as we shall shortly see) captured Sarekat Islam, which thus began to lose its Muslim peasant support – their successors were always inspired by the belief that there could be mass movements of a kind that had hardly ever happened here before; henceforth their leaders, that is, lived in the confidence that it was well within the bounds of possibility to draw upon countrywide support for their cam-

[3] R. McVey, *The Rise of Indonesian Communism*, Ithaca, 1965; F. Robinson, *Separatism among Indian Muslims*, Cambridge, 1976; J.M. Brown, *Gandhi's Rise to Power*, Cambridge, 1972; W.R. Roff, *The Origins of Malay Nationalism*, New Haven, 1967.

paigns. Such confidence came to their contemporaries in some of the other Asian countries only later on. Because indeed the Muslim movements in India and Indonesia had no counterpart in the Philippines, or in China, or in Vietnam, the course which events took there differed significantly. For example, it is striking that while by the 1920s the days of all but unalloyed elitist nationalism in India and Indonesia were already past, in Vietnam – where there was no Muslim movement because there were no Muslims – elitist nationalism persisted, and eventually reached its climax with the unsuccessful violent uprising in 1930 of the recently formed elitist Vietnamese nationalist party, the VNQDD.

While these post-First World War Gropings constituted an important step forward, none of them secured any great success. Following the explosion of the Russian Revolution of 1917, there developed alongside as well a further set of Gropings that eventuated in the creation of a number of small communist movements in all of these countries which soon drew some of the more ardent spirits into their ranks. Naturally a good deal of interest was taken in these first communist movements in Asia both by the Comintern and by the intelligence services of the imperial powers.

The first Dutch communist had arrived in Indonesia in 1913. By the end of the First World War the original Indonesian communist supporters were well on their way to securing control of Sarekat Islam. The first Communist Association of the Indies was formed in 1920; the Partai Kommunis Indonesia in 1924. In China the first congress of the Chinese Communist Party was held in Shanghai in July 1921. During the mid-1920s various communist organisations were formed in India; the Communist Party of India itself in 1927. In 1930 in Vietnam an Indochinese Communist Party was created, and in that year a Philippines Communist Party was formed as well. Some of the most important individuals who were caught up early on in these movements became, in due course, major figures in their countries: Mao Zedong, Ho Chi Minh, Tan Malaka, Musso, M.N. Roy. There was here a further Groping indeed.

One striking fact, however, about the 1920s in Asia was that the various communist initiatives which ensued soon suffered severe setbacks. The Dutch regime in Indonesia very easily crushed the communist-led rural revolts in Java and Sumatra in 1926–7. Sun Yat-Sen after having established a new base for his Kuomintang (Nationalist Peoples State Party) in Canton in the early 1920s made a United Front there with the embryonic CCP. But in 1927 his successor, Chiang Kai-shek, treacherously wheeled upon it and destroyed four-fifths of it (principally in the cities). Soon afterwards in 1929 the British, via the long-winded Meerut Conspiracy Case, swept the Indian communist leadership into jail. During the following two years the French in Vietnam ruthlessly crushed a rash of peasant revolts with which the Vietnamese communists had become associated in the provinces of Ha Tinh

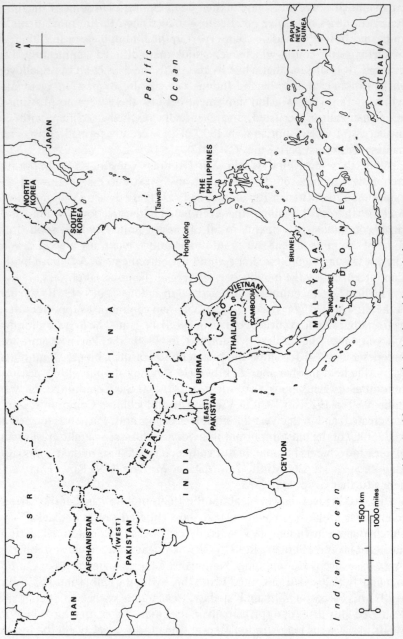

Map 1   Monsoon Asia in the mid twentieth century

and Nghe An; whilst in 1933 the Americans declared the Philippines Communist Party a subversive group and incarcerated all of its leaders it could catch.

By that time, however, a further, different set of Gropings had been mounted by those who saw themselves not as communists but as secular nationalists. In 1927 the VNQDD, as we have seen, was founded in Vietnam against the French. In that same year the Indonesian Dutch-educated elite joined with the young engineer Sukarno, who had formed the Partai Nasional Indonesia, to mount a radical nationalist coalition against the Dutch; while in India Gandhi and the new Congress peasant-oriented leadership of such men as Rajendra Prasad, Rajagopalachari, Vallabbhai Patel, and Abdul Ghaffar Khan, along with several younger leaders like Jawaharlal Nehru and Subhash Bose, were soon leading a major new campaign against British dominion in India – knowing that they had done this once already in the Khilafat/Non-Co-operation movement of 1920–2.

In the early 1930s, however, it was soon made clear that almost all of the regimes that were still paramount in Asia were not only determined to crush the communist movements by which they were confronted, but any and every movement that in any way sought to expel them. Thus the French White Terror of 1930–1 was directed as much against the VNQDD as against the Indochinese communists (upwards of 700 Vietnamese nationalists and communists were executed by the French in the early 1930s). The Meerut Conspiracy Case against the communists in India was soon overshadowed by Britain's eventually unremitting repressions of Gandhi's two Civil Disobedience movements (1930–1, 1932–4). In 1930 the British energetically suppressed the Saya San rebellion in Burma as well. Meanwhile, first in 1929 and then more particularly in 1933, Sukarno was arraigned by the Dutch, who the second time around exiled him and his like ostensibly for life, and all but destroyed the rising Indonesian nationalist movement altogether. In these very same years, moreover, in the course of the so-called Five Encirclements, Chaing Kai-shek, flatly opposed to any more radical revolution in China, pressed hard upon the remnants of the Chinese communists in the countryside, and eventually squeezed Mao out of his southern redoubt in Kiangsi onto his Long March to Yenan away in China's north-west. When indeed one looks about one in the mid-1930s for the major figures of a decade or so later, not only does one see Mao cooped up in Yenan and Ho in exile in Moscow, but Nehru in Dehra Dun prison and Sukarno banished to Flores.

Thus while both the pre-, and the first of the post-First World War Gropings had all eventually petered out, both the subsequent communist and secular nationalist thrusts of the mid 1920s to the early 1930s were severely blunted by the imperialist powers and the Kuomintang as well. To all appearances there was still a long way to go before any major change of regime looked like being secured.

Yet in a quite remarkable way the mid-1930s saw a very significant array of more positive developments. The most striking of these was in the Philippines. There in the first two decades of the twentieth century the American regime had always been much more liberal towards its local nationalists than any other imperialist power. Throughout the 1920s, under the Republicans Coolidge, Harding and Hoover, and their successive nominees, Wood, Stimson, and Welles, the prospects for Filipino nationalism had never looked dimmer. But with Roosevelt's accession to the American Presidency in 1932, the outlook changed, and out of the to-ing and fro-ing of the Hare-Hawes-Cutting Act of 1933, its rejection by the Filipino oligarchy and legislature, followed by Quezon's support for the Tydings-McDuffie Act, there came into being the Commonwealth of the Philippines under Quezon's presidency in 1935, with a promise of full independence ten years later.

Then in the following year, 1936, the advent of the Popular Front Government in France led to a momentary revival of some political freedoms in Vietnam, which the newly formed Indochinese Communist Party used in a highly skilful way to develop its first cadres both in the cities and in the countryside. In December 1936 the Sian Incident gave Mao and the Chinese communists a quite new standing as allies of Chaing Kai-shek's Kuomintang against the Japanese, of which over the ensuing decade they made spectacular use. In the early part of 1937 the Indian National Congress, having for the time being abandoned civil disobedience, successfully capped its recent series of electoral victories by winning control of eight of the eleven provincial governments of India. In that same year 'responsible government', as the British called it, came to Burma too, with Ba Maw becoming his country's first prime minister. Only in Indonesia was there still no movement, with only the collaborating parties being free to operate.

Taken together, these various developments in the 1930s were to be of singular importance for the future. For while they entrenched the Filipino oligarchy (the only national leadership which had so far secured a clear promise that it would shortly take over from its imperial rulers), they everywhere else undermined the existing regime's local supporters. They gravely weakened most of the non-Congress parties in India; the collaborating Gerindo and Parindra parties in Indonesia; the Constitutionalist Party in Vietnam; even the supporters of the Kuomintang in China. At the same time they were of great importance on the other side as well. For while they saw Mao firmly established as the prime Chinese communist leader; the Indochinese Communist Party now effectively replaced the VNQDD as the leading Vietnamese nationalist party; despite patent British hostility the

Indian National Congress had successfully displayed its convincing ability to win a massive electoral victory; in Indonesia Sukarno's pre-eminence as a nationalist leader, was also well on the way to becoming entrenched; while in Burma, Aung San and U Nu were already being seen as up and coming nationalist leaders for the future too. The casts were already chosen for the larger dramas of the 1940s.

With change in the wind, this fifth set of Gropings seemed at last to be making a great deal more headway than anything which had eventuated previously. Yet before their full effect could be felt the Second World War had supervened. This (in truth) began when open war finally burst forth between Japan and China in 1937; but by 1939 western Europe was at war as well. In 1941 first Russia and then the United States became involved too, and by the turn of that year war had spread to all of Southeast Asia also.

As in China – with the creation in 1937 of the second United Front between the communists and the Kuomintang against the Japanese – the war very directly cut across all the older confrontations, and raised some quite new possibilities for their resolution. Whilst the Vichyite French stayed on in Vietnam – but only at the mercy of the Japanese – the British were soon driven from Malaya and Burma; the Dutch from Indonesia; the Americans from the Philippines; and at one stage it even looked as if the Japanese would soon be marching into India. The previous apparent inviolability of the western imperial regimes was quickly broken, where indeed it was not destroyed altogether.

In these circumstances the future for the nationalist and radical movements in Monsoon Asia was all the same most unclear. Should they resist the Japanese? Collaborate with the Japanese? Or what? There was much debate as to the best way to grope forward, and in every case there was a marked division in the ranks. Given the stark intensity of the moral-political issues which the onslaughts of the Japanese posed, it was of considerable moment that in the upshot Mao did not break at this time with Chaing; that Osmena, the Philippines president's prime rival, stuck with Quezon and went into exile to America with him; and that Ho with his Viet Minh in Vietnam, Nehru and his like in India, and Sjahrir and others in Indonesia, stood out against the Japanese so unrelentingly.

But there were others who took a different course, perhaps out of expediency, perhaps in an effort to hold on to their existing gains, perhaps because they could see no end to the Japanese occupation. Thus, as early as 1940, the erstwhile Chinese revolutionary and one-time leftist leader, Wang Ching-wei, became premier of a Japanese puppet government in Nanking. A few months later Subhas Bose, who had long been Nehru's rival for the plaudits of the younger Indian nationalists, joined the Axis powers, and in due course formed the Indian National Army to support the Japanese. In the Philippines, Vargas, President Quezon's former secretary, very soon headed up a Philippines Executive Commission to cooperate with the Japanese; in Indonesia both Hatta and Sukarno, now at last released, readily agreed to collaborate with them; while shortly afterwards Ba Maw, prime minister of Burma under the British, agreed to serve as his country's head of state under the Japanese as well. One can readily see the Gropings in this further phase taking many different forms.

As the war turned against them so the Japanese attempted to exploit this situation further. In August 1943 they made Ba Maw prime minister of an allegedly more independent Burma. In October 1943 they established a new Republic of the Philippines under the presidency of yet another Filipino oligarch, José Laurel. In that same month Subhas Bose established under their auspices a Provisional Government of Azad Hind (Free India). Then in March 1945, having eventually turned upon the Vichyite French, the Japanese elevated the young Emperor Bao Dai to be head of an independent Vietnamese state; and in the following months started to move towards assisting with the creation of an independent Indonesian republic also.

The ambiguities which suffused these situations could be traced out in some detail. It is fascinating to note, for example, the skill with which some of those who walked the knife-edge managed to survive the Japanese defeat – Sukarno for a start, chairman of PUTERA under the Japanese, President of the Indonesian Republic after their defeat. Likewise the first president of the Philippines was none other than Manuel Roxas, a collaborator with the Japanese during the war, but the protégé of (the American) General MacArthur following their defeat. Similarly, Aung San, who originally had collaborated with the Japanese, successfully linked up with the British commander-in-chief, Lord Mountbatten, and placed himself in unrivalled position to lead Burma into independence thereafter.

As these examples serve to illustrate, such delicate feeling of the way could, if fortune smiled, open doors that had hitherto been closed. Caution born of hard, protracted Gropings generally, however, prevailed for just a little longer. Thus when the war ended with the decisive defeat of Japan and the opportunity that provided to the former dominant regimes to reassert their control, the leaders of the new nationalist and radical forces opposing them not only moved with great circumspection. They very often actually entered into negotiations with them. They all began by feeling, that is, that there was probably more to be gained at this stage by *diplomasi*, as the Indonesians called it, than by *perjuangan* (struggle).

So it was that Chou En-lai and Mao parleyed with Chaing in 1945–6; that Nehru and the other Indian leaders met the British Viceroy, Lord Wavell, at Simla in the following year; that in Vietnam Ho Chi Minh signed the 6 March Agreement with Sainteny, and attended the Fontainebleu Conference in Paris in 1946; and that in November 1946 the Indonesian nationalist leaders signed the Linggajati Agreement with the Dutch, and early in 1948 the Renville Agreement with them as well.

THE GREAT ACHIEVEMENTS

It was in the aftermath of these negotiations that so many of these situations suddenly changed quite dramatically, when all of a sudden the long protracted Gropings often quite unexpectedly gave way to the long-striven-for Great Achievements, that at long last seemed to make so many of the earlier efforts so decidedly worthwhile. For in just less than four years, in all but one of the countries with which we are concerned, a major change of regime now ensued. In 1946 the Americans granted the Philippines the formal independence they had promised it just a decade previously. In 1947 the British transferred power to an independent India and an independent Pakistan, and likewise in 1948 to Burma and Ceylon. In 1949 the Dutch finally acknowledged the independence of the Indonesian Republic; and on 1 October of that year Mao proclaimed the establishment of the People's Republic of China. Only in Vietnam did the future still remain uncertain.[4]

In view of the climactic importance of these events they warrant closer scrutiny than earlier or later developments receive. Once that is embarked upon, however, it very soon transpires that whereas it is the commonalities in these Asian stories up until the end of the Second World War which are most worth emphasising, here it is certain of the differences that particularly call for comment. Two arrays of these warrant special notice. In the first place, amidst a great torrent of events in the late 1940s one can fairly easily discern a series of paired contrasts in the experiences of different groups of countries which, moreover, constituted a pronounced sequence. What is then especially striking is not only that the poles of these pairs of contrasts cumulatively fell into two quite distinctive sets of positions, but that to a quite extraordinary degree the major differences in the experiences of two different (and in some respects almost randomly composed) groups of countries were governed by which of these two sets of positions fell to their lot. Thereafter, there is a second and quite different array of contrasts to be noticed concerning the distinctive socio-political configurations in various of these countries which characterised the means by which transfers of power were effected in them. In reviewing the events attending the final approaches to the Great Achievements some consideration of each of these will be made in turn.

Striking contrasts of the first kind began to appear at the very moment of the Japanese surrender in August 1945, in terms of the extent to which the formerly controlling powers did or did not exercise full control over their former territories. As early as 1944 the Americans had re-established their

[4] See generally R. Jeffrey (ed.), *Asia. The Winning of Independence*, London, 1981.

control of the Philippines. Remarkably in 1945 the British once again secured control of Malaya, virtually unopposed (and hereafter some allusions to the Malayan story will become warranted). They were still just in control of India, and had lately recovered Burma. But, even several months after the war was over, the Dutch to their fury were still not back in full control of Indonesia; nor the French of Vietnam; nor the Kuomintang of China.

Thus while the Americans in the Philippines and the British in India and Malaya, could still very largely (in the short run at least) determine the course of events in the territories which they claimed as theirs (as the nationalists in each of these cases generally understood), the Dutch found themselves confronted in August 1945 by Sukarno's proclamation of the independent Republic of Indonesia; the French by Ho Chi Minh's declaration in September 1945 of the independent Democratic Republic of Vietnam; and the Kuomintang by Mao's control of large numbers of communist 'Liberation Zones' in China. What was scarcely less portentous, both Ho and Sukarno already controlled some of their countries' major cities, while Mao stood athwart Chaing's road to the crucial industrial region of Manchuria.

In each of these cases we can then see the imperial powers seeking to establish regimes with which they could hope to live subsequently. In 1947 Mountbatten in India made his settlements with Gandhi and Jinnah, Nehru and Patel. In Burma, Rance cut Britain's losses, and transferred power to Aung San. In Malaya after a shaky start the British managed to reaffirm their existing alliance with the Malayan elite. Meanwhile, as we have seen, MacArthur's choice, Roxas, became the first president of the post-war independent Republic of the Philippines.

D'Argenlieu in Vietnam for his part tried a variant on these themes, but with a significantly different purpose. Inherently hostile to the Viet Minh, and to its communist core in particular, he energetically strove to reinstall the former Emperor, Bao Dai, in the hope that France could then live with a regime which he headed, and certainly elbow Ho Chi Minh aside. For some years this policy seemed to be promising; but only at the cost of mounting conflict with the Viet Minh.

In Indonesia Van Mook took a similar line. Despite Musso and Tan Malaka the Indonesian nationalists were never led by their communists. But they were led by a man whom the Dutch (understandably seared by their experience of the German occupation) considered a quisling. Because of this the Dutch wanted to thrust the radical Indonesian nationalists aside as well. Accordingly Van Mook tried to mobilise the non-Javanese in Indonesia into a Federation under the Dutch Crown so as to confine the Indonesian Republic to its Javanese heartland.

Meanwhile General Marshall and other American representatives sought to bolster up the Kuomintang, or at all events ensure that it should be entrenched as the dominant partner in any future Chinese coalition. They failed, of course.

What is striking here is that even within this apparent set of commonalities, sharp contrasts developed between, on the one hand, those who were ready to use the breathing space which Asian *diplomasi* gave them to accommodate themselves to a new regime's advent, and, on the other, those who so resolutely sought to resist any such conclusion.

These contrasts then coincided with a further pair of contrasts which quite precisely matched these earlier ones. For whereas in 1946 the Americans were ready to grant independence to the Philippines and the British had decided to depart from all of South Asia, the Dutch (convinced, quite wrongly, that control of their Southeast Asian empire was crucial to the well-being of their home economy) were set upon recovering their position in Indonesia; the French (who were all but united in believing that the retention of their empire was vital to the restoration of their gravely damaged position as a great power in the world) were similarly determined to recover Indo-China; while Chaing Kai-shek showed himself as little prepared to share power with the CCP as he had been in the late 1920s and early 1930s. As a consequence, there were strict limits both for the Indonesian and the Vietnamese nationalist leaders and for the Chinese communist leaders as to the efficacy of the *diplomasi* upon which they had embarked in 1946; and before very long armed conflict had broken out in all three countries.

It then happened that these successive contrasts fortuitously meshed with a further one. For it now transpired that those movements (in the Philippines and South Asia) which did not need to take military action against the formerly dominant regimes (the USA, Britain) were those which had not had an opportunity during the war to develop their own military forces; while those that did need to take military action against the older regimes (the Dutch, the French, and the Kuomintang) did happen in one way or another to have had such an opportunity to build up a nucleus of their own military forces during the war. Thus in Indonesia the Japanese had encouraged the creation of PETA, which became the starting point for the Indonesian republican army against the Dutch. In Vietnam, Ho and Giap had been able to develop a key military base for their revolutionary army in northern Tonkin; while in China Mao had been able to build up the Red Army to an impregnable position in many of the central and northern parts of the country. (The intriguing exception here lay in Burma where Aung San and his 'Thirty Comrades' had formed the nucleus of the Burma National Army, which upon the reconquest of Burma by the British could, as the British very soon realised, have launched a brisk campaign against them – but in the event did not need to do so. Such exceptions, however, were far from common.)

Seen upon a larger scale the most dramatic of the events which then followed – the Great Achievements, as they are called here – occurred in China. There, in 1946, protracted attempts to create a coalition government between the Kuomintang and the communists finally broke down, and major civil war between them followed. This first took the form of a struggle for Manchuria, where the Russians, astonishingly, at the end of the Second World War had transferred control of the cities to the Kuomintang. The CCP's Peoples Liberation Army (PLA) eventually, however, overran the Kuomintang's forces there. This was followed by Lin Piao's great victory in the Huai-hai campaign in central China – whereupon the victorious PLA swept southwards to Canton. Raging inflation, which the Kuomintang could not control, led to widespread erosion of such lingering support as the Kuomintang retained, and before very long Chaing Kai-shek fled to Taiwan. The climax here came on 1 October 1949 when Mao Zedong proclaimed the establishment of the People's Republic of China in Peking. These massive events provided the ever-present backdrop to contemporary developments elsewhere in the region, particularly in Southeast Asia.

They were, however, not readily replicated elsewhere. For, except in Vietnam, none of the other colonial territories had suffered the extensive collapse of an ordered society to the extent that China had; none of them saw the decisive military overthrow of the previous dominant regime which China did; and none of them experienced the establishment of a communist regime at this time as China did.

This was not for lack of activity on the part of communist, or at all events leftist, movements elsewhere. In the middle and late 1940s there were considerable leftist revolts in India (in Telengana, Kerala and Bengal); in the Philippines (by the Huk); in Indonesia (under the Moscow returnees, Tan Malaka and Musso); while by the end of the Second World War the Malayan Communist Party was probably the most powerful in the country, and in 1948 took to armed revolt. Nehru's India, however, repressed all of the Indian outbreaks. American support for the Filipino oligarchs led to the suppression of the Huks in the Philippines. The incautious precipitancy of the Madiun affair in September–October 1948 thwarted the hopes of the Partai Kommunis Indonesia – for the time being at least; while in 1948 the British declared the Malayan Emergency, and by 1954 had successfully reduced the largely Chinese Malayan communists to a marginal minority ekeing out a living in the forests. Only Ho Chi Minh, with his 'Yenan' in northern Tonkin, managed to survive the post-war onslaughts against the communists and their like in the ex-colonial territories, and even there Giap's great victory at Dien Bien Phu in 1954 did not come until five years after Lin Piao's in northern China, and even then secured control of only North Vietnam.

Of the other stories canvassed here perhaps the most straightforward meanwhile took place in the Philippines. There, from the days of their takeover from the Spaniards, the Americans had maintained the Filipino oligarchs in power. This elite managed to hold on to its position throughout the Japanese occupation; and after the war authority was transferred to it remarkably smoothly by the Americans. For this the Americans reaped their reward in the special commercial and military privileges which they enjoyed in the Philippines in the decades that ensued. As a consequence the Philippines continued to have one of the most unreconstructed social orders in Asia. While there was a modicum of land reform (as we shall see), power still continued to be held by those who owned its well-entrenched estates.

In the immediate post-war years a transfer of power was similarly effected without any armed conflict between the British and each of the nationalist movements in South Asia. But by contrast with the Philippines, the transfer of power in India saw not the entrenchment of a landholding oligarchy, but the coming to power at national level of those who had long held power at village level.

India's attainment of independence was indeed in every respect the outcome of a much more strenuous struggle than in the Philippines. It depended greatly on the extraordinarily magnetic leadership of Gandhi. His prime achievement had been to bring into the nationalist movement tens of thousands of activists from the towns and villages of India, who eventually secured hundreds of thousands of supporters. During the period from 1917 to 1937 the tactic the British primarily employed against the Indian nationalist movement had been to extend the franchise for the provincial legislatures in British India beyond the bounds of those groups from which the Indian National Congress had so far drawn support. By enfranchising something like 4–5 per cent of the population the British were relatively successful in maintaining their position in the years between 1920 and 1935; the provincial legislatures of British India, and the executives partially linked to them in the 'Dyarchy' period, generally withstood the Congress onslaught. At the same time the British deflected the thrust of Congress-led peasant agitations, first by making concessions, and then by displaying a determination to confiscate land when concessions proved ineffectual. But their extensive use of police repression against Congress' two major Civil Disobedience campaigns of 1930–34 nevertheless alienated many of those with influence. As a result, when in the mid-1930s the British sought once again to undercut the nationalist movement by extending the franchise to around 12 per cent of the population, they found the Congress had by now undercut them. The consequence was (as we have seen) that at the provincial elections of 1937 Congress not only achieved a dramatic electoral victory. Because of the provisions of the new Government of India Act of 1935 it went on to secure control of eight of the eleven provincial governments in India.

It is true that during the Second World War there seemed to be a marked conservative reaction in British Indian policy. But as Churchill's appointee in 1943 to the Viceroyalty, Field Marshall Lord Wavell, immediately appreciated, Britain's interest in maintaining its empire in India was now distinctly fading. British preferences as well as British trade with India were no longer what they had been. India indeed was now proving costly for the British (the Indian Army, for example, was no longer the inexpensive asset which it once used to be). Accordingly in 1947, Mountbatten, Wavell's successor, took energetic steps to transfer power to those who at the elections of 1946 had amply demonstrated the very considerable political support they possessed in various parts of India. Since the preceding decade had seen in the movement for Pakistan the most striking case of the classic end-of-empire dispute about how power should be disposed upon the actual attainment of independence, the eventual transfer ultimately entailed the appalling trauma of Partition between the two successor states of India and Pakistan. But as between Britain itself and the leaders of these states, the transfer was scarcely less smooth than it had been in the Philippines. It was smoother still in Ceylon.

By contrast, the transfer of power in Indonesia involved substantial armed conflict. Although the Dutch had created a small *Volksraad* (assembly), they had never made any significant constitutional concessions to the Indonesian nationalists. Ultimately this precipitated Sukarno's unilateral declaration of Indonesia's independence in August 1945. In Java the defence thereafter of the embryoninc Indonesian Republic regularly involved violent confrontations, often of an heroic kind, as, for example, against the British-led forces assisting the Dutch at the Battle of Surabaya in November 1945. That, and various other events which followed, brought about the Linggajati Agreement of November 1946 by which the Dutch agreed, not, it is true, to Sukarno's independent Indonesia, but to the establishment of a federal Indonesia of which Sukarno's Java would be simply one part. But since there were soon different interpretations as to what all this entailed, the Dutch in July 1947 eventually sought to settle the issue by mounting their First Police Action against the new Indonesian state. This only precipitated, however, intervention by the United Nations through a Good Offices Committee, which patched up the precarious Renville Agreement in January 1948. Later that year, in the course of the ill-fated Madiun affair, Sukarno's nationalists overran the Indonesian Communists. But, still dissatisfied, the Dutch then mounted their fatal Second Police Action. This, however, roused such strong United Nations, and particularly American, support for the Indonesian nationalists – who had just prevailed at Madiun over their communist associates – that international pressure soon forced the Dutch to transfer sovereignty before the end of 1949 to the United States of Indonesia.

Vietnam in some significant respects had a like experience. Back in 1941 Ho Chi Minh, building upon the communist experience in Vietnam in the late 1930s, had formed a united front nationalist organisation, the Viet Minh. Under Vo Nguyen Giap's remarkable military leadership this formed a military base in northern Tonkin during the Japanese military occupation. Following the Japanese defeat in 1945, Ho dramatically proclaimed the independence of Vietnam. But during the course of the first Indo-China War (1945–6), the French nevertheless re-established themselves in south and central Vietnam, and in March 1946 forced Ho to accept Vietnam's participation in the newly formed French Union, in exchange for French recognition of his Viet Minh government. But such compromises, as in Indonesia, very soon collapsed, and before 1946 was out, full-scale war – the second Indo-China War of 1946–54 – had broken out between France and the Viet Minh.

In the years that followed the Viet Minh forces steadily increased their hold upon Vietnam's northern countryside. But unlike the Indonesian nationalists, they won next to no support in the west, particularly when following the victory of the Chinese communists in 1949 they more openly proclaimed their communist attachments. French arms, moreover, were more substantial than Dutch ones. The French were able to play on communist control of the Viet Minh to hold at least some Vietnamese nationalists to their side; and as we have noted, they once more made the former Emperor Bao Dai head of a Vietnamese puppet state. In the end, however, the Viet Minh forces wore down the French, and at Dien Bien Phu in 1954 delivered their brilliant *coup de grâce*. By then the Geneva Conference on Indo-China had been called, in which all the main world powers played an important part, and that gave full control over North Vietnam to Ho Chi Minh and his Viet Minh.

The contrasts were thus plain. In the Philippines the Americans transferred power to the Filipino oligarchy which readily provided them with a continuing commercial and military presence. In South Asia the British accepted the legitimacy of the Indian, Pakistani, Ceylonese and Burmese nationalist leaderships, and thankfully clutched at the readiness of the first three to remain members of the (British) Commonwealth of Nations. In both these major cases, transfers of power were accordingly effected without armed conflict.

But it was very different elsewhere. After the defeat of Japan, Chaing Kai-shek, holed up for most of the war in his Chungking retreat, not only failed to recover effective control of China's main cities, but quite failed to prevail over the now well entrenched CCP. A huge and bitter civil war thereupon followed. Meanwhile the Dutch, for their part, would not accept the right of what they saw as the Javanese quisling, Sukarno, to rule Indonesia, and they had no confidence that he and his regime would uphold the Dutch notion of an Indonesian federal state within the 'Realm' of the Queen of the Netherlands. Armed warfare accordingly followed here too. Likewise, many Frenchmen not only abhorred the Viet Minh leadership in Vietnam for its communist attachments, but questioned still more whether it would really accept Vietnam's place in the French Union. So war followed here as well.

Linked to these sets of paired contrasts was yet one more. For where there was no armed conflict, and peaceful transfers of power did occur – as in the Philippines and in all of South Asia – there were thereafter to be all sorts of continuities with the past. The Indian independence constitution, for example, owed a great deal to Britain's Government of India Act of 1935; while the Philippines' oligarchy was now once again confirmed in its place of power. Where, however, armed conflict did break out, there was (to a greater degree than we ordinarily encounter here) substantial revolutionary change, and (for all the important cultural continuities which may be noted) a major break with the past. This was palpably true of Communist China and North Vietnam. It was to a large extent also true of Indonesia.[5]

The intricacies of these successive contrasts are well exemplified in the Malayan case. There in a situation where the native state structure had been maintained by the imperial power, a strong nationalist movement had been as slow to develop as it had been in the Indian Princely states, or in many of the outer islands of Indonesia. Because of the openings for able Malays in the state bureaucracies, many ambitious young Malays had found their energies and abilities adequately provided for in the colonial era. During the Second World War they were by no means enamoured of the Japanese. Upon the Japanese defeat their leaders became particularly anxious, however, lest the most active of the anti-Japanese elements, the Malayan communists, should inherit the future. By trying in 1946 to impose an impolitic Malayan Union upon the country (in which the immigrant Indians and Chinese would have had full citizenship rights) the British nearly botched the whole affair. But they soon reacted positively to vehement Malayan opposition to this, and thereupon fashioned a much more acceptable Federation of Malaya (in which, through the upholding of their Sultanates, the Malays were assured of their primacy). The alliance between the British and the Malayan elite which this restored thereupon thrust the largely Chinese Malayan communists, who during the years of the Japanese occupation had developed a strong forest base, into violent opposition. War (euphemistically termed the Emergency) then ensued in 1948 between the British and the Malayan communists till the mid 1950s.

[5] See ch. 5 below.

But by contrast with the position of the Dutch in Indonesia, and of the French in large parts of Vietnam, the British in Malaya managed to hold a majority of the local population to their side; and by combining successful military operations against the Malayan communists with steady constitutional concessions to the Malayan elite (and its Malayan Chinese and Indian allies as well), they were eventually able, to a degree the French never were, to defeat the communist threat. They then transferred power to a right-of-centre independent Malayan regime which, upon achieving independence in 1957, remained within Britain's Commonwealth – and retained many continuities with the past.

Beyond this first set of differences concerning the manner in which the Great Achievements were attained, there was (as we noted earlier) a second array of differences which warrants attention too. This did not have the sequential character of the contrasts just considered. It was a good deal more procedural. The differences here turned on a number of highly significant contrasts in the socio-political circumstances which conditioned the means by which the Great Achievements were secured.

There were four cases where – rhetoric and irritation and from time to time frustration aside – no overwhelming struggle with the imperial power occurred, but where, as things transpired, there were relatively smooth transfers of power to well-entrenched elites. This was obviously the case in the Philippines – as later in Malaya in 1957. But it was also the case in Pakistan. For reasons which have still to be spelt out, control of Pakistan at independence passed into the hands, not of the numerically predominant Bengalis, but of the military-bureaucratic-landed elite principally based in the Punjab.[6] Likewise power in Ceylon was transferred at independence to the western-educated western-oriented elite of what was known (from the quarter in which many of them lived) as 'Colombo 7'.

Elsewhere things were very different. Following upon the example of the Russian Revolution of 1917, it had long been expected by a great many of those involved that independence in the colonial world, and a further change of regime in China, would most probably come, not through some amicable agreement over a transfer of power, but through a leftist, almost certainly communist, revolution. The expectation, moreover, was that in accord with both Marxist doctrine and communism's European precedents this would assuredly come in the cities. That, however, proved, for the most part, not to be the case.

Here the example of the Communist Party of India is particularly suggestive as to what happened. In the two decades up to the Second World War, the CPI was probably the most substantial urban Communist Party in Asia. In the 1920s it had secured a remarkably strong base in Bombay; by the early 1940s it was strong as well in other cities like Calcutta. In 1929 its

[6] See D.A. Low (ed.), *The Political Inheritance of Pakistan*, London 1991.

leaders were imprisoned by the British, as we have seen, in the aftermath of the long-drawn-out Meerut Conspiracy Case. But by contrast with what occurred elsewhere, in China, Indochina and Indonesia, the leaders of the Communist Party of India were not largely destroyed by their ruling power. During their imprisonment they relied on the Comintern to maintain their position, and on their release in 1933 mainly returned to their old party bailiwicks in the cities.[7]

Paradoxically that constituted their first major setback. It needs to be remembered that unlike their counterparts in Indonesia, Indochina and China, they were not involved in the 1920s and early 1930s in a countryside revolt. Indeed the collapse of these elsewhere may well have reinforced their proneness to concentrate upon the cities. But to confine themselves, as they very largely did, to the cities was to limit themselves to less than 15 per cent of India's population. Even in the cities, moreover, they at no time held a monopoly of the available radical impulses. They always had to share these with the very different Indian National Congress; and they were never in fact able to mount a communist revolution sprung from the urban bases which they had secured.

Then from the mid-1930s onwards the CPI was caught in two further difficulties, one of which climaxed in a prime disaster. At this time the doctrine of its mentors in the Comintern called for 'united fronts'; in India that meant muting its ideological conflict with the Congress governments, who in the late 1930s held power in so many British Indian provinces. There then ensued (following the Soviet entry on the western side in the Second World War) the enormously damaging period of 'People's War', when, just as the Indian National Congress was mounting its final 'Quit India' movement of August 1942 against the British, the CPI aligned itself in effect with the British. It never fully recovered from this, and by the time the more revolutionary Zhdanov line was being propounded by the Comintern in the late 1940s, any opportune moment for a revolutionary upheaval in India had clearly passed. With the coming of independence all the levers of power in India had passed into the hands of the anti-communist Congress.

The key failure of the CPI seems in retrospect, and by comparison, to have lain in its failure to 'go rural'. It should be emphasised that this occurred, not simply because of its prevailing ideology and its close involvement with its urban bailiwicks, but more particularly because the position in India's rural areas made it very difficult for it to do so. For, speaking generally, patterns of political authority at the village level in so many parts of India were at this time still remarkably intact, and leftist

---

[7] R. Stuart, 'The Formation of the Communist Party of India, 1927–1937', PhD dissertation, Australian National University, Canberra, 1978.

movements accordingly encountered great difficulties, as they continued to do, in securing entry there.

The importance of this consideration is most illuminatingly exemplified by the case where, in the 1930s, the Communist Party in India did in fact 'go rural'. In north Malabar in southwestern India, during the transition of the previously dominant Nayar caste from matrilineal to patrilineal succession, a breakdown of the structure of authority in the rural areas had occurred. As a consequence, significant numbers of younger, western-educated Nayars became seriously alienated from their society, and moved into the leadership of a communist movement in the countryside.[8] Elsewhere in India such developments were most unusual.

Against this particular background the characteristics of the communist movements in Indonesia, Indochina and China – and the later developing Malayan movement – become the more apparent. As we have seen, by the early 1930s the first three had all had their experience of a largely rural communist revolt, which thereafter stuck in their memories. All three, moreover, had suffered the virtual elimination of their urban parties. All that was open to the remnants that survived, or so it seemed, was long-term exile.

For the Indonesian communists there was never to be very much relief to this. In 1945 Sukarno magically established the Republic of Indonesia, and made it possible for them to return. But they then tried to press their case too quickly – in 1946 and in 1948 – not merely against the much better established republican leadership, but before their leaders had really restored their position after their long years abroad. Whilst under Aidit in the 1950s and in the early 1960s the PKI did eventually achieve some substantial support in the countryside, its ability to 'go rural' was ultimately always as constrained as its ability to hold on to Sarekat Islam's earlier Muslim peasant support had been in the 1920s.

In the early 1930s the ability to 'go rural' of the Communist Party of China and of the Indochinese Communist Pary was much restricted too. But since – unlike the CPI – they had been decimated in the cities, their only hope if they were to operate at all, was in fact to 'go rural', and as it happened the opportunities to do this were marginally more favourable than for their counter-parts in Indonesia. As is well known, the inability of the Kuomintang government to control effectively the whole of China in the 1930s allowed the CCP to establish a rural base in Yenan. The corresponding opportunity in Indochina came first with the advent of the Popular Front Government in France in 1936 and then with the Japanese invasion in 1941, which allowed the ICP to develop its rural cadres and its rural base sooner than might otherwise have occurred. In both these cases, moreover –

[8] R. Jeffrey, 'Matriliny, Marxism and the Birth of the Communist Party in Kerala 1930–1940', *Journal of Asian Studies*, 38 no. 1 (1978), 17–20.

by contrast with the Indian and the Indonesian ones – the communist
movement came to enjoy a substantial hold on the radical tendencies in
their two countries: in China, as the Kuomintang moved politically to the
right; in Vietnam, following the French extermination in the early 1930s of
the VNQDD.

But more to the present point, in both China and Vietnam (in contrast to
so much of India, and for that matter Indonesia and Malaya), the ability of
the CCP and ICP to 'go rural' seems to have been substantially assisted as
well because both countries experienced serious breakdowns in the structure of authority at rural level during the crucial period. The circumstances
were very different from those in Malabar. But in China there were the
ravages of warlordism on the one side, and social banditry on the other,
while in Vietnam there was the serious dislocation of patterns of authority in
the rural areas caused by the sustained French assaults upon the rural
scholar-gentry. In both instances the way was opened for communist
intrusion into key positions of rural leadership.

In both instances, moreover, there was no question of their being caught
at a critical moment on 'the wrong side' of the pre-eminent local issue, as the
CPI had been in India in August 1942, the PKI in 1946 and 1948, and the
Malayan Communists in the late 1940s. Mao joined Chiang in fighting the
Japanese; Ho Chi Minh and Vo Nguyen Giap fought similarly. Both parties
were at the same time able to hold on to their rural bases, in Yenan and in
northern Tonkin (as the Huks never could in the Philippines in central
Luzon); while the CCP in particular seems to have benefited greatly from its
ability to provide succour to those devastated by the Japanese army's rural
rampages. In the event, an armed communist-led revolution was eventually
effected in both these countries, though at the cost of a major war in China
and a grotesquely protracted one in Vietnam.

There were, therefore, successful communist revolutions in Asia. But
they did not occur everywhere, and (despite the ICP's initial victories in the
cities in 1945) the communist revolutions in Asia which did succeed were
essentially rural ones, not the urban ones so many had expected.

But what of Indonesia, and of India? In neither of them did a transfer of
power take place to a formerly well entrenched elite; nor was there a
communist revolution either. So what happened?

Indonesia had its own distinctive story. It is important to note that there
were many indications that the structure of power at rural level in Indonesia
was kept largely intact during the Dutch period. Indeed, the 'agricultural
involution' of which Geertz wrote, may well have served to reinforce the
position of the *pamong desa* (village officials) at the head of the grievously
hard-pressed, but much interlocked Indonesian village society, in Java
particularly. Certainly the ability of the PKI to 'go rural' was, as we have
seen, always much restricted. It would also seem that in the 1920s and 1930s

the Indonesian nationalists of Sukarno's ilk did not 'go rural' either – not even to the extent that Sarekat Islam had done before them. Herein no doubt lay one of the major weaknesses of Indonesian nationalism, which would seem to explain why it was so much more easily crushed by the Dutch in the 1930s than Indian nationalism was by the British.

Accordingly, it would seem highly significant in the present context that when in 1945 the opportunity for Sukarno and his associates did eventually come, it was powered by a ferment (nationalist as distinct from communist) *in the cities*, particularly amongst younger men. In the course of the Indonesian Revolution Sukarno and his associates had to be careful not to be outmarched on the left. They were not, however, unsuccessful in this, as the events of the late 1940s were to show. To some extent in their armed conflicts with the Dutch, rural support was of some importance; that of many smaller towns a good deal more so. But the evidence is that the eventually highly successful Indonesian nationalist movement owed its critically important initial thrust to a series of well co-ordinated non-leftist urban revolts in which young activists were to the fore in the Javanese cities of Jakarta, Bandung, Yogyakarta, Surabaya, etc., along with some corresponding upheavals in Sumatra and Makassar. It was these outbursts that formed the base from which Indonesia's Great Achievement came to be secured.

The Indian case was quite distinctive too. In terms of the argument outlined here, the central facts are these: whilst the CPI, as we have seen, did not for the most part 'go rural', the Indian National Congress in the 1920s and 1930s under Gandhi's leadership clearly did. But it did not do so in a situation where the structure of power at rural and village level had broken down; but rather, and very precisely, through an association with those whose power at village level remained intact. In the years between 1919 and 1945, the British successfully repressed both urban and rural revolt in India. The Indian National Congress nevertheless edged its way to power, first by securing the support of leading urban and then rural elements, and then (as these became enfranchised) by winning the elections the British instituted at local, provincial and eventually national levels. In marked contrast to the Indonesian case, the Indian nationalists themselves took steps in the 1940s to damp down urban revolt. Despite events in Kerala, Telengana and elsewhere, they had little to fear from forces of the left. It was essentially therefore a Congress increasingly linked to urban and rural powerholders that won India independence in 1947.

Once again the Malayan case underlines the various points to be made. The Malayan Communists did in a sense 'go rural'. They came to base themselves in the forests, and it required a good deal more effort on the part of the British in Malaya to destroy their influences than it did, for example, for the Indian government to destroy the leftist movements in Bengal and

Telengana. But the Malayan communists, who were largely ethnic Chinese, were unable to move out of their forest redoubts and effectively secure control of the countryside, because Malay rural society remained very much intact, and highly resistant to communist leadership. Malaya's elite nationalists, moreover, very successfully established their political connections not only in the towns but in the various rural areas of Malaya, and thus procured as effective a power base as the Congress had in India before them. They eventually secured their own Great Achievement, when Malaya finally became independent of the British as we have seen in 1957.

The ways in which the Great Achievements were thus attained differed quite substantially. Yet there were a number of distinct patterns into which these distinctions fell, and if we are to probe the whole experience of Monsoon Asia's 'general crisis' we need to take careful note of them.

THE RECTIFICATIONS

Despite the momentousness of these events for so many of the countries concerned, it warrants emphasising, however, that they did not constitute the sum total of the revolutions (in the sense employed here), through which so many of them have passed in the twentieth century. Whilst the events of the 1940s assuredly remained their Great Achievements, during the decades which followed there continued to be a great deal of political turbulence in these countries, and much of this seems to have involved the further working out of their 'general crisis'.

There could be many ways in which the major events which followed could arguably be conceived. The principal suggestion to be offered here is that just as in the first half of the twentieth century significant popular forces in so many of these countries passed through a remarkably common sequence of developments, there came to be a further common sequence in the second half as well. Whilst the first half saw what we have termed the Gropings, the second saw a series of what we may call the Rectifications. These fell, moreover, into three successive phases, which we may call, respectively, the Renovations, the Second Starts, and the Conservative Outcomes (the last of which seems, as of this writing, in some instances at least, to have faced a 'Democratic Challenge'). As the detailed information which is readily available for the post-1950 decades is so much more abundant than for the pre-1950s period, the major occurrences here can be much more briefly outlined.

Upon the attainment of the Great Achievements, mainly in the late 1940s, the initial part of the first purpose generating the 'general crisis' in Monsoon Asia – the determination to expunge imperial rule – had very largely been secured. Clearly, however, a great deal remained to be done. There were still the dual concerns – to create modern nation states and establish more equitable and appropriate social orders – to be pursued. These pursuits were now to find a further range of expressions.

There was at the outset some general readiness to allow that once the Great Achievements had been attained there had to be a settling in period. In much less than a decade, however, a good number of influential people in quite a number of these countries began to feel that what had thus far been accomplished was still somehow unsatisfactory, inadequate, and far from comprehensive in effect.

The nature and extent of this prevailing sense of unease varied greatly, of course, both within and between different countries, and given the considerable variations in each case, it can readily be argued that no real commonalities can be discerned running through them. But there is a case to be offered on the other side as well. Despite all the striking differences, a plethora of contemporaneous attempts was made during the 1950s and 1960s by influential groups in all of these countries to try to put to rights what they saw to be the inadequacies of the developments that had ensued upon the Great Achievements.

There was to begin with a series of what we here call the Renovations.

The first of these seems to have been essayed in the Philippines by Ramon Magsaysay, when in the aftermath of his leadership of a successful campaign against the eventually communist-led and very substantial peasant-generated Huk Rebellion, he became president of the Philippines in 1953, and began to institute an extensive programme of land reforms. These were soon cut short by his death in 1957, but they probably constituted much the most substantial programme of land reforms which, for all the rhetoric employed by his successors, the Philippines has seen in this century.

In the meantime a second, and rather different, Renovation had taken place in 1956 in Ceylon, when S.W.R.D. Bandaranaike and his People's United Front won a dramatic victory at the polls over his former colleagues from 'Colombo 7' and their United National Party, who had at once masterminded and benefited from Ceylon's extraordinarily smooth progress towards independence just eight years previously. Bandaranaike's success clearly stemmed from his perception that independence on the terms the elitist politicians had blocked out was not what most of his countrymen wanted. They required a great deal more emphasis upon their country's Sinhalese and Buddhist character. A number of steps were accordingly taken to this end.

Two years later two more Renovations, of a still more different kind, were attempted in two other South Asian countries. In Pakistan in 1958 the military-bureaucratic elite finally clamped its hold upon what they saw as a disintegrating polity racked by squabbling politicians, when Ayub Khan proceeded to establish Pakistan's first military dictatorship. In that year

General Ne Win stepped in to hold the political centre in somewhat similar circumstances in Burma too.

These were the years as well of important changes in Indonesia. During the early and mid 1950s Indonesia had seen seven insubstantial coalition governments in just seven years (and a major revolt in Sumatra too). Accordingly, between 1957 and 1959, with the full support of both the army and the communists, President Suharto now gave himself full presidential powers, and instituted what he called his 'Guided Democracy'; a Renovation surely.

Meanwhile in China these were the climactic years of the CCP's rural collectivisation programme; the Hundred Flowers campaign; and Chairman Mao's 'Great Leap Forward'; a sustained attempt to improve upon the original Revolution of just a decade previously, and a clear attempt at Renovation too.

Whilst it happens that there was no such focussed set of developments in India, in the resolutions which Nehru moved in favour of a more socialistic pattern of society in India at the Avadi Congress in 1955 and then at the Nagpur Congress in 1959, and more particularly in his attempt to secure a crucial Seventeenth Amendment to the Constitution (so as to ensure the establishment of ceilings on land holdings), and in the institution of the Kamaraj Plan in 1963 (when a number of leading Congressmen were required to step down from their ministerial positions so as to revivify the party), one can readily discern the same sense of unease, and of a desire to effect a Renovation, which lay behind these other events elsewhere.

However, within a very short span of years there was not merely unease – more particularly in the more radical quarters in these countries – but open anxiety over the uncertain rate of progress towards a new and better order which seemed to be in train. For all their importance the Renovations of the late 1950s soon seemed to very many people to have been very insufficient. Something a great deal more extensive was now urgently required. As a consequence what had previously been bent so as to form a new shape was now frequently to be broken so as to create a substantial new order.

The characteristic examples of this second array – the Second Starts as they are called here – began, or so it would seem, in Burma, with Ne Win's second *coup d'état* in 1962, his assumption of state power, and his associated decision at that time to turn Burma into a militarily governed socialist state committed to 'the Burmese Way to Socialism'; a paradigm case, it would appear, of a Second Start.

There was then a still more striking case in Indonesia. There by the early 1960s the Partai Kommunis Indonesia (despite its second defeat during the late 1940s, following its first disasters in the late 1920s) had by peaceful means built up a very large following, and was clearly edging towards creating a Communist Second Start in Indonesia as soon as this could be achieved. To that end it was vigorously supporting Sukarno's *Konfrontasi* with the ex-imperial power Britain and its alleged accomplices in Malaysia – which greatly redounded to its advantage as compared to the more limited support for this of its chief rivals, the Indonesian army. The PKI embarked, moreover, on an aggressive campaign for a more equitable land redistribution scheme in the countryside. But they were then overtaken by a huge disaster. In 1965 there was a botched army coup by a leftist '30th September Movement'. This immediately provoked a counter coup by other and larger elements in the Indonesian army under General Suharto, who then seized the opportunity to destroy their foremost rivals. This produced a quite disastrous result for the PKI. For at the hands of an outraged army, along with numerous better-off Muslim peasants, half a million or so of the PKI's followers were massacred; and thereupon a Second Start of a very different sort was instituted in Indonesia. President Suharto, as he shortly became, pushed Sukarno to the wall, and established what he called a 'New Order' for Indonesia – of a distinctly rightist kind.

Meanwhile China had become embroiled in much the most momentous of all the Second Starts – Mao's Great Proletarian Cultural Revolution (GPCR); a tremendous new thrust towards creating some quite new orientations for Chinese society, even, for a time, at the cost of considerable damage to the principal girder of Mao's regime, the Chinese Communist Party itself. From the mid 1960s to the early 1970s this wracked and nearly overwhelmed Mao's China; it required the intervention of the PLA to bring it to a halt.

Yet this was by no means the unique occurrence that those whose concerns are with China only have tended to imply. For to begin with, by the late 1960s, the East Pakistanis had eventually united themselves against their subordination to West Pakistan, and thereafter via the trauma of an election, a bloody repression, a populist *hijrah* and uprising, and an Indian military invasion, eventually achieved in 1971 the Liberation of Bangladesh; a Second Start surely. As a consequence the military regime established in Pakistan in 1958 collapsed, to be replaced by a civilian regime under Prime Minister (later President) Z.A. Bhutto; a Second Start again.

Meanwhile in India the Congress had split in 1969, roughly along a right/left axis, after which Mrs Gandhi then proceeded to lead the winners into a decisive electoral victory in 1971 on the slogan of *Garibi Hatao* (Abolish Poverty): yet one more attempt, surely, at a Second Start. That year, 1971, Sri Lanka became embroiled, to most people's surprise, in a violent attempt to introduce a quite new order there as well, in the abortive uprising of the JVP (the Janata Vimukthi Peramuna, or People's Liberation Front). And then in 1972 the ever wily President Marcos finally cut across an obviously deteriorating situation in the Philippines to assume dictatorial powers, and catching the spirit of the times adventitiously proclaimed his 'New Society' in the Philippines.

For two or three years around the turn of that decade, it seemed possible (especially amid the wider fall-out from China's Great Proletarian Cultural Revolution) to imagine that *soi-disant* Maoist revolutions might well now be effected in several other parts of Asia too. Certainly the Naxalite uprisings in various parts of India were impelled at this time by this aim, as was the JVP in Sri Lanka. There were those, moreover, who hoped for, and those who feared, that such an outcome would erupt from the Bangladesh struggle. The moment, however, passed, and in South Asia no such change occurred.[9]

But it was soon to be very different in Indochina. There victory in the (third) Vietnam war finally went in 1975 to the communists, and shortly afterwards all of Laos, Cambodia and South Vietnam fell into their hands. The Vietnamese story does not readily stretch to the pattern outlined here (for reasons which have been suggested earlier). There the Great Achievement did not finally occur until 1975. Its concurrence, however, with the Second Starts arguably merged these stages there. Certainly the denouement followed a very similar course; and certainly too the quite horrendous case of the Pol Pot regime in Kampuchea gave some idea of what a quite unrestrained Second Start might entail.

It is interesting to note that following the Great Achievements, there was a certain convergence amongst the new Asian regimes, symbolised perhaps by the Bandung Conference of Non-Aligned Powers in 1955. However, to some extent following the Renovations, and certainly by the time of the Second Starts, that convergence had noticeably diminished – as the India–China war of 1962, the massacres of the Indonesian communists in 1965–6, and Marcos' campaign against the Philippines communists' New Peoples' Army, variously illustrated. As its 'general crisis' spun out its course, Monsoon Asia did not become anything like as united as had once appeared likely.

A close convergence did, however, mark the sequel, and in terms that were very different from any expected earlier. During the late 1960s (when not merely Monsoon Asia but large parts of western Europe and the United States were scored by millenarian outbursts in search of some great new ordering of society) it would have been very difficult to imagine in how short a while a further major Rectification would now have taken place in Monsoon Asia, and of a very different kind as well. Yet that is precisely what occurred. For in the mid-1970s the previously long-evolving revolutionary propensities in Monsoon Asia quite suddenly came to a halt, and were extensively succeeded by what we here call the Conservative Out-

[9] E.g. K. Gough and H.P. Sharma, *Imperialism and Revolution in South Asia*, New York, 1973.

comes. Why this should have happened needs probing further. At the level
of the analysis offered here it looks as if in the aftermath of the heady days of
the Second Starts, a large number of people in these countries came to one
bald conclusion – that a halt had to be called to the hitherto prevailing idea
that social redemption for their societies could only be achieved by some
great, ideologically propelled political upheaval, before irreparable damage
was done to them.[10]

The third Rectification probably had its beginnings in the core
experiences through which so many people had now lived. For three
quarters of a century almost all the most energetic leaders of these countries
had constantly played on the theme of the urgent necessity for a great new
thrust towards a future that would be altogether brighter and better. There
had been a good deal of warrant for what they had originally promised. New
and better futures (it could readily be allowed) had in many cases come to
pass. Yet once one had passed through one great *bouleversement*, then seen a
deliberate Renovation attempted, and then a Second Start made, the old
thesis began to pall, if the full millennium did not come, as in most cases it
did not. Significantly people now ceased to believe that one more change of
regime in Bangladesh, or one more purge of officials in the Philippines,
would make any real difference to the situations in their countries. Few
continued to dream that an armed uprising in India, or for that matter in
Indonesia, would in the near future bring into existence a radical, leftist
regime there. Nothing was more palpable, moreover, in India in 1974 and
1975 than the emptiness of the 'J.P.' movement's rhetoric. Jayaprakash
Narayan's talk (it was little more than that) of 'Total Revolution' lifted the
revolutionary decibels for very many people well out of their earshot.
Likewise in China in 1974–5 the anti-Confucius and anti-Lin Piao campaigns clearly represented very little more than a pale, half-hearted,
perhaps even desperate attempt to relive the heyday of the GPCR. Perhaps
those in 1976 who demonstrated in Tienanmen Square in the centre of
Peking on the death of Chou En-lai were making the now essential point.
Not only were they protesting at the denigration meted out to him
personally by the *fin de siècle* Maoist regime. They were apparently
determined to hammer home that they had had enough of its revolutionary
antics as well.

The death of Mao in 1976 shortly afterwards; the enthusiasm in China
which greeted the fall of his *soi-disant* radical successors, the Gang of Four;
and the ensuing early rehabilitation of their erstwhile adversary, Deng
Xiao-ping, quickly wrote *finis* to further revolutionary predilections in
China. Thereafter the Conservative Outcome followed there on an ever
widening scale. The 'Four Modernisations' came to be adopted; the

[10] Contemporary events in Monsoon Asia are most helpfully reported over the years in the *Far
Eastern Economic Review* published in Hong Kong.

Commune system was steadily abrogated – to be replaced by the 'responsibility' system; the surviving victims of the Cultural Revolution were ostentatiously rehabilitated; the hero-worshipping of Mao was brought to an end; and Deng Xiao-ping thereupon embarked upon his very pragmatic campaign to free China from its Maoist past.

Whilst, no doubt, the Chinese case was the most dramatic example of the mid-1970s switches to a Conservative Outcome, the striking fact is that, once again, it in no way stood upon its own. It looks indeed as if once more a widespread change of temper was now taking place in much of Monsoon Asia.

Already (intriguingly in an impassioned reaction to a threat to her personal position from Jayaprakash Narayan's impulsive rhetoric about 'Total Revolution') Mrs Gandhi in 1975 had proclaimed her Emergency in India. Whilst she was impelled to bring this to an end in 1977, and thereupon immediately lost the ensuing election,[11] two years later she was back in 1979 as India's domineering prime minister once again. But this time there was no further talk from her of *Garibi Hatao* or anything at all like it. The limp socialism of her father, and her own earlier flirtations with it, had been relegated to a now discarded past.

Elsewhere the Conservative Outcome was soon apparent too. There had once been a time, and not so long since either, when over-ardent observers had regularly implied that Presidents Marcos and Suharto, those two right-wing dictators who had so skilfully exploited the rhetoric of the Second Starts, would very soon be toppled. But Marcos soldiered on into the mid-1980s, and Suharto for two decades and more; while in Burma General Ne Win remained its long reigning president as well. No less strikingly, in 1975 Bangladesh's 'Father', Sheikh Abdur Rahman, was murdered in a military *coup*. Two *coups* later it looked as if a (Pakistani-like) military regime had effectively superimposed itself upon so many of the hopes of Bangladesh's Liberation of just half a decade previously. Then in 1977, the civilian President Bhutto found himself swept aside in Pakistan as well (and in due course arraigned on a murder charge and executed) by his country's third soldier-president, General Zia al-Huq. And in the following year, 1978, a Gaullist constitution was instituted in Sri Lanka, with an active head-of-state president, whereby any electoral opportunities for any leftist coalition were quite palpably curtailed.

Soon, indeed, across all of East, South, and South-east Asia, the Conservative Outcome was all but complete – surely a remarkable denouement to seven decades and more of long persistent strivings for some deep seated restructurings both of state and of society. Against it old-style revolutionaries, where they could be found at all, could do little more than shake their fists in vain.

[11] See ch. 6 below.

During the 1980s pragmatic, growth-oriented, often authoritarian, regimes prevailed right across the region. They were well represented both on the left and on the right. Deng Xiao-ping's regime in China maintained both its opposition to old style Maoism, and its commitment to its authoritarian ways. Over to the right, Suharto's regime in Indonesia continued on its course as well. In the Philippines the communists' New Peoples Army kept up its military action against the Philippines' elitist landlordist regime, but with little more success than for several decades past. In Sri Lanka in the late 1980s a resurgent JVP ran a terrorist campaign once again, but failed to check the democratic election of a new president and parliament.

The notable fact then is that where there were new stirrings they now displayed a quite different character from that expressed previously. No longer did they focus on some reordering of society. Nor did they challenge the non-revolutionary mood the Conservative Outcomes represented. Their principal concerns were – much more narrowly – to curb the excesses of authoritarian regimes, and champion democratic ones.

There was an early example of this in the Janata 'wave' against Mrs Gandhi in 1977, that was capped in 1979 when India's exasperated voters expelled her ill-composed successors. The new emphases became a great deal more widespread from the mid 1980s onwards. The main group of stirrings could variously be seen – and still more significantly, some governmental accommodation of them – even in two of the most staunchly authoritarian regimes in East Asia, South Korea and Taiwan. Under a variety of popular pressures in the former, a new military president, Roh, clearly decided to trim the authoritarian sails of his three ironhanded predecessors – Rhee, Park and Chun; while in the latter, Chaing Kai-shek's son and long-reigning successor spent some of his final years paving the way for a somewhat less dictatorial regime there. Likewise, the most recent of the military Presidents in Bangladesh, Ershad, evidently felt it would be wise to handle his (much divided) democratic opposition there with a good deal of circumspection. More strikingly, in 1986 Cory Aquino in the Philippines mobilised 'People Power' to topple President Marcos, and put herself in his place. Two years later, following President Zia's (unexplained) assassination in Pakistan, a similar populist convulsion swept Benazir Bhutto, daughter of the executed President Z.A. Bhutto, to the prime ministership of a, once again, Pakistani civilian government; while comparable propulsions lay behind the movement which that year nearly toppled the ageing Ne Win's regime in Burma. The new Democratic Challenge was most dramatically represented in the Pro-Democracy Movement in China which reached its peak in Beijing in May 1989. Elsewhere in those places where democratic elections persisted throughout these years – India, Sri Lanka and Malaysia – the authoritarian propensities their heads

of government periodically displayed generally seem to have been moder-
ated by this now widespread public mood. A bloody assault, however, was
used to suppress the Burmese movement, and in China the now essentially
gerentocratic regime first declared martial law, and then on 4 June 1989
sent an army corps with its tanks to crush the student demonstrators in
Tienanmen Square in an altogether barbarous manner. The Burmese and
Chinese repressions at the instance of the two octogenarians, Ne Win and
Deng Xiao-ping, alongside the more liberal developments elsewhere
pointed to yet one more period when the more general political complexion
of the Monsoon Asian region would once more be problematic.

All of which amounts to saying that in the first half of the twentieth
century, Monsoon Asia saw the largest and most widespread uprising
against the dominion of western imperial powers that the world had seen
before or since. Thereafter there were extensive attempts to work out some
more deep-seated revolutionary impulses to the full, so as to create much
more 'modern' political systems and much more equitably and efficiently
structured social orders. The first of these purposes called for many a long
year of sustained and valiant strivings; but was then for the most part quite
suddenly, and mightily, achieved. Thereafter the pursuit of the further
objectives that remained turned out to have a much more problematic
outcome; partly because as the prescriptions polarised and various ideological formulations came to be tried out, there was not only much
disputation, but not all that much result; but partly too because as people
wearied of the whole struggle several previously half-noticed phenomena
began to take on a greater prominence. The Green Revolution in agriculture turned not red, but greener yet. Asia, against the odds and so many
earlier prognostications, did not starve; it looked indeed as if it would now
feed itself. Furthermore, in the Asian 'Tigers' – Japan, Taiwan, South
Korea, Singapore, Hong Kong – there proved to be economic growth, of a
kind, to an extent, and at a rate, no one had expected, and the hope became
widespread that this could be repeated elsewhere. At other levels, strong
political and economic alliances between increasingly prosperous urban
and peasant elites were now extensively entrenched (and dictatorially and
ideologically oriented regimes were having increasingly to accommodate
themselves to them). Thus, from the perspective offered here – and there
are, of course, many others – Monsoon Asia's political concerns as the
twentieth century neared its end displayed few of the apocalyptic guises
they had previously avowed. As in the European general crisis of the
seventeenth century there was plenty to suggest that the continuing struggle
still lay between 'the country' and 'the court'. But the detailed agenda had
now been much transformed. The revolutionary impulses of an earlier date
had, it seemed, lost their potent thrust.

SELECT BIBLIOGRAPHY

Burma

J.F. Cady, *A Modern History of Burma*, Ithaca, 1958; U Maung Maung, *From Sangha to Laity. Nationalist Movement of Burma 1920–1940*, Canberra, 1980; R. Burwell, *U Nu of Burma*, Stanford, 1963; H. Tinker, *The Union of Burma: A Study of the First years of Independence*, London, 1961; R. Taylor, *The State in Burma*, London, 1987.

China

M.C Wright (ed.), *China in Revolution. The First Phase 1900–1913*, New Haven, 1968; L. Bianco, *Origins of the Chinese Revolution 1915–1959*, Stanford, 1971; E. Snow, *Red Star over China*, New York, 1938; J. Chen, *Mao and the Chinese Revolution*, London, 1965; J. Chesnaux, *Peasants' Revolts in China, 1840–1949*, London, 1973; J. Chesnaux, *China. The People's Republic 1949–1976*, London, 1979; C.A. Johnson, *Peasant Nationalism and Communist Power*, Stanford, 1962; M. Selden, *The Yenan Way in Revolutionary China*, Cambridge, Mass., 1971; B. Schwartz, *Chinese Communism and the Rise of Mao*, Cambridge, Mass., 1951; S.R. Schram, *Mao Tse-Tung*, Harmondsworth, 1966; C.P. Fitzgerald, *The Birth of Communist China*, Harmondsworth, 1964; S. Pepper, *Civil War in China. The Political Struggle 1945–1949*, Berkeley, 1978; R. Macfarlane, *The Origins of the Cultural Revolution*, 2 vols., London, 1974, 1983; T.W. Robinson (ed.), *The Cultural Revolution in China*, Berkeley, 1971; M. Meisner, *Mao's China*, New York, 1977;

India

S. Sarkar, *Modern India 1885–1947*, Delhi, 1983; J.M. Brown, *Modern India; the Origins of an Asian Democracy*, Oxford, 1984; J. Gallagher, G. Johnson and A. Seal (eds.), *Locality, Province and Nation. Essays on Indian Politics, 1870–1940*, Cambridge, 1973; B.R. Nanda, *Mahatma Gandhi*, London, 1958; S. Gopal, *Jawaharlal Nehru. A Biography*, 3 vols., London, 1975–84; R. Kumar (ed.), *Essays on Gandhian Politics. The Rowlatt Satyagraha of 1919*, Oxford, 1971; D.A. Low (ed.), *Soundings in Modern South Asian History*, London, 1968; D.A. Low (ed.), *Congress and the Raj. Facets of the Indian Struggle 1917–1947*, London, 1977; D.A. Low (ed.), *The Indian National Congress. Centenary Hindsights*, Delhi, 1988; R.J. Moore, *The Crisis of Indian Unity*, Oxford, 1974; R.J. Moore, *Escape from Empire*, Oxford, 1983; C.H. Philips and M.D. Wainwright (eds), *The Partition of India*, London, 1970; F. Frankel, *India's Political Economy 1947–77*, Princeton, 1978; H.C. Hart (ed.), *Indira Gandhi's India*, Boulder, 1976; M. Shepperson and C. Simmons (eds), *The Indian National Congress Party and the Political Economy of India 1885–1985*, Aldershot, 1988; R. Sisson and S. Wolpert (ed.), *Congress and Indian Nationalism*, Berkeley, 1988; J. Masselos (ed.), *Struggling and Ruling: The Indian National Congress 1885–1985*, New Delhi, 1987.

Indonesia

M.C. Ricklefs, *A History of Modern Indonesia*, London, 1981; C. Geertz, *Agricultural Involution*, Berkeley, 1963; R. van Neil, *The Emergence of the Modern Indonesian Elite*, The Hague, 1960; B.R.O'G. Anderson, *Java in a time of Revolution: Occupation and Resistance 1944–1946*, Ithaca, 1972; H.J. Benda, *The Crescent and the Rising Sun*, Bandung, 1958; B. Dahm, *Sukarno and the Struggle for Indonesian Independence*, Ithaca, 1969; J. Ingleson, *Road to Exile. The Indonesian Nationalist Movement, 1927–1934*, Canberra, 1979; G.McT. Kahin, *Nationalism and Revolution in Indonesia*, Ithaca, 1952; J.D. Legge, *Sukarno*, London, 1972; R. McVey, *The Rise of Indonesian Communism*, Ithaca, 1965; J.A.C. Mackie, *Konfrontasi. The Indonesia-Malaysia Dispute, 1963–66*, Kuala Lumpur, 1974; A.J.S. Reid, *The Indonesian National Revolution*, Hawthorn, 1974; R.J. McMahon, *Colonialism and Cold War. The United States and the Struggle for Indonesian Independence 1945–49*, Ithaca, 1981; H. Feith, *The Decline of Constitutional Democracy in Indonesia*, Ithaca, 1962; R. Mortimer, *Indonesian Communism under Sukarno*, Ithaca, 1974; H. Crouch, *The Army and Politics in Indonesia*, Ithaca, 1978; B. May, *The Indonesian Tragedy*, London, 1978.

Malaysia

L.Y. and B.W. Andaya, *A History of Malaysia*, London, 1982; R. Emerson, *Malaysia: A Study in Direct and Indirect Rule*, London, 1937; W.R. Roff, *The Origins of Malay Nationalism*, New Haven, 1967; Cheah Boon Kheng, *Red Star over Malaya*, Singapore, 1983; A.J. Stockwell, *British Politics and Malay Politics during the Malayan Union Experiment 1942–1948*, Kuala Lumpur, 1979; A. Short, *The Communist Insurrection in Malaya 1948–1960*, London, 1975.

Philippines

P.W. Stanley, *A Nation in the Making: The Philippines and the United States*, Cambridge, Mass., 1974; G.A. May, *Social Engineering in the Philippines*, London, 1980; R.C. Ileto, *Pasyon and Revolution*, Quezon City, 1979; T. Friend, *Between Two Empires: The Ordeal of the Philippines*, New Haven, 1965; U. Mahajani, *Philippines Nationalism*, St Lucia, 1971; D.J. Steinberg, *Philippine Collaboration in World War II*, Ann Arbor, 1967; D.R. Sturtevant, *Agrarian Unrest in the Philippines*, Ohio, 1969; D.R. Sturtevant, *Popular Uprisings in the Philippines, 1840–1940*, Ithaca, 1976; B.J. Kerkvliet, *The Huk Rebellion*, Berkeley, 1977; F.L. Starmer, *Magsaysay and the Philippine Peasantry*, Berkeley, 1961; D. Rosenberg (ed.), *Marcos and Martial Law in the Philippines*, Ithaca, 1979; M. Turner (ed.), *Regime Change in the Philippines. The Legitimation of the Aquino Government*, Canberra, 1987.

Sri Lanka (Ceylon)

K.M. de Silva, *A History of Sri Lanka*, Berkeley, 1981; W.H. Wriggins, *Dilemmas of a New Nation*, Princeton, 1960; A.J. Wilson, *Politics in Sri Lanka 1947–1979*, London, 1979; J. Manor (ed.), *Sri Lanka in Change and Crisis*, London, 1984; J. Manor, *The Expedient Utopian. Bandavanaike and Ceylon*, Cambridge 1989.

Vietnam

J. Buttinger, *Vietnam. A Dragon Embattled*, 2 vols., New York, 1967; S. Karnouw, *Vietnam. A History, New York*, 1903, W.J. Duiker, *The Rise of Nationalism in Vietnam, 1900–1941*, Ithaca, 1976; W.J. Duiker, *The Communist Road to Power in Vietnam*, Boulder, 1981; D.G. Marr, *Vietnamese Anticolonialism, 1885–1925*, Berkeley, 1971; D.G. Marr, *Vietnamese Tradition on Trial*; J. Lacouture, *Ho Chi Minh: A Political Biography*, New York, 1968; E.J. Hammer, *The Struggle for Indochina, 1940–1955*, Stanford, 1954; J.T. McAlister, *Vietnam. The Origins of Revolution*, New York, 1970; A.B. Woodside, *Community and Revolution in Modern Vietnam*, Boston, 1976; B.B. Fall, *Streets Without Joy. Insurgency in Vietnam 1946–1963*, Harrisberg, 1963; F. Fitzgerald, *Fire in the Lake*, Boston, 1972.

3

India and Britain: the climactic years 1917–1947

In 1936 Rajendra Prasad, president that year of the Indian National Congress, remarked that

from being at one time an organisation of a small number of persons educated in schools and colleges [Congress] has now become the largest organisation of the common people drawn very largely from the village population and counting amongst its members lakhs of peasants and cultivators and a sprinkling of industrial and field workers.[1]

From an early date the Indian National Congress was supported by a small number of individuals drawn from a wide spectrum of Indian communities.[2] It was only in the decades following the First World War that it won substantial rural support. In the early 1930s Congress and British sources seemed to agree that 'the Congress standing army is at most one lac' (100,000);[3] and although in 1936 Prasad was writing 'lakhs' in the plural, he still did not claim 'millions' or 'crores' (10,000,000). He drew a clear distinction, moreover, between 'peasants and cultivators' on the one hand, and 'industrial and field workers' on the other. The main support for Congress, he asserted, came from the former.

In the course of some lectures in Patna in 1971, Professor Nurul Hasan compared the structure of mediaeval India to a pyramid, with the emperor at the apex, below him the 'chieftains', and below them the 'intermediaries'. Then, at the base, superimposed upon a 'considerable body of agricultural labourers', were those he called 'primary zamindars'. These, he said,

---

[1] Prasad's draft for Mass Contacts Committee's report, 1936, Prasad P. IX. 36.4. Nehru Memorial Museum & Library, AICC papers G30(a) 1937.
[2] Dr Gopal Krishna emphasised this point in conversation.
[3] Sri Prakash to Sita Ram, 20 May 1933, Sita Ram P. 29(106); Williamson's note, 16 Feb. 1934, National Archives of India, Home Department (hereafter H) Poll 4/4/34.

were for all practicable purposes the holders of proprietary rights over agricultural as well as habitational lands. In this class may be included not only the peasant proprietors who carried on cultivation themselves or with the help of hired labour, but also the proprietors of one or several villages. All agricultural lands in the empire belonged to one or the other type of primary zamindar. The rights held by the primary zamindar were hereditary and alienable. . . . The Mughal state considered it its duty to protect the rights of these zamindars.[4]

Given the vastness of India, every such generalisation requires detailed qualification as to time and place. It has nevertheless been deliberately affirmed by Professor Béteille that 'the Indian village is often highly differentiated and generally stratified',[5] and in the present context it is of considerable importance that, despite innumerable variations, Professor Hasan's 'primary zamindars' seem broadly to correlate with those whom British administrators have called 'the village brotherhood', anthropologists 'the dominant caste', economists 'rich peasants', some political scientists 'elite proprietary castes' (others, variously, 'kulaks', 'rural middle class', 'jotedars', 'maliks', 'dominant rural strata', etc.).[6] They seem to correlate too with those whom Rajendra Prasad specified as 'peasants'. Here they will be called 'dominant peasants'. It is clear that they have persisted in many parts of India over the last several centuries[7] and that by various methods of 'patronage and exploitation'[8] they have dominated the lives of the poorer peasants in the half million villages in which most Indians have lived. It is increasingly clear too that at the core of the conflict between the Indian National Congress and the British Raj in India in the 1920s and 1930s, there raged a battle for their political allegiance.

Professor Hasan's picture of a multi-layered society is reminiscent of Professor Cohn's well-known account of the several levels in the body politic of the Banaras region in northern India in the eighteenth century, and with Professor Shah's of Gujarat in western India at the same time.[9] It looks, moreover, as if the British conquests did not much alter these

[4] Saiyid Nurul Hasan, *Thoughts on Agrarian Relations in Mughal India*, (New Delhi, 1973, pp. 30–1.
[5] André Béteille, *Six Essays in Comparative Sociology*, Delhi, 1974, p. 49.
[6] The literature on modern India abounds with such references.
[7] E.g. Bernard S. Cohn, 'Structural Change in Indian Rural Society', and Burton Stein, 'Integration of the Agrarian System of South India', in R.E. Frykenberg (ed.), *Land Control and Social Structure in Indian History*, Madison, 1969; Rajat and Rathna Ray, 'Zamindars and Jotedars: A Study of Rural Politics in Bengal', in *Modern Asian Studies*, 9 no. 1 (Feb. 1975), 81–102; D.A. Washbrook, 'Country Politics: Madras 1880–1920', in John Gallagher, Gordon Johnson and Anil Seal (eds.), *Locality, Province and Nation. Essays on Indian Politics 1870–1940*, Cambridge, 1973.
[8] See the admirable study of some south Gujarat villages by Jan Bremen under this title, (Berkeley, 1974). See also A.C. Mayer, *Caste and Kinship in Central India*, London, 1960; André Béteille, *Caste, Class and Power*, Berkeley, 1965, etc.
[9] Bernard S. Cohn, 'Political Systems in Eighteenth Century India: The Banaras Region', in *Journal of the American Oriental Society*, 23 no. 3 (July–Sept. 1962), 312–20; A.M. Shah, 'Political System in Eighteenth Century Gujarat', in *Enquiry*, 1 no. 1 (Spring 1964), 83–95.

Map 2   India before 1947

structures. For the most part they merely involved the supersession of traditional Indian rulers who held power at their upper levels by alien British bureaucrats. The new rulers were ranked in a new hierarchy of viceroy and governor-general at the apex; governors, lieutenant-governors and chief commissioners at the next level down; with, below them, several successive layers of commissioners of divisions, district magistrates, collectors, etc.[10] In the past, the links between these various levels had frequently been tenuous. During the British period those at the upper levels were greatly strengthened. But underneath the old weaknesses persisted, and throughout their time the British were perennially haunted by anxieties over their connections, not so much with their innumerable Indian subordinates, but, more particularly, with the dominant peasants in the

[10] Philip Woodruff, *The Men who Ruled India*, 2 vols., London, 1954.

countryside beyond.[11] It is a prime feature of the present account that the major decision the British ultimately made to begin to bring these people within their new electoral politics following the First World War entailed in the upshot the supersession of the British Raj in India by what was appositely called Congress Raj.

In 'British India' the British tended at first to thrust aside those whom Professor Hasan called the 'chieftains'. They frequently retained, however, those he called the 'intermediaries'. Though there were great regional variations, these evolved into the landlords of British India, who, together with the dominant peasants, became the chief elements to whom the British looked to maintain an ordered society under their rule. The main day-to-day British administrative effort was always expended indeed upon the highly complex land revenue administrations through which these connections were nurtured and elaborated.[12]

As, however, in the latter half of the nineteenth century the British became increasingly conscious of the fragility of their dominion, they set about welding into the middle and upper levels of the Raj a series of additional supports which were to be characteristic of it until well into the twentieth century. For a start – to a degree they had not done previously – they cultivated the 'chieftains' who remained, the Indian princes. These came to be honoured as key figures at imperial durbars,[13] and the views of the ablest of them were treated with considerable deference. When, later, in the twentieth century, national agitations erupted, strenuous efforts were made to keep these princes loyal. In 1909 Sir Harcourt Butler's policy of *laissez faire*, which involved the reduction of some of the previous curbs upon their independence, was officially adopted.[14] In the 1920s the more important princes were cobbled into a Chamber of Princes, and then stitched into a blocking third of conservative votes in the Federation proposals of the 1930s.[15]

The ultimate bulwark of the Raj which the British exercised in India was

[11] This subsumed their perennial concern for the levels of peasants' rents, their indebtedness to money lenders, and the alienation of their lands, which led to such legislation as the Deccan Agriculturalists Relief Act of 1879, the Punjab Land Alienation Act of 1900, and a whole series of Rent Acts.

[12] Major studies include Elizabeth Whitcombe, *Agrarian Conditions in Northern India*, Berkeley, 1972, and P.H.M. van den Dungen, *The Punjab Tradition*, London, 1972.

[13] J.C. Masselos, 'Lytton's "Great Tamasha" and Indian Unity', in *Journal of Indian History*, 44 no. 3 (Dec. 1966), 737–60.

[14] Butler to his mother, 15 Dec. 1909. 27 Jan. 1910, Butler P. 7; Butler's handing over report, 15 Nov. 1910, Butler P. G7; Minto's Udaipur speech, 1 Nov. 1909, Lady Minto, *India, Minto and Morley 1905–10*, London, 1934, pp. 342–5; D.A. Low, '*Laisser Faire* and Traditional Rulership in Princely India', in R. Jeffrey (ed.), *People, Princes and Paramount Power. Society and Politics in the Indian Princely States*, Delhi, 1978, pp. 372–88.

[15] R.J. Moore, *The Crisis of Indian Unity*, Oxford, 1974, *passim*; B. Ramusack, *The Princes of India in the Twilight of Empire. Dissolution of a Patron–Client System, 1914–1939*, Columbus, Ohio, 1978; S.R. Ashton, *British Policy towards the Indian States*, London, 1982.

always, however, the 'Army in India'. Following Kitchener's reforms in the
first decade of the twentieth century, this was divided into the field army
(for war beyond the frontiers); covering troops (for operations on the
frontier); and internal security forces. By 1925 the whole was found by
57,000 British troops, and an Indian Army of 140,000.[16] The internal
security forces (which were calculated in terms of what would be required
to hold India for the British during any absence by the field army)
comprised by the 1920s twenty-two of the hundred established Indian
infantry battalions, along with twenty-eight battalions of British infantry,
and some cavalry, artillery and armoured car units. These were stationed so
as to guard essential communications, protect scattered European communities, and overawe turbulent cities and towns. (It is some indication of their
role that the Bombay Government should have protested successfully in
1927 at the proposed removal of one of the two battalions at Santa Cruz
where they were located within three miles of the Bombay mill area.)[17]
After 1923 the British always had an agreed Martial Law Ordinance in
draft. On a number of occasions martial law was in fact declared (for
example, in Sholapur in 1931).[18] Military forces, moreover, were quite
frequently called out 'in aid of the civil power', particularly to suppress
communal disturbances.[19]

Yet, in the wake of the Jallianwallah Bagh massacre in 1919, the British
were very reluctant to use the army to suppress nationalist agitations, and
particularly reluctant to impose martial law on a widespread scale. Their
prime arm came to be the police, some of whom had firearms, most of
whom were trained to wield lathis and batons. In the 1930s there were
200,000 police in British India, 33,000 of them in the United Provinces, the
majority of them under British officers.[20] All over India, moreover, there
was provision for 'Additional Police' to be posted upon 'recalcitrant'
communities at their own cost.[21] When in 1931 the world slump reached
India, the only official salaries which did not suffer a 10 per cent cut were
those of ordinary policemen. Since concurrently there was a price fall, this
amounted to a wage rise. No wonder – it was the time of the Civil
Disobedience Movement – police recruitment had never been better.[22]

[16] V. Longer, *Red Coats to Olive Green*, Bombay, 1974, pp. 179, 187; Philip Mason, *A Matter of Honour*, London, 1974, p. 456.
[17] H. Poll 79/30; Indian battalions had 766 officers and men, British battalions about 150 more, Longer, *Red Coats*, pp. 188–9.
[18] H. Poll 376–24, 209/31.   [19] E.g. Mitra's note, 3 Nov. 1928, H. Poll 79/30.
[20] Irwin to Police Conference, 19 Jan. 1931, H. Poll 152/31; IGP, UP, 3 Sept. 1930, H. Poll 259/30; Sir Percival Griffiths, *To Guard My People. The History of the Indian Police*, London, 1971, especially appendix 2.
[21] E.g. H. Poll 33/31.
[22] H. Police 106/I/32, especially report of Viceroy's meeting with Indian Police Association, 11 June 1932, 58/IV/32. See more generally D. Arnold, *Police Power and Colonial Rule. Madras 1859–1947*, Delhi, 1986.

For the ordinary administration of the country the British chiefly relied, however, upon the Indian members of the subordinate bureaucratic 'Provincial Services'. Many of these were drawn from local landed families and/or elitist 'service' communities which had served traditional rulers in this capacity in the past. Particularly as extra assistant commissioners, deputy collectors, tehsildars, mamlatdars, talukdars, etc., they provided the critical link between the alien British superstructure and the landlords and dominant peasants in the countryside.[23] Such men had their heyday during the British period since the curbs upon them at that time were by no means always effective.[24]

The British realised, however, that (for all their own passion for data collecting) the information about Indian attitudes and desires which flowed up these bureaucratic channels, and the public connections which their Indian subordinates formed, were inadequate for the purpose of securing their imperial rule.[25] As a consequence they developed the practice of what may be called 'neo-darbari' politics.[26] This involved a multiplicity of initiatives to associate non-official Indian 'notables' with the workings of the higher levels of the Raj so as to extend the linkages through which Indian society could be controlled. This entailed at one end an elaborate system of honours and titles;[27] at another the practice of arranging periodic interviews between British officials and 'leading Indian gentlemen'.[28] More systematically, it led, from Frere's minute in 1860 onwards, to the appointment of 'prominent' Indians to the imperial and provincial legislatures,[29] and to such institutions as the new university senates. (In the 1930s this culminated in the appointment of British-chosen Indian 'leaders' to the Round Table Conferences in London.) It led too to the introduction on narrow franchises of elected municipal and district and sub-district boards.[30]

Yet this was only the half of it. For in the vacuum left by the widespread

---

[23] Z. Islam and R.L. Jenssen, 'Indian Muslims and the Public Service 1871–1915', in *Journal of the Asiatic Society of Pakistan*, 9 no. 1 (1964), 85–148; Patricia A. Thompson, 'The Provincial Service in the Punjab in the late Nineteenth Century', MA dissertation, University of Sussex, 1968.

[24] E.g. R.E. Frykenberg, *Guntur District 1788–1848*, Oxford, 1965.

[25] Dr Benedikte Hjejle has made this point in conversation.

[26] '. . . the Provincial Advisory Council . . . comes as near as present times admit to associating the spirit of the Durbar system with the circumstances of our methods of rule', Adamson's note, 2 Aug. 1908 on Meed to Adamson, 27 July 1908, H. Public 156–165B Oct. 1908.

[27] Bernard S. Cohn, 'Representing Antiquity in Victorian India', in his *An Anthropologist among the Historians and Other Essays*, Delhi, 1987, pp. 632–82.

[28] E.g. Alexander–Sita Ram correspondence 1919, Sita Ram P. 29; Fremantle to Sita Ram, 30 Oct. 1920, *ibid.* 28/9.

[29] Minute of 16 Mar. 1960, H. Public, 31 Jan. 1861, No. 76; and see Thomas R. Metcalf, *The Aftermath of Revolt, 1857–70*, Princeton, 1964, ch. 7.

[30] Hugh Tinker, *The Foundations of Local Self-Government in India, Pakistan and Burma*, London, 1954.

destruction in British India of traditional rulerships, various tendencies converged by the end of the nineteenth century to foster the creation of some quite new corporate entities based upon class, community, and interest. The most illuminating example of this widespread process comes from the princely state of Travancore, where, in the eighteenth century, the conquering Maharajah, Martanda Varma had disposed of most of the local chieftains. A century and half later – following the extensive spread both of literacy and of new communications – statewide communal organisations burgeoned, the most famous being the SNDP Yogam, and the Nair Service Society.[31] Such developments did not proceed with quite the same speed and comprehensiveness in the always much less literate British India; but by the beginning of the twentieth century there were many new associations of this kind, such as all those which tried to see Montagu, the British Secretary of State for India in 1918,[32] or hammered on the doors of the All-Parties Convention in Calcutta a decade later.[33] Many of these were artificial and insubstantial bodies; most were contrived. Perhaps the most fateful example of this whole process, and of its ready legitimation by the British Raj, occurred in 1906 when the viceroy, Lord Minto, received the famous deputation that claimed to represent 'the Mahomedan community' of India, and promptly conceded to it the most extreme form of communal voting – separate electorates.[34] Along with the involvement of individual 'notables', neo-darbari politics rested indeed quite explicitly upon the incorporation into the formal and workaday structure of the Raj of *soi-disant* spokesmen of such 'classes and interests'.[35] (Even in the 1940s British viceroys still painfully allocated the seats in their Executive Councils amongst the highly artificial, or quite minute, categories of 'Caste Hindus', 'Muslims', 'Scheduled Castes', 'Sikhs', 'Europeans', 'Christians', and 'Parsis'.)[36] From an early date these new aggregations were not, of course, confined to religious categories. They included landlord and commercial associations, and such 'public bodies'[37] as the Indian Associations (in Calcutta and Lahore), the Bombay Presidency Association, the Poona

---

[31] Eric Miller, 'Caste and Territory in Malabar', *American Anthropologist*, 56 no. 3 (June 1954), 410–20; Robin Jeffrey, 'The Social Origins of a Caste Association, 1875–1905: the Founding of the S.N.D.P. Yogam', in *South Asia*, 4 (Oct. 1974), pp. 39–59; Robin Jeffrey, *The Decline of Nayar Dominance, Society and Politics in Travancore, 1847–1908*, London, 1976.

[32] Anil Seal makes the point in his 'Imperialism and Nationalism in India', in *Locality, Province and Nation*, pp. 19–21.

[33] AICC API 1928.

[34] M.N. Das, *India under Morley and Minto*, London, 1964, ch. 5, b; Syed Razi Wasti, *Lord Minto and the Indian Nationalist Movement 1905 to 1910* (Oxford, 1964), ch. 5; Stanley A. Wolpert, *Morley and India 1906–1910*, Berkeley, 1967, ch. 8.

[35] E.g. Minto to Lawley, 15 June 1908, H. Public 116–146A Oct. 1908; Meston to Wheeler, 1 Jan. 1913, Meston P.3; Craddock to Meston, 30 Aug. 1916, *ibid.* 4.

[36] P.N.S. Mansergh, *India, The Transfer of Power*, vol. 3, London, 1971, *passim*.

[37] J.C. Masselos, *Towards Nationalism*, Bombay, 1974.

Sarvajanik Sabha, and the Madras Mahajana Sabha. It was men from these quarters that in 1885 came together to create the Indian National Congress – the association of the intelligentsia, and the apical construct of this whole development.[38]

In so many respects Congress at first, like so many of its lesser contemporaries, accepted the political structure of the Raj as by the end of the 19th century the British had fashioned it. Not only did its leaders frequently avow their 'loyalty'.[39] They ran a protracted campaign, not to destroy the mainly British-occupied Indian Civil Service, but to secure increased Indian access to it.[40]

It was, even so, the Indian National Congress – rather than, say, the army, or the princes, or large numbers of dominant peasants – which led the way in breaking loose from its allegiance to the framework the British had constructed. At first its leaders dared little more than declare that British rule was 'un-British' in character.[41] In due course, however, a radical critique of the British exploitation of India began to be advanced,[42] which was soon reinforced by more strictly political concerns. In particular, Congress supporters in Bengal, Maharashtra, and the Punjab became affronted by the campaigns of the Viceroy, Lord Curzon – against the Municipality and University in Calcutta;[43] against Tilak and his supporters in Poona;[44] against local 'non-agricultural castes' by the Punjab Land Alienation Act of 1900.[45] The key break came in 1905 in reaction to Curzon's partition of Bengal, and in Dadabhai Naoroji's declaration in his presidential address to the Calcutta Congress in 1906 that the ultimate objective of the Indian National Congress was now *Swaraj* (self rule).[46]

Many of the details of the ensuing story have been recounted elsewhere, and need not detain us. In 1906 the ultimately highly important All-India Muslim League was formed.[47] Nationalist agitations were at first confined, however, to particular provinces, and to minorities within them;[48] and in 1907 Congress split along a Moderate–Extremist divide that was fomented

[38] Anil Seal, *The Emergence of Indian Nationalism*, Cambridge, 1968; S.R. Mehrotra, *The Emergence of the Indian National Congress*, Delhi, 1971; R. Suntharalingam, *Politics and Nationalist Awakening in South India, 1852–91*, Tucson, 1974.
[39] E.g. Khaparde's speech to the Central Provinces and Berar Provincial Conference, April 1905, H. Public 217–227A, Oct. 1906.
[40] B. Pattabhi Sitaramayya, *History of the Indian National Congress*, vol. I, Delhi, 1935, pp. 30–2.
[41] Dababhai Naoroji, *Poverty and Un-British Rule in India*, London, 1901.
[42] B. Chandra, *The Rise and Growth of Economic Nationalism in India. Economic Policies of Indian National Leadership, 1880–1905*, New Delhi, 1966.
[43] Christine P. Furedy, 'Municipal Politics in Calcutta: Elite Groups and the Calcutta Corporation, 1874–1900', DPhil thesis, University of Sussex, 1970.
[44] Stanley A. Wolpert, *Tilak and Gokhale*, Berkeley, 1962.
[45] Norman G. Barrier, *The Punjab Alienation of Land Bill of 1960*, Durham, 1966.
[46] R.P. Masani, *Dababhai Naoroji*, London, 1939, ch. 33.
[47] Das, *India under Morley and Minto*; Wasti, *Lord Minto*, ch. 2.
[48] D.A. Low (ed.), *Soundings in Modern South Asian History*, London, 1968, Introduction.

by a factional dispute in Bombay.[49] Because during the next ten years the
Moderates held control of Congress, and the British somewhat enlarged
their neo-darbari system with the Morley–Minto reforms of 1909 (which for
the first time conceded unambiguous, if still limited, provincial elections),[50] Congress became a tame affair. Eventually, however, in 1916,
Moderates and Extremists joined hands once again, and even effected the
memorable Lucknow Pact on communal representation with the Muslim
League.[51] By this time 'Home Rule Leagues' of a more vociferous kind
were showing how agitations in different provinces could be linked up with
each other;[52] and when eventually in 1919–20 Congress fell under Gandhi's
sway, he soon showed how the Khilafat and Punjab 'wrongs' could be
turned into all-India 'wrongs', in a way the Bengal partition had never quite
been.[53]

Accounts of Gandhi's practice of satyagraha, and the manner in which this
became the chief *modus operandi* of the Congress are readily available
elsewhere.[54] Recent discussions have illuminated the manner in which the
extension of government activity from the late nineteenth century onwards
had disrupted local patterns of power and interest, made the Raj more
obtrusive and disliked, provided new issues and arenas for the ambitious to
fight over, and started to link up provincial centres and peripheries as never
before.[55] They have also shown how the dominance of British Managing
Agencies based upon Calcutta had by the turn of the century gone far to
crush the economic life out of the landholding classes of eastern India, and
thus fuelled the vehemence of Bengal nationalist politics;[56] because in some
respects this vehemence was premature, it fell over its own heels in the
1920s to the galling frustration of several generations of its participants.[57]
Here, however, we shall dwell upon some rather different aspects of the
ensuing struggle, and in the first place upon the intriguing similarities
between the three major phases of nationalist agitation against British rule

---

49 Gordon Johnson, *Provincial Politics and Indian Nationalism. Bombay and the Indian
  National Congress 1880 to 1915*, Cambridge, 1973, ch. 4.
50 Das, *India under Morley and Minto*; Wasti, *Lord Minto*; Wolpert, *Morley and India*.
51 Hugh F. Owen, 'Negotiating the Lucknow Pact', in *Journal of Asian Studies*, 21 no. 3 (May
  1972), 561–87,
52 H.F. Owen, 'Towards Nationwide Agitation and Organisation: the Home Rule Leagues,
  1915–18', in Low (ed.), *Soundings*, pp. 159–95.
53 Judith M. Brown, *Gandhi's Rise to Power, Indian Politics 1915–1922*, Cambridge, 1972.
54 Brown, *Gandhi's Rise to Power*; Joan V. Bondurant, *Conquest of Violence*, Princeton, 1958.
55 Gallagher, Johnson and Seal, *Locality, Province and Nation*; C.J. Baker and D.A.
  Washbrook, *South India. Political Institutions and Political Change 1880–1940*, Delhi, 1975;
  C.A. Bayly, *The Local Roots of Indian Politics. Allahabad 1880–1920*, Oxford, 1975.
56 E.g. Rajat K. Ray, 'The Crisis of Bengal Agriculture, 1870–1927 – the Dynamics of
  Immobility', *Indian Economic and Social History Review*, 10 no. 3 (1973), 244–79.
57 J.H. Broomfield, *Elite Conflict in a Plural Society: Twentieth Century Bengal*, Berkeley,
  1968.

in India through which Gandhi led the great Indian national movement in the years that followed. The first of these ran from about 1917 to 1923; the second from 1927 to 1934; the third from 1939 to 1946.[58]

Each began with a fairly protracted agitational run-up, especially propelled on each occasion by some great affront to Indian feelings: in the first case by a combination of Annie Besant's internment in 1917[59] and the Rowlatt Bills of 1919; in the second, by the appointment of the 'all-white' Simon Commission in 1927 to determine India's future over India's head; in the third by the Viceroy Lord Linlithgow's declaration in 1939 that India was at war before any Indian public body had even been consulted. In each instance there was then a first Gandhi-led agitational campaign: on the first occasion the Rowlatt satyagraha of 1919; on the second the first Civil Disobedience campaign (the so-called salt satyagraha) of 1930; on the third the 'individual' satyagraha campaign of 1940–1.

Thereafter there followed upon each occasion a striking mid-course break, when important figures in the leadership of the movement all but made a settlement with the British. During the first period, Gandhi proposed at the Amritsar Congresss in December 1919 that Congress should accept, and not boycott, the new Legislative Councils which were being established by the British under the Montagu–Chelmsford reforms; during the second he himself in March 1931 concluded the memorable Gandhi–Irwin Pact; while the third time around, in March 1942, two of his closest associates, Maulana Azad and Jawaharlal Nehru, came within an ace of reaching a settlement with the British minister, Sir Stafford Cripps.

Yet every time these attempts at some mid-course settlement (which on the Congress side all entailed attempts to hold the movement back) were swept aside by a profound undertow of unfulfilled expectations which then erupted in a second agitational campaign: on the first occasion, in the Non-Co-operation movement of 1920–2; on the second, in the renewed Civil Disobedience movement of 1931–2; on the third, in the 'Quit India' campaign of 1942.

Thereafter three developments occurred concurrently. In the first place, when these second campaigns had broken, or – as on the second and third occasions – been broken by the British, there was no third campaign: agitational propensities seemed to have become exhausted. At this point Gandhi was careful to dramatise his own moral authority so as to prevent the integrity of his movement from breaking asunder: he did this in 1922 by the speech at this trial; in 1932–4 by the Poona Pact and his Harijan

---

[58] This section is at once a digest and an elaboration of D.A. Low, *Lion Rampant. Essays in the Study of British Imperialism*, London, 1973, pp. 153–72. The easiest general introduction to the period is now S. Sarkar, *Modern India 1885–1947*, 2nd ed., London 1989.

[59] E.g. Meston to Chelmsford, 20 June 1917, H. Poll 86–106A, Aug. 1917.

campaign; in 1943 by his 'epic' fast.[60] On each occasion there was at the same time a highly significant move towards 'Council entry' – towards, that is, participation in the legislatures, and later the executives, which the British were cautiously instituting. This process was clearly at work – in 1923, in 1934, and in 1945.[61]

Caution is obviously required in adhering too closely to this analysis. It takes no account, for example, of the differences in the concurrence of each phase with a world war, with the absence of war, and with the immediate aftermath of war (to read the sequence backwards); equally the first phase displayed less adherence to the pattern than the later ones. It nevertheless serves to underline not only the switchback quality of the protracted encounter between the Indian national movement and the British, but also the fact that the Congress leaders were rarely at a loss about what to do next.[62] They played upon the two themes of agitation and Council entry alternatively, and thus successfully maintained themselves in the public eye throughout. It should be emphasised, moreover, that both themes became part of the national movement's legacy, to an extent, particularly as regards 'Council entry, that has never quite been sufficiently allowed.

Seen in this sequence the probable importance of economic influences can be readily signalised. The first agitational phase was fairly certainly propelled by the great price rise that accompanied the ending of the First World War and the subsequent price collapse; the second was clearly boosted by the price fall that marked the onset of the world slump; the third was impelled by wartime shortages, and more especially by a particularly sharp price rise in the summer of 1942. The differential impact of these reverses has still to be spelt out, but on each occasion many from a variety of strata were afflicted.

There can be little doubt that the third time round many of those involved in the encounter appreciated its likely dynamics. There was, for example, a clearly ritualistic quality to the individual satyagraha campaign of 1940–1; Gandhi no longer banked on the British making a settlement with him (as in the light of his original South African experience,[63] he had done ten years earlier); while his awareness that the British had only to put into operation the measures they had successfully taken against the renewed Civil Disobedience campaign in 1931–2, seems to have made him hesitate to embark upon a further mass satyagraha in 1940. But it looks too as if in 1942, in the light of the fate of his 1931 Pact with Irwin, he realised that the

---

60 Francis Watson, *The Trial of Mr Gandhi*, London, 1969; ch. 4 below; Mansergh, *Transfer of Power, 1942–47*, vol. 3.
61 The process only became full blown in 1926, 1937 and 1946.
62 E.g. Gandhi was talking in April 1937 of the next satyagraha. Notes of Working Committee 26–8 April 1937, AICC Misc. 42 1936 [sic.]. There was, of course, often protracted argument on such occasions.
63 W.K. Hancock, *Four Studies in War and Peace*, Cambridge, 1961, ch. 3.

settlement which Cripps had come to India to offer could not be sustained, and that because of the relative tameness of the already curtailed individual satyagraha campaign of 1940–1, the almost certain renewal of agitation, which came later in 1942, would probably lead to the greatest outburst ever.

Others were learning as well. Some understood that a dramatic collapse of the British position would not come about easily, and that the mere repetition of a previous campaign could very well be costly. Others calculated on the other hand, that if anything tangible was to be achieved, the previous campaigns would have to be substantially outdone: mass violence could not therefore be any longer eschewed.[64] The British were also learning. During the first phase their response had been conditioned by their concern to uphold the allegiance of the Indian Moderates;[65] in the second they were chiefly preoccupied with the 'loyalty' of their subordinate Indian police and bureaucracy (some of whom had given them cause for concern in 1919–22).[66] On both these occasions their stance proved sufficient. But they were then caught out, both in 1940 when the agitation was much milder, and in 1942 when it was far greater than they had anticipated. Yet towards the end the implication was clear. As their use of well over fifty battalions of troops against the 'Quit India' movement of 1942 illustrated, at moments of crisis they were being steadily pushed back upon their ultimate, military, bulwark.[67]

Their initial response to the successive Gandhi-led campaigns had, however, been to promulgate declarations of policy on future constitutional reforms, and if one plots the moments when these were issued the results are striking. The British made their declarations of future constitutional intent, either before the first agitational campaigns had begun, or at those very significant mid-course breaks. This is true, under the first head, for the Montagu declaration of 1917, the Irwin declaration of 1929, and the August offer of 1940; and under the second, for the decision to implement the Montagu–Chelmsford reforms in 1919, the Macdonald 'responsibility-at-the-centre' statement of 1931, and the Cripps offer of 1942. It is interesting that the first declarations were all initiated by the Government of India. From the start, however, every one of them was damaged by its treatment in London. (Because of the wartime crisis, the 1917 declaration was dangerously delayed in the British War Cabinet. In 1929 there was an extremely

---

[64] Francis G. Hutchins, *India's Revolution, Gandhi and the Quit India Movement*, Cambridge, Mass., 1973, records some of the details; for an interesting insight, see Apa Pant, *A Moment in Time*, London, 1974, p. 31.

[65] D.A. Low, 'The Government of India and the first Non-Co-operation Movement', in R. Kumar (ed.), *Essays on Gandhian Politics*, Oxford, 1971, pp. 298–324.

[66] E.g. Petrie's note, 31 July 1929, H. Poll 237–29; Griffith to Collins, 29 May 1930, H. Poll 257/V/30; Irwin to Police Conference, 19 Jan. 1931, H. Poll 152/31; H. Poll 78/34. There had been problems earlier in, e.g. Andhra, Madras City, Bombay.

[67] 'Statement made by the Honourable the Home Member to the National Defence Council . . .', 8 Sept. 1942, H. Poll (i), 3/26/42)2).

damaging parliamentary outburst against the Irwin declaration. In 1940 Churchill emasculated the 'August offer'.)[68] The second declarations on the other hand were all originally conceived in London – which was tardily beginning to learn the seriousness of the situation: this is true for the Montagu–Chelmsford Reforms of 1919, the Macdonald statement of 1931, and the Cripps offer of 1942.

When one plots these declarations on the graph of Gandhi's campaigns, it immediately becomes clear that their primary purpose was to head off a first agitational campaign or secure good grounds for checking its renewal. (The fruitlessness of the Muddiman Reforms Enquiry Committee of 1924 indicates that without the direct threat of agitation, or of a renewed agitation, such declarations were not made.)[69] None of the declarations succeeded, however, in halting either a first or a second campaign. But equally, no second agitational campaign ever succeeded in extracting a third declaration from the British. At this stage the most that the British in India would do (often in the teeth of London opposition) was to press on with the Reforms already adumbrated. In 1923 Willingdon, as governor of Madras, proposed the early introduction of Responsible Government in his province;[70] as viceroy a decade later, he persistently urged London to press ahead with the making of the new Government of India Act;[71] while ten years afterwards Wavell, to Churchill's fury, deliberately embarked upon winding up the British Raj altogether.[72] The significance of all these developments should be emphasised. As the whole sequence unfolded, so the British successively enlarged their concessions until by the end they had nothing of very much significance to offer.

British rule in India was in very many respects a self-regarding autocracy which displayed crude racist attitudes, a strong propensity to distort India's economic circumstances for its own imperial ends, and an unwarranted assurance in the efficacy of British remedies for India's ills.[73] This was why strong nationalist sentiments were generated against it. But it was always subject as well to criticism in the British Houses of Parliament, and that made it a flexible autocracy. In illustration of one characteristic British attitude here, we may cite R.A. Butler, son and nephew of British governors, under-secretary of state for India from 1932–7, and later, of course, a prime figure in the British Conservative Party. Writing in May

68 R. Danzig, 'The Announcement of August 20th 1917', *Journal of Asian Studies*, 28 no. 1 (Nov. 1968), pp. 19–39; Moore, *Crisis of Indian Unity*, p. 59, sqq; R.J. Moore, 'British Policy and the Indian Problem, 1936–40', in C.H. Philips and M.D. Wainwright (ed.), *The Partition of India*, London, 1970, pp. 90–1.
69 Muddiman note, 4 Mar. 1925, H. Public 166/II/24.
70 Willingdon to Vincent, 1 July 1922, H. Poll 418/22.
71 For example, Willingdon to Hoare, tel. 19 April 1934, Templewood Papers 12.
72 Penderel Moon, *Wavell, The Viceroy's Diary*, London, 1973; Mansergh, *Transfer of Power*, vol. 3.
73 Francis G. Hutchins, *The Illusion of Permanence*, Princeton, 1967.

1937 to his contemporary and close personal friend, Lord Brabourne, Governor of Bombay, Butler declared:

I have always thought that British Government in India should depend, as Sam Hoare saw so quickly, upon firmness combined with what loosely can be described as progress. It is always when these two qualities are equally balanced that India has had her most tranquil periods, and our policy never is the most successful when one or the other is uppermost . . . Minto seemed to me to combine the two qualities better than any other ruler of India. He said, you will remember, that the English were as passengers in a strange land and must keep moving on . . . In Chelmsford's day progress was too much to the front, leaving a legacy to Reading who, being a lawyer, fenced with Gandhi . . . Irwin's period definitely weighed down the balance against order to an extent that has frightened the Administration today . . . Consequently Willingdon's regime put off the real problem of preparing the Hindu community to pass from fifty years in opposition to one of creative construction, and what is now needed is a return to the balance of order and progress.[74]

Such an attitude was suffocatingly lofty; but it was pliant as well; and as 'liberal' British opinion of this kind took the strain of the Indian struggle, it responded positively as well as negatively. It was embarrassed by the furore which Gandhi's agitations caused, and dismayed that the repression of lawlessness should entail suspending the rule of law.[75] It instinctively sought refuge in Britain's own tradition of piecemeal constitutional reform with its uniquely time-laden commitment to the solvency of electoral politics. The Montagu–Chelmsford reforms of 1919 were thus in due course overtaken by the Government of India Act of 1935.[76] By the 1930s it was the British Labour Party which was beginning to make the running here.[77] But *The Times*, London's premier newspaper, was never far behind, and by the early 1940s many such influences in Britain were quite fully committed to India's early independence.[78]

But the rundown did not come at all smoothly. For simultaneously the government of India ran the gamut of its successive modes of repressing India's nationalist movement, and the conservative forces in Britain its sequence of rearguard actions. The indecision that characterised the government of India's policy towards nationalist agitation between 1903 and 1919 eventually had its horrifying denouement in the Jallianwallah

[74] Butler to Brabourne, 21 May 1937, Brabourne P. 21.
[75] On the awareness of people in India of the importance of British opinion see, e.g., Hailey to Crerar, 7 Jan. 1930, H. Poll 98/30; Alexander to Miss Slade, 24 Dec. 1930, H. Poll 21/31. It is of some significance that while the Dutch used to speak of 'peace and order', the British always spoke of 'law and order'.
[76] Moore, *Crisis of Unity*, records the details; see also D.A. Low, 'Sir Tej Bahadur Sapru and the first Round Table Conference', in Low (ed.), *Soundings*, ch. 10.
[77] Partha Sarathi Gupta, 'British Labour and the Indian Left, 1919–39', in B.R. Nanda (ed.), *Socialism in India*, Delhi, 1972, pp. 69–121; Nanda, *Imperialism and the British Labour Movement 1914–64*, London, 1975.
[78] John A. Wheeler-Bennett, *King George VI*, London, 1958, p. 703.

Bagh. Thereupon the government of India switched to the much more cool-headed policy (which was fashioned by Sir William Vincent) of giving Gandhi's movement all the rope it needed to hang itself. Since by 1922 this had succeeded from the British point of view in effecting the collapse of the Non-Cooperation movement,[79] Vincent's policy dominated British thinking for the rest of the decade. But it was much less successful against the Civil Disobedience movement, and in 1931–2 the government of India accordingly found itself propelled towards its third position – to the policy of swifter and longer proscriptions and imprisonments of Congress and its leaders – that dominated its mind till the end.[80] This had to be modified in response to the milder 'individual' satyagraha campaign of 1940–1; but it was then massively supplemented, especially in eastern India by military action – though interestingly enough still not by martial law[81] – in 1942. With that, however, the expedients were running out.

So they were, by then, in London too. Until the First World War the 'conservative' elements in British politics had attempted to deny that self-government, except at the local level, was at all appropriate to India. When, by the end of that war, such a position had become untenable, they bent their efforts to confining substantial constitutional advance to the provincial level. They were outraged by Irwin's declaration in 1929 that India could some time have Dominion Status, and thereupon gave their minds to effecting a new holding position whereby, even if there should be 'responsibility' at a Federal centre, there would be a guaranteed conservative blocking third of members in the Federal legislature nominated by the Indian princes. But in 1940 this expedient collapsed too, through the eventual refusal of the princes to join the Federation.[82] So they fastened instead on the dogma that further constitutional advance would have to await the ending of the war. Thereafter the cogitations of Linlithgow, Amery, Churchill and their like,[83] which were characterised by an almost frenetic search for still further expedients, were chiefly eloquent of the degree to which these conservative British elements had by now reached the end of their tether.

These political erosions had some fairly precise economic parallels.[84]

---

[79] Low, 'First Non-Cooperation Movement'.

[80] D.A. Low, '"Civil Martial Law": the Government of India and the Civil Disobedience Movements, 1930–34', in Low (ed.), *Congress and the Raj. Facets of the Indian Struggle 1917–47*, London, 1977, pp. 165–98.

[81] Dr David Arnold draws attention on this point to H. Poll 3/42/42. There was not even martial law in the Punjab in August 1947.

[82] Moore, *Crisis of Indian Unity*, *passim*; C. Bridge, *Holding India to the Empire. The British Conservative Party and the 1935 Constitution*, Delhi, 1986.

[83] Mansergh, *Transfer of Power*, vols. 1–3.

[84] On these I have benefited greatly from conversations with Dr Elizabeth Whitcombe. See A.D.D. Gordon, *Businessmen and Politics. Rising Nationalism and a Modernising Economy in Bombay 1918–1933*, Canberra, 1978; A.G. Bagchi, *Private Investment in India, 1900–39*,

Ever since 1857 the British had found themselves in an almost impossible financial position in India because of the need they felt for a strong army and a well paid bureaucracy.[85] Together, however, these took a high percentage of the available revenue, which could not be increased without grave risk – without, that is, having to increase the size of the army and the bureaucracy still further. During the First World War this situation dramatically worsened. Supply costs and the public debt rose steeply. Reliance upon land revenue no longer sufficed. For the first time it became necessary to impose large customs and income taxes. This, however, merely served to underline the fundamental dilemma. For, as we shall see, the introduction of progressive taxation stoked the radicalisation of the Indian merchant communities.

Simultaneously, between 1913 and 1938, British exports to India halved in value, and by the 1930s British investment in India was declining as well. During the First World War the Indian import duty on piecegoods had been enhanced, and in 1925 the Lancashire cotton industry lost the benefit of a countervailing duty. By this time its Indian market was falling prey to Japanese competition; in 1931 it was forced to concede that it could no longer interfere with India's tariff policy; and when a system of preferences was finalised in the Mody–Lees Agreement of 1933, its further decline was only temporarily arrested.[86] By 1939 Britain was having to buy half a million bales of Indian raw cotton to maintain any preference at all. Through 1930–1, moreover, the Governments in Delhi and London fought a critical battle over monetary control. During the financial crisis of 1931 a weak rupee was tied to sterling's minuet with gold. With the creation, however, of the Reserve Bank of India under the 1935 Act, real control over monetary policy in India came to be placed within India itself. Furthermore, in spite of the 'home charges' the financial benefits brought to the British Isles from India were constantly diminishing during the inter-war period; while in India itself the British never had available anywhere near enough surplus revenue to make extensive 'development' possible. In view of all this the long-standing doubts in some quarters as to whether the Indian Empire was worth the trouble it gave began by the 1930s to spread. The *coup de grace* came in the Second World War when Britain's largest financial stake in India, the sterling debt and its interest, disappeared, to be replaced by Britain's rupee debt to India.[87] With that, Britain's prime economic reason for remaining in India during the interwar period evaporated.

It was in some respects the same story with the Army in India. Although

Cambridge, 1972; I.M. Drummond, *British Economic Policy and Empire, 1919–39*, London, 1972.

[85] S. Battacharyya, *Financial Foundations of the British Raj*, Simla, 1971.
[86] E.g. *The Times*, 14 Jan. 1938.
[87] Mansergh, *Transfer of Power*, vols. 1–3.

defence expenditure had actually dropped from 34 per cent of the total
expenditure of the Government of India in 1914 to 27 per cent in 1933, the
Garran Tribunal in 1933 laid down that Britain should now pay £1.5 m. per
annum towards the maintenance of British troops in India; while as a
consequence of the Chatfield Committee in 1939 Britain became responsible for much of the cost of the Indian Army's modernisation. Despite all
the talk of the 'eastern barracks', the main attack on the Japanese was then
made, not by the British from India, but by the Americans from across the
Pacific. At the same time, because of increased recruitment during the
Second World War, the proportion of British to Indian officers fell from
10:1 to 4:1. Like so many of the newer entrants to the Indian Civil Service,
these were being increasingly drawn, moreover, from the urban intelligentsia and entrepreneurial rather than from the more traditional landed
families.[88] So yet another sea-change was on its way.

Yet two central facts in this whole story remain. Despite the herculean
efforts of the Indian national movement, it never once broke the hold of the
British Raj over India. Many critical decisions were made in Britain; but
there was never a traumatic collapse there of the will to govern India
either.[89] If this suggests that for further enlightenment one has to look more
closely within India itself, that indeed seems the path of wisdom. For when
one does so, it soon becomes apparent that, alongside the protracted conflict
between Congress and the British, which has understandably dominated
existing accounts, there was the no less significant process by which
Congress captured the Raj in India from the British by supersession. This
chapter is not merely concerned, that is, with the conflict between Congress
and the British Raj. It discusses as well the manner in which the Indian
National Congress became the Raj.

Before considering this rather more directly, it is necessary to review a
number of the components here. In the twentieth century, in response to
the way the Raj itself operated, Congress, in its institutional organisation,
sought to parallel the Raj rather precisely. Thus at the all-India level it came
to have its president and Working Committee, the All-India Congress
Committee, and the annual Congresses. As the conflict sharpened, so it
developed its more informal, but much more powerful, High Command.
Beneath these stood the Provincial Congress Committees; and beneath

---

[88] N.C. Sinha and P.N. Khera, *Indian War Economy: Supply, Industry and Finance*,
Combined Inter-Services Historical Section India and Pakistan, 1962, p. 229 sqq; Longer,
Red Coats, passim, e.g. p. 212. Stephen P. Cohen, *The Indian Army. Its Contribution to the
Development of a Nation*, Berkeley, 1971, p. 138 sqq; J.H. Voigt, *India in the Second World
War*, Delhi 1987. D.C. Potter's argument in 'Manpower Shortage and the End of
Colonialism: the case of the I.C.S.', *Modern Asian Studies*, 7 no. 1 (1973), 47–73, seems
ill-conceived: the British went on recruiting public schoolboys for their colonial empire for
another fifteen years.
[89] Low (ed.), *Congress and the Raj*, ch. 12 (Moore).

them City, District, and sometimes Taluka, Ward and Village Congress Committees, with their Presidents and officers as well.[90]

When in 1920 under Gandhi's influence the Congress provinces were redrawn they accorded rather better with indigenous linguistic divisions and helped pave the way for the recruitment of new categories of supporters; but since this entailed misalignments with the provinces, presidencies and princely states maintained by the Raj, it also made for problems. Some Congress Committees straddled 'British' boundaries.[91] Sometimes several Provincial Congress committees jostled within the confines of a single British province.[92] Throughout, indeed, Congress, like the Raj, had to fend with all the complexities of a political system which possessed a multiplicity of levels. Some of its links here were strong. For thirty years after the foundation of Congress in 1885, the bonds between the Bengal Congress and the All-India Congress were close. Thereafter, however, they atrophied. In the days of Gokhale and Mehta, the Bombay and the All-India Congress were intimately associated, as were the UP PCC and the AICC from the time Jawaharlal Nehru first became General Secretary in 1921.[93] By contrast in all the years before independence the bonds between the Mysore Congress and the All-India Congress (not to mention those between the Mysore Congress and any kind of major rural base) were tenuous indeed, while the weakness in the authority of the UP PCC over the local Congress leadership in Rohilkhand was marked until as late as the mid-1940s.[94] There were other matters besides. Elsewhere it has been shown how factional conflicts at the Bombay provincial level lead to the Congress split at Surat in 1907 at the All-India level, and how factional struggles became rampant in the Bengal PCC in the 1920s and 1930s.[95] It is all too easy to point to other examples of this – in the Punjab, UP, and Madras,[96] to mention only three. Such strife was very often found at district levels too.[97] Congress leaders at higher levels generally attempted to leave such matters to be dealt with within their own local arenas; but there were strong tendencies at lower levels to appeal to higher levels for supporters and/or arbitrators, and a reluctant readiness by higher levels to despatch arbitrators in response.

[90] Gopal Khrisna, 'The Development of the Indian National Congress as a Mass Organisation, 1918–23', *Journal of Asian Studies*, 25 no. 3 (May 1966), 413–30.
[91] E.g. the Mysore Congress.
[92] E.g. in the Central Provinces, and in the Madras Presidency.
[93] Sitaramayya, *History of INC*, I.
[94] Low (ed.), *Congress and the Raj*, chs. 13 (Manor) and 15. (Brennan).
[95] Johnson, *Provincial Politics and Indian Nationalism*, ch. 4. J. Gallagher, 'Congress in Decline: Bengal, 1930–39', in Gallagher, Johnson and Seal, *Locality, Province and Nation*, pp. 269–325.
[96] Punjab report, 15 Dec. 1938, Andhra report, 22–31 Dec. 1938, AICC G28 1938/9; Sri Prakash to Prasad, 2 Dec. 1935, Prasad P. III/35/4.
[97] For a striking example, see Sri Prakash's report on Partabgarh, 25 Dec. 1937, AICC P20 (i) 1937; see also Sri Prakash to Prasad, 31 Oct. 1935, Prasad P. III/35/3.

The relationship between levels within the structure was of great importance. There could, for example, be 'level-jumping', when a Congress committee of one category sought elevation to another[98] – a process that paralleled the creation of new provinces on the British side (Bihar and Orissa in 1911; Sind, etc. in 1935). Those holding power at one level could furthermore be turned to good use at another level. Vallabhbhai Patel's national importance stemmed from his provincial position; Rajagopalachari's provincial importance depended considerably upon his national position. But there could be difficulties here: Patel's national pre-eminence was not easily established, whilst Rajagopalachari's was always locally resented.[99] Just as the Raj had special problems in bonding its levels together (governors could disagree with viceroys;[100] they sometimes had as much difficulty in controlling their subordinates as Gandhi), so did Congress. The purpose of its elaborate construct was primarily of course to build a movement with which to assault the Raj at all the levels it commanded as soon as this became possible. It has to be emphasised that a concerted assault was never readily mounted.

In all this Congress was greatly helped even so by four important circumstances – some of which have tended to be overlooked. In the first place the spread of education in English provided a common language, and much common understanding, for its all-India leadership.[101] Next, the extensive cross country railway system, most of which had been built by the beginning of the twentieth century, not only meant that Congress leaders, beginning with Gandhi himself, could, in their efforts to stir the populace and control the Congress organisation, move about quite easily; it meant in particular that he and his associates could meet at very short notice to thrash out their next moves (with the coming of the bus and the motor car these conveniences were redoubled). Then there were the postal and the telegraph systems; one has only to dip into Gandhi's *Collected Works* to realize how invaluable to him and his movement both of these were. Above all there was the huge number of newspapers: a few of them in English, with an extra-provincial readership; many of them in a vernacular with large provincial readerships; others more confined to a community or a district; some especially produced as agitational bulletins; most of them supplemented at times of crisis by a large pamphlet and broadsheet literature.[102] These

98 E.g. Draft Report of Constitution Committee [Aug. 1937], AICC G28 1937.
99 Gandhi to Mahadev Desai, 22 Sept. 1929, *Collected Works of Mahatma Gandhi*, XLI,p. 453; Durga Das (ed.), *Sardar Patel's Correspondence 1945–50*, Ahmedabad, 1972, II, ch. 4.
100 Low, 'First Non-Co-operation Movement', p. 310 sqq.
101 Aparna Basu, *The Growth of Education and Political Development in India 1898–1920*, Delhi, 1974; J.C. Butler, 'Educational Administration in Bombay Presidency, 1913–37', MPhil thesis, University of Sussex, 1973.
102 E.g. G. Pandey, 'Mobilization in a Mass Movement: Congress 'Propaganda' in the United Provinces (India), 1930–4', *Modern Asian Studies*, 9 no. 2 (April, 1975), pp. 205–26. The

ensured that all of the major (and most minor) political events were not only reported, but widely discussed as well. It needs to be remembered too that the readership of these newspapers greatly exceeded their circulation figures, while subsequent verbal reporting of the news they carried very soon spread important information further still. It was one consequence that where local political controllers of one kind or another were locally very powerful, their subordinates could not be long kept in ignorance of developments elsewhere. It was another, and much more important, result that the ideology of the movement was very readily bruited abroad, and soon stood on the lips, if not of millions, then of many hundreds of thousands of India's people.

It must nevertheless be underlined (though this should not now need much labouring) that the great national agitations were always patchy occurrences. This has been amply demonstrated for the Rowlatt satyagraha;[103] it was clearly true of the Quit India movement 23 years later.[104] Equally, the actual force of agitations varied within provinces over time as well as space,[105] especially perhaps as between the Non-Cooperation and the Civil Disobedience movements: the former seems to have been much more multi-faceted, but less widespread, than the latter.[106] It is of prime importance to remember too that whilst many Muslims were to the fore in the Non-Co-operation movement, most of them actively abstained from Congress' agitations thereafter. One must indeed be wary of postulating linear developments here.[107] Rohilkhand in UP was up, for example, in 1920–2 to a much greater degree than in 1930–2, while the Patidars of Gujarat were vigorous participants in the first Civil Disobedience movement, but mostly abstainers in the second. A similar contrast can be drawn between east Bengal in the early 1920s and in the early 1930s.[108] Likewise, in the early 1930s Malabar pulsated, but stood still in 1942.[109] Bihar on the other hand was relatively quiet in 1931, but exploded extensively eleven years later.[110] There were marked variations too in the response of leading individuals; consider the fluctuating careers of, for example, B.C. Pal, G.S. Khaparde, Srinivasa Iyengar, even the great hesitations of Jawaharlal Nehru in midsummer 1942 as compared with his vigorous campaigning a decade previously. Consider, on the other hand, the contrasts in the career

Government's annual reports on newspapers are voluminous, e.g. for 1930, H. Poll 229/31; for 1931, H. Poll 230/32.

103 Kumar, *Essays on Gandhian Politics, passim.*
104 G. Pandey (ed.), *The Indian Nation in 1942*, Calcutta, 1988.
105 E.g. IGP UP, 3 Sept. 1930, H. Poll 259/30.
106 E.g. Baker and Washbrook, *South India*, p. 98 sqq.
107 E.g. Keith Ogborn, 'The Development of Nationalist Politics in the Assam Valley 1920–39', PhD thesis, University of Western Australia, 1982.
108 Low (ed.), *Congress and the Raj*, chs. 15 (Brennan) and 1 (Hardiman).
109 Gallagher, 'Bengal 1930–39', *Locality, Province and Nation*, pp. 288–9.
110 Low (ed.), *Congress and the Raj*, chs. 9 (McDonald) and 10 (Harcourt).

of Morarji Desai: deputy collector under the British in the 1920s; their satyagraha prisoner in the 1930s and 1940s.[111]

A central issue here affecting the operations of the movement concerns the part played by local agitations within the larger national agitations. As Seal has neatly put it, the former often ran upon their own clocks.[112] There can be no doubt that there were a great many agitations that to the participants at least had a quite localised significance, and that many of these originally unfolded quite regardless of Congress.[113] But as Congress became stronger, more particularly from the First World War onwards, its leaders had increasingly to decide whether they would 'nationalise' local agitations – weld them, that is, into a nationalist programme of action. It was only one of the later agitations that was 'nationalised' in Champaran in 1917 – and even then only in retrospect. In 1918 the Kheda agitation was no more than 'half' nationalised.[114] The Eka movement in UP in 1921, the Akali movement in the Punjab, the Bombay strikes of the late 1920s, and many later Kisan Sabha movements, were among those that were never 'nationalised.[115] By contrast the formidable Bardoli agitation in 1928, the forest Satyagrahas in Bombay and CP in 1930, the no-rent campaign in UP in 1931, and the Rajkot agitation in 1939, were prime examples of those that were nationalised.[116]

There was the obverse here too in the 'localisation' of national agitations. It was towards this that the Congress leaders bent so many of their efforts. Gandhi's hope for the salt satyagraha of 1930,[117] to take a prime example, was that through the local and illegal manufacture of salt a dramatic defiance of the Raj could be mounted in innumerable local areas. His initiative was faithfully followed on the Maharashtrian coast, in Malabar, in Tamilnad, in Andhra, in south-west Bengal, in parts of UP, and elsewhere. In many other areas, however, it was technically very difficult to effect the illegal manufacture of salt since the necessary ingredients were not locally present. So, forest satyagrahas, and no-revenue campaigns, were emphasised instead; and in most centres chief use came to be made in the end of the movement's stock-in-trade – boycotts, hartals, processions, speeches,

111 Morarji Desai, *The Story of My Life*, vol. 1, Delhi, 1974.
112 *Locality, Province and Nation*, p. 26.
113 Baker and Washbrook, *South India*, p. 29 sqq.
114 Brown, *Gandhi's Rise to Power*, ch. 3; D. Hardiman, *Peasant Nationalists of Gujarat, Kheda District 1917–1934*, chs. 1–6; S. Henningham, *Peasant Movements in Colonial India: North Bihar 1917–1942*, chs. 1–2.
115 W.F. Crawley, 'Kisan Sabhas and Agrarian Revolt in the United Provinces 1920 to 1921', *Modern Asian Studies*, 5 no. 2 (1971), 95–109; chs. 2 and 9 below; Khuswant Singh, *A History of the Sikhs*, Princeton, 1966, II, ch. 13; B.B. Chaudhuri, in Nanda, *Socialism in India*, pp. 219–29.
116 S. Gopal, *The Viceroyalty of Lord Irwin, 1926–31*, Oxford, 1957, ch. 3; chs. 6 and 7 below; John R. Wood, 'Indian Nationalism in the Princely Context: the Rajkot Satyagraha of 1938–9' in Jeffrey (ed.), *People, Princes and Paramount Power*, ch. 7.
117 Dr David Dalton is making a detailed study of this.

flag-raisings, picketings, and such like – since it was by these (soon time-honoured) means that national agitation could be most readily localised.[118]

From the start the core support for Congress had come from the western-educated intelligentsia – from successive generations of college students; from the 'lawyer class'; from teachers, and from the new professions generally.[119] It was from their ranks that there came the main organisers, the speech makers, the newspaper editors and the most active party workers. The commitment of the intelligentsia to Congress was nevertheless very uneven. It came early and strongly from Bengal, more hesitantly from UP, tardily from Gujarat (perhaps because of the availability of service posts in the neighbouring princely states); it was delayed in the Hindi-speaking areas of the Central Provinces until the 1920s.[120] There were very many of the intelligentsia, moreover, who were never active in Congress; who never resigned their posts; who never went to gaol. There were many indeed who were actively opposed to Congress, especially when its agitations threatened their status quo. Even those who approved of these were happier when they were at some distance – in Champaran, or Rae Bareli, or Kheda. In any case their discontents did not necessarily coincide with other peoples'. Large numbers of the intelligentsia do seem even so to have followed the fortunes of the Congress movement very closely, participated emotionally and vicariously in its agitations, mourned its failures, rejoiced in its successes, and – what eventually mattered most – then voted for it.[121] Some of the leading edges went off into socialism and communism;[122] but in the end very many maintained their support for the Congress, because of its unswerving commitment to Indian independence, particularly once it showed itself to be a well-organised, but non-revolutionary, party.

It has been shown elsewhere that before and after the turn of the century the Congress activists were not often their own men, but were primarily spokesmen for local notables in the towns and countryside.[123] Clearly Congress came to depend a good deal upon the various nexuses between the

---

[118] E.g. Sec. Maharshtra PCC to A/Pres., Indian National Congress, 28 July 1930, AICC G148 1930; Report of the Satyagraha movement in Tamil Nadu, 4 Oct. 1930, AICC G189; and information from Drs Jeffrey and Barun De.

[119] Seal, *Emergence*; Suntharalingam, *Politics . . . in South India*, etc.

[120] Broomfield, *Elite Politics*; C.A. Bayly, *Local Roots*; David Hardiman, 'Baroda State' in Jeffrey (ed.), *Princely States*; D.E.U. Baker, 'The Rowlatt Satyagraha in the Central Provinces and Berar', in Kumar (ed.), *Gandhian Politics*, ch. 5.

[121] For one point of view see Percival Spear, 'A Third Force in India, 1920–47; a Study in Political Analysis', in Philips and Wainwright (ed.), *Partition of India*, ch. 24.

[122] Nanda, *Socialism in India*, ch. 1.

[123] C.A. Bayly, 'Patrons and Politics in Northern India, 1880–1920', *Modern Asian Studies*, 7 no. 3 (1975), 349–88; D.A. Washbrook, 'Country Politics: Madras 1880 to 1930', *Locality, Province and Nation*, pp. 186–7.

intelligentsia and the commercial communities.[124] Some members of the merchant communities were with Congress from the beginning. After the First World War such communities increasingly adhered to it. This was partly because the massive profits which Indian capitalists secured during the wartime boom, together with an elaborate promise of 'fiscal autonomy' for India, fired their ambitions to replace the British as India's capitalist class. They were incensed by the interference in the Indian economy of Lancashire and the City of London; by the failure of the longed-for industrial renaissance to take place; by the extent to which European capitalists remitted their excessive profits home; and by the manner in which British interests upheld what they considered to be a most adverse rupee–sterling exchange rate. Several prominent Indian capitalists became as a consequence leading Congress paymasters.[125] But there were many smaller entrepreneurs who were also now radicalised, in part because of their incorporation for the first time in an alien income tax system (which, to meet their rising costs, the British imposed during the First World War); in part too because they felt themselves to be the unheeded victims of inequitable wartime controls. They found in Congress an ideal outlet for their vexations, in Gandhi a bania of their kind[126] and (an important matter for some of them) a welcome religious leader too. Many of them now became riveted to the Congress, especially from amongst the Marwaris in Calcutta and elsewhere, and the Gujaratis of Ahmedabad and Bombay.

Yet such people could from time to time be a drag upon the movement. The industrialists did not much like its use of trade boycotts,[127] and were always careful to keep some of their connections with the British for fear of losing their economic privileges (it can be said indeed that when Congress was relatively quiet, leading industrialists could be vehement; but when Congress became vociferous, such men trimmed).[128] Both they and the merchants were strong opponents, moreover, of anything that smacked of social revolution. Gandhi, so Ambalal Sarabhai once remarked, was the best guarantee against communism which India possessed.[129] With the radicalisation of the Bombay commercial community, contemporaneously with the emergence of a communist leadership amongst the Bombay working class in the late 1920s, Bombay city could, just conceivably, have exploded (as it was the British had great difficulty in maintaining their control over it).[130] But by definition these two classes were in sharp

124 Gordon *Businessmen in Politics*, and see ch. 4 below.
125 E.g. Petrie's note on Congress funds, 26 May 1930, H. Poll 5/40/31; unsigned note, 7 April 1931, H. Poll 136/31.
126 For a most interesting commentary see Kaka Kalelkar's introduction to *Jamnalal Bajaj Ki Diary*, Allahabad, 1969.
127 E.g. Thakurdas to Patel, 22 July 1930, AICC G56 1930; AICC 29 1930.
128 C. Markovits, *Indian Business and Nationalist Politics 1931–39*, Cambridge 1985.
129 Monteath to Government of Bombay, 2 May 1932, H. Poll 14/28/32.
130 Haig's note, 25 Mar. 1932, H. Poll 5/82/32.

opposition to each other; Gandhi for his part was fearful that he could not control working class leaders; and when in 1929 the British conveniently removed the communist leadership from Bombay and elsewhere to appear in the Meerut Conspiracy Case, the Congress leadership was relatively perfunctory in its protestations.[131] In 1930–2 there were in fact actual clashes in Bombay between Congress supporters and proletarian mill workers; while Congress in the city was now fast becoming a largely middle class party.[132] It was much the same in Calcutta, and elsewhere. In Madras, for example, there were in 1930, at the height of the Civil Disobedience Movement, proletarian strikes which the Congress leaders deliberately disregarded.[133]

Linked with the intelligentsia – often indeed overlapping with it – the commercial classes had by 1930 swung very largely to Congress.[134] Together they and their clienteles made the cities and towns the main foci of Congress agitations. 'The net impression left on my mind is that the Police reigns but Congress is ruling in Calcutta', a member of the Viceroy's Council declared in June 1930.[135] Such by then was the case in a great many Indian cities. There were, all the same, strict limits to the propulsion which large numbers of either the intelligentsia or the commercial communities would allow to nationalist agitations, and this clearly blunted the movement's thrust.

But what of the countryside? Here 'landlords' overwhelmingly stood with the British. Some formed landlord parties that participated in the legislatures.[136] Most were so locked into the British land revenue system that they rarely gave the British cause for concern. The British were not much perturbed either with the feelings of the vast mass of agricultural labourers. Such people, they told themselves, were ignorant of politics. (The essential fact was that without a licence from those immediately superordinate to them, poorer peasants were always hesitant to move.)[137]

Uncertainty centred upon the dominant peasants. It should be emphasised that dominant peasant communities were often internally differentiated and physically dispersed. It should be stressed as well that the actions of prominent individuals from amongst them did not necessarily commit their fellows. They, nevertheless, signified a trend. And it now begins to

---

[131] There is an interesting honours thesis by J.D. Redenback on 'Gandhi's Attitude to Communism 1917–32', La Trobe University 1974.

[132] Petrie's note, 9 Oct. 1929, H. Poll 257/I/30; H. Poll 5/82/32.

[133] Tamilnadu Archives G.O. 1366 (1–5) 1707–L, 1930, 1686–L, 1931. Public Works and Labour. (Dr Arnold's notes).

[134] H. Poll 14/28/32.

[135] Mitter's note, 15 May 1930, H. Poll 248/II/30. Cf. CP Marathi Congress report, AICC 24 1930.

[136] E.g. P.D. Reeves, *The Landlords and Governments in Uttar Pradesh. Studies in their relations until Zamindari abolition*, Delhi 1990.

[137] H. Poll 4/28/32, *passim*.

look as if one central theme stretching through the three decades 1917 to 1947 lay in the successive adherences to Congress, not just of the intelligentsia and the commercial classes, but of major segments of the dominant peasant communities we noted at the outset.[138] With many a caveat in mind, one can indeed now begin to discern some elements from these communities swinging to Congress from about 1918 onwards. Certain Patidars and Bhumihars and other dominant peasants from Gujarat and Bihar seem to have led the way, followed very soon by some Rajus, Kammas and Reddis from the Andhra delta (who thus ensured that it would not just be a north Indian movement), together with some Ahirs, Kurmis and Rajputs from several of the eastern UP districts, some Mahisyas from west Bengal, Muslim 'Jotedars' from east Bengal, Nayars from Malabar, and others besides.[139] Then, in 1930, quite dramatically, a number of Muslim Pathans from the Frontier Province, organised as *Khudai Khitmadgars*, and soon dubbed the 'Red Shirts', threw in their lot with Congress when the Muslim League refused to help them in their local clash with the British.[140] Thereafter, we now have specific stories from the mid-1930s of the recruitment to Congress of certain Gounders of Coimbatore in Tamilnad;[141] of the fruitful collaboration by this time between the Maharashtrian Congressman, N.V. Gadgil, and the non-Brahmin leader Jedhe,[142] together with similar developments leading to the recruitment to Congress of non-Brahmin leaders in Berar and the Marathi-speaking parts of CP, along with the adherence to Congress of many Kanyakubja Brahmins in Hindi-speaking CP.[143] Ten to fifteen years later 'Haryana' Jats, Nayars in Travancore (when Mannam suddenly switched), Vokkaligas and Lingayats in Mysore, Rajputs and Jats in Rajasthan, all swung in large numbers to Congress as well.[144]

[138] E.g. Utkal report, p. 16, 27 Sept. 1930, AICC 24 1930.

[139] Low, *Congress and the Raj*, Chs. 1 (Hardiman), 3 (Stoddart), 6 (Pandey), 9 (McDonald), 14 (Jeffrey); G. Pandey, *The Ascendency of the Congress in Uttar Pradesh 1926–34*, Delhi 1978; Hardiman, *Gujarat*; Henningham, *North Bihar*; Ray, 'Masses in Politics: the Non-Cooperation Movement in Bengal 1920–22', *Indian Economic and Social History Review*, 11 no. 4 (Dec. 1974), 333–410. I am indebted too for information about UP to Professor Urmila Phadnis and Dr D.N. Pannigrahi.

[140] D.G. Tendulkar, *Abdul Ghaffar Khan*, Bombay, 1967, p. 50 sqq; Khalid B. Sayeed, 'Pathan Regionalism', *South Atlantic Quarterly*, 63 (Autumn 1964), 488–96. Hallett's note, 20 Apr. 1934, H. Poll 4/4/34.

[141] David Arnold, 'The Gounders and the Congress: Political Recruitment in South India, 1920–37', *South Asia*, 4 (Oct. 1974), pp. 1–20.

[142] Gail Omvedt, 'Non-Brahmans and Nationalists in Poona', *Economic and Political Weekly*, Annual Number 1974, pp. 201–16; R. O'Hanlon, 'Acts of Appropriation: Non-Brahmin Radicals and Congress in early Twentieth Century Maharashtra', in M. Shepperson and C. Simmons (eds.), *The Indian National Congress and the Political Economy of India 1885–1985*, Aldershot, 1988, pp. 102–46.

[143] D.E.U. Baker, *Changing Political Leadership in an Indian Province. The Central Province and Berar 1919–1939*, Delhi, 1979.

[144] Imran Ali, 'Relations between the Muslim League and the Panjab National Unionist Party 1935–47', *South Asia*, 6 (1976), 51–65; Low (ed.), *Congress and the Raj*, chs. 13 (Manor) and 14 (Jeffrey); R. Sisson, *The Congress Party in Rajasthan*, Berkeley, 1972, p. 136.

In UP in the early 1920s (as in Arambagh in Bengal under Atulya Ghosh and P.C. Sen in the 1930s) Congress looked as if it might in places just perhaps become a poor peasants' party.[145] There were many tribals in Madras and the Central Provinces who were amongst the most active of the satyagrahis whenever a major agitation occurred;[146] while from 1917 onwards Malaviya, Tandon and others were forming Kisan Sabhas and Kisan Sanghas in eastern UP and elsewhere.[147] But in fact they and their like built upon the networks of proponents of Hindi against UP's Urdu-using elite, and operated along the Brahmin linkages radiating from Benares and Allahabad to the holders of temple-owned land beyond.[148] This had the typical consequence that Congress in UP, despite – indeed in many respects because of – its initial association with the rural disturbances of the early 1920s in the province, became not a poor, but a dominant peasant party, typified, not so much by the self-styled socialist, Jawaharlal Nehru, but by Charan Singh of Meerut, who in the 1930s mobilised for Congress the powerful Jats of western UP.[149]

It is of major significance that unlike most of their predecessors (certainly Naoroji, Mehta, Gokhale, Aurobindo, even Das, though arguably not Tilak) the new Congress leadership from the First World War onwards was largely characterised by its responsiveness to the needs for links with these dominant peasant communities.[150] This began with Gandhi – even if he himself never sought exclusive links with any groups in the countryside. It was true of his prime lieutenants, Vallabhbhai Patel, the Patidar lawyer from Gujarat; Rajendra Prasad, the small landowner lawyer from Bihar; Rajagopalachari, the small town lawyer, not from Madras City, but from Salem in Tamilnad; not to mention Abdul Ghaffar Khan, the educated small landowner from the Frontier. It was true too of so many others besides: Sasmal, Tandon, Sampurnanand, Ranga, Prakasam, Hardikar, Shukla, Sri Prakash, Mohanlal Saxena, Morarji Desai.

It must be emphasised that the initiative for these connections very often came from within these dominant peasant communities themselves. It was their spokesman from Champaran and from Kheda who first sought out

---

[145] Low, *Congress and the Raj*, ch. 6 (Pandey); and information from Dr Barun De and his associates.

[146] E.g. Hindustani PCC, CP, report, 19 Sept. 1930, AICC G9 1930; D. Baker, '"A serious time": Forest Satyagraha in Madhya Pradesh', *Indian Economic and Social History Review*, 21 no. 1 (1984).

[147] E.g. See UP Kisan Sangha to Gen. Sec. Swaraj Party, 10 Dec. 1924, AICC F23, 1924; R. Gordon, 'The Hindu Mahasabha and the Indian National Congress, 1915 to 1926', *Modern Asian Studies*, 9 no. 2 (April 1975), 159, 177–9.

[148] Bayly, *Local Roots*, pp. 219–21, 267; Bengal to Home Dept. 25 Aug. 1926, H. Poll 187/26.

[149] Low (ed.), *Congress and the Raj*, ch. 6 (Pandey), and information from Dr D.N. Pannigrahi and Mr K.C. Pande.

[150] It is a major theme of Sumit Sarkar's *The Swadeshi Movement in Bengal 1903–8*, New Delhi, 1973, that this did not happen at that time there.

Gandhi in 1917–18.[151] It was Abdul Ghaffar Khan who led the Red Shirts into Congress in 1930.[152] It was local Andhra leaders who made the running in the delta in the 1920s and early 1930s – as in UP so often throughout.[153] It was Sasmal the Mahisya who originally mobilised the agitations in Midnapore and its surroundings in West Bengal.[154] It was factional leaders from these communities who, sensing the wave of the future, so often hitched their fortunes to the Congress star in the 1930s.[155]

It begins to look too as if many of those from amongst these dominant peasant communities who came into Congress at this time were 'upwardly mobile' – increasingly involved, that is, in a cash economy, acquiring land, linked to a wider world by new communications, generally more oriented to the market than in the past, and with a largely new access to western style education. The Patidar story has been related by Hardiman, that for the Andhra delta by Stoddart, while Sir Olaf Caroe writes for this period, in his book on *The Pathans*, of 'The Pathan Renaissance'.[156] The Mahisyas of Midnapore were both expanding their agricultural lands, and sending some of their sons to Calcutta University.[157] Kurmis and Ahirs in eastern UP, Jats in western UP, Syrian Christians in Travancore, Mahrattas in Maharashtra, were likewise elbowing their way to a more satisfactory livelihood, as were others of their kind. They were beginning to produce men, moreover, with the qualifications and skills of the old 'service' communities, but who, when they took to the towns, nevertheless maintained their rural links. One thinks here of Vallabhbhai Patel in Gujarat in the 1920s, of Y.B. Chavan in Maharashtra in the 1940s, and so many others. In due course they became the Congress' vital link.

It was of great importance that elements from such communities could turn sharply radical when they felt themselves frustrated – by their rivalry with indigo planters, as in Champaran; by a too unrelenting revenue system, as in Gujarat; by panicky repression, as on the Frontier; by a new *chaukidari* tax (and draconian police activities) as in Contai and Tamluk in Midnapore; by the application, at a time when economic conditions were worsening markedly, of a new settlement originally made in relatively good circumstances, as in the Andhra delta;[158] and so on.

151 J. Pouchepadass, 'Local leaders and the Intelligentsia in the Champaran Satyagraha (1917): A Study in Peasant Mobilization', *Contributions to Indian Sociology*, ns 8 (1974), 67–85; Henningham, *North Bihar*; Hardiman, *Gujarat*.
152 Tendulkar, *Abdul Ghaffar Khan*.
153 Low (ed.), *Congress and the Raj*, ch. 3 (Stoddart).
154 Secretary, Bengal PCC, to Doulatram, 16 Aug. 1936, Prasad P. IX/36/3; Ray, 'Masses in Politics', p. 367 sqq.
155 E.g. Washbrook, 'Madras', *Locality, Province and Nation*, p. 205 sqq.
156 London, 1958.
157 Information from Dr Barun De and his associates.
158 Pouchepadass, 'Local Leaders'; Tendulkar, *Abdul Ghaffer Khan*; *Law and Order in Midnapore 1930*, H. Poll5/31.

The patterns varied greatly, and have still to be fully traced out. But where, for example, as in Monghyr district in Bihar, so many at all levels were Bhumihars,[159] or in Midnapore, where so many were Mahisyas,[160] a sustained rural revolt against the British could, it seems, be most readily mounted, with violence in no way ruled out (more especially if the British picked off the leaders!). The British were fortunate perhaps, and the more ardent nationalists disadvantaged, that this was not more widely true. Where, however, caste cleavages reinforced class cleavages – which elsewhere was the more common pattern – any propensity to violence was sharply resisted. Where dominant peasants had no landlords positioned above them, but themselves sat above landless labourers, as for instance in Gujarat, a Congress satyagraha could secure much dominant peasant support, precisely because – but only so long as – it did not threaten widespread violence. Where, however, landlords were found, as in UP, the position was compounded, for when agitation erupted here, uncontrollable violence broke out fairly easily, and for fear of a wholesale collapse of the status quo, Congress' essentially unrevolutionary leaders soon found themselves engaged in damping it down.[161] In all these cases, Congress' actions were very evidently determined by dominant peasant interests.

In many parts of India, changing local concerns (not least as a consequence of the increasing penetration of local arenas by the Raj) were generating a myriad of local conflicts, some of which were characterized by factional rivalry, others by quasi-class or communal conflict, others by direct confrontation with local officialdom.[162] In such circumstances many leading individuals, and not least from amongst the dominant peasant communities, began to look to Congress as the appropriate vehicle for their rising political aspirations. This was true for certain Bhumihars, Patidars, Pathans, Mahisyas, Reddis, Rajus; some UP Rajputs, Kurmis, Ahirs, Jats; certain CP Kanyakubjas, Lodhis and Marathas;[163] and so on.

But this tendency was by no means universal. For in some areas Congress was long thought to be not a vehicle for upwardly mobile rural communities, but the preserve of provincial elites who sat above or, at all events, away from them. It was upon this feeling that the Justice Party traded in its opposition to the Congress in the 1920s and 1930s.[164] It was this belief that kept the non-Brahmin leaders of the Maharashtrian areas of Bombay Presidency and CP away from Congress until the 1930s. It was primarily

159 Gil McDonald kindly showed me his notes on B & O, Political Dept., Special, 32/31.
160 Ray, 'Mass Politics', *passim*; Ray, 'Zamindars and Jotedars', pp. 101–2; Gallagher, 'Bengal', *Locality, Province and Nation*, pp. 293–4.
161 Low (ed.), *Congress and the Raj*, chs. 1 (Hardiman) and 6 (Pandey).
162 Baker and Washbrook, *South India*, and Bayly, *Local Roots*, *passim*.
163 See fn. 139 above.
164 Eugene F. Irschick, *Politics and Social Conflict in South India, The Non-Brahman Movement and Tamil Separatism*, Berkeley, 1969; Low (ed.), *Congress and the Raj*, ch. 8 (Arnold).

because in the latter case Gandhi's lieutenants were able to work upon the antipathy towards the local 'Tilakite' Congress that in the end many were persuaded to join the 'Gandhian' Congress.[165] But concurrently there was increasing hostility between the Mahisya Congressmen of Midnapore and its environs, who saw themselves as standing close to Gandhi, and the *bhadralok*-dominated Bengal Provincial Congress Committee, which could be very hostile to Gandhi.[166] This was a most serious impediment since it probably halted the spread of the uniquely disruptive Midnapore agitations which the British acknowledged to be the most serious local threat they encountered anywhere in India.[167] As early as 1923, moreover, Congress in Bengal, dominated by its Hindu elite, had already lost the support it had earlier had amongst Bengal's Muslim Jotedars.[168]

If these checks to dominant peasant recruitment to Congress had been more widespread, its advance would have been seriously curtailed, as the Punjab story illustrates. There, in the heartland of British power from which the Indian Army was chiefly drawn (and in the Canal colonies so assiduously succoured),[169] the Hindu intelligentsia and commercial communities were always in strong support of Congress.[170] But they never threw up a Gandhian-type leadership, and never effectively crossed the non-agriculturalist/agriculturist divide into which the Punjab had been fixed by Curzon's Punjab Land Alienation Act of 1900. As a consequence the Punjab Congress remained all but confined to the urban Bania, Khatri, Arora elite; and from the early 1920s to the early 1940s, the dominant rural peasantry of the Punjab, especially the Jats of all three religious communities, Muslim, Sikh and Hindu alike, gave their support, not to Congress, but to that remarkable trans-communal party, the Unionist Party. First under the leadership of Fazli Husain,[171] later under Sikander Hyat Khan,[172] this was highly successful in winning support from the Hindu Jats under their robust leader, Chhotu Ram. Had this situation been extensively replicated elsewhere, Congress would have continued to be the small, frustrated, politically ineffectual, urban party which it was in the Punjab until independence.[173]

---

165 Low (ed.), *Congress and the Raj*, ch. 7 (Baker); cf. Berar report, 23 July 1938, AICC G28 1938/9.
166 Communications from Drs Rajat Ray and Barun De and his associates; Gallagher, *op. cit.* p. 318.
167 Emerson's note, 20 June 1931, H. Poll 14/8/31.
168 E.g. Bose to J. Nehru, 12 July 1928, AICC Misc. 1 1928. Information from Dr R.K.Ray.
169 Imran Ali, *The Punjab under Imperialism 1885–1947*, Princeton, 1988.
170 E.g. Satyapal to J. Nehru, 27 Jan. 1930, AICC G13 1930; Hardeo Sahai to Prasad, 22 Nov. 1932, AICC G9 1934.
171 Azim Husain, *Fazl-i Husain*, Bombay, 1946.
172 R. Coupland, *Indian Politics 1936–42*, London, 1943, ch. 5.
173 Duni Chand to J. Nehru, 31 Mar., 9 Apr. 1937, 8 Dec. 1938, Mangal Singh to J. Nehru, 9 Apr. 1937, J. Nehru to Satyapal, 3 Aug. 1937, Satyapal to J. Nehru, 27 Sept. 1937, AICC P17 1937; Satyapal to Bose, 8 Dec. 1938, AICC PL10 1937–9; Gerald A. Heeger, 'The

Even as it was, it was by no means certain as late as the mid-1930s that the great majority of these dominant peasant communities across the length and breadth of British India were ready as yet to give their support to Congress. As with the intelligentsia and the commercial communities (with whom through various religious, professional, commercial, educational and marital connections they were so often linked) there were not many of them who were ready to chance their all in nationalist agitations. Up to this point Congress, as it well recognised, was in very many areas almost as marginal to Indian existence as the Raj itself. It now looks as if by the 1930s competition for the allegiance of the dominant peasant communities stood at the heart of its conflict with the British.[174] The Congress rhetoric spoke of mobilising the masses; the British of instituting further constitutional reforms. It is on these latter years which we should now focus.

Back in the 1910s some of Britain's rulers had begun to feel that to continue to rely upon their 'neo-darbari' controllers to secure their rule would no longer suffice.[175] Their anxieties had become more urgent after 1916 as the Congress Moderates began to slip into the Extremist camp.[176] As they saw things, the Montagu–Chelmsford Reforms were then designed to pull these Moderates back to support of the Raj.[177] But they also hoped that by enfranchising up to 4 per cent of the population they could bring the 'smaller landed gentry', who had been among their prime supporters, within 'constitutional' politics, and thereby 'furnish a useful and independent contingent to the legislative bodies of the future'.[178] In the continued belief that 'the strength and virtue and sanctity of India still lie in her innumerable small zamindars and occupancy tenants', the Raj, they felt, should 'call in the old world to balance the new.'[179]

Growth of the Congress Movement in the Punjab, 1920–40', *Journal of Asian Studies*, 32 no. 1 (Nov. 1972), 39–51; Stephen Oren, 'The Sikhs, Congress, and the Unionists in British Punjab, 1937–45', *Modern Asian Studies*, 8 no. 3 (July 1974), 397–418.

[174] E.g. Ch. Sec. UP to Commissioners etc., 12 Feb. 1918, Meston P. 15; GoI to LGs, 24 June 1929, H. Poll 179/29; B.N. Sen to J. Nehru, 29 Oct. 1929, AICC G40 (ii) 1929 II; Emerson to Haig, 3 Jan. 1930, II. Poll 98/30; Rajputana and Central India PCC Report, 22 Sept. 1930, AICC 24 1930; Berar PCC to J. Nehru, 25 Sept. 1930, AICC 30/30; Mahakoshal report, 29 Jan. 1931, AICC G9 1930; Willingdon to Hoare, 11 Nov. 1934, Templewood P. 8; GoI to LGs, 21 Jan. 1935, H. Poll 3/16/34; Shillidy to Knight, 7 May 1935, Knight to Hallett, 20 May 1935, H. Poll 3/8/35; M. Desai to Nehru, 6 Sept. 1935, JNP Gandi file; Craik to Governors, 12 June 1936, H. Poll 4/8/36. Above all see H. Poll 14/28/32, and J.P. Narayan P. 116; Prasad P. IX/36/4; AICC G30(a) 1937.

[175] Note by Meston, 21 July 1913, Meston P. 15; Meston to Chelmsford, 19 Aug. 1916, Meston P. 1.

[176] E.g. Meston to Chelmsford: 11 Jan. 1917, Meston P. 1; 7 Feb. 1917, Meston P. 17; 21 May 1917, Meston to Chhatari, 8 July 1917, Meston P. 4.

[177] E.g. Robertson to Meston, 18 July 1917, *ibid.*

[178] *Report on Indian Constitutional Reforms* (Montagu–Chelmsford), Calcutta 1918, p. 95.

[179] Morris to Meston, 24 Sept. 1917, Meston P. 19.

Thereafter for nearly twenty years, until indeed as late as 1934,[180] Britain's rulers in India sought to split the nationalist ranks with a view to creating a working entente with its less vehement sections. They knew this would entail further concessions. They gambled, however, upon the hope that further extensions of the franchise would provide them with greater support. Progress along these lines was chequered in the 1920s, but, thanks to the inducements which the 'dyarchy' regime offered to those who chose to participate in it, it was only in Bengal that a collapse of the Montagu–Chelmsford constitution threatened – and there Muslim votes were very successfully mobilised to spike the nationalist guns.[181] (In the Central Provinces when there were similar threats, they were dispelled by the elevation first of Tambe and then of Raghavendra Rao.)[182] When, therefore, a further round of reforms was called for by the late 1920s, the British were by no means unhopeful that their earlier policy could simply be taken a step or two further. The ideas of 'the small landholders and the more substantial peasantry', so the Government of India opined in 1930, did not 'necessarily coincide with those of the corresponding urban classes'. Even civil disobedience, they believed, 'had left the rural districts but little affected'. They were ready therefore to 'take some risks' in extending the franchise to around '10 per cent of the total population' – so long, they insisted, as there was 'due regard to the respective claims of urban and rural areas'. 'We attach great importance,' they declared, 'to securing genuine and effective representation of rural interests.'[183]

It is rather . . . as a source of potential political influence [so the Simon Commission had lately remarked] than as a means of satisfying a demand for reform that the vote must be regarded in India . . . If a new Act of Parliament is to confer powers of self-government on the provincial councils, it should at the same time provide means for securing that these councils will in time rest on wider popular support than they can at present, so that the transferred powers may not remain in the hands of an oligarchy.[184]

The political calculus as authoritative British opinion saw it was thus explicitly stated.

It was clear to most of those concerned that (until the mid-1940s at least) the British were strongly placed to crush a widespread insurrection. The events of 1942 were ultimately to confirm that, as 1858 and 1919 had twice

---

[180] E.g. Haig's note, 30 Mar. 1934, H. Poll 4/4/34.   [181] Broomfield, *Elite Politics*, ch. 7.
[182] D.E.U. Baker, 'The Art of Governing: Sir Montagu Butler, the Central Provinces and Berar, India, 1925–33', cyclostyled paper, Perth, 1975.
[183] GoI, *Despatch on Constitutional Reforms*, Simla, 1930, pp. 4, 9, 23, 24.
[184] *Report of the Indian Statutory Commission*, Calcutta 1930, vol. 2, pp. 90, 94. Cf. '. . . we should go on quite definitely with the Bill . . . for I am still convinced that the great majority of the people of the country, though inarticulate, are not in favour of Congress and wish us to go forward steadily towards responsible government', Willingdon to Hoare, 19 Nov. 1934, Templewood P. 8.

done previously. The British had little fear too from a rural revolt. They successfully suppressed the Moplahs in 1921,[185] the Red Shirts in the early 1930s, and even the Midnapore uprisings then and later. Certainly between 1931 and 1935 they were deeply worried by the Bengal terrorists.[186] Asked in 1933 about the incidence of terrorism in UP, Clay, the chief secretary, remarked that although it had not spread there yet, it would do so shortly if constitutional reforms were delayed much longer.[187] It took Britain's two past-masters in these situations, Sir Charles Tegart[188] and Sir John Anderson,[189] to curb the terrorism in Bengal. But it was done.

The British were for a time greatly perturbed about rural agitations. They were especially careful to forestall these in the Punjab. In 1907 Minto vetoed the much disliked Canal Colonies Bill; in the 1920s the Governor, Sir Malcolm Hailey, handled the Akalis with considerable circumspection; while in 1931 his successor was swift to make revenue concessions of 24 per cent when the world slump hit.[190] They persisted, moreover, with their earlier attempts at agrarian reform in such places as UP.[191] But in 1928 Sardar Vallabhbhai Patel outwitted the Bombay Government with his satyagraha against a new revenue settlement in Bardoli and the British were forced to retreat.[192] About this Irwin, the viceroy, was deeply disturbed. In May 1929 he called a meeting of all the provincial Revenue Members and insisted that nothing like this should happen again;[193] the unpopular new revenue settlements that contemporaneously were creating an agitation in the Andhra delta were, as a consequence it seems, now held up.[194] This, however, was only one part of the government's response and when, at the height of the first Civil Disobedience Movement, the Bombay Government asked if they could have an unequivocal assurance that they could institute irrevocable forfeitures of land against those who participated in a purely political no-revenue campaign, they were immediately given the undertakings they sought.[195] Irwin, moreover, successfully resisted all Gandhi's

185 R.N. Hitchcock, *A History of the Malabar Rebellion*, Madras, 1925.
186 Willingdon to Hoare, 20 Dec. 1931, Templewood P. 5.
187 Clay to Hallett, 11 Sept. 1933, H. Poll 45/17/33.
188 Sir Charles Tegart, *Terrorism in India*, Royal Empire Society, London, 1932.
189 J.W. Wheeler-Bennett, *John Anderson, Viscount Waverley*, London, 1962, ch. 5
190 N.G. Barrier, 'The Arya Smaj and Congress Politics in the Punjab 1894–1908', *Journal of Asian Studies*, 26 no. 3 (May 1967), 375. Khuswant Singh, *History of the Sikhs*, II, p. 211; Noyce to Emerson, 20 May 1931, H. Poll 33/9/31.
191 Walter C. Neale, *Economic Change in Rural India, Land Tenure and Reform in Uttar Pradesh, 1800–1955*, New Haven, 1962.
192 Gopal, *Irwin*, ch. 3; Ghanshyam Shah, 'Tradition Society and Political Mobilization: The Experience of the Bardoli Satyagraha (1920–1928)', *Contributions to Indian Sociology*, ns 8 (1974), 89–107.
193 Proceedings of Conference at Simla, 1 May 1929, H. Poll 138/29.
194 Cf. Patel to J. Nehru, 19 Nov. 1931, AICC G60 1931; Patel to Emerson, 21 Nov. 1931, AICC 53 1931.
195 Ch. Sec. Bombay, to GoI, 17 June 1930, GoI to Ch. Sec. Bombay, 3 July 1930, H. Poll 214/30. Cf. AICC G80 1930.

attempts to have the lands so confiscated in Gujarat in 1930 restored as part of the Gandhi–Irwin Pact.[196] With the consequence that in 1932 when civil disobedience resumed, rural agitation in Gujarat never effectively revived.[197]

UP in 1931 saw the new two-pronged British response to rural agitations exemplified very clearly. With the onset of the economic crisis, the government of UP, unlike the Punjab Government, was initially slow in making revenue remissions, perhaps because Hailey, who had now become governor here, was away on leave.[198] Congress had early on become involved in a no-rent campaign. On his return, Hailey, in response, promptly set about securing some finely judged rent remissions; since he knew these to be inadequate (he was seriously perturbed about a probable revenue shortfall), when the no-rent campaign persisted, he soon showed himself ready to work for some more detailed concessions in the Allahabad area. But when these too failed to halt the agitation, he declared a state of emergency, and swiftly imprisoned the Congress leaders; whereupon, at long last, the agitation did collapse.[199] The British still remained highly sensitive, however, to rural agitation. When in 1933 a no-revenue campaign threatened in Andhra for example, the government of India told the government of Madras in no unmistaken terms that it must make extensive remissions promptly. They did so, and the agitation evaporated.[200] The Raj's remarkably successful post-Bardoli policies against rural agitations were then neatly summarised in 1936 as:

(a) to rectify grievances,
(b) to deal firmly with illegal, subversive or seditious activities carried on under cloak of *bona fide* action for meeting local grievances.[201]

It is of considerable significance that in the great anti-British agitations of the 1940s no-rent and no-revenue campaigns scarcely figured at all.

The problem here, as Gandhi seems to have realised, was that whilst the actions characteristic of Congress agitations in towns – hartals, processions, flag-raisings, etc. – could lead to broken bones and periods of imprisonment, they did not often threaten anyone's long-term livelihood. But in the countryside no-rent and no-revenue campaigns did: ejectments and confiscations could be literally disastrous for those who participated in them, because in defence of the land revenue system – the central citadel of the Raj

196 Cf. Bombay to GoI, 25 Mar. 1931, H. Poll 33/I/31; Surat police report, 5 May 1931, H. Poll 33/III/31.
197 Patel to J. Nehru, 21 July 1931, AICC G60 1931; Emerson's note 18 Apr. 1932, H. Poll 14/17/32; Maxwell to Hallett, 19 July 1934, H. Poll 50/I/34.
198 Emerson to Prasad, 28 Mar. 1931, Hailey to Emerson, 27 Apr. 1931, H. Poll 33/XI/31.
199 Hailey to Crerar, 8 May 1931, H. Poll 33/XVI/31, 33/24/31, 33/36/31; AICC 63 1931.
200 H. Poll 4/20/33, especially GoI to Madras, tel, 30 Nov. 1933.
201 Hallett's note on 'Congress and the Agrarian Problem', 5 May 1936, H. Poll 4/8/36.

– the British could be as adamant as they were in defending their army and police. Gandhi showed himself ready to support such campaigns where there were specifically identifiable grievances and/or extensive preparations; but despite considerable pressure from such as Vallabhbhai Patel and Jawaharlal Nehru, he never made them the chief prongs of his nationalist campaigns.[202]

The critical years for the Indian national movement came as the 1930s opened. Bardoli had been immensely encouraging, but would clearly be very difficult to repeat. Congress had failed to capture, let alone destroy, the reformed Legislative Councils. The British were making a strenuous effort, not only – with their promise of a Round Table Conference in London – to split the nationalist forces, but to outmarch them again; while, to Gandhi's dismay, there were clear signs of a slippage on the Congress side into violence.[203]

It was in these circumstances that in 1930, in the aftermath of his own recruiting tours in the 1920s, Gandhi eventually determined to seize the initiative once again; strove to effect a demonstration of national unity by holding together as much of the movement as he could; and launched, not a no-revenue, but a salt satyagraha, as a great symbolic defiance of the British. Thousands, he believed, could personally participate in this, and thereby give vent to the frustrations and anger they felt, without resorting to the socially fragmenting violence which he dreaded.[204] By the time of his arrest in May 1930 he had the movement solidly behind him – the factions and futilities of the 1920s being pushed aside. By June he had the British badly frightened.[205] By the following February he was in personal negotiations with the Viceroy.

In the aftermath of the ensuing Gandhi–Irwin Pact an extraordinary situation obtained.[206] During this fascinating interlude the British looked to Gandhi to control the forces he had unleashed, while Gandhi pushed his claims that Congress represented India, and that over any matters in dispute the British should work through its leaders. This, as so many appreciated, presaged a *bouleversement*; but since the British would not recognise Gandhi's more extensive claims, while Gandhi himself found it increasingly difficult to control his followers (particularly during his visit to London in late 1931), the Pact collapsed, conflict resumed, and between

202 E.g. *Young India*, 5 Sept. 1929, *CWMG*, 41, 214; *Bombay Chronicle*, *re* Vallabhbhai Patel, 9 July 1929; Patel to J. Nehru, 25 Nov. 1931, AICC G60 1931.
203 D.A. Low, 'The Purna Swaraj Decision 1929; New Potentialities for Indian Nationalist Biography' in Wang Gungwu (ed.), *Self and Biography: Essays on the Individual and Society in Asia*, Sydney, 1976, ch. 7.
204 Low (ed.), *Congress and the Raj*, ch. 4 (Brown).
205 V to SoS, tel, 2 June 1930, H. Poll 483/30.
206 E.g. AICC 1931, 2, 3, 17, 22, 32, 53, 75; H. Poll 33/I/31, 33/II/31, 33/III/31, 33/19/31; Gopal, *Irwin*, ch. 6.

1932 and 1934 the police effectively repressed the ensuing agitation.[207] But through the Poona Pact Gandhi entrenched the unity he had secured. Throughout these years it was, moreover, of prime importance that there were countless clashes between police and various crowds of Congress supporters, and a good many beatings and ill-treatments in gaol. For as a consequence (or so it eventually appeared) the moral authority of the British Raj became mortally undermined; common memories and overarching loyalties were created amongst very many Congressmen; and the British clearly lost much of their political hold over the towns and cities of India.[208] The renewed Civil Disobedience campaign was nevertheless very effectively repressed; the British were not forced to their knees;[209] they now became increasingly niggardly over constitutional concessions; Gandhi, for his part, began to see himself as no longer so relevant to the Congress cause; while, on the available evidence, the support for the Congress of many dominant peasants was still by no means assured.[210] The British had now become exceedingly careful not to squeeze such people any longer; and by giving their leading edges the vote, they were for the first time according them a substantive position within the public realm.

At this critical juncture it was the Tamil Congress leader, Rajagopalachari (who had formerly been a staunch 'no-changer' but had now turned 'pro-changer') who above all articulated the way forward.[211] In April 1934 he pleaded with Gandhi 'that the parliamentary programme [to which the British were now pushing the Congress leadership] be done in the name of the Congress' rather than in that of a miscellany of swarajist parties. 'If the magic of the Congress name and memory of its past sacrifices are utilised', he argued, then a position of 'prestige and confidence among the masses' could be established, and 'whatever the [new] constitution may be it can give us the power' which the Congress had enjoyed at the time of the Gandhi–Irwin Pact.[212]

To the dismay of the British and their supporters, and the surprised delight of the Congress camp, so it eventuated.[213] Congressmen, now released from prison, soon became not just leaders of a political movement

---

[207] E.g. *CWMG* 55–8, *passim*; H. Poll 33/IV/31; Emerson's note, 7 Apr. 1931, H. Poll 33/I/31; Garrett to Ch. Sec. Bombay, 22 Apr. Hailey to Emerson, 2 May 1931, H. Poll 33/XI/31.

[208] E.g. Rajputana and Central India PCC report, 22 Sept. 1930, AICC 24 1930; H. Poll 14/13/31; AICC P35 1932, 3, 1933.

[209] Low (ed.), *Congress and the Raj*, ch. 5.   [210] H. Poll 50/I/34, 31/III/34, *passim*.

[211] For his skill at the time of the Gandhi–Irwin Pact see H. Poll 33/9/31, 33/30/31; Low (ed.), *Congress and the Raj*, ch. 8 (Arnold).

[212] Rajagopalachari to Gandhi, 21 Apr. 1934, H. Poll 4/4/34; Gallagher, *Locality, Province and Nation*, pp. 301–2, 306; for the opposite point of view, see Prasad to Kripalani, 9 Aug. 1935, Prasad P. III/35/2.

[213] Low (ed.), *Congress and the Raj*, ch. 5.

but cadres of a political party seeking to win elections.[214] In so doing they were able to draw on the moral authority which Gandhi and their own participation in his satyagraha campaigns had won for them[215] (and on the discontent which now existed with the 'dyarchy' regimes),[216] with the result that the British, who had pushed Congress away from civil disobedience and into constitutional politics, now found themselves hoist with their own petard. Whereas the last elections Congress had fought in 1926 (still on a very narrow franchise) had produced, so far as the Congress was concerned, some very ragged results,[217] Congress overwhelmingly won the Central Legislative Assembly elections on a similar franchise in 1934.[218] It went on to win innumerable district board elections in the next two or three years; and in 1937, at the end of what was a long three-year campaign, eventually secured legislative majorities in the provincial elections in seven of the eleven provinces of India.[219] For these the British had introduced new property franchises which had extended the electorates to 11.5 per cent of their population. 'The great majority of electors in the rural areas were certainly cultivators or landholders, as the primary franchise qualification was almost always the payment of a certain level of land revenue, of rent, or of tax.'[220] Since a high proportion of seats were also 'General Rural', it can reasonably be said that the dramatic Congress victories in 1937 now showed that despite the understandable hesitations of so many dominant peasants to commit themselves unequivocally to Congress' agitations, large numbers of them had eventually (in addition to so many in the intelligentsia and commercial classes) given their political allegiance to the Congress in the less dangerous context of the ballot box. They had certainly been wooed. Vallabhbhai Patel had made himself busy with a campaign of plague amelioration in Borsad.[221] Rajendra Prasad had organised earthquake relief in Bihar.[222] Congress in UP had dropped much of its poor peasant rhetoric, and turned itself into a dominant peasant party.[223] Even the *bhadralok*-dominated Bengal Congress had given some of its energies to rural

---

[214] For British tributes to Congress electoral organisation in 1937, see UP, Bihar, *FR*1 Feb. 1937, H. Poll 4/9/37. For details on the 1934 elections see Ansari P. on the 1937 elections, Prasad P.

[215] E.g. Prasad to Ansari, 26 Dec. 1934, Prasad P. III/35/2.

[216] D.A. Washbrook, 'Madras', *Locality, Province and Nation*, p. 205.

[217] Richard Gordon, 'The Hindu Mahasabha and the Indian National Congress', pp. 145–203.

[218] AICC G9 1934.   [219] AICC P20 (pt. 2) 1938.

[220] David Taylor, 'The Reconstruction and use of the Statistics of the Provincial Elections of 1937', *Bulletin of Quantitative and Computer Methods in South Asian Studies*, 2 (March 1974), p. 20.

[221] Shillidy to Knight, 9 May, Knight to Halliday, 20 May 1935, H. Poll 3/8/35.

[222] Hallett to Tallents, 9 Feb. 1934, H. Poll 133/34; R. Prasad, *Autobiography*, Bombay, 1957, chs. 76–7.

[223] G. Pandey, *The Ascendency of the Congress in Uttar Pradesh 1926–34*, Delhi, 1978; Sec. UP PCC to Doulatram, 28 Aug. 1936, Prasad P. IX/36/3.

recruitment;[224] while the right-wing Congress had resolutely stood its ground against the new left-wing forces.[225] The interest of influential local leaders in the fruits of full responsible governments in the provinces, which the new Government of India Act of 1935 now provided, was, moreover, assiduously fostered.[226] The control this allowed over land revenue administration was particularly emphasised.[227] Above all the straightforward nationalist arguments against the immoralities of foreign rule were vigorously propounded. The whole campaign was managed indeed with quite singular dexterity;[228] and the dominant peasant voters responded fully. It was commonly reported that

many villagers observed fast on the day of polling and broke it after exercising their franchise in favour of the Congress candidate . . . village voters bowed before the Congress candidate boxes as a mark of respect to Mahatma Gandhi.[229]

It was this which was Congress' greatest, unimpeachable victory over the British for, in a way the Congress agitations had of themselves failed to do, it registered in terms the British allowed as legitimate the uniqueness, strength and range of its political support in India. This was very soon acknowledged in Britain – by the Labour Party leaders and, in essence, by many Conservatives as well.[230] It was recognised too by senior British officials in India, who now set aside their earlier, long-standing, policy of trying to split the nationalist forces, and moved over to a new policy of collaborating with the Congress provincial leaders (as they had nearly done with Gandhi in 1931) in the quite pragmatic hope that, following the electoral demise of their earlier political associates, Congress would now become the new controller of India's political forces under their aegis.[231] The later close association at the national level between Mountbatten and Nehru has long been recognised. Both the British and the Congress archives reveal that between 1937 and 1939 there were similar relationships at the provincial level between Erskine and Rajagopalachari in Madras,

---

[224] 'Brief Summary of Political Events in . . . Bengal . . . 1937', H. Poll 132/38; Humaira Momen, *Muslim Politics in Bengal, A Study of Krishak Praja Party and the Elections of 1937*, Dacca, 1972, p. 66.
[225] E.g. Patel to Nehru [8 Jan. 1937], AICC E14 1936; Birla to Thakurdas, 20 Apr. 1936, Thakurdas P.
[226] E.g. Rajagopalachari to Prasad, 24 Feb. 1936, Prasad P. viii/36.
[227] E.g. Bihar *FR*1 Feb. 1937, H. Poll 4/9/37.
[228] Kripalani to Prasad, 20 Nov. 1935, Prasad P. III/35/4; Ch. Sec. Bihar to Maxwell, 16 Feb. 1937, H. Poll 4/3/37, AICC Gen. Sec. report 1937, AICC G47 1937.
[229] Deputy Central Intelligence Officer, Nagpur, 24 Feb. 1937; see also Bihar, UP, CP *FR*1 Feb. 1937, H. Poll 4/9/37.
[230] Nehru's 'Notes for Working Committee', 30 July, 6 Sept. 1938, JNP; Cripps to Nehru, 16 Nov. 1939, *ibid.*, Cripps file; Zetland to Linlithgow, 20 Dec. 1939, Zetland P. 11.
[231] For an interesting commentary on this, see Linlithgow to Zetland, tel, 30 Jan. 1940, Linlithgow P. 19.

Haig and Pant in UP, Lumley in Kher and Bombay, and elsewhere too.[232] This move largely succeeded from the British point of view in holding the potentially disintegrating political forces in India in check. (The land revenue apparatus was tinkered with by the new Congress governments, but left essentially intact.) The arrangements were satisfactory too to the Congress leaders. From the beginning of 1936 they had known that their followers would insist that they should seize the levers of provincial power which the new constitution offered to them.[233] After a largely ritualistic delay, during which they demonstrated the effective authority of the Congress leadership, they agreed to accept office under the chairmanship of British governors. Their great electoral triumph allowed them to call most of the tunes. Having already laid hands on so many district and municipal boards from which the British had long since relinquished control,[234] they were now able to seize power at the provincial level without going through the trauma of a further frustrating agitation. As a consequence Congress in the provinces all but became the Raj. The shrewdest amongst its leaders were quite satisfied, moreover, that although India itself was as yet by no means independent, a short period in provincial office (in order to ensure that what was now the Congress 'Party' would be seen amongst its voters as India's eventual independent Government) could readily be followed by a renewed agitation for a final push if that should be required.[235]

But it was not merely the British and Congress who quickly appreciated the significance of the Congress victories.[236] The most arresting evidence of their importance can be seen in the very large increase in Congress membership at this time;[237] in the shock-wave that went through the Muslims in India that led to the marked revival of the Muslim League;[238] and in the burgeoning of 'Praja Mandals' in the princely states.[239] It was of central importance that so many of those who had hitherto tuned their activities to the dictates of the British, now began to look to Congress as the

---

[232] Congress Working Committee proceedings, 14–17 Aug. 1937, AICC Misc. 42 1936; Lumley to Linlithgow, 3 Apr. 1938, NAI Reforms 113/38G; and communications from Drs Arnold, Brennan and David Baker.

[233] Kripalani to Prasad, 15 Feb. 1936, Prasad P. III/36/1; for the pressures, see Prasad to Dalvi, 24 Sept. 1935, Prasad P. III/35/3.

[234] E.g. Bayly, *Local Roots*, p. 244.

[235] Report on remarks by Rajendra Prasad by Deputy Central Intelligence Officer, Nagpur, 24 Feb. 1937, H. Poll 4/9/37.

[236] For some details in one locality see Harold A. Gould, 'The Emergence of Modern Indian Politics: Political Development in Faizabad, part II, 1935 to Independence', *Journal of Commonwealth and Comparative Politics*, 12 no. 2 (July 1974), 157–88.

[237] It rose from 6.36 lakhs in 1936 to over 3 million in 1937, Congress General Secretary's report for 1937, AICC G47 1937.

[238] For a general account, see P. Hardy, *The Muslims of British Inia*, Cambridge, 1972, ch. 9.

[239] Low (ed.), *Congress and the Raj*, chs. 13 (Manor), and 14 (Jeffrey); Phadnis, *Integration*, ch. 7; Sisson, *Congress in Rajasthan*, chs. 3 and 4; Menon to Mehta, 2 Apr. 1938, All-India States Peoples Congress P. Gp I/5/1935–42.

political force to which they should chiefly relate.[240] Amongst the Muslim
elite in the Muslim-minority provinces a state of near panic led them to raise
the cry of 'Islam in danger' – successfully, because their co-religionists
could no longer look to them to safeguard their interests; while in the
princely states many in their often miniscule elites suddenly realised that
political power had now passed to their counterparts in the provinces of
British India, while they themselves were still subject to the autocratic rule
of Maharajahs and Dewans.

It is certainly true that the British lorded it over India for another ten
years. It is no less true that there was, for a time, a strong conservative
reaction in British policy towards India; that between 1942 and 1945
Congress itself was resolutely repressed; and that this clearly demonstrated
that the British still had the power to change the rules of the political conflict
if they so chose. These were, of course, the years of the Second World War
– and that introduced a major variable.[241] Congress leaders rightly sensed
that the wartime emergency was being used by some of Britain's Conservative leaders to cloud their profound reluctance to transfer power to
Congress at the all-India level. Many more Britishers believed that it was
necessary to take a strong line against Congress when its consequential
hostility coincided with the great crisis for humanity, which, as the British
saw it, now confronted the world. In these circumstances some British
Conservatives were active in exploring ways by which Britain might retain a
dominating strategic position in India in the post-war period. There can be
no doubt too that Muslim separatism was now encouraged. This in turn
fuelled the megalomania of the Viceroy, Lord Linlithgow, that only the
British could solve India's problems, and that it would be in the country's
best interests if Congress could be 'crushed' (a view which by 1940 was no
better than a *pis aller* from the bankruptcy of Britain's all-India policies now
that the Federation idea had collapsed). Such an idea was contested in the
Cabinet in London as early as 1940.[242] It was contested again early in 1942.
It sufficiently prevailed, however, in Delhi to mastermind both the
draconian suppression of the 'Quit India' movement in August 1942, and
the viceroy's adamant stance against Gandhi's 'epic' fast early the next year.
With consummate, aristocratic fortitude, Linlithgow held the line, and the
bitterness in the conflict between Congress and the Raj reached its peak.[243]

But with the war going in the Allies' favour, Wavell, Linlithgow's
successor, field marshal and Churchill's appointee though he was,
brusquely discarded in 1943 such wartime fantasies, and set his mind to

240 Baker, *Central Province*; D. Arnold, *The Congress in Tamilnad. Nationalist Politics in South
    India 1919–1937*, Canberra, 1977.
241 Low (ed.), *Congress and the Raj*. ch. 11 (Voigt).
242 H. Poll (I) 6/13/40 especially, Linlithgow to Governors, 8 Aug. 1940.
243 On all this, see Mansergh, *Transfer of Power*, vols. 1–3, and John Glendevon, *The Viceroy
    at Bay*, London, 1971.

arranging a British withdrawal from India as soon as the war was over. This, he was convinced, was what British public opinion now desired. He retained the wartime tenderness of the British for India's Muslims – which seemed justified by the Muslim League's capture for the first time of most of the Muslim seats at the 1946 elections. The impact of the events of 1937 then once more surfaced in Wavell's proposals for a solution of the final crisis through a British withdrawal from India province by province. Wavell became so fixated on a British withdrawal that he fumbled his relations with the Congress leaders, and neither resisted, nor prepared for, the partition into two states which now stood in the offing.[244] Because Britain's parlous position in the immediate post-war years made such indecision intolerable,[245] he had eventually to be replaced by Mountbatten – who established a firm association with the Congress leaders (because they headed a solid political edifice to whom power at the centre could effectively be transferred); opted promptly for partition (so as to mitigate country-wide civil war); and carried through swiftly the ensuing transfers of power.[246]

Some have been tempted to suggest that in the end a good deal turned on the Indian National Army trials, the Bombay Naval mutiny, and such like. They overlook the basic reality that by this time the British had decided to leave.[247] As a consequence of their experience in 1937 most Congress leaders now knew, moreover, (especially after 1942) that the future chiefly turned on their winning the next elections. For them a revolution had become all but unnecessary. They could have the substance of their desires through the transfer of power which in principle the British were offering them. And so, in the end, it transpired. One thinks especially here of Vallabhbhai Patel, who long thought (through the years of the Non-Co-operation movement, the Bardoli satyagraha, and the Civil Disobedience movements) that the way to proceed was by sustained dominant peasant satyagraha, but who, following the Congress victories in 1937, and the threatening upheavals (for him) of 1942, came out of prison in 1945, not to organise yet another agitation (he was a prime figure in defusing the Bombay mutiny), but to organise efficiently the upcoming elections. At these, outside the Muslim-majority areas, Congress outdid its 1937 successes (the earlier, remaining patchiness had gone). Patel's was then the prime voice that spoke for Congress' acceptance of office in a national government in mid-1946, because, in an otherwise potentially revolution-

244 Moon, *The Viceroy's Diary, passim*, esp. ch. 1 and p. 62.
245 Paul Simpson, 'Imperial Mendicancy and Resource Diplomacy: Transfers of Power and Independence for Britain', Honours thesis, University of New South Wales, 1974.
246 H.V. Hodson, *The Great Divide*, London, 1969; Philips and Wainwright, *Partition of India*.
247 In some respects the most illuminating evidence lies in the British reluctance to assist the Dutch to recover Indonesia, S.L. van der Wal, *Officiele Bescheiden Betreffende de Nederlands–Indonesische Betrekkingen 1945–1950* 's-Gravenhage, I, 1971, e.g. p. 310; II, 1972, e.g. p. 458.

ary situation, he saw all central power here within his grasp.[248] Congress could now, in fact, become the Raj.

In some of the princely states revolution was rather nearer the surface. In Mysore there was indeed a political revolution – muted here because to save his reputation the Maharajah meekly bowed before it. In Travancore there was another one too, staunched only because the Congress leaders feared a real left-wing revolution, such as shortly exploded in parts of Hyderabad.[249] Here and elsewhere Butler's earlier notion of making the states a bulwark against the nationalist storm (which British officials had painfully discarded a few years previously)[250] met its denouement. For some decades strong Indian Dewans had satisfied both Indian pride and British requirements.[251] But, especially after 1939, and more particularly in August 1942 – when Dewans followed strong British hints that they should incarcerate their Congressmen as well – Dewani regimes had become conspicuous for their bitter opposition towards local politicians. As a reward for their dedication to the causes of nationalism and democracy, these politicians now began to gather wider support (not least from amongst their states' dominant peasants); and, as the British showed signs of departing, these Princely/Dewani regimes either tardily made concessions that undermined them anyway, or wriggled ineffectively to defy their fates. In one or two instances (Travancore, Hyderabad) *laissez faire* led in its last stages to some desperate bids for separate independence. But when the British departed, most of the 'bulwarks' were but jetsam on the beach.[252]

By then the Indian political left was driftwood too. For decades nationalism had avowed the cause of the masses. The rise of the Congress Socialists in the 1930s had signalled that many were sceptical that this had much meaning.[253] In 1936 there was within Congress itself a classic confrontation between those who were anxious to organise a multi-class peasant revolt with which to destroy the British position, and by extension inaugurate a more egalitarian order, and those who feared that, while not effecting the first, it could all too easily bring on the second.[254] The flash point here was Bihar, and the right wing Congress leadership desperately sought to defuse it. Up until 1942 they were largely successful; but Bihar and its environs then erupted. It was of great significance that when it did so it was not the right-wing Congress leaders who were faced with having to

[248] *Sardar Patel's Correspondence*, II; Moon, *Viceroy's Diary*, p. 29.
[249] Low (ed.), *Congress and the Raj*, chs. 13 (Manor) and 14 (Jeffrey).
[250] By 1939, and still more by 1940, many in the Political Department of the Government of India had given away the princes as a lost cause, communication from Dr I.F.S. Copland.
[251] Such people as Sir Mirza Ismail, Sir Akbar Hydari, Sir Khrishnaswamy Aiyar, Sir C.P. Ramaswamy Aiyar.
[252] V.P. Menon, *The Story of the Integration of the Indian States*, Calcutta, 1936. See also various contributions in Jeffrey, *Princely States*.
[253] H.K. Singh, *History of the Praja Socialist Party 1934–59*, Lucknow, 1959.
[254] J.P. Narayan P. 116; Prasad P. IX/36/4; AICC G30(a) 1937.

suppress it, but the British, and the British could do so with impunity, since the explosion occurred at the height of the Second World War when they could employ massive violence against it without the world protesting. Rarely have revolutionaries chosen a more unpromising moment.[255] Given, moreover, that the electoral franchises in 1946 were still virtually as limited as in 1937, the policies of the Congress governments that came to power at state and national level as independence dawned were quite unrevolutionary. As these were still much dependent on dominant peasant votes they were naturally opposed to very large landlords and soon set about carrying through Zamindari Abolition Acts: but since their supporters were equally opposed to real social revolution, the new governments soon set about curtailing as well the Tebhaga movement in Bengal, the Communist threat in Kerala, and the Telangana revolt in Hyderabad.[256] Because none of these had any of the force of the 1942 uprising, they were very soon checked.

The basic essentials in all of these issues can be readily captured in one striking personal example. After independence Morarji Desai became chief minister of Bombay, finance minister at the centre, and a long term aspirant for India's prime ministership, which he eventually attained in 1977. In 1936 as secretary of the Gujarat Prantik Samity he roundly responded to a formal questionnaire from the Congress 'Mass Contacts Committee' by saying that his committee felt strongly that class conflict should not be introduced into the Congress structure.[257] In his autobiography he castigated the Congress Socialists for their underhand ways and their disloyalty to the Gandhian principles of truth and non-violence. For a person of his background, a former deputy collector in British service, and an Anavil Brahmin – and as such a member of an important dominant peasant community in south Gujarat – imprisonment as a Gandhian satyagrahi began by being a vexatious ordeal. But the Gandhian way presaged a means by which to destroy British dominion in India without endangering the status quo in any other respect; and (to one of his readers at least) it accordingly appears that such a person set about training himself to suffer imprisonment according to Gandhian principles as the prime means of securing his nationalist objectives without setting loose a violent social upheaval.[258]

---

255 Low (ed.), *Congress and the Raj*, ch. 10 (Harcourt).
256 R. Jeffrey, 'India's Working Class Revolt: Punnapra-Vayalar and the Communist "Conspiracy" of 1946', *Indian Economic and Social History Review*, 18 no. 2 (1981), 97–122; Sunil Sen, *Agrarian Struggle in Bengal 1946–47*, New Delhi, 1972; and D.N. Dhanagare, 'Social Origins of the Peasant Insurrection in Telangana (1946–51', *Contributions to Indian Sociology*, ns 8 (1974), 125; Carolyn M. Elliott, 'Decline of a Patrimonial Regime: the Telangana Rebellion in India, 1946–51', *Journal of Asian Studies*, 34 no. 1 (Nov. 1974), 27–47.
257 M. Desai to Doulatram, 28 July 1936, Prasad P. IX/36/2.   258 Desai, *My Life*, I.

India, it has to be said, was never physically wrenched from the hands of the British. The British were increasingly concerned however that this might happen. They knew better than most that agitations could not ultimately be stopped by simply adopting an unyielding stance. They accordingly made a series of attempts to enhance the role of those who might still be mobilised in support of a British regulated regime. Given their own unusually strong commitment to parliamentary institutions, this entailed successive instalments of constitutional 'reforms'. Ironically, but quite logically, the denouement then turned, not upon the success of any major revolt against them, but upon the eventual ability of the Congress leaders (building upon their record of sacrifice, and upon much hostile reaction against British repression) to win over to their side, within the arena of electoral politics the British held so dear, those dominant peasants and others whom, in their latter-day attempt to hold the nationalists at bay, the British in the 1930s had decided to enfranchise. Once this had happened, most dramatically by 1937, only those blinded by their own personal prejudices could fail to see the demise of the British Raj stamped on the wall.

To the end the apparatus of the Raj maintained by the British remained intact, and was never physically destroyed. Rather, a trifurcated Raj was then yielded to the leaders of the two political parties, the Indian National Congress, and the Muslim League who, in distinct parts of India, had demonstrated through the ballot box the strength of the political support they possessed, more especially amongst the recently enfranchised but, as we began by noticing, very long standing dominant peasant communities. Once the allegiance of large numbers of the latter had swung openly to the nationalist cause, the game, in the terms the British had determined it, was up. Despite grievous last-minute alarums and excursions, the transfers of power inexorably ensued.

4

The forgotten Bania: merchant communities and the Indian National Congress

In studies of the history of the Indian National Congress a good deal of attention has been given to the manner in which different categories of India's population became, or did not become (or ceased to be) in association with it. This is, no doubt, a blunt approach that allows far too little for all the innumerable nuances that characterised the Congress' support (or shortfalls in support) that close, detailed, investigations reveal. Yet the broad brush was the fairly regular instrument of those who described these matters whilst the struggle with the British *Raj* was on. When, for example, in 1936 Rajendra Prasad wrote of the support which Congress enjoyed by that time, he specified 'those who had been to school and college' and 'peasants and cultivators' as its principal adherents, whilst listing 'industrial and field workers' as not as yet having come into its ranks in any significant numbers.[1] The British similarly employed very broad categories when they came to identify both their principal supporters (e.g. 'landlords') and their opponents (e.g. 'the student and teacher class').[2] As we shall see, it is noteworthy that in his listing in 1936 of supporters of the Congress Prasad did not specifically mention 'the commercial communities', whereas in the lists the British made these figured very largely. For in neglecting the commercial communities Prasad was anticipating the short shrift they have received from the majority of the modern generation of Indian historians – the present author amongst them.[3]

A great deal of research has been devoted to the processes by which there came to be enlisted in the Congress and in its support those who, in Prasad's phrase, had 'been to school and college' – the 'western educated'. The

[1] Prasad's draft Mass Contacts Committee's Report, 1936, National Archives of India Prasad papers, IX, 36,4.
[2] See below, footnote 45.
[3] A welcome exception is S. Sarkar, *Modern India 1885–1947*, Delhi, 1983.

participation of goodly numbers of them in the various Associations which sprang up, particularly in the major cities of India, through the middle of the nineteenth century and prior to the founding of the Congress in 1885, is now well known.[4] The role of such people in the foundation of Congress has been extensively explored,[5] and the part they played in its first twenty-five years as well.[6] There have been particular studies too of the activities before and after the First World War of the largest concentrations of them in Bengal,[7] and in Bombay,[8] while their counterparts in Madras have had their historians for these years as well.[9] Their activities during the First World War have then been variously recounted,[10] and the considerable part they played between the two World Wars figures very largely in most standard accounts of the major agitations which Gandhi led in those years.[11] Their participation, moreover, in nationalist politics at provincial level has been extensively recounted for that later period, in Madras particularly.[12] If detailed studies are not quite so abundant for other areas, there is nevertheless considerable information on the part they played in UP,[13] CP,[14]

[4] A. Seal, *The Emergence of Indian Nationalism: Competition and Collaboration in the Later Nineteenth Century*, Cambridge, 1968; S.R. Mehrotra, *The Emergence of the Indian National Congress*, Delhi, 1971.

[5] S.H. Mehrotra, *Emergence*; B. Martin, *New India, 1885*, Berkeley, 1969.

[6] J.R. Mclane, *Indian Nationalism and the Early Congress*, Princeton, 1977; S.A. Wolpert, *Tilak and Gokhale*, California, 1962; B. Chandra, *The Rise and Growth of Economic Nationalism in India. Economic Policies of Indian National Leadership 1881–1915*, Delhi, 1966; B.R. Nanda, *Gokhale, the Indian Moderates, and the British Raj*, Delhi, 1977.

[7] J.H. Broomfield, *Elite Conflict in a Plural Society: 20th Century Bengal*, Berkeley, 1968; L.A. Gordon, *Bengal: The Nationalist Movement 1876–1940*, Delhi, 1974; S. Sarkar, *Swadeshi Movement in Bengal 1903–1908*, New Delhi, 1973; R. Ray, *Social Conflict and Political Unrest in Bengal 1875–1925*, Delhi, 1984.

[8] G. Johnson, *Provincial Politics and Indian Nationalism. Bombay and the Indian National Congress 1880–1915*, Cambridge, 1973; R. Cashman, *The Myth of the Lokamanya; Tilak and Mass Politics in Maharashtra*, California, 1975.

[9] R. Suntharalingam, *Politics and Nationalist Awakening in South India 1852–91*, Arizona, 1974; D.A. Washbrook, *The Emergence of Provincial Politics: Madras Presidency 1870–1920*, Cambridge, 1976).

[10] H.F. Owen, 'Towards Nationwide Agitation and Organization: The Home Rule Leagues 1915–1918', in D.A. Low (ed.), *Soundings in Modern South Asian History*, London, 1968.

[11] Particularly J.M. Brown, *Gandhi's Rise to Power. Indian Politics 1915–1922*, Cambridge, 1972, and *Gandhi and Civil Disobedience: The Mahatma in Indian Politics*, Cambridge, 1977.

[12] E.F. Irshchik, *Politics and Social Conflict in South India: The Non-Brahman Movement and Tamil Separatism 1916–1929*, California, 1969; C.J. Baker, *The Politics of South India 1920–1937*, Cambridge, 1976; D.A. Arnold, *Congress in Tamilnad: Nationalist Politics in South India 1919–37*, Delhi, 1977; B. Stoddart, 'The Structure of Congress Politics in Coastal Andhra 1925–37', in D.A. Low (ed.), *Congress and the Raj. Facets of the Indian Struggle 1917–1947*, London, 1977.

[13] G. Pandey, *The Ascendancy of the Congress in Uttar Pradesh 1926–34. A study in Imperfect Mobilization*, Delhi, 1978; L. Brennan, 'From one Raj to Another: Congress Politics in Rohilkhand, 1930–50', in Low (ed.), *Congress and the Raj*.

[14] D.E.U. Baker, *Changing Political Leadership in an Indian Province: the Central Provinces and Berar 1919–39*, Delhi, 1980.

Bihar,[15] and even Orissa[16] and Assam.[17] We have been given a clear picture as well of the various stances of the many 'western educated' who were not fully-fledged members of the Congress but who nevertheless periodically gave it much support – strong when its actions tallied with their interests, weak, sometimes in the extreme, when it did not: a characteristic of all such categories, as we must note.[18]

Latterly much attention has also been given to the progressive accretion of support to the Congress of well-to-do peasant communities across most – though not all parts – of India from around the end of the First World War to the end of the Second. Broadly this seems to have begun in parts of Bihar.[19] That was soon paralleled in Gujarat[20] and in West Bengal.[21] Similar support then came dramatically from the Khudai Khitmatgars in the Muslim-majority Frontier Province around 1930 (a story which now possesses its professional historian),[22] and around that time too or shortly afterwards in places as far flung as UP,[23] CP,[24] Madras,[25] Maharashtra[26] – though not, importantly, from the Punjab.[27] There were then later accretions in the princely states as these came to be absorbed in the mainstream of Indian and Congress politics as well.[28]

The two principal sources of support for Congress which Rajendra Prasad identified in 1936 have now therefore been extensively studied – though clearly there are many deeper studies to be made than the first generation of scholars who have worked on these subjects could reasonably have been expected to cover.

[15] G. McDonald, 'Unity on Trial: Congress in Bihar, 1929–39', in Low (ed.), *Congress and the Raj*.

[16] U. Mahanty, *Oriya Nationalism*, Delhi, 1982.

[17] A. Guha, *Planter Raj to Swaraj: Freedom Struggle and Electoral Politics in Assam 1826–1947*, Delhi, 1977.

[18] P. Spear, 'A Third Force in India 1920–47: A Study in Political Analysis', in C.H. Philips and M.D. Wainwright (eds.), *The Partition of India. Policies and Perspectives 1935–1947*, London, 1970.

[19] Brown, *Gandhi's Rise to Power*, J. Pouchepadass, 'Local Leaders and the Intelligentsia in the Champaran Satyagraha (1947): A Study in Peasant Mobilization'; *Contributions to Indian Sociology*, no. 8, 1978; S. Henningham, *Peasant Movements in Colonial India: North Bihar, 1917–1942*, Canberra, 1982.

[20] D. Hardiman, *Peasant Nationalists of Gujarat; Kheda District 1917–1934*, Delhi, 1981.

[21] H. Sanyal, 'Congress in Southwestern Bengal', in R. Sisson and S. Walpert, *Congress and Indian Nationalism*, Berkeley, 1988, Ch. 16.

[22] S. R. Henberg, *Ethnicity, Nationalism and the Pakhtuns. The Independence Movement in India's North-West Frontier Province*, Durham, NC, 1988.

[23] See Pandey, *Ascendancy*; Brennan, 'One Raj to Another'.

[24] See D. Baker, *Changing Political Leadership*.

[25] See Arnold, *Congress in Tamilnad*; C. Baker, *Politics of South India*.

[26] G. Omvedt, *Cultural Revolt in Colonial Society: The Non-Brahman Movement in Western India 1873–1930*, Bombay, 1976.

[27] Prem Choudry, *Punjab Politics. The Role of Sir Chhotu Ram*, Delhi, 1984.

[28] J. Manor, *Political Change in an Indian State: Mysore 1917–55*, Delhi, 1977; R. Jeffrey, 'A Sanctified Label – Congress in Travancore Politics, 1938–48', in Low (ed.), *Congress and the Raj*; R. Sisson, *The Congress Party in Rajasthan*, Berkeley, 1972.

Congress, of course, at the end of the First World War and through the Gandhi-led Rowlatt satyagraha and Non-Co-operation movements also enjoyed the powerful co-operation of a great many Indian Muslims who were intent on pursuing their contemporaneous Khilafat movement.[29] One of the major facts of South Asian history in the subsequent period is, of course, that Congress lost that support.[30]

This was not the only category of Indian society, however, that came to be much dissociated from the Congress. The 'subaltern' school, as well as others, has begun to eludicate one of the dimensions to the story here.[31] The disjunctions between the separately propelled concerns and agitations of various UP peasants and those of the principal Congress leaders and their supporters in that province have been recounted,[32] and likewise those in Bihar.[33] These disjunctions were clearly very much more wide-spread than traditional accounts have allowed. They were present in CP, Gujarat, Maharashtra, and West Bengal,[34] quite apart from those areas where the Communist Party was to become very influential, such as Kerala.[35]

There were corresponding disjunctions between the strikes and agitations of urban workers and the campaigns of the Congress. This was particularly the case in Bombay in the late 1920s and early 1930s;[36] but it was also the case in Madras.[37] These divergencies tallied very closely with Rajendra Prasad's acknowledgement in 1936 that Congress had by then

29 Brown, *Gandhi's Rise to Power*; F. Robinson, *Separatism among Indian Muslims: The Politics of the United Provinces' Muslims 1860–1923*, Cambridge, 1974; A.C. Niemijer, *The Khilafat Movement in India*, The Hague, 1972; G. Minault, *The Khilafat Movement, Religious Symbolism and Political Mobilization in India*, Delhi, 1982; U. Kaura, *Muslims and Indian Nationalism*, Delhi, 1977.
30 Philips and Wainwright (eds.), *Partition*, passim; D. Page, *Prelude to Partition: All-India Muslim Politics 1921–32*, Delhi, 1981.
31 R. Guha (ed.), *Subaltern Studies, Writings on South Asian History and Society*, vols I–VI, Delhi, 1982–9.
32 See Pandey, *Ascendancy*; M. Siddiqi, *Agrarian Unrest in North India. United Provinces 1918–22*, Delhi, 1978.
33 See Henningham, *Peasant Movements*; W. Hauser, 'Bihar Provincial Kisan Sabha 1928–1942', PhD, University of Chicago, 1961.
34 See Guha, Hardiman, Omvedt, and O'Hanlon; D. Baker, '"A Serious Time": Forest Satyagraha in Madhya Pradesh 1930', *Indian Economic and Society History Review*, 21 no. 1 (January–March 1984); S. Sarkar, 'Primitive Rebellion and Modern Nationalism: A Note on Forest Satyagraha in the Non-Cooperation and Civil Disobedience Movements', in K.N. Panikkar (ed.), *National and Left Movements in India*, Delhi, 1980.
35 R. Jeffrey, 'Peasant Movements and the Communist Party in Kerala 1937–57' (mimeo).
36 R. Kumar, 'From Swaraj to Purna Swaraj: Nationalist Politics in the City of Bombay 1920–1932', in Low (ed.), *Congress and the Raj*; R. Chandavarkar, 'Workers' Politics and the Mill Districts in Bombay between the Wars', in C. Baker, G. Johnson, A. Seal (eds.), *Power, Profit and Politics; Essays on Imperialism, Nationalism and Change in 20th Century India*, Cambridge, 1981; R. Newman, *Workers and Unions in Bombay 1918–1929*, Canberra, 1981.
37 E. Murphy, *Unions in Conflict; A Comparative Study of Four South Indian Textile Centres*, Delhi, 1981.

only managed to secure support from 'a sprinkling of industrial and field workers'.

One further category of supporters of the Congress has also now been closely studied – India's commercial and industrial capitalists.[38] They became increasingly important to it in the last decade or so before independence, as they distanced themselves the more steadily from the British, and allied themselves the more closely with the Congress 'right'. Like the 'western-educated', and like the richer peasantry, they numbered amongst them those who could not be relied upon to support Congress wholeheartedly when the going was difficult;[39] but they were very clearly a powerful addition to the Congress, as its struggle with the British reached its climax.

In these studies of the involvement of India's capitalists in Congress politics there is frequent reference to the fact that they themselves rose out of, and maintained close connections with, India's merchant communities. It is freely acknowledged too that the generality of these merchant communities were ordinarily much more staunch in their support for the Congress than the wealthier, increasingly distinguishable, capitalists. But it is upon the activities of the latter that such studies are ordinarily focussed, and it is hard to find any study that discusses to the degree that acknowledgement would seem to call for (or much evidence would seem to demand) the support for the Congress of the generality of the merchant communities themselves. There are important studies of them in the period prior to their extensive involvement in Congress politics,[40] but the most we seem to have at the moment for the later period is one study of them in Bombay,[41] which usefully distinguishes between 'marketeers' and 'industrialists', and gives as much space to the political activities of the former as of the latter. This present account cannot hope to make up for these shortcomings. All it can attempt to do is to draw attention to them, and reinforce its admonition by presenting one corpus of evidence of a very broad-brush kind, and another that reinforces a developing explanation.

In 1929 the Indian National Congress at its Lahore Congress committed itself to a campaign of Civil Disobedience against the British under

[38] V. Pavlov, *Indian Capitalist Class*, Delhi, 1964; B. Chandra, *Nationalism and Colonialism in Modern India*, Delhi, 1979; R. Ray, *Industrialization in India: Growth and Conflict in the Private Corporate Sector 1914–47*, Delhi, 1979; C. Markovits, *Indian Business and Nationalist Politics 1931–39*, Cambridge, 1985.

[39] See Spear and Hardiman; S. Sarkar, 'The Logic of Gandhian Nationalism', *Indian Historical Review*, July 1976.

[40] C. Dobbin, *Urban Leadership in Western India: Politics and Communities in Bombay City 1840–85*, London, 1972; J. Masselos, *Towards Nationalism: Public Institutions and Urban Politics in 19th Century Bombay*, Bombay, 1974; C.A. Bayly, *The Local Roots of Indian Politics: Allahabad 1880–1920*, Oxford, 1975; R. Ray, *Urban Roots of Indian Nationalism, Pressure Groups and Conflict of Interests in Calcutta City Politics 1875–1939*, Delhi, 1979.

[41] A.D.D. Gordon, *Businessmen and Politics: Rising Nationalism and a Modernising Economy in Bombay 1918–1933*, Delhi, 1978.

Gandhi's-leadership. This was launched early in the next year by his Dandi march. There followed the largest agitation against the British since the combined Khilafat/Non-Co-operation movement of 1920–2. It extended through the rest of 1930.[42] But early in 1931 it was called off, partly under pressure from the merchant communities who had originally participated strongly but were now seeing their trade endangered, and partly as a consequence of some marginally hopeful signs that were emanating from the first Round Table Conference in London.[43] The upshot was the Gandhi–Irwin Pact of March 1931. But that did not hold. During the Pact's currency a great many British officials came to feel very deeply that their previously dominant position was being seriously undermined, and by expressing their concerns to successive viceroys, Irwin and Willingdon, they secured their agreement to the proposition that if there was any renewal of Civil Disobedience British repression would be swift and comprehensive. Following the Gandhi–Irwin Pact Gandhi had agreed to go to London and attend the second Round Table Conference. But on his return at the end of 1931 Civil Disobedience was erupting spontaneously in more than one part of India, and early in January 1932 the Government of India held to its word to its principal officials, declared a countrywide state of emergency, and swiftly incarcerated the Congress leaders and many of their chief supporters. It was to be some months before the back of the renewed campaign was broken, but in due course such was its fate even so.[44]

Before that had happened the Government of India had become increasingly concerned at the suggestions that were being made, chiefly in Britain, that all they had managed to do was to generate an immense 'sullen resentment' against British rule in India. They accordingly decided to enquire of their principal subordinates whether such was the case. 'It will be very valuable to have at this time', so the Home Member of the Government of India, Sir Harry Haig, ordered in March 1932, 'an authoritative appreciation of the state of public opinion'; and in a way that was entirely characteristic of the procedures of the British Government of India a circular letter was thereupon despatched to its provincial governments in which they were asked to report whether or not India was 'sullen'. The replies to this enquiry prove on investigation to provide a great deal more information than this rather banal question might on its own have evoked. For, more importantly for our present purposes, the provincial governments were also asked not only to report on a number of other

[42] Brown, *Gandhi and Civil Disobedience*.
[43] Sarkar, 'Logic of Gandhian Nationalism'; D.A. Low, 'Sir Tej Bahadur Sapru and the First Round Table Conference', in Low (ed.), *Soundings*.
[44] D.A. Low, 'Civil Martial Law: the Government of India and the Civil Disobedience Movements 1930–34', in Low (ed.), *Congress and the Raj*.

matters too, but in particular on 'the classes of the people which are (a) sympathetic with and (b) opposed to the civil disobedience movement'.[45]

It cannot be very often that an imperial power has attempted such a systematic survey of those who support it and those who oppose it, but this enquiry had essentially that purpose. It needs no emphasising that imperialists' views of who may or may not be their supporters can be all too frequently myopic. But there would seem to be less reason to be quite so sceptical when they have counted their opponents. It is not particularly gratifying to have to acknowledge that one has opponents. It is important that they should be precisely identified; and as nationalist movements became very active they could usually be fairly easily discerned. Our present interest lies in noting that in the replies to the Government of India's circular a great many British officers gave far more prominence to the range, strength and importance of the support for the Congress and its cause among the merchant communities of India than is ordinarily specified in later accounts. They placed this fully on a par with that of 'the teacher and lawyer' class and significantly ahead of that of well-to-do peasants (upon whose support for the Congress at this time they were interestingly equivocal).

The nature of the replies to the questionnaire from the Government of India was principally determined by the great relief amongst its principal officers that the anguish they had felt whilst the Gandhi–Irwin Pact was in operation was a thing of the past. Interestingly some British officers clearly believed that whilst the short-term value to their position of the subsequent repression was not to be denied, it would soon be necessary to effect some significant measure of constitutional reform in India, if only to retain upon their side numbers of those who for the time being at least continued to lend them their support. Other officers, however, the majority perhaps, were prone to give vent to some rather more stereotypical feelings. Sometimes indeed in colourful language.

All were in no doubt that there were important figures in the country, and in many cases large parts of the population, who stood firmly on their side in being directly opposed to Civil Disobedience and its Congress architects. The characteristic list of such supporters included landlords, retired military and civil officers, and (to a notable degree considering the number of times they were specifically mentioned) 'Mussalmans'. This evidence confirms indeed that Muslim support for the Congress and its works was by the early 1930s near to minimal, and that the close alliance between the Congress and very large numbers of India's Muslims of a decade previously had now essentially disappeared. The detailed evidence upon this score

---

[45] The detail in this and the ensuing fifteen or so paragraphs is drawn from National Archives of India, H. Poll. 4/28/32.

which the returns provide will not be set out here. It is, however, both abundant and emphatic.

British calculations as revealed by the returns concerning the attitudes towards the Congress and its agitations of India's huge rural populations were, as we have remarked, decidedly and interestingly equivocal, and since the evidence they provide about these make an important contrast to that which they offer concerning the support for them from the merchant communities, it will be illuminating to canvass it.

Some British officers seemed in no doubt early in 1932 that they had their rural area firmly under control. To the District Magistrate of Muttra, for example, the issue of whether Congress enjoyed widespread support in his area hardly arose. 'Villagers as a whole', he reported, 'want nothing more than peace and order. They have no proper appreciation of what the meaning of *swaraj* is'. His Muslim colleague writing from Mainpuri was equally assured. 'So far as these provinces are concerned,' he remarked, 'the policy of Government in granting liberal remissions of rents and land revenue to tenants and zamindars, respectively . . . has gone a long way to allay agrarian discontent and to induce feelings favourable to the Government among the rural population'. From Sitapur came a similar story. 'The position in the rural areas', so the deputy commissioner put it, was 'excellent'. The district magistrate in Kolaba was supremely confident as well. 'The masses as a whole', he reported, 'particularly the agriculturists, are loyal'. Whilst his counterpart in Thana put it differently, the substance of his report was the same: 'in rural areas people are so backward and poor that the vast majority do not understand politics'. Elsewhere hereabouts their colleagues wrote very similarly and merely added some particular details. In Ahmednagar, for example, 'the majority of the classes', the district magistrate averred, were indifferent to the Congress agitation; 'under this head come the agricultural classes in general, such as the Marathas, Wanjaris, and Dhangars'. And his sub-divisional magistrate concurred: 'the Maratha agriculturists . . . are not only loyal but are indifferent to any agitation against Government'. The UP government summed up the position in the rural areas as it saw this by including 'the better class villagers' in the list of those whom it reckoned were 'strongly opposed to the civil disobedience movement'; while the government of Madras was still more olympian. 'The first point on which this Government would wish to lay special emphasis', it declaimed, 'is that in this Presidency the vast majority of the rural population, probably 95 per cent, take little or no interest in the civil disobedience movement . . . This is particularly true of poor and backward areas which at no time have given any trouble'.

All the same the Madras government had to qualify this. 'The one important exception', it was obliged to state, 'is the rich deltaic area included in the Telugu districts of east and west Godaveri, Kistna and Guntur . . . One mainly agricultural caste, the Kamma, has been specially prominent in its hostility to the Government . . . Taking the Presidency as a whole it may be said that civil disobedience has been an active force in four Telugu districts, five Tamil districts . . . and the two West Coast districts'. There was likewise some frank reporting from Kaira district, in Bombay presidency. Here, as the district magistrate reported, 'high caste Hindus and most of all the Patidar cultivators from which class hail the Patel brothers who also have their home in this District are generally' supportive of the Congress; 'even the elderly Patidar folk seem to be very largely disaffected'. The government of the Frontier Province felt it necessary to be candid too: 'in the rural areas of the Peshawar District', it wrote, '. . . the bulk of the menial non-landowning classes and non-occupancy tenants together with a number of the smaller land owners' were prominent among those supporting the Congress. In Peshawar district the villain of the piece was, of course, the 'Frontier Gandhi', Abdul Ghaffar Khan. In the Pali sub-division of Almora district, so the deputy commissioner reported, the ring-leader was Har Govind Pant. 'Here I must admit', he wrote, 'that there is a considerable amount of Congress feeling . . . [in] certain villages mostly in the Ramganga valley and the salt pattis, but a good many in other pattis as well.'

On closer investigation the pervasive impression is in truth that many British officers were finding it extremely difficult to judge their standing in the rural areas at all correctly. For example, while the seemingly very confident district magistrate in West Khandesh emphasised more than once that 'Khandesh is rightly described as a very loyal, contented and prosperous part of the Presidency', he also stated: 'I cannot help feeling that the Congress preaching has permeated deep down in the rural state . . . There is of course no open defiance but the cultivators are prepared to show their annoyance when it can be quietly and safely done'. And the government of Bihar and Orissa reflected this view: 'if restrictions are removed', it wrote, 'and the Congress party begins to function again, as it will do, the people, generally, will support them for the same reason as before, because they are organised and can reach the villages and can make active opponents uncomfortable, and because any other party cannot and will not do so'. From Rae Bareli there then came a report from a young deputy commissioner which his commissioner called 'by far and away the best appreciation' he had seen. This stated:

I now come to a class which I am not prepared to include unreservedly either amongst those sympathetic with or opposed to the civil disobedience movement. This is the cultivating class, mostly Hindu, and forms of course the greater part of the population of this district. I would say that in the case of 90 per cent or over of the individuals of this class, there is no outward sign of opposition to Government . . .

The *kashtkar* and agricultural labourer, and with these may be included the petty proprietor, does not oppose the civil disobedience movement, nor unless he be actively stirred up by some agitator, does he actively support the movement. If he does actively support it, his motive is economic rather than national or political. He feels that times are hard, and if some one, such as the trained literate Congress agitator, promises him some pecuniary or material advantage, he is prepared to support civil disobedience. To some extent also an appeal to his religious feelings may win his support on either side. There is no doubt that there is a latent respect for Gandhi in his mind – whether he looks upon him as a saint or practically as a deity.

This degree of uncertainty imbues almost all of the more thoughtful accounts which British officers produced of peasant support for Congress in the early 1930s. Nevertheless it seems a reasonable conclusion that while there were clearly places where the Congress could claim a very substantial measure of support in the rural areas – for example, in parts of Madras and Bombay presidencies, and in the North West Frontier Province – and while the British position was clearly in doubt in a much larger number of other such places, nevertheless, whatever their apprehensions, the British were still by no means fully convinced in the early 1930s that they had lost the acquiescence in their rule of the vast rural expanses of India taken as a whole, and felt indeed that, by and large at all events, they just about still had the situation there under control.

This picture is worth portraying since although it is possible to find some similar equivocation in the reporting by British officers in early 1932 of their impressions of the attitudes of the merchant communities towards the Congress and its activities, the general impression which the returns provide on this score is strikingly different. Throughout the merchant communities were ordinarily placed very firmly amongst those who supported and/or sympathised with the Congress and its activities. It is important to note in this connection that the assessments which British officers provided in 1932 were given of a period when the Congress leaders were all in jail and when the Congress movement was suffering from one of its gravest setbacks. In these circumstances the pervasiveness of the support for the Congress from the merchant communities, as perceived by India's British administrators, becomes all the more notable.

In a good number of the responses to the questionnaire the merchant communities appear as a matter of course with the professional classes amongst those who were most sympathetic towards the Congress and its works. Those who were 'openly so', wrote the district magistrate from Poona, comprised 'Konknastha Brahmins (mostly Chitpawans), Gujaratis, Marwaris'. In Belgaum, the district magistrate put it: 'Generally speaking the professional and trading classes and educated persons in general', were all staunch Congress supporters; 'the distribution being of course very much more urban than rural'. And the general picture as seen by the British was depicted by the government of Bombay when it declared that the Congress 'naturally appeals most to the professional and educated classes and to the Hindu commercial communities'. To this the UP government simply added a few elaborated details. Those supportive of the Congress movement were, it said: '(a) the student and teacher class; (b) the petty intelligentsia of the towns; (c) the Hindu shopkeepers, moneylenders and businessmen; (d) the better educated middle class population, such as lawyers and politicians; and (e) the unemployed and loafer class both in town and country'. For the most part other respondents generally aggregated similarly.

Given the fact that the extent of the support for the Congress is not often detailed – at all events to the extent that such testimony suggests can occasionally be done – it is permissible perhaps to set out at some length some of the specifics which these returns contain. Fortuitously two sets of district officers' responses to the Government of India's questionnaire that were sent on to it are readily to hand, and it is from these that the more detailed testimony can be drawn. One of these came from UP.

From this a remarkably consistent picture emerges. L.M. Stubbs, the commissioner of Kumaon, for example, expressed himself as being in no doubt that 'the educated or professional classes and the mercantile community' in his division were strong in their support for the Congress. And he went on:

There can, I think, be no doubt that the state of the world's trade has given great strength to the movement of discontent, and that if trade had been good one would have heard less of civil disobedience. The commercial community feel as do the educated unemployed that things could hardly be worse and that any change must be for the better . . . The next consideration may not seem at first sight to be a strong one but I really think it has importance. Gandhi is a Bania and the commercial class is predominantly ruled by Banias . . . Propaganda on the side of Congress has been extraordinarily astute and it has not I think been generally recognised how deep that propaganda has penetrated. It is at least three years ago that I was told by the late Nawab of Rampur that the jewellers of Delhi with whom he had an extensive acquaintance had assured him that they were prepared to face any risk or loss of business in the event of a real *swaraj*. That they should express an opinion of this kind in the face of so confirmed a reactionary as His Highness was, I think, a remarkable illustration of the depth of their feeling.

Stubbs's colleagues had reached very much the same conclusions. The deputy commissioner of Naini Tal put the matter curtly: 'the lawyers, educated and Bania classes' seemed to him 'all pro-Congress in sympathy'. His counterpart in Almora detailed a similar impression; 'the shopkeepers of Bageswar and Someswar', he wrote, 'have always been sympathisers of Congress'. In Bulandshahr the district magistrate was evidently a blusterer.

In pungent terms he set forth his view of the similarities between Banias and Jews. 'The connection of this caste', he wrote, 'with Congress activity is well-known, and it has been suggested that most of the political agitation is a tremendous ramp to enable the Brahman to regain and strengthen his old social and religious power and to enable the Bania to make even larger profits than he does at present'. The deputy commissioner from Sitapur was rather more measured. 'In the urban area', he found 'the attitude of the Hindus difficult to gauge'. Yet (he added) 'I should say that a large majority of them are really in sympathy with the Congress and what it stands for. In this city there have been constant *hartals* . . . I have reason to believe that most of the Hindu shopkeepers and traders are still subscribing secretly to Congress funds'. His colleague, the deputy commissioner in Rohilkhand, was inclined to think 'the Hindu shopkeeper element' were not always 'whole hoggers'. All the same he included them in a now all but conventional list of likely 'Congressites'. For his part the commissioner of Allahabad had no such hesitations: 'the Hindu of the city', so he intoned, 'be he trader or an ordinary professional man' – and we may note the recurring conjunction – 'is in sympathy with the Congress aims which includes the creation of the Hindu *Raj*, and his sympathy with the aims of Congress is stronger than his dislike of Congress methods'.

And so it was upon similar lines that virtually all the UP returns reported. 'Traders, moneylenders and the moneyed classes generally', came the refrain from the Commissioner of Fyzabad, 'includes many who sympathise with Congress, notably among town dwelling Hindus'. To the district magistrate of Muttra it was clear that a principal

class sympathetic with the movement is the small shopkeeper class of the Vaish and Kayastha communities. This class is always resentful of taxation, and hopes to obtain remission of taxation through the Congress . . . He feels that a Congress *raj* with Mr Gandhi at the head will be favourably disposed to the Vaish community . . . the Vaish community appreciate immensely the glamour with which Mr Gandhi has surrounded himself as the Mahatma. He is the first Vaish to come into prominence, and the community is proud of this.

This emphasis upon Gandhi's particular importance to the merchant communities figures as well in the other cache of provincial returns which is readily available, more particularly since this comes from Bombay presidency. Hardly surprisingly, in view of Gandhi's long association with the city and the region, the District Magistrate from Ahmedabad reported that there 'the influence of Mr Gandhi is very great indeed amongst the urban population of the District. Large numbers of almost all communities regard him as little less than a deity and would be unwilling to oppose actively any programme he might sponsor, even though it were opposed to their business interests.' And from Thana there came the corresponding report that 'the younger generation . . . seems convinced that Mr Gandhi's is the only method for achieving political freedom within the shortest possible time the younger generation which includes professional as well as business men is generally in favour of it.'

The message from the Southern Division was more generalised, Congress' supporters included there, so the return ran, 'a proportion of the well-to-do trading class'. And from Ahmednagar came a similar report: the sympathisers with Congress here included 'most of the trading classes', Gujaratis and Marwaris in particular. The same was reiterated from West Khandesh: 'amongst the Hindus themselves in the mercantile community, which consist very largely of the Gujarathis and Marwadis sympathy with the Congress propaganda and methods is very widespread'. Whilst the 'hard-hearted Deccanies' might be more hesitant, 'the logic of the mercantile community at the present time', so the district officer averred, 'is very muddled and there seems no possibility of producing in their minds anything like an intellectual conviction of the soundness of the Government position in the present struggle'. So it was in Poona too: 'in Cantonment', the district magistrate remarked, 'the Gujarathi trader class are still sympathetic with Congress and in City I believe many of the shopkeepers support Congress demonstrations with money subscriptions. In the District Gujar trading classes are in one or two places notably Paud and Saswad continuing to support Congress'. And from Sholapur came a similar account: 'practically all Gujarathis (who are of course immigrants in the Deccan)', so the district officer expressed it, 'are either openly or secretly in favour of the movement'. The same was said of Bijapur, and of Kolaba too. The Collector of Ratnagiri seemed to sum up the case. Along with the usual array of 'educated' supporters 'those sympathetic to the C.D. movement' were, he said, the 'Wanis: who are usually small merchants and moneylenders. They believe they would be better off with swadeshi trade, and with greater opportunities for more profitable money lending under Congress auspices. They also think that their casteman Mr Gandhi cannot do without their assistance in his movement against Government.'

Yet it was the Commissioner of Police from Bombay who penned the most perturbed report. He was in no doubt that Bombay had emerged from the situation a year previously when 'Congress activities were allowed such license . . . that the expression grew that Congress was a mightier force than Government'. But now in April 1932, after four months of emergency rule, it was, he bemoaned, 'my opinion that Congress still has greater power in certain parts of the City than Government has'. Whilst there were some signs of business interests revolting against it, none the less

where these business men are Gujeratis their sympathies naturally are with Mr Gandhi and Congress, and if they are beginning to smart under the tyranny of Congress, as I believe they are, their opposition to the Ordinances must grow colder and colder until finally they may be glad to seek their protection. But this is not going to happen rapidly. Congress is still powerful, and men who have 'posed as staunch patriots cannot easily turn for protection to the very power that Congress is seeking to destroy.

In the face of all this evidence of how it appeared to the British – each officer writing quite independently of his colleagues – it seems essential to grant the merchant communities of India a principal position in the front ranks of India's nationalists in a way that does not seem to have been sufficiently allowed to them hitherto. Whilst in the longer run the more prosperous peasant communities were to be perhaps of even greater importance to the Congress, the merchant communities more generally seem to have been earlier upon the scene. In 1936 even Rajendra Prasad underestimated their importance – though perhaps inadvertently.

What lay behind this development by 1932 of such strong and extensive support for the Congress from the Hindu merchant communities of India has still to be explored with the specificity historians have accorded to the other adherences to the Congress. All that can be attempted here are one or two pointers. We should begin by recalling that there is now a strongly argued case that especially in the eighteenth century India's merchant communities grew in strength, cohesion and wealth. At the same time they were always strong in their adherence to their Hindu religious values and practices, and in particular gave very freely of their wealth to religious and charitable foundations. They then became closely associated with the British conquests of India, not only by providing the finance and the provisions the British needed, but through the benefits they themselves obtained, from, for example, greater security for their trade.[46] Thereafter some of these trading communities much extended their reach, sometimes outside India, but not least within India itself, the Marwaris above all, and into Calcutta especially.[47]

Superimposed upon the peasant economy of India which centred about agricultural production and weekly and bi-weekly markets and periodic fairs, these merchant communities conducted the very much wider 'bazaar' market which came to spread throughout the subcontinent. They rarely exercised very much direct control over peasant production itself. Rather, they managed the seasonality of Indian agricultural production by means of loans to and purchases from peasants; stored the grain, oil seeds, fruits, etc. which this produced; and then marketed these not only locally but sometimes to quite distant places as well. Within the networks all this entailed they traded gold and silver, and increasingly piece goods and other

[46] C.A. Bayly, *Rulers, Townsmen and Bazaars; North Indian Society in the Age of British Expansion*, Cambridge, 1983.
[47] T.A. Timberg, *The Marwaris*, Delhi, 1978.

retail items also. In these connections many of their members acted as bankers and commission agents, and not infrequently conducted trade upon a large and extensive scale, using in particular the long established system of credit notes, *hundis*. By 1930, 35 out of the 38 million tons of rice, wheat and linseed produced in India were being marketed in this manner, and goods of this kind that were being carried by rail within India itself comprised nine times the amount exported overseas.[48]

In the cities and towns of India leading members of these merchant communities were always closely involved in urban politics, and not least during the latter part of the nineteenth century.[49] They soon became variously represented as well at the Congress' annual meetings.[50] But characteristically they were much more cautious in its early years in giving vent to strong nationalist aspirations than the more actively nationalist 'western educated'. Many of them were wary, it seems, of breaking their links with their British rulers, with whom they had long been associated, and from whom they continued to derive a number of benefits. Whilst the Banias, Aroras and Khatris of the Punjab fell into conflict with the British at the turn of the century over the Punjab Land Alienation Act, and men like Lala Lajpat Rai figured very largely thereafter in the Congress movement, even here the adherence of the merchant communities to the Congress continued to be highly problematic, at all events until around the end of the First World War.[51]

It would seem to have been very largely the effects of that War which brought about the crucial change, since thereafter large numbers of the merchant communities across the length and breadth of India did throw in their lot with the Congress, often indeed extremely vigorously. Here contradictory processes had a mutually reinforcing effect. In some places the huge rise in War and post-War profits seems to have triggered one change of considerable dimensions. For some of the more successful of these merchant communities now felt themselves to be fully capable of generating considerable wealth without having to hold on to their former British connections – and indeed were now finding that British policies were curbing rather than assisting their activities.[52] Elsewhere, however, it was commercial failure that more often turned members of merchant communities against the British. For simultaneously many other members

[48] R. Ray, 'The Bazaar' (unpublished monograph).
[49] Dobbin, Masselos, Bayly, *Local Roots*; K. Gillion, *Ahmedabad: A Study in India's Urban History*, California, 1968; K. Jones, *Arya Dharma: Hindu Consciousness in 19th Century Punjb*, California, 1976.
[50] P.C. Ghosh, *The Development of the Indian National Congress 1892–1909*, Calcutta, 1960, p. 24, Chart B.; G. Krishna, 'The Development of the Indian National Congress as a Mass Organisation 1918–1923', *Journal of Asian Studies*, 25 no. 3 (May 1966).
[51] Jones, *Arya Dharma*; N.G. Barrier, 'The Arya Samaj and Congress Politics in the Punjab, 1894–1908', *Journal of Asian Studies*, 26 (3 May 1967).
[52] Ray, *Urban Roots*; Gillion, *Ahmedabad*.

of these communities were being very seriously afflicted, by inordinate government interference in their trade during the War, by the inflation that occurred during and after the War, and by the disastrous slumps, for example in the cloth trade, that accompanied these.[53]

All this was then compounded by the heavy increases in taxation which the British imposed upon those they thought could afford to help finance the War. Not merely did these give rise to significantly enhanced customs and excise duties, but more especially to a much more burdensome income tax and even super tax. Each of these fell particularly heavily upon the merchant communities. They were then especially affronted by the culturally abhorrent intrusion into their personal affairs which the newly enlarged income tax collection entailed. And in this and other connections many of them became particularly concerned at the moves by the Government of India to extend the extraordinary judicial powers it had secured under the Defence of India Act during the War by means of the so-called Rowlatt Act of 1919. Gordon and Ferrell have elaborated upon these issues, principally on the basis of the evidence from Bombay and Delhi.[54] A look at some further evidence from an otherwise often quoted source will serve to underscore their points.

In 1919, thanks in part to the deep antipathy towards its urban communities of Sir Michael O'Dwyer, its draconian governor, the Punjab witnessed the largest urban disturbances in India in the immediate post-War period. Whilst O'Dwyer's government blamed their onset principally upon 'the professional classes', they also set out, in a submission to the Disorders Inquiry Committee their view that 'they [the professional classes] would, however, have achieved little success in the agitation but for the ready support of the shop-keeping and trading classes. It was the adhesion of this class', it declared, 'which secured the success of the agitation. In many cases the hartal of 6 April appears to have owed little to direct organisation of public men; so ready were the trading classes to accept the suggestion for a universal demonstration that the closure of shops appeared to many to be almost spontaneous'.[55]

On one of the major sets of issues which lay behind this ('the new Income-tax Act and the more searching methods of enquiry recently introduced') the Punjab's Financial Commissioner, the very distinguished Sir John Maynard, gave the enquiry a revealing note. 'Ancient Hindu policy', he stated, 'recognised the taxation of traders . . . Historical accident and economic theories prevalent in Britain at the time of the annexation of the Punjab led to the condemnation of existing methods of

53 Gordon, *Businessmen and Politics*; D.W. Ferrell, 'The Rowlatt Satyagraha in Dehli', in R. Kumar, ed., *Essays on Gandhian Politics, The Rowlatt Satyagraha of 1919*, Oxford, 1971.
54 Gordon, *Businessmen*; Ferrell, 'Rowlatt Satyagraha'.
55 Disorders Inquiry Committee, *Evidence Taken Before the Disorders Inquiry Committee*, London 1920, vol. 4, p. 100.

taxing traders . . . For years they escaped all taxation'. Whilst in due course income and excise taxes did come to be imposed, 'the burden was light . . . the system of assessment . . . took the line of least resistance and treated the rich and influential very gently'. But then a new Super Tax in 1917, a new Income Tax in 1918, a new Excess Profits Tax in 1919, and above all a very considerable increase in the numbers and power of the tax collecting staff changed all of that fundamentally. Tax collectors were now empowered to conduct house to house surveys. They were empowered too to use any information they secured to determine an assessee's income. No assessee could object to the rate set unless he himself had made a full return, and any income that escaped tax, or had been assessed at too low a rate, could be reassessed in a following year. As a consequence in 1918–19, so Maynard reported, tax returns in Lahore city went up by 30 per cent, in Amritsar by 55 per cent, and in the other urban areas of the Lahore Division by on average no less than 217 per cent![56] It is scarcely surprising that India's merchant communities were now becoming very seriously alienated from the British when this was only one of the new afflictions being imposed upon them.

There was at the end of the War another consideration. In its aftermath the leadership of the Indian national movement passed into the hands of Mahatma Gandhi, and on at least four related counts that was of major importance for the adherence to it of India's merchant communities. The points are well known, but they warrant underlining. Gandhi himself was a Bania; Indian nationalism's principal figure was thus now one of their own. He was in addition a deeply religious figure. Given the importance of their religious commitments in the culture and values of these merchant communities, adherence to him accordingly involved not only a political but a religious involvement. That proved to be especially important for the powerful, wealthy and now very extensive Marwari community, which was especially influential in Calcutta. Two of its principal leaders, Birla and Bajaj, soon established highly personal associations with him of a quasi-filial and religious character.[57] But this consideration was important for the Gujaratis as well. On his return to India in 1915 Gandhi had made his base amongst them at this Sabarmati Ashram in Ahmedabad, and from there had established very close associations not only with Gujarat's principal commercial figures, but through them with the major Gujarati trading community in Bombay, and elsewhere too. In this and other connections it is perhaps worth stressing that whereas in relation to Congress' growing association with India's well-to-do peasants, the role of link figures (such as

[56] *Ibid.* p. 235.
[57] G.D. Birla, *In the Shadow of the Mahatma*, Bombay, 1953; Birla, *Bapu – a Unique Association – Correspondence 1940–47*, Bombay, 1977; Kaka Kalelkar, *Jamnalal Bajaj Ki Diary*, Allahabad, 1969.

Patel, Abdul Ghaffar Khan, Prasad, Rajagopalachari and many a somewhat lesser figure) was often of great importance, so far as the merchant communities were concerned the link with Gandhi was far more direct, and was not shared to anything like the same degree with any other prominent leader. That was one (sometimes overlooked) reason for his dominance over the movement as a whole.

The immediate upshot in the post-First World War years was to be found in the heavy involvement of many members of merchant communities, as in the Punjab, in the Rowlatt satyagraha of 1919, which in these terms marked the major breach in the hitherto longstanding nexus between so many of the commercial classes and the British.[58] Thereafter there were all manner of variations in the now largely new association between the merchant communities and the Congress. Beyond those considerations just mentioned, four others flowed. In the first place Congress could now ordinarily be assured of having access to adequate financial resources. Secondly, the extensive, often intimate, commercial networks across the length and breadth of India which the merchant communities operated for their commercial purposes soon began to be used for their new nationalist purposes also. Thirdly, merchant supporters of the Congress, in the innumerable towns of India, were not only singularly well placed to organise nationalist activities in them. Their extensive commercial interactions with the local peasant economy in their immediate vicinity provided them with a readymade connection as they and others, under the leadership of Gandhi and some of his leading lieutenants, sought to respond to the nationalist impulses of well-to-do peasants and associate them with the national movement too.

There were thereafter a number of special variations in the active role played by the merchant communities in the Indian national movement. These were the more particularly displayed first in the major thrust they provided to the first Civil Disobedience movement of 1930, and most dramatically in Bombay, and then in the check their leading spokesmen put upon this in 1931 when its elongation threatened to destroy their trade.[59] A similar oscillation was exemplified when Civil Disobedience was renewed in 1932. But, as the British recognised (and as we have seen), and as subsequent electoral processes soon confirmed, to a very considerable extent the commercial communities were now wedded to India's nationalist cause as never before, and the large majority of Hindus amongst them to the Congress in particular. Some scattered information is available on these matters – but it would now seem timely to seek for more.[60]

As over a rather longer period and by other means (some of which have

[58] Brown, *Gandhi's Rise to Power*, Kumar, *Rowlatt Satyagraha*.   [59] Sarkar, 'Logic'.
[60] E.g. Gordon, *Businessmen*; Pandey, *Ascendancy*; Sarkar, *Modern India*; Baker, *Changing Political Leadership*; Brennan, 'One Raj to Another'.

been spelt out, but others of which remain to be fully related),[61] well-to-do peasant communities came to adhere in large numbers to the Congress as well, oo the alliance was created between the professional classes, the commercial communities, and the richer peasants in so many parts of India that for the rest of this century has so engrossed its life. Whilst that has been sufficiently emphasised, what perhaps has not – and in any event calls for closer comparative consideration – is the apparent unusualness of so large a role being played in the development of a country's anti-colonial nationalism by its merchant communities. Some fleeting examples of this could be found from Africa, especially West Africa (and one thinks of Oginga Odinga in Kenya too).[62] But perhaps the most striking comparison is with Indonesia, where, for a variety of reasons, no similar involvement by its merchant communities in the nationalist cause seems to have occurred, principally no doubt because the counterpart merchant communities there were mainly alien Chinese.[63] At the same time it may be too (as Ray has suggested) that indigenous traders in Indonesia were at this stage little more than peddlers;[64] they did not know the credit note and all which that involved; and thus had none of the expertise and range of connections which their Indian counterparts had to hand. If this is so then it becomes all the more important for historians to probe the more extensively the particularities of the adhesion of the merchant communities to the Indian National Congress. This sketch remains a plea for more study to be made of these matters, by way of a modest contribution to its discussion on the basis of presenting the evidence that many of India's imperial rulers on the ground had clearly come to believe, by 1932, that this was at least as great as that by the longer associated professional classes; and noticeably more so – for the time being at least – than by the majority of India's well-to-do peasants.

[61] Low (ed.), *Congress and the Raj.*
[62] J.S. Coleman, *Nigeria, Background to Nationalism*, Berkeley, 1958; Oginga Odinga, *Not Yet Uhuru*, London, 1967.
[63] J.A.C. Mackie, *The Chinese in Indonesia; Five Essays*, Melbourne, 1976.
[64] C. Geertz, *Peddlers and Princes. Social Change and Economic Modernization in Two Indonesian Towns*, Chicago, 1963.

5

Counterpart experiences: India/Indonesia 1920s–1950s

India's national day is 26 January; Indonesia's 17 August. They point to a difference. 26 January derives from the Indian National Congress' decision at its Lahore Congress in December 1929 to launch a Civil Disobedience movement against the British Government in India. Jawaharlal Nehru as Congress' President arranged that the first step would be for thousands of Congress rank and file to join together on 26 January 1930 to take the Independence Pledge. This declared that since 'it is the inalienable right of the Indian people . . . to have freedom, . . . if any government deprives a people of those rights . . .the people have a . . . right to . . . abolish it . . . We recognise, however, that the most effective way of gaining freedom is not through violence. We will, therefore, prepare ourselves by withdrawing, so far as we can, all voluntary association from the British Government and will prepare for Civil Disobedience.' From that moment onwards 26 January has been India's Independence Day, though when it was first held India's independence still stood 17 years away. The celebrations have thus come to link post-independent India with the feats of the Indian national movement which for so many years pursued the strategy of civil disobedience, and which, despite a series of intervening fits and starts, is seen to have been crucial to its success. For India the heroics of its freedom struggle lie, that is, in its elongated pre-independence past, of long years of humiliating harassment and costly commitment. They are not much associated with the final run up to independence. With the emphasis rather upon the earlier, principally Gandhian years, of protests and processions, of proscriptions and prison, the final transfer of power is not seen, moreover, as comprising a traumatic break with the past, but as the logical climax to all that had gone before. The direct continuities between the pre- and post-independence periods in India in these respects are accepted as a central part of its national heritage.

The contrasts with Indonesia could not be greater. As Indonesia's national day 17 August derives from the declaration on 17 August 1945 by the largely self-designated President Sukarno and Vice-President Hatta of the nascent Republic of Indonesia, before a small audience outside Sukarno's house in Jakarta, and to the accompaniment of the raising of a flag stitched up by Sukarno's wife, of little more than the bald statement that 'We the people of Indonesia hereby declare the independence of Indonesia'. Even that much – pronounced eleven days after the first atomic bomb had been dropped on Hiroshima – had virtually to be dragged out of Sukarno, following his abduction by a small group of excited young men, because of his Janus-headed fear that any such declaration might needlessly provoke the still present Japanese, or, if made whilst the Japanese were still physically in control, irretrievably damage the shoe-string Republic in the eyes of the advancing Allies. The contrasts between the large public assemblies in India on 26 January 1930 and the furtive gathering in Indonesia on 17 August 1945 would be difficult to exaggerate.

Yet it is from 17 August 1945 that the great national eruption of the Indonesian Revolution has ever afterwards been seen to have stemmed. Unlike India's the heroics embedded in the Indonesian memory of their winning of Independence are not those of earlier, and mostly pre-war, decades, but of the middle and late 1940s. The break, moreover, with the past is seen to have been at once sudden, sharp and traumatic, and in no way a logical conclusion to a long sustained campaign. Whilst in historical reality negotiations with the Dutch pervaded Indonesia's tumultuous story in the late 1940s, the principle memory of it is not of *diplomasi*, let alone of anything approaching civil disobedience, but of *perdjuangan*, struggle – in the first place of the *permuda*, the youth, heroically seeking to uphold the independence declaration, resisting the return of the Dutch, and in particular withstanding day after day, often with quite inadequate weapons, and at an unaccountable cost to their lives, the newly arriving occupying forces of British-led Indian troops, especially at the well-nigh fanatical battle of Surabaya in September–October 1945. Other memories extend beyond this to details of the immense confusion within and across the largest archipelago that ever sought to become a nation; to the aspirations and uncertain commitments of armed bands roving the countryside (only some of whom merged with any organised army); to the plethora of parties and groups and leaders, none of whom could be certain of the extent of their support, and some of whom fared disastrously in the melee; and withal, to the Dutch attempts to create in this maelstrom a Dutch dominated federal state in which Sukarno's Java-based Republic would be only one of the parts; to two major Dutch armed attacks upon the nascent Republic, and finally to much international peacemaking that not until five years had passed since the original 17 August declaration, eventually managed to bring the Republic the wide international recognition which was essential to its persistence. There were several major post-independence Indonesian leaders whose political roots stretched into the past well behind these events. But whereas for most independent Indians their political heritage belonged to a protracted experience of long braved non-violent agitation, the political roots for most Indonesians have lain in the frenetic, disorganised, inchoate violence of the radical break with most that had gone before that comprised the close-knit Indonesian Revolution. Twin gateposts at the roadside in many parts of Indonesia heavily inscribed '17' and '8' (17 August) and sometimes '45', have no counterpart in India. While India saw a long worked for denouement in a non-revolutionary transfer of power, Indonesia witnessed the swift and seething turbulence of a bloody and bewildering political revolution.

MUSLIMS AND COMMUNISTS

The contrast was once far from being anything like as sharp. As compared with the distinctly differing scenes at the end of the Second World War, those in the two countries at the end of the First World War had in one importantly formative sense been remarkably similar. Both countries had had elite nationalists already; India more so that Indonesia. But politics in both countries were in the late nineteen teens principally marked by Muslim movements that were Monsoon Asia's first modern mass movements. Sarekat Islam – the Islamic Union – had originally been formed in Indonesia in 1912. It had its origins in some particular elite Indonesian Muslim concerns with the commercial success of the Chinese in Indonesia. But it soon became a much larger, and far more widely supported movement for the defence of Indonesia's Muslim society much more generally. It won extensive rural support (as few other Indonesian movements were to do until the communists rural explosion in the late 1950s), and it was led from early on by a long-lasting leader, Tjokroaminoto.

Muslims in Indonesia were of course in an overwhelming majority. Outside Bengal and all of India's north-west, India's Muslims were on the contrary a decided minority, divided and fearful both of the British and of their far more populous Hindu countrymen. Principally in the north central United Provinces, from which general region Muslim dynasties had for centuries once lorded it over a great many Hindu subjects, the position of Muslims who now ruled no longer in an overwhelmingly Hindu India had been earnestly debated from the mid nineteenth century onwards. In fortuitous conjunction with a particular concern that the defeat in 1918 by Britain and her allies of the centuries old Ottoman empire looked to be leading to the sacrilegious destruction of the Khalifate of Islam, in the person of the Ottoman's emperors, a great wave of commitment to a

Khalifat movement came to express, as the First World War came to its end, an impassioned search for a coherent Muslim identity for the much fragmented Indian Muslim community in a seemingly increasingly Hindu dominated India.

Neither country – nor it may be emphasised any other Asian country either – had hitherto seen movements of this kind with such wide support, all the way from the humble to the elite. To an important degree they gave the political conditions in both countries a momentarily similar appearance. Above all they demonstrated that political movements with large popular support could be aroused in their countries; a prospect which would-be politicians in both of them always henceforward held clearly in view, to an earlier and greater degree than their counterparts elsewhere in Asia.

These earlier similarities do not end there. In the 1920s both Sarekat Islam and the Khalifat movement atrophied markedly, and in Muslim circles their like was not to be seen again until Masyumi first arose in Indonesia in the early 1940s and the Muslim League dramatically revived its fortunes in India during those very same years. (These chronological similarities are beyond the calls of this account; indeed they seem as yet beyond the current expertise of those expert in Islamic affairs.) In the meanwhile Sarekat Islam persisted through the twenties and thirties, for long still under Tjokroaminoto's leadership. The Khalifat movement finally collapsed, however, when in 1924 the Turks themselves abolished the Khalifat, and thereafter all-India Muslim politics entered their doldrum years.

It is nevertheless noteworthy that at their peak others not of their persuasion thought both Sarekat Islam and the Khalifat movement warranted capture – a telling tribute to their substance and force during their heyday. In India it seemed crucial to Gandhi in the aftermath of the First World War that the thrust of the Khalifat movement should be joined – indeed should be used to impel – the non-co-operation movement he was set upon mounting against the British. Almost alone of the leaders of the overwhelmingly non-Muslim Indian National Congress he strove to effect this conjuncture, and eventually succeeded in being accepted by the Khalifat leaders as their leader as well. The Khalifat movement might sooner or later have broken apart in any event, but its supporters always thereafter believed this originally occurred largely because of Gandhi's decision in February 1922 to call off the combined Khalifat/Non-co-operation movement when the frenzied overrunning of the police station at Chauri Chaura in the United Provinces by a crowd of its supporters seemed to contravene appallingly his absolute commitment to his non-violent creed. Despite his many palpably heartfelt attempts in the coming decades once more to join together his Congress supporters with India's Muslims, most of the latter refused henceforth to commit their destinies to him ever again; and in due course the total separation of India's Muslim majority areas from the rest of the sub-continent was, of course, to take place.

The seekers after Sarekat Islam's support in Indonesia were, meanwhile, strikingly different. The first cell of communists in Indonesia had gathered about a Dutch refugee from Holland, Hendrik Sneevliet, a few years before the Russian Revolution made communism at once exhilarating and notorious. Thereafter they gathered to themselves an Indonesian coterie as well. In Semarang especially leftist activists soon developed Indonesia's trade unions, and in due course precipitated a number of industrial strikes. In 1920 the PKI (the Indies Communist Party) was formed, the first formally constructed Communist Party in Asia. Looking for still larger support, its leaders had already started to infiltrate Sarekat Islam, and within a few short years had actually succeeded in taking much of it over – though that hardly did them very much good, for as the nature of the takeover became manifest, the support for Sarekat Islam amongst the traditionally religious wilted away; and just as most of India's Muslims henceforth would have nothing to do with Gandhi, so most of Indonesia's Muslims (and that could mean much of its overall population) became determinedly opposed to its communists as well.

The PKI's penetration of Sarekat Islam had at the same time one portentously fateful consequence. For because of its initially successful takeover of what at its apogee had been a highly popular movement, especially in the Indonesian countryside, too many PKI activists deluded themselves into thinking that they could with ease enlist like forces in their cause as well. The communist hierarchy, not least at Comintern level, was persistently wary of any such proceeding. But as in the mid 1920s in more than one Asian country the most ardent of Asia's first communists dreamt of a swift repetition in their part of Asia of Lenin's achievement in Russia, so their urge towards setting alight a communist revolt became exceedingly difficult to curb. Contemporaneously with the first Chinese communist attempts at rural revolt in the mid-1920s, communist hustlers in 1926–7 precipitated in Java and Sumatra a handful of rural revolts, contrary to clear orders from their anxious superiors, and without either concerted preparation or effective coordination. The Dutch turned upon these with resolute ardour, and not simply were they vigorously suppressed; apart from a few shadowy wanderers abroad, and some later avowed secret supporters, no communist presence was to be seen again in Indonesia for another two decades.

By the mid 1920s there were a few communists in India as well, and despite the worst fears of its British rulers they ultimately proved as little threatening to the British as after 1927 the PKI was to the Dutch. The early Communist Party of India did not have any close association with a movement with rural connections such as the PKI had had with Sarekat

Islam. Throughout it was overwhelmingly wedded to India's cities and their urban proletariats. In the late 1920s – by which time the urban-based Communist Party of China had been decimated by Chiang Kai shek, and the Indochinese Communist Party was about to be trapped in some rural revolts as well – the CPI had probably become the most powerful urban communist party in Asia. It certainly showed in 1928 that it could mastermind a major mill-workers strike in Bombay. If there was now not much chance of a major conjunction of Muslims and Hindus in India, the British were fearful that the CPI might nevertheless forge a link with the Indian National Congress. They were accordingly exceedingly careful in the steps they took as they sought to curb the CPI, and eventually they arraigned its leaders on what proved to be an inordinately longwinded conspiracy case. This was so managed, however, that (apart from inducing some largely ritualistic support from the Congress for the communists on trial) the conjunction the British had feared between the CPI and the Congress never took place. Thereafter the British neither banned the CPI nor set about slaughtering its leaders, as the French were doing meanwhile in Vietnam; and indeed by 1933 most of the CPI leaders had been released from jail. They then returned to the cities whence they had come, and, whilst resolutely watched, showed themselves largely uninterested in extending their support into the countryside where the majority of Indians lived, and where the Indian National Congress for its part was becoming increasingly active. Thereafter the major disaster for the CPI came in the Second World War when, tied to Moscow, and to the Moscow line after mid 1941 – that with the German attack on Russia the imperialist war had become a people's war – the CPI fatally sided with the British at precisely the moment when the Indian nationalist movement mounted its largest ever onslaught against the British in the Quit India movement of 1942. For this treachery the CPI was never to be forgiven in India, and by 1945 it was in almost as parlous a state as the PKI had long been in Indonesia.

So to an altogether remarkable degree two forces that had earlier had some prospect of being of prime political importance in these two countries – activist Islam and marxist communism   had in the crucial decades before the end of the Second World War run themselves, or been run by others, into the sand. The earlier, sometimes dramatic, Muslim movements had by the mid-1920s largely evaporated. They were each to revive in new forms, but except upon one great but nevertheless passing issue – the partition of India – were never to be of such central importance again. To a still greater extent the hopes of the earlier communists had likewise been dashed in both these countries, and – once again with the short-lived exceptions of the PKI's emeute at Madiun in 1948, and its great expansion prior to its final disaster in 1965 – were never to be revived again. In ways that had earlier been by no means assured the main force in the political development of both India and Indonesia in the mid twentieth century came instead from their secular nationalists.

SECULAR NATIONALISM

The oldest, most substantial expression of these was the Indian National Congress which had been founded in 1885. It had a prehistory in various lesser organisations going back into the mid nineteenth century. It originally consisted very largely, as one of its later presidents was to put it, of 'persons educated in schools and colleges'. Its earlier fluorescence, as compared with anything comparable in Indonesia, would seem to have stemmed from the much earlier development of schools and colleges by the British in India than by the Dutch in Indonesia. For its first twenty years or so, despite the hostility of a succession of British viceroys, its principle interest had been in improving the access of the small westernised Indian elite to India's existing corridors of power. In the present context its most notable achievement was to have created a single political organisation from the largest parts of India that included people from all its main cities, and thus from all its principle regions, north and south, east and west. In 1906 it began to call for Swaraj, self-rule. In 1907, however, it broke apart into a 'moderate' wing, which was determined to stick to previous procedures and came out on top, and an 'extremist' one which demanded forcible agitation, and on its fringes was ready to take to violence. This division was aggravated by factional conflict, and in the years preceding the First World War led to a marked decline in Congress activities.

During the First World War, however, a conjunction of forces (including the deaths of the two leading moderates, Gokhale and Mehta, and the return from deportation of the most prominent extremist, Tilak) led not only to the reunification of the two nationalist wings, but at Lucknow in 1916 to a formal Pact between the Congress and the Muslim League over the longstanding matter of communal representation in the Indian legislatures. At the same time somewhat separate Home Rule Leagues were founded of a kind that elsewhere have sometimes undermined older nationalist movements – one thinks of Nkrumah's creation in 1949 of the Convention People's Party in Ghana at the expense of the older United Gold Coast Convention. It chanced, however, that one principal Home Rule Leader, the vociferous Englishwoman Annie Besant, having first stirred many young enthusiasts, then pulled in her horns, and soon slipped from its leadership, whilst her counterpoise in the movement, the former extremist leader, Tilak, also lost his way (and then in 1920 died). In their place the former longstanding leader of the Indians in South Africa, M.K. Gandhi emerged in the years following his return to India in 1915, not only to take over the leadership of the withering Home Rule movement, but to give a dramatically new and hugely successful leadership to the still extant Congress itself. Towards the end of the First World War some former moderates left the Congress, eventually to form the Liberal party, but very few went with them; and it soon proved to be a special feature of Gandhi's political genius that his ardent commitment to programmes of non-violent agitation, while meeting the desires of many instictive extremists for some more positive action, at the same time allayed the fears of many instinctive moderates lest this should slip into violence. As we have seen, during the first great wave of Gandhi led agitations, from 1918 through to 1922, Gandhi was also able, for a brief moment at least, to enlist the potent Khalifat movement in his cause as well.

But as we have seen too, in 1922, (following mob killings of policemen at the police station at Chauri Chaura in the United Provinces) Gandhi, to most people's astonishment, called off his by then combined Khalifat/Non-co-operation movement. There was a great deal of subsequent debate as to the form the Indian nationalist movement should then take, and out of this emerged separate Swaraj, and Nationalist parties, which by no means all Congressmen (not Gandhi himself for a start) were to join. But when one compares these Indian complexities with the fragmentations that were shortly to overtake the Indonesian nationalist movement, the fact that all these Indian constructions did not entail any further split within the Congress itself, not even to the extent of that effected by the now near moribund Indian Liberals, constituted a political achievement of quite singular moment. Coupled with the enduring fact, from the days of the earliest Congress onwards, that the Indian National Congress had support in most major parts of the country – despite the existence of the Justice Party in Madras, the Unionists in the Punjab, and some other single province organisations too – this meant that it had an unequalled claim to wide national support of an order no Indonesian party ever obtained. Gandhi's singlehanded decision to call off his first great agitation in 1922 certainly lost him the support of most of India's Muslims for ever; but it preserved the overarching integrity of the Congress itself – and deprived the British of any plausible excuse to proceed vigorously against it. By the early 1920s, moreover, the essential core of its support amongst those 'educated in schools and colleges' had been decisively enlarged (principally following, it would seem, the adverse financial effects of the exigencies of Britain's war and post-war economic policy in India) by the adhesion to it of the greater part of the strategically placed mercantile communities of all the small as well as the large towns of India. As members of the same 'bania' community from which Gandhi himself was drawn, they saw in him both one of their own, and a political leader whose non-violent style posed no threat to their interests, and a saint of the kind they traditionally revered. Henceforth they were amongst his most ardent supporters (and his principal paymasters) even when their business interests necessarily placed checks upon their ultimate agitational commitments. By the early 1920s, moreover, thanks to Gandhi's own peculiar talents in providing by his non-violent satyagraha doctrine procedures which could be used by communities of peasants who were urgently seeking to have some particular local disability remedied, Congress was joined as well by the first cohorts of better off peasants who were to be so crucial to its eventual success.

By the late 1920s the post 1922 inclination of some Congressmen to see if participation in the legislatures in British India, whose powers, especially at provincial level, the British had lately enlarged by their Government of India Act in 1919, might prove a fruitful proceeding, was rapidly declining, and coupled with the new urgency of another generation, epitomised by such younger leaders as Jawaharlal Nehru and Subhas Bose, a new and still more powerful agitational thrust than Congress had mounted in the early 1920s was gathering momentum. This led between 1930 and 1934 to the two major waves of Gandhi-led Civil Disobedience movements. By means to which we must return these were each halted by the British, and in the aftermath there was a further flowering of Swaraj and Nationalist parties, including for the first time the creation of a Congress Socialist Party. But once again these all continued to stand under the wide umbrella of the long-persistent Congress, and the significance of the earlier break away of the Liberals had by this time come to lie principally in its being the last such separation that occurred in all the years before India became independent. What was more during the course of the Civil Disobedience movements, and despite – though perhaps because of – Britain's successful checking of them, many more peasant communities, especially of the better off, now began to swing behind the Congress as well. Even from the overwhelmingly Muslim Frontier province there came such support under the so-called Frontier Gandhi, Abdul Ghaffar Khan, while, more enduringly, in the mid 1930s, the leaders of Maharashtra's majority non-Brahman movement, which had formerly been hostile to Congress as the preserve of the elite Tilak-led Brahmans, swung their support behind the Congress as well. By the mid-1930s, as events were shortly to show, the unity and reach of the Congress (which was still very much under Gandhi's ultimate leadership) had become both remarkably powerful and very extensive.

The contrasts with Indonesia can then be readily set down. It too had had its embryonic nationalist movements prior to the First World War. But they did not have so lengthy a history. Budi Utomo was founded in 1908 principally as a society for cultural and educational advancement. In 1912 there was founded as well the Indische Partij, a more overtly political, indeed revolutionary party, largely at the outset under Eurasian leadership. This was soon transformed under Dutch government pressure into a more moderate party, Insulinde, which like Budi Utomo continued to operate for a number of years. But neither attained any greater muscle than the pre-Congress organisations that India had seen before it was founded in 1885, and the principal development in Indonesia in the following years was rather to be found, as we have seen, within Sarekat Islam. This by Indian comparisons, even as compared with the Khalifat movement, was in its heyday a far more extensively supported movement than anything India was to see until the 1930s. But as we have seen too, Sarekat Islam's force was gravely reduced by the competition within it after the First World War of the communists, and, more particularly following the communist defeats in the mid-1920s, it was only then that the way was decisively opened, in so largely a Muslim country, for secular nationalism.

This had more than one genesis. It came to be led by Sukarno, a qualified engineer educated only in Indonesia, who was thus one of the tardy products by Indian standards of the delayed Dutch commitment to some Indonesian higher education. He was of much the same generation as Nehru and Bose in India, and in a number of obvious ways was to display some of their key characteristics. But initially there was a more potent group of Indonesian secular nationalists which in most respects had no counterpart in India. These were those who, in the absence of sufficient facilities in Indonesia, had gone to the Netherlands for further education. There were certainly some Indians who had been educated in Britain – Jawaharlal Nehru for a start – but despite a variety of Indian student organisations there they never formed any organisation that was nearly as influential as Perhimpunan Indonesia, the political organisation of Indonesian students in the Netherlands. Judging from the aftermath, PI fostered three streams of thought; first, a fervent commitment to secular nationalism for Indonesia; second (though varyingly) a belief that this should properly be combined with a purged nationalist version of the Dutch doctrine of 'peace and order'; and third (perhaps still more varyingly) an interest in the socialist as distinct from the communist doctrines that were internationally in such vogue at the time. The last two streams can each be especially associated, together emphatically with the first, with the names of Hatta and Sjahrir respectively.

These developments became more generally salient in Indonesia itself first with the formation of a miscellany of Study Groups in the middle 1920s, and then more precisely in Sukarno's formation of the Partai Nasional Indonesia in 1927.

Sukarno had lived with, indeed had married the daughter of, Tjokroaminoto, the long surviving leader of the now much reduced Sarekat Islam. In part perhaps as a consequence he never lost sight of the fact that this was principally a Muslim country. Yet PNI was not to be, as Sarekat Islam had been before it, a primarily Muslim organisation. Sukarno's principal gift –

in which he had no equal either in Indonesia or in India – was his oratory. He could capture and stir huge audiences in a way no other leader – certainly not Hatta – ever did, and this he combined not merely with a considerable personal nationalist fervour but with acute political sensitivity as well. That led him not only to create PNI and enlist many PI returnees in its ranks, but to form PPPKI, a congress of all the wide variety of Indonesian political parties, as well. By 1929–30 the wary Dutch administration arrested him and some of his principal associates and put them on trial for attempting to undermine their colonial authority. Hatta meanwhile had also been arraigned, in 1929 – though in Holland, to which he had returned. By contrast to Hatta's, Sukarno's spirited defence at his trial in 1930 did not secure his immediate release. But it very well served his nationalist purposes; and a year later he was set free by the Dutch when even they realised that the force of the case advanced against him was, to say the least, questionable.

Upon his release Sukarno found, however, not only that his old PNI had formally ceased to exist, but that its supporters had divided into a new PNI, PNI Baru, and another party, Partindo. His efforts to conjoin these were now unsuccessful, as were his further attempts to make the full range of Indonesia's extant parties cohere once again in a revived PPPKI; and when he eventually chose to join Partindo he found that his authority within it was never to be as great as it had once been in PNI. Whilst he steadily resumed his old oratorical heights and thus reattained not only his old popular public primacy but the renewed hostility of the Dutch, by Indian standards not only did the Indonesian nationalist movement now lack the overall organisational unity of the Indian National Congress. It was still almost wholly confined to the cities of Java. Even there it did not enjoy – as the Indian Congress had now come to do – the active support of prominent merchant communities, for these were in Indonesia chiefly Arab or Chinese. It was as well, moreover, in no sense archipelago-wide; and since its SI heyday it had never developed (aside from the limited fateful involvement of the PKI in the mid 1920s) any significant rural roots of the kind that the Indian Congress was now so promisingly establishing. Indeed it was hardly ever to do so. Larger contrasts with the Indian case it would be difficult to conceive.

IMPERIALIST RESPONSES

These weaknesses may well have made Indonesian nationalism an easier prey for its opponents in the Dutch administration to confront than the very much stronger Indian National Congress was for the British. It should be emphasised that in their liberal minds Dutch administrators could be at least as accommodating as the British ever were. There had been a much more sympathetic welcome to Budi Utomo from Governor-General Van Heutsz than was ever accorded to any Indian development once Lord Ripon had ceased to be viceroy of India in 1884; while in the 1920s Governor-General De Graeff (1926–31) later attempted to pursue 'a policy based on creating trust' that was ultimately to be responsible for Sukarno's release in 1931.

But apart from the more general imperialist instinct to resist colonial nationalism of any form, three impulses, which had few counterparts in the Indian case, seem to have been very important to the Dutch. First, there was always a much larger Dutch community, relatively speaking, in Indonesia than there ever was a British one in India. This was divided, again in a way that had no counterpart in India, between the supporters of two propagandist organisations. There were on the one hand the hardliners, represented by the *Vaderlandsche Club*, the lobby for the unending primacy of Dutch interests; and on the other the 'softer liners' – of which the last Dutch Lieutenant Governor-General Van Mook was throughout his career a distinguished exponent – in the so-called Stuw movement. (This latter sought a more independent and integrated regime in the Netherlands East Indies in which the Indonesian born Dutch would have a full place along with all the other inhabitants of the islands.) Whatever their emphases, the relatively large numbers of Dutch residents were all but unanimous, however, on the need for a firmly restraining check upon any liberalisation of the Dutch position in Indonesia, of an order that was never similarly to be found influencing British policy in India. This was then reinforced by the very direct influence of Dutch capitalists upon Dutch policy in Indonesia. This had early been exemplified by their founding and financing of professorships in Indies studies at the University of Utrecht as a conservative counterweight to the earlier and much more accommodating school at the University of Leiden – as epitomised by the great Dutch Islamic Indonesian scholar-adviser, Snouck Hurgronje. It was then displayed the more especially in the appointment of De Jonge as governor-general of the Dutch East Indies (1931–6), and of the hold over Dutch policy there of Colijn, Minister for the Colonies (1933–7), both of whom were former directors of Dutch Shell. Never did British capitalists come anywhere near so close to holding the key British offices concerned with India.

There was a third distinctive circumstance to the making of Dutch policy in the interwar period, as compared with British policy towards India, as well. Nothing ever occurred in India to compare with the communist revolts in Java and Sumatra in 1926–7. The British were always wary of communists, and of revolt. They vigorously repressed the Muslim Moplahs in south India in 1921, and the Redshirts (no communists these, but Frontier tribesmen who dyed their shirts to a rust colour) in 1930. But during the interwar years the British never lived with the fear, as after 1927 the Dutch always did, that armed insurrection against the very basis of their rule, having lately occurred once already, could well occur again. That made them much more prone than the British ever were to take the draconian course.

All of this, following the liberal uncertainties of the Governor-General De Graeff period, eventually added up to an emphatic determination during the De Jonge's days, strongly backed by Colijn, to have no dealings at all with Indonesian nationalism. 'We have ruled here', so De Jonge was quoted as saying, 'for 300 years with the whip and the club and we shall be doing it in another 300 years.' Sukarno was accordingly arrested again in 1933 and this time without trial was banished for life. His realisation that this could be for him the end of any purposeful existence precipitated his pathetic pleas to be released on condition that he retired from political life altogether. But these were to no avail, and shortly afterwards Hatta and several others were incarcerated likewise, whereupon Indonesia's strongly voiced secular nationalist movement fell into ruins.

The British stance was significantly different. Whilst they imprisoned India's nationalist leaders too, all told for a great many years, they never did so *ad infinitum*. Their weasel words, promising, in 1917, self-government, and, in 1929, Dominion Status, were all heavily circumscribed by being only applicable in a long distant future; but at least they had been uttered. They held, moreover, in 1930–33 Round Table conferences with 'representative Indians' in London. Whilst these were principally notable for fashioning constitutional reforms that were explicitly designed to prevent the Indian National Congress from securing control of India's central government, at least they eventually led to Congress control of most of the provincial governments in India.

Yet, against all this, it was scarcely surprising that after over two frustrating decades of seeking a real *swaraj*, Congress should in 1929 have committed itself to attaining *purna swaraj*, complete independence, and have thereupon launched, under Gandhi's extraordinarily inspirational leadership, the two successive Civil Disobedience movements of 1930–1 and 1932–4.

To these the British responded by harassments, arrests and imprisonments. Finding themselves hard pressed late in 1930, but with some superficial movement at the First Round Table Conference in London, they fashioned the compromise that became the Gandhi–Irwin Pact of 1931, by which both the movement and the imprisonments were called off on condition that Gandhi would go, as he did, to the Second Round Table Conference in London later that year. But since that effected no basic change in the situation, confrontation was resumed at the end of the year. This time, however, such was the new efficiency of Britain's police action that the second Civil Disobedience movement was brought to a halt early in 1932 without resort either to armed conflict or to indiscriminate executions.

These contretemps had meanwhile provoked the largest debate that was ever to be held in Britain upon India's affairs. During the early 1930s this engrossed British politics to an extraordinary degree. It was primarily a debate within the British Conservative Party. Winston Churchill led the 'diehards', adamantly opposed to any relinquishment of the British Empire, and vehemently hostile to any 'betrayal' of 'the Indian masses' to the interests of 'a few Brahman agitators'. Upon the other side no radicals were to be found but only some rather more liberal Conservatives, displeased with the seeming need for repressions, and fearful of any repetition of the appalling saga of Britain's earlier battle over Irish independence, who were looking within the tradition of Britain's consti- tutional development for some more presentable holding mechanism. Fortuitously the Conservative party leader, Baldwin, stood in this latter camp, and that tipped the balance in his party. He would, he said, 'not have another Ireland in India.' 'We have taught [India] the lesson', so he averred as the debate reached its climax, 'and she wants us to pay the bill.'

For all the deliberate obstructiveness of the proposed federal sections of the Government of India Act 1935 that then ensued, the debate's outcome made for a crucial difference between India and Indonesia. Whilst Colijn's view prevailed in the Netherlands, Churchill's failed in Britain, and although Churchill's later position as prime minister led to a considerable diehard reaction during the Second World War, that proved to be no more than a passing, if for the time being very serious, occurrence. For the great debate of the early 1930s in Britain over India was never really resumed, and the future accordingly lay, represented as electoral chance would have it by Britain's post Second World War Labour Government, who by then had become fully committed to India's early independence.

In the meanwhile during the late 1930s the crucial difference between Indonesia's experience and India's could be more readily discerned in contrasting events within the two countries themselves.

Since 1918 Indonesia had had a *Volksraad*. There had been some hope at an earlier stage that it might soon secure an Indonesian majority and develop into an embryonic Parliament. But as these hopes evaporated those from such organisations as Sarekat Islam, Tjokroaminoto especially, whom the Dutch wanted to appoint to it, increasingly declined to serve upon it. There was, scarcely surprisingly, never any question of the secular nation- alists, Sukarno, Hatta and their like, either being asked, let alone actually doing so. But upon their banishment and all which that implied the *Volksraad* seemed to be the only arena in which any kind of Indonesian nationalist opinion could be expressed, and as a result leaders of the new collaborating parties, Gerindo and Parindra, accordingly decided to work within its confines. In 1936 the point was reached when the *Volksraad* submitted to the Dutch government the so-called Soetardjo Petition (named after its designer) that very modestly sought a little further constitutional advance in their country by means of a joint conference of representatives of the Netherlands and the East Indies. For fifteen months this received no answer, and when it came it was simply a curt rejection. Dutch diehardism remained supreme.

By contrast in India whilst there was no effectual constitutional advance at the centre in the 1930s, the Government of India Act of 1935 did provide for full 'Responsible Government' in the provinces. Provincial elections were accordingly held in 1937, and at these Congress unequivocally demonstrated its potency by winning the largest number of seats in seven of the eleven provinces of India, backed above all by its rich peasant and merchant community supporters who were crucial to its success. After some hesitation it then formed 'responsible' governments in each of these provinces. That was a position of which Indonesia's nationalists of whatever colour could as yet scarcely dream.

As it chanced this denouement did not last. As the Second World War opened this Indian outcome collapsed in an outburst of hostility with the British over the role Indian nationalists should play in support of the war; and through two variations of the old Civil Disobedience procedures the Indian National Congress, with Gandhi once more at its head, thereupon embarked upon its third great series of nationalist agitations against the British – 'individual satyagraha' in 1940–1, and the mass 'Quit India' movement in 1942. This time the conflict was aggravated by the liaison which the British established with the reviving Muslim League; by the grave exigencies for the British of the war; and by the lesser grasp that the Congress leadership found it now had over some of its most volatile supporters. As it happened the Quit India revolt of 1942, though short, was far more eruptive than the Congress leadership desired, and was repressed with far greater vehemence by the British than they had customarily employed since the notorious Amritsar Massacre of 1919. But in the midst of all this Churchill's Labour colleagues in his wartime coalition, together with a sufficiency of non-diehard Conservatives, put into the public record, by means of the so-called Cripps Offer of 1942, an all party undertaking that at the end of the War Britain would very soon end its dominion in India. Since, having made such pronouncements, the British had always held to their word, there was henceforth a strong prospect that Independence could be won for India without revolution.

There could be no such prospect in Indonesia. Further pressure in 1939 from a new, still moderate, nationalist gathering, GAPI, had again yielded no result, and even after the Germans had in 1940 overrun the Netherlands, banishment was still the lot of Indonesia's leading nationalists. Nevertheless following the flight of Queen Wilhelmina's government to London at that time, the Dutch government came under such pressure from the United States to renounce its empire that in 1942 it made two declarations promising a constitutional conference after the war. These simply promised, however, no more than that this would lead to a reconstruction of the different territories of the Kingdom of the Netherlands into a Commonwealth in which each would 'participate, with complete self-reliance and freedom of conduct for each part regarding its internal affairs, but with the readiness to render mutual assistance' – which in truth amounted to next to nothing. Indeed given the context and the actual attitude when the war ended even (by Dutch standards) of the liberal Lieutenant Governor-General Van Mook (let alone his more conservative superiors and critics, such as Gerbrandy or Beel), very little short of a successfully mounted revolution against Dutch rule held out any hope for Indonesians of the early independence the Indians could now be well confident of achieving from the British very shortly.

The near miracle was that amid great anguish and trauma and much pulling this way and that Indonesia's nationalists nevertheless did win their independence within two years of India's.

REVOLUTION AND TRANSFER OF POWER

Their opportunities began with the Japanese conquest of South-east Asia during 1941. The seemingly all-powerful Dutch were thereby dashed from their pinnacles, and a first crisis arose. How would the Japanese treat Indonesia's incarcerated nationalists? How might these respond to any Japanese overtures? It is notable that the main response of Indonesia's nationalist leaders did not follow the path of their Indochinese counterparts, nor that of the Communist Party of Malaya, both of which during the war years strongly resisted the Japanese. Nor did they follow that of the more radical Burmese nationalists in first allying with the Japanese when the war went Japan's way, and then deserting them for the British when the war's fortunes turned. The actual alignments of the Indonesian nationalists (along with some remarkable strokes of fortune) sometimes very directly determined the subsequent seminal course of events, and need to be picked out very precisely.

At the outset the Japanese very soon set the Indonesian nationalist leaders free. The key figures then arranged among themselves that they should hedge their bets whilst maintaining their contacts with each other. As became those of a more decidedly socialist, and thus anti-fascist, cast of mind, Sjahrir and Amir Sjaffaruddin went underground to lead such anti-Japanese movements as might be formed there. Sukarno and Hatta meanwhile made themselves available to work with the Japanese. This kind of cleavage in nationalist ranks was a commonplace elsewhere. In China Chiang and Mao went one way, Wang Ching-wei the other. In the Philippines Quezon and Osmena withdrew to America, whilst Vargas, Laurel, Roxas and others stayed behind to work with the Japanese. Even in India the younger leaders divided. Nehru was adamantly hostile to the Japanese fascists. His contemporary, Subhas Bose, by contrast threw in his lot with the Japanese, and in association with them was soon masterminding the anti-British Indian National Army. (If the Japanese had conquered India as they conquered Indonesia, Bose could easily have become India's Sukarno, whilst Nehru might well have found his career ending a quarter-century before it did.) What was distinct in the Indonesian case was that the two wings remained in close alliance with each other.

For the most part the Japanese occupation of Indonesia lacked nothing in brutality. They maintained, however, the existing Indonesian powers-that-were who had previously served the Dutch, and with great deliberation brought together the varied Muslim organisations into a single Muslim association, Masyumi. Then in 1943 they placed Sukarno and Hatta at the head of the newly formed Putera (Centre of People's Power) to be the principal instrument for enlisting popular support for their occupation regime. Although this did not last very long it gave Sukarno a unique opportunity to resume the primacy he had previously held in the halcyon years 1927–9. For he was now free to move around the country and become the principal spokesman once again for his people. In these circumstances a special role came to be played by some of the urban youth who following the tardy expansion of the Dutch system of education which was unmatched by any increase in jobs, still stood in the first flush of their frustrated enthusiasms, much as the supporters of the 'extremists' and then of Gandhi had done in India both before and after the First World War. For the most part these youth – *pemuda* – at first aligned themselves more with Sukarno then with Sjahrir, and the underground campaign accordingly languished – certainly as compared with its counterpart in Malaya.

Crucially in 1944 the Japanese went one step further. Fearful that the war was now turning against them they moved to training and arming companies of young Indonesians as auxiliary defenders of the Japanese position against an allied invasion. Some of these were placed under the auspices of an overtly Muslim organisation, Hizbullah. But the principal creation was Peta (Protectors of the Fatherland). Drilled, trained, and imbued with Japanese notions of loyalty and heroism, the Peta recruits – and not least its Indonesian officers – were thereby inducted into a military career in a way that was to have major consequences for Indonesia's history, till our own day at least.

As the Allies advanced, so the Japanese sought to win greater support in their conquered territories by installing Japanese sponsored governments, first in Burma, then in the Philippines, and later in Vietnam. In May 1945 a preparatory committee to create a self-governing Indonesia was eventually formed in Indonesia too, with Sukarno and Hatta amongst its principal members. There were by now no Indonesian figures at home or abroad to challenge their primacy. They had the support of the networks of Hokko-kai, the later, more tightly Japanese controlled version of Putera; and they had to hand companies of preliminarily trained Indonesian troops who – unlike the armed anti-fascists in Malaya – were in no way committed to the western Allies. The Indonesians were especially careful at this time not to establish contacts with the Dutch (as their Burmese and Malayan counter-parts were doing with the British) since they were understandably fearful of the likely atttitude of the Dutch at this time – and thus early on revealed the deftness they could display as the swiftly developing crisis unfolded.

In August 1945 the Second World War cataclysmically ended in Asia when the two atomic bombs were dropped on Japan. The Japanese were then unclear as to whether they should encourage the Indonesian nation-alists to declare their independence in advance of a Dutch return (as indeed were both Sukarno and Hatta themselves). A major step the Japanese did take was to disarm and disperse Peta and its counterparts. But in the event, when, as earlier described, Sukarno and Hatta under immense *pemuda* pressure declared the independence of Indonesia on 17 August 1945 the Japanese decided not to stand in their way. The Dutch for their part, war-stricken as they were, assumed that the British and their Indian divisions would shortly assist them in restoring Dutch rule in Indonesia, as the British were simultaneously – and, let it be emphasised, astonishingly – restoring their own in Malaya and Borneo and as the Americans had already restored theirs in the Philippines. In view of such expectations the Dutch had no intention of giving place to those whom they saw as Indonesia's quislings, Sukarno, Hatta and others of their kind; and thus the prospects of conflict became patent.

The nascent Republic of Indonesia was at first a most fragile entity. Its leaders had already bent before the pressure of a mob; its bureaucratic underpinnings were largely non-existent; and what might have been its army had just been disbanded. However, there were still enough former Peta and other recruits around, and enough international support too for the declaration of independence, to make some British commanders hesitate to crush it, to the fury of the Dutch; and when others showed themselves less cautious, they often found themselves quite fanatically confronted by *pemuda* and former Peta and other forces that were now regrouping into new formations, and not least into the embryonic Indo-nesian Republican army. But fearful of the fragility of their own position the Republican leaders nevertheless long attempted to negotiate with the

Dutch. To this end it soon seemed better that Sjahrir, the underground leader, and now a primary spokesman for the *pemuda*, should head the executive government, since he could in no way be accused of being a collaborator. That entailed a departure from the presidential system of government whose establishment had followed upon the original republican declaration, and that in turn called for a national council representing the now emerging parties: Sukarno's old PNI, Masyumi for the Muslims, PSI for the socialists, and, from out of the woodwork, the long since exiled PKI.

The turmoil of the ensuing five to six years cannot be rehearsed here. What is striking is the sharp contrast between the immediate post-war attitude of the British in South Asia and the Dutch in Indonesia. It is tempting to explain Britain's departure from India by reference to its exhaustion at the end of the Second World War, and its inability to hold India for very much longer. But when the Dutch story in Indonesia is brought into consideration both explanations need major review. For a start, whilst the British had successfully withstood the major Quit India revolt against them in 1942, the Dutch were never able to suppress the forces of Indonesia's nascent Republic. The British may have been war torn; but scarcely to the extent that the Dutch were. It is arguable that the Dutch economy depended more upon its investments in Indonesia than Britain's did upon its involvements in India – especially since by the end of the Second World War Britain had, for the first time, become massively India's creditor. There does seem, moreover, to have been more commitment in the Netherlands to the notion that its possessions in the Indies were crucial to its economic recovery than to any counterpart notion in Britain; and this was no doubt reinforced by the much higher proportion of Dutch who saw themselves as citizens of the East Indies than of British who saw themselves as principally belonging to India. The fact that the subsequent economic histories of the two former imperial countries scarcely bore out the Dutch conviction at the time in no way detracts from the strength with which it was held.

There were other considerations as well. The events of the 1920s and 1930s had made it easier for the Dutch to argue that radical Indonesian nationalism was a mere will o' the wisp than it was for the British to believe likewise in India. Indonesia's nationalists had been divided and relatively easily elbowed aside. By contrast the Indian National Congress had for nearly three decades proved to be a much more substantial foe to the British; and whatever Britain's success against the Quit India movement, the experience of it had made it seem highly unlikely that after the war they could successfully repress the still larger revolt they could be expected to confront if, like the Dutch, they showed themselves unwilling to depart. These subtler considerations that would seem to have governed the thinking in Britain and in the Netherlands in the thirties and early forties, and the accompanying differences in the stance of their respective ruling circles towards their Asian dominions, were, by the time the war came to an end, generally palpable. The great debate in Britain in the early 1930s over their possessions in South Asia had prepared the ground for Britain's clear decision to depart from India so soon as the Second World War was over. The Dutch determination, at least from Colijn's years onwards, that they should stay, led them by contrast to gird themselves as the war ended to return to the Indies and if necessary fight there to restore their previous dominance.

The attitude of the Dutch – in sharp contrast to that of the British in all of South Asia – thus veered between no concessions at all to the Republic and Lieutenant-Governor Van Mook's Dutch Indonesian-born notion of a federated East Indies in which the Republic would be at best no more than one constituent part of a Federation that would be one of the two main Realms of the Dutch Crown, in which the other, the Netherlands, would, of course, be dominant. Twice, in the Linggadjati agreement in 1946 and the Renville agreement in 1948, a settlement along the lines Van Mook long desired seemed to be mutually agreed. But on both occasions the Republicans dragged their feet since they were deeply suspicious of the Dutch for inordinately pressing the quite uncertain small print. Twice in turn these hesitations led the Dutch (indeed Van Mook himself, and not just the harderliners) into launching 'police actions', i.e. military attacks, first in 1947, and again in 1948, so as to bring the nascent Republic to its knees; but twice these attempts were halted. Meanwhile twice, in the July 1st affair in 1946, and more especially in the Madiun affair in September 1948, the Republic faced attempts by the leftists within it – and at Madiun by the PKI more deliberately – to overthrow its existing leadership because of its apparent readiness to compromise with the Dutch. Twice, however, these moves were suppressed by a combination of a dramatic radio appeal by the ever eloquent Sukarno, which was then backed by action by dominant forces within the steadily evolving, and in the circumstances increasingly anti-communist, Republican army. Twice, moreover, the United Nations (fairly certainly stretching its mandate) intervened to halt the Netherlands' pressure upon the fragile Republic, first through a Good Offices Commission in Indonesia itself, of which the United States, Belgium and Australia were members, following Van Mooks first 'Police Action' in 1947, and then, more forcibly, by direct American diplomatic and economic pressure on the Netherlands itself following the second 'Police Action' in 1948. For as a consequence of the young Republics' resoluteness in resisting its communist detractors it assured itself of American support; and thanks to the accumulating experience of four years of conflict, and now six years of some experience of military discipline, the increasingly confident Republican Army, and its associated plethora of less disciplined irregulars, were able to frustrate the Dutch the second time around even more than they had the first. In the upshot the Dutch agreed to call a round table conference at The Hague during 1949 at which Hatta led the Republican delegation, and there secured, for 27 December 1949, all but full independence for a Sukarno-led 'United States of Indonesia' – a concession to the residuum of Van Mook's federal plans which within a year gave way to an essentially unitary Republic of Indonesia, as Indonesia's Java-based nationalists had always desired. In the new regime Hatta, whilst remaining vice-president, became prime minister of a coalition party government under the overall presidency of Sukarno that in liberal democratic terms was now held to be responsible to a still not yet nominated multi-party parliament.

The death toll during Indonesia's revolutionary years from 1945 to 1949 is impossible to tabulate. It was almost certainly less, however, than that which contemporaneously occurred in India. In one respect that is paradoxical since as between Britain and India there was at this time no military conflict. Despite some twistings and turnings the British after the war clearly held to their Cripps commitment in 1942 to leave India at its end, as indeed they went from Burma and Ceylon as well. The crisis which did occur came not therefore over the issue of whether the British were prepared to go, but over what kind of place would then be left when they did for India's now rearoused Muslim minority.

Since 1940 the Muslim League had increasingly demanded the creation of a separate state of Pakistan. The Congress for its part could not contemplate the partition this would entail. That dispute led among other things to the breakdown of Viceroy Wavell's Simla Conference in 1945. In 1946 a three-member British cabinet mission tried to fashion an acceptable compromise whereby one set of Hindu and two sets of Muslim majority provinces would be constitutionally grouped under a rather weak overall centre. But that attempt collapsed amidst much rising hostility, and since the British now increasingly feared that they could not maintain their position in India for very much longer, they in the first place determined to leave the country by a fixed date in 1948, and then brought this forward summarily to coincide with a Partition in August 1947 that would leave Pakistan with less territory than its leaders had always sought, indeed with no more than those portions in which the Muslims unarguably held a majority. It was in the course of this crisis that terrible communal killings started to occur. They were nothing, however, to those which, following Partition and Independence on 14/15 August 1947, overwhelmed India's north western province, the Punjab, which was not only divided in a manner the Muslims especially had never expected, but in which the warlike Sikhs, who had finally opted for India, were scattered throughout. As the 1940s came to their end both Indonesia and India, and of course Pakistan also, were appallingly traumatised by the crises which had struck them.

DIFFERING OUTCOMES

Yet the contrasts, between India and Indonesia at least, were once again major. Each had won its independence after a long, persistent struggle. Each saw its independence – as the Filipino elite to whom in 1946 the Americans had also granted independence could never do – as the fruit of their peoples' heroic endeavours. Each new regime as it happens had by 1950 successfully resisted communist insurrections – in 1948 the PKI was militarily and politically routed at Madiun, and shortly afterwards the CPI was vanquished in Telangana – just at the time when Mao Zedong's communists were winning their victories in China, and when Ho Chi Minh's communists were establishing themselves as Vietnam's principal nationalist leaders.

But while one country, Indonesia, owing to the unbending resistance of the Dutch had, as it felt, won its independence by means of a sudden, sharp and often bloody revolution, the other, India, owing to the eventual readiness of the British to leave, had in the end, as it knew, secured its independence by means of a long sought non-revolutionary transfer of power.

As a consequence in India the law of the land upon the attainment of independence rested in the main upon Britain's Government of India Act of 1935, which was then only somewhat upgraded into India's independence constitution of 1950. Along with this went continuity in legal minutiae, in bureaucratic practices and bureaucratic membership, and in countless other respects as well. This was true too as concerned the practice of parliamentary government, which in 1937–9 had been in operation in the provinces of India all but to the full, and which now revived both there and at the centre as well. Continuity was found too in the persistence in the Indian Administrative Service of so much that had characterized Britain's former Indian Civil Service. At Partition, moreover, whilst the Indian Army was, of course, divided, it too retained after Independence direct continuities with the British formed Army that had existed in India for well over a century.

In Indonesia on the other hand, the roots of the constitution went no further back than the work of the preparatory committee set up by the Japanese in May 1945. Upon the declaration of the Republic in August 1945 a system of presidential rule under Sukarno as president was speedily instituted. But in October 1945 this was superseded by a system of prime ministerial rule, in the first place under Sjahrir, in which Sukarno was relegated to an essentially figurehead presidency. That arrangement was eventually incorporated into the independence constitution of 1949 for the short-lived United States of Indonesia, which then gave way to the ultimate unitary Republic of Indonesia. In Indonesia constitutional democracy thus had negligible roots in its pre-republican history, and was then much buffeted about by the markedly differing aspirants for power during the revolutionary years. Here in the post-independence years was already one marked contrast with India. But there were others as well.

The contrast between a revolutionary and a non-revolutionary experience was mirrored in the sidelines where traditional rulers, rajas and their like, wound their ways. It is sometimes forgotten that as independence came to India there were precipitate, fundamental political changes in some of its Princely States that amounted to an (albeit largely non-violent) political revolution. Mysore and Travancore would be cases in point here (Hyderabad was soon to be another story). But for the most part India's princely states were not the bloodied victims of a revolutionary upsurge. They simply underwent slow political strangulation in the course of the next two decades or so. It was very different in several parts of Indonesia. Not merely were village officials put to death in considerable numbers. There were a great many killings of traditional rulers, both large and small, especially in Sumatra. An actual revolution often entails murderous attacks upon those who have formally been greatly privileged; and so it was in Indonesia in a manner that had no counterpart in non-revolutionary India.

Revolution imbued Indonesia's bureaucratic heritage as well. Hatta, in accordance with his strong personal concern for a new 'peace and order', wished to maintain in Indonesia some Dutch bureaucratic and Dutch managed enterprises, so as to keep the new republic from running aground on administrative and bureaucratic shoals. But such expatriates were always on a short leash, and within a decade the Dutch were rudely expelled. In the meanwhile one of the largest difficulties had lain in the merging of those Indonesian officials who had continued to serve under Van Mook and his briefly fostered non-republican federal state with those who, under still greater difficulties, had from the outset thrown in their lot with the Republic. In India the transfer of power meant that the bureaucracy, shorn of its expatriates, continued very much as before. Revolutionary independence in Indonesia meant rather that former bitter opponents had somehow to learn to work with each other.

Beyond this the contrasts are still more palpable. While India had an assured, disciplined, army, that had lately enhanced its already great reputation upon several major battlefronts in another World War – and in no way saw itself as politically involved but essentially as a great servant of its state – Indonesia had an army of uncertain size, and uncertain discipline, whose activities had always been confined to its own homeland, where it saw itself not so much as the secure, respected servant of the state, but rather as its heroic, ill-buffeted, undervalued saviour, without whom it would never have survived the threats against it, either from the Dutch or from the communists – and which was thus fully entitled to play a predominant part in the shaping of its future.

In Indonesia there were in addition, from the establishment of the embryonic Republic in 1945 onwards, an abundance of political parties, all of them with aspirations to power, with ideologies as elaborated as that of the Islamic religion on the one hand to Stalinist marxism on the other, and with more than one such position in between. In India there was a Communist Party; and soon after independence the Congress Socialists departed from the Congress to set up fully on their own as well; and there were several other minor groupings too. But, in major contrast to Indonesia, in India, following on the Partition and the consequential removal of its major rival in the Muslim League, the Indian National Congress bestrode the scene essentially alone as the colossus it had now become. Whereas, moreover, in Indonesia Sukarno as president lacked executive power, but was nevertheless by far the most active, articulate and acclaimed expositor of the ideology of the new Indonesian state (whilst the hard task of government lay in the hands of what proved to be a swift succession of short-term prime ministers presiding over various insecure coalitions), once Gandhi had been killed, at an assassin's hands, and the masterful Patel lay dead as well – and Nehru had in 1951 routed the attempt by his right wing critics to foist Purushottamdas Tandon upon him as president of Congress – Nehru combined in himself (and essentially in much happier circumstances, for at least he did not have a still highly politicised army to contend with) the position of Sukarno as the ideologue of the state, with the prime ministership of his country, at the head of a cabinet that was not only drawn solely from his own Congress party but was invariably composed of his own choosing as well. All this was then backed by a loyal bureaucracy – no doubt with its weaknesses – that was never so riven, at least at the top, as its Indonesian counterpart. The concentration of substantial power in India in a single pair of hands – Nehru's – was quintessentially what Indonesia in the post independence years most grievously lacked.

The consequences could be clearly seen in the steady breakdown of constitutional democracy in Indonesia during the 1950s. The Wilopo Cabinet (1952–3) tried to stem the tide, but failed to do so. All of Indonesia's now successive short-term governments were invariably made up of various fluctuating non-communist alliances. The first sequence of cabinets sought to legitimise the whole of the constitutional democratic regime. Later ones simply tried to establish their own particular legitimacy within the constraints of an increasingly strident nationalist, as distinct from democratic or constitutional, regime. The position was in no way alleviated by the general elections of 1955 which merely reinforced the existing multi-party uncertainty. In the event, amid clashing ambitions within the Army, which were in part accompanied by serious revolts, not least in Sumatra, against the Republican regime, Sukarno moved step by step (from 1957 to 1959) towards his conception of a Guided Democracy, and, eventually with Army and, as it happened, communist support, reestablished the original 1945 constitution that gave prime executive power to him as president instead of to the prime minister. That eventually gave him formally even greater power than Nehru had all along enjoyed in India, but by a bumpy, circuitous route that had not been encountered in India.

In India Congress had comfortably won the general elections of 1952 and 1957. There were serious crises over the structuring of the body politic, but through the various stages of what was called States Reorganistion many of the worst tensions were relieved. Certainly there was no breakdown in the post-independence political position as there soon was in Indonesia.

Whilst Indonesia's political post-independence troubles were not therefore much replicated in India, nevertheless the widespread sense in Monsoon Asia in the later 1950s that the expectations aroused by the triumphs of the 1940s had not been fulfilled, of which Sukarno's move towards Guided Democracy was only one expression, had more counterparts in India than is perhaps ordinarily realised. These were principally expressed by Nehru's own moves to secure the support of his Congress for the development in India of a more 'socialistic pattern of society'. He secured successive resolutions to this end at its meetings at Avadi in 1954 and Nagpur in 1959. He then sought to take reform still further by adopting the so-called Kamaraj plan in 1962 which (somewhat like Sukarno's Guided Democracy) was an attempt to renovate the disappointments that had suffused the post-independence era. But just as Sukarno was to find himself in the 1960s at the end of his career overwhelmed by the conflicts that his Guided Democracy had propelled, so Nehru found himself checkmated in the end by the hostility within his own party which his socialist tendencies had always provoked, that was finally exemplified by his humiliating inability in 1963 to secure a quorum of his own party for his proposed seventeenth amendment to the constitution that was designed to clear the way forward for really effective land reform.

In the intervening years both Nehru and Sukarno had become major world figures, not least within the Non-aligned Movement of which they were amongst the chief sponsors. Nehru had been a principal participant in Sukarno's remarkable Bandung Conference in 1955, which has never since been fully paralleled. They had both been involved as well with deeply offensive imperialist residues. India at Nehru's instance eventually invaded Portuguese-held Goa in 1960. The year following Indonesia under Sukarno's impassioned leadership (and via some egregious devices under United Nations auspices) finally wrested West Irian from the Dutch who had fruitlessly held on to it since 1949.

But if there were these passing similarities in the experiences of the two countries at the end of this story, it is still the contrasts that figure most largely; the overall discontinuities in Indonesia, the overall continuities in India; the fragile regime in Indonesia; the ordered state in India.

There was one final contrast in the post-independence years which calls for mention, and here the centre of attention begins in India. There proprietary landlordism had been upheld by the British, and in some ways the largest discontinuity between British ruled and independent India was signalised by the great effort which after 1947 was put by the Congress leadership in India into Zamindari (landlord) abolition. It is not difficult to show that this had its beginnings in the pre-independence period; that it never involved any radical reform of a communist variety; and that even within its invariably narrow limits it was frequently circumvented. It nevertheless symbolised the strong shift that did occur in India towards a rich peasant dominated rural society which all major commentators on India's post-independence years have remarked upon.

There was no such realignment in Indonesia. Landlords of the Indian kind were never so widely prevalent there. The Dutch had made the priyayi principally a salaried rather than a landed elite. What was more they had systematically maintained the *pamong desa* (the village officials) with the *lurah* (the village headman) at their head. Despite the killings of many particular headmen during the revolution, and the immense turbulence that the revolutionary years unleashed, the system of Indonesian village government, which the Dutch had so entrenched, outlived the revolution notably intact. There were long established parallels in India. But as a system of rule they had hardly been so extensively articulated there in the past, and only took their later twentieth-century forms after Independence once landlord abolition, *panchayati raj*, and other reforms had been promulgated. To an overseas visitor there appeared to be significant likenesses between an Indian *sarpanch* and an Indonesian *lurah*, but one was constantly aware too that the latter had deeper roots and enjoyed far more effective power than his apparent Indian counterparts. So one needs to conclude with the comment that whatever the disjunctions that occurred at Indonesia's apex – and they assuredly were extensive – there seems even so in the structuring of Indonesian rural society to have been a formidable continuity that India did not quite match.

Both countries none the less shared in the end one characteristic that was of preeminent importance. In both cases the better-off in the countryside were the crucial underpinnings of the superordinate structure: in India by providing the crucial base for both state and national powers-that-be through the operations of the parliamentary electoral system that is still of critical importance to the Indian polity; in Indonesia through the operations of the unwritten concordat by which, in return for much well backed local standing and authority, village officialdom gave effect to the dictates of the bureaucrats and military men manning the Republic's superstructures. The effect was to entrench in both countries regimes of an ever increasing right-of-centre kind, while leaving their remaining leftists wringing their hands in vain.

SELECT BIBLIOGRAPHY

An essay of this kind is necessarily based upon a large number of monographs and textbooks. A selection of these would be:

Indonesia

S. Abeyasekere, *One Hand Clapping: Indonesian Nationalists and the Dutch 1939–1942*, Clayton, 1976.

B.R.O'G. Anderson, *Java in a Time of Revolution: Occupation and Resistance, 1944–1946*, Ithaca, 1972.

H.J. Benda, *The Crescent and the Rising Sun: Indonesian Islam under the Japanese Occupation, 1942–1945*, The Hague, 1958.

H. Crouch, *The Army and Politics in Indonesia*, Ithaca, 1978.

B. Dahm, *Sukarno and the Struggle for Indonesian Independence*, Ithaca, 1969.

H. Feith, *The Decline of Constitutional Democracy in Indonesia*, Ithaca, 1962.

M. George, *Australia and the Indonesian Revolution*, Melbourne, 1980.

D. Hindley, *The Communist Party of Indonesia 1951–1963*, Berkeley, 1966.

J. Ingleson, *Road to Exile: The Indonesian Nationalist Movement 1927–1934*, Singapore, 1979.

R.F. Jay, *Religion and Politics in Rural Central Java*, New Haven, 1963.

G.McT. Kahin, *Nationalism and Revolution in Indonesia*, Ithaca, 1952.

J.D. Legge, *Sukarno: A Political Biography*, London, 1972.

D.S. Lev, *The Transition to Guided Democracy: Indonesian Politics 1957–1959*, Ithaca, 1966.

A. Lijphart, *The Trauma of Decolonization: The Dutch and West New Guinea*, New Haven, 1966.

R. McVey, *The Rise of Indonesian Communism*, Ithaca, 1963.

M. Nakamura, *The Crescent Arises over the Banyan Tree*, Yogyakarta, 1983.

A. Nagazymi, *The Dawn of Indonesian Nationalism*, Tokyo, 1972.

D. Noer, *The Modernist Muslim Movement in Indonesia, 1900–1945*, Singapore, 1973.

Nugroho Notosusanto, *The Peta Army during the Japanese Occupation of Indonesia*, Tokyo, 1969.

A.J.S. Reid, *The Indonesian National Revolution 1945–1950*, Hawthorn, 1974.

A.J.S. Reid, *The Blood of the People: Revolution and the End of Traditional Rule in Northern Sumatra*, Kuala Lumpur, 1979.

M.C. Ricklefs, *A Modern History of Indonesia*, London, 1981.

J.R.W. Smail, *Bandung in the Early Revolution 1944–1946*, Ithaca, 1964.

H. Sutherland, *The Making of a Bureaucratic Elite: The Colonial Transformation of the Javanese Priyayi*, Singapore, 1979.

A. Taylor, *Indonesian Independence and the United Nations*, London, 1960.

R. van Niel, *The Emergence of the Modern Indonesian Elite*, The Hague, 1960.

C. van Dijk, *Rebellion under the Banner of Islam: The Darul Islam in Indonesia*, The Hague, 1981.

Yong Mun Cheong, *H.J. van Mook and Indonesian Independence*, The Hague, 1962.

India

D. Arnold, *The Congress in Tamilnad,, 1919–1937*, Delhi, 1977.

C.J. Baker, *The Politics of South India 1920–1937*, Cambridge, 1976.

J.H. Broomfield, *Elite Conflict in a Plural Society: Twentieth Century Bengal*, Berkeley, 1968.

J.M. Brown, *Gandhi's Rise to Power: Indian Politics 1915–1922*, Cambridge, 1972.

J.M. Brown, *Gandhi and Civil Disobedience: The Mahatma in Indian Politics 1928–1934*, Cambridge, 1977.

C. Bridge, *Holding India to the Empire: The Conservative Party and the 1935 Constitution*, Delhi, 1986.

D.N. Dhanagare, *Peasant Movements in India 1920–1950*, Delhi, 1983.

F.R. Frankel, *India's Political Economy 1947–1977*, Princeton, 1978.

S. Gopal, *Jawaharlal Nehru: A Biography*, 3 vols., London, 1975–1984.

R. Guha (ed.), *Subaltern Studies: Writings on South Asian History and Society*, vols I–VI, Delhi, 1982–89.

D. Hardiman, *Peasant Nationalists of Gujarat*, Delhi, 1981.

S. Henningham, *Peasant Movements in Colonial India; North Bihar 1917–1922*, Canberra, 1982.

A. Jalal, *The Sole Spokesman: Jinnah, the Muslim League and the Demand for Pakistan*, Cambridge, 1985.

R. Kumar, *Essays in the Social History of Modern India*, Delhi, 1983.

R. Kumar, *Essays in Gandhian Politics: The Rowlatt Satyagraha of 1919*, Oxford, 1971.

D.A. Low (ed.), *Congress and the Raj: Facets of the Indian Struggle 1917–1947*, London, 1977.

G. Minault, *The Khilafat Movement*, Delhi, 1982.

W.H. Morris-Jones, *Parliament in India*, London, 1957.

R.J. Moore, *The Crisis of Indian Unity*, Oxford, 1974.

R.J. Moore, *Escape from Empire: The Attlee Government and the Indian Problem*, Oxford, 1983.

R. Newman, *Workers and Unions in Bombay*, Canberra, 1981.

G.D. Overstreet and M. Windmiller, *Communism in India*, Berkeley, 1960.

D. Page, *Prelude to Partition: The Indian Muslims and the Imperial System of Control 1920–1932*, Delhi, 1982.

G. Pandey, *The Ascendancy of the Congress in Uttar Pradesh 1926–34*, Delhi, 1978.

F. Robinson, *Separatism among Indian Muslims*, Cambridge, 1974.

S. Sarkar, *Modern India 1895–1947*, Delhi, 1983.

M.H. Siddiqi, *Agrarian Unrest in North India 1918–22*, Delhi, 1978.

B.R. Tomlinson, *The Indian National Congress and the Raj 1929–42*, London, 1976.

B.R. Tomlinson, *The Political Economy of the Raj 1914–1947: The Economics of Decolonisation in India*, London, 1979.

6

Emergencies and elections in India

When I was on a visit to India in the mid-1970s, I flew one morning from Delhi to Jaipur. After we had all settled back into our seats a short, dapper, moustached man in an ordinary western suit, climbed into one of the front seats. At Jaipur he was the first off the plane, and was met at the foot of the steps by several army officers, with much saluting and clicking of heels. It happened that when I flew back the next day he was on the same plane once again; and at Delhi airport I eventually realised who he was. He was met there by several members of his well-dressed family, and was shown to his huge car by his seemingly even larger, magnificently turbaned, driver. He was, I realised, Sam Maneckshaw, the Indian Army's only Field Marshal since Independence, the hero of its spectacular victory in the Bangladesh war, now, very evidently, living in enviable, luxurious, much honoured retirement.

What a contrast to those political generals, the house-bound ex-presidents of the day, Ayub Khan and Yahya Khan, in Pakistan next door! What a contrast too to Generals Ne Win, Suharto, Zia and others of their ilk still wrestling with the intractable problems of their countries.

That day, what I saw of Sam Maneckshaw neatly symbolised the remarkable abstention of the Indian Army from any direct control over India's politics in all the thirty years and more since Independence.

For some time now various scholars have been making a range of new enquiries into India's political history of the late nineteenth and twentieth centuries. From these studies it is now beginning to be possible to make some suggestions about how the Indian body politic actually operates. The purpose of this chapter is to canvass one feature of this – one which links the maintenance of parliamentary government in India, based on periodic democratic elections, to its handling of political emergencies. The fact that, unlike so many of its Asian neighbours, India has not seen a military takeover is related to these circumstances; so is its astonishingly persistent adherence to universal suffrage, open elections and governments based upon majority electoral support; so too, it will be suggested, were Mrs Gandhi's remarkable decisions in the years 1975–7, not merely to impose a national state of emergency in mid-1975, but her even more remarkable decision to hold national elections early in 1977. It is beginning to be possible to see how all these exemplify the distinctive ways in which the Indian body politic functions. Ultimately the issues relate to the relationship in India between the holding of elections and the management of what those at the apex of its political system see as political emergencies.

There are, however, four preliminaries to be considered first.

To begin with, there is the fundamental fact of the relative depth in India of the acceptance of the legitimacy of superordinate political authority. There are many ways in which this can be illustrated. Perhaps the most striking is by reference to the persistence in India, over two millennia and more, of the notion of the *chakravartin*, the supreme ruler. Supreme rulership in India has by no means always been actually in operation, and its writ has only rarely been comprehensive. But from the dynasty of the Mauryas, through the Guptas, to the Moguls, the British, and the Congress, the dominance of a supreme, overall, political authority has periodically come close to being operational in India, and that has served to keep the notion of its legitimacy healthily alive. The system has readily allowed, moreover, for several layers of rulership underneath: in its heyday – beneath the Emperors – Nawabs and Nizams, Maharajas and Rajas, Viceroys and Governors. And the prevalence of the idea of rulership all the way down to the lowest levels of the political structure is well exemplified by the common address of 'Maharaj' to any superior even at village level. The legitimacy indeed of political authority all the way up to and down from Delhi is, as Max Weber would have put it, deeply traditional in India. Though the particulars are significantly different one could say the same of China. but one could not say the same – if the contrast may be emphasised – of Africa whose countries, and capitals, are so often entirely new, and, by the same token, unsupported by such traditions; not even (to the same extent at least) of Islamabad, Dacca or Rangoon.

That is the first point to bear in mind. In India the authority of superordinate political power is not much in question, and this has major implications for the way the body politic actually operates.

The second point to note is that we should be in no doubt that, whatever may be a commentator's interest in elections at state and national levels in India, and the emergencies which have punctuated their history, these only quite marginally affect what happens at village level. There, in the half million and more villages in which the overwhelming majority of Indians live, the body politic has its own distinctive ways of working. There (if one may generalise over a vast array of particular variations) one witnesses, in so many cases, what the anthropologists have called the dominance of the dominant castes. At the apex of Indian village society, that is, there are numbers of more prosperous peasants who have economic, ritual and social preeminence and who possess a position of political primacy which, if periodically challenged, is only very rarely undermined. In many areas these dominant peasants come from only one caste. Their ownership of land per head of household is well above the village average; and they tend to live in the brick-built rather than the mud-built houses in the village. Though their leaders frequently quarrel amongst themselves, and factionalism is indeed a feature of their interaction with each other, the prevalence of village factionalism chiefly reflects the very dominance which the richer peasants hold within it. For if this dominance were not secure, these dominant peasants would – and do – soon close ranks.

Contrary to the general belief, the middle echelons of village social structures are, moreover, highly variegated, and thus fluid. Accordingly they provide ready recruiting grounds for prosperous peasant faction leaders who are looking for subordinate supporters. Underneath all of these are the agricultural labourers, often of untouchable caste, and generally fixed in their misery. Only very rarely can they influence village politics, and, even then, very often only as the paid hirelings of their superiors.

This is a situation at village level across the length and breadth of India which now seems for the most part fixed hard. From above decrees may go out for land reform; but they do not succeed in lowering the ceilings upon any single individual's ownership of land below 20–30 acres – for at that point they encounter the impermeable resistance of the richer peasants. From below there may, from time to time, be attempted eruptions. But the richer peasants can afford guns, and can also afford to employ one group of impoverished labourers to suppress another group of impoverished labourers, and do so. The 1970s showed in particular – especially in the experience of the violent, revolutionary, Naxalite parties – that those who have sought to organise rural revolutions against this system can make little headway. Only in Kerala, where different circumstances apply (for example, because settlement, as the geographers would say, is not nucleated but dispersed) has this situation been somewhat ameliorated under the impact of a succession of marxist influences on the State government. In the years after 1977 a marxist government ruled in Bengal. It was exceedingly careful, however, particularly after the unhappy experiences of two United Front Governments in the 1960s, not to upset the prevailing order in the villages of Bengal too abruptly, lest it ran its head prematurely against the brick wall of rural rich peasant dominance there too.

Most Indian political parties, of whatever formal designation, have reflected this rural situation in their make-up since at least the 1930s. In 1979 the hold of rich peasant dominance upon the Indian political system was neatly symbolised at national level in the persons of two prime ministers and the leader of the opposition. For all the differences between them, Morarji Desai – an Anavil Brahmin from south Gujarat – Charan Singh – the ideologue of the north Indian Jats for over thirty years – and Y.B. Chavan – a quintessential dominant caste Maratha from Maharashtra – all had strong rich peasant backgrounds, and their actions reflected this.

So, while the first point to underline is the depth of the acceptance in India of the legitimacy of political authority all the way up to and down from Delhi itself, the second is the persistence of the dominance of the dominant rich peasant communities both at the village level where so many Indians live, and all the way through several political layers up to the national Parliament itself. Elections in India may come and emergencies may go, but both operate in an arena which is bounded by these two parameters, is dependent upon both of them, and has little or no effect upon either.

Into this arena the Indian Army has never so far marched. This is not to say that the Army has had no political involvement in India. On the contrary, its role has in certain respects been critical. Some of the specifics will explain the case.

Perhaps the starting point lies in the profundity of the shock for the British when in 1857 their Sepoy army mutinied. The British repressed that mutiny, and its accompanying rebellions, with great ferocity; and from that moment onwards they paid very careful attention to the role which the army should play in the structure of the Indian state. Under the British for long afterwards Indian troops were not allowed to man fieldguns, and for most of the remaining years of their rule the British maintained in India large numbers of British troops to buttress their position.

In the course of the army reforms they instituted in India in the first decade of the twentieth century (at a time when Lord Kitchener was British commander-in-chief), the Army in India – as the combination of British and Indian troops came to be called – was quite explicitly (and for our present purposes very significantly) divided into three categories: the field army, for service beyond the frontiers of India; the covering troops, for service in the frontier regions; and the internal security forces. By the 1920s the internal security forces were composed of fifty battalions of British and Indian troops. These were carefully positioned, moreover, at strategic points about India, particularly near railway junctions, from where they could be swiftly despatched to overawe, more especially the towns and cities of India, whenever these turned turbulent.

It needs to be emphasised that in the British period there were numerous occasions when the Army was called out, as the classic phrase had it, 'in aid of the civil power'. This was frequently done in order to suppress communal disturbances. The Army was massively employed, moreover, by the British against Gandhi's last, and greatest, civil disobedience campaign (the so-called Quit India campaign of August 1942) when the British used well over fifty battalions of troops against it.

It is not therefore that the Indian Army has had no tradition of employment for political ends. It has been frequently used indeed for these purposes, both before and after Independence. It has been calculated, for example, that the Indian Army was called out in aid of the civil power between 1961 and 1970 no less than 476 times. It has often seemed, moreover, as if in Bihar and Bengal significant parts of the Indian Army have been openly stationed so as to provide a perpetual reminder, and on occasion an actual expression, of the fact that the existing social and political order in India is only to be challenged by its critics at their direst peril.

Its role in such matters has long been supplemented, moreover, by para-military forces of armed policemen. These have their origins in three quarters. It may be recalled that for centuries there have been 'social bandits' in India; armed groups, on the fringes of settled societies – the famous (or infamous, according to one's choosing) *dakaits*. Against them most provincial and later state police forces have for a century and more despatched remarkably intrepid specially trained, armed police. To the extent that *dakaits* in particular situations have periodically merged with the more deliberately revolutionary groups, the role and size of special police forces has been enlarged as well. In certain areas special police forces were explicitly formed as such. The violent uprisings of the Muslim Moplah community in what used to be Madras Presidency under the British (and is now part of Kerala) led the British, back in the 1920s, to create the Malabar Special Force. We have noted already that the British also mobilised special forces to guard India's borderlands.

In independent India these various elements were in due course developed into such well known para-military forces as the Central Reserve Police and the Border Security Force. These have generally been commanded by army officers, and amounted at one count to 800 000 men, or the equivalent of two-thirds of the size of the regular Army. After the metal-tipped-stave-armed police they became indeed the Government of India's prime line of attack against disruptive forces; and against these there has been very little hesitation in using them.

Coercive force, that is, has been at once a latent and an actual element in the workings of the Indian body politic, to a degree that has sometimes been underestimated.

But the earlier point remains. Thus far at least, the Indian Army has never sought to be the arbiter, let alone the controller, of the country's political affairs (nor the Central Reserve Police either).

There is one further preliminary to mention too. This concerns the

Indian bureaucracy. Since independence the seniormost Indian administration – represented quintessentially by the Indian Administrative Service has been at once very unBritish and very British. In the first place it really has, of course, no counterpart in Britain itself; nor in the white Dominions either. For there is nothing there to resemble the centrally appointed generalist official/magistrate with large responsibilities over one of the many districts into which the country has long since been divided, who remains the key agent in exercising the power that the Indian government possesses. But in the second place the Indian administration has at the same time been in many ways very British indeed, since the highly elitist Indian Administrative Service, which dominates its central and local bureaucracies, is in every sense the direct descendant of the premier Indian Civil Service that the British created. Its members are trained, moreover, as their predecessors had been, to rule, and when called upon – for example during political emergencies – very readily proceed to do so.

Nevertheless, for all that has been said so far, the fundamental fact remains that at the core of India's changing politics there have since Independence been rulers who have made the key day-to-day political decisions, who have been politicians who have regularly competed with each other at contested elections at the head of political parties at which they have won electoral majorities. This is a sufficiently rare phenomenon in any country, let alone in one which is as large, and which has been as economically impoverished, as India, to call for some substantial explanation; and to this we shall now turn rather more directly.

Let it be emphasised straight away that elections to legislatures in India have been very frequent, and that they are accordingly a remarkably well-established part of its regular political routine.

There are several reasons for this. To begin wtih, the system of electoral politics was not introduced into India at, or shortly before, Independence, as in so many other newly independent countries. It has a very much longer history than that. Nowadays studies are frequently made of contemporary Indian elections. There are also detailed studies, however, of provincial elections in India back in 1912 and even earlier. Those early elections were fought, moreover, with all the energy to which the studies of more recent elections have now accustomed us. Such evidence points to the fact that open parliamentary-style elections have been part of the political life of large areas of India for most of the twentieth century.

This consideration is reinforced by a further consideration which is all too frequently overlooked. The popular version of the history of India's national movement in the first half of this century is primarily associated with the person of Gandhi and his successive civil disobedience movements. His and their importance is not to be gainsaid. Without them the

Indian national movement would have been much less vigorous than it was, whereas, compared with its counterparts elsewhere in Asia, it was for thirty years quite extraordinarily substantial. It has, nevertheless, to be said that none of the three great Gandhi-led phases of nationalist agitation – between 1919 and 1922; 1929 and 1934; 1940 and 1943 – ever succeeded in overthrowing the British. These agitations certainly made the British very uncomfortable, and their position periodically precarious. They succeeded too in advancing the cause of Indian nationalism amongst Indians themselves. But they did not succeed in wresting political control over India from the British. That only came when the Indian National Congress started to win elections.

Congress, to begin with, had a strong tendency to boycott elections. It did so in 1920 at the onset of Gandhi's first non-co-operation campaign (there are signs that this was because it was not confident at that time that it would win them). When in 1923, and more particularly in 1926, many members of the Congress contested the legislative elections after all, they were not as successful as one might well have expected the leaders of a vigorous nationalist movement would have been.

The turning point here came in 1937 when, after the collapse of the civil disobedience campaigns of the early 1930s, Congress decided it would, once again, contest the upcoming elections, and, to everyone's surprise, proceeded to win a majority position in seven of the eleven provincial legislatures of India. Shortly afterwards, in accordance with the provisions of the new Government of India Act of 1935, and despite Congress' own initial hesitations, it took control of the provincial governments in all of these Provinces.

That outcome had a major effect. For when, after a further – again initially abortive – agitation against the British during the Second World War, the Congress leaders came out of prison once again, they promptly set about organising, not a nationalist revolt, nor a further vehement agitation, but rather a major campaign for the state and national elections which were called in 1946. When in the non-Muslim majority areas, they won these overwhelmingly, their course became firmly set in the direction of the transfer of power from the British which occurred in August 1947.

As a consequence of these experiences – which had few parallels elsewhere in Asia – the Indian nationalist leadership was in no doubt that its success in parliamentary elections had played a vital role in India's attainment of independence; and, as a result, their commitment to parliamentary-style elections was strongly reinforced.

It happened that the franchise for the 1937 and the 1946 elections was based on property qualifications and was limited to something between 11 per cent and 14 per cent of the population, or in other words, in the rural areas, to the dominant peasants mentioned earlier. These comprised the bulk of those who could afford to give their time and their money to electoral politics. When, after independence, universal suffrage was introduced, the already established patterns of electoral activity were not, it seemed, greatly changed. Accordingly, the political elite, with the powerful dominant castes at their core, remained happily staunch in their commitments to them.

Since independence there has as a consequence been a continuous succession of elections in the Indian States. There were, for example, twelve in 1978; six more in 1979.

At national level there has also been an all but systematic succession of parliamentary elections too. Following upon the first general elections in 1952, general elections occurred with an orderliness which puts those of us who have lived in Australia (with four general elections between 1972 and 1977 in five years) to shame. With two slight, but self-adjusting exceptions, these regularly took place every five years. In 1971, in the aftermath of the Congress split in 1969, and following her triumphs in the Bangladesh war, Mrs Gandhi called the election a year early. Because of the way she handled the national emergency in 1975, she did not then call the next general election until nearly a year late; but she did then hold it early in 1977. And with that the succession of Indian parliamentary elections appeared to move back on its orderly quinquennial course. It did not, of course, turn out that way. Half way through its ensuing term the new Janata Government, which was elected in 1977, broke apart, in circumstances which in most other new democracies would surely have put paid to parliamentary government. In India, however, in 1979 there was the astonishing spectacle of a considerable political crisis being handled by a calm decision to mount new general elections four months later. All in all it has been, by any standards, an extraordinary record.

It is buttressed by the further fact that, for a century or so, there have in many places in India been growing traditions of remarkably open elections at city, town, district, and even at village level. One might be tempted to wonder indeed whether India has not lumbered itself with more than its fair share of elections, particularly if one is sceptical, as many observers would be, as to whether they really make any difference at all to the lot of most ordinary people. But India is a large country, and it can be persuasively argued that such a plethora of elections serves to relieve some of the strains in an otherwise aching social and economic system. Such elections certainly reinforce the commitment of the Indian body politic to the regular testing of the electoral support of those holding superordinate political power at its various levels; and their succession continues.

The central point to be made here is, however, that such a commitment to electoral politics might nevertheless not have sufficed to hold India to its continuing systems of parliamentary government, had India not also had its own special methods for dealing with political emergencies – or at all events with what the powers-that-be conceive to be political emergencies. For these have certainly occurred, and on a scale which, had this been Africa, would – I venture to suggest – long ago have wrecked the institution of parliamentary government in India, for all that can be said about the attachment of so many there to it.

The expedients which have been employed in India to deal with such circumstances would seem to be all but unique; and it is upon these that we may now dwell.

They are more easily understood as they operate at the State level of politics. Here the method employed is known as 'President's Rule'. The general form of its application is written into the Indian Constitution, and stems, as so much of that Constitution does, from the British Government of India Act of 1935. Section 93 of that Act was designed to deal with a situation in which the British government had come to believe that a locally elected provincial government was not fulfilling its functions in accord with the declared law of the land. In such circumstances it allowed for a governor appointed by the British to take over charge of the government of his province, notwithstanding that a transfer of power to an elected government had previously taken place. Section 93 of the 1935 Act was in fact used in several of the provinces of British India during much of the Second World War, mainly because the Congress governments previously elected to power in them had resigned in protest against Britain's wartime policy towards India.

After a good deal of anxious debate in the Indian Constituent Assembly after Independence, much of the essence of Section 93 of the British Government of India Act of 1935 was translated into Sections 356 and 357 of the Indian Independence Constitution. Section 356 of this Constitution has since then provided that:

If the President, on receipt of a report from the Governor . . . of a State or otherwise, is satisfied that a situation has arisen in which the Government of the State cannot be carried on in accordance with the provisions of this Constitution, the President may by proclamation . . . assume to himself all or any of the functions of the Governor of the State . . .

Because these powers are formally assumed upon such occasions by the president himself, their operation is now generally known as President's Rule. The president does, as it happens, come into the business personally, since he is required to be the recipient of the formal report which needs to be submitted before President's Rule can be brought into operation; and he then has to sign the necessary proclamation. But in practice the president acts, of course, upon the advice of the government of India, and it is thus the central government of India which assumes authority over the government of a state when President's Rule is instituted there. Under President's Rule the governance of a state is, however, to a greater or lesser extent, actually conducted by the governor of the state, who ceases *pro tem* to be the 'constitutional monarch' he is otherwise expected to be. To say here 'to a greater or lesser extent' is deliberate; because, according to whether or not a particular governor has himself had significant administrative experience, there has been an increasing tendency to provide him with experienced administrative advisers who, in one way or another, perform the tasks previously undertaken by state ministers. Such advisers have usually been drawn from the senior ranks of the Indian Administrative Service. Their capacity and their readiness to take charge on such occasions, as has been earlier indicated, is not in doubt, so that under President's Rule orderly government has been readily maintained, where indeed it has not actually been restored.

While, almost by definition, the proclamation of President's Rule entails the dismissal of the State executive, it does not necessarily involve the immediate dismissal of the state legislature – even though this often occurs. However, under the provisions for President's Rule the functions of the state legislature nevertheless fall to be exercised by the national parliament. This provision has had a somewhat chequered history; but increasingly such functions have come to be delegated by the national parliament to a consultative committee presided over by the central minister for home affairs. That committee has generally been composed of national parliamentary members from the state in question, broadly in proportion to their party representation in the national parliament. The detailed operation of President's Rule has thus become extensively elaborated.

All manner of arguments have, of course, surrounded every imposition of President's Rule. But its operation has long since become a quite familiar feature of the Indian political system. In the ten years after 1967 there was never, for example, a moment when one or other Indian State was not under President's Rule. Up to 1977, when an authoritative count was done, all but five of the Indian states had been subjected to President's Rule on at least one occasion since the Constitution was first promulgated in 1952. Between 1952 and 1977 President's Rule was imposed around forty times. On five occasions it persisted for up to six months; on ten occasions for between six months and a year; on eight occasions for over a year.

The intriguing point then is that upon every occasion, once political heels had cooled – and the time necessary for this varied of course a good deal – new elections to the State legislature were invariably called; a new government was formed; President's Rule was brought to an end; and parliamentary-style government was then restored.

It cannot be said that the emergencies which led to the proclamation of President's Rule were all deep-seated. There have been occasions when it was simply introduced to meet the convenience of the government in New Delhi, either because its own party in the state was in some kind of disarray, or because the government in New Delhi was anxious to bring down the government of the opposing party whose control of a state it wished to end. Three kinds of crisis can be more generally discerned from the multiplicity which have led to President's Rule. It has been proclaimed when a state government has been defeated, in a situation where there seemed to be no early prospect of a successor government being installed. It has been proclaimed where there has been such extensive floor-crossing in the state legislature that stable government has become an unlikely prospect. It has been proclaimed when grave allegations of corruption have been advanced.

When one looks through any list of the occasions and the causes of President's Rule, one soon has good reason to believe that, but for its existence, parliamentary government in many Indian States would long since have broken down irredeemably. One has the impression too – if the earlier point may be underlined – that had the president of the Organisation of African Unity had anything like the powers possessed by the President of India, the breakdown in Africa of parliamentary government would not have been anywhere near so widespread.

One also has the impression that the existence and the use of President's Rule has been as vital – perhaps even more vital – to the maintenance of electoral politics in India as the relatively strong tradition in India of electoral politics itself.

There is at first sight no similar system for dealing with comparable political emergencies at the national level. The main point to be made here, therefore, is that in the light of the events of 1975–7, one may, however, suggest that there exists a great deal more of a system for dealing with what the powers-that-be see to be a great crisis at the national level than the Constitution or common understanding have hitherto suggested.

To explain this proposition it is necessary to retrace one's steps once again back to the British period, and consider first the history in modern India of the expedient of 'Preventive Detention', since the present provisions for this stretch back in a fairly direct line to the famous Regulation III of 1818 of the British administration in Bengal. This was used by the British throughout the nineteenth century to lock up those they wanted out of the way, but against whom they could not readily bring criminal charges.

Then, as nationalist forces gathered momentum in the two opening decades of the twentieth century, and some few terrorist groups came to be formed, the British Government of India began to feel that Regulation III was an altogether too ineffectual weapon for their needs. They required, so they believed, some much more substantial methods for dealing with what they soon came to term 'Revolutionary Crime'; and in due course they decided to establish Special Tribunals before whom existing rules of evidence, advocacy and appeal were not to obtain. These arrangements were then embodied in the so-called Rowlatt Bills of 1919 – named after the British judge who presided over their formulation; and it was against the British Government of India's promulgation of these that Gandhi led his first great nationalist campaign, the so-called Rowlatt Satyagraha of 1919. That, combined with various other upheavals in the Punjab, precipitated the great Punjab disturbances of April that year. Confronted by these, both the British Government of India and the British Government of the Punjab made the critical decision to call in the Army, and in a spine-chilling communiqué issued in April 1919, the British Government of India emphatically expressed the view that:

It remains for the Governor-General in Council to assert in the clearest manner the intention of Government to . . . employ the ample military resources at his disposal to suppress organized outrages, rioting, or concerted opposition to the maintenance of law and order.

Martial Law was thereupon declared in the Punjab, and in full accord with the government's declared doctrines as there set out, there immediately followed the notorious massacre at the hands of General Dyer of a large political meeting in the Jallianwallah Bagh at Amritsar in the Punjab.

The shock of that outrage put the British regime back on the defensive; and they reconsidered furiously. Against the next Gandhi-led agitational wave, the so-called Non-Co-operation Movement of 1921–2, they were not only very careful not to use the Army; they deliberately refrained for as long as they possibly could from taking action against the leaders of the movement, until the leaders themselves, with Gandhi at their head, became so concerned at the way the movement was slipping into violence, that they themselves brought it to an end.

For the purpose of the present argument the crucial developments came ten years later. In opposing the next great Gandhi-led agitation, the British began once again by taking the line of least resistance that had served them so well in 1921–2. But this time, such was the strength of the agitation against them, that they very soon began to feel that their authority in India was in real danger of being seriously undermined. With memories of the massacre in the Jallianwallah Bagh in 1919 still hanging over them, they were very reluctant, however, to call in the Army. What they needed was a quite new approach; and this they proceeded to create.

The new policy which the British fashioned, and which it is here suggested Mrs Gandhi followed, almost to the letter, in 1975, was first unveiled on 4 January 1932 – when the British put into widespread operation against the Indian National Congress what one British official engagingly called '*civil* martial law'. Its essentials can be readily specified. There were to be no deliberate political killings; no dramatic political trials;

no suspension of the Constitution; no dismissal of the legislatures; no employment of the Army. Rather, there was an immediate declaration of a state of emergency and the assumption of substantial emergency powers by the government, which was promptly accompanied by widespread, unannounced, arrests by police of a carefully prepared list of political opponents, who were then imprisoned without trial for quite indeterminate periods. It is significant that some care was taken to see that the conditions of imprisonment for some of the leading figures were a good deal better than for ordinary prisoners. Care was taken, that is, to reduce the danger of creating political martyrs.

In the upshot, however, all of this was only the half of it, and in due course the other half unfolded. For as the air cleared a series of unannounced releases of lesser figures then occurred spasmodically over a period of several months. In due course even the leading figures themselves were released from detention. And then new legislative elections were called, so that the country's politics could be put back once again on what the government believed to be its proper rails. This system, it will be noted, while different from President's Rule, has several important similarities with it.

During the 1930s, 'civil martial law', as it may be termed, served Britain's immediate political purposes in India remarkably well. Not only was Gandhi's great civil disobedience campaign effectively halted; but first in 1934 and then more particularly in 1937, Congress, instead of boycotting, set about contesting the legislative elections which the British then called.

At the same time details of the new system were being committed to printed handbooks in case they should be needed again. The new policy was in fact employed by the British ten years or so later, first in 1940 and then in 1942, against Gandhi's last two great agitational campaigns; and with similar results – though given the widespread rural revolt in northeastern India in 1942 it had to be supplemented on the latter occasion, as has been mentioned earlier, by massive army intervention.

During the first twenty-five years or so after Independence, because of the persistent one-party dominance of the Nehru-Gandhi Congress, no similar crisis seemed to threaten India's polity at its apex. The expedient of 'civil martial law' was, however, employed against the Indian communists in the 1960s, and then, in a notable instance in 1974, against a national strike of railway workers.

This is not the place to rehearse the details of the onset of the grave emergency which Mrs Gandhi believed she saw overtaking her in 1975, nor the ensuing Emergency itself. There is already a large literature upon it, beginning with the proceedings of the Shah Commission and typified in such understandably polemical books as David Selbourne's *An Eye to*

India. The Unmasking of a Tyranny or Michael Henderson's *Experiment with Untruth*. The point to be made here is that when – like the British rulers of India early in the 1930s and again in the 1940s before her – Mrs Gandhi believed she saw in June 1975 a threat to the very stability of the supreme political authority which she exercised over India being mounted, she set to work to act precisely as they had done. She did not turn to the Army; nor did she dismiss Parliament. Rather, she sent the police to arrest her political opponents, and put them into preventive detention for indeterminate periods. None of them was shot. None of them – with the rather particular exception of Mr George Fernandes – was put on trial. And just as in 1942 the British incarcerated Gandhi in the Aga Khan's not uncomfortable home in Poona, so in 1975 Morarji Desai and some of the other opposition leaders were sent to the really rather pleasant Haryana State Tourist Centre just above the hot springs at Sohna southwards of Delhi. Though the press was seriously curbed, rioters were suppressed, an emergency was declared, and in a good many prisons quite appalling brutalities were inflicted, there was neither martial law nor military intervention.

This suggests that, like it or not (and most of it no one does), the Indian body politic seems to have at its disposal a well-tried method for dealing with perceived crises at the political centre which is scarcely less potent and patent than is provided by President's Rule for the states. This system has been openly used during this century upon four successive occasions: in 1932, 1940, 1942, and 1975. It has its own distinctive characteristics. It turns upon action, not by the Army, nor by firing squads, nor by special tribunals, but by the Police and then the prison services.

There is confirmation for the view that what was witnessed in 1975–7 is on the way to becoming an established method by which crises at the political centre in India may be handled in the future in the similarities between the developments that occurred subsequent to the onset of the Emergency. For precisely in four stages, as the British had before her, Mrs Gandhi began to set free her lesser opponents from prison; in due course she authorised the release of their leaders too; about the same time she decided that the only way by which the national political system could be placed back on its rails was to hold an election; and she then wholly miscalculated – as the British had done before her – the strength of the hostile reaction her Emergency had evoked. As a consequence, just as in the aftermath of the first imposition of 'civil martial law' in 1932–4, supporters of the British lost heavily in the ensuing 1934 and 1937 elections, so in the 1977 elections supporters of Mrs Gandhi lost heavily as well.

It was not merely therefore that the emergency measures she employed were those fashioned by the British; her way out of them followed very precisely the pattern which they had set as well.

Perhaps some of the threads here can now be brought together. What all this is suggesting is that the 1975–7 Emergency in India, placed in a longer and wider context, served to indicate that the government of India – whoever may be in control of it – now has at its disposal an established means of managing a perceived crisis at the political centre, which is now as notable a feature of the way in which the Indian body politic actually operates as President's Rule itself. Let it be reiterated that this does not call for intervention by the army; nor for political killings; nor for political trials. It calls in the first place for a now well-tested police operation against carefully listed political opponents.

But, as with President's Rule, there seems to be as well a propensity within the operation of 'civil martial law' towards bringing it to a conclusion by then holding elections. This is no doubt a tribute to the widespread commitment to the electoral process which exists in India: it may indeed be said that this would now seem to be strong enough to make new elections appear in India to be the best way out of the impasse into which authoritarian rule almost inevitably finds itself drawn. All of which then implies that while over the longer run the existence of emergency procedures actually assists in maintaining the commitment to elections in India, so the relatively very strong sense there that only those willing to submit themselves to an election within a reasonable time span have a legitimate right to hold governmental office, serves to check the prolongation of such an emergency once this has been declared. In quasi-technical language there is a two-way functional association, that is, in India between emergencies and elections.

There remains the irony of the evidence that the longer such elections are delayed, and the more stringent the conduct of the Emergency, the greater the chance that the electorate will vote against the supporters of those who declared the Emergency. This could lead to one of two conclusions. Either the next employers of 'civil martial law' will call an election sooner than Mrs Gandhi did in 1977, so as to avoid her defeat upon that occasion; or, fearing a like defeat, they will brazen out their position for very much longer as at one stage some observers thought that she would do. Should any future declarers of an emergency really take the latter course, the Indian body politic will have abandoned its moorings (as it has not, it is here suggested, done so far) and would then enter some quite new seas. The 1980 election may have made this even less likely than before. For it may be suggested that it showed that in India a leader who loses badly in one election, and is severely hounded for his pains in the aftermath, can in fact be back in an even stronger position just three years later. Here one has only to contrast the return of Mrs Gandhi to power with the execution of Mr Zulfikar Ali Butto in Pakistan to obtain some appreciation of the distinctive characteristics which the Indian body politic seems to display.

It would of course be foolhardy to suggest that the system of 'civil martial law' could never be discarded. But the essential point remains, and it brings us back to the issue with which this chapter opened. A major reason why the Army has not up to this point moved in to take control of India's political system – as its counterparts have in so many other countries in Asia and elsewhere – is, it may be suggested, because, very unusually, India has evolved systems both at state and national levels for handling what the powers-that-be see to be crises in the working of parliamentary government. These systems have many harsh, brutal, and worse features. But, as they have operated so far, they have always ended with a new start in the holding of new elections.

Parliamentary government has persisted in India, that is, not merely because it has been an important part of the country's political life for quite a while now, but because at its apex India has developed methods for the management of political emergencies that have the special features that they allow for the reintroduction of parliamentary government once the immediate emergency has apparently receded. Emergency President's Rule is now all but routine for the States. Emergency Prime Ministerial rule, or 'civil martial law', or whatever one may term it, seems to be a no less readily available expedient at the centre as well.

SELECT BIBLIOGRAPHY

Granville Austin, *The Indian Constitution: Cornerstone of a Nation*, Oxford, 1966.
Stephen P. Cohen, *The Indian Army*, California, 1971.
Percival Griffiths, *To Guard My People: The History of the Indian Police*, London, 1971.
Harry C. Hart (ed.), *Indira Gandhi's India: A Political System Reappraised*, Boulder, 1976.
Michael Henderson, *Experiment with Untruth*, Delhi, 1977.
D.A. Low, 'The Government of India and the First Non-Cooperation Movement 1920–1922', *Journal of Asian Studies*, 25 (2 February 1966), 241–59.
D.A. Low (ed.), *Congress and the Raj: Facets of the Indian Struggle 1917–1947*, Delhi, 1977.
S.R. Maheswari, *President's Rule in India*, Delhi, 1977.
Philip Mason, *A Matter of Honour*, London, 1974.
David Selbourne, *An Eye to India: the Unmasking of a Tyranny*, Harmondsworth, 1977.
Philip Woodruff, *The Men Who Ruled India*, 2 vols., London, 1974.

7

East Africa: towards a new order 1945–1963

(co-authored by J.M. Lonsdale)

In 1945 East Africa was under British rule. Many pressures exerted in the inter-war years had prevented it from passing irrevocably under the control of its small European population. But there were still a few who looked to Kenya's future as a 'white man's country'; and European unofficials exercised a large influence over its neighbours too. Within less than twenty years there was revolutionary political change. By 1963 independence had come to all four of the territories of East Africa, Tanganyika, Uganda, Kenya and Zanzibar, as part of the vast process in which dependencies of Europe have emerged as the Third World. It is difficult to discern an equivalent revolution in their economy and society. Their tripartite caste structure was as yet little modified by the upward mobility of Africans in the political and administrative fields. Europeans still controlled large-scale production; Asians still serviced industry and agriculture by craftsmanship and trade; most Africans remained peasant farmers. Nor are the processes of change within African society itself easily susceptible of theoretical analysis. A nationalist historiography, for instance, must confront the lack of territorially organized national movements prior to the decades covered here. In sharp contrast to other parts of the Third World, there was no significant span of time during which nationalist groups and their ideologies might have affected the patterns of mobility or the boundaries of community. The nationalist impetus had to depend, instead, upon the successful meshing by tiny literate minorities – rarely possessed of independent means or professional status – of their own aspirations with the groundswell of discontents among the rural and urban populations. And these cannot be described straightforwardly as peasantry and proletariat, nor yet the elites as a bourgeoisie. A marxist analysis, therefore, which would stress not the achievement of independence but the unfinished business of class conflict, is as difficult to formulate. For the historical experience of these years is too rich in variety. Its more obvious aspects, the imperial recession or the nationalist upsurge, may be the easiest to delineate in the pages which follow; but in future perspectives they may be of least importance. Deeper processes may prove to be of more enduring significance. This chapter will try to explore the complex moral and social dimensions of individual and corporate innovation in change, and to draw together some of the threads which underlie the more detailed histories of the countries concerned. It will end with a brief overview of the politics of the final phase of East African decolonisation.

IMPERIAL RECESSION

The ending of British rule was, as in other parts of the world, a synthesis of imperial decision and nationalist pressures. Its East African application was, however, not a simple replay of other peoples' experience. It came, of course, in the wake of Britain's leading decision to relinquish empire in Asia, and then in West Africa and the Caribbean. But in most British minds these precedents offered no guide to the future of East – or Central – Africa: on the contrary, their European and Asian minorities made these areas entirely different.[1] However much their local African nationalisms might draw strength from the success of similar movements elsewhere in Africa and in other parts of the world, for much of the period under review the imperial authorities could not accept what the nationalists had to assert that the Third World was one. This British attitude was grounded in traditional sentiment; it was much reinforced by the strategic requirements of the Cold War, and by the new economic importance attached to Africa in assisting the post-war reconstruction of Britain. The local European population was the most reliable collaborator in both military and economic purposes. This global metropolitan perspective – and it was the view from the defence and economic ministries rather than the Colonial Office[2] – shaped the local political framework in two decisive ways. First, inter-territorial organisations were created as the sturdier successors of the instruments of wartime co-ordination. Secondly, the careful contrivance of 'partnership' or 'multi-racialism' was erected against the claims of African nationalism. It followed that governmental intervention against this growing force was much more determined than in the West African colonies.

The official hardness of heart owed much to the fact that eastern Africa overlooked the Indian Ocean, on the further shores of which the certainties of Empire were giving way to the diplomacies of Commonwealth. The

[1] D.A. Low, *Lion Rampant: Essays in the Study of British Imperialism*, London, 1973, ch. 6, provides an outline account.
[2] Illustrated perhaps by the absence of maps on the Secretary of State's room walls until Lyttelton took over in October 1951: Viscount Chandos, *The Memoirs of Lord Chandos*, London, 1962, p. 346.

Second World War had seen this empire on the march; no contingents had been more ubiquitous than those from India. The Indian Ocean's eastern gateway had also witnessed the empire's most crushing defeat, at Singapore in 1942. The consequences of military unpreparedness against the Japanese were painfully demonstrated in the losing battles by Dutch and French to re-establish themselves in Indonesia and Indochina, and by Britain's long fight against the communist guerrillas in Malaya. Nearer at hand, by 1948 India, Pakistan, Ceylon, and Burma were all independent, the last having slipped almost unnoticed out of the Commonwealth. And in June of that year Britain abdicated from her Palestine Mandate. Yet the eastern Mediterranean, once the route to India, retained immense strategic importance; the Suez military base must now take over from the Indian subcontinental barracks the task of guaranteeing to Britain her access to Persian Gulf oil. But in 1951, barely two years later, no force was used at Abadan in defence of the Anglo-Iranian oil company against Mussadiq; and the Canal base itself was soon to be under Egyptian siege following the Wafd government's abrogation of the Anglo-Egyptian treaty of 1936. Suez, far from being its nerve centre, became a 'concentration camp' for a large proportion of the British Army.[3] The strategic artery of late-Victorian empire was at risk; the Imperial General Staff looked to its flanks, to Cyprus (after the loss of Palestine) and the Arab lands on the one hand and, on the other, to East Africa, which had owed its British connections in part at least to its position as an outlying picket on the way to India.[4] In 1947 acres of Suez stores had been shipped to Mackinnon Road, inland from Mombasa.[5] Then in 1950 British and French military discussions in Nairobi had stressed the need to maintain a southerly air route across equatorial Africa. Wider talks in the following year, again in Nairobi, had involved the other colonial powers and South Africa; these had been more concerned with the defence of Africa itself.[6] Kenya, with its naval and air facilities, was pivotal to both designs. In contemplating the next, the planners were no doubt re-fighting the last war. Then, the three mainland territories of East Africa, besides providing base facilities for the Middle East theatre, had raised twenty-nine battalions of King's African Rifles; these, with units from Britain, West and South Africa, had helped to drive the Italians out of Somalia and Ethiopia; they had also operated against the Vichy French in Madagascar and the Japanese in Burma; one battalion did garrison duty in

[3] In the words of John Strachey, onetime Secretary of State for War, *Hansard*, 5th series, H. of C., 524, c. 2477, 11 Mar. 1954.
[4] Ronald Robinson and John Gallagher, with Alice Denny, *Africa and the Victorians*, London, 1961.
[5] Elizabeth Monroe, *Britain's Moment in the Middle East*, London, paperback edn., 1965, pp. 157–8; Negley Farson, *Last Chance in Africa*, New York, 1950, p. 64.
[6] J.M. Lee, *African Armies and Civil Order* London, 1969, p. 28; Eric A. Walker, *A History of Southern Africa*, London, 1964, p. 824; also Admiral R.L. Conolly, 'Africa's Strategic Significance', in C. Grove Haines (ed.), *Africa Today*, Baltimore, 1955, p. 58.

Egypt and Palestine.[7] Thereafter, men from East Africa were called upon to help to fill the yawning gap in imperial manpower caused by the departure of India. A Kenya battalion saw service in the Malayan Emergency (it was followed by a similar unit from Central Africa), and in the 1950s East African Pioneers replaced Egyptian labour in the Suez Canal base.

British East and Central Africa stood, then, at the western end of the great Indian Ocean arc which reached east to Singapore, and on the southern fringe of the Middle East. However much the relative importance of these two spheres might shift in imperial strategies, East Africa's supporting role would remain unchanged. Eastern Africa also occupied much the same position on the African continent. Within all these three interlocking zones of British influence it was seen as a firm base which underpinned the more flexible and realistic policies pursued elsewhere in Britain's readjustment to the post-war world. To some metropolitan minds and interests this readjustment looked uncommonly like retreat. Old habits of behaviour demanded that however much the area of direct British authority might contract, the degree of British influence in the world ought to remain as far as possible unimpaired. Yet by the early 1950s it was already apparent from the Asian experience that British influence would be most strongly rooted through a flexible accommodation to local nationalisms. The rupture between Holland and Indonesia, the catastrophe of French arms at Dien Bien Phu, were clear enough illustrations of the alternative which the British themselves had so nearly had to face in India. India's republican membership of the Commonwealth had, after all, gone against the grain of both the existing British conventions of association and extreme opinion within Congress. A decision which proved to be the turning-point in the evolution of the post-war Commonwealth, and of critical significance to later British policies in Africa, might so easily have turned in the opposite direction. As late as 1946 Congress had been committed to secession, in reaction to its thirty years of recurrent conflict with the Raj. There were many reasons for Nehru's reversal of this stand; none was more important than his desire to hedge his non-alignment against the threat of isolation in an uncertain and potentially hostile world.[8] In Indian eyes the friendship offered by the Commonwealth connection was composed of many intangibles; the British could persuade themselves that it was valued for their own palpable military presence in the area, as Nehru himself seemed to acknowledge in his understanding of the British position in Malaya.[9] And in Ceylon, at the centre of Britain's Indian Ocean arc, the two policies of accommodation to nationalism and retention of military potential had coincided; Britain continued to enjoy the use of the Trinco-

[7] Lt.-Col. H. Moyse-Bartlett, *The King's African Rifles*, Aldershot, 1956, part 5.
[8] Michael Brecher, *Nehru: A Political Biography*, London, 1959, pp. 317, 413–18.
[9] Brecher, *Nehru*.

malee naval base until 1957. In the British view of South Asia as a whole, the presence of bases provided insurance in a world of local nationalisms; but it was a successful nationalism which ensured the local security of the base.

The same combination of conciliating nationalisms when necessary and falling back upon prepared military positions where possible – a conditioned reflex rather than a long-term policy – was practised by the British when facing the changing circumstances of the Middle East and Africa. Eastern Africa was directly involved in both spheres; in British minds the boundary between them lay along the northern frontiers of Uganda and Kenya.

We have indicated how Kenya was by 1947 already involved in the extension of the military options available to the British in the Middle East. The way in which this process interlocked with the momentum of local nationalisms must now be outlined, for it was to be paralleled in sub-Saharan Africa. In both spheres the story unfolded against a triangle of forces. In the Middle East the triangle was formed by Egypt, the country in which Britain had the greatest interest and whose nationalism was accordingly the least tractable; by the Sudan, representative of areas of lesser British interest; and by Cyprus – supplemented by Kenya – the secondary position available after the first, Egypt, had become untenable. Anglo-Egyptian relations had been chronically bad for decades, crossed by the twin conflicts over Britain's military requirements and the status of the Sudan. British dealings with Sudanese political leaders had been conditioned by a competition with Egypt for their future affection.[10] Britain's agreement in 1953 to a three-year transitional period before self-determination was her final and, it appeared, successful throw in the game. This same reliance upon peripheral Middle Eastern nationalisms as potential counterweights to the latent influence of Egypt at the centre was apparent in Britain's readiness to depart from the former Italian possessions of Libya, Eritrea, and Somalia; and her hesitation over progress in British Somaliland reflected her desire to conciliate the more ancient nation of Ethiopia. Once the British government had accepted that the Suez base was more of a liability than an asset, and once the Free Officers had taken power in Egypt, it was even possible to predict an era of good feeling in Anglo-Egyptian relations.[11] Yet old military habits of thought died hard. Egypt was once again alienated when Britain consolidated her alliance with the states on the Middle East's northern periphery by joining the Baghdad Pact in 1955. But the disconcerting way that even a contracting military potential could jeopardise the friendly relations, by which alone Empire

---

[10] For details see L.A. Fabunmi, *The Sudan in Anglo-Egyptian Relations*, London, 1960; M. Al-Rahim, *Imperialism and Nationalism in the Sudan*, London, 1969.

[11] Monroe, *Britain's Moment in the Middle East*, pp. 175 sqq.

could safely be replaced, was more dramatically shown in the armed resistance which now flared on the island colony of Cyprus. In 1950 the Colonial Secretary had claimed that 'in our Colonial Territories the movement for political and constitutional advance never checks, never pauses'.[12] Four years later, with the British army withdrawing to Cyprus from Egypt, a junior minister declared the contrary, that in view of its strategic importance the island could 'never' expect to be fully independent. This slip, which came out in reply to questioning, heralded the onset of the Cyprus emergency.[13] In relation to their wider setting, there was much resemblance between EOKA and Mau Mau.

BRITAIN'S CHOICES IN AFRICA

The parameters of British policy in Africa were well illustrated by a series of events in 1948. Against the menacing background of the Berlin crisis, the year witnessed the Christiansborg riots in the Gold Coast, Malan's victory over Smuts in the South African elections, the acceptance in official British circles of the desirability of federation in Central Africa[14] and, on 1 January, the institution of the East Africa High Commission for the co-ordination of inter-territorial services. As British authority and influence were challenged in the west and south, measures were being taken to consolidate them elsewhere.

In 1940 black troops from the Gold Coast had fought side by side, as good comrades indeed, with whites from South Africa in the Abyssinian campaign. By 1951 South Africa was denouncing the Gold Coast's progress towards self-government.[15] For Britain, some foresaw a future need to choose between association with the white supremacist south or the emergent 'Gold Coast democracy'.[16] But for the British government this was a choice between sentiments; to the national interest the nationalisms of West and South Africa were almost equally risky. It is true that after the 1948 riots the Gold Coast moved swiftly towards independence; to protests

[12] James Griffiths, *Hansard*, 5th series, H. of C., 477, c. 1380, 12 July 1950.
[13] For the government's embarrassment over the statement see Chandos, *Memoirs*, p. 436. An equally momentous statement on Uganda was to be made in similar unguarded circumstances. See D.A. Low, *Buganda in Modern History*, London, 1971, ch. 4.
[14] Claire Palley, *The Constititional History and Law of Southern Rhodesia, 1888–1965, with Special Reference to Imperial Control*, London, 1966, p. 333.
[15] Walker, *History of Southern Africa*, pp. 824–5; see also Gwendolen M. Carter, *The Politics of Inequality: South Africa since 1948*, London, 1984, p. 202, for the influence of the Gold Coast and Mau Mau upon the 1953 South African general election.
[16] P.N.S. Mansergh, *The Multi-racial Commonwealth: Proceedings of the Fifth Unofficial Commonwealth Relations Conference, held at Lahore, Pakistan, March 1954*, London, 1955, quoted in Mansergh, *The Commonwealth Experience*, London, 1969, p. 357; see also Margery Perham's letter to *The Times*, 4 Aug. 1950 and her article, 'The British Problem in Africa', *Foreign Affairs* (July 1951), both reprinted in her *Colonial Sequence, 1949 to 1969*, London, 1970, pp. 20 sqq., 26–39.

from a Kenya settler in 1951 the Colonial Secretary, James Griffiths, replied: 'And what was the alternative, man? Bloody revolution, that's what it was'.[17] The Indian government had risked this alternative three times in as many decades. It was a measure of the force of the Indian example no less than of the comparatively smaller British stakes in West Africa that the Labour government would not take similar risks in Accra. The principle of the devolution and eventual transfer of power, which had been translated so reluctantly from the white to the brown empire, was now to be applied without further argument to the black African dependencies; but only to the western ones, at least for the time being. It was difficult to argue that the people of the Gold Coast shared, with the white Dominions, the traditions and culture of Britain; but neither, now, did the ruling circles in South Africa. In the political and economic fields indeed, the Gold Coast seemed to be the more reliable. Many of the Gold Coast elite had graduated from British universities, and even the London School of Economics seemed preferable to the former theological seminary of Stellenbosch. The Gold Coast's Cocoa Marketing Board continued to earn dollars for the Sterling Area. South Africa, by contrast, withdrew from the Area's dollar pool; the Nationalist government had to recall Smuts' gold loan to Britain; British capital, nervous of take-overs, ceased if only for a time to flow to South Africa. It found fresh outlets in the Rhodesias.

This trend of events in the south played a major role in converting the Attlee government to reluctant support of federation in Central Africa. The scheme appeared to hold clear economic advantages. And had not Cripps, Britain's new Chancellor of the Exchequer, given as his opinion to the African Governors' Conference in 1947 that 'The whole future of the sterling group and its ability to survive depends . . . upon a quick and extensive development of our African resources'?[18] Any political scruples were countered by the fear that, without federation, Southern Rhodesia might take up the option offered in 1923 and join the Union; already one-fifth of its white voters were Afrikaners, and some observers thought they might dominate the country within a decade.[19] In bundling protesting Africans into the federation while simultaneously refusing to hand over to the Union their fellows in the three High Commission territories, Britain was but repeating her nineteenth-century encirclement of the Boers. Nkrumah's nationalism – if it could not be Danquah's – was less alarming than Malan's; that of Sir Godfrey Huggins was positively to be welcomed.

This discrimination between nationalisms, of whatever colour, could be rationalised by a modern form of the old prejudices over racial competence

[17] Sir Michael Blundell, *So Rough a Wind*, London, 1964, p. 83.
[18] Rita Hinden, *Common Sense and Colonial Development*, Fabian Colonial Bureau, London, 1949, p. 9.
[19] Chandos, *Memoirs*, p. 387.

in government. Lugard's appreciation of the Fulani as 'born rulers . . . incomparably above the negroid tribes in ability[20] is well known. Later comparisons were also made, always unfavourable to eastern Africans, most of whom (and it was no coincidence) were perceived as a working class. Whereas a British official in the Gold Coast for instance, remarked how in 1948 his official colleagues were all, 'in varying degrees, good nationalists', there can have been few such in East and Central Africa at that time. Apart from the difficulty in choosing between rival nationalisms there, white and black, the Negro peoples of West Africa seemed to belong to 'a quite different stock from the Bantu of Central Africa, and they seemed to be of higher calibre . . . these people were no more like the Central Africans than we are like the Eskimos.[21] And in eastern Africa itself the 'Hamitic hypothesis', that there was 'a positive correlation between the amount of Hamitic blood in a people's veins and the degree of their political evolution',[22] still enjoyed currency in European circles; there is evidence to suggest that it may have conditioned Kenya's official mind when it faced the claims of 'negroid tribes'.[23] Those with closer experience of the Hamitic Somalis were more impressed with the fact that they were virtually ungovernable;[24] nevertheless, the peoples to whom the British had ceded independence in North-East Africa were either Hamites (Cushites more properly speaking) or Arabs, most markedly so in the Sudan. Racially as well as strategically, this area was conceived as part of the Middle East, not Africa, or *Afrique noire* as the French unapologetically called it. Historical perspective has obediently decreed that the translation to independence of Ghana, not its earlier achievement in the Sudan, should mark the start of sub-Saharan Africa's path to freedom.[25]

Such rationalisations conspired with the strategic argument to foster the belief that the tides of nationalism could be checked within geographical compartments. This reluctance to admit the force of precedents elsewhere could be more demonstrably justified by the presence or absence of a local 'political class'.[26] The Gold Coast elite was recognised as such by the British, the handful of African literates in East and Central Africa was not.[27]

[20] Margery Perham, *Lugard: The Years of Authority, 1898–1945*, London, 1960, p. 47.
[21] Sir Kenneth Bradley, *Once a District Officer*, London, 1966, pp. 148 sqq.
[22] B.A. Ogot, 'Kingship and Statelessness among the Nilotes', in J. Vansina, R. Mauny, and L.V. Thomas (eds.), *The Historian in Tropical Africa*, London, 1964, p. 284.
[23] See the discussion of the incidence of 'Mau Mau' among Masai whose 'pure strain' had been diluted by Kikuyu blood, in *Historical Survey of the Origins and Growth of Mau Mau*, by F.D. Corfield, Cmnd. 1030 (1960), pp. 208–9.
[24] Sir Richard Turnbull, 'Djibouti: Last French Dependency in Africa' (review article), *Geographical Journal*, 135 no. 2 (June 1969), 240.
[25] And in the largest territory in colonial Africa, Nigeria, there is little doubt that British sympathies with the Muslim North played a disproportionate part in influencing the structure of the federal government.
[26] J.M. Lee, *Colonial Development and Good Government*, London, 1967, *passim*.
[27] Chandos, *Memoirs* p. 389.

The political class was there provided by the local Europeans and, as was more grudgingly acknowledged, by the leaders of the Asians.

The immigrant groups have also been described by a former official as 'economic man incarnate'.[28] And in British business circles the political implications of colonial Africa's new economic importance appeared to be plain enough. In 1948 Colonel Ponsonby, MP, Chairman of the Joint East Africa Board, stated that

up to a year or two ago the policy was 'Africa for the Africans'. . . . Now the opposite course is being pursued. In order to increase the world's production of raw materials, the word has gone out, 'Full speed ahead,' which means that the natives gradually must continue to come less and less under the rule of the chief and more and more to be a part of an active European organisation. . . . This is probably best for the African in the long run, but the Government must say so quite frankly and not wrap it up in pious hopes about Africans taking over the management or becoming the owners of great enterprises . . .[29]

Neither British political party could have accepted the full logic of this argument at any time in the post-war years. Both Labour and Conservatives flatly refused to concede to Huggins and Welensky the amalgamation of the two Rhodesias.[30] There was nevertheless more than a streak of this kind of thinking in the Central African Federation scheme as finally adopted.

And East Africa's Groundnut Scheme was hailed by the *Economist* of London as an example of 'the sort of economic planning which is needed to change the face of the colonial empire'.[31] Apart from the fact that its disastrous failure subsequently vindicated the advocates of increased African peasant production, the scheme had three features which bear directly upon our argument. First, its scale; the British government invested no less than £36 million in an attempt to coerce mechanically the barren scrubs not only of Tanganyika but also – had the original plans materialised – of Kenya and Northern Rhodesia, into producing edible fats for the metropolitan housewife. Secondly, overall responsibility lay with the British Ministry of Food, with the United Africa Company as its agent, not with the territorial government or the Colonial Office. Finally, one of the chief attractions of the selected areas was the paucity of Africans upon them.[32] And the logic of this large-scale economic development did appear to carry over into the politics of regional co-ordination. As the Groundnut Scheme opened, so London published its revised proposals, 'Colonial 210', for the composition of the East African Central Legislative Assembly. In

28 N.S. Carey Jones, *The Anatomy of Uhuru*, Manchester, 1966, p. 73.
29 In a letter to *The Times*, 31 Mar. 1948.
30 Even then it must be remarked that Britain was as much concerned for the control of the strategic mineral copper as for the welfare of the Africans who mined it.
31 The *Economist*, 1 Mar. 1947.
32 S. Herbert Frankel, *The Economic Impact on Under-Developed Societies*, Oxford, 1953, pp. 141–53.

deference to settler protest, these marked a significant retreat from the equality of racial representation originally proposed. The arguments for administrative co-operation between the three mainland East African territories had been greatly strengthened by their recent wartime experience; and the Labour government insisted that it was thinking in terms of continued administrative efficiency only, and not about political federation. But the controversy over the East African Assembly had shown how contentious was the attempt merely to provide a constitutional basis for the operation of the common services. Had there been a stronger local political will for closer union, as among the whites of Central Africa, had East Africa had the same economic potential, it is very possible that the global priorities of military strategy and economic reconstruction would have prevailed against the lengthy Colonial Office tradition of territorial autonomy. It was not until late in 1950 that the Secretary of State publicly concluded that it would be best to pursue constitutional change 'separately in each territory rather than on a general East African basis', and even then with the qualification, 'for the time being at at any rate'.[33]

THE SECOND COLONIAL OCCUPATION

The Colonial Office tradition of territorial autonomy did indeed come much closer to political reality after the Second World War. Although the scale of British economic planning was now global, the institutional sinews of development remained firmly embedded in each territory. In this as in other contexts the Groundnut Scheme was an aberration, for the close interrelationship between economic and political development was now the topic of Empire.[34] Some political change was recommended by the conventional canons of business efficiency. The general concept of representative government as a successor to 'administration', and its specific application by Sir Philip Mitchell to Kenya in the 'membership system', are cases in point.[35] But there was also a new awareness that the rank and file as well as the captains of the colonial economies must be associated, if only at the local or district level, in the making and implementation of policy. From the first, all administrative officers had known that without African co-operation nothing would ever get done; there was now much more to do. From the late 1940s there was a great intensification of government activity throughout British Africa; in contrast to earlier years, and to the recent war period when territories were drained of staff, this access of official energy amounted to a second colonial occupation. It had a variety of causes.

Its origins lay in the 1930s when the world depression generally and the

[33] James Griffiths, *Hansard*, 5th series, 482, c. 1167, 13 Dec. 1950.
[34] Lee, *Colonial Development and Good Government*, *passim*.
[35] G. Bennett, *Kenya: a political history* London, 1963.

West Indies riots in particular crystallised a new set of attitudes to Britain's dependent Empire. The Colonial Development and Welfare Act of 1940 codified the growing opinion that Britain must play a much more active role in promoting the welfare of her colonial peoples; it broke with the old convention of territorial self-sufficiency in finance. The conception of purposeful state action was then applied in Britain – an expedient during the war, the prime tool of the Labour administration's social engineers thereafter – and subsequently exported to the dependencies. Innovatory paternalism, the leverage required before a people internalised the desirability of change for themselves, received a powerful new ideological support. It was buttressed in the colonies by two further considerations. First, large human and economic investments were held to be necessary before Africans would be 'fit for self-government'. Secondly, and more negatively, it was believed that as Africans became 'detribalised', so governments would in any case be obliged to assume the social welfare functions formerly performed within the tribes.[36]

What chiefly distinguished this post-war period from earlier years was the availability of development funds. For the most part these were provided by the territorial governments, which enjoyed buoyant revenues until the sustained boom in primary commodity prices finally ended in the mid-1950s. The metropolitan Colonial Development and Welfare funds were perhaps more important for their institutional than for their directly economic contributions. They were granted in aid of Ten-year Development Plans devised by the local bureaucracies, not by Whitehall. Further, such grants were conditional upon the recognition of trade union rights within a colony.[37] And the secretary of state's 1947 circular on local government stressed the need to secure full benefits from development moneys at least as much as further political education; local governments had to be 'efficient', not 'democratic' merely.

All levels of activity in the colonial world were now much more firmly interlocked. Great Britain's own needs had, for instance, prompted the transfer to Africa of the long-term bulk-purchasing contracts which had long featured in her trading relations with the old white Commonwealth.[38] And the local contracting parties, the commodity marketing boards, gave to territorial governments an immense discretion in economic affairs. At the same time the territorial governments in Africa were, for all the signs of

[36] A. Creech-Jones, 'British Colonial Policy, with Particular Reference to Africa', *International Affairs*, 27 no. 2 (Apr. 1951), 178, 182. The formulation foreshadowed that of Karl Deutsch in his 'Social Mobilization and Political Development', *American Political Science Review*, 55 no. 3 (Sept. 1961), 492–514.
[37] B.C. Roberts, *Labour in the Tropical Territories of the Commonwealth*, London, 1964, pp. 187–8.
[38] P.H. Ady, 'Britain and Overseas Development', in G.D.N. Worswick and P.H. Ady (eds.), *The British Economy, 1945–1950*, London, 1953, p. 558.

imperial recession elsewhere in the world, intervening increasingly in what had hitherto been local concerns. They did so in the name of the efficiency which would raise African production, protect African land from erosion or Africans themselves from disease, and in search of the democratic supports without which no project, however expert, could be implemented. It was here, at the local rather than at the territorial or global levels, that the decisive strains appeared in the colonial relationship as it applied to East Africa.[39]

It was no accident that East Africa's most ambitious rural development scheme – apart from the special case of land consolidation in Kikuyuland – was prosecuted in the Sukuma area of Tanganyika's Lake Province, the territory's experimental laboratory for local government reform.[40] But it was no accident either that what may well have been the precipitating crisis in Tanganyika's early achievement of independence also occurred in Sukumaland.[41] The political history of Uganda and Kenya in these years likewise centred upon their local crises, in Buganda and Kikuyuland. These were exceptional in their intensity only, typical in that their origins lay in great measure in the frustration of local interests by an increasingly purposeful territorial government. For the complementary halves of the Colonial Office policy – to raise the level of efficiency in African production while widening the incidence of popular participation in development – only too often fell into mutual opposition on the spot.

The district teams of administrative and technical officers pursued efficiency, the African councils with whom they worked took up their stand upon the bruised principle of participation. It was partly that officials found economic development a more concrete, more congenial task than political education, partly that there were many more officials, of the technical variety especially, than ever before.[42] The understaffing of the colonial service was a perpetual cause of concern to parliament, but it was deficient only when measured against the new range of government duties. The perspective from below was rather different. Just as measurable numbers of Africans were acquiring the necessary professional skills, so their contribution and their ambition was engulfed by the swelling numbers of expatriate officers, by raised levels of technical knowledge, and by a tendency for the planning of quite parochial schemes to vanish into the

[39] By contrast with, say, Algeria and the Belgian Congo, both of them cases where the involvement of metropolitan politics and metropolitan sensitivity to world opinion were of much more direct consequence. See Crawford, 'Decolonization in Africa', in L.H. Gann and Peter Duignan (eds.), *Colonialism in Africa, 1870–1960*, Stanford, and London, 1970, II, pp. 467–79.

[40] G. Andrew Maguire, *Toward 'Uhuru' in Tanzania: The Politics of Participation*, London, 1969; for the flavour of official enthusiasms at the time see Elspeth Huxley, *The Sorcerer's Apprentice: A Journey through East Africa*, London, 1948, pp. 171–81.

[41] For the 'Geita crisis', see Maguire, *Toward 'Uhuru'*, pp. 196–234.

[42] Lee, *Colonial Development and Good Government*, pp. 35 sqq., 86, 144.

higher reaches of government. If this new generation of secondary-school-leavers and graduates felt themselves insufficiently recognised, the older intermediary leadership of chiefs and mission teachers was being actively displaced, not only in the local arena of the district council, but in the parochial ones within it, the chiefdoms. Before the war this intermediary leadership had enjoyed very considerable control over the political resources and rewards available at both levels, for the colonial governments had occupied a comparatively small portion of the political space which lay beyond the centre. But the central governments were now attempting to penetrate the remotest corners of their political territory. Their officials, most of whom were those same new Africans already mentioned, made direct demands upon individual family heads, in breach of the previous unspoken contract with the parochial intermediaries. If the one were to achieve an autonomous political role or the other to regain its lost political ground, both sets of African leadership, together or in competition, would have to parallel the new intensity of government themselves by linking up the parochial, district, and territorial levels of authority and their associated arenas of political competition.

INDIVIDUALS IN A TURNING WORLD

At this point it becomes important to explore further what was happening at the local levels rather more generally. Indeed if the drama of these years is to be portrayed in the round we must begin with the fact that the experience of the last two decades before independence was as much that of men as individuals as of men in their more corporate capacities. It is only possible here of course to be illustrative, but our purpose will be served by being at once quite particular and quite general.

Mpuga and Kihara, it is reported, were two somewhat ordinary Amba villagers. Their homeland lay below the western slopes of Mount Ruwenzori right upon the western edge of Uganda.[43] In the past their people had lived in villages, each of which had very largely been an independent political unit. In the first half of the twentieth century, however, they had found some of the people with whom they intermarried becoming subject to the dominion of the 'Congo', while they themselves became part of a 'county' of neighbouring Toro, which was one of the kingdoms of the British 'Protectorate' of 'Uganda'. They became subject indeed to a Toro 'county chief' and to three Toro 'sub-county' chiefs placed under him. Ineluctably the Amba found themselves submitting to this new political

---

[43] This section is based on Edward H. Winter's three publications, *Bwamba: A Structural-Functional Analysis of a Patrilineal Society*, Cambridge, 1956; *Bwamba Economy*, East African Studies No. 5, Kampala, 1955, and *Beyond the Mountains of the Moon: The Lives of Four Africans*, London, 1959. The biographical portraits are drawn from the last.

superstructure and even, through those Amba who became 'parish' and 'sub-parish' chiefs at its base, participating in it. As a consequence during a few short decades the world in which they lived underwent a political transformation. No longer was it an almost isolated entity. Its 'scale' enlarged to an extent which was unique in its history.[44] In the recent past an Amba village had simply been part of the Amba social system. Now it was being linked in a myriad of ways to all sorts of other systems. Cultivation, moreover, was now increasingly not just for subsistence or for local exchange. In the 1920s the overarching British administration had introduced the cultivation of coffee into Bwamba country for the world market, and in the 1930s cotton as well. The most conspicuous symbol of the vast new world to which Amba society was now being actively linked had come in 1938 with the opening of the road around the north end of the mountains to Fort Portal, the capital of Toro.

In some ways Mpuga and Kihara were a little more prosperous than their neighbours. In the mid-1950s, when it was reckoned that annual incomes were around the Sh. 120 mark, Kihara earned roughly Sh. 250 (mostly from selling coffee and cotton), while Mpuga had about Sh. 350 (since he occasionally secured a paid job). They were nevertheless still primarily involved in those things which preoccupied most other Amba – dealing with their wives, arguing with their neighbours, coaxing their children, worrying about sickness, busying themselves with their cultivation, going off to market. Kihara himself was a serious, but in certain respects disappointed, man. In the early years of British rule his father had held a prominent position locally, and he himself had once worked as a sub-parish chief under Toro overlords. His promotion, however, had been blocked because he had never learned to read and write. His neighbour Mpuga had been a church teacher. More recently he had been an employee at the locally established though short-lived Yellow Fever Research station. By all accounts he was a staunch Christian. He believed, for example, that the biblical account of the creation of the world was strictly factual. He had not of course dismissed the beliefs in local powers and local spirits which were still held by the majority of his fellow countrymen, for how could he know that they did not coexist with the God of whom Christianity spoke, and that in certain specific circumstances their influence might not be more efficacious? He was convinced, however, that Christianity was the gateway to the larger world which was now pressing in upon him, and he was quite clear that to be like Kihara and remain a 'pagan' was to allow the opportunities which that new world had to offer – as Kihara himself had discovered – to pass him by. He was faced even so by a serious problem. Because he had three wives living in his household, the representatives of the Christian

---

[44] Godfrey and Monica Wilson, *The Analysis of Social Change*, Cambridge, 1945, esp. chs. 2 and 6.

Church told him he was 'living in sin'. He himself did not see it that way, but because the Church did he could not participate in its activities as fully as he would have wished. Like a great many other East Africans at this time he was thus caught in a vortex, and was finding it difficult to make his way out of it.

Personal adjustments were nevertheless being made, even in very unpromising circumstances. Towns were growing very rapidly in East Africa by the 1950s. It was estimated for example that while in 1943 Dar es Salaam, Tanganyika's capital, had some 43,000 people, fourteen years later it had grown to 129,000. Here for numbers of ordinary people the physical environment was very largely new; so was their work situation; so was their style of life.

Hasan [J.A.K. Leslie noted of an inhabitant of Dar es Salaam in 1956] is a youngish man in his thirties, of some dignity and personality, though perhaps inclined to give himself more airs than his elders would allow him . . . He lives in Buguruni where he built in 1950, and has his own house, a low-roofed three-roomer, whitewashed and with painted doors and lintels, all in a little need of redoing. There are two lodgers, both young men like himself, each with one room and paying 10 Shs. a month to him . . . He was born near Kitunda, that is beyond Mbezi to the north, in a bit of bush where houses are scattered and few. Some of his family are still there, but both parents are dead . . . He worked for the military in Dar es Salaam during part of the war; once he was a Public Works Department daily paid labourer on the roads; several times he had periods of up to a year with various Europeans as laundryman and houseboy . . . [Recently] he has had a death in the family, which meant a whipround among fellow-tribesmen and relatives both here and in the home village a few miles out on the Kawe road; whether he made something on balance out of the funeral, or whether it meant that he came into a bit of property I do not know. Anyhow he has taken out a Shs 20. licence to be a trader at the Shark Market and he buys tables and chairs from local artisans, cash down, and sells them on the never-never in the Shark Market, making a margin for himself. He says it is a good living.[45]

These eventualities were being experienced not just by individuals but by whole societies, and some of them developed a sophisticated language in which to discuss them. Five hundred miles north-west of Dar es Salaam, and perhaps four hundred miles eastwards of Bwamba country, where the boundary between the British territories of Kenya and Tanganyika reached down to the eastern shore of Lake Victoria, lay Kuria country.[46] Up to the late 1920s, it had seen little European administration. But by about 1930 schools, Christian missions, technological improvements in agriculture, external trade, and closer British administration had come to it, and by the

45 J.A.K. Leslie, *A Survey of Dar es Salaam*, London, 1963, pp. 138–9.
46 This section is based on M.J. Ruel, 'Religion and Society among the Kuria of East Africa', *Africa*, 35 no. 3 (1965), 293–306, and on an unpublished typescript on the Kuria which Dr Ruel has generously allowed us to use.

1950s their impact was beginning to be very intense. The Kuria, it seems, were not an especially religious people. Nevertheless ritual actions and requirements, it has been stated, 'figure very large in their life and in the planning activities', and in these were to be found 'a tight cluster of ideas and symbolic actions', in which 'the ideas of life, well-being and "straightness"' were involved but in which there was also a correspondence sought between 'the ordered growth of natural things and that of people in society'. By the 1950s, however, 'straightness' and 'ordered growth' were becoming increasingly difficult to sustain. Increasingly Kuria were being confronted by what they called *chomba* – by that which was introduced, modern, non-Kuria, and non-African. By *chomba* they meant in the first place any area or place of development: Nairobi, Mombasa, Mwanza, Kisumu, the tea estates of Kericho and so on. Even neighbouring Kisii and Migori were called *chomba* when mentioned in this context. It was also the place from which the Europeans and Asians had come; and to which Kuria migrant labourers now went. *Omochomba*, a '*chomba* person', was the term originally applied to the Arabs who had come to the country, and then to the Europeans and Asians who followed them.

Most often it was used with the derogatory, indeed inhuman, prefixes, *iri/ama*, rather than with the personal ones, *omo/aba*. By *amachomba*, '*chomba* things', Kuria came to mean all people of alien culture – including those Kuria who associated with it – mission converts, European employees, chiefs, headmen, and even the elders who sat in the new councils and courts. All were seen as inhuman, alien, and threatening; and in naming them *chomba* the Kuria conceptualised their disdain for, and fear of, the whole new world which was now impinging upon them. The opposition between 'traditional Kuria' and '*chomba* things' was not however just conceptual. There was practical opposition as well – to the building of roads, to the erection of a dispensary, to the recruitment of labour. Fairly distinct cultural classes, moreover – 'traditionalists' and 'new Kuria' – were now appearing in a society which previously had been both homogeneous and markedly conformist. More seriously, a kind of social hiatus had opened up in Kuria society in which traditional forms of organisation and social status had disappeared before they had been fully or effectively replaced.

The explosive invasion, that is, which for men like Kihara and Mpuga away in Bwamba country had brought periodical tension and strain, or for Hasan in Dar es Salaam had involved some swift-footed readjustments, was here bringing conflict and cleavage. Sometimes it even opened chasms. In one form or another the Kuria experience was widely shared amongst the peoples of East Africa.[47] On occasion indeed the breakdown in pre-existing

[47] See e.g. J.H.M. Beattie, 'Bunyoro through the Looking Glass', *Journal of African Administration*, 12 no. 2 (Apr. 1960), 85–94.

patterns of social organisation occurred with extraordinary swiftness. In 1935, it has been reported, 'the traditional rituals celebrated by the lineages and chiefdoms [of the Nyakyusa peoples down near the north end of Lake Nyasa in south-western Tanganyika] formed a coherent system. They were directed towards the shades and the heroes.' 'By 1955 [however] the ritual cycle was nowhere celebrated in full; what remained were "bits and pieces" of ritual none of them fully intelligible without reference to the complete cycle.[48] Sometimes the disintegration could be very disruptive indeed. In 1952 a lifelong observer, Dr. L.S.B. Leakey, described the effect upon Kikuyu marriage and socialisation patterns (and so much that went with these things) of the flow of migrant labour to Nairobi and the 'White Highlands'.[49] Other observers, of the Luo, for instance, of Kenya's Nyanza province, reported similarly. Particularly where there was large-scale migrant labour, families were left without their male head. Wives found themselves in an uncertain position. Elderly parents suffered neglect. Boys were left free to roam around as they wished. Girls lacked the protection their fathers could provide. Social obligations were fairly easily reneged upon; and disputes festered.[50]

'*Comba iri ni ijire.*' 'The Europeans arrived.' So said, not just the Kuria (though the term is the same as theirs), but the Meru of Mount Kenya; and the ensuing sense of malaise could often be acute. Sometimes it brought internal conflict. 'You are not as we were', a Meru elder remonstrated with a young literate fellow-tribesman, 'you always quarrel, and the reason is that you do not respect your elders.' In the old days, another inveighed,

the young initiates were told to behave properly; the elders were expected to do the actions of elderhood and not of childhood. The only man to suffer in those days was the one who did not want to do like the others. We say that if our chief *munene* – the Mugwe, would come back, we would not like to be dominated by the present state of affairs, *comba iji iri ku nandi*.[51]

On so many occasions indeed the buttresses of society, both social and ideological, looked as if they were about to collapse. Despite the attempts of men like Jomo Kenyatta,[52] or Kabaka Daudi Chwa of Buganda,[53] back in the 1930s to make readjustments, existing value-systems seemed to be singularly inadequate to meet the exigencies of the changing milieux. The Mugwe (the chief ritual figure of the Meru), Father Bernardi has recorded, was by the 1950s 'a failing prophet', 'a figure of the past', 'as an institution

[48] Monica Wilson, *Communal Rituals of the Nyakyusa*, London, 1959, p. 211.
[49] L.S.B. Leakey, *Mau Mau and the Kikuyu*, London, 1952, pp. 74–7.
[50] M.G. Whisson, *Change and Challenge: A Study of the Social and Economic Changes Among the Kenya Luo*, Nairobi, 1964.
[51] B. Bernardi, *The Mugwe: A Failing Prophet*, London, 1959, pp. 170, 174–5.
[52] See J. Kenyatta, *Facing Mount Kenya*, London, 1938.
[53] Kabaka Daudi Chwa, 'Education, Civilization and Foreignization', in D.A. Low (ed.), *The Mind of Buganda*, London, 1970, pp. 104–8.

[the Mugweship had] lost its significance with the people and its influence on the social structure.'[54] The integrity of existence looked to be falling apart.

THE POSITIVE RESPONSE

The great fact was, however, that for all the stresses and strains, it was in East Africa only very occasionally that substantial disintegration occurred.

Some people deliberately sought to resist innovation. The Masai, for instance, and some other pastoralists, like the Samburu, maintained their deep disdain for outsiders throughout. Having adjusted themselves reasonably successfully to the sparse ecology of their homeland areas, they found little in the outsiders' contrivances to attract them. Status in such societies was generally ascribed, so that there was not much personal benefit to be had from education, or from financial success, or from entering a modernised elite. The pastoralists' pre-eminence in war had given them a cultural prestige amongst some of their neighbours which had led to a widespread adoption of certain pastoralist values.[55] Now, however, some of these neighbours found themselves obliged to break ranks, enter the modern cash economy, and start to adapt – in the case of the Arusha of northern Tanzania largely because of a sharp population increase and a consequent land shortage.[56] Even so there was never a breakdown – the mechanisms of social control could, it seems, be adapted in time.[57] In a multitude of ways indeed the response of most Africans to the radical changes to which they found themselves subject was at once flexible and fertile. Hardly any of them went the way of the Northern American Indian, the Australian aborigine, or the South African bushman.[58] Very few turned their faces to the wall. But then those who had developed a full subsistence agriculture and were not deprived of their land were relatively well-placed to maintain their footing. Amongst the Kuria, for example – for all their clear-sightedness about the threat to the ordered growth of their society – there were steady readjustments,[59] especially where their political units retained

---

[54] Bernardi, *The Mugwe*, p. 182. For further examples of the general phenomenon discussed here, see *inter alia* John Beattie and John Middleton, *Spirit Mediumship and Society in Africa*, London, 1969, pp. xxix, 161, etc.

[55] P.H. Gulliver, 'The Conservative Commitment in Northern Tanzania: The Arusha and Masai', in Gulliver (ed.), *Tradition and Transition in East Africa: Studies of the Tribal Element in the Modern Era*, London, 1969, pp. 223–42. Paul Spencer, *The Samburu*, Berkeley, 1965.

[56] P.H. Gulliver, 'The Arusha; Economic and Social Change', in Paul Bohannan and George Dalton (eds.), *Markets in Africa*, New York, 1965, pp. 250–84.

[57] P.H. Gulliver, *Social Control in an African Society*, London, 1963.

[58] This large subject does not as yet appear to have been systematically considered. One starting point would be C.D. Rowley, *The Destruction of Aboriginal Society*, Canberra, 1970.

[59] Ruel, 'Religion and Society among the Kuria', 293–306.

their 'traditional' boundaries.[60] Amongst the Basoga,[61] the Tiriki,[62] and a great many others, there was similar accommodation. Time and again, moreover, this process of adaptation moved with the half dozen or so positive ingredients which were usually in the offing.

Few were of greater importance than the continued vitality, despite all sorts of vicissitudes, of the economy and society of the rural areas.[63] These things might undergo 'development' and change. Their continuance might be seriously threatened. But by and large men were not chased from their hearths. And even when they were it was often feasible to rebuild them in similar form elsewhere. Perhaps of particular importance was the persistence of the previously elaborated social structures. The clans to which men belonged remained in being. 'The very vagueness of its functions may have permitted the clan to become a symbol of important values', it has been said. It 'stood to the people as a recurrent reminder of the basic verities of their heritage and of their membership in some large community.[64] At the same time, although men's consciousness of their subjecthood within a rulership, or of their personal progression through an age-grade organisation, might now present them with novel problems, for the most part the scaffoldings by which the social order was upheld seem to have borne remarkably successfully the strain which the enlargement of scale brought about. Rarely were they so brittle as to break.

A prime consideration here was the striking openness of most East African societies. For a start, many 'tribes' had never been hard and fast communities;[65] the inflow and outflow of people amongst them – and not just at their edges – had been marked. One thinks, for example, of the merging frontiers of the Masai people, of Rwanda migrants turning themselves into Ganda, or of the readiness of the Nyamwezi to assimilate strangers.[66] Equally, it had long been common practice for the institutions of one people to be adopted by another – age-set organisations, for example, had spread on both sides of the Rift Valley region, as had rulership in Alur

[60] For a discussion of this phenomenon in India see L.I. and S.H. Rudolph, *The Modernity of Tradition*, Chicago, 1967.
[61] See especially Lloyd A. Fallers, *Law without Precedent: Legal Ideas in the Courts of Colonial Busoga*, Chicago, 1969.
[62] Walter H. Sangree, *Age, Prayer and Politics in Tiriki, Kenya*, London, 1966.
[63] See W. Allen, *The African Husbandman*, Edinburgh, 1967, especially chs. 9–12, 18, 22.
[64] Elizabeth Colson, 'African Society at the Time of the Scramble', in L.H. Gann and Peter Duignan (eds.), *Colonialism in Africa*, Cambridge, 1969, I, p. 55.
[65] Ronald Cohen and John Middleton, *From Tribe to Nation in Africa: Studies in Incorporation Processes*, Scranton, 1970.
[66] Julian H. Steward (ed.), *Contemporary Change in Traditional Societies*, London, 1967, I, pp. 164, 286; A.I. Richards (ed.), *Economic Development and Tribal Change*, Cambridge, 1954; R.G. Abrahams, *The Political Organization of Unyamwezi*, Cambridge, 1967, pp. 151–5.

country westwards of Lake Albert.[67] Such contacts could lead moreover to the adoption of major social values – witness the spread of Masai-like *laibon* through the Kalenjin peoples;[68] and there could be a wide dispersion too of religious movements such as that of the Yakany in the regions west of the Nile.[69] Since for most people the processes of adaptation were as much a matter for those in the spirit world as for those whom one could see and touch, the issues here were essentially religious issues; and despite all the vicissitudes of the time the widespread assumption that there were matters here of quite fundamental importance was scarcely ever shaken. If the existing conceptions seemed to be inadequate, then the new ones that were on offer were carefully investigated. If these also seemed to have their drawbacks, the quest was rarely abandoned: most usually it now moved into its most creative and adaptive phase. If the world was out of joint – so it seemed that people were saying – that was no reason for renouncing it: the need for them to wrestle with their destinies was all the more vital.[70]

THE NEW AGGREGATIONS

There were two broad processes that we may consider here with which these constructive forces seem to have worked. In the first place, they frequently found concrete expression within the multiple forms of aggregation which were occurring in East Africa during the colonial period. They also found expression in developments in the new religion, Christianity.

Modern tribalism is often characterised as a means to reduce the outside world to a manageable size; but here we would emphasise its positive side.[71] Not only did Africans frequently manage their world with some success, but in order to do so they enlarged rather than diminished the range of their social relationships. In the past, many East African societies had been essentially small-scale, yet they commonly shared with their neighbours some cultural or linguistic affinity. These clusters we may call latent societies; now they were increasingly becoming actual. To take three

---

67 See e.g. A.H.J. Prins, *East African Age-Class Systems*, Groningen, 1953 and Robert LeVine and Walter H. Sangree, 'The Diffusion of Age-Group Organisation in East Africa: A Controlled Comparison', *Africa*, 22 no. 2 (Apr. 1962), pp. 97–110; and for the Alur, Aidan W. Southall, *Alur Society*, Cambridge, 1956.

68 Robert A. Manners, 'The Kipsigis of Kenya', in Steward, *Contemporary Change*, I, 262 sqq.

69 John Middleton. 'The Yakan or Allah Water Cult among the Lugbara', *Journal of the Royal Anthropological Institute*, 93 no. 1 (1963).

70 See *inter alia* Beattie and Middleton, *Spirit Mediumship and Society* and David B. Barrett, *Schism and Renewal in Africa: An Analysis of Six Thousand Contemporary Religious Movements*, Nairobi, 1968, *passim*.

71 For many of the insights and case studies which inform this section, see Gulliver, *Tradition and Transition in East Africa*, and especially Gulliver's introduction; Cohen and Middleton, *From Tribe to Nation*; and June Helm (ed.), *Essays on the Problem of Tribe*, Seattle, Wash., 1968 – especially the paper by Elizabeth Colson.

examples only: the Luo-speaking peoples were becoming the Luo people, Nyakyusa-speakers the Nyakyusa people, Lango clans the Lango people.

These processes of social aggregation altered the self-image of quite large communities in relation to the outside world in general; but the myriad initiatives which went to extend the boundaries of community were taken by individuals, and for specific purposes. As people engaged in an increasingly varied range of new occupations, so they needed a wider range of associates on whom they could rely or whose assumptions they could understand. Farmers who took new crops to market; small traders who found that two men's social circles more than doubled the opportunities which were available to one; teachers who were posted to a school beyond the neighbouring ridge; workers who stepped, uncertain, off the bus that took them to town – all needed to establish their acceptability beyond the knowable bounds of kin. These fluid social boundaries – generally expanding but contracting sharply on occasion – did not enclose mere operational groups or contestants. They also defined social arenas, that is, spheres with generally recognised (if not always honoured) rules of right behaviour and a set of cultural referents which might serve both as points of departure for deviant factions and as rallying points for larger unities. Indeed, the peoples who mastered the new situation with the greatest confidence seem often to have been those – like the Ganda, or the Kikuyu, or the Chagga – whose cultural distinctiveness was most assiduously fostered.[72]

It is true that even in the nineteenth century, along with the social disruption and economic diversification which had occurred in these parts, there had been aggregation as well.[73] What made this process so much more rapid, substantial – and its outcome perhaps more durable – in the twentieth century was the super-imposition of vastly larger political structures by the colonial powers. These actively influenced the expansion of social scale in two quite distinct ways. First, each administrative level – in East Africa typically the 'district' – not only transmitted the external demands which prompted peoples to aggregate with their neighbours, but gave them, if often unintentionally, the political resources which helped

[72] Our understanding of the relationships between different levels and arenas of political authority and competition has been refined by the following works in particular: F.G. Bailey, *Tribe, Caste and Nation*, Manchester, 1960, and *Politics and Social Change*, Berkeley, and Bombay, 1963; Fredrik Barth (ed.), 'The Role of the Entrepreneur in Social Change in Northern Norway', *Arbok for Universitetet I Bergen, Humanistisk Serie* (1963), No. 3, Bergen, 1963; Marc J. Swartz (ed.), *Local-Level Politics*, Chicago, 1968; London, 1969; Martin Staniland, 'Single-party Regimes and Political Change: the P.D.C.I. and Ivory Coast Politics', in Colin Leys (ed.), *Politics and Change in Developing Countries*, London, 1969, pp. 135–75; and Bernard S. Cohn, 'Political Systems in Eighteenth Century India: the Banaras Region', *Journal of the American Oriental Society* 82 no. 3 (July–Sept. 1962), 312–20.

[73] E.g. amongst the Nandi.

them to do so: the district councils which were instituted in order to give to the framework of administrative planning the underpinning of popular consent and the lubricant of a local rate; district appeal courts whose ruling came to affect judgements in the smaller units, the chiefdoms; co-operative unions created to market the cash crops whose geographical distribution so often justified the designations 'coffee district', 'cotton district'; and in some places a standardised district vernacular – used in pulpit or council chamber, if not in the home – originally designed to promote economies of scale in education. The control of these and other local political resources became the first object of competition among men who were concerned for the well-being of their society. New social aggregations thus merged with new politics,[74] and political arenas developed both to govern access to the rewards offered by the administrative system, and to check its demands.

There were several levels of authority in the world of colonial East Africa. The lowest which concerns us here we may for convenience label the parochial level – in Tanganyika the chiefdom, in Kenya the location, the county in Uganda. Above this stood what may be defined – again somewhat arbitrarily – as the district level; and above this again the provincial. The district was always a substantial entity, the province rarely so, either in terms of administrative concentration or of African community. The two levels higher still, the territorial and the inter-territorial or regional, represented in 1945 planes of regular social intercourse or responsibility for only a handful of East Africans. But – and this was the second contribution of the overarching colonial institutions to the processes of social aggregation – such levels did provide a stable frame of reference within which African societies might place both themselves and a much wider range of neighbours, or rivals, than previously. As societies gained new instruments of internal articulation, so also they came to be in greater need of solidarity against forces external to them.

Although from above the parochial units might appear to be sub-units beneath the district levels, they often in fact had an autonomy of their own; and within them important aggregations were occurring. Following their incorporation into Tiriki location, for instance, the Tiriki clans of Western Kenya became transformed under their chief Hezron Mushenye into a single society, self-consciously distinct from its neighbours.[75] Reporting upon the Sebei, a small cluster of Kalenjin-speaking groups to the north of Mount Elgon, Walter Goldschmidt remarked upon a similar development:

---

[74] For further examples see Audrey Richards (ed.), *East African Chiefs*, London, 1960, e.g. on the Soga, p. 93; Goran Hyden, *TANU Yajenga Nchi: Political Development in Rural Tanzania*, Lund, 1968.

[75] Sangree, *Age, Prayer and Politics*, *passim*.

The word Sebei refers to a group of formerly independent but closely interrelated tribes living on the northern and north-western slopes of Mount Elgon (and on the plains below) in Eastern Uganda. The term has come into use in modern administration parlance and these people now identify themselves as Sebei. Etymologically, *Sebei* (variously Sabei, Sapei, etc.) is a corruption of Sapin (the name of one of the tribes that constitutes modern Sebei).[76]

Similarly the Luguru, to take an example from eastern Tanganyika, were becoming increasingly conscious of themselves at this time as Luguru. Like the Tiriki and the Sebei they were a parochial unit, both within the larger cultural region of related peoples to which they had long belonged, and at the administrative level of Morogoro District within which they were now incorporated. In the past the clan and the still smaller unit, the lineage, had been the principal groupings in which their social relations had operated; they had had no tribe-wide organization nor any concept of 'tribal' unity. The distinctions between Luguru and the Kaguru and Nguru to the north, and the Kutu and Zaramo to the east had, moreover, been very uncertain. By the 1950s, however, the Luguru were becoming a more cohesive entity: and when some of them moved to other areas, so the census counts showed, they described themselves as Luguru who were living outside the Luguru area.[77]

Larger-scale district units were being activated as well. At a time of uncertain change the possibility of aggregating within a wider latent system so as to create a larger actual system was often seized upon as the most effective mode for meeting the new challenges. The common terms for these, 'district tribes' and 'tribal districts', well illustrated the close relationship between social and administrative levels and arenas. But in the kingdom areas, where larger political entities had existed before the creation of the colonial bureaucratic structures, similar developments were also occurring; peripheral areas were now being increasingly tied in with the larger kingdoms, as in Ankole,[78] or, as in Busoga, formerly separated state structures within a single cultural region were being newly amalgamated.[79] The whole process created social and cultural bases which possessed the triple merits of matching with many peoples' pre-existing social networks; of seeming firm enough to face the more concrete demands of the larger political superstructures, colonial and then national; and of enjoying legitimacy in the eyes of those who commanded the apex of these superstructures – at least while the latter were still Europeans. Thus it was that corporate groups like the Luhya, Gusii, and Kamba in Kenya; the

---

[76] Walter Goldschmidt, *Sebei Law*, Berkeley, 1967, p. 7.

[77] R. Young and H.A. Fosbrooke, *Land and Politics among the Luguru of Tanganyika*, London, 1960, pp. 39 sqq.

[78] Richards, *East African Chiefs*, pp. 156 sqq.

[79] Lloyd A. Fallers, *Bantu Bureaucracy*, Cambridge, n.d..

Chagga, Haya, and Zaramo in Tanganyika; the Acholi, Teso, and Gisu in Uganda, and many more besides, now became substantially more than their component parts.[80] Not all such aggregations were effected smoothly, and the relationship between parochial and district units often differed considerably through space and over time. But where, as in the instances just quoted, the district arena substantially encompassed the parochial, it provided both a polity and a focus of identity for several hundreds of thousands of people who had previously seen themselves as principally involved in much smaller groups. Important tribal units were coming into existence to comprise the major elements in the East African scene.

The most substantial of them were those that comprised aggregations of provincial dimensions, specifically Buganda, Kikuyu, and Sukuma. While their actual articulation varied, it was no coincidence that they each became the scene of the most serious political crises which the three mainland administrations encountered in the decade or so before independence. These societies had a solidity which in East Africa was without parallel.[81] And – a point to which we shall return – they were also distinguished by the standing discrepancy between the provincial size of their African arenas and the district-level institutions upon which the British mainly concentrated.

At the territorial level the situation was different. Here the colonial rulers had created a relatively formidable structure of political, economic, and even cultural power. Here was the apex of an array of modern institutions – courts, schools, public works departments and so on, as well as the command of police, central prisons, and troops.[82] Given the concern of African political leaders to establish African control over the destinies of East Africa's peoples, it was inevitable that these should become the target for their strivings, particularly when they saw that aggregations upon this scale would provide the means for establishing their own people's equality with the other peoples of the world, many of whom were formed into internationally-recognised independent nation-states, often of no greater size. By the same token, the comparatively slender political resources of the regional level invited relatively less attention from African politicians.

But lest it should be felt that this way of looking at what was afoot was alien to the peoples of East Africa themselves, it is worth considering a

[80] See for instance the chapters on the Gisu by J.S. La Fontaine and on the Chagga by Kathleen M. Stahl, in Gulliver, *Tradition and Transition*.

[81] See, e.g. D.A. Low, *Buganda in Modern History*, London, 1971, introduction; C.G. Rosberg and J. Nottingham, *The Myth of Mau Mau*, New York, 1966; Maguire, *Toward 'Uhuru'*. Aggregation on this scale was ssometimes sought by others, e.g. the Kalenjin and Mijikenda of Kenya, see Gulliver, *Tradition and Transition*, p. 23; Manners, 'Kipsigis', in Steward, *Contemporary Change*, I, 323–7.

[82] If only because of their post-imperial significance these institutions deserve more study than they have received.

report by two foreign observers upon the perspectives of a small community in Kisii country in Western Kenya in the mid-1950s.[83]

The social universe as Nyansongans see it [they wrote] is made up of units of increasing size and inclusiveness from the family to the nation, all of them referred to by the same term, *egesaku*, and all composed of a group of men who recognize a common patrilineal ancestor and occupy a common territory. *Egesaku* in its most general sense thus means 'lineage', although it can refer to the group of father and sons in a single homestead, a lineage at one of four levels between family and clan, a clan, one of the seven Gusii 'tribes', the Gusii people as a whole as contrasted with other ethnic groups (each one of which is also termed *egasaku*), or a nation such as Kenya, the United Kingdom or the United States. Each unit within the Gusii ethnic group is spoken of as *egesaku* when considered as a separate entity, but when considered as one of several segments of a larger social unit, it is called *enyomba*, 'house'. Thus each social unit is thought of as sub-divided into 'houses', a pattern based explicitly on the polygamous extended family . . .

It was precisely indeed because there were people who could see their socio-political positions in these terms that there were such remarkable positive responses to the larger aggregations which were evolving. Whilst such an outlook did not preclude some concentration upon one particular 'level', if this seemed necessary, it effectively postulated an ever-enlarging series of social universes within which men could perceive themselves. At the same time it recognised that there were distinctions between coexistence and aggregation. An *egesaku* might persist as an *egesaku* (as, given the peculiar heterogeneity of its peoples, Bukedi District in Uganda, for example, saw before independence).[84]

Sometimes the developing process of aggregation would itself provoke opposition from a peripheral group: thus the Sebei insisted that they should be separated from Bugisu District in Uganda,[85] and the Konjo of Mount Ruwenzori, who by the time of Uganda's independence had become bitterly opposed to being incorporated in neighbouring Toro, resorted to arms.[86] An *egesaku* might also, however, turn itself into an *enyomba* – a component part of a larger whole. Since, moreover, the whole concept was explicitly based upon the workings of the polygamous extended family, it encompassed one further feature as well. Gusii recognised that polygamous wives along with their offspring were prone to quarrel. Accordingly they took steps to keep them physically apart. Yet for many operational purposes

[83] Robert A. and Barbara B. LeVine, *Nyansongo: A Gusii Community in Kenya*, New York, 1966, p. 18.

[84] F.G. Burke, *Local Government and Politics in Uganda*, Syracuse, 1964.

[85] Uganda Government, *Exchange of Despatches between His Excellency the Governor and the Secretary of State for the Colonies concerning the Creation of Sebei District*, Entebbe, 1962.

[86] Uganda Government, *Report of the Commission of Inquiry into the Recent Disturbances amongs the Baamba-Bakonjo People of Toro*, Entebbe, 1962; Martin R. Doornbos, 'Kumanyana and Rwenzururu: Two Responses to Ethnic Inequality', in Robert I. Rotberg and Ali A. Mazrui, (eds.) *Protest and Power in Black Africa*, New York, 1970, pp. 1,088 sqq.

they also saw them as being ideally linked together in successive pairs.[87] In this way such an outlook encompassed the tendency towards internal division within a single *egesaku* or *onyomba* – within, that is, any social entity – which (if we may take three examples from Uganda) could be seen, at a parochial level, in the division between Mukirane and the splinter group in Ruwenzori who in 1963 refused to countenance violence,[88] in the division at a district level between the Iseera and the Ngoratok in Teso District,[89] and more generally at the territorial level between Bantu and Nilotic. It was precisely because that way of looking at all these processes was in terms of the replication, at a number of successive levels, of some locally familiar principle[90] that there was both a ready adaptation to the multiple demands of a rapidly changing environment, and so much vehemence, not only about the newly emerging forms of co-operation, but over the new axes of conflict as well.

THE SPREAD OF CHRISTIANITY

The other phenomenon of these years with which the constructive forces seem to have worked was the spread through much of East Africa of Christianity. Although many avowed Christians held on to their old anchorages in pre-existing religious practices, there was surprisingly little syncretism. It looks as if the new religion spread in ways that indigenous cults had ordinarily done; along kinship routes, in response to particular small-group tensions – all much like a bush fire; taking on, moreover, particular local emphases (much as previous cults had, and concurrent ones were still doing). Christianity's diffusion was now, however, on a much larger scale than that of even the most wide-ranging of these other movements, such as the Chwezi cult in southern and western Uganda.[91] If by western standards its local resources might still seem exiguous, in East African terms they were clearly formidable. It was not just that its material resources were larger. Even the smallest of its missionary societies generally possessed a directing strategy of an order that no indigenous cult could

---

[87] LeVine, *Nyansongo*, pp. 67 sqq.

[88] Kirsten Alnaes, 'Songs of the Rwenzururu Rebellion: The Konzo Revolt against the Toro in Western Uganda', in Gulliver (ed.), *Tradition and Transition*, pp. 249, 261.

[89] Uganda Government, *Report of the Commission of Inquiry into the Management of the Teso District Council*, Entebbe, 1958.

[90] The Lugbara of north-western Uganda provide another example. Amongst them, it is reported, '*suru* has the meaning of a group of people who consider themselves and are considered by others to form a group because they share a territory and have ties between them based on common ancestry . . . Thus *suru* refers to major lineages and sections, clans, subclans and subtribes. The term is also used in a wider sense as the *suru* (peoples, tribes) of Madi or Europeans . . .', John Middleton, *The Lugbara of Uganda*, New York, 1965, p .39; while Dr. Anne King tells us that her informants discussed the two World Wars in terms of *Suru germani* and *Suru britishi*.

[91] See Luc de Heusch, *Le Rwanda et la civilisation interlacustre*, Brussels, 1966.

mount. It mobilised, trained, and posted its evangelists in a far more systematic way. It did not, moreover, have to create its own rituals or its own doctrines as most of the cults had to do, for it had its own long-matured stores of tradition to draw upon. In addition, for all the narrowness which some of its expositors displayed, its concern for the human state vis-à-vis both society and the divine could be profound. Its written scriptures for instance provided, as it seems many people found,[92] immense stores of guidance for all sorts of human situations. Furthermore, it displayed a capacity that no cult possessed to comprehend the new world into which so many people were moving at such breakneck speed. In particular it offered a value-system, an ideology, a vision of the true end of man, that could claim to interpret the greatly enlarged frame of existence with which the peoples of East Africa were increasingly forced to come to terms. Given that there was no such indigenous conspectus; that in this period, outside certain restricted areas, it had no substantial competitor; that it was vigorously preached; and that through its associated school-system it provided the main point of entry into the higher-level roles which were rapidly opening up within the developing new order, it is hardly surprising that it attracted large numbers of new adherents.[93]

There were at the same time sustained efforts to develop its African character. If the intellectual and social resistance to its adoption was – by Indian standards for example – inconsiderable, there was soon a keen intellectual and social desire to relate it to African conditions. Nowhere was this more true than in the evangelical revival movement which spread through many of the Protestant churches during this period: it was, for all the alien analogies which might be adduced, emphatically an African movement.[94] More specifically there were some who came to feel that only if they broke with the mission churches and created churches of their own could a satisfactory nexus between the needs of their society and the Christianity they had made their own be secured. The real significance of such men, we may suggest, lay not in their numbers; as compared with those who stayed in the mission churches these have tended to be exaggerated. Rather it was that they were frequently the first to give

---

[92] Barrett, *Schism and Renewal in Africa*, pp. 127 sqq.

[93] On Christianity in East Africa see, e.g., R.A. Oliver, *The Missionary Factor in East Africa*, London, 1952; Lloyd W. Swantz, *Church, Mission, and State Relations in Pre and Post Independent Tanzania 1955–1964*, Program of Eastern African Studies, Syracuse University, Occasional Paper No. 19; Monica Wilson, *Communal Rituals* part 2; J.V. Taylor, *The Growth of the Church in Bugunda*, chs. 12–13, London, 1958, part 2; Edward H. Winter and T.O. Beidelman, 'Tanganyika: A Study of an African Society at National and Local Levels, part 2, Ukaguru: The Local Level', in Steward (ed.), *Contemporary Change*, I, 166–88; Sangree, *Age, Prayer and Politics*, chs. 5–6. On the cults see David J. Parkin, 'Medicine and Men of Influence', *Man*, 3 no. 3 (1968), 424–39, and references there cited.

[94] Max Warren, *Revival: An Enquiry*, London, 1954; Winter and Beidelman, 'Ukaguru', in Steward, *Contemporary Change*, I, 181–2.

expression to the key issues of Africanisation, of African independence, of 'a place of one's own', which the nationalist politicians only took up later.[95] It is arguable indeed that the political developments in East Africa at this time should in a very real sense be seen as no more than the political expression of a larger endeavour which related to men's place in the world generally.

That the cleavage with the mission churches was not more widespread was partly because those who moved into them in the decades immediately preceding independence still found the new experience all-engrossing; while upon other fronts there was probably just enough sensitivity to African proclivities for fresh dispositions – for example the new welcome in the 1950s for the Revival in Uganda, or the consecration of African bishops there and elsewhere – to be made in time.

All these issues were plainly of immense importance. No feature of people's thinking (as revealed by a survey of opinion in the cosmopolitan Buhaya district in north-western Tanzania shortly after independence) seems to have been more substantial than their belief that their 'fate is in the hands of God'.

The local word that is expressing their opinion on this question is *omugisha* – blessing. It has always been a common belief in Buhaya that a human being needs *omugisha* – blessing by the supernatural powers – in order to succeed.

Almost nine out of ten respondents said as much. God might be conceived of in different ways – as the Christians conceived of Him or otherwise. But that the order which He, or at all events one or other manifestation of the divine, had determined was the one with which before all else men had to make their peace seems to have been a view which was widely held.[96]

LEADERS AND THE WELL-BEING OF SOCIETY

In most areas the leadership in the two enterprises we have just considered – the elaboration of larger politico-cultural entities, and the adoption of Christianity – lay with the members of a new elite. They constituted indeed the two chief processes by means of which it evolved. Where there was already a pre-existing elite within a particular society there was sometimes an uneasy relationship with the newcomers: very often, however, the new men were the old elite's sons. Characteristically most of them had been at mission schools and had thereby secured a literary education. They

[95] F.B. Welbourn, *East African Rebels*, London, 1961; F.B. Welbourn and B.A. Ogot, *A Place to Feel at Home*, London, 1966; Sangree, *Age, Prayer and Politics*, ch. 7; Barrett, *Schism and Renewal*; T.O. Ranger, 'The African Churches of Tanzania', *Historical Association of Tanzania*, Paper No. 5 (Nairobi, n.d.).

[96] Hyden, *TANU Yachenga nchi*, p. 215; but see also *inter alia* John Middleton, *Lugbara Religion*, London, 1960.

generally included those who were leaders in the churches – priests, pastors, evangelists, school-teachers. They numbered as well those who entered most warmly into elaborating the new political and cultural institutions, both by entering the district or parochial administration, and by developing new extra-governmental activities, including some secular cultural ones. Most strikingly these men tended to develop a new style of life – in clothes, in house-patterning, in work roles, in their preoccupation with the education of their own and their kindred's children, and in a new sensitivity to extra-parochial, extra-local issues. In Tanganyika such people were widely linked by their common use of Swahili. In many places they were linked as well by their common experience of a particular mission school. By mid-century they were in most areas immediately recognisable as the district elite.[97]

Two features were crucial to their position. First, however distinct they may have become from their rural background, the tendrils by which they were attached to it possessed a quite remarkable elasticity. And secondly in the virtual absence in East Africa of anything which could as yet be called a national elite – of the kind which in many West African countries had long been present – such people had a peculiar special significance not just in their own local areas but, potentially at least, as the source from which those who would take the lead on a yet larger plane would be drawn.

Of vital importance here was the phenomenon of what, if we may adopt the Kikuyu term, we may call the *muthamaki* tradition amongst so many of the peoples of East Africa – the tradition which acknowledged the existence of 'prominent men'.[98] Its foundations lay in the fact that few East African societies had previously had any rigid social stratification. Where there was at the same time little hereditary fostering of specialised skills, there was very often room for men with particular personal skills to prove themselves as leaders and pioneers, more especially vis-à-vis those outside the local society.[99] When, in the first half of the twentieth century, that which was originally right outside the local society came to impinge increasingly upon it, this tradition came to express itself in new terms. Jomo Kenyatta had revealed his own relationship to it back in 1942 when he had published a small pamphlet entitled *My People of Kikuyu and the Life of Chief Wangombe* (a turn-of-the-century Kikuyu *muthamaki*). As the twentieth century advanced there was an efflorescence of this previously established tradition.

[97] Winter and Beidelman, 'Ukaguru', in Steward, *Contemporary Change*, I, *passim*; L.A. Fallers, *The King's Men*, London, 1964, esp. chs. 3 and 4; Middleton, *The Lugbara*, pp. 91–2.

[98] See, e.g. H.E. Lambert, *Kikuyu Social and Political Institutions*, Oxford, 1956, pp. 105–6; Peter Marris and Anthony Somerset, *African Businessmen*, London, 1971, ch. 2.

[99] Such a person was called a 'laiguenan' amongst the Samburu, an 'ntwale' amongst the Nyamwezi, an 'opi' amongst the Lugbara. Spencer, *Samburu*, p. 181; Abrahams in Cohen and Middleton, *From Tribe to Nation*, p. 104; Middleton, *The Lugbara*, pp. 40–1.

That meant both that there were men who felt free to provide leadership for excursions into the new openings which the new century brought to East Africa, and more especially that political leaders with a traditionally legitimized authority were available when the political situation suddenly started, as it did in the less than two decades covered by this chapter, to change very rapidly. In the first category one can name William Nagenda, the Balokole leader from Buganda, Bishop Mathew Ajuoga of the Church of Christ in Africa, Bishop Obadiah Kariuki of the Anglican Church in Kikuyu country, or a Muganda farmer such as Leonard Basudde. In the second one thinks of Hezron Mushenye, Chief of Tiriki; of Tom Mboya, a highly effective trade union leader when he was still in his mid-twenties; of Oginga Odinga with his Luo Thrift and Trading Corporation; of Eridadi Mulira, the Uganda schoolmaster who became a politician and newspaper publisher; and of several of those many who became active in agricultural co-operatives before moving into politics more centrally – George Magezi, for instance, and Felix Onama in Uganda, or Paul Bomani and Nsilo Swai in Tanganyika. In addition to Kenyatta himself one thinks as well of Milton Obote, of Julius Nyerere, and even of that startingly dramatic figure 'Field-Marshal' Okello.[100]

It must be remembered that substantial numbers of the new elite managed to find considerable personal fulfilment from participating in the parochial, district, and Christian arenas into which they moved. Paulo Kavuma for example, sometime Katikiro of Buganda, was no anxious, uncertain, disenchanted man, despite the trauma of his time in that office in the early 1950s. Though the winds of fortune beat upon him, he never lost his inherent composure; and as behoved a long-experienced former chief clerk to the British Resident in Buganda, he was an efficient bureaucrat as well. Always, moreover, a staunch Muganda according to his own personal lights, he remained a man who was calmly proud of the way he believed he had served his people (and he always seemed to fit a western-tailored suit better than anyone else in Uganda). Kosia Shalita stood likewise. Living as bishop in a former missionary's house where he had once been a house-boy, and looking back upon his time as pastor of so many churches at once that only he could be expected to remember their number, he had, in the

---

[100] On Ajuoga see Welbourn and Ogot, *A Place to Feel at Home*; on Mushenye see Sangree, *Age, Prayer and Politics, passim*; on Mboya, see his own *Freedom and After*, London, 1963; on Odinga, his own *Not yet Uhuru*, London, 1967; on Magezi and Onama, see Crawford Young in E.A. Brett and D.G.R. Belshaw, *Public Policy and Land Development in East Africa*, Nairobi, 1972; on Bomani, see Maguire, *Toward 'Uhuru', passim*; on Swai see Anton Nelson, *The Freemen of Meru*, Nairobi, 1969, *passim*; on Obote see Cherry Gertzel, *Party and Locality in Northern Uganda, 1945–1962*, London, 1974; on Nyerere, see Judith Listowel, *The Making of Tanganyika*, London, 1965; on 'Field-Marshal' Okello, see his own *Revolution in Zanzibar*, Nairobi, 1967. Information upon Nagenda, Kariuki, Basudde, and Mulira is from personal recollections. See also Marris and Somerset, *African Businessmen, passim*.

aftermath of a year of study at Wycliffe Hall, Oxford, become the principal Protestant figure in his own and a couple of neighbouring districts in south-western Uganda. As father of a large family he was a much respected figure, unpretentious, active, a reconciler who was always unquestioningly serene in his personal religious faith. There were others like him; the schoolmaster James Aryada, for instance, first of his small tribe (the Samia of the Uganda–Kenya border) to go overseas – again to Oxford, but in his case for a mathematics degree. As compared with that of most of his compatriots his style of life was clearly elitist. His kinship links however were strong. He was at his happiest, moreover, when he had a piece of chalk in his hands and a roomful of boys in front of him. But he also displayed a shrewder knowledge of all levels of school education than anyone else in Uganda, and could talk about them with unassuming authority.[101]

There were men like this not only in Uganda but in the other territories as well. Tribal state, Christian church, and school, all provided for some of those who worked within them both their major commitment and a steady contentment.

So much indeed was this the case that when numbers of other men of lesser serenity saw a threat to the order within which they moved, they tended to react in a highly protective manner; one thinks here of the defiant actions of Kabaka Mutesa II of Buganda through much of the 1950s and 1960s, or of those African clergymen who would have no truck with Africanising their vestments – because they saw here the symbol of a great betrayal – and clung tenaciously to liturgies which by this time, even in the original, were patently archaic. The assured ones may have been a minority. Certainly there were acute conflicts afflicting many a parochial or district situation, both internally and in relation to the colonial government superimposed upon them. The split between the Iseera and Ngoratok in Teso District in northern Uganda is but one example of the first, the Meru land case of the second.[102] What seems so often to have accompanied them was a keen desire to take part in some grouping with a cause to advance, so as to thrust aside the atomizing propensities of the changes which were occurring. In Kamba country in the 1950s even the British administration could mobilize a popularly acceptable movement against sorcery when this became widespread;[103] while as independence neared, not only Legio Maria, the breakaway movement from the Roman Catholic Church in Kenya, but the Kamcape movement in south-western Tanganyika, and a series of movements among the Mijikenda peoples of the Kenyan coast all sought to provide through religious renewal both individual security and

---

[101] Information upon all the examples quoted in this section is from personal recollection.
[102] *Inquiry into . . . Teso District Council*; Nelson, *Freemen of Meru*.
[103] J.C. Nottingham, 'Sorcery among the Akamba in Kenya', *Journal of African Administration*, 11 no. 1 (1959), 2–14.

the renovation of society.[104] The chief appeal at this time of the independent churches was precisely indeed that they offered some people what Welbourn and Ogot have neatly termed 'a place to feel at home'; while the sudden alarm which shot through Kipsigi country on the eve of independence in Kenya exemplified the convulsion that a threat of alienation could effect.[105] Such concerns pervaded the Bataka movement in Buganda in the 1950s, the Luguru rioters in 1955, and the Geita disturbances in 1958.[106] They were close to the centre too of the precipitation towards violence upon the slopes of Mount Ruwenzori in the Rwenzururu movement in the early 1960s, and in Nairobi in the early 1950s,[107] as they were of course to Mau Mau generally. And as Mau Mau – or for that matter the Bataka movement in Buganda – showed, they were especially prevalent where the sense of political, economic, social, and cultural deprivation was most acute. This was particularly the case where, as with the Kikuyu, an enterprising and unhide-bound people constantly found itself being confined to what the regime above it saw to be the norm for Bantu Africans in the first half of the twentieth century – that of a labouring proletariat. Amid the torrent of unco ordinated change, and within the plethora of all these separated movements, there were those whose focus was narrow or who believed that life was concerned with more things than politics. But there were nevertheless increasingly those who saw the chief threat to their individual and social integrity in outside forces – in particular in the persistence of the alien colonial regime in East Africa, most fearfully because it supported the privileged position which the domiciled European population had attained, and the powerful economic hold which the domiciled Asians had secured.

POLITICAL LEVELS AND ARENAS

If ever they were to present an effective challenge to the alien regimes, those Africans who did see the issues in these political terms would have to learn how to influence the various levels of authority in East Africa. They would have to do more: to deploy the assets they accumulated within East Africa at still wider levels if they wished to bring additional pressure to bear upon the Imperial government. At the 'global' level, East African politicians made use of the United Nations forum, most effectively those from Tanganyika for whom access to this level was formally provided through the

104 Audrey Wipper, 'Prophets, Priests and Protests', PhD thesis, University of California, 1968, ch. 5; R.G. Willis, 'Kamcape: An Anti-Sorcery Movement in South-West Tanzania', *Africa*, 38 no. 1 (1968), 1–15.
105 Manners in Steward, *Contemporary Change*, 327–9.
106 *Commission of Inquiry into Civil Disturbances in Buganda in April and May 1949*, Entebbe, 1950; Young and Fosbrooke, *Land and Politics, passim*; Maguire, *Toward 'Uhuru'*, ch. 7.
107 Doornbos in Rotberg and Mazrui, *Protest and Power*, pp. 1,088 sqq.; Rosberg and Nottingham, *Mau Mau*, ch. 7.

Trusteeship Council and its three-yearly Visiting Missions. The 'African' or continental level also had its uses which, after the All African Peoples' Conference of 1958, confounded the myopic belief of many colonial administrators in the political impermeability of territorial frontiers. More immediately important was the 'regional' or inter-territorial level, for which the Pan-African Freedom Movement for East and Central Africa (PAFMECA) was founded in the same year. It faced in two directions. It attempted to represent Eastern Africa as a group within the continental, African arena. But at the same time, like the Imperial government, PAFMECA used its authority to mediate between contenders at a lower level, most notably between the Nationalist and Afro-Shirazi Parties in Zanzibar.[108] It was on the 'territorial' level however – once again in replication of the imperial authority – that African nationalism mainly concentrated. Until the 1950s Africans had been permitted to exercise power only at the still lower levels which we have called 'parochial', and it was here that they acquired their political expertise. Organised nationalism was thereafter the means through which Africans converted the supports which they had accumulated at these subordinate levels into resources which could be staked against the expatriate power-holders at the territorial level. And it was as the hold of the colonial governments relaxed that the territory became increasingly available to Africans as an arena for their own political competitions.

The political processes involved were here, as everywhere, made up of a complex interplay between the needs of societies and the desires of men. East Africa experienced, however, a particular stimulus to this widening of political activity which was perhaps peculiar to the colonial world – namely, an increasingly irreconcilable discrepancy between arenas and levels. The concerns and rivalries, that is, which preoccupied the subject peoples tended to diverge ever more insistently from those political institutions which the colonial power had either ratified or created to deal with them.

It is important to remember that this divergence had been continuous throughout the colonial period, at the parochial level particularly, where every demand for the subdivision of a chiefdom, for the establishment of additional village headmen – or, conversely, for the recognition of a senior chief – was evidence that some Africans at least thought that the existing institutions prejudiced their chances in parochial competition. In success-fully pressing any of these demands a group climbed to a higher political level. Such competitive level-climbing could also occur at the district level, especially where cultural or linguistic discontinuities between groups

[108] PAFMECA began as a regional grouping within the framework of the All African People's' Conference. Its first meeting at Mwanza in Tanganyika in September 1958 was attended by African leaders from Tanganyika, Kenya, Uganda, Zanzibar, and Nyasaland. There were later meetings in Moshi in 1959, in Mbale in 1960, and in Nairobi in 1961. See Richard Cox, *Pan-Africanism in Practice*, London, 1964.

served as symbols of confrontation for the African actors, and justification to their white rulers for the creation of a new district. In this way, as we have seen, the Kalenjin-speaking Sebei peoples of Mount Elgon both came together in a new grouping and secured their own district in order to deny administrative advantage to the Bantu Gisu, more than ten times their number, who by a similar process of aggregation had come to dominate the district which they had formerly shared. To the south of the same mountain, the Bukusu were able to use a much slighter cultural variation from their fellow Bantu-speakers in Kenya's North Nyanza district in order to define a separate district which would ensure for them the more exclusive enjoyment of their large maize revenues. When 'Elgon Nyanza' was created for the Bukusu in 1956, and Sebei District in 1962, two parochial-level aggregations had climbed to the district level.

In these and in similar cases, then, discrepancies between arenas and levels were overcome by adjusting the levels. The terms of formal access to the structures of power were revised, and with them the balance of resources available for competitive activity. To the colonial authorities, such readjustments were consistent both with a philosophical predisposition towards matching the scale of government with what was thought to be the proper scale of African society, and with the maintenance of overall control. They did not affect the fundamental concordat of colonial coexistence by which, in return for acceptance of its monopoly of power at the territorial level, the alien government allowed a degree of autonomy to its native supporters at the lower levels. As long as the political ambitions of African leaders and their followings were focussed primarily upon parochial-level rewards such as chiefships – which often conferred access to district-level power through *ex officio* membership of a district council – or upon the satisfactions available to the district elites, so long did each colonial territory maintain a comparative political stability. This is not to imply that before, say, the 1940s all African social arenas were encapsulated in chiefdom or, at most, district. On the contrary, large numbers of Africans played a part in various other arenas associated with their employment, trade, or religious affiliation, which could extend much further afield, even at times beyond the limits of their colonial territory.[109] But such arenas were only fitfully the scenes of political activity, either because the rewards which they offered were too uncertain to support any structured and enduring competition between Africans themselves, or because – in direct contrast with the situation pertaining at the parochial and district levels – political contests between Africans and the colonial

[109] For instance, the migrant labour experiences of the Rwanda, the Luo or Nyakyusa; or the Kikuyu settlers on Mount Kilimanjaro; or the Somali cattle-traders throughout East Africa; or the independent churches which came in to southern Tanganyika from further south.

authority could not be long sustained, for lack of any mutually accessible set of intermediary political institutions. When one or both of these conditions ceased to apply, the monopoly of the rulers at the territorial level was very soon challenged.

We may identify three historical processes as the collective cause of such a change, in which new political arenas crystallised out of those social arenas which bridged the gap between the local and territorial levels of power, and in so doing critically curtailed the colonial governments' room for readjustment.

The first process, the colonial government's penetration of the myriad localities at the parochial and district levels, was, as we have suggested, greatly accelerated during the 'second colonial occupation'. While the funds and powers transmitted through these levels were greatly increased, their autonomy, never absolute, was further reduced at the parochial level especially. The growing number of agents of improvement, the instructors of every kind, were often insensitive to the moral pressures of local politics; and their goodwill might have to be won by breaking local ranks, especially in those periods when the government was focussing its hopes upon individual 'better farmers'. The chiefs, or at a higher level the white district commissioner or African district secretary-general, were no longer the only keepers of the gates which opened on to other levels; and against the press of traffic the gates could no longer be kept closed.[110]

This situation underlined what was already apparent to many Africans, particularly in Kenya – the failure of what has been called the 'politics of local focus',[111] in which the main prizes had been district-level office whose prime obligations had been to secure a more advantageous allocation of resources from the central government and the curtailment of central powers. It was no accident that the community which leant most heavily upon the central government, the white settlers, was also the most agile in jumping levels, able to influence policy equally in their district councils in the Highlands, in the Standing Finance Committee of Kenya's legislature, or in Britain's House of Lords. By the post-war period, not a few Africans saw clearly that interests which remained tied to local levels were unlikely to be well served, and determined to act accordingly.

The second of the processes which we are considering here was the sharpening during the post-war period of the long-standing rivalry between two groups who were readily identifiable within most of the district elites of

---

110 For a case study of comparable developments in the Southern Rhodesian context, see *Report of the Mangwende Reserve Commission of Enquiry*, Salisbury, 1961, on which is based J.F. Holleman, *Chief, Council and Commissioner*, Assen and London, 1969.

111 J.M. Lonsdale, 'Some Origins of Nationalism in East Africa', *Journal of African History*, 9 no. 1 (1968), 119–46; but see also the discussion of 'fourth-phase political institutions' in D.A. Low, 'Political Parties in Uganda', reprinted in *Buganda in Modern History*, London, 1971, pp. 167–266.

East Africa. On one side were those to whom government officers often referred as the district establishment – the chiefs, the older generation of schoolteachers, the more senior district councillors, many of whom had served in some branch or other of government earlier in their careers. These men's district-level power was in most cases a consequence of their parochial leadership which, in turn, they commonly owed to their formal intermediary role between parochial society and such 'territorial' institutions as the administration, the missionary societies or (as co-operative society officials) the statutory crop-marketing boards. Their rivals were as heterogeneous in origin – younger teachers, independent traders, traditional leadership groups which had since been displaced – and alike only in their shared sense of exclusion from formal power. Some of these men were preoccupied with long-standing parochial-level intrigues. But, increasingly, there was an 'unofficial' district elite whose primary social and economic networks were at the district level – often in the local township – and whose major interest lay in the decisions of the district licensing authority or in the district council's allocation of school building contracts. Some of these men found that district-level power was denied them for lack of a parochial base; such an impasse could be a powerful reason for canvassing the existence of a new 'district tribe', greater than its component chiefdoms.[112] Others managed to secure election to the district council and tacit recognition as the established opposition.

Whether or not they were councillors, the unofficial district elite tended to have a much more pressing interest than did the district establishment in testing the political potential of association with actors in other district arenas, and to be more realistic in their perception of the limitations of local-focus politics. Both dispositions now accentuated the district rivalries from which they had taken their origin. For if, as we have just suggested, the district establishment's power sprang from its members' simultaneous occupation of roles at different levels, then its maintenance required that those levels be kept apart, with intercommunication limited to the official networks which they themselves controlled.[113] But political associations – even those whose membership was circumscribed by the district arena – aspired to become an alternative means of bridging the gap between levels; and political parties thereafter appeared to hold over the district establishments the ultimate threat of closing the gap altogether by compressing the various levels into one nation.

Much of nationalism's inspiration, and certainly the incidence of the

112 As in the case of Luhya, a name coined by district-level opponents of the chiefs of Wanga, Maragoli, Tiriki, and so on, to distinguish the 'district tribe' from its parochial components. See J.M. Lonsdale, 'Political Associations in Western Kenya', in Rotberg and Mazrui (eds.), *Protest and Power*.
113 For a theoretical discussion of this point see F.G. Bailey, *Stratagems and Soils*, Oxford, 1969, pp. 144–82.

nationalist parties' early support, can be traced to the internal district rivalries which ensued. But the nationalisms of East Africa gathered weight and mass as part of a third process. This involved the continuing drama of social change in directions dictated largely by the colonial economies, but with a critical new element. There was a growing awareness by those Africans who were now committed to change, that they were now pressing hard against the limits of that 'improvement' which had previously made change bearable for many and welcome to the few.[114] For an increasing number of people, the aspirations of nationalism filled the gap between expectation and fulfilment which the colonial governments were also striving to bridge through the developmental policies of the second occupation.

The constraints on improvement were apparent to rural producers and urban wage-earners alike. While producer prices did indeed rise almost continuously from the early years of the Second World War until the mid-1950s and many new areas were therefore brought into production, it is nevertheless probable that opportunity ceased to expand for the more ambitious farmers in older centres of production such as Chaggaland or Bugisu or southern Kikuyu. Population pressure made the further extension of a man's holding costly and contentious, if indeed it was still possible. Declining soil fertility or inability to find the capital with which to pay labourers limited the returns from the land which was available. Amongst all classes of producer it seemed possible to detect a rather general sense of unease as they appreciated the likelihood of fundamental changes in the general egalitarian pattern of rural life.[115] Rural opposition to specific government measures – these were based during the 1950s upon the desirability of an increase in social differentiation which was regarded as in any case inevitable – was like an occasional eddy indicative of the much deeper groundswell beneath. But at the same time the growing, in some places clamant, interest in co-operative marketing organisations or in obtaining credit, fertiliser, or technical advice, all of them services supported or provided by government, was a potential political resource of great value to any organisation which promised African control over government's decisions.

In the rapidly growing towns, African distress was more immediate than in most rural areas; workers' discontent reached a peak in the late 1940s, with general strikes in 1947 at Mombasa and along the lines of rail in Tanganyika, when other workers followed the lead given by the Dar es Salaam dockers.[116] More needs to be known about how conditions varied

114 See J. Iliffe, 'The Age of Improvement and Differentiation', in I.N. Kimambo and A.J. Temu (eds.), *A History of Tanzania*, Nairobi, 1969.
115 C.C. Wrigley, *Crops and Wealth in Uganda*, Kampala, 1959, p. 80.
116 J. Iliffe, 'A History of the Dockworkers of Dar es Salaam', *Tanzania Notes and Records*, 71 (1970), 119–48.

for different categories of worker, but all were adversely affected by wartime and post-war price inflation, the pressure of increasing numbers of job-seekers upon a relatively static labour market, and an adequate – in Dar es Salaam's case even a contracting – stock of urban housing. Under some circumstances at least, workers were acting together as a working class. And the 'territorial' political consciousness which this activity projected (save in Uganda where so many African workers were of immigrant origin) was further sharpened by the tendency of strikers' demands to be settled in negotiation with government officials or government-appointed tribunals, rather than with often ineffectual employers' organisations; and in the 1950s by governments' close involvement in the developing machinery of industrial relations.[117]

If the beginnings of a territorial African community could be most visibly detected in the trade unions, the tribal unions which grew alongside them preserved within this community the principle of segmentation.[118] These tribal unions strove to meet all the individual and social hazards of migrant labour – death far from home, the abandoned wife, the unchaste daughter; but also to promote the welfare of the 'tribal' community in education, in employment opportunity, or on the sports field – highly political activities all. Tribal unions were rarely strong organisations; their existence did nevertheless indicate that for some peoples their rural, district, social arenas now substantially encompassed town and plantation as well. And there were two specific elements in the wider environment, aside from the normal differences of opinion over ways to advance social welfare, which demanded that this enlarged social arena should also be a field of political activity. First, the urban authorities tended to regard tribal affiliation as the natural constituency for the representation of resident African opinion. Tribal unions could thus attempt to control access to formal urban office, whether this was membership of a social centre's committee of management or a seat on the municipal council. Secondly, the rivalries which split the district elites were projected on to the urban and even more the national levels by governments' application there of the selection procedures used at the district level. In 1945, for instance, two up-country chiefs were successfully used as intermediaries in a strike at Mombasa.[119] More remarkable was the extent to which African officials were the first representatives of their community at the territorial level. The first three African

[117] For government involvement see Iliffe, 'History', pp. 133–4; Mboya, *Freedom and After*, p. 32. For trade unions more generally, William H. Friedland, *Vula Kamba: The Development of Trade Unions in Tanganyika*, Stanford, 1969; Roger Scott, *The Development of Trade Unions in Uganda*, Nairobi, 1966; and postgraduate theses on the Kenya trade unions at the University of Sussex by R.J. Sandbrook and by Margaret Kiloh.

[118] For these, see David Parkin, *Neighbours and Nationals in an African City Ward*, London, 1969.

[119] Rosberg and Nottingham, *Myth of 'Mau Mau'*, p. 209.

members of the Tanganyika Legislative Council were all chiefs; their counterparts in Uganda were officials of their kingdom or other local governments. And at the inter-territorial level even Kenya, which accorded to chiefs much less importance than its neighbours, sent as one of its first members in the Central Legislative Assembly the Luo chief, Paul Mboya.

The leaders of organised nationalism therefore not only had to move between political levels; in so doing – as many had already learned in the district arenas – they faced direct competition with African officials who had reached up from their generally parochial bases to the territorial level of representation and beyond.[120] In this competition the nationalists – who were recruited rather more often from the unofficial district elites than from the establishments – were handicapped by the discrepancy in size between the political arena and the levels of authority into which it was divided. The arena was the colonial territory, or at least the jointly rural and urban environment which now supported the life of most 'district tribes'. But the decisive institutions of authority remained at the district level, at the disposal of the district establishments. It was not until the late 1950s that direct elections to Legislative Council in all the territories superseded indirect methods of selection based upon the district and eliminated this discrepancy; or rather, with civil servants debarred from party-political activity, reversed it to the nationalists' advantage.[121]

PATTERNS OF NATIONALISM

The relative strengths of local government institutions clearly had an important influence upon the course of nationalism in each of the territories (and, subsequently, upon the character of the post-independence regimes). A scale can be constructed on which Tanganyika's local government system was the least and Uganda's the most strongly developed in the post-war period.[122] Tanganyika's district administrations found it difficult to adjust the elaborate and very personalised native authority system which had been handed down from the time of Sir Donald Cameron's governorship. Where early experiments in conciliar forms were essayed, as in Sukumaland, they were crippled by their complexities. While Tanganyika's start in representative local government had some need of the stimulus provided by the Creech-Jones despatch of 1947, Kenya's district councils could well have served as the model for that despatch, in their representative qualities at least, if not in the extent of their powers. Some of them had been

---

[120] In Tanganyika the government for a time placed some reliance upon a territorial-level convention of chiefs as a counterweight to the nationalist politicians; see below.

[121] For striking examples, see Gertzel, *Northern Uganda, passim*.

[122] For information on local governmental developments see Stanley Dryden, *Local Administration in Tanzania*, Nairobi, 1968; Burke, *Local Government and Politics in Uganda; Report of Local Government Commission of Enquiry*, Nairobi, Govt. Printer, 1967.

inaugurated as early as 1925. Chiefs had been accustomed to sharing these local forums with unofficial councillors right from the start; by the late 1940s many councils had a majority of elected members, a nucleus of experienced men who could serve as paid local government officials, expanding revenues and some power to spend them to local advantage. In Uganda such councils were a somewhat later growth, but they soon overhauled Kenya's in terms of power, largely because the Buganda kingdom's government and Lukiko (council) provided the model to which they all aspired to rise. A brief reference to the careers of three national leaders will serve further to illustrate the differences between the territories.

Paul Bomani's career in Tanganyika provides an outstanding example of the politician's special skill in using the resources of different arenas in order to exercise power at several levels.[123] He helped to organise the Sukuma cotton-growers in their villages and the traders in Mwanza town; he helped to found the co-operative federation which spanned all Sukuma-land and thereby provided one arena for what was formally five districts or forty chiefdoms. His nomination to the Tanganyika Legislative Council in 1954 recognised and reinforced his local position. But peculiar to Tanganyika was the apparent absence of any selection process at the local level prior to Legislative Council nomination and correspondingly, the virtual inability of the administration – save in the exceptional area of Kilimanjaro – to offer any real political prizes at the district level. In consequence, there were no significant mediatory institutions to soften any clash between the Tanganyika African National Union (TANU) when it entered the political arena, and the territorial government. It was already 1960 when local governments which approximated to those in Kenya were set in train in Sukumaland; not only did Bomani as the local Member of Legislative Council advise upon their constitution, but the majority of TANU's candidates, many of them without previous local government experience, were elected unopposed in the wake of the party's landslide victory at the national level.

In western Kenya, by contrast, a whole generation of Luo politicians found local government office more attractive than any prizes offered by the Kenya African Union. Oginga Odinga's early political career, in some ways similar to Bomani's, differed from the Sukuma leader's in having to confront this obstacle.[124] When he first entered Legislative Council in 1957 he did so as the elected representative of the district opposition, victorious over the champion of the district establishment (and Kenya's first African minister), Apolo Ohanga.

123 Maguire, *Toward 'Uhuru'*, *passim*.
124 For Odinga's career, see *Not Yet Uhuru*; B.A. Ogot, 'British Administration in the Central Nyanza District of Kenya, 1900–1960', *Journal of African History*, 4 no. 2 (1963), 249–73; Cherry Gertzel, *The Politics of Independent Kenya*, Nairobi and London, 1970.

Milton Obote's entry to the Uganda legislature later in the same year was
the outcome of a different pattern again.[125] He was the choice of his Lango
District Council, sitting as an electoral college. The Lango council had
already witnessed something like a transfer of power from one establishment generation to the next (to whom they were not infrequently
related), which had emerged as the established opposition with the opening
of a local branch of the Uganda National Congress. During this period the
districts were arenas of much greater consequence than the territory; they
even controlled the appointment of chiefs, a power which, although it was
to be short-lived, was much in excess of any enjoyed by Kenya's African
district councils, let alone Tanganyika's.

It cannot be claimed that these three experiences are to be taken as
archetypes of the relationship between local-level politics and the developing nationalism of their respective territories; there was too wide a variation
between districts in all three territories for that. It is not easy however to
imagine the circumstances of any one of these contests being replicated in
either of the neighbouring territories.

Yet for all the many territorial differences, the politics of East Africa
during the period of growing nationalist opposition to colonial rule did have
one common characteristic. Political allegiance, whether to the territorial
governments or to their opponents, became much more jealous in its
demands upon individuals' thoughts and energies.[126] This was partly
because the political stakes were much higher than before, in that nationalists appeared to offer not only independence but an entirely new way of
life. It was also a direct result of the new interplay between different levels
and arenas, where so much political activity was concerned with exploring
unfamiliar ground or with testing alliances which, perforce, had to be
struck with strangers. Uncertainty naturally bred suspicion of anything
other than total commitment to a political leader and his cause and helped to
give to East Africa's, as perhaps to all nationalisms, much of their forward
impetus.

THE FORMULAE OF PARTNERSHIP

The political field on which in East Africa this rising African consciousness
encountered the general thrust of imperial policy was governed by the local
rules of multi-racialism or partnership. The contest centred upon the
relative degrees of influence which the several racial communities should

---

[125] See Gertzel, *Northern Uganda*, ch. 4.

[126] This applied to Europeans as much as to Africans, as may be seen not only in such a
well-known incident as the reception of Blundell as a traitor by the settlers on his return to
Nairobi after the 1960 Kenya Constitutional Conference, but in the more general
sharpening of animosities in small upcountry communities, largely composed of officials,
between those sympathetic and those opposed to African nationalism.

exercise in government and so, more critically, over the whole social and cultural fabric of existence. Communal fears were in no way diminished by the Imperial government's long refusal to commit itself to any policy on the timing and direction of constitutional change. As a matter of principle British governments, of whatever political hue, were reluctant to interfere in what they felt should be the organic development of a colony. In the affairs of East and Central Africa, the explosive possibilities latent in the divergence between their inherited policies of imperial trusteeship towards Africans and local responsibility for Europeans demanded an abnormal reticence. And Conservative governments, in power from 1951 until after the last of the East African territories achieved independence, had compelling party reasons for imprecisions of statement, as was shown by the growth of the settler lobby after 1959, when equivocation between the 'West African' and 'South African' traditions of policy could no longer be maintained.[127]

It was in this context that the partnership concept was so attractive to British policy-makers. It was flexible and imprecise, as the old doctrine of native paramountcy which it supplanted was not. Partnership could be interpreted either as an end in itself, as, in effect, the preservation of privilege for the European minorities upon whose strategic loyalty and economic dynamism the imperial government placed such reliance; or it could be taken as a means for negotiating the difficult transition to majority rule.[128] If the latter, then in its various stages it might imply the partnership of senior and junior – like the Central African rider and horse; collaboration subsequently between equals; and, finally, an unequal partnership again but with the former roles reversed. The concept and the rhetoric remained the same.[129] But for all its conceptual flexibility, partnership was an artificial political system, responsive less to politicians' rhetoric than to a slide-rule; a slide-rule moreover which measured the communal pressures upon a colonial government to a degree that it would never have done upon an African one.[130] Partnership had, then, two flaws. The first was that the majority of the local Europeans (in Kenya certainly) and virtually all Africans, at least until the later 1950s, took it to be an end which as things turned out it could not be; and the mutual mistrust which this belief engendered compounded the second, which was that as a means for easing the passage of white privilege (and thus of imperial control) its inherent

127 David Goldsworthy, *Colonial Issues in British Politics, 1945–1961*, London, 1971, pp. 306–9, 364–72; Dan Horowitz, 'Attitudes of British Conservatives towards Decolonization in Africa', *African Affairs*, 69 no. 274 (Jan. 1970), 9–26.
128 Cf. W.P. Kirkman, *Unscrambling an Empire*, London, 1966, p. 55.
129 Creech-Jones, 'British Colonial Policy, with particular reference to Africa', p. 180; and compare the discussion on the concurrent concept of administrative partnership in David E. Apter, *The Political Kingdom in Uganda*, Princeton, 1961, pp. 223–4.
130 Cranford Pratt, '"Multi-racialism" and Local Government in Tanganyika', *Race*, 2 (Nov. 1960), 37.

stress upon communal difference and minority interests inhibited the creation of a well-structured successor regime.

For rather more than a decade after the end of the war, the colonial
governments continued to use the perspectives of the social engineer.
Their sequence of priorities was to foster the economic growth which was
needed to underwrite the more equal society in which, in turn, a lasting
political partnership between the races might prosper. They set their face
against any political pressure which appeared to threaten this careful and
always incomplete structure. East African governments regulated the political arena with a force and frequency sanctioned neither by general principle nor by the precedents of British West Africa, where African politicians were but rarely imprisoned and their parties were never banned. In
Kenya, not only was war levied against large sections of the Kikuyu
people, but African political organisations at the national level were outlawed for six years from 1953. In Tanganyika some TANU branches were
closed, and the African Congress was denied registration. In Uganda too,
African parties were banned in the 1940s and again in 1959, and the strong
separatist drive of the kingdom of Buganda was more than once halted.
Government action against immigrant political opinion was rare, and taken
only against individual newspaper editors or owners – Indians who were
too friendly, Europeans who were too rude to Africans.[131]

The racial disparity in these restraints upon political expression reflected
in the late 1940s the official preoccupation with economic development
and, in subsequent years, the difficulties in changing the political arrangements under which continuing European and Asian investment had then
been encouraged. The practice of representative government, as it developed in the British colonial territories, had had two purposes: to secure the
co-operation of the colonial community as a whole and to harness the commercial expertise of specific interest groups; but in East Africa the
economic priorities of the day lent a preponderant weight to the second
objective, and so to the representation of the immigrant minorities. As
representative principles took hold, moreover, so the colonial government's capacity to act authoritatively to determine the rules and rewards of
the political arena at the territorial level was weakened by its need to hold
its own there as a competitor on its own account. The political history of
the 1950s certainly seemed to justify the fears expressed earlier by metropolitan critics, that the conjunction of multi-racialism and representative
government would give to the immigrant communities, as the currently
'senior' partners, additional political resources which would unnecessarily

---

[131] For examples in Kenya, see Felice Carter, 'The Asian Press in Kenya', *East Africa Journal*,
6 no 10, Nairobi, 1969, pp. 30–4, and 'The Kenya Government and the Press, 1906–60',
Hadith, 2, Nairobi, 1970, 243–58; George Bennett and Carl Rosberg, *The Kenyatta
Election: Kenya 1960–1965*, London, 1961, p. 96.

complicate, if not prevent, any future revision of the terms of partnership.[132]

The similar fears entertained by Africans were compounded by the impact of the second colonial occupation. While the Kenya government, for instance, appointed a leading settler to the quasi-ministerial post of Member for Agriculture, it doubted whether Africans were competent even as peasants;[133] such doubts in Tanganyika had argued for the mechanised Groundnut Scheme. It was not until midway through the 1950s that governments began to act on the belief that prosperous African farmers could be raised up as the professional and political partners of the white settlers. Until then the African partners-presumptive had been pre-eminently the agricultural and veterinary assistants and, to a lesser extent, the schoolteachers who graduated from Makerere College. But however much these might participate in the second occupation, especially in the campaign against soil erosion,[134] they did so as the skirmishers of a visibly European army. Although Europeans generally and some Asians were being co-opted into government,[135] Africans were now finding themselves governed as never before.

While a few percipient settlers, even at the peak of their post-war confidence, foresaw that the Imperial government might later regard them as merely the economic midwife for a political revolution in which they would have little place, Africans could not be so certain.[136] Their campaigns to secure firm assurances from London on political advance were launched within the separate territories. But, in contrast to West Africa where British colonies were not contiguous, there was also in East African decolonisation an inter-territorial flow of political currents. This may best be charted by watching the course of what we call the 'symbolic formulae' of multi-racial representation in the colonial legislatures and executives.[137]

The key indicator was the composition of the legislatures, and here there were three basic formulae. There was 'primacy', either European primacy, as when in Kenya and Tanganyika the white unofficials had a clear majority over those of other races, or African primacy in the years immediately

---

[132] As was foreseen by Uganda's wartime governor Sir Charles Dundas: see Apter, *The Political Kingdom*, p. 221 sq.; for criticisms of Creech-Jones' policies on this score, Goldsworthy, *Colonial Issues* pp. 19 sqq., 155 sqq.

[133] M.P.K. Sorrenson, *Land Reform in the Kikuyu Country*, Nairobi, 1967, p. 55.

[134] A condition which seemed to some Europeans proof of peasant incompetence. Robert Chambers, *Settlement Schemes in Tropical Africa*, London, 1969, p. 22.

[135] Most obviously so during the Kenya Emergency, not only at the War Council level but also on the ground, with young white settlers mobilised in the Kenya Regiment or employed as assistant district officers and (with some Asians) in the Police Reserve.

[136] George Bennett, *Kenya: A Political History*, London, 1963, p. 106 sq.

[137] The symbolism of the period extended beyond these formulae into government statements. The sequence in announcing a territory to be 'multi-racial', 'non-racial', 'predominantly African', and 'primarily African' is one example of what Tanganyikan officials referred to as magical cantrips (witches' spells).

preceding independence. There was 'parity', also European or African, when the members from one community balanced the other two (or three in the case of Kenya with its Arab members). And finally there was 'equal representation', briefly in Uganda in the 1940s and in Tanganyika a decade later, when each community had the same number of representatives. These permutations could be modified almost indefinitely by adding in the balance of unofficials on the executive councils or by counting heads among assistant ministers.

After the promise of the late 1940s – with the 1947 Local Government Despatch revealing London's nervous preparedness for a torrent of post-war change – the formulae of representation from the African viewpoint worsened quite perceptibly, until by the early 1950s the terms of partnership appeared to have congealed into a pattern from which Africans might never emerge as the senior. There was a retreat from equal representation in the inter-territorial Legislative Assembly. Governor Twining's proposals for African parity in Tanganyika's legislature were diluted into equal representation. In Uganda Sir John Hall's rhetorical declaration in 1946 that 'Primarily, the development . . . must be by the African, for the African,'[138] (which was based upon the old peasant production), had been superseded by 'partnership', whose virtues were pressed even upon this most 'West African' of the East African territories by the Colonial Secretary, James Griffiths, in 1951. And in the background were the preliminaries of Federation in Central Africa. By 1950, six years after the first African had entered any of the territorial legislatures, there was European parity on the unofficial benches in Kenya and Tanganyika. African parity in Uganda.

The gap between the last two narrowed when, in 1952 and 1954 respectively, Uganda first instituted and Tanganyika enlarged its Executive Council. By comparison with their unchanged legislatures the former retreated, the latter advanced, each to arrive – among the unofficial members of their Executive Councils – at equal representation, 2:2:2 being the formula for balancing the races. Mathematical juggling was relatively simple in these two territories, where all the unofficial legislators were still nominated by the governor. In Kenya, where the settler representatives were elected and experienced, it was quite different, as the Secretary of State discovered in 1951. European parity was at that time secured by the formula 11:4:5:2 for Europeans, Africans, Asians, and Arabs respectively. Following Kenyan African demands, Griffiths agreed to increase African representation to six, while the rift between Muslim and Hindu argued for another Asian member too. But in order to preserve European parity – even though he was careful not to accept this as a permanency – Griffiths

138 Kenneth Ingham, *The Making of Modern Uganda*, London, 1958, p. 228.

increased the unofficial European membership to fourteen;[139] a concession of two to Africans had occasioned a European advance of three. It is small wonder that few Africans trusted the calculus of partnership.[140] In the nationalist view, the terms of partnership would never change unless they were given a jolt and the symbolic formulae unhinged.

TOWARDS A NEW ORDER

The first African jolts were administered not by territorial nationalist movements but in convulsions within two strategic localities which had long been close to crisis – Kikuyuland and Buganda. It is true that at the time of the Kikuyu convulsion there was already in existence in Kenya the most powerful political movement in East Africa, the Kenya African Union, and that it was not confined to Kikuyuland. But the Kenya government was genuinely confused between the identities of KAU and 'Mau Mau', and of one thing it was certain: 'Mau Mau' was a Kikuyu affair. And it was in reaction to 'Mau Mau', not KAU, that Kenya Africans were first admitted to a limited partnership in government. For all his refusal to see 'Mau Mau' as anything other than a reversion to barbarism, the new Conservative Secretary of State, Oliver Lyttelton, saw that African confidence in government was the only alternative there to rule by force; he made it clear moreover that the settlers could not continue to wield sole political power. And so by the terms of the 'Lyttelton constitution' of March 1954 the partnership principle was extended from the legislature to the new Council of Ministers. European parity was retained there in the formula 3:2:1, but that 1 was portentous: the first African in East Africa had a ministerial portfolio.[141]

Two months later, discussions of still greater import opened on Namirembe Hill in Kampala.[142] These aimed at the resolution of the crisis which had blown up in Buganda in the previous year over the kingdom's internal administration and its external relations with the rest of Uganda. Both problems had been amplified by the multi-racial mould prescribed both for Uganda and East Africa as a whole which, so an unguarded remark

139 Statement on Kenya Constitution (Discussions) in *Hansard*, 5th series, H. of C., 488, cc. 408–10, 31 May 1951.
140 A point graphically illustrated in Vicky's *Evening Standard* (London) cartoon 'Bingo!', showing a bemused Kaunda sitting while the figures of Macleod (with his concealed playing-card), Sandys, Welensky, Lords Beaverbrook and Salisbury cavort with their successfully completed cross-racial voting cards during the 1961 negotiations on the Northern Rhodesian constitution: Kenneth Kaunda, *Zambia Shall be Free*, London, 1962, facing p. 91.
141 The importance of the symbolism in the formula is seen clearly in Blundell's account of the negotiations. See *So Rough a Wind*, pp. 144–59, and for Lyttelton's view, Chandos, *Memoirs*, p. 406 sq., and *Hansard*, 5th series, H. of C., 525, cc. 880–5, 22 Mar. 1954.
142 For a full discussion see Low, *Buganda in Modern History*, ch. 4.

by Lyttelton implied, might one day emulate the newly launched Central African Federation. Only after there had been some solid confirmation that Uganda would after all develop as an African state were Buganda's problems resolved, temporarily as it subsequently proved. But the profound difference of view on this point between Uganda's governor and the Colonial Office meant that Lyttelton's assurance, that Uganda's future was to be 'primarily as an African state with proper safeguards for minorities', had to be drawn from him, as his questioner Eirene White put it, 'accidentally by intervention in debate'.[143] Well might the Secretary of State have refrained from including this declaration in his earlier statement on the Kabaka's deportation: it marked the initial breach in the partnership line drawn about East and – ultimately – Central Africa. It remained for the Namirembe conferences to unhinge the symbolic formulae of partnership. By late 1954 it was agreed for Uganda not only to allow an overall African majority in a legislature which still retained a semblance of multi-racial balance on its unofficial benches, but to remove all traces of arithmetical elegance from the unofficial side of the Executive Council. There equal representation was to be supplanted by African primacy with the decisive ratio of 5:1:1.

By early 1956, when these reforms were implemented, the initiative in change had veered back to the region's two ruling minorities, the Zanzibar Arabs and the Europeans in Kenya. During the two years from 1954 influential sections among them, led by Sheikh Ali Muhsin and Michael Blundell respectively, reached the conclusion that their continued survival depended upon their transforming their communities from a closed caste into the elite among a non-racial political class.[144] The Arab initiative was the more determined of the two. It was also, until a month after independence, successful.[145] What is important here is that the Arab Association deliberately abandoned the protection of communal representation under Zanzibar's own version of the multi-racial formula and, in direct opposition to the British constitutional proposals of 1955, went for a common roll. Blundell's much more hesitant steps in the same direction succeeded only in splitting European opinion, but this was a prerequisite for any further political movement;[146] and in the end, his wedge of liberal opinion was to

[143] *Hansard*, 5th series; H. of C., 521, cc. 1268–9, 2 Dec. 1953.

[144] For Blundell's thoughts on the problem see *So Rough a Wind*, pp. 148, 160, 178 especially. See also *Round Table*, (Sept. 1956), 405–8.

[145] Michael F. Lofchie, *Zanzibar, Background to Revolution*, Princeton, 1965, especially pp. 127–80.

[146] As was quickly recognised by the Labour MP, James Johnson, in commenting upon Lyttelton's constitutional proposals. *Hansard*, 5th series, H. of C., 525, c. 884, 22 Mar. 1954. See also Margery Perham, letter to *The Times*, 31 Dec. 1954, reprinted in *Colonial Sequence, 1949 to 1969*, p. 100.

prove Macleod's most valuable lever in the constitutional conference of 1960.[147]

All these developments kept the East African terms of partnership in motion, decisively so in the case of Uganda. They did little to question the continuation of imperial control. The United Nations Visiting Mission of 1954 had suggested a target of 20 to 25 years for Tanganyika's self-government. Nyerere accepted this estimate. While government rejected it in principle, subsequent remarks by the Colonial Secretary left little doubt as to the real objection: the timetable was too short.[148] As it turned out, even the lower of these estimates was cut by two-thirds. For the upward thrust of Tanganyikan nationalism was to coincide with, and provide the first East African test of, a new realism towards the African residue of Empire – now its emotional core – which was forced upon Britain by fresh crises in the eastern Mediterranean.

The Suez invasion of November 1956 was designed to secure very specific western interests in Egypt. But in the minds of the colonial powers, Nasser was also the personification of all the perils immanent in decolonisation. The French joined the invasion to stop up the back door of the Algerian revolution; Belgium's foreign minister foresaw 'a long series of retreats' for the west, the British prime minister feared the reaction of Africa (personified in a Nigerian Muslim chief) 'if Nasser were allowed by the world to seize his spoil and keep it.'[149] Radio Cairo's broadcasts were already the bane of the East African governments; its *Sauti ya Uhuru* (Voice of Freedom) attempted to give the impression of originating from a mobile transmitter in the Mount Kenya forests. And in the background was the fear of a Russian penetration of Africa via Egypt. Had not the 1955 Simonstown Agreement described southern Africa's defences as lying 'not only in Africa but also in the gateways to Africa, namely in the Middle East'?[150] The upshot of the invasion, however, changed all this. Under the thermo-nuclear umbrella, the next year's Defence White Paper sounded the retreat.[151] Compulsory military service in Britain was to be ended within three years, and the strength of the armed forces to be almost halved. Colonial garrisons were to be reduced, even if East Africa was still indicated as a base for the defence of the Persian Gulf. In July 1957 the new prime minister, Harold Macmillan, in some little-noticed passages of a speech at Bedford, talked of the need to accommodate African nationalism in terms

---

147 See Macleod's review of Blundell's memoirs, in 'Blundell's Kenya', *The Spectator*, no. 7082 (20 Mar. 1964), p. 366.
148 *Speech by the Rt. Hon. Alan Lennox-Boyd, . . . at a Luncheon in the Karimjee Hall, Dar es Salaam . . . October 28th 1957*, Government Printer, Dar es Salaam, p. 4.
149 Sir Anthony Eden, *Full Circle*, London, 1960, pp. 458, 443.
150 *Exchange of Letters on Defence Matters between the . . . United Kingdom and the Union of South Africa, June 1955*, Cmd. 9520, July 1955.
151 *Defence, Outline of Future Policy*, Cmnd. 124, Apr. 1957.

very similar to his 'Wind of Change' oration of 1960.[152] It would be wrong to conclude that the British government had decided to relinquish the remainder of its African empire. Not only was the withdrawal from Cyprus a sensitive enough reversal of policy for the moment,[153] but it lent added military importance to Kenya, where the building of barracks for a brigade of the British strategic reserve began in 1958. But Suez did help to crystal-lise a growing acceptance – in Whitehall if not in Africa – of Britain's dim-inishing capacity for guiding the social and economic developments by which colonial policy had hitherto been measured. And in 1955 the East Africa Royal Commission's report[154] had shot away even the economic case from under the privileges of the local guarantors of the imperial inter-est, the Kenya settlers. The official powers of guidance would now have to be harnessed increasingly to the motor of African nationalism – once it had generated sufficient momentum to become not merely a rival but a potential successor to the settlers.

And it was now that Tanganyika, seen conventionally as the territory least well-equipped to fend for itself, began to set the pace. There, TANU's hotly debated decision in January 1958 to contest rather than boycott the forthcoming elections enabled the party to demonstrate that political power took little account of even the most carefully contrived of multi-racial constitutions. The new legislature might have equality of representation, 10:10:10, on its unofficial benches, but almost all the new members, of whatever race, owed their presence to TANU support. The multi-racial United Tanganyika Party was as empty as its Swahili acronym, *utupu*, had proclaimed. Though the assurance seemed revo-lutionary enough at the time, the new governor, Sir Richard Turnbull, was only stating the obvious when in October 1958 he opened the new Council session by declaring that at independence the country's government would be 'predominantly African'.[155] What was genuinely revolutionary was the speed at which Tanganyika now moved towards that goal. TANU's electoral victory was won against the background of European fears of vio-lence, and perhaps some African fears too. At times in Tanganyika, as in comparable periods elsewhere, nationalist elite and colonial government seem to have joined in a tacit defensive alliance against those uncertainties of rapid change by which they, no less than ordinary individuals, were

[152] The speech did later achieve some notoriety, but for a different reason – the first use of the phrase, We (or you) have 'never had it so good'. See Harold Macmillan, *Riding the Storm, 1956–1959*, London, 1971, pp. 350 sqq; and for comparisons between the two speeches, Horowitz, 'Attitudes of British Conservatives', pp. 15 sqq.

[153] Goldsworthy, *Colonial Issues*, pp. 306–16, 365.

[154] *East Africa Royal Commission Report*, chairman Sir Hugh Dow, Cmd. 9475 (London, HMSO, 1955), ch. 17 especially.

[155] *Address by His Excellency the Governor at the Opening of the 34th Session of the Tanganyika Legislative Council on Tuesday, 14th October, 1958*, Govt. Printer, Dar es Salaam, 1958.

beset.[156] In the districts it seemed that TANU's local cadres were strong enough to disrupt the processes of rural administration, but were disturbingly deficient in the disciplines required of a potential party of government. Officials contemplated the possibility of an Emergency with a good deal of pessimism. There were very few police; in contrast to Kenya virtually every tribe would have become involved; it would be like Cyprus, without the Turks. The governor had therefore to act quickly, to help to convert a crumbling colonial order into a stronger nationalist one.[157] Two important elements in former policy and the chief issues of political contention – the multi-racial local councils and vigorous land utilisation schemes – were fundamentally modified, but accelerated constitutional advance was the only political resource now available to augment the authority of TANU over its followers; the Tanganyika government had little option but to put to the test the thesis being increasingly accepted by Blundell in Kenya that the only solid safeguard for the immigrant minorities could be the goodwill of the majority, not the constitutional devices of multi-racialism. It was able to move ahead rapidly since Tanganyika was not split as were both Uganda (between Ganda and non-Ganda) and shortly Kenya as well (between KANU and KADU).

By the middle of 1959 Kenya was isolated.[158] The general position taken at the Chequers conference of January 1959 between the Secretary of State and the East African governors – that nationalism should be subject to imperial restraint for a further decade[159] – had been cut away. Power could not be held for that long in suspense.[160] Tanganyika did not, like Kenya, have its Hola camp or Uganda's trade boycott, or Nyasaland's full-blown Emergency, but the lesson seemed clear; the perils of going too fast were as nothing to the perils of going too slow – even if the Imperial government had a somewhat exaggerated impression of the current fragility of colonial authority.[161] Kenya's isolation was magnified moreover as one looked out beyond East Africa. Ghana had been independent for two years already, Nigeria would be in 1960, and so also would be Somalia on Kenya's

---

156 Cf., Maguire, *Toward 'Uhuru'*, pp. 234, 253–6; and Tom Mboya's article in the *Observer*, (14 Dec. 1958), reprinted in *The Challenge of Nationhood*, London, 1970, p. 38.

157 For a well-informed guide to Turnbull's relations with the nationalists see Judith Listowel, *The Making of Tanganyika*, London, 1965, pp. 340 sqq., 348–57.

158 As was recognised by the Colonial Editor of *The Times* (27 Jan. 1959), in the second of a series of three articles, 'African Nationalism Spreads Apace'. This view he repeated on the following day to a gathering of 250 members of the civil service, the professions, and industry, organised by the Royal African Society: *The Africa of Today and Tomorrow*, London, 1959, p. 26 sq.

159 Chequers conference reported in *The Times*, 26 Jan. 1959, under the headline 'Nationalism sweeps East Africa: Urgent Need for a Colonial Policy'; Blundell's account, *So Rough a Wind*, p. 261 sq., is corroborated in Roy Welensky, *Welensky's 4000 Days*, London, 1964, p. 139.

160 Cf. Margrey Perham, *The Colonial Reckoning*, p. 79 sq.

161 Goldsworthy, *Colonial Issues*, pp. 361 sqq.; Macmillan, *Riding the Storm*, pp. 734, 737.

borders. Still more startling changes in French Africa culminated in a rush of independences in 1960. The Belgians then announced their imminent withdrawal from the Congo; and de Gaulle's determined handling of Algeria demonstrated both the possibility of resolving the problems of settler Africa and the bitter consequences of leaving them until too late. At a deeper level, Britain's economic interests now seemed to depend more upon the future of Europe than of Empire. So, fortified by his election victory in 1959, Macmillan travelled to Africa early in 1960 and reiterated in Accra and Cape Town what he had said three years earlier at Bedford. This time people took notice. Kenya's constitutional conference was already in session at Lancaster House; after a month's negotiation Macleod announced that a new legislature with an African majority would be elected early in 1961, with African 'parity' among the unofficials in the Council of Ministers being obtained with the formula 4:3:1 (the one being an Asian). For all the maintenance of this multi-racial façade – and it was intended to last for some years – it was clear at last that in Kenya the direction now lay towards African predominance. Within weeks of the end of the conference the African deaths at Sharpeville seemed to provide in South Africa tragic confirmation of the alternative.

Tanganyika went on to achieve independence in 1961, Uganda in 1962. Before Kenya's turn came in 1963, the global and territorial levels of British policy had one last opportunity to interact. For the final timing of Kenyatta's release from restriction in August 1961 owed something at least to the British need for political calm around the Kenya base from which troops were then operating to defend imperial interests in the Persian Gulf state of Kuwait.[162] A local nationalism was once again being conciliated in order to preserve a continuing military capability elsewhere; the strategic priorities demonstrated in this case were a clear indication that the imperial camp was about to be struck in this part of Africa. With it went the devices of multi-racialism, whose winding up was made visible in the buying out of many white farmers in Kenya and the offer of British citizenship to Asians. In the British view, if these commitments were the price of disengagement it was not, at the time, expensive. For Africans they marked merely the start of a search for the political, not symbolic, formulae which might foster a new social order.

[162] Patrick Keatley, *The Politics of Partnership*, Harmondsworth, Middlesex, 1963, p. 388 sq.

8

Africa Year 1960

At the beginning of 1960 British newspapers and the British Labour Party dubbed 1960 'Africa Year'. Subsequent events soon justified that description. Perhaps two of them stand out as pre-eminently important: the shooting dead of seventy-eight Africans at Sharpeville and Langa in South Africa in March and the later protracted crisis in the Congo.

The former epitomised for the watching world the tragic issues that had still to be resolved upon the last major battleground for racial equality. Racial discrimination, of course, existed elsewhere; but in no other country was it any longer elevated so purposefully to be the touchstone of national life. Sharpeville turned the meeting of Commonwealth prime ministers in May 1960 into the most electric thus far of the whole series of such meetings that stretched back for half a century and more. It precipitated a clear definition of the Commonwealth as pre-eminently a multi-racial society, and it hastened the departure from the Commonwealth of a member state (and a 'white' one at that) against its own declared wishes after having been a full participant for over half a century. For the world's only close-knit cross-continental club that was an eventuality of major significance.

The crisis in the Congo, which followed its attainment of self-government on 30 June 1960, obviously had even greater repercussions. It precipitated in particular not only the most ambitious political operation ever undertaken up to that date by the United Nations, but the establishment of the growing number of independent African countries as a world political force in their own right.

These events were only the most dramatic of a whole series which in 1960 thrust Africa upon the consciousness of a largely unsuspecting world. Beneath them there subsisted a single common theme.

It needs to be remembered that Africa had at that time a total population of something over 220 millions. Of these less than 15 millions lived in the Union of South Africa. The real centre of interest, therefore, lay to the north where the remaining 200 millions and more lived. At the beginning of 1960 considerably less than half of these lived in non-self-governing African states: by the end of 1960 considerably more than half lived in self-governing nation states. This major transformation was the starting point for Africa's propulsion during 1960 to the centre of the world's stage. It intimately affected, for example, the congeries of developments which surrounded both the Sharpeville incident and the crisis in the Congo. For the attainment of independence in the latter could only be properly understood within the context of (and by contrast with) similar, concurrent, attainments of self-government by numerous other African countries which are near neighbours to it; whilst the Sharpeville incident symbolised the pressures which were piling up in Africa wherever the attempt was being made to dam up the onward swirling waters of African independence. Political independence for Africans – its attainment and its denial – engulfed African affairs in 1960 to a quite tumultuous degree. Why?

In the first place it needs to be recalled that in a number of instances the attainment by African countries of political independence in 1960 had for several years been a pre-arranged and widely-expected conclusion. Somalia, the Italian Trust Territory, and former Italian colony, in the north-eastern horn of Africa, became self-governing on 1 July 1960, in accordance with the mandate which the Italian Government received from the United Nations in 1950 at the end of a long international wrangle about the territory's future. The Italian trustees were then granted ten years in which to complete preparations for Somali independence. They fulfilled their mandate in the letter and the spirit. There were many arguments advanced against the setting of time tables for independence. They deserved to be seriously reconsidered in the light of the Italian achievement in Somalia. For few colonial countries ten years before attaining independence were quite so 'backward' in the possession of embryonic self-governing constitutional, political and administrative instruments, or the local citizens to man them. Yet knowing that there was a bare decade in which to accomplish the allegedly impossible, the Italian administration buckled themselves to their task, and, having within six years held countrywide elections to the first Somali parliament, felt ready in 1956 to grant a measure of autonomy to the first Somali government; with the consequence that, thanks to Italian application, there existed in Somalia at the transfer of power not only a local administration wholly composed of Somalis, but an indigenous parliament, cabinet and structure of government with a modicum of experience behind them. The Italians had, in short, shown that there was nothing to make colonial rulers think and plan more urgently or more perceptively like the fixing of a term to their stay a good way ahead. A very large part of Africa's story in 1960 derived from the myopic failure of other colonial powers to emulate the crystal gazing which the Italians had forced upon them. That is not to say that Somali independence carried with it no problems: Somalia was not economically self-supporting, and its leaders were keenly anxious to wrest from neighbouring Ethiopia Somali-occupied areas which lay within Ethiopian borders – an ambition which Ethiopia plainly indicated she would resist: but the smooth attainment of independence under a long-regulated pro gramme by so backward a country suggests that there was little that was unavoidable about, for instance, the Congo crisis.

The attainment of self-government in 1960 by three other territories, all of them in West Africa, was also in accordance with prearranged plans. Two of these had likewise been Trust Territories, both this time of France. On 1 January 1960, as the herald of so many others to follow, Cameroons, which comprised a large part of the once German colony of Kamerun, became self-governing. It was followed on 27 April by the similar but smaller one-time German colony of Togo. Neither had been incorporated by the French into their large administrative Federations of French West and French Equatorial Africa. Because of the Trust agreements which France held with the United Nations for them they were not subject either to the long persistent French plans for organic connection between their colonial territories and metropolitan France itself. They were accordingly free to tread untrammelled the path to national independence on their own. Neither, however, upon the attainment of independence, was a particularly flourishing country. Cameroons lay in thrall to a civil war in which one faction had control of the Cameroons government, whilst the other enjoyed the patronage of the most active of the self-governing African powers – the United Arab Republic, Ghana and Guinea. As for Togo, which was so small and tribally so artificially compounded that it was obviously in danger of incorporation by more formidable neighbours, within a few weeks of its independence it was the target of some verbal ranging shots upon this very objective by President Nkrumah of neighbouring Ghana. Both Cameroons and Togo thus contributed their meed to the quicksilver of African politics in 1960.

Within six months, however, the fourth planned attainment of self-government in 1960 was accomplished on 1 October in much more promising circumstances when Nigeria joined the ranks of the world's independent nations. Nigeria is the African giant. While Ghana had then a population of no more than five millions, Nigeria had a population variously estimated as between 35 and 40 millions. No African country south of the Sahara had even half that number. If it were to hold together it was securely placed to take the political leadership in Africa. It was constitutionally divided under a Federal regime into three Regions. Each of these had thrown up its own dominant political party and its own distinguished leaders. There was naturally rivalry between them. Yet it then seemed so obviously to Nigeria's advantage to hold together, so as to be able to claim the leadership of the whole continent, that the fissiparous tendencies which it contained had heavy odds against which to contend. Upon the attainment of self-government, moreover, the three powerful regional political movements seemed very neatly dovetailed into the federal structure. The prime minister was Sir Abubaker Tafawa Balewa, the federal leader of the Northern People's Congress, which shared power in the Federal government with the National Council of Nigeria and the Cameroons. The NCNC, which was dominant in the Eastern Region, supplied the head of state too – the governor-general, the veteran Nigerian nationalist leader, Azikiwe; while the Action Group, which was dominant in the Western Region, supplied the Leader of the Federal opposition, whose party shortly before the attainment of independence had once again won the regional elections in the region which surrounded the Federal capital at Lagos. The Nigerian government did not seem to be in any particular hurry to lay claim to the leadership of Africa which its power warranted. That leadership throughout the preceding decade had lain fairly firmly with Ghana and its Dr Nkrumah. The Congo crisis coming so soon before Nigeria's attainment of self-government gave an unbudgeted, last-minute boost to Ghana's leadership in Africa. It was Ghana which represented sub-Saharan Africa amongst the neutralist 'five' that tried to secure a vote in the UN Assembly in September to bring President Eisenhower and Mr Khrushchev together. But as soon as Nigeria wished to assume the purple which Ghana had worn in Africa hitherto, it could probably have shouldered it for the asking. In view of its size and position Nigeria had too as rightful a claim to be heard in the counsels of the Commonwealth as the older members. It was no mean phenomenon that the leading independent power of Africa should now have joined the leading non-communist power of Asia in its inner circle. These happenings alone would have made 1960 a memorable year.

One other major occurrence in Africa in 1960 had also been foreseen – the review of the constitution in the Federation of Rhodesia and Nyasaland. This had been fixed for 1960 in a joint communique issued at the end of talks between the British and Rhodesian governments in 1957. It was then assumed that the review would be primarily directed towards the establishment of Dominion status for a Federation which would be European dominated. In the event that relatively simple formula had to be completely jettisoned, primarily because of the unheralded concourse of events which crowded the African year in 1960.

The expected occurrences in Africa in 1960 were, in all conscience, considerable enough. They were soon almost completely overshadowed, however, by those which had not been widely foreseen. These included not merely such considerable steps as the holding of a referendum for the establishment of a Republic in both the first white and the first black Commonwealth Dominions in Africa – in South Africa and in Ghana – but the collapse of a long-nurtured French policy in west Africa and Madagascar, of a long-nurtured Belgian policy in the Congo, and of a long-nurtured British policy in east and central Africa, as well as the addition to UN membership not just of four but of seventeen new African countries.

The key to this swift and radical concourse of events lay in the main in the destruction of the illusion that any one part of Africa was immune to events elsewhere in the continent. It used to be thought by European colonial administrators that it was possible for them to handle their colonial territories each in their own distinctive way and each at its own distinctive pace. Thus French policy had one set of priorities, Belgian another, British a third, Portuguese a fourth, and so on. It was assumed too that whatever might happen in British West Africa, it could have no immediate impact upon British East, Central or South Africa. Was there not (it was implicitly argued) a whole decade separating the independence of India from the independence of Malaya? Would there not be a similar interval between, say, the independence of Nigeria and the independence of Tanganyika? It was such shibboleths as this which in 1960 were rudely demolished. Events in one corner of the continent had prompt repercussions everywhere else. Africa, in this respect, was shown to be one single whole. There was almost everywhere a burgeoning forth of the more strident African nationalism – in places as widely separated as Basutoland, British Somaliland and French Sudan, to take just three examples almost at random. One precipitating cause was certainly the relatively sudden growth over the immediately preceding years of Pan-African assemblies which drew African leaders from non-self-governing territories into concert with African leaders of independent nations. But in addition to this, it is important to remember that African demands for independence were aggravated in a large number of the still non-self-governing territories by the persistence within them of colonial policies which had become very largely anachronistic; and more particularly that Africa, as the last major preserve of colonial rule, had now attracted the concentrated attention not only of the anti-colonial forces of the Communist, Arab and Asian worlds, but of the western world itself. These now gave their full moral support to the clamant demands of African leaders that Africa's colonial regimes should be liquidated without more ado. In the face of these cumulative pressures three of the four major colonial powers were in no mood to resist. More than one of them had progressively so reduced the timescale for the changes which they thought should precede self-government that they no longer had any satisfactory grounds for holding out against still further reductions. No longer were they as concerned as before with their self-imposed task of nation-building; their prime desire was now to establish friendly post-independence relations with their former colonies; they accordingly vied with each other in displaying a generous spirit, and for this purpose suppressed any latent qualms. The logic behind the former idea, moreover, that countries should attain self-government when they were 'ready' for it was now put to mockery; the succession of countries attaining self-government bore no relation whatsoever to their relative viability. The question in one form or another which Africans all over the continent were now asking was: 'if Ghana (or the Sudan, or Somalia, or Guinea, or Liberia) can have self-government, with a seat in the UN, why cannot we too?' To this there was no final answer. The floods had risen up. The banks had worn thin. Soon the waters poured through.

The *bouleversements* were countless. Even the British, who had often prided themselves on their skill in these matters, were critically affected. In British Somaliland, which was neighbour to (Italian) Somalia, little note was taken until 1958 of the UN mandate to the Italians to grant independence to Somalia in 1960, and it was not until February 1960 that the first elected majority was introduced into the British Somaliland Legislature; yet in May 1960 at a constitutional conference held in London the British government agreed that British Somaliland should become self-governing on 26 June 1960 (five days before Somalia) because the two peoples (as had long been clear) were anxious to amalgamate. This was even more precipitate than the Belgian handover in the Congo.

It was not, however, just the pace of events in 1960 which overturned all previous assumptions. Whole policies were washed away too. The French, to begin with, had always planned to maintain some organic link between their colonial territories and the metropolitan country; their Algerian policy had only been the most extreme example of this. In the immediate post-war period they formulated plans for a French Union incorporating their colonial territories. By the time President de Gaulle came to power this had been officially reconstituted as the French Community; but the essential purpose remained. It looked at one moment as if in sub-Saharan Africa it might triumph. By contrast with British colonial and constitutional practice the French had long had colonial representatives in their own parliament in Paris. For four years before de Gaulle came to power in 1958 one of the vice-premiers in the French governments was an African, M. Houphouet-Boigny, the leader of the powerful Rassamblement Democratique Africain which had a substantial following in several French African territories. Houphouet was a strenuous advocate of the organic link with France, which, given the environment of French colonial and constitutional practice, was no more extraordinary than Nkrumah's advocacy of the Commonwealth. When de Gaulle put this policy to its first serious test in 1958 – when he held the referendum on his accession to power, and gave the African territories the option of enjoying what the British would call 'responsible government' within the Community, or separated independence – only one French African territory, Guinea, out of thirteen chose the latter alternative. Thereafter de Gaulle was assiduous in giving French African leaders an honoured place in France's international relations; four African leaders, for instance, became in 1959 Ministers Advisory to the French delegation to the United Nations.

But in 1960 the whole project for organic links between France and its African territories collapsed. African leaders in power as Premiers of their territories saw no good reason to curtail their independence. The French failure to resolve the Algerian war undermined African confidence. Guinea's success in strutting across the world's stage once it had severed its links with France, Ghana's self-confident nationhood, the prospect of the Cameroons, Togo, Nigeria and the Belgian Congo securing independence in 1960 all proved to be too beguiling. The world's predilection for self-governing nation-states proved too powerful for French Africans, even Houphouet, to withstand for very long. In a speech at Dakar in December 1959 President de Gaulle gave evidence of his awareness of the coming change. The only hope now for France was to seek the establishment of a transformed French Community on the model of the British Commonwealth. Immediate incorporation in such a creation was the wish to those in the Mali Federation in West Africa and in Madagascar who at the beginning of 1960 were the first to slip loose. In April 1960 the necessary constitutional instruments with France were signed. Both states became self-governing in June, Mali on 20 June, Malagasy (as Madagascar was renamed) on 26 June. By that time the four territories of French Equatorial Africa and Mauretania in French West Africa had decided to follow suit, and the four remaining territories of French West Africa, momentarily caught out on a limb, then decided to go one better and demanded that they be granted independence in advance of any commitment to joining the Community. These four became self-governing in August, Dahomey on the 1st, Niger on the 3rd, Upper Volta on the 5th, Ivory Coast on the 7th; they were followed by the Equatorial territories, Chad on 11 August, Central African Republic on the 13th, Congo (the French Congo, that is) on the 15th and Gabon on the 17th. The last of the series, Mauretania, followed in November.

It was these events which caused the sudden fragmentation of this part of Africa. For the assumption in French Africa from 1956 onwards was that internal political authority would be devolved upon the 13 different territories of French Africa, and that since they would maintain organic links with metropolitan France, the former Federations of French West (eight territories) and French Equatorial Africa (four territories; Madagascar alone lay on its own) could be allowed to be whittled down to the bone.

In consequence the French and French Africans never steeled themselves to create something comparable to the British West African Federation of Nigeria. But in 1960 the organic links with France were broken so that there only remained the former constituent French African territories, now elevated to be nation states on their own. There were three attempts to check this result, but each of them failed. The Mali Federation of French West Africa, formed in 1959, originally consisted of Senegal, French Sudan, Upper Volta and Dahomey. Ivory Coast soon procured the secession of the last two, and with them and French Niger established the Conseil de l'Entente. This, however, never developed into a constitutional union; while shortly after the truncated Mali Federation attained independence it split (as a result of a quarrel between its leaders) into its two component parts, French Sudan reserving to itself the Mali name, Senegal procuring independence on its own. Meanwhile the four territories of French Equatorial Africa first discussed the possibility of a customs union and then of a Union of Central African Republics. But Gabon, the richest though the smallest, refused to join the Union. French Congo was soon preoccupied by the proximity of untoward events in the former Belgian Congo and, by the time independence was upon them, no effective union had been created. It was these events which, by making out of French Africa not three or four but thirteen independent nations, gave the African bloc in the UN the extra ten seats which made it the largest single bloc in the organisation.

If French plans for their African colonies had to be radically transformed during 1960, two successive Belgian plans were destroyed in as many years. It had always been the Belgian assumption that if they placed sufficient emphasis upon social and economic development, political upheaval could be postponed. They certainly did more to create an African artisan class than any other colonial power in Africa, primarily because by contrast with West Africa there was no long-standing economic contact with Europe, while by contrast with East Africa there were no Asiatics and by contrast with South Africa too few Europeans. So consistent was their policy of holding down precipitate political advancement that they restricted the political rights of the Europeans in the Congo hardly less than those of Africans. But in view of events in British West Africa and then more especially in view of the establishment of African territorial governments in neighbouring French Africa, it was abundantly clear by the end of 1958 that Belgian policy would have to undergo a radical transformation. Near the mouth of the Congo river, for instance, some members of the Bakongo tribe in French Congo now enjoyed local autonomy; it would have been impossible to deny this for very much longer to the members of the same Bakongo tribe within the Belgian Congo without using force. At this point it is of first importance to recall Belgium's position in Europe, with France to the south and Holland to the north. For both of these neighbours had faced similar situations elsewhere and the Belgians had seen both of them suffer in a manner which they did not wish to see repeated on themselves. Fundamentally Belgian policy during 1959 was to avoid in their relations with the Congo a French–Algerian situation on the one hand and a Dutch–Indonesian situation on the other. They wished to establish a Belgo–Congolese Community of a Commonwealth type on the British–Indian, British Ghanian model. The Belgians eventually concluded, however, that such was Congolese estrangement (aggravated as it was by Congolese political inexperience) that nothing short of precipitate independence had any chance of winning for them any accord with the Congolese politicians. As a result the Belgian Government agreed in February 1960 to grant independence to the Congo on 30 June 1960. Had their hope of thus creating a mutually acceptable Belgo–Congolese Community been fulfilled, the subsequent crisis in the Congo which faced the United Nations need never have occurred. The world now knows that the hope was not justified. But wishful thinking, unfortunately, had long been the bane of capricorn Africa.

Throughout the preceding decade it dominated official British thinking about British East and Central Africa. In 1951 a British Labour Colonial Secretary spoke in Uganda about 'partnership' as the official British policy for this as well as other British territories in the region. The idea in origin was, no doubt, noble; it suggested that men of different races should co-operate in partnership. But as it came to be translated into constitutional formulations it generally displayed one fatal flaw, for in practice it was used in defence of constitutional expedients designed to give non-African minorities in these territories a political preponderance which their small numbers did nothing to justify. In the end it probably did serious harm to such contrivances, for it provoked a cynical edge to African protests against them. Except in one last but critical instance – the Federal constitution of Rhodesia and Nyasaland – 'partnership' was relegated in 1960 to the limbo of lost causes along with French plans for organic union and Belgian plans for a Belgo–Congolese Community.

The *coup de grace*, as it chanced, was given by Harold Macmillan, the British Prime Minister, himself. 'The winds of change', he said in his justly famous speech in Cape Town in February, 'are blowing through Africa'. This statement had an immediate impact upon the Commonwealth, the Conservative Party in Britain, and on the Union. It was no coincidence that the Sharpeville episode followed a month later. Mr Macmillan's words about creating a society 'in which individual merit and individual merit alone, is the criterion for a man's advancement, whether political or economic' were translated along with the rest of his speech into numbers of South African languages. But it needs to be remembered too that these words were of no less immediate significance to the British territories further north. They allowed the British colonial secretary Macleod, at a constitutional conference in February to break the coalition between the Kenya Government and the Kenya Europeans which for several years had dominated events in Kenya, and so open the way to African domination of the country's government. They enabled him to repeat the performance for Nyasaland in July, and for Northern Rhodesia thereafterwards. Both Tanganyika and Uganda had already circumvented the old formulation of the 'partnership' doctrine: the former when Julius Nyerere, the leader of the Tanganyikan African National Union, discovered that the particular constitutional formulation of the partnership doctrine in Tanganyika was not so loaded against Africans as elsewhere, won the elections of 1958, and emerged as the dominant leader of an allegedly partnership framed legislature; the latter when the 'Wild' constitutional committee of 1959 broke with impunity its restricted terms of reference on the establishment of a common roll with special safeguards for minorities. After Macmillan's speech in Cape Town Tanganyika and Uganda once more found themselves back within the ranks of the orthodox, for partnership in its initial formulation had disappeared. With the Congo to the west, Somalia to the north, and Malagasy to the east – all shortly independent African nations – this was only just in time. Tanganyika bid fair, under Nyerere's leadership, to secure self-government shortly amid an aura of friendliness. Kenya and Uganda would no doubt follow, though each was plagued, to an extent that Tanganyika was not, by deep political divisions among its African populations. The question for them was not whether they would before long become self-governing; it was rather the *locus* of power when they did.

Immediately to the north of the capricorn line the colonial demise was thus by the end of 1960 virtually complete. Southwards there remained five bewildering situations. First there was the undetermined future of the three British Protectorates – Bechuanaland, Basutoland, and Swaziland. Embryonic self-governing institutions were being introduced in all three, but their future awaited the resolution of the fate of their neighbours. Secondly, there was the question of the status of South-west Africa; the Union's persistent refusal to transform its mandate from the League of Nations into a trust agreement with the United Nations continued to provide a legalistic basis for its continued refusal to countenance any external interference with its regime there. Thirdly there was the situation in the Union itself; it seemed at the end of 1960 that the position there would become even more forbidding before it could improve, and that the next critical occurrence would not be so much its possible expulsion from the Commonwealth, as the establishment of a South African Government-in-exile on the Algerian (one almost might say the de Gaullist) model. (That, however, did not occur.) Fourthly, there were the Portuguese territories of Angola, Mozambique and Guinea Bissau. Officially they were part and parcel of metropolitan Portugal. There were, however, well authenticated reports from them of troop movements and even of massacres of dissidents. The Portuguese had apparently decided not to emulate the Belgians and quit. They still, after all, occupied Goa; yet Goa was far smaller (and its population far more assimilated) than any of the territories in Africa. There seemed here the makings of Congo crises worse than the Congo's.

Lastly there was the Federation of Rhodesia and Nyasaland. It was the scene of the head-on collision of two classic British colonial policies. Under the one, political power was granted to white colonists despite the paucity of their numbers; under the other, political power was transferred to the indigenous peoples, despite their inexperience in handling British constitutional instruments. Events elsewhere in Africa suggested that here too the eventual outcome could not be in doubt. The African majority would be content with nothing less than their own nation state, or nation states. Nothing short of that had prevailed anywhere else in Africa. There was nothing to suggest that Africans even in Southern Rhodesia would be satisfied unless it prevailed there. It used to be suggested that Southern Rhodesia, the European stronghold in Central Africa, which claimed sixty years of freedom from racial violence, might be immune to changes accruing elsewhere, but riots in Salisbury and Buluwayo after the middle of the year put paid to that illusion. In October the Monckton Commission, in its published report, recommended a series of reforms which, given the tenor of previous official British and Rhodesian policies in Central Africa, were little short of revolutionary. However, the only fundamental question which remained in the Rhodesias was whether the transition from European dominance to African control would be smooth, and the outcome free from tragedy. Already by the end of 1960 the rule of colonial powers in Africa was virtually over. That left the citadels of colonist domination – in Algeria, in the Portuguese territories, in the Rhodesias, in the Union – perilously isolated.

9

The end of the British Empire in Africa

Domino theories have been much in issue, and much in dispute, in the post-Second World War history of Southeast Asia. They seem decidedly applicable to the post-Second World War history of tropical Africa. As was well understood, there were in Africa various territorial differences of some magnitude. There were differences too between the policies of its different imperial powers and, indeed, between the policies of the same imperial power in different parts of Africa. But, aside from the partial exception of Egypt and the clear exception of Algeria, there were, in broad terms, three successive sequences to the independence of Africa outside the Union of South Africa, and domino theories were applicable to all three of them.

The first sequence extended from the independence of Libya in 1951, through the final withdrawal of British troops from Egypt in 1955, to independence for Morocco, Tunisia, and the Sudan in 1956. Algeria's exclusion from this first sequence precipitated one of the two colonial wars[1] of the first two sequences; but, apart from Algeria, by the mid-1950s all of North Africa had as a consequence become independent. It was widely anticipated that if there were to be further chain reactions in the attainment of African independence, there would be upwards of at least half a dozen of them. There were in fact just two. The more extensive one (the second of the three sequences) involved the precipitate fall of a whole string of colonial regimes right across the middle of tropical Africa – thirty of them all told – in one quite unexpected collapse. The other, mostly in South-Central Africa, was then delayed for a decade or more, but eventually overtook four territories that had escaped the earlier onrush. It is on these last two sequences that we shall focus in this chapter, and more especially on the British involvement in them.

[1] Mau Mau was the other.

The violence that accompanied the third sequence, in South-Central Africa, surprised hardly anyone. Everyone, however, was surprised by the speed and extent of the second. At the end of World War II it would have been a bold prophet who would have forecast the precipitancy with which so much of tropical Africa was to win independence in the course of the second sequence. As the war ended the British would very shortly transfer power in all of South Asia, while the Dutch were soon to be chased out of Indonesia and the French from Indochina. But in one way or other the nationalist movements in all these countries had had a history that stretched back continuously to at least the opening of the century, and in each case, despite their variations, there was a long-fought and often bitter struggle.[2] Resistance movements had reared their heads in Africa, and nationalist aspirations had certainly in some people's minds come to the surface. But with few exceptions there were as yet next to no specifically nationalist movements in most of tropical Africa's many colonial territories as the Second World War drew to a close, and certainly no expectation in their colonial masters' minds that independence for any of them might be an early eventuality.

Nevertheless, the three major imperial powers across the tropical African midriff, Britain, France, and Belgium, had each been learning some crucial lessons in Asia. They knew that nationalism could erupt suddenly, forcefully, and disconcertingly, so they each gave their minds in the postwar years to how they could fend off such eruptions in Africa.

The British, as represented by their Colonial Office, sought to fashion the most elaborate mechanisms to these ends. Under the leadership of the Labour secretary of state for the colonies, Arthur Creech-Jones (1946–1950), and impelled by the nervous energy of the head of its African branch, the young Andrew Cohen, the Colonial Office evolved one general set of British policies for Africa and then one specific set, which it believed would enable it to guide its colonial territories and prepare them for an ultimate independence without the kind of trauma the British and others had variously but usually encountered in Asia. Britain's ultimate commitment was to 'responsible self-government . . . a goal towards which His Majesty's Government will assist them with all the means in their power'. It was characteristic of the British that while they often gave their minds to bringing or holding together in federations several groups of territories, they always held to the notion of the separated independence of the entities they ruled from Britain itself, while always allowing for some continued relationship within the Commonwealth. They never contemplated – except oddly at one time as regards Malta – any direct involvement by their

[2] D.A. Low, 'The Asian Mirror to Tropical Africa's Independence', in Prosser Gifford and Wm. Roger Louis (eds.), *The Transfer of Power in Africa: Decolonization 1840–1960*, New Haven, 1982, pp. 1–30.

colonies in Britain's own institutions in London. The Colonial Office was thus clear in the post-war years that independence would sometime eventually come to each of the territories for which it held responsibility, and quite unusually (but not uniquely, as we shall see), it accordingly set about seeking to prepare for this.

Since there was now in Britain both a commitment to establishing the welfare state and some awareness of the debilitating effects of the depression and the war upon the colonies, so it was also now British policy, as the Labour colonial secretary put it in 1946, 'to develop the Colonies and all their resources so as to enable their people speedily and substantially to improve their economic and social conditions'.

Thus there was to be a sustained programme of colonial development, covering agriculture, transport, education, and much else besides. At the same time universities were to be started, within which an elite would be developed to provide enlightened educated leadership for the future. Then in a striking about face it was planned to supersede the former British dependence upon collaborating chiefs – as expressed in the principal British African colonial policy of indirect rule – by the development of an 'efficient and democratic system of local government'. There were four purposes in mind here. First, to secure more developmentally oriented instruments of native administration than were provided by traditional chiefs. Second, to develop the basic building blocks for a new governmental system built up from below which, through a sequence of indirect elections by lower elected bodies, would lead on to the construction of higher legislative and executive bodies. Third, by this means in particular to compel prospective nationalist politicians to go out and compete with local worthies and win their political laurels close to the mass of their countrymen. It was hoped that nationalist politicians would thereby be deflected from operating at the national level only. Their co-operation was at the same time to be actively sought. And then, fourth, by such means it was planned to sow democratic traditions in African minds. Additionally, the long-standing British commitment to a steady progression from Crown Colony status to representative government to responsible government and finally to Dominion status and independence was to be very significantly replaced by a much more flexible, and numerous, series of possible constitutional changes that would avoid the sharp disjunctures between elected legislatures and official executives, as well as the rigidities and delays that had characterised the old progression. These distinct yet co-ordinated positions were then variously embodied in Britain's successive Colonial Development and Welfare acts (1945, 1950, 1955), in Creech-Jones's notable Local Government dispatch of February 1947, in the Caine–Cohen Report on African Policy of May 1947, and in the discussions at the African Governors' Conference at Queens' College, Cambridge, in

August 1947 (where several of these positions met a frosty reception from some of Britain's most senior African governors).[3]

But if all this now composed Britain's more general policy in Africa, there was a further, specific one as well. For in the British mind there was a fairly sharp distinction between those African colonies, largely in West Africa, where there were no European settlers, and those, in Central and East Africa, where since the beginning of the century numbers of European settler immigrants had made their homes. Here by the Second World War there had been a persistent confrontation between settler politicians and the Colonial Office. The settlers had long sought for an assurance that they would in due course enjoy as much self-government as their fellow European settlers in, for example, Australia, New Zealand, and South Africa. The Colonial Office, subject to a great deal of missionary and British liberal influence, insisted that, notwithstanding those precedents, where there was an African majority (as there invariably was here), African interests and not European settler interests had to remain 'paramount'. In Southern Rhodesia, where the South African Act of Union of 1910 had allowed the alternative prospect of incorporation into South Africa, the Europeans had won full internal responsible government for themselves in 1923. Elsewhere, particularly in Northern Rhodesia and Kenya, the settlers, while rigorously denied this right, nevertheless steadily advanced their positions, especially during the Second World War.[4] But then as South Africa swung sharply toward Afrikaaner nationalism and apartheid following the elections in 1948, the Colonial Office became increasingly fearful that without some new moves on their part, the influence of South Africa – already important for the economies of the two Rhodesias – would soon spread north much more powerfully than before and blow all the bulwarks supporting African 'paramountcy' disastrously asunder.[5] (Following South Africa's plans for a 'pax Pretoriana' in the 1970s and 1980s, that possibility looks a good deal less fanciful than it seemed to many critics of British policy in the 1950s and 1960s).

Out of these concerns there evolved in the Colonial Office mind the

---

[3] The literature on all this is growing, e.g., Robert D. Pearce, *The Turning Point in Africa: Decolonization Policy, 1938–1948*, London, 1982; Ronald Robinson, 'Sir Andrew Cohen: Proconsul of African Nationalism (1909–1968)', in L.H. Gann and Peter Duignan (eds.), *African Proconsuls, European Governors in Africa*, New York, 1978. For a contemporary, pithy, authoritative summary, see Arthur Creech-Jones, 'British Colonial Policy with Particular Reference to Africa', *International Affairs*, 27 (April, 1951), 176–83.

[4] See still W.K. Hancock, *Survey of British Commonwealth Affairs*, vol. 2, *Problems of Economic Policy, 1918–1939*, part 2, London, 1942, pp. 90–127. Also Ronald Robinson, 'The Moral Disarmament of African Empire, 1914–1918', in Norman Hillmer and Philip Wigley (eds.), *The First British Commonwealth*, London, 1980, pp. 86–104.

[5] There are some interesting details on this in Brian Lapping, *End of Empire*, London, 1985, pp. 460–3.

proposition that the right way for British policy to proceed in East and Central Africa would not be to try to hold to the old policy of 'paramountcy' but to develop the new policy of 'partnership' between the races, so as to create 'multi-racial' societies there and thus obviate the spread of South African influence and apartheid northward by obfuscating the issue of racial rivalry, indeed of conflict, over the local distribution of political power. The partnership doctrine could be – and indeed was – extensively propagated as a noble ideal. It enjoyed the support of an old war horse of 'paramountcy', J.H. Oldham, and from 1949 onward was ideologically fostered by Colonel David Stirling's Capricorn Africa Society.[6] It was at first, moreover, at least as assiduously propounded by Britain's Labour government before 1951 as by its Conservative successor thereafter. On 13 December 1950, for example, Creech-Jones's successor as Labour colonial secretary, James Griffiths, appealed to all concerned, in a major statement on British policy in East Africa, 'to work together towards that goal of true partnership on which the future prosperity and happiness of all in East Africa must depend'.[7] Thereafter the formal policy of partnership found hugely complex expression in all those racial formulas for the composition of legislatures and executives with which Britain's Eastern- and Central-African territories came to be plagued during the 1950s and early 1960s.[8] In its idealist form it lent respectability – in much of Britain at least – to the major creation in 1953, initially with Labour-party support, of the settler-dominated Federation of Rhodesia and Nyasaland, as well as to some people's hopes of a similar federation in East Africa too. In the British mind the application of 'partnership' doctrines clearly distinguished East and Central Africa from British West Africa. To the settlers it was acceptable as an alternative to the South African Afrikaaner's doctrine of apartheid, because (as the Federation's first prime minister bluntly described it) it entailed the partnership of European rider and African horse.

Indeed, so confident did the settlers now become that in the partnership doctrine they had in their hands an up-to-date justification for their claims to Dominion status, and so committed did the new Conservative government after 1951 become to it, that in 1957 the two governments jointly agreed not only to reduce the remaining curbs on the Federation's independence but also to bring forward by three years, to 1960, the decennial constitutional-review conference (that was already agreed),

[6] J.H. Oldham, *New Hope in Africa*, London, 1955.
[7] 'Statement about Colonial Territories in East Africa', 13 December 1950, *Hansard* (Commons) 1950–1951, vol. 482, cols. 1174–5; see also David Goldsworthy, *Colonial Issues in British Politics, 1945–1961*, Oxford, 1971, pp. 214–30, and Creech-Jones, 'British Colonial Policy'.
[8] D.A. Low and Alison Smith, *History of East Africa*, vol. 3, Oxford, 1976, app. 2.

which it was widely understood would lead to the white-dominated Federation's full independence.[9]

The British were not alone in the deliberateness of their African policies following 1945. French policy for tropical Africa after the Second War was no less carefully fashioned. France committed itself as Britain did to a programme of colonial economic development on an extensive scale. It set its face unequivocally, however, as the Brazzaville Conference in January and February of 1944 put it, against 'any idea of autonomy or any possibility of evolution outside the block of the French Empire, or self-government even in the distant future'. There were all the same to be representative assemblies in each of France's colonial territories as well as in its two federations, French West Africa and French Equatorial Africa. In total contrast to the stance of the British, there was also to be increased African representation in France's own National Assembly in Paris, and much more extensive representation after 1946 in the assembly of the new 'French Union'. France's formal commitment to the processes of elite assimilation to, and intimate association with, France itself now indeed became marked, and despite their experience in Indochina the French believed that these contained all the ingredients needed to hold rampant colonial independence movements at bay.[10]

The Belgians' position was meanwhile simplicity itself. Like the two other imperial powers, they were strongly committed to programmes of economic development and social welfare in their African colony of the Belgian Congo. But far from seeking to assimilate the Congo's emerging elite to Belgium's own society, the Belgians believed that the most efficacious way to check the propensity of colonial peoples to espouse anti-imperialism was in the first place to do nothing to facilitate the growth of a westernised colonial elite; in the second, to make anything that even verged on nationalist politics in their colony impossible to conduct; and in the third, to preclude even their local colonial whites from mounting any specifically political activity. They believed arrantly that along these lines they could endlessly outlaw the colonial anti-imperialism that had so invariably erupted against their much less perspicacious fellow imperialists.[11]

The central development right across the tropical-African belt in the 1950s and early 1960s was, however, that *all* these prescriptions were abruptly blown away. African nationalism proved to be no respecter either of the distinction the British sought to draw between British West and

[9] Robert Blake, *A History of Rhodesia*, London, 1977, chs. 20–3; R.I. Rotberg, *The Rise of Nationalism in Central Africa*, Cambridge, Mass., 1965, chs. 9–10.

[10] See e.g., Elikia M'Bokolo, 'French Colonial Policy in Equatorial Africa in the 1940s and 1950s', in Gifford and Louis (eds.), *Transfer of Power*, pp. 190–200.

[11] Jean Stengers, 'Precipitious Decolonization: The Case of the Belgian Congo', in Gifford and Louis (eds.), *Transfer of Power*, pp. 305–18.

British East and Central Africa or of the distinction the French drew between their tropical-African colonies and the British ones, let alone the distinction the Belgians drew between their colony and every other one.

The onset of this whirlwind needs little reiteration. It was first precipitated in the British colony of the Gold Coast. There in 1947 the United Gold Coast Convention was formed, with Kwame Nkrumah (lately returned from studies in America and a sojourn in Britain) as its paid secretary. The critical event took place in February 1948 when an outbreak of rioting, in Accra and elsewhere, left twenty-nine dead. Before the kind of pressure this represented, Britain's Labour government was now quite deliberately and regularly bending elsewhere (not least in the Middle East at the instance of its formidable foreign secretary, Ernest Bevin), and it now did so in West Africa too.[12] Propelled, moreover, in the Colonial Office by the influential Andrew Cohen (now suddenly anxious that Britain's wider reforms in Africa stood at risk), the British thereupon took the crucial decision to step ahead in both the Gold Coast and Nigeria, lest they should fatally lose the initiative (as they saw it) to West Africa's nationalists. 'The most important thing' (so Britain's chief secretary in Nigeria, Sir Hugh Foot, propounded it) 'is to take and hold the initiative [and] not to allow frustration to set in'.[13] As it happened, Nkrumah and the Gold Coast's radicals were not to be easily assuaged. In 1949 he and his followers formed their breakaway Convention Peoples Party and in January 1950 embarked on a campaign of 'positive action' for 'self-government now'. Strikes and violence and looting ensued. A state of emergency was declared, and arrests, of Nkrumah in particular, quickly followed. But elections were then held in 1951, which the CPP quite handsomely won.

A new governor, Arden-Clarke, who had lately served in Sarawak amid the nationalist maelstrom of Southeast Asia, thereupon released Nkrumah from jail to become without delay the Gold Coast's Leader of Government Business. Britain's timetable in the colony was thereby substantially speeded up. But it was not yet blown away. Further elections came to be held in 1954; and when it then transpired that there was a good deal of opposition to the CPP from the principally Ashanti-supported National Liberation Movement, the British insisted on a third election in 1956. The CPP, however, won this too, and short of turning about, which the British were not minded to do, independence for the Gold Coast could no longer be denied. Independence came in 1957, when its name was changed to Ghana. Britain thereby secured the rewards it had been seeking – no further open conflict with West African nationalism; wide recognition of Britain's

---

[12] Wm. Roger Louis, *The British Empire in the Middle East*, Oxford, 1984.

[13] Sir Hugh Foot, *A Start in Freedom*, London, 1964, p. 106. Again there are some interesting details in Lapping, *End of Empire*, pp. 370–8; and see Robinson, 'Moral Disarmament of African Empire'.

genuine commitment to colonial independence; and Ghana's willing membership of the British-sponsored Commonwealth of Nations.[14]

This relatively well-ordered denouement was greatly assisted by the separation of Britain's several African colonies from each other: the Gold Coast, that is, did not have to wait for the rest of Britain's Africa to move along the decolonisation path, as Bengal had so disastrously had to wait for the rest of British India. Western and Eastern Nigeria, however, did have to wait for the more conservative Northern Nigeria with which they were bound up in the larger Federation of Nigeria. The former secured regional self-government in 1957 – at the time of Ghana's independence; Northern Nigeria's self-government was put off until 1959. The accompanying negotiations, moreover, were far from easy. But thanks, not least, to two successive liberally minded governors-general, Sir John Macpherson and Sir James Robertson, and to the considerable aplomb of Britain's bullish Conservative colonial secretary, Oliver Lyttleton, and his successor, Alan Lennox-Boyd, it was eventually agreed that Nigeria should have its full independence on 1 October 1960.[15] Sierra Leone followed closely behind, moving into independence in 1961.[16]

It had in the meanwhile been arranged with the United Nations that three other colonies should become independent in 1960 as well – the French United Nations Trustee Territories of Cameroons and Togo and the Trust Territory of Somalia, granted to the former colonial power, Italy, under a commitment in 1950 that it should be systematically prepared – as was done nowhere else – for full independence ten years later. In the event, however, these were by no means the only independences secured in 1960.

Back in 1954 France had suffered its humiliating defeat at Dien Bien Phu in Indochina, and all but simultaneously was then finally chased by the Geneva Agreements from its dominion there. Morocco and Tunisia – as we have seen – embarked on their full independence just two years later. As Algeria was denied this, since to so many French it was part of France's homeland, a major colonial war of liberation ensued from 1956 to 1962, which throughout these years constituted the anguished backdrop to all that occurred everywhere else in Africa.[17]

That left the future of France's other colonies in Africa in a state of considerable uncertainty. In response to this the French position was marginally adjusted. The *loi cadre* of 1956 allowed the creation of African-dominated executives there in addition to the existing African-dominated

---

[14] Denis Austin, *Politics in Ghana, 1946–1960*, London, 1966; David Rooney, *Sir Charles Arden-Clarke*, London, 1982.

[15] There is nothing still to surpass James S. Coleman, *Nigeria: Background to Nationalism*, Berkeley, 1965. See also *The Memoirs of Lord Chandos*, London, 1962, chs. 18–22.

[16] Martin Kilson, *Political Change in a West African State*, Cambridge, Mass., 1966; J.D. Hargreaves, *The End of Colonial Rule in West African*, London, 1979.

[17] See Alistair Horne, *A Savage War of Peace: Algeria, 1954–1962*, London, 1977.

legislatures. But larger changes soon followed. For when de Gaulle returned to power in 1958, propelled by the major upheavals the Algerian war created in France itself, he was keenly aware of the pressures that Ghana's independence in the previous year, and British policy elsewhere in West Africa, were putting on the French Empire. He accordingly proceeded to dismantle the two French federations of West and Equatorial Africa and transformed the now somewhat battered French Union into the French Community. While strongly committed as before to France's continuing purpose of closely associating its African territories with metropolitan France itself, and eschewing all ideas of following where the British had led before in preparing its colonies for independence within its Commonwealth, de Gaulle now made this a voluntary association. In 1958 he thus required that all of France's colonies, in Africa especially, should decide by referendum whether they wished to continue as members of the French Community or not. When twelve of France's African colonies thereupon voted yes, but Guinea voted no, Guinea was immediately cast into independence by France in an abrupt, dismissive, and avowedly exemplary manner.

But these gambits quickly failed. The larger proportion of West Africans had either now already won independence or were shortly to do so. Africa's European boundaries had never before looked quite so arbitrary. Some tropical African leaders were now playing parts on the world stage from which others were arbitrarily excluded. Guinea, moreover, soon looked more of a model to follow than an example to be avoided. In an effort to stem the now rapidly advancing tide, de Gaulle appointed four African leaders in 1959 to be ministers advisory to the French delegation to the United Nations. However, in a speech in Dakar in December that year he moved toward acknowledging that there was no further possibility of stopping the skittles from falling over each other. The French Community could now at best hope to be little more than the equivalent of Britain's Commonwealth.

The Mali Federation (of Senegal and French Sudan) and Madagascar were the first to slip the rope. The necessary constitutional instruments for their independence were signed in April 1960. The Mali Federation became independent on 20 June 1960, the Malagasy Republic on 26 June. The race was then on to beat even Nigeria into independence, while keeping pace with the Trust Territories of Cameroons and Togo and, as we shall see, the Belgians' Congo. August 1960 thereupon saw eight French territories attaining their independence: Dahomey on 1 August, Niger on the 3rd, Upper Volta on the 5th, Ivory Coast on the 7th, Chad on the 11th, the Central African Republic on the 13th, the French Congo on the 15th, and Gabon on the 17th, while Mauritania followed a few months later in November. With all this the last-minute African substitutes for France's

West African and Equatorial African federations also soon collapsed – the two successive, contracting, Mali federations; the Conseil de l'Entente; and the Union of Central African Republics. Since France's prime attention had been focussed on the links between its tropical African territories and France itself, the federations, being geographically amorphous, had never been determinedly welded together.[18] Nigeria remained as West Africa's one viable federation (with its greatest traumas yet to come).

All these bouleversements had meanwhile brutally wrenched the Belgians from their former, superior, complacency. Having no previous experience of how to decolonise, they found themselves at a special disadvantage. Even as late as 1956 the very suggestion that Congolese independence could perhaps be attained in thirty years' time had been brushed aside by their leaders as ludicrously inconceivable. But in December 1958 Patrice Lumumba had formed the Mouvement National Congolais. In January 1959 there was fierce rioting in Leopoldville, and the Belgians now awoke from their dreams to discover that they no longer controlled key areas of their colony. Alert to the Netherlands' fruitless conflict with its former Indonesian colony (now rising to yet another peak in the continued dispute over West Irian); keenly aware of the appalling cost to their other neighbour France from its violent entanglements in Algeria; and riven by a violent domestic campaign against the dispatching of Belgian troops to the Congo (which in the case of conscripts was under the constitution dependent upon their – improbable – consent), dire decisions were swiftly taken in Belgium itself that extensive repression of its colonial nationalists could not conceivably be contemplated. Without any of the necessary timely preparations, leaves were now torn from Britain's book. An outside chance was sought of granting immediate independence to the Congo in the grim hope of thereby evoking a cordial last-minute nationalist response and so maintaining the essentials at least of their colonial state; it was calculated that with continued Belgian control of the army, the administration, and the economy, this might just prove feasible. In December 1959 a precipitate independence was thus swiftly propounded. June 1960 saw it being speedily proclaimed – but only to be followed by the disastrous mutiny of the still Belgian-officered Force Publique, the swift slide into the Congo's disintegration thereafter (which led in turn to a mass exodus of its Belgian settlers and administrators), and then to the fateful intervention of the United Nations before the year was out. That in turn generated a seismic fear among other whites – not least in East and Central Africa – at what some further such precipitancy might portend for them.[19]

[18] Ruth Schachter Morgenthan and Lucy Creevey Behrman, 'French Speaking Tropical Africa', in Michael Crowder (ed.), *The Cambridge History of Africa vol. 8, From* c. *1940 to* c. *1975*, Cambridge, England, 1984, pp. 611–73, is probably the latest authoritative summary.

[19] M. Crawford Young, *Politics in the Congo*, Princeton, 1965.

It is well to remember that the swiftest scuttle in Africa was not, however, by the Belgians from the Congo, but by the British from British Somaliland. There, likewise, next to nothing stood ready. Not until February 1960 was there an elected majority in the legislature. When its leaders then sought union with their Somali neighbours, whose long Italian-prepared independence would reach consummation in mid-year, the British tumbled over themselves to make this *pis aller* work. A conference in London agreed in May 1960 that British Somaliland should become self-governing on 26 June, a bare five days before Somalia itself was due to become independent, and on 1 July 1960 – to Britain's intense relief – a united independent Somalia did, remarkably, come into being.[20]

What had happened?

The western world's imperial clamps had first been loosened and then wrenched apart in Asia. By 1954 North Vietnam, by 1957 Malaya (and soon afterward Singapore too), had gone the way of all the larger countries. British (and French) attempts to shore up collaborative governments in the Middle East had mostly failed as well (as the Iraqi revolution and the murder of Britain's ally, Nuri as-Said, had very recently shown in 1958).[21] West European imperialism was generally on the run.

In Britain there was never as it happened any major debate over whether its West African colonies should be granted independence (as there had been in the 1930s over whether Britain should grant more autonomy in India). Sheet anchors were now no longer employed. Slipping ropes were simply wrapped around bollards. The most powerful advocates now spoke, moreover, almost wholly on one side. There were a number of movements on the left, in particular (after 1954), the Movement for Colonial Freedom (though its influence is hard to assess).[22] Initially the Labour party's Fabian Colonial Bureau was the most important lobby. The Rev. Michael Scott's Africa Bureau came, however, to occupy the most prominent place and, small as it always was, became remarkably effective, particularly by securing a hearing for African nationalist leaders visiting London in some of the places that mattered – private meetings, for example, in the House of Commons. The churches were important as well. Canon Max Warren, general secretary of the Church Missionary Society, Canon John Collins of Christian Action, the archbishop of Canterbury, Dr Geoffrey Fisher, and other Church leaders, especially in Scotland, such as George Macleod of the Iona Community, all firmly argued in favour of African freedom.[23]

[20] I.M. Lewis, *A Modern History of Somalia*, 2nd rev. edn, London, 1980, pp. 139–65.
[21] Louis, *Middle East*; Lord Birdwood, *Nuri As-Said*, London, 1959; Majid Khadduri, *Independent Iraq, 1932–1958*, London, 1960.
[22] Fenner Brockway, *Towards Tomorrow*, London, 1977, chs. 23–27.
[23] W. Purcell, *Fisher of Lambeth*, London, 1969, ch. 11; F.W. Dillistone, *Into All the World. A Biography of Max Warren*, London, 1980, *passim*.

Margery Perham, doyenne of British Africanists and Oxford don, was sometimes more cautious; but her magisterial, and keenly awaited, letters to the *Times* always upheld Britain's commitment to independence and could devastatingly rebuke obfuscating checks.[24] The *Times*'s colonial editor, Oliver Woods, and its later Africa correspondent, W.P. Kirkman, the *Guardian*'s Patrick Keatley, the *Economist*'s Roy Lewis, and above all the *Observer*'s Colin Legum, each ensured that London's quality press kept a close watch on the developing scene and insisted that there should be sensitive hands on its tillers. Legum's characteristic attitude was best displayed by his book *Must We Lose Africa?*,[25] half devoted to an attack on the liberally minded Sir Andrew Cohen (now governor of Uganda) for not being liberal enough. Other newspapers, as varied as the *Scotsman* and the *Daily Mail*, also strongly supported the African cause.

Perhaps the most potent factor, however, was the concurrence over African independence of first the Conservative opposition, and then after 1951 the Conservative government, with their Labour opponents – at least where there were no white immigrants to complicate the scene. Prior to 1951 Conservative MPs had been predominantly empire minded. With the 1955 entry there was an even more marked change: the more European minded now outnumbered the empire men by two to one.[26] At the 1959 election half the Conservative candidates never mentioned the Commonwealth in their manifestoes at all.[27] During the late 1940s the Conservative colonial spokesman, Oliver Stanley, had largely supported Creech-Jones's initiatives. Throughout the 1950s, certainly in West Africa, Lyttelton and his successor as Conservative colonial secretary, Alan Lennox-Boyd, both held firmly to the course their Labour predecessors had set.[28] By the mid-1950s the Labour party was moving on to a commitment to one man one vote in the colonies,[29] and by the end of the decade this was being espoused by the influential Conservative Bow Group as well.[30]

Yet, in spite of all this public support in Britain for African freedom and the Colonial Office's urgent planning in the middle and late 1940s, it is false to believe it was Britain that made the running in Africa's decolonisation. British preoccupations in these matters principally served to prepare Britain itself to meet rather more surefootedly than it might otherwise have

---

[24] For example, Iverach McDonald, *The History of The Times*, vol. 5, London, 1984, ch. 14; Patrick Keatley, *The Politics of Partnership*, Harmondsworth, 1963; W.P. Kirkman, *Unscrambling an Empire*, London, 1966.

[25] Colin Legum, *Must We Lose Africa?*, London, 1954.

[26] S.E. Finer, H.B. Berrington, and D.J. Bartholomew, *Backbench Opinion in the House of Commons, 1955–59*, London, 1961, pp. 86–90.

[27] Miles Kahler, *Decolonization in Britain and France*, Princeton, 1984, p. 158.

[28] On all this, see Goldsworthy, *Colonial Issues, passim*.

[29] Goldsworthy, *Colonial Issues*, p. 386.

[30] The impressions of the Kenyan European leader about this are in Michael Blundell, *So Rough a Wind*, London, 1964, pp. 255–6.

done the nationalist onrush with which it was shortly confronted. As its officials and ministers discovered, they had not framed, as they thought, mechanisms for fostering independence creatively and deliberately but, in the upshot, expedients to which to turn in their hurry as their colonialist feet slipped out from under them. It was, for example, highly convenient that they should have fashioned a whole new sequence of multiple constitutional steps forward (in place of the old stately three-stage progression from Crown Colony to Dominion status) before they confronted Nkrumah's insistent demand for 'self-government now', even if they found themselves forced to speed these along a great deal faster than they had ever originally contemplated. It was that availability which enabled them to permit Nkrumah after 1951 to move swiftly from 'leader of government business' to chief minister, to prime minister, and to full control of the Gold Coast's internal government by means of 'tactical action' rather than his earlier vociferous 'positive action'. That in turn helped to reinforce the impression that it could well prove possible to move the British (as they had ultimately been moved in South Asia) by a Gandhi-like oscillation between active agitation and temporising accommodation, rather than by resorting to armed conflict as had so fruitlessly been done by the Mau Mau in Kenya.[31]

In three other respects, however, Britain's new policies of the late 1940s fairly certainly made their task very much harder than it might otherwise have been – at any rate if one considers their experience in Africa taken as a whole. In the first place their concern with development led to a great increase in the number of British officials, especially of departmental and technical officers, in the capitals and district centres of their colonial territories. It led also, to an often striking degree, to a variety of authoritarian measures, particularly in respect of what they believed to be rural reform: better cropping patterns, cattle inoculation, anti-erosion terracing. This mounted to a second colonial invasion that was deeply resented by, and frequently deeply offensive to, its colonial peoples. The well-meaning attempt to assuage the economic consequences of the depression, the war, and their aftermath thus regularly backfired.[32]

Second, the fostering of democratically elected local councils often backfired too. There was little commitment there to all the development purposes they were meant to serve. Their prospective role as electoral colleges was soon abandoned. More seriously, their early politicisation led to a fateful undermining of the power of the formally collaborating chiefs. As a result these chiefs ceased to be the instruments of imperial diktats, and, in the absence of anything in their place – the great increase in European

---

[31] Austin, *Politics in Ghana.*
[32] For example, see chapter 7 above; *Report of the Nyasaland Commission of Inquiry* (the Devlin Report), Cmnd 814, London, 1959, p. 19; R. Young and H. Fosbrooke, *Land and Politics among the Luguru of Tanganyika*, London, 1960, ch. 7.

administrative officers in Kenya in the Mau Mau and post-Mau Mau years during the 1950s suggests the possible alternative – imperial control of so many a local area was soon being quite simply lost.[33] And then third, whereas in the aftermath of a spate of strikes all over Africa during the late 1940s the British made considerable efforts to foster functionally separated, organisationally circumscribed trade unions, African leaders frequently came to employ these as organs of anti-colonial protest, as Tom Mboya's career in Kenya (and Sékou Touré's in Guinea) so strikingly illustrated.[34] These various ingredients then variously coalesced. Protests against well-intentioned but harshly imposed soil-conservation measures conjoined, for example, with widespread dismay at the enlarged European presence; and whereas representative councils and assisted trade unions had been planned to moderate volatile elements, they more often provided vehicles for articulating and spearheading unassuaged discontents and rising ambitions all the more vigorously.[35]

But in searching for the propellants of Africa's insistent nationalism in the post-Second World War years one must look in three further directions as well. If the experience of African troops during the Second World War outside their home areas and often outside tropical Africa itself may not have bred quite the crucial cohorts of African nationalists that was once suggested, it assuredly provided one of the many channels through which Africans' increasing awareness of the independence that was coming to others would have travelled. All these channels, in ways hard to count, will have helped generate the powerful combination of excitement at what might be attained and dismay at what was still being endured that were the principal components of Africa's nationalisms, as of so many others.

Nationalism was fuelled too, to a degree that has not perhaps been sufficiently appreciated, by a long-gathering and widespread discontent. This had already reared its head in the 1930s in strikes and coffee holdups in many urban and rural centres. These discontents were the seemingly unremitting consequences of the world slump in the 1930s, which were then compounded by the dislocations and deprivations of the Second World War and the inflation and persisting shortages thereafter. If we consider only the remarkably detailed evidence of the malaise all this set up in the minds of West Africa's colonial administrators, it takes little imagination to visualise the still deeper discontents it generated in so many African minds even before one goes on to consider the abundant evidence of strikes, riots, demonstrations, *et hoc genus omne* following the war. Paradoxically, these

[33] For example, *Report of the Commission of Inquiry into the Management of the Teso District Council: Report of the Commission of Inquiry into Disturbances in the Eastern Province, 1960*, Entebbe, 1960.
[34] David Goldsworthy, *Tom Mboya*, Nairobi, 1982.
[35] For example, Cherry Gertzel, *Party and Locality in Northern Uganda, 1945–1962*, London, 1974.

animosities were then given a substantial stir by the passing euphoria that accompanied the Korean War boom in the early and mid-1950s, only to be greatly compounded once again by the sharp economic downturn when the boom collapsed.[36] The accompanying discontents were extensively expressed in Africa's innumerable nationalist parties, of which the Rassamblement Democratique Africain founded in French West Africa in 1946 was at one time the most extensive.

Yet by contrast with their most powerful Asian counterparts, such as the Indian National Congress, or the Communist party of China, or smaller movements such as Sukarno's Partai National Indonesie, these African nationalist parties were often markedly less substantial than the eruptive movements propelling them forward. Upon this matter detailed studies of the lower Congo, the Geita district in Tanganyika, some villages in Northern Rhodesia, and other places besides, provide clear evidence that by the late 1950s vibrant rural radicalism with a decidedly nationalist thrust had become widespread.[37] There was considerable urban radicalism too (of which Ghana's much-noted 'verandah boys' had been only one expression). But in essence this turbulence was essentially 'subaltern' (as, after Gramsci, it is now being termed in Indian studies).[38] It was not principally, as imperial rulers were apt to claim, an elite contrivance. It could be narrowly confined (in place or issue), spread over a larger area, more generally suffused, or concentrated in one category of persons, episodic or persistent. Induced by the surge of hopes and angers now sweeping through Africa, it was essentially a populist, often a disaggregated, phenomenon. What it meant was that by the late 1950s African nationalist leaders were not having to mobilise cowed, apathetic, or disinterested populaces (as the Asian movements certainly sometimes needed to do). Rather, their largest concerns were frequently to establish some measure of control over a multiplicity of populist expressions of anti-colonial ambition and discontent that were now pullulating in Africa, so as to utilise these to promote their centrally focussed nationalist cause. It was as much in an effort to capture such forces as to advance them that Nkrumah so trenchantly exclaimed: 'Seek ye first the political kingdom and all the rest shall be added unto you.' In the immediate post-independence years the authoritarianism to which so many nationalist leaders succumbed owed a great deal to their baffled anxiety to hold the lid on the plethora of localised agitational propensities

---

[36] For example, A.G. Hopkins, *An Economic History of West Africa*, London, 1973, ch. 7; J.D.Y. Peel, 'Social and Cultural Change', in *Cambridge History of Africa*, vol. 8, ch. 4.

[37] Herbert Weiss, *Political Protest in the Congo*, Princeton, 1967; G. Andrew Maguire, *Towards 'Uhuru' in Tanzania*, Cambridge, England, 1969; Thomas Rasmussen, 'The Popular Basis of Anti-Colonial Protest', in W. Tordoff (ed.), *Politics in Zambia*, Manchester, 1974, ch. 2; D.A. Low, *Buganda in Modern History*, London, 1971, ch. 5; Gertzel, *Northern Uganda*.

[38] Ranajit Guha (ed.), *Subaltern Studies*, vols. I–VI, Delhi, 1982–9.

that were then surrounding them. In the terminal colonial years the daunting prospect of having to contain the profusion of disturbances now confronting them in Africa baffled, dismayed, and ultimately quite threw off balance their British, French, and Belgian predecessors.

It was certainly in response to the palpable evidence of such continent-wide eruptions in the late 1950s that Harold Macmillan, Britain's Conservative prime minister, echoed the words of his predecessor, Stanley Baldwin, over India in 1934, and repeated his own remarks at Bedford in England in 1957, when he declared to the South African Parliament in February 1960 that 'the wind of change is blowing through this Continent'.[39] At larger levels, both Nkrumah and the South African prime minister were by now seeking to turn their countries into free-standing republics. In the months thereabouts, de Gaulle was bending before the wind in West Africa (as Macmillan quickly appreciated) and was evidently preparing to pull out of Algeria as well. The Belgians were battling with the sudden storm overwhelming them in the Congo. The British themselves were already yielding to pressures even in tiny British Somaliland. In East Africa, despite having suppressed Kenya's Mau Mau revolt, the pressures against them were in many ways building up as never before. There were major popular disturbances in both Uganda and Tanganyika and serious riots in all three of Britain's Central African territories.[40] Guerrilla attacks were beginning to be launched in Portugal's African territories; while dramatic encounters were soon occurring in South Africa too, at Sharpeville and Langa especially. 'We have seen the awakening of national consciousness', Harold Macmillan told the South African Parliament in February 1960, 'in peoples who have for centuries lived in dependence on some other power. Fifteen years ago this movement spread through Asia . . . Today the same thing is happening in Africa . . . In different places it may take different forms. But it is happening everywhere.'[41]

All of which now entailed major problems in sustaining control over the agitational forces that had been loosed. These were indeed affecting both the imperialists and many nationalist leaders alike (as Kaunda in Central Africa among others was soon to discover). While to some repression seemed the only sensible answer – the Portuguese were shortly to take this line in Angola as, momentarily, did the Central African Federation's prime minister too – all Asian experience, and all the killings in Algeria and later in Portuguese Africa and Rhodesia, unarguably demonstrated that ulti-

[39] K. Middlemas and J. Barnes, *Baldwin*, London, 1969, p. 713. The essentials of Macmillan's February 1960 speech are in N. Mansergh (ed.), *Documents and Speeches on Commonwealth Affairs, 1952–62*, London, 1963, pp. 347–51.
[40] Maguire, '*Uhuru' in Tanzania*; Low, *Buganda*, pp. 156–8; Rotberg, *Nationalism in Central Africa*, pp. 282ff.
[41] Mansergh, *Documents and Speeches*, pp. 347–51.

mately this was an appallingly worthless course.[42] Sharper minds accordingly calculated that if searing debacles were to be avoided the wiser course would be to grant early independence and leave the upshot to Africa's impatient nationalists.

The supreme irony now was that it was principally the British, who had hitherto preened themselves on being the first to respond to these pressures, and had not therefore fallen into the traps others had dug for themselves, who now faced the largest crisis in Africa. For while they had just about successfully managed to keep themselves ahead of the waves of disorder they might have faced in West Africa, from which France in West Africa had just escaped too, but which were now overwhelming the Belgians, the persistence of British rule in East and Central Africa, particularly under the increasingly specious banner of 'partnership', now left them uniquely exposed to the winds of change there in precisely the manner they had always hitherto assiduously sought to avoid. There had been some hope, indeed an expectation, that, rather as there had been a ten-year hiatus between independence in South Asia and independence in Malaya, so, at the very least, there would be a similar interlude between independence in British West Africa and independence in the rest of British Africa. But it was not to be. The dominoes were continuing to fall. Along the East African coast Somalia became independent in 1960, as did the Malagasy Republic too.

Britain's appalling miscalculation rested on its failure to appreciate three if not four immensely potent circumstances. First, as we have implied, it was just not the case that post-war African nationalism was principally a West African phenomenon. It was simultaneously erupting right across the continent. That was hardly to be wondered at. Even in the 1940s nationalist agitation had been as vigorous in Kenya, for example, as in the Gold Coast. By any standards Kenyatta stood senior to Nkrumah in the nationalist cause. The point was then underlined by the weight of East and Central African attendance at Nkrumah's All African Peoples' Conference in Accra in December 1958. Second, the fact that by 1960 so much of West Africa had become independent naturally intensified the dismay in the rest of the continent that in order simply to meet the inordinate ambitions of the European settlers, East and Central Africa were to be treated differently. That in turn brought into even sharper focus the dire fact that the overwhelming reason for this distinction was quintessentially racial; as the British Somaliland outcome pinpointed, where there were no white settlers in East Africa, the British could bring themselves to grant independence as precipitously as anyone. And fourth, far from having reached its apogee with the upheaval in the Congo, the momentum of change that had spread

---

[42] D. Birmingham and T. Ranger, 'Settlers and Liberators in the South', in D. Birmingham and P.M. Martin (eds.), *History of Central Africa*, London, 1983, II, pp. 341–5.

outward from Ghana was still, if anything, mounting to its peak. In particular in Northern Rhodesia and Nyasaland the fear was now rampant that the federal constitutional-review conference lately advanced to 1960 would lead to the clamping of white supremacy over its black population forever, unless they were now to erupt against this. The altogether disconcerting fact was that for all Britain's hitherto remarkably successful attempts in its confrontations with African nationalism to be quick off the mark, there were now much greater threats of anti-colonial violence in Eastern and Central Africa than it had ever encountered in West Africa.[43]

By 1959–60 the British in East and Central Africa accordingly found themselves caught badly out on a limb with dangerous deeps below it. Their 'partnership' doctrine in particular was under the severest possible challenges. Were it to be held to, the cover it provided for special privileges for those of white skin would be brutally hounded at home and abroad; African rebellion against it would be assured of global applause. Yet were it to be abandoned, imprecations of treachery, cowardice, and worse from the whites in Africa would ring in the Conservative government's ears. Another Congo-type collapse would certainly be laid at its door. The white minorities might, moreover, take the law into their own hands. (That had already been threatened more than once; Macmillan became keenly anxious about the possibility of a Central African Boston tea party).[44]

The situation was made none the easier because of other surrounding circumstances. Once the fateful attempt to impose Britain's will upon Colonel Nasser's Egypt had decisively collapsed in the disastrous Suez affair in 1956, Britain's policy makers were neither of a mind nor in a state to advance strategic or commercial reasons why Eastern and Central Africa should be held at whatever cost. Kenya's settler leader, Michael Blundell, was told by a friendly Conservative that 'the British Cabinet lost its collective nerve after Suez and decided to climb out of any situations which might involve them in critical escapades overseas'.[45] It would have been closer to the mark to have said that following the Suez aberration the Conservative government saw the wisdom of its Labour predecessor's 'grand strategy' of nonintervention and the conciliation of the moderate nationalists which British policy makers had previously consistently held to, even through the major Anglo–Iranian crisis of 1951.[46] To that, as early as May 1959, Macmillan added the warning to Blundell that 'the only possible policy was a liberal one . . . any Government of Great Britain could not carry with it for long the people on any policy which had not a strong moral conviction in issues of this sort'.[47] The issue, moreover, could no

[43] Rotberg, *Nationalism in Central Africa*.
[44] Blundell, *So Rough a Wind*, pp. 262–3; Clyde Sanger, *Central African Emergency*, London, 1960, pp. 246–7.
[45] Blundell, *So Rough a Wind*, p. 267.   [46] Louis, *Middle East*, p. 5.
[47] Blundell, *So Rough a Wind*, pp. 262–3.

longer be baulked. Macmillan no doubt had part of his mind elsewhere – on Europe, the British nuclear deterrent, and the American alliance.[48] 'But what remains in my mind', he later wrote, 'is the immense amount of time and trouble taken over the future of the African territories amidst so many other baffling problems, internal and external.'[49]

Already on the ground the erosion of Britain's partnership commitments in East Africa had by 1959 incrementally proceeded far. As early as 1952 Uganda – gratuitously hustled under the 'partnership' banner just a short while previously – had to be acknowledged as 'a primarily African country', even if there were still to be special safeguards for minorities. By the time of the so-called Namirembe Agreement with Buganda in 1954 it was clear that Uganda could look forward to African majority rule, and in 1959 its Wild Committee on constitutional reform delivered the *coup de grâce* by advocating a common roll in which Uganda's Europeans and Asians would be swiftly submerged.[50] In the meantime, in 1955, in small but symbolically important Zanzibar, Britain's attempt to maintain even there the multiracial ideal by providing special representation for the hitherto governing Arab minority was totally undermined when the younger Arab nationalists, early perceiving the long-term dangers in any such arbitrarily protected role, and gambling on their ability to hold their own in the future, forcefully demanded that common-roll elections should be introduced in Zanzibar too, and in the years that followed eventually had their way.[51]

Meanwhile Tanganyika, under its imperious governor, Sir Edward Twining, was in the throes of a sustained British attempt to press it into an equally balanced, multiracial 'partnership' mode, with one European and one Asian for every African representative despite the huge population disparities. But as a consequence, by the late 1950s there was in Tanganyika more overt opposition to British colonial rule there than anywhere else in East Africa. The Tanganyika Africa National Union had been founded in 1954. In 1958 its leader, Julius Nyerere, then seized on the fact that in the impending legislative elections it would be possible for TANU to win a complete ascendency if, instead of boycotting their multiracial procedures, it exploited the fact that Africans could vote for the candidates required of other races so as to ensure that only those who supported its larger cause would win their seats. TANU's triumph along precisely these lines drove a coach and four through Twining's multiracial concoction. By 1959 the new governor, Turnbull, despite being an old Kenya hand, was insistent that he had no power to resist the ensuing demand for African majority rule.[52] By

[48] R.F. Holland, *European Decolonization, 1918–1981*, London, 1985, pp. 204–7.
[49] Harold Macmillan, *Pointing the Way, 1959–61*, London, 1962, p. 150.
[50] Low, *Buganda*, chs. 4–6.
[51] Michael F. Lofchie, *Zanzibar: Background to Revolution*, Princeton, 1965.
[52] John Iliffe, *A Modern History of Tanganyika*, Cambridge, 1979, chs. 15–16.

then Kenya alone of Britain's East African territories remained formally enmeshed in the multiracial web; and at the beginning of 1959 its African members began a concerted boycott of its Legislative Council.

That year then saw the foundations of Britain's East and Central-African policies being shaken as never before by two occurrences that unnerved even its most conservative supporters. The largest upheaval against British rule in Africa had been by Kenya's Mau Mau revolt that had broken out openly in 1952. Since its supporters had shown themselves ready to kill, British public opinion had generally supported the use of military force against them, and by 1956–7 its back had been largely broken. But by 1959 numbers of Mau Mau supporters remained in detention, and in Kenya's Hola camp there was an appalling case of killings by brutal and insensitive warders. When the news leaked out, Britain's parliamentarians, from the left to the right, were deeply outraged: perhaps the most potent denunciation was made by the former Conservative minister Enoch Powell.[53] Meanwhile in the same year there had been, as we shall see, widespread riots in Nyasaland to the south. A report by the Devlin Commission subsequently criticised the colony's administration for overreacting and accused it of creating a 'police state'.[54] These two events together served to supercharge the major debate that was now being generated in Britain (of an order that its African decolonisation story had never seen previously) over the whole future of its former commitment to multiracial regimes in East and Central Africa, particularly as these entailed extraordinary privileges for white settlers. For if continued British dominion in East and Central Africa entailed consequences like these, the British people were increasingly disinclined to have any more of it. Books, especially on the Central African situation, came tumbling from the press where they line the shelves as testimony to the debate's intensity.[55] Almost uniformly they argued in support of the position of the churches, the quality press, and even significant sections of the Conservative party that without further ado Britain should now carry through in East and Central Africa what it, France, Belgium, and Italy were already completing everywhere else in Africa.

Early in 1959 the Conservative government's second colonial secretary, Lennox-Boyd, had summoned his East African governors to a meeting at the prime minister's country house at Chequers. They knew very well by

[53] *Hansard* (Commons) 1959, vol. 610, cols. 232–7; Charles Douglas-Home, *Evelyn Baring: The Last Proconsul*, London, 1978, ch. 29.

[54] Cmnd 814, *Nyasaland Commission of Inquiry*.

[55] E.g., Philip Mason, *Year of Decision*, London, 1960; R. Gray, *The Two Nations*, London, 1960; Edward Clegg, *Race and Politics*, Oxford, 1960; C. Leys and C. Pratt, *A New Deal in Central Africa*, London, 1960; Sanger, *Central African Emergency*; C.E. Lucas Phillips, *The Vision Splendid*, London, 1960.

then that a change of pace was required in East Africa. By all reports they agreed that they should now plan on Tanganyika's becoming independent in about 1970, Kenya in 1975, and Uganda sometime in between. They agreed too that any head-on collision with African nationalists that might involve the use of force must be avoided.[56]

In October 1959 there was a general election in Britain that returned the Conservatives to power. Lennox-Boyd now retired, and he was succeeded by an able, ambitious, younger Tory, Iain Macleod. Although new to colonial issues, Macleod immediately sensed that such were the tides now flowing in Africa that the Chequers timetable of just a few months previously was already almost hopelessly out of date. He was later to write:

The situation in autumn, 1959 was grim . . . Perhaps the tragedy of the Hola camp, even more than the 'murder plot' emergency in Nyasaland, was decisive . . . It has been said that after I became Colonial Secretary there was a deliberate speeding up of the movement towards independence. I agree. There was. And in my view any other policy would have led to terrible bloodshed in Africa . . . Were the countries fully ready for independence? Of course not . . . [But] we could not possibly have held by force our territories in Africa . . . The march of men towards freedom can be guided, but not halted. Of course there are risks in moving quickly. But the risks of moving slowly were far greater.[57]

For British policy makers the position in which they now found themselves was deeply humiliating: not merely were they being left far behind those they had always believed to be much less sensitive and skilful decolonisers. ('Do you know what that means?' Macleod remarked when he heard that the Belgians had decided to quit the Congo. 'We are going to be the last in the colonial sphere instead of the first.')[58] They were now faced by nationalisms whose especially vehement impatience was being angrily driven by being denied, for principally racial reasons, a legitimate outlet. There was every prospect, moreover, of violence erupting on a scale the available British forces would be stretched to control, or regime collapses whose possible human costs were dreadful to contemplate, or both. Above all they were being forced to jettison all that remained of their careful planning in the late 1940s for an orderly progression toward decolonisation. In October 1959 one governor wrote to another: 'It looks to me as though we have "had" Africa'; it only remained to 'do all we can to make them ready between now and then; and then leave them to the denizens and to the human misery that will result for most of them'.[59] Given the main thrust of

56 The *Observer*, 1 Feb. 1959; Blundell, *So Rough a Wind*, pp. 261–2; Douglas-Home, *Evelyn Baring*, p. 283.
57 *Weekend Telegraph*, March 12, 1965; *Spectator*, Jan. 31 1964. On this whole issue, Dan Horowitz, 'Attitudes of British Conservatives towards Colonization in Africa', *African Affairs*, 69 (Jan. 1970), 9–26.
58 Blundell, *So Rough a Wind*, p. 271.
59 Crawford to Baring, in Douglas-Home, *Evelyn Baring*, p. 285.

the public debate now being conducted in Britain (and in African, American, and international quarters as well), that meant they had now to face not simply the abandonment of the policy of partnership to which they had been strongly committed for a decade past. They had actually to contemplate rolling this back in the face of bitter recriminations by those white political leaders, especially in Kenya and the Rhodesias, who were quick to denounce any such volte face as unabashed treachery, and who were understandably dismayed at seeing all that they had worked for – and had, even quite lately, confidently expected to obtain – being wrenched from their grasp by men of whose stance they could no longer be sure and whose word they soon found difficulty in trusting.[60] For Britain's Conservative prime minister and his successive colonial secretaries the general position then became still more troublesome because of the growth after 1960 of a small but influential group within their own party that was increasingly hostile to the course they themselves felt impotent to avoid. While there were those in the Conservative party who generally felt the settlers should fend for themselves (as one Bow Grouper crudely put it, 'What do I care about the f . . . ing settlers, let them bloody well look after themselves')[61] there was also the fact, as Macmillan himself remarked, that 'Lord Salisbury and Lord Lambton would easily rally a "settler" lobby of considerable power'.[62]

Given this context it was Macmillan's 'wind of change' speech, primarily direct at the South African regime, that provided the lifeline for Macleod and allowed him to do what he now believed had to be done. 'A series of Dunkirks, of gallant, prolonged, bitter rearguard actions' would, he believed, be futile.[63] 'The fences will get higher', he averred, 'if we do not take them now'.[64] In April 1959 his predecessor, Lennox-Boyd, had said he could not foresee any date 'at which it will be possible for any British Government to surrender their ultimate responsibilities for the destinies and well being of Kenya'.[65] Having finally terminated in January 1960 the emergency under which Kenya had been living since the Mau Mau outbreak seven years before, later that month Macleod presided over a constitutional conference on Kenya at Lancaster House in London. There, on 1 February 1960, he eventually took the bull by the horns and outlined changes that could only ensure that before very long African majority rule would replace the white-dominated multiracialism in Kenya and that independence for Kenya on these lines would not be indefinitely delayed

---

[60] This is the burden of Roy Welensky, *Welensky's 4,000 Days*, London, 1964.
[61] Blundell, *So Rough a Wind*, p. 266.
[62] Harold Macmillan, *At the End of the Day, 1961–1963*, London, 1973, p. 290.
[63] Nigel Fisher, *Iain Macleod*, London, 1973, p. 145.
[64] Sanger, *Central African Emergency*, p. 311.
[65] *Hansard* (Commons) 1959, vol. 604, col. 563.

thereafter.[66] Two days later Macmillan sanctioned this approach when he told the South African Parliament: 'The growth of national consciousness in Africa is a political fact and we must accept it as such. This means, I would judge, that we must come to terms with it'.[67] Blundell, the Kenya settler leader, explained to the Central African Federation's prime minister, Welensky, that 'developments around us in Tanganyika, the Congo, Uganda and British Somalia make it almost impossible for us to hold back'.[68] He was soon conceding, however, to Macleod that in Kenya 'all the jealous racial questions have just gone . . . the alternative to Lancaster House for Kenya was an explosion'.[69] There were still problems over Kenya to come – the conflict between KADU and KANU; the debate and delay over the release of Kenyatta; a further Lancaster House conference in London in 1962; and a pre-independence election in 1963. In December 1961 Macmillan was chafing over the dilemma that 'if we have to give independence to Kenya, it may well prove another Congo. If we hold on, it will mean a long and cruel campaign'.[70] But in fact it was neither. It was immensely important to the outcome that, in Kenyatta, Kenya had a widely supported nationalist leader, who even held out an olive branch to the settlers, and at the end of 1963 Britain gratefully transferred power to him.

By then Tanganyika and Uganda were independent too, and Zanzibar's independence was to follow very shortly. Seeing Nyerere and TANU now comfortably entrenched as Tanganyika's single nationalist party, Macleod was anxious to press ahead there as swiftly as he could. Further elections were held in Tanganyika in September 1960. A final constitutional conference was called (unusually, outside London) in Dar-es-Salaam in March 1961, and independence for Tanganyika eventuated in December that year. Uganda was more complicated, owing to the determination first of the Baganda and then of the other southern Ugandan kingdoms to establish a federal constitution. There were talks in London in September 1960, and a full constitutional conference just a year later. The arrangements made had little to commend them, but Uganda became independent on 9 October 1962. Zanzibar had serious internal problems too that were in no way settled by the time independence came to it. But it likewise had a Lancaster House conference in London in 1962 and became independent at the end of 1963.[71]

Having by 1960 re-established Britain's credibility as a responsive decoloniser, in particular by having finally broken white settler dominance in Kenya, Macleod secured just a little more leverage, and time, for the unscrambling of Britain's East African empire than the Belgians had had in

[66] Fisher, *Macleod*, pp. 144–8; Goldsworthy, *Mboya*, pp. 131–6.
[67] Mansergh, *Documents and Speeches*, pp. 347–51.
[68] Blundell, *So Rough a Wind*, p. 279.   [69] Fisher, *Macleod*, p. 148.
[70] Macmillan, *End of the Day*, p. 291.
[71] Low and Smith, *History of East Africa*, vol. 3, chs. 1–4.

the Congo. Most of the earlier ideas of preparing colonies for independence went by the board. The opportunity was principally used to settle a little more securely, by means of national elections (more than one if necessary), the successions to power at independence. In both Uganda and Zanzibar the conclusions reached soon disastrously collapsed, in the Zanzibar revolt of January 1964 and in Obote's *coup* in Uganda in 1966.[72] But at least, from the British point of view, there was not (as yet) widespread disaster on the Congo's scale. The principal danger of this, as Macmillan had seen, had been in Kenya, where a widespread African grab for land, and a precipitate departure by Kenya's whites, might together have created the kind of Congo-type disaster that would have threatened the very future of the Conservative government among its own supporters (Maudling, Macleod's successor as colonial secretary, feared there might be 'a bloody shambles').[73] Late in 1960 a grievous twist in the Congo crisis, centring on Katanga's possible secession, gave Macmillan his most anxious days during these years. He dreaded their repetition in a Kenyan collapse. Accordingly, and well nigh uniquely, several millions of British taxpayers' money was made available to a Kenyan Land and Settlement Development Board to enable it to act as a broker between land-hungry blacks without resources and settlers demanding cash for their properties. This arrangement triumphantly served the government's dual purpose of preventing a Congo crisis in Kenya and the bitter conflict within the Conservative party that would certainly have ensued.[74]

Yet East Africa had never been the centre of Britain's African crisis. Macleod's principal test had in the meanwhile been in Nyasaland.[75] In June 1958 Hastings Banda had returned there after forty-two years abroad to assume the leadership of the Nyasaland African Congress. Its primary objective was to secure Nyasaland's secession from the white-dominated Federation. By early 1959, because Britain was seen to be dragging its feet over constitutional reforms within Nyasaland itself, demonstrations and riots were spreading there. To halt these Welensky, the Federation's prime minister, decided in February 1959 to fly in Southern Rhodesian troops to Nyasaland.[76] On 3 March Banda and some 200 of his supporters were arrested and soon accused of plotting to murder Nyasaland's whites. In the accompanying disturbances, more than fifty blacks were killed. It was a crucial moment. For Welensky was demonstrating that conceptually there was an alternative to the policy the British government was pursuing: force

72 Lofchie, *Zanzibar*, pp. 257–81; Low, *Buganda*, ch. 7.
73 Macmillan, *End of the Day*, p. 291, and *Pointing the Way*, ch. 16.
74 Gary Wasserman, *Politics of Decolonization: Kenya Europeans and the Land Issue, 1960–1965*, Cambridge, England, 1976 – though this seems to me to miss the main point: see, e.g., Blundell, *So Rough a Wind*, pp. 276, 286, 307.
75 Sanger, *Central African Emergency, passim.*   76 Welensky, *4,000 Days*, pp. 118–21.

could be used to repress nationalist movements (as the much more impoverished Portuguese were to do so harshly in Angola just two years later).[77] But as the immediate outcry in Britain against any such proceeding (that came to be embodied in the Devlin Report on the Nyasaland disturbances)[78] made very plain, Macmillan and his colleagues found themselves in no position to take the Welensky route, even if they had wanted to (which they did not). 'I cannot guarantee', Macmillan shortly informed Welensky, 'that British troops would undertake the kind of duties that would be necessary'.[79]

Macleod's crucial move then came in April 1960 when he released Banda from prison, invited him to London, and entered into negotiations with him. By August 1961 the renamed Malawi Congress Party overwhelmingly won Nyasaland's ensuing general election. In November 1962 there was one of the now customary Lancaster House conferences in London, and a month later the British conceded that Nyasaland might secede from the Federation. Six years to the day since he had returned to his country, Banda saw Malawi become independent on 6 July 1964.

As we have noted, an agreement had been reached back in 1957 to hold a review of the Federation's constitution in 1960. Following the disturbances not only in Nyasaland but elsewhere in the Federation early in 1959, Macmillan decided to establish first an advisory commission, eventually under Lord Monckton's chairmanship, to report on the situation before this review was undertaken.[80] He tried to appoint some Labour members to it, but since, in deference to Welensky, he declined to allow it to consider dismantling the Federation, the Labour party refused to cooperate.[81] Monckton and his colleagues thereupon began work in February 1960 and reported in the following September. 'African distrust' of the Federation, they then wrote, 'has reached an intensity impossible, in our opinion, to dispel without drastic and fundamental changes', and they went on, despite Mamillan's original curb upon them, but in full accord with the considerable slippage in British attitudes at the time, to insert the fateful recommendation 'that Her Majesty's Government should make a declaration of intention to consider a request from the Government of a Territory to secede from the Federation'.[82] It was this that opened the door to Nyasaland's eventual departure just two years later.

From Welensky's point of view Nyasaland's departure was a bad precedent, but its participation was in no way crucial to the Federation's

---

[77] E.g., Gerald J. Bender, *Angola under the Portuguese*, London, 1978, ch. 6.
[78] Cmnd 814, *Nyasaland Commission of Inquiry*.
[79] Welensky, *4,000 Days*, p. 324.
[80] Lord Birkenhead, *Walter Monckton*, London, 1969, chs. 3–5.
[81] Philip Williams, *Hugh Gaitskell*, London, 1979, pp. 483–5, 679–82.
[82] *Report on the Advisory Commission on the Review of the Constitution of Rhodesia and Nyasaland*, London, 1960, Cmnd 1148, paras. 74, 300.

continuance. Northern Rhodesia's was. Without it there would be no wealth to be drawn from its extensive copper mines, and the Federation would be confined to Southern Rhodesia only. The principal battle of these years accordingly turned on whether or not Northern Rhodesia would remain in the Federation.

From before the inception of the Federation African opinion there had been strongly aroused against it. But Northern Rhodesia's nationalist forces were not only overridden; during the 1950s they became all but fatally divided. Nevertheless, by March 1959 there were widespread disturbances, and leading officials of Northern Rhodesia's Zambia Congress were arrested. As early as January 1960, however, their release was ordered, and Kenneth Kaunda then set about welding together the new United National Independence Party as no other Northern Rhodesian African party had ever been before – and no Southern Rhodesian African party was ever to be thereafter. In December 1960 he was persuaded to attend the federal review conference in London, pursuant upon the Monckton Commission's report, on condition that the existing Northern Rhodesian constitution would at the same time be reconsidered. That precipitated the major encounter over Northern Rhodesia which spread through all of 1961 and beyond.[83]

Reconsideration of Northern Rhodesia's constitution was now of central importance. For if this were to end with the existing white domination being maintained, the Federation might just survive, but there would almost certainly be a major black upheaval. If on the other hand white domination could be crucially undermined, black majority rule and the Federation's collapse were well nigh assured (though, as always, Rhodesia's whites might well take the law into their own hands). As the issues became joined, so the tensions rose, and not least in the minds of Britain's decision makers. The federal review conference soon proved abortive. The Africans simply walked out. There was then much to-ing and fro-ing between central Africa and London, and at one stage Welensky mobilised Southern Rhodesia's white territorial troops as a threat against London. Meanwhile there was mounting opposition towards Macleod in the Conservative party. In February 1961 Lord Salisbury denounced him in the House of Lords for 'being too clever by half', and in the Commons an 'early day motion' was put down by a former Conservative minister that implicitly criticised Macleod by calling for Northern Rhodesia's 'nonracial' representation to be maintained; at one stage it attracted the signatures of more than a hundred Conservative MPs.[84] But there were loud voices on the other side too. On 14 February the *Times*, for example, declared that

[83] Rotberg, *Rise of Nationalism in Central Africa*, *passim*.
[84] Fisher, *Macleod*, pp. 170–3; Finer, Berrington, Bartholomew, *Backbench Opinion*, pp. 125–6; Kahler, *Decolonization*, p. 146.

'for the British Government the path of wisdom in this era of revolutionary change in Africa lies in going ahead, coolly and inflexibly'.

On 15 February 1961 Harold Macmillan began his weekly letter as prime minister to the queen: 'Since I last wrote to your Majesty on 7 February', he told her, 'I have had to devote nearly all my time to the Northern Rhodesian Constitutional Conference', and elsewhere he recorded:

If we lean too much to the European side,
1. [African] confidence in Her Majesty's Government will be undermined.
2. There will be serious disorder in Northern Rhodesia, perhaps spreading throughout the Federation.
3. [Some Ministers] will resign.
4. Our Government and party will be split in two.

If, on the other hand, we make a decision which, without satisfying African demands, goes in their general favour,
1. Europeans will have no faith left in Her Majesty's Government.
2. Sir Roy Welensky will declare Federation to be 'independent' and will try to take over Government of Northern Rhodesia by force or bluff or both.
3. If the Governor defends his position, there will be civil war – Europeans versus British officials, troops and Africans.
4. [Other Ministers] will resign.
5. Our Government and party will be split in two.[85]

In the event, Macleod on 21 February announced proposals that went the African way. Yet by 24 February Macmillan was deeply troubled. 'We are preparing', he wrote, 'for the worst event in Rhodesia – that is open rebellion. We are drawing up the necessary . . . plans, if the worst should occur.'[86] But they did not occur, essentially because the government now bent before the pressure which, with much Conservative support, Welensky mobilised against it; and on 26 July Macleod was obliged to issue new proposals that went Welensky's way. In the run-up to these Macmillan recorded: 'By a miracle, we have achieved a solution of the immediate crisis. Both Sandys [the Commonwealth secretary] and Macleod have agreed and so – under pressure – has Welensky. So the Conservative Party . . . are calm and united on the issue.'[87] No doubt they were; but Northern Rhodesia's blacks, correctly understanding what had now happened, erupted as never before. Government buildings, such as schools and workshops, were set alight. Bridges were cut. Roads were blocked. Northern Rhodesia was fast slipping out of colonial control. Thanks to Kaunda's pleas, no whites other than the security forces were attacked. But three thousand arrests were made, and 2,500 blacks were sent to prison. To Welensky's fury, however, since he could readily sense what was implied,

[85] Macmillan, *End of the Day*, p. 309.　　　[86] Macmillan, *End of the Day*.
[87] Macmillan, *End of the Day*.

Macleod on 13 September then announced that only when such disturbances ceased would the constitutional proposals be considered further.[88]

In October Macmillan promoted Macleod to the leadership of the House of Commons and put Maudling in his place. 'Had I thought there would be some relief in the pressure from the Colonial Office,' he was later to record, 'I was doomed to disappointment . . . in some respects he seemed *plus royaliste que le roi.'*[89] The Northern Rhodesian disturbances had clearly left their mark. It was soon apparent that the government's July proposals could not be held to, except at a cost Britain was not prepared to pay. So in February 1962 Maudling finally announced some marginal changes in the new constitution for Northern Rhodesia that did contain the possibility of an African majority. In a House of Commons motion forty Conservative MPs still denounced any such moves; but among the rest of them the Northern Rhodesian disturbances had hit their target. There were two more general elections in Northern Rhodesia, in 1962 and 1964; but on the last day of 1963, following a winding-up conference at the Victoria Falls in the previous July, the Federation disappeared, and in October 1964 Zambia finally became independent.[90]

Throughout these years colonial issues – if one may judge from the regular national opinion polls – were never preeminent in the minds of the British generally. But they did arouse more public interest than usual, and for the most part public opinion seems by this measure to have supported the government's actions.[91] These clearly entailed a wrenching apart of so much that had been fashioned before. That required a determination which probably cost Macleod the leadership of the Conservative Party. It required as well all the soothing skills that Macmillan himself could muster and eventually made him call on his second-in-command, R.A. Butler, to head a special Central Africa Office in March 1962.[92] It also involved the anathemas of Welensky and other white Rhodesian leaders. The outcome ultimately turned on Kaunda's mobilisation of a cohesive UNIP; on the positive impact of the Northern Rhodesian disturbances of late 1961 on the Conservative party; and on Welensky's eventual decision not to take the law into his own hands.

Thus, in that part of Central as well as East Africa where direct British colonial rule had persisted, the British in the end, under mounting African pressure, hastily granted independence as they and others had already done in West Africa. They followed this by granting independence (as they were concurrently doing in the West Indies and elsewhere) to the Gambia in 1965, to Botswana and Lesotho in 1966, and to Swaziland and Mauritius in

[88] D.C. Mulford, *Zambia: The Politics of Independence* (London, 1967).
[89] Macmillan, *End of the Day*, p. 318; Reginald Maudling, *Memoirs* (London, 1978), ch. 7
[90] Mulford, *Zambia*; Lord Alport, *The Sudden Assignment* (London, 1965).
[91] National Opinion Polls Ltd, *Political Bulletin*, passim, for these years.
[92] Lord Butler, *The Art of the Possible* (London, 1971), ch. 10.

1968. With that the second sequence in the tropical African transfer of power was concluded.

There remained, besides the Portuguese territories and of course South Africa, Southern Rhodesia. In 1961 it had obtained a new constitution that, many British Conservatives averred, provided better opportunities for its large black majority, albeit within a country still under white settler control, than they could otherwise have expected. While in London, Joshua Nkomo, Southern Rhodesia's principal nationalist leader at this time, initially agreed to work within the 1961 constitution, but since his associates would have none of this, he eventually joined them in boycotting the ensuing 1962 elections. These were won by the new right-wing white party, the Rhodesian Front, of which Ian Smith became leader in 1964. On the break-up of the Federation, Welensky retired from the fray. Rhodesia, as Southern Rhodesia now became, thereupon inherited most of the Federation's armed forces and under Smith's leadership demanded the total independence that the African countries to its north had now secured. Three British prime ministers in succession, Macmillan, Douglas-Home, and Wilson, made it abundantly clear, however, that without further provision for major advances in the prospects for Rhodesia's blacks there was no chance of any British government granting independence. When in October 1964 the Labour Party came into office under Harold Wilson, a spate of fruitless negotiations was undertaken, but on 11 November 1965 Ian Smith eventually proclaimed Rhodesia's Unilateral Declaration of Independence.[93]

The tortuous story of the years between 1975 and 1980 on this issue can only be summarised here. In the present context several considerations may nevertheless be emphasised. There were no internal black upheavals in the mid-1960s in (Southern) Rhodesia to turn the tables; Zimbabwe's nationalists were much at odds with each other. From 1964 on their various parties were banned and their leaders imprisoned indefinitely. The Labour government contemplated transferring the issue to the United Nations but found several reasons against this. From the outset Wilson signalled that he would not use force. It has been suggested that Britain's military would have refused to obey him if he had done so, but no evidence has been advanced. During 1964–6 Wilson's majority was paper thin, though he did not change his tune when it was enlarged in 1966. There was some huffing and puffing within the Cabinet[94] (and there are indications that if Gaitskell had lived to be Labour's prime minister rather than Wilson he would have

[93] J.P. Barber, *Rhodesia: The Road to Rebellion*, London, 1967.
[94] On this and other such matters see Harold Wilson, *The Labour Government, 1964–1970*, London, 1971; Richard Crossman, *The Diaries of a Cabinet Minister*, 3 vols. London, 1975–7; Barbara Castle, *The Castle Diaries, 1964–70*, London, 1984, *passim*.

been far more resolute).[95] But the basic consideration seems to have been that British public opinion was determinedly hostile to the use of force in Rhodesia. When the archbishop of Canterbury suggested that if the government should use this they would deserve public support, there was an outcry against him.[96] In October 1965 a national opinion poll recorded that only 2 per cent of the British public supported the use of armed force against Rhodesia; a further poll in September 1966 showed that this figure had risen to only 16 per cent.[97] Throughout Wilson knew that on this issue the new Conservative leader, Edward Heath, could and would divide the country against him. That would have been a Labour Suez. As it was, in December 1965 the Conservatives ignominiously split three ways over mild sanctions: for and against, with the leadership abstaining.[98] There is no reason to doubt that these conclusions were imbued with a large element of racism: the British would not support the use of their own troops against their own kith and kin. 'They are prepared to see us standing up for what is right', the Labour minister Crossman put it at the time, 'but they wouldn't tolerate a war against fellow whitemen who are also British subjects'.[99] It remains true that in the unwinding of empire the British used troops only against communists (in Malaya) or against those who made it their business to kill (Mau Mau, EOKA, Aden's NLF). The Rhodesians were not ab initio in that league.

But if the British were not to use troops, what then about sanctions? Here Britain's response was decidedly half hearted. Some attempt was made to draw up a government 'war book',[100] but on the sanctions issue the Labour cabinet contained doubters on three scores. Would sanctions really work? Was it sensible to introduce sanctions that others would simply circumvent? Would sanctions not inflict immense damage on the already feeble British pound?[101] When some sanctions were imposed, the government sought to check the flow of oil to Rhodesia by means of the navy's Beira patrol; but nothing was done when it became known that some British oil companies were breaching its rules.[102]

The principal onslaught on Britain's backsliding came instead from the newly enlarged Commonwealth. At the time this was an unexpectedly potent force. Especially during the years when Britain had been impelled to cut its colonial ties in a tearing hurry and to renege on its apparent commitments to its fellow whites on the partnership score, comfort was

---

[95] Williams, *Gaitskell*, p. 785.   [96] See Crossman's comments, *Diaries*, I, p. 361.
[97] *National Opinion Poll Bulletin*, Special Supplement 1, Rhodesia, Oct. 1965; *ibid.*, Sept. 1966.
[98] Philip Norton, *Dissension in the House of Commons, 1974–1979*, Oxford, 1980, p. 455.
[99] Crossman, *Diaries*, I, p. 361.   [100] *Castle Diaries, 1964–70*, pp. 28, 60.
[101] For example, Crossman, *Diaries*, III, pp. 69, 91, 142, 698, 744.
[102] Martin Bailey, *Oilgate, the Sanctions Scandal*, London, 1979; T.H. Bingham and S.M. Gray, *Report on the Supply of Petroleum and Petroleum Products to Rhodesia*, London, 1978.

taken in Britain from the decisions of most of the swiftly decolonised to join the Commonwealth. Macleod (so his liberal Conservative biographer was shortly to write) 'saved Africa for the Commonwealth'.[103] In the crucial Commonwealth Conference in 1961 when the future of South Africa's membership of the Commonwealth stood at issue, and Nyerere made it plain that Tanganyika would not join if South Africa remained a member, Macmillan regretfully decided to prefer the new black African membership to continued white South African membership. No Labour government could now turn that choice around, and Wilson found himself in the new Commonwealth's line of fire over Rhodesia.

The ranging shots had been fired at the June 1965 Commonwealth Conference, when Nyerere unsuccessfully pressed Wilson to use force against Rhodesia. Soon after UDI Wilson imposed a few selective sanctions. But they did not bite, and to save the day a special Commonwealth Conference – the first to be called outside London – was held in Lagos in June 1966. Wilson only survived this with the statement (which he believed at the time) that sanctions would work in 'weeks rather than months'. Three months later when they again had not, the bitterest conference of all gathered in London. Wilson was called a racist and felt himself in a vice. He now promised that if Smith did not settle soon, Britain would move for mandatory sanctions against Rhodesia at the United Nations and commit itself to no independence until majority rule had been achieved.[104]

On three major (and innumerable lesser) occasions British governments then negotiated with Ian Smith: on *HMS Tiger* in December 1966, on *HMS Fearless* in October 1968, and in the Home–Smith talks of 1971. Though they felt increasingly frustrated and irritated over the Rhodesian issue, they were seeking the impossible. They needed both to entice Smith into a settlement and uphold their verbal commitments to the Commonwealth. They nevertheless successfully trimmed the small print so as to come within reach of meeting Smith's determination to have no black majority in Rhodesia in his lifetime. As early as November 1966 Labour ministers were calculating that over such a settlement Wilson 'would have at most fifty abstentions [in his own party] and he would have the whole Tory party solidly behind him and the whole country as well'.[105] Confident that he was not losing, Smith twice rejected Wilson's offer, on *Tiger* and on *Fearless*, and in March 1970 declared Rhodesia an independent republic. In the end, in November 1971 he made an agreement with Sir Alec Douglas-Home, Britain's Foreign and Commonwealth secretary in the new Conservative government elected in 1970. Home believed that the terms which were then

[103] Fisher, *Macleod*, p. 198.
[104] J.D.B. Miller, *Survey of British Commonwealth Affairs: Problems of Expansion and Attrition, 1953–69*, London, 1974, chs. 9, 10; Arnold Smith, *Stitches in Time*, London, 1981, ch. 4.
[105] Crossman, *Diaries*, II, p. 139.

reached were so favourable to Rhodesia's blacks that 'had we not agreed to a Commission to test opinion, I should have had no hesitation in asking them then and there for the support of the British Parliament'.[106] But a test there had to be, and, as the Pearce Commission early in 1972 quickly found, Rhodesia's blacks would not succumb to the proferred terms. It was estimated that, with luck, these might have brought majority rule to Rhodesia in AD 2035.[107]

'This time', Home wrote, 'it was the Africans who turned down a settlement which could have averted war.'[108] But that was to be myopic. The Smith–Home agreement principally signalled that there was no real alternative for Rhodesia's blacks to the use of force. Britain had reached the end of its line. Opinion polls now showed that while more than one third of British opinion believed Smith could not be trusted, a decisive majority wanted Rhodesia's blacks to accept the Home–Smith terms.[109] When they did not, Britain bowed out, and even the Commonwealth concluded that a return to their earlier assault could make no difference. In Wilson's memoirs of his final term in office during 1974–6, Rhodesia scarcely figures at all.[110]

It was guerrilla war, primarily in the Portuguese territories, that now turned the scales. Again the details cannot be fully specified here. With the Portuguese unmoved by the decolonisations of the British, the French, and the Belgians, and largely impervious to the earlier Asian precedents as well, it was clear that force alone would shake them. Nationalist warfare against them was least successful in Angola, most successful in Guinea, and partially successful in Mozambique. But all told it cost Portugal 45 per cent of its budget, the deployment of 200,000 Portuguese troops, and eight thousand dead. This was soon too much even for its military leadership in Africa. In April 1974 Portugal's Armed Forces Movement overthrew its long-entrenched dictatorship and decreed the ending of Portugal's empire. Guinea became independent in September 1974, Mozambique in June 1975, and Angola in November 1975.[111] Zimbabwean nationalists, much

---

106 Lord Home, *The Way the Wind Blows*, II, London, 1976, p. 257.
107 Details in A. Verrier, *The Road to Zimbabwe 1890–1980*, London 1986; Blake, *Rhodesia*; Robert C. Good, *UDI*, London, 1973; Elaine Windrich, *Britain and the Politics of Rhodesian Independence*, London, 1978; Martin Meredith, *The Past is Another Country: Rhodesia, 1890–1977*, London, 1979; Miles Hudson, *Triumph or Tragedy: Rhodesia to Zimbabwe*, London, 1980; David Martin and Phillis Johnson, *The Struggle for Zimbabwe: The Chimurenga War*, London, 1981.
108 Home, *Way the Wind Blows*, pp. 257–8.
109 Polls reported, *Evening Standard*, 10 December 1971, *Daily Telegraph*, 13 December 1971; see Windrich, *Politics of Rhodesian Independence*, p. 176.
110 Harold Wilson, *Final Term: The Labour Government, 1974–1976*, London, 1979.
111 J. Marcum, *The Angolan Revolution*, 2 vols., Cambridge, 1969, 1978; B. Munslow, *Mozambique: The Revolution and Its Origins*, London, 1983; Patrick Chabal, *Amilcar Cabral*, Cambridge, England, 1983.

riven among themselves and checked by hope against hope that the British might pull off a miracle, only started mounting effective attacks on the Rhodesian regime after 1972. But following Mozambique's independence in 1975 their base areas could be doubled. The third group of skittles was beginning to tumble over.

Portugal's collapse evoked a striking realignment. Nationalist South Africa had so far seen its outward defences lying in white-dominated Angola, Rhodesia, and Mozambique. The first and the third were now overrun, and the second was left dangerously exposed. An alternative possibility had meanwhile suddenly appeared. President Banda of Malawi had long since sought South African assistance, and not been denied it. In so many ways the former British Protectorates, Lesotho, Botswana, and Swaziland, now independent, were from the start South African satellites. Subsequently preparations were made to create in South Africa 'independent' African homelands, Transkei (1976), Bophuthatswana (1977), and so on. A 'pax Pretoriana' comprising South Africa's assistance to new and insecure rulers against their rivals in return for an assurance that their countries would not be used for guerrilla bases against South Africa now emerged as a powerful option.

In 1974 Vorster, South Africa's prime minister, accordingly embarked upon his brief era of 'detente'. Its aim was to fill the post-Portuguese power vacuum in Central Africa with regimes that would be neither communist nor Soviet allied. In the event it did not last, for in 1976 South African forces were attacking just such a regime in Angola. The intervening opportunity was, however, employed by President Kaunda of Zambia to induce Vorster to force Smith to negotiate with the Zimbabwean nationalists. As it happened, the South Africans had very little time for the Rhodesians. They had always been careful to maintain their links with Britain and had invariably declined to recognise Smith's illegal regime. Vorster's entourage, moreover, took the view that Rhodesia should have joined the Union by its referendum in 1923. The consequences of having stood out on its own could not now be baulked. After 1974 South Africa's support for the Rhodesian regime could no longer be relied on.[112]

Back in July 1973 Smith had talked vaguely to Bishop Muzorewa, chairman of the African National Council formed at the time of the Pearce Commission in 1971. But under pressure from Vorster, who was now keenly anxious for a settlement to his north, in November 1974 Smith first allowed Nkomo to meet Kaunda, Nyerere, Machel (of Mozambique), and Khama (of Botswana) – the so-called front-line presidents – in Lusaka and then in December released the Zimbabwe nationalist leaders entirely. There followed, at Vorster's and Kaunda's joint instance, the extraordinary

[112] Deon Geldenhuys, *The Diplomacy of Isolation: South African Foreign Policy Making*, Johannesburg, 1984, especially pp. 39–41.

meeting in a railway carriage on the bridge at the Victoria Falls in August 1975 that Vorster, Kaunda, Smith, and the Zimbabwean nationalist leaders all attended. But it quickly aborted. The nationalists inevitably demanded majority rule. Rhodesia, however, had hitherto not only successfully defied sanctions; it had also so far not been much infiltrated by Zimbabwean armed forces. So Smith was not yet of a mind to settle on other peoples' terms. Late in 1975 and into 1976 he talked to Nkomo alone, but to no better result. The whole position was meanwhile impeded because the split among the Zimbabwean nationalists now released from detention (which in essence dated back to 1963) had become greatly aggravated. In 1975 the Rhodesian security forces murdered Herbert Chitepo, whom they believed to be the most threatening among them, and had the satisfaction of seeing this blamed on some of his rivals.[113] One of the Zimbabwean parties, ZANU, was thereupon expelled from Zambia. In 1976 there was actually internecine fighting between them. All that in turn made it very difficult for Vorster to impose a settlement on Smith, since in front of his own electorate he could not be seen to be encouraging any repetition of the internecine conflicts in which he was fast becoming embroiled in Angola. When, however, in August 1976 Rhodesian forces made a damaging raid, against South African wishes, on a Zimbabwean base in Mozambique, Vorster to Smith's dismay did decide to withdraw the assistance that South Africa had been providing since 1967, and which had been of such importance to the Rhodesian regime.

For by that time (much to Vorster's initial gratification) a larger actor had entered the scene. In 1976 came the intervention in Central Africa of the American secretary of state, Henry Kissinger, troubled as America now was by Cuban troops supporting the marxist regime in Angola, by another marxist regime in Mozambique, and by potentially increased Russian influence over the whole area. After meetings with the British government, with Vorster, and with Nyerere and Kaunda and the front-line states, Kissinger flew to Pretoria in September 1976, where he forced Smith to make a public commitment to majority rule in Rhodesia. Though in the event this intervention was entirely fruitless (Smith simply did nothing about his undertaking), it nevertheless signalled that the tide was turning.[114] Among other things the pressure of the newly fashioned Zimbabwean liberation armies on white Rhodesia was now mounting. Thanks to Smith's release of the principal leaders, their coming together in the new Popular Front late in 1976, the addition of friendly Mozambique bases from which to operate, and the adoption of Maoist policies of first

---

[113] Mr Ken Flower of the Rhodesian security services made this clear to the author. See his *Serving Secretly*, London 1988.
[114] For this and the next four paragraphs see footnote 107 above.

winning over the rural population to their cause, they were now becoming a formidable adversary.[115]

The British, lately quite pitiful in their self-inflicted impotence but still feeling a residual responsibility, now awoke to the fact that the parties might not be quite so far apart as before, and – much prodded from all sides – ventured back to the fray.[116] Labour's representative at the United Nations, Ivor Richard, thereupon presided over the lengthy Geneva Conference beginning in October 1976, which ground to a halt in December, and in September 1977 Labour's young foreign secretary, David Owen, brought in President Carter's envoy, the black Andrew Young, to produce the Anglo–American proposals, for a brief interim British colonial administration prior to the prompt establishment of black majority rule. Again the details reflected the larger fact that Ian Smith's world was remorselessly shrinking.

By 1978 Smith had come to believe this too. But he still wanted a settlement on his own terms, not those of the nationalists' armed forces. So in March 1978 he made his 'internal settlement' with Bishop Muzorewa. Muzorewa's African National Council thereupon won the national elections in April 1979, and Muzorewa himself became prime minister of Zimbabwe-Rhodesia.

The denouement began to shape up in May 1979 when the Conservatives in Britain were returned to office under Margaret Thatcher. Since a black majority had already voted in the 1979 elections within the terms of the internal settlement, she was minded to think they accepted it. In November 1978 the largest breach in her own party's ranks since the Second World War had occurred when the former (once liberally minded) colonial secretary Reginald Maudling had led more than 40 per cent of its MPs to vote against the continuance of sanctions, on an occasion when the leadership itself abstained.[117] There was no possibility that the Conservatives would tolerate any further extension of Rhodesia's sanctions thereafter. Indeed, their election manifesto clearly implied that they would very soon recognise the Muzorewa–Smith regime.[118] Mrs Thatcher was pushed away from this conclusion from three directions: by evidence that neither the Americans nor the French nor most other countries would recognise a Zimbabwean regime established on that basis; by the sudden threat to Britain's overseas interests in Nigeria's now intimidatory nationalisation of British oil installations; and by a well-nigh united Commonwealth Conference in Lusaka in August 1979 at which the Liberal (that is, conservative)

[115] T. Ranger, *Peasant Consciousness and Guerilla War in Zimbabwe*, London, 1985; David Lan, *Guns and Rain*, London, 1985.
[116] Barbara Castle, *The Castle Diaries, 1974–76*, London, 1980, records some of the details in the Labour cabinet.
[117] Norton, *Dissension in House of Commons*, pp. 455–6.
[118] Hudson, *Triumph or Tragedy*, pp. 148–58.

Australian prime minister, Malcolm Fraser, played a principal role against her.[119] The details of the internal settlement had clearly left white Rhodesians in many seats of power and in no way represented real majority rule By now, moreover, the Zimbabwean liberation forces were destroying the underpinnings of the Smith–Muzorewa regime – at an all-told cost of around 20,000 lives. White conscription had become extensive, and it was increasingly uncertain whether Smith could hold out much longer. Back in September 1978, after secretly but fruitlessly seeking a settlement with Nkomo, he had started to declare martial law (on one day, 31 May 1979, sixty-four violent incidents were recorded). During 1979 he extended it to 90 per cent of the country.

Following the Commonwealth Conference in Lusaka, the climax was reached in yet one more of Britain's innumerable end-of-empire Lancaster House conferences. With several thousand liberation fighters now operating within Rhodesia, this occupied much of the rest of the year. The British chairman, the foreign and commonwealth secretary, Lord Carrington, had to cajole and bluster the delegates toward an agreement; but eventually – as by Macleod and others before him – the deed was spectacularly done. Carrington was crucially assisted by Kaunda and, above all, Machel, the hosts of the Zimbabwean base areas, who both badly wanted a settlement. It entailed the dispatch to Salisbury of a last British governor, Winston Churchill's son-in-law, Lord Soames. There were some anxious weeks while the liberation forces came in from the bush. But new elections were held in February 1980, and in March Mugabe, the principal leader of the Patriotic Front, was installed as prime minister of Zimbabwe; on 17 April 1980 the now well-honed flag-lowering-and-raising independence ceremony then took place.[120]

With that the third sequential collapse of the colonial regimes in Africa ended. In striking contrast to the second, it had in every case required an anti-colonial war.

Two or three pertinent comments may be added. In these East and Central African colonies two British colonial policies that ultimately stemmed from the same source (from Durham in Canada in 1839) were bound to clash – the policy of giving self-government to British settler communities without much regard to their numbers and that of granting self-government to non British peoples when their claims became irresistible. In Africa the second decisively prevailed over the first. In Rhodesia this was principally the work of the liberation forces that were eventually mustered against it. Britain in the end took some pride in the outcome. But it had only come about because, in addition to the dedication of guerrillas, Portugal had collapsed, South Africa had double-somersaulted, and the British had been saved, more than once by the Commonwealth, more than

[119] Smith, *Stitches*, pp. 227–50. [120] Lapping, *End of Empire*, pp. 522–34.

once too by Ian Smith himself, and decisively in 1971 by Rhodesia's own Africans from clinching a settlement that scarcely anyone else would have accepted. They gave no thanks to the Commonwealth or the others for their pains. The sheer protraction of the Rhodesian crisis, paralleled as it was by *coups*, killings, one-party regimes and economic collapse elsewhere in Africa, had by this time induced in Britain a great ennui with the Commonwealth and with Africa of an order Macmillan and Macleod, not to mention Creech-Jones and Cohen, would never have dreamt. For them it had been 'make or break'. It proved instead to be, or so many Britons came to feel, 'hear no evil, see no evil, speak no evil'.

It has lately been suggested that international pressures and domestic constraints were at least as important as colonial pressures in propelling the west's former imperial powers to decolonise. This now seems scarcely tenable. For a start, the reality of international pressure can be seriously overdrawn. International moral support was no doubt valuable to nationalist leaders, but in practical terms it amounted to very little. Financial assistance to Tom Mboya in Kenya from the International Confederation of Free Trade Unions was certainly helpful. Overseas scholarships for Kenyans and others,[121] and arms and military back-up elsewhere were no doubt valuable too. But of what good was even the redoubtable Henry Kissinger? At most, all of this support was very incidental. International pressures on colonial powers could be irritants. But the ease with which the Portuguese and Smith regimes brushed them aside for so long serves to underline their ineffectiveness. Such an argument fares no better when one asks whether international pressures (as distinct from other precedents) exercised significant influence earlier over the Belgians' decision to hasten from the Congo or eventually that of the French to concede independence to their African colonies. Harold Macmillan spoke eloquently of 'the great issue in this second half of the twentieth century' being 'whether the uncommitted peoples of Asia and Africa will swing to the east or the west'.[122] Yet it was not that which provoked Britain's suddenly accelerated decolonisation after 1959. It was above all the fervour in the nationalisms they were still confronting. If this had not been displayed it is unimaginable that Britain's Conservative government after 1959 would have embarked on all that was entailed from their political and emotional point of view in dismantling the Central African Federation.

As for the importance of the opinions with influence within the imperial countries themselves, the moral of the tale told here has surely been that the positions adopted there, even when these openly contemplated decolonisation (which was not often the case outside Britain), were invariably broken asunder by the force of nationalist developments within Africa itself. There are some suggestions that once Europe had made its post-war

[121] Goldsworthy, *Mboya, passim.*   [122] Mansergh, *Documents and Speeches*, p. 348.

recovery, control of colonial resources could be dispensed with and the remaining colonies released. But the deliberate decision of the Labour government not to use force in the Anglo–Iranian oil crisis of 1951 – in full accord with Ernest Bevin's well-honed policy of 'nonintervention'[123] that, apart from the Suez aberration, was the evident precursor to subsequent Conservative policy right across Africa – clearly indicates that even where major economic interests were at stake the British would not use military power against nationalist forces, so long as these were neither communist nor deliberately violent, in the way the French did in Indochina and Algeria, the Dutch in Indonesia, and the Portuguese in Africa. (It seems highly unlikely, for example, that after the war the British would have used force in Malaya – vital though its contributions were to Britain's lifeline, the sterling bloc – if the opposition there had been nationalist and not communist).

Where imperialist stances did indubitably count was in fashioning the response that each imperial power successively made toward the colonial pressures to which it was subjected. This has been the principal burden of this chapter. Here the British position was compounded of the contradiction between their deep-seated desire to stay, for prestigious, economic, strategic, and, it must be allowed, certain altruistic purposes, and their long-standing commitment, to themselves and in their empire, to popular self-government. It was that contradiction which created the continuing tensions in their minds when they came to face nationalist forces. Ultimately, if painfully, these were always resolved in the latter direction. But to elevate such conclusions to a primary place in the great terminal decisions of empire is to give them precisely the place they did not have. For without nationalist pressure the contradictions would never have been confronted, let alone resolved. More generally, where under nationalist pressure imperialist reactions were or became accommodating, non-violent transfers of power could mostly occur; where under nationalist pressure these became adamantine, war – in Algeria, the Portuguese colonies, and Zimbabwe – invariably followed. Either way domestic imperial concerns were never primary determinants. Wherever one looks, nationalist upheavals against imperialist rule set the pace: in the Gold Coast indubitably, in French and Belgian Africa too, and palpably in Portuguese territory. Had they been less, or later, than they were in East and Central Africa, as the British fondly expected, perhaps the 'partnership' regimes there might have been the better able to congeal. Since they were not, the British were caught out in a position they found both singularly embarrassing and exceedingly tiresome to handle. Much always turned on how well nationalist movements were welded together: Nkrumah, Nyerere, Banda, and Kaunda were so much more adept here than Awolowo, Nkumbula,

123 Louis, *Middle East.*

Nkomo, and Sithole. All of which then raises the pervasive question of what the ingredients were that precipitated African nationalism and fashioned its varying expressions. A number of suggestions about this have been made above, but it is still a topic requiring much deeper investigation.

10

History and independent Africa's political trauma

The study of tropical Africa's politics has passed through a number of phases since shortly before independence came to the greater part of the continent in the early 1960s. To begin with, a great deal of pioneering work was done on the emergence of African nationalism, party formation, charismatic leadership, and the like.[1] This was later to be much criticised for advancing too simplistic a 'modernisation' thesis, but it remains an invaluable source of important data. There was then a great spurt of neo-marxist analysis, with its accompanying 'dependency' theory. At its best, in Colin Leys' study of Kenya, it could be very illuminating.[2] Its empirical work was not always, however, solidly based; its implicit, and sometimes explicit, prescriptive notions were frequently falsified by events; and there came a stage when it was difficult to keep track of the scholarly internecine feuding which it soon provoked.[3]

[1] For example, T. Hodgkin, *Nationalism in Colonial Africa*, London, 1956; D.E. Apter, *The Gold Coast in Transition*, Princeton, 1955, and *The Political Kingdom in Uganda*, Princeton, 1961; G. Almond and J.S. Coleman (eds.), *The Politics of Developing Areas*, Princeton, 1961; I. Wallerstein, *Africa; The Politics of Independence*, London, 1960; F.M. Bourret, *Ghana: The Road to Independence*, London, 1960; R.L. Sklar, *Nigerian Political Parties*, Princeton, 1963; R. Lemarchand, *Political Awakening in the Belgian Congo*, Berkeley, 1964; J.S. Coleman, *Nigeria. Background to Nationalism*, Los Angeles, 1958; C. Young, *Politics in the Congo*, Princeton, 1965; B. Dudley, *Parties and Politics in Northern Nigeria*, London, 1968; J.P. Mackintosh (ed.), *Nigerian Government and Politics*, London, 1966; C.S. Whittaker, *The Politics of Tradition. Continuity and Change in Northern Nigeria, 1946–1966*, Princeton, 1970.
[2] C. Leys, *Underdevelopment in Kenya*, London, 1975. See also G.W. Kitching, *Class and Economic Change in Kenya; The Making of an African Petit Bourgeoisie*, New Haven, 1980.
[3] For example, S. Amin, *Neo-Colonialism in West Africa*, Harmondsworth, 1973; G. Arrighi and J.S. Saul, *Essays on the Political Economy of Africa*, New York, 1973; J. Rweyemamu, *Underdevelopment and Industrialisation in Tanzania*, Nairobi, 1973; P.C.W. Gutkind and I. Wallerstein (eds.), *The Political Economy of Contemporary Africa*, Beverly Hills, 1976; T.M. Shaw and K.A. Heard, *The Politics of Africa*, Harlow, 1979. For four Uganda examples see: M. Mamdani, *Politics and Class Formation in Uganda*, London, 1956; D.W. Nabudere,

Intertwined with some of this and parallel with most of it were a number of studies of Africa's military *coups*.[4] A good deal of the empirical work here has stood the test of time, and remains of particular importance. There were then some very important studies, especially by Hyden, Bates and Hart, of state–peasant relations in Africa,[5] a matter which still warrants further elaboration by others. Twenty years after independence there came a further sheaf of studies, of Ghana, Zaire, Cameroon, Nigeria, the Horn etc., which often centred on accounts of state patrimonialism in its various guises.[6] These were as solidly informative as anything which had been produced previously. They ranged from accounts that reported little but disaster to a glimmering here and there of just possibly some better things to come. Alongside all of these there has always been a fairly constant stream of symposia and summarising textbooks,[7] along with a sprinkling of

Imperialism and Revolution in Uganda, London, 1980; J.J. Jorgensen, *Uganda: A Modern History*, London, 1981; T.V. Satyamurthy, *The Political Development of Uganda 1900–1986*, Aldershot, 1986.

[4] For example, H. Bienen (ed.), *The Military Intervenes*, New York, 1968, and *Armies and Parties in Africa*, New York, 1978; J.M. Lee, *African Armies and Civil Order*, New York, 1969; C.E. Welch (ed.), *Soldier and State in Africa*, Evanston, 1970; R. First, *Barrel of a Gun: Political Power in African and the Coup d'Etat*, London, 1970; A.A. Bebler, *Military Rule in Africa: Dahomey, Ghana, Sierra Leone and Mali*, New York, 1973; W.F. Gutteridge, *Military Regimes in Africa*, London, 1975; D. Austin and R. Luckham (eds.), *Politicians and Soldiers in Ghana 1966–72*, London, 1975; S. Decalo, *Coups and Army Rule in Africa*, New Haven, 1976; S. Baynham (ed.), *Military Power and Politics in Black Africa*, London, 1986. See also a number of articles by scholars employing quantitative methods, e.g., R. Jackman, R. O'Kane, T. Johnson, P. McGowan and R. Slater, 'Explaining African Coups d'Etat', *American Political Science Review*, 80 no. 1 (March 1986), 225–49.

[5] G. Hyden, *Beyond Ujamaa in Tanzania. Underdevelopment in Tanzania*, London, 1980; R.H. Bates, *Markets and States in Tropical Africa*, Berkeley, 1981 and *Essays on the Political Economy of Rural Africa*, Cambridge, 1983; K. Hart, *The Political Economy of West African Agriculture*, Cambridge, 1982.

[6] J.C Willame, *Patrimonialism and Political Change in the Congo*, Stanford, 1972; N. Chazan, *An Anatomy of Ghanian Politics, 1969–1982*, Boulder, 1983; C. Young and T. Turner, *The Rise and Decline of the Zairian State*, Madison, 1985; T.M. Callaghy, *The State–Society Struggle. Zaire in Comparative Perspective*, New York, 1984; J.-F. Bayart, *L'Etat au Cameroon*, Paris, 1979; R.A. Joseph, *Democracy and Prebendal Politics in Nigeria*, Cambridge, 1987; W.D. Graf, *The Nigerian State*, London, 1988; J. Markakis, *National and Class Conflict in the Horn of Africa*, Cambridge, 1987; C. Clapham, *Transformation and Continuity in Revolutionary Ethiopia*, Cambridge, 1988.

[7] The more recent ones include J. Dunn (ed.), *West African States: Failure and Promise*, Cambridge, 1978; D. Austin, *Politics in Africa*, Hanover, 1978; W. Tordoff, *Government and Politics in Africa*, London, 1984; R. Hodder-Williams, *An Introduction to the Politics of Tropical Africa*, London, 1984; A.A. Mazrui and M. Tidy, *Nationalism and New State's in Africa*, London, 1984; R. Sandbrook, *The Politics of Africa's Economic Stagnation*, Cambridge, 1985; G.M. Carter and P. O'Meara, *African Independence: The First 25 Years*, Bloomington, 1985; P. Chabal (ed.), *Political Domination in Africa*, Cambridge, 1986; P. Duignan and R.H. Jackson (eds.), *Politics & Government in African States*, Stanford, 1986; Z. Ergas, *The African State in Transition*, London, 1987; N. Chazan, R. Mortiner, J. Ravenhill and D. Rothchild, *Politics and Society in Contemporary Africa*, London, 1988; W.O. Oyugi, E.S.A. Odhiambo, M. Chege and A.K. Gitonga, *Democratic Theory and Practice in Africa*, London, 1988; L. Diamond, J.J. Linz and S.M. Lipset, *Democracy in Developing Countries*, Boulder, 1988.

biographies, of, for example, Nyerere, Cabral and Mboya.[8] Thirty years on there is a good deal to which one can turn.

All the same when one looks at the literature on the first three decades of tropical Africa's independence there remains a matter of major importance which if rarely overlooked – it would be difficult to do so – is frequently underplayed. This relates to what must surely be a major question about tropical Africa in the years after independence: why was so much of it so grievously afflicted by so many extremely serious political ills? Whilst this question constantly hovers in the background, there is a notable tendency either to shy away from it because it appears too difficult to tackle directly, or address it in terms that some ready comparisons quickly reveal to be seriously deficient. There are even attempts to pass it off as the inevitable travails of 'the early modern state'. All this is the more serious since there is an accompanying tendency to imply that the general political situation in tropical Africa could not be significantly altered because it arose inexorably from some quite impervious circumstances.[9] Since it is precisely this argument which has so much less warrant than is ordinarily assumed, the fateful prognoses that rest upon it are fortunately almost certainly flawed as well.

There are matters here of very considerable moment. A number of the accompanying elements can be readily indicated. Of the world's poorest thirty-four countries, twenty-one are in Sub-Saharan Africa. It is the only region in the world where per capita food production has in the 1980s actually fallen. Unless something is done about this 1/3 of Africa's food requirements will need to be imported by the end of the century. Life expectancy at an average age of forty-seven is here the lowest for any region in the world. One fifth of Africa's babies die before they are one year old. Whilst the growth in the world's population is running at 2.3 per cent per annum, Africa's stands at 3.2, and Kenya's at over 4. By the turn of the century Africa's population will be half as large again as in the mid-1980s. More than half its population is under sixteen and the proportion is rising steadily. Africa's towns have at the same time been growing at the rate of 6 per cent per annum. In 1960 Sub-Saharan Africa had only three cities with populations of half a million; by 1980 there were twenty-eight; by the year 2000 half of its greatly increased population could well be crowded into cities of 200,000 and more.[10]

[8] C. Pratt, *The Critical Phase in Tanzania 1945–1968. Nyerere and the Emergence of a Socialist Strategy*, Cambridge, 1976; P. Chabal, *Amilcar Cabral*, Cambridge, 1983; D. Goldsworthy, *Tom Mboya*, London, 1982.

[9] I fear this alas is true not least of such otherwise extremely interesting studies as Sandbrook, Callaghy, and Linz et al. (footnote 7). The most helpful guide is R.B. Collier, *Regimes in Tropical Africa: Changing Forms of Supremacy, 1945–1975*, Berkeley, 1982.

[10] These, and other such statistics can be most conveniently traced in the World Bank's *World Development Report* now published annually. See also World Bank, *Accelerated Development in Sub-Saharan Africa: An Agenda for Action*, Washington, 1981.

In the 1980s all this became compounded by drought. This was sometimes bad in the 1960s. It was periodically bad again in the 1970s, and in the 1980s became in parts extremely serious. In 1984 thirty of Africa's states were drought-stricken. Rainfall along the south Saharan belt was 60 per cent less than the mean for 1931–60. The Nile discharge in the northern Sudan was lower than for several centuries. Lake Chad had shrunk in size from 25,000 square kilometres in 1960 to 3,000 in 1985. In places the Niger had been reduced to a mere trickle.[11] For this and a number of other reasons more than half of the world's refugees had come to be numbered in Africa.

As if all this were not enough tropical Africa's economic circumstances soon became quite appalling as well. It was not always thus. From early in the 1950s until the mid-1970s there was economic growth in Africa which by Africa's historic standards was very considerable. It owed a good deal to the more general world boom which had gathered momentum from about 1942 onwards. In the period between 1945 and 1960 the economies of colonial Africa grew from a low base at an annual rate of between 4 and 6 per cent per annum, whilst the growth in Kenya, Gabon and Zaire, at between 6 and 11 per cent per annum ranked amongst the highest in the world. Sophisticated manufactured goods became available as never before. Production expanded. External capital was often readily available. In 1980 Africa's external loans were nine times larger than they had been in 1970. Of course all this entailed a great deal of neo-colonialism at the hands of the former colonial powers, and there was much dependence upon the world capitalist system, but we misconstrue events if we imply that Africa's independence was accompanied or immediately followed by economic recession.

The trouble was that the main changes stemmed principally from a considerable increase in the amount of land under production rather than from any structural alterations or improved productivity. A very large part of the proceeds went into huge increases in public expenditure on health, communications, education, and general welfare upon a scale it was difficult to sustain. There was inordinate public consumption too – State Houses, Parliament Buildings, airlines, embassies, armies. Africa's arms purchases rose from US $300m per annum in 1973 to US $3bn in 1978 and on thereafter upwards. All that was then compounded by overambitious plans for import substitution where available markets were hopelessly small, and was soon accompanied by high levels of corruption, and low prices to farmers (which increasingly acted as a disincentive to production). On these last two matters some West African examples are not untypical. Between 1966 and 1982 Ghana had four (politically motivated) major

[11] For example, A.T. Grove, 'The State of Africa', *Geographical Journal*, 152 No. 2 (July 1986), 193–203.

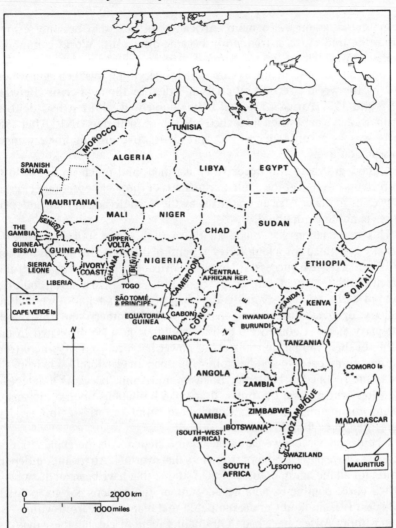

Map 3   Africa 1975

commissions of inquiry into corruption, with little or no effect. Tax avoidance in Nigeria in these years ran out of control. In 1956–7 Ghana cocoa farmers were paid US $355 per ton when the world price stood at US $530. In 1965–6 they were getting US $133 per ton when the world price stood at US $290. The rest was withheld by the state. Naturally the farmers started to opt out of cocoa production. There were similar stories to be told elsewhere.

As a consequence, despite the growth which had often occurred, the economic situation in so many African countries soon became serious. From the mid-1970s it frequently became disastrous. World commodity prices, on which so many tropical African countries depended, first dropped and then sometimes plummeted. Everything was then aggravated, first by the world's second oil crisis and then by the debt crisis. Between 1973 and 1977 Africa's external debt doubled. By 1982 it had doubled again. Sudan's debt when it reached US $7bn equalled its GNP. After 1983 there was as a consequence widespread negative growth in very many African countries.

A good deal here still needs to be clarified, and much no doubt to be corrected as well. Yet the acute parlousness of the socio-economic circumstances in so many African countries by the third decade of their independence is not to be doubted.[12]

This degradation was made all the worse, where indeed it was not actually generated, by a long series of political disasters. By mid-1985 there had been sixty-five successful coups in Africa, no more than a handful of which could be termed 'salutary'.[13] Soon little more than a dozen countries had not had a military *coup*. By 1984 half of Africa's regimes were either military or quasi-military in character; of the others one third were one-party states. Competitive politics could at most be discerned in one eighth of them. So far no transfers of power had occurred anywhere from one governing party to another following upon an election. Aside from the grotesque regimes of Nguema, Bokassa and Amin, preventive detention measures, curbs upon the press, draconian limitations upon criticisms of incumbent regimes, and harsh devices to suppress intra-regime rivalry, were often to be found.

Whereas, however, we can attach some credence to the explanation as outlined above of the economic disasters that overtook Africa after independence, for all the innumerable political studies that have been made, we still lack a correspondingly tenable account of the reasons for its political debacles. It is no doubt understandable that many, both from within and from without Africa, have had their qualms about discussing these matters. It has frequently been impolitic if not, indeed, dangerous to do so. Yet it is high time that the questions were squarely faced. It should properly be recognised that some countries – Senegal, Ivory Coast, Cameroon, Kenya, Tanzania, Zambia, Botswana for example – have been less afflicted than others – Ghana, Nigeria, Sierra Leone, Togo etc. – and that these have been less traumatised than Guinea, Zaire, Chad, Sudan, Ethiopia, Mozambique or Angola, let alone in these years Uganda, the Central African Republic

[12] On so much of this, see D.K. Fieldhouse, *Black Africa 1945–1980. Economic Decolonisation & Arrested Development*, London, 1986.
[13] See C.E. Welch, 'The Military and the State in Africa: Problems of Political Transition', in Ergas, *African State in Transition*, ch. 8, Appendix, pp. 214–15.

and Equatorial Guinea. The downward spiral of political intolerance, political repression and political violence has all the same been dreadful to behold – and so much worse to suffer. We may take our charter for boldly probing these matters from the courageous, forthright, anguished outcries by so many of Africa's leading literary figures, Wole Soyinka, Chinua Achebe, Ngugi wa Thiongo, Cyprian Ekwensi, Ayi Kwei Armah most notably perhaps among them.

The conventional explanation for Africa's political traumas since independence began to be propounded at a very early date, and can be readily listed. Africa's new nations, it was correctly stated, are wretchedly poor and had been very arbitrarily demarcated. 'They inherited the plenitude of autocratic power possessed by the departing colonial government, with few institutionalised restraints upon its exercise. Divisive and separatist tendencies, unchecked by any countervailing sense of national loyalty, threatened the geographic integrity and the internal security of the state, and even the authority of government itself.' 'The exposure to pluralistic democracy was relatively brief.' The 'staggering problem of nation building and modernization requires a central and unitary organisation within the state'.[14] And so on.

Yet, taken on their own, such explanations do not pass muster. For very many of them could be very easily checked off against a profusion of similar conditions in other impoverished, newly independent countries such as India, Malaysia, Mauritius, Jamaica, Trinidad, several of the other Caribbean islands, and so many of those in the Southwest Pacific too where, for all the harshnesses of politics, things have never quite reached the pass that had become commonplace in Africa. One needs to be careful here. There are important countervailing histories of political longevity (of more than one kind) in a number of these countries. It is by no means the case, moreover, that political disturbances, political terrorism indeed, are unknown there; that their governments work effectively; that all is sweetness and light: frequently, on the contrary. These and much worse conditions have variously been found, moreover, in a number of European states, and extensively in Latin America. None the less, all too many of the explanations ordinarily advanced for the political traumas that afflicted tropical Africa after independence remain far too blinkered and do not stand up to comparative evaluation.

If, therefore, there is to be a convincing explanation of the political havoc that occurred in so much of tropical Africa after independence (with all its economic, social and human consequences), it is necessary to be much more discriminating. The primary requirements would seem to be, first, to search out those circumstances that made African countries prone to slip

[14] J.S. Coleman and C.G. Rosberg (eds.), *Political Parties and National Integration in Tropical Africa*, Berkeley, 1964, 'Conclusions', p. 655 sqq.

down the spiral of political disaster – but which they share with a number of not dissimilar countries that to the same degree have not done so – and then to identify those that tipped the balance and were arguably unique to Africa. The indications are that it is especially profitable here to look into that critical period immediately before and immediately after tropical Africa's independence, and that it is in the distinctive history of that period that the principal clues to the fashioning of Africa's fateful political high culture in the years after independence are to be found.

One must nevertheless begin with the fundamentals, since there can be little doubt that these generally created an exceedingly difficult situation for Africa's new nationalist leaders to handle – even if with the caution that henceforward one must be alert to their ultimate inadequacy as a sufficient explanation of why it was that political developments in independent Africa went so fatefully awry.

As with so much else, the starting point must be to recall that as recently as the late nineteenth century it would have been possible to count in Africa, on one calculation 6–800, on another 1,500, on Professor Oliver's reckoning 10,000, politically distinctive 'autonomous units'. During the colonial years, and not least during the move towards independence, these came to be reduced to a mere fifty or so. That was not the process of fragmentation and balkanisation that is so often referred to, but an astonishing, extremely bewildering, and often very painful process of amalgamation.

The blame for the principal anomalies in this process is usually attached to the quite arbitrary fashioning of Africa's territorial boundaries upon the green baize tables of European Foreign Offices in the late nineteenth century. It is perfectly correctly stated that this took no account of the 'tribal' or cultural connections and differences which existed on the ground. That was certainly the case in a great many instances, and some of Africa's most serious post-independence crises – for example in the Horn and in the Sudan – have very directly followed upon that. But it would be well to be cautious here. For if new nations were to be carved out in Africa at all, it was hardly possible to avoid putting together into one polity a variety of peoples who in the past had in no way seen themselves as constituting a single community. With a rather better informed, more sensitively crafted drawing of the maps some of the more egregious misalignments might have been avoided. Yet we delude ourselves if we imagine that the majority of the strains that the amalgamation process of the last hundred years entailed in Africa would somehow thereby have been avoided.

Those strains proved in one respect to be peculiarly serious, principally because by the time independence came a critically important process had ordinarily only reached a half-way stage. Within the arbitrary political boundaries which the European colonial powers clamped upon Africa, it is now well appreciated that processes of social and political aggregation gathered momentum during the first half of the twentieth century and beyond.[15] Networks of small separate communities began to link up locally together in something of a larger entity. Groupings of what had previously been largely separate, small, even tiny rulerships; polities with little or no concentration of coercive force or of elites ruling over them; communities with still less differentiation in power and status within them, variously proceeded to club together; often enough at the instance of their imperial rulers (who for their own ideological and administative purposes required this to happen); often enough too as a means of providing within novel and uncharted circumstances for a modicum of mutual protection against the pressures which both colonial rule and the ambitions of other comparable groups were exerting, or were threatening to exert against them; often enough as well as a means of avoiding internal local class conflicts and divisions at a time of very rapid change and a considerable enlargement of interactive scale.[16] As a consequence there was in Africa during these years an extensive process by which ethnic solidarities that were aggregates of longer-existing, smaller-order, communities began to be established, and new 'tribal' entities and identities came to be created. Thus the Igbo-speaking peoples became the Igbo tribe, the Kikuyu-speaking peoples the Kikuyu tribe, the various Shona groups the Shona people, the citizens of the plethora of Yoruba towns the Yoruba, the Tongan peoples the Tonga, and so on *ad infinitum*.[17]

The serious matter for the post-independence saga was that with relatively few exceptions this process of aggregation had not by the end of the colonial period proceeded much beyond the local level. Little or no such developing sense of community identity had developed at the level of the territories which the colonial rulers had fashioned and which upon independence became the new nations of Africa. The years since Africa had been carved up into its fifty or so new 'territories' had been far too short for any such thing to have occurred – and in any event was often deliberately hindered by the colonial rulers themselves. Moreover, there were not as yet in Africa that plethora of other larger-than-local identities that one finds, for example, in India, which allow people to shift their preoccupations, depending on the situation, so as not to be torn by too close an attachment to any one of them. Upon independence the leaders of the new African nations thus found themselves having to deal with congeries of new, disparate and ordinarily very localised entities, which were often still in their first flush of creation, acutely sensitive to the manifold uncertainties of their novel situation, with many of their own internal linkages still in a raw state, and

[15] See ch. 7 above.
[16] This point retains its importance, G. and M. Wilson, *The Analysis of Social Change*, Cambridge, 1945, esp. chs. 2 and 6.
[17] R. Cohen and J. Middleton, *From Tribe to Nation in Africa*, Scranton, 1970, provides a good starting point.

with very little of that multiplex of associations which elsewhere knitted societies together much more substantially. They were, inevitably, an exceedingly unruly flock to have to try to shepherd into a new fold.

The problems here were made especially difficult by a particular legacy of the European takeover. When that had first been mooted, the European powers involved, often deeply suspicious of each others' intentions, had agreed amongst themselves (principally at the Congress of Berlin in 1884) to recognise each others' new African colonies so long as they were represented on the ground by 'effective occupation'. As none of them was prepared to expend much of its own resources upon these new colonies that meant that whilst they soon claimed dominion over the whole of each of those which came their way, they set about doing this with an absolute minimum of administrative personnel: to begin with, indeed, many of them even devolved their responsibilities to a 'chartered' company. That situation was never, moreover, fundamentally altered, despite the subsequent increases in colonial personnel, particularly following the Second World War. When independence came to Africa its new national leaders inherited therefore a state apparatus which lacked a number of crucial attributes. Territory-wide government was generally still an exceedingly exiguous construct; little related to the social realities over which it was superimposed; in no way bedded into any popular conception of an established 'national' arena; and with next to no roots in any indigenous political culture. Clearly it was an exceedingly formidable task to have to ensure that a nation state functioned in these circumstances when very little more than the bare outlines of a nation state structure actually existed. To have to do this, moreover, with a randomly composed assembly of newly politicised entities would have been enough to tax anyone's abilities. Nation states in Europe, so it has been argued, either began as nations within which a state could be created, or as a strong state within which a nation came to be formed. In Africa at the time of independence there were scarcely any nations and hardly any states.

The major point, however, which has then to be disinterred is that at the time of independence the largest fear amongst both Africans and Europeans alike was that the most likely consequence of this doubly difficult state of affairs was not that the new independent regimes would collapse from within – to begin with many of them looked in the circumstances to be unexpectedly robust – but that the separatist tendencies that the arbitrary nature of so many of the African boundaries were generating right across the continent was bound sooner rather than later to lead many of them to fragment.

Despite the prevalent, high-pitched rhetoric of African unity at the time of independence that fear was only too well grounded. For a start several of the federations which the colonial rulers had formed during the colonial years quickly broke up around the time of independence into their territorial components. French West Africa, French Equatorial Africa, the Federation of Rhodesia and Nyasaland, all split along the territorial boundaries within them, as did the less closely linked East African Community, and the Mali Federation, the Conseil de l'Entente, and the Union of Central African Republics which, in a number of last minute efforts to salvage something from the wreck, several of the francophone West African states had hastily formed. These breakups took place, moreover, despite the considerable efforts of a number of African nationalist leaders to prevent them.

Then, at or soon after independence, the three most extensive European-fashioned territories in Africa became embroiled in large-scale civil wars, each of which centred on the resolve of major regions within them to secure their separated independence. In 1956 the first southern revolt against its northern rulers erupted in the Sudan just as independence dawned. Between 1963 and 1972 this developed into a persistent civil war. Immediately upon independence in 1960, Zaire dissolved into four years of civil war. Within weeks of independence first the Katangan region and then South Kasai declared their separated independence. By 1967 major civil war had broken out in Nigeria too, as Biafra declared its independence. There followed three hard-fought years before this reached its conclusion.

Beyond these major events it was patent that there were a great many demands for some kind of separated existence elsewhere. Back in 1953 Buganda had sought to break away from Uganda. In 1960 it declared it was doing so. Whilst in the short term that was to be of no avail, its vociferous demands for privileged treatment thereafter tore at the very vitals of the new Ugandan state. Likewise the Barotse made special claims for themselves in Zambia. There were threats to the integrity of Guinea from the Foula; to Ghana from the Ashanti; while in both Kenya and Ethiopia between 1964 and 1968 Somali minorities took to violence in support of their demand for transference to neighbouring Somalia. All in all it was a most unnerving prospect.

Yet the astonishing, and all too often neglected, fact is that the very considerable fear which all this generated in Africa was in a relatively short time put to rest. The crucial event here was the triumph of the Nigerian federal government in its civil war with the breakaway state of Biafra. That turned out to be the test case. Whilst Katanga's secession had been successfully brought to an end in Zaire with United Nations help in 1963, the Biafran secession looked as if it might succeed thereafter. Biafra could advance as good a claim to its own separate nationhood as many an existing African state. It made a certain amount of ethnic sense (since it originally encompassed chiefly the Igbo and some related peoples). Its territory was compact. It enjoyed access to the sea. Its agriculture and oil revenues made it look economically viable. Its excision, moreover, would not have left a hopelessly disjointed Nigeria (such as Uganda would have been if Buganda had been separated from it); northern Nigeria would still have had access to the sea through western Nigeria (were northern Nigeria itself subsequently to separate, it would still have been at least as well found as the other interior West African states; whilst, with or without northern Nigeria, western Nigeria would have been just as viable as its neighbouring seaboard states).

Biafra secured a good deal of sympathy both in Africa and elsewhere for these and other reasons. In particular it won recognition not only from Tanzania and Zambia. Since there was a certain amount of francophone interest in seeing the very large anglophone West African state of Nigeria being dismembered, it secured recognition too from the Ivory Coast and Guinea; and because France could see other advantages in its existence, a good deal of French assistance also.

Nevertheless, an overwhelming majority of the African countries, in accordance with their strong support of articles II and VI of the Organisation of African Unity's Charter of 1963, came down decisively against any acknowledgement of Biafra's independence, both because so many of them were plagued in one way or another by secessionist threats of their own, and because they knew only too well that once a precedent had been set for any such breakaway serious consequences could all too easily have ensued elsewhere. They therefore resolutely supported the Nigerian federal government in its war against Biafra, and made no protest against the external assistance which it received.[18]

In view of the considerable world-wide attention the Biafran war aroused, Biafra's defeat by 1970 had very considerable repercussions. For with it separatism in Africa, for a crucial period at least, suffered a fatal blow. Following Biafra's demise only one separatist movement succeeded anywhere in the world for at least the next twenty years. That was in the quite special case of Bangladesh, where the two parts of Pakistan were divided by the whole of India in a way that had no counterpart elsewhere (and where, if one looks at the details, it was arguably West Pakistan that broke away once it looked, after twenty years of independence, as if it would be dominated henceforward by its hitherto repressed East Pakistan majority). In different parts of the world a number of other new states had separatist movements too (for example, in Papua New Guinea, in both Papua and the North Solomons). If Biafra could not succeed, however, it was going to be very difficult for these others to do so. Turkey alone recognised Turkish Cyprus; the campaign for a Sikh state of Khalistan was

[18] S.K. Panter-Brick (ed.), *Nigerian Politics and Military Rule: Prelude to the Civil War*, London, 1970; A.H.M. Kirk-Greene (ed.), *Crisis and Conflict in Nigeria. A Documentary Sourcebook, 1966–69*, Oxford, 1971; J. de St Jorre, *The Nigerian Civil War*, London, 1972.

vigorously resisted by India; while the Kurds were as trapped as ever. With so many new states having votes at the United Nations and so many of them concerned not to establish any tenable precedent, international recognition for breakaway states ceased, for a time at least, to be an option. Whilst African states might be internally weak, in the event they became juridically, in respect of their territorial integrities, extremely strong.

Astonishingly, therefore, the European-drawn boundaries of Africa's new nations now became entrenched. There continued to be a number of international wars in Africa: Somalia versus Ethiopia; Tanzania against Uganda; Libya versus Chad; Mali versus Burkina Faso. However, considering the other problems Africa confronted after independence there really have not been very many of these. There continued to be civil wars – in Angola, Mozambique, Sudan, Chad, Ethiopia and Morocco. Yet, with the possible exceptions of Eritrea and Saharawi (for the altogether outlandish reason that their cases rest principally upon the claim that unlike Africa's other countries their right to independence within their 'colonial' boundaries has been quite arbitrarily denied to them) there is at present no conceivable chance that any of them can be resolved except by some internal settlement.

One kind of nightmare that did make its appearance in Africa in the years after independence thus came to be expunged to an extent that no one at the outset had any good reason to expect.

It is all the more notable, therefore, that, in major contrast, one-party states, military rulerships, internal disruptions, dictatorships and sometimes a good deal worse beside came to possess independent Africa in a way that generally no one had anticipated. This is the more striking since – contrary to much popular and, one has to say, much Africanist scholarly, perception – these things have not been nearly so uniformly common in other comparable situations as is still too frequently suggested.

There have in essence been two sides to what characteristically happened politically in Africa in this respect after independence.

The first arose from the development in Africa of the notion of the 'one-party state'. Several streams merged here. Significantly (as we shall notice again) the idea first seems to have been championed in a number of the new francophone West African states even before independence in 1960. The idea was soon eagerly taken up in neighbouring Ghana. Following the collapse of Zaire it naturally had great attractions there; and before very long it came to be adopted in East and Central Africa too – where the principal challenge had come from white settler-led parties who had stood in the way of the crucial advance to black majority rule. The qualms about the full-blown doctrine of the one-party state which were variously displayed there – which one can see exemplified in, for example, Nyerere's opposition to the all too readily accompanying doctrine of the 'vanguard' party – led to several ingenious modifications upon that side of the continent, particularly the provision for vigorous 'primary' elections within parliamentary constituencies for the positions of party candidate.[19]

Yet there and elsewhere the doctrine of the one-party state soon became entrenched. It was widely argued that a one-party state was an essential prerequisite for the creation of national unity; that only a single dominant party could create the necessary moral community; that the highest priority had to be given to creating a single popular will; that poorly institutionalised states could not afford the luxury of multi-party democracy; that it was necessary to avoid conflict in a new state; that it was essential to support order and rationality; that it was intolerable to have to accept the senseless wranglings of political oppositions; that the obvious shortcomings of multi-party systems were not to be endured; that in new states – poor, ill-equipped and faced with a host of fissiparous tendencies – no other course was possible. At the same time marxists and their like argued the case for a vanguard party; whilst many insisted that a one-party system was a perfectly proper African variant of democratic principles. There was a good deal of intellectual support for these propositions.

The doctrine thus propounded did not, however, for very long stand upon its own. For in almost every case those nationalist leaders who espoused it soon displayed a fateful tendency to employ it in support of a series of moves to entrench their own personal positions, hamstring their opponents, clamp authoritarian control over their national domains, and even set up their own despotic regimes. Nkrumah, for example, very soon gave himself over to such practices – by means of a Deportation and Emergency Powers Act in 1957, a Preventive Detention Act in 1958, a Constitutional Amendment Act in 1959, and his own elevation to an executive Presidency in 1960. In 1964 he capped all this by declaring Ghana to be a one-party state.[20]

In the Ivory Coast, Houphouet-Boigny proceeded along similar lines. Prior to the immediate post-independence elections in November 1960 his party newspaper announced that 'the Ivory Coast will unanimously elect M. Felix Houphouet-Boigny president of the Republic and the seventy candidates of the PDCI deputies to the National Assembly'. He thus became the first of Tropical Africa's new executive presidents. Thereafter he proceeded to bring both unions and youth movements under firm government control. In 1963 he conducted a purge of plotters against his regime. By 1965 his party's slogan announced quite simply its commitment to: 'A single party, for a single people, with a single leader'.[21] Similar

[19] For example, A.R. Zolberg, *One-Party Government in the Ivory Coast*, Princeton, 1974; L. Cliffe, *One Party Democracy. The 1965 Tanzanian General Elections*, Nairobi, 1967.
[20] On much of this see D. Austin, *Politics in Ghana 1946–1960*, London, 1964, ch. 8; H. Bretton, *Rise and Fall of Kwame Nkrumah*, London, 1966.
[21] Zolberg, *Ivory Coast*.

developments were occurring simultaneously in Senegal, Guinea, Mali, Niger, Benin, Togo and Mauritania. They were taking place too upon the other side of the continent. A one-party state was formally established in Tanzania in 1965, along with government control over unions and co-operative societies, and a fairly free use of 'preventive detention';[22] and there were comparable moves in Kenya[23] (though it was not formally declared a one-party state till 1982). As a consequence not only had the doctrine of the one-party state become by the mid-1960s well established as a predominant part of independent Africa's high political culture. There had come to be established as well a sustained thrust towards highly centralised, highly personalised, highly authoritarian, even paranoic dictatorships.

That would have been grievous enough. Yet it was soon to be only the half of it. For there then supervened, soon in nearly countless cases, the further phenomenon of the political coup, and more especially the military *coup*. The triggers here were dual. First, there was the Sudan officer-led army *coup* in 1958. Then in 1960 the mutiny of the 'other ranks' in Zaire – Congo (Leopoldville, later Kinshasha) as it was called at the time – against their (Belgian) officers. To the significance of both of these we must return.

The now notorious major sequence of *coups* in Africa began more particularly eighteen months later in Togo in January 1963, when some veteran soldiers, angry at being excluded from the new order which independence had brought to their country, killed its first head of state. In August 1963 a *coup* was mounted in Congo (Brazzaville), and in October 1963 one in Benin (then called Dahomey). There followed in 1964 the successful anti-Arab revolution in Zanzibar, and in each of the three adjacent East African countries army mutinies as well, which, for the first and last time, the British helped to check. That year there was a further *coup* in the Sudan.

The main sequence of *coups* then gathered momentum in 1965. In 1965 there were *coups* in Zaire, Benin (ex-Dahomey) and Algeria; in 1966 in Upper Volta, Nigeria (twice), Ghana, the Central African Republic, Burundi and Uganda; in 1967 in Togo, Benin (once again), and Sierra Leone; in 1968 in Mali, Sierra Leone (again), and Congo (Brazzaville); and so it went on throughout the 1970s and into the 1980s. Between 1960 and 1972 Benin had six changes of ruler. Soon the Sudan had had its fourth *coup* since Independence, Ghana, Nigeria and Uganda had each had their sixth.

This is not the place to enlarge upon the extensive literature upon these *coups*.[24] They were generally mounted not by the police or the air force, but

---

[22] Pratt, *Critical Phase*, esp. ch. 7.
[23] C. Gertzel, *The Politics of Independent Kenya*, London, 1970.
[24] See fn. 4 above. The best single study is still R. Luckham, *The Nigerian Military*, Cambridge, 1971.

by the army. Variously, they were led by locally trained officers; by those
who had attended overseas military academies, such as St Cyr, Sandhurst or
Mons; but at times too by 'other ranks'. They often stemmed from the
resentful disaffection of people (Zairean other ranks, Nigerian officers,
northern Ugandans) who felt themselves to have been marginalised –
deprived, that is, of the prestige and the pickings which independence had
brought to others. But propelling these upheavals more generally was a
good deal of personal ambition and ordinary human avarice. Yet sometimes
too there was a flickering sense, even if a self-regarding one, of a duty to save
the state from itself. Highly trained officers in particular could persuade
themselves of their unique qualifications to guide the nation. In disturbed
and uncertain circumstances those with arms could, of course, make their
will prevail – and with increasing frequency proceeded so to do. Moreover,
both prior to and subsequent upon a military *coup* army command
structures could often be of some assistance. Yet one army *coup* could very
easily be followed by another. Army officers and personnel were not
necessarily any more politically adept than their civilian counterparts; nor
better able to deliver socio-economic benefits; nor better placed to curb
factional, ethnic and other political rivalries. Army *coups* generally therefore settled very little. More seriously, once the genie of the military coup
had been loosed from the bottle, it proved all but impossible to push it back
there once again.

Whereas, therefore, separatist breakaways ceased to be an inherent part
of Africa's political high culture after independence, one-party states, and
in so many instances military coups and military regimes, soon engrossed
its very core. Both, moreover, quickly developed an appalling tendency to
transmute themselves not simply into authoritarian regimes, but, in all too
many cases, into regimes that were grasping, avaricious, brutal, and
sometimes quite incapable of maintaining any viable civil order. The
appalling consequence for large numbers of ordinary Africans soon became
incalculable.

In trying to understand, however, why the descent into the abyss of so
many regimes took place it will no longer suffice to parade the customary
explanations in the traditional way. For that obfuscates the particulars that
cry out for attention. More especially they ordinarily neglect the crucial
developments over a relatively short period of time which principally
fashioned this development. More careful consideration suggests that it is of
first importance to distinguish carefully between what we may call the
conditioning factors which occasioned the outcome and the determining
ones that so fatefully decided it.

As to the first, it warrants re-emphasising that there were a number of
seriously debilitating circumstances that the first African nationalist leaders
had to contend with upon independence. As has been laboured above, they

now found themselves having to preside over new states whose boundaries had been often quite arbitrarily demarcated; within which there was generally a multiplicity of quite unrelated peoples who felt little or no affinity with each other (indeed often saw themselves as rivals); who somehow had to be welded into a single national community that would readily recognise the legitimacy of those who held overarching political office within it. Such states were predominantly rural; were pervaded by poverty; were suffering the strains of runaway birth rates and galloping urbanisation; were often riven by uneven development between centre and periphery, the coast and the hinterland; and were grievously weak too in institutional sinews. Despite the economic growth that had occurred, they had to endure, moreover, an absolute shortage of resources in high international demand; a crippling dependence upon the vagaries of the world market; a debilitating deficiency in infrastructural development; all too little provision for the greater part of the population; and inadequate revenues for their governments to expend.

The difficulties here were all the more serious since at the time that independence came to Africa the air was thick with ebullient expectations, fervid aspirations and much enhanced demands.

For a start there was widespread impatience amongst the population very generally. This was not simply the corollary of the natural expressions of joy that the colonial regime had gone and 'self-government' had come. It stemmed from a more profoundly based concern that was rooted in the frustrations of several preceding decades.[25]

By the opening years of the present century many Africans had moved into cash crop production for the growing urban and the wider world market. That had seemed to offer considerable new economic opportunities. But after about 1922 there was a marked drop in the prices they received for their agricultural products, and the position worsened thereafter during the world slump in the 1930s. Whilst the Second World War sometimes brought some relief, it brought shortages and controls as well. These troubles persisted into the post-war decades and were then aggravated by inflation. There was a certain amount of euphoria at the time of the Korean war boom, and, as we noted earlier, the economic trends during the next two decades did continue upwards. But they did not move fast enough for so many of those whose hopes had first been whetted and then frustrated. And the result was to be seen in all the rural and urban disturbances that studded the histories of so many of Europe's African colonies before and after the Second World War.

In the course of these disturbances, substantial proportions of the African populace became politically radicalised, and by no means chiefly at the

[25] Interestingly, much the best analysis of all this is in A.G. Hopkins, *An Economic History of West Africa*, London, 1973, ch. 7.

hands of any elitist leaders. This process became intensified as all sorts of rural people now moved into new roles whose actualities all too rarely matched their expectations: teachers, clerks, clergymen, traders, shop-keepers, commission agents, artisans, contractors, lorry owners. The widespread, and much disaggregated, pullulation that then resulted eventually became much too difficult for Africa's colonial rulers to control without resorting to the draconian repression they knew their metropolitan electorates would not support. So in the end the colonial administrations scrambled to hand over responsibility for controlling these situations to the hands of Africa's eager nationalist leaderships. Yet after a brief honeymoon they too were faced with all the problems of having to control the highly volatile populaces over which they now presided[26] and they soon found their effervescent aspirations all but impossible to meet.

That problem was all the worse because it went with one other. Hitherto few parts of Africa had had established elites, while the colonial powers had generally done their utmost to keep aspirant bourgeoisies in check. With the advent of nation statehood elite positions suddenly, however, became available upon a much larger scale than ever before, and a second, African scramble for Africa then ensued, as all manner of aspirants pushed and elbowed their way towards the new elite positions which were now opening up. The newly western-educated assumed that they had a special claim to such positions. That meant that in the absence of a well-developed private commercial sector, they were able to gain control of those parts of the public sector that had money and positions to offer. After independence (as indeed sometimes before) there was as a consequence an intensive fight to become the insiders here – within the new public corporations, marketing boards, government departments, and the like that were now looking for African operators. In the struggle for access to the quite unaccustomed wealth that such positions had to assign – and the revolution in the circumstance of their own kith and kin which could thereby be effected – the scrambling elite often found themselves propelled by much familial pressure from behind. As total resources were far from being abundant, the competition for their control could accordingly become exceedingly sharp, if only because an opportunity once let slip might not necessarily recur. The elite politics of scarcity were accordingly tumultuous to behold and generally exceedingly difficult to contain.[27]

These things were the more fateful because of the position so frequently adopted by Africa's principal nationalist leaders themselves. Not only were they generally avid players in this second scramble. They were often dazzled by the vistas which suddenly opened before them. When one thinks

---

[26] See ch. 9 above.
[27] For a memorable account of an early example of all this see K.W.J. Post and G.D. Jenkins, *The Price of Liberty. Personality and Politics in Colonial Nigeria*, Cambridge, 1973.

of the speed with which so many of them had in the end triumphantly led their countries through the seemingly impenetrable barriers of colonial rule, it is not at all surprising that so many of them should have been carried away by the spectre that they had of an historical mission to fulfil. When, moreover, after long years of colonial rule, colonial exploitation, and colonial denigration they suddenly found themselves having to represent their own new nations both to their people beneath and to the world beyond, it is not surprising either that so many of them should have come to see themselves as the human, symbolic, heaven-born embodiments of the very existence of their countries. When to this was added the inordinate responsibilities they had placed upon them to push the substantial economic and social development of their countries forward; to meet the surging aspirations of so many of their people, and to keep atop the contests for position and place that were now raging, it is scarcely to be wondered at too that they were hugely impressed by the dimensions of their task, frequently evinced a hegemonic imperative to shape their country's destiny, and displayed a hubris which soon engulfed them.[28]

To all this was then added the inevitable rivalries between men at the top – in Senegal between Senghor and Mamadou Dia, in Ghana between Nkrumah and Gbedemah, in Zaire between Lumumba, Tshombe, Mobutu and so many others, in Kenya between Mboya, Odinga and Kenyatta, in Tanzania between Nyerere and Kambona, in Malawi between Banda and Chipembere, in Zambia between Kaunda and Kapwepwe. A prodigal recipe for political turmoil thus resulted.

The difficulties in coping with this febrile, rampant ferment were in all conscience huge. For a start the instruments to hand were quite inadequate. Despite the enthusiasm lately generated for anti-colonial nationalism, it was difficult to find a strong nation-wide political party in independent Africa that was tempered in the face of preceding adversity, and could act as a new state's principal prop. Not only was there scarcely anything to compare with, for example, the Indian National Congress or the Chinese Communist Party. It was even difficult to find in Africa after independence any great effort being expended upon maintaining the party formations that did exist.

Bureaucracies were generally quite inadequate too – in size, experience, and the length and strength of their traditions. There was little in Africa to compare with the bureaucratic machinery, bureaucratic numbers, traditional 'service' communities that existed in India, and still more in China. Such bureaucracies as did exist were often spatchcocked together as independence came, and were seriously short not merely of trained and experienced managers, but of skilled administrators too.

The tax base for the new African states was, moreover, grievously

---

[28] For an elaborated discussion of the range of categories here see R.H. Jackson and C.G. Rosberg, *Personal Rule in Black Africa. Prince, Autocrat, Prophet, Tyrant*, Berkeley, 1982.

limited. That was an old story. In pre-colonial Africa there had never been much industry at all to tax, while population pressures had rarely been so great as to enable a land tax to be collected. Characteristically, early colonial regimes were able to do very little more than levy a poll tax. The one available source for a reasonably remunerative taxation system in Africa was, as ever, commerce. That had been widely the case in pre-colonial Africa.[29] During the colonial years the opportunities here were considerably improved. Production for the world market increased both in tropical agricultural products and in minerals. Then, following the extensive development of state monopoly marketing boards, especially during the Second World War, it became possible for colonial governments not merely to levy sizeable export taxes upon such products, but to raid the reserves the marketing boards originally built up with a view to keeping producer prices stable as world prices slumped. Given the extremely parlous economic and budgetary situations which usually obtained, such mechanisms generally presented a major temptation first to colonial governments and then to independent regimes to exploit. Arguably this was done in the good cause of national development, but in due course it was done at least as much in the cause of elite aggrandisement and for the financing of patronage networks. The consequences could be very serious. The one financial resource which was available now came to be so much abused as to destroy its dependability. Since it entailed the forced exploitation of peasant farming, peasant and other producers – who benefited too little from the projects which it financed, and were the principal losers from these proceedings – soon sensed what was happening and, so as to ensure that they were fleeced no more, took one or more of the exit options: operating a black economy; smuggling across a convenient boundary; ceasing to produce for the urban and world market upon the scale the national leadership required. Governments thereupon had to learn the hard way that peasants needed governments less than governments needed peasants.[30] The mishandling of this made the new governments' tasks all the more difficult.

In addition to the heightened tension which these various strands generated, two further inputs contributed to the outcome. One was the dual heritage of African politics. It is periodically forgotten that up until the end of the nineteenth century, and into the first decade or so of the twentieth, political violence in most parts of Africa (aggravated in East, North-east, Central, West, and West-central Africa by all the various slave trades; there and elsewhere by territorial disputes, territorial expansionism, and much else besides) had become all but endemic. That is abundantly clear from the briefest of glances at the pre-colonial history of almost any part of the

[29] See especially A.G. Hopkins, 'The World Bank in Africa: Historical Reflections on the African Present', *World Development*, 14 no. 12 (1986), 1,473–87.

[30] Hyden, *Beyond Ujamaa*; Hart, *Political Economy of West African Agriculture*.

continent.[31] Such violence then reached its climax in the piecemeal conquest of so much of Africa by its colonial powers.

It warrants emphasising that these traditions of violence had not all that long been buried by the time of independence. A single instance must suffice: Houphouet-Boigny, the long-standing post-independence president of the Ivory Coast, was just three years old when the French conquered the area in which he was born. By definition his father was by that time an adult, who would not only have lived through the conquest by the French, but through the local, violent conflicts rife in his region. One finds a contrast here with India – indeed with the West Indies too – where for a century and more before independence the colonial state's monopoly of coercive force had prevailed, and local warfare of a kind so commonplace in Africa had passed to a greater degree out of folk culture. Political violence in post-independence Africa has more roots in this pervasive feature of a not so distant past than is generally allowed. It is no coincidence, for example, that the cultural roots of the notorious President Amin of Uganda lay in the rampant slave raiding in the nineteenth century southern Sudan, or those of the Ethiopian Dergue in the armed expansion of nineteenth century Abyssinia. There could be other examples too.

Political violence on the earlier scale ceased once colonial rule was finally established, but this was by no means true of the political activity that had gone with it – at least, to judge from some well attested cases.[32] There persisted the rivalries, conflicts, alignments, and realignments which are the stuff of politics everywhere – as classes strive for primacy, and elites compete for power – and before long all of these spread into the new 'tribal' and national arenas that came to be formed by the middle decades of the twentieth century. As independence came, Africans, that is, were already hardened practitioners in political struggles, as so many of them were shortly to confirm.

But it was not just the heritages of African politics that permeated the situation. There were the heritages of African government as well. In pre-colonial times, along with so much sophisticated structuring, there had been a good many polities that were both volatile and fragile, and others which were predatory, innured to violence, and even sometimes the insecure creatures of a despotic individual.[33] Pre-industrial polities were generally governed by a high degree of institutional coercion, and Africa's polities were no exception. The successor colonial regimes ordinarily established much more extensive political frameworks and more effective

[31] See the evidence summarised in all the regional chapters of R. Oliver and G.N. Sanderson, *The Cambridge History of Africa*, vol. 6, 1870 to 1905, Cambridge, 1985.

[32] For example, J.D.Y. Peel, *Ijeshas and Nigerians. The Incorporation of a Yoruba Kingdom, 1890s–1970*, Cambridge, 1983; D.A. Low and R.C. Pratt, *Buganda and British Overrule 1900–1955*, Oxford, 1960.

[33] For example, *Cambridge History*, vol. 7, *passim*.

control over the use of coercive force. Yet characteristically they too were inherently authoritarian, periodically draconian, frequently exploitative, as well as being highly centralised and ultimately very personal – not merely at the level of the district officer, but more especially in the person of the territorial governor. They were often, moreover, highly statist and some-times corporatist as well. Some attention was given in the terminal colonial years to the much lauded principles of democratic government, but not only were these markedly at odds with the continuing practice of Africa's colonial rulers, when it was finally decided to start to institutionalise them that could only be done very hurriedly as the colonial rulers set about departing. Had the preparations for independence been as protracted as some colonial governments had originally planned; had democratic habits been steadily built up over a number of decades from the local level upwards as some had intended, they might have put down roots of the kind that, despite numerous vicissitudes, they did both in India and in the West Indies – where the gestation periods were so very much longer. As it was, Africa's much older traditions of despot rulers, political violence and aggressive politics soon became meshed with colonial gubernatorial prac-tices, political detention systems, and a neurotic concern over the control of coercive force, so as to recreate in a new guise too many of the noxious characteristics of traditional African kingdoms and of the successor colonial states as well. These dual but complementary legacies had a great deal to answer for.

One could go on in this way piling up the list of circumstances that conditioned the political development of so many of Africa's new nations in the aftermath of independence and made them prone to the authoritarian-ism, *coup* fever, violence and so much worse besides that variously came to overtake so many of them. The fact, however, is that with next to no exceptions the circumstances listed above can be readily identified as applying elsewhere, and not least in the ten new states of the South-west Pacific. For those, after all, were just as newly formed; just as impover-ished; at least as denied a developed bourgeoisie; just as arbitrarily demarcated; just as divided (e.g., between highlanders, Papuans, Tolai etc. in Papua New Guinea, or francophones and anglophones in Vanuatu); at least as internally differentiated (the different languages in PNG and Vanuatu run into hundreds); no less plagued before and after independence by secession movements (e.g., the North Solomons and Papua in PNG); just as afflicted by avaricious elites (as the stories of forestry concessions and mineral studded islands illustrate); at least as deficient in taxable resources; equally endowed with traditions of political violence; just as bereft of helpful traditions of government; similarly compromised by their colonial pasts; and in several instances led by larger-than-life individuals too. Whereas Nkrumah was 'Osagyefo' and Kenyatta 'Mzee', Somare in PNG has always been 'The Chief', whether in or out of office; whilst Ratu Mara in Riji had invariably exhibited a keen sense of mission – to secure the position of the indigenous Fijians. These countries all became independent, moreover, during essentially the same period as the greater part of Africa – beginning with Western Samoa in 1962 and ending with Vanuatu (despite the French) in 1980 (the same year as Zimbabwe).

And yet, apart from the late-in-coming Fiji *coup* (which had none of the bloodshed so common in Africa, and to which we must return), none of them has seen the establishment of an authoritarian one-party state, nor a coup, nor a military takeover. None of them has resorted, moreover, to the preventive detention, censorship of the press, suppression of opposition, or authoritarian rulership so common in Africa. On the contrary, they have seen twenty and more peaceful changes of government by well established constitutional means, following general elections, parliamentary motions of no confidence, even decisions by alien chief justices against incumbent prime ministers – a host indeed of democratic, peaceful, constitution-respecting proceedings which so much of the commentary on independent Africa far too quickly suggests cannot reasonably be expected of such countries.

Certainly the populations of these South-west Pacific countries are often significantly smaller – sometimes indeed quite tiny – as compared with those in Africa. Yet there are quite a number of African countries with similarly sized populations. That, however, has not insulated them from the continent's malaise. There can of course be no guarantee that the South-west Pacific countries will persist in their original course. Whatever the peculiar circumstances of Fiji – where the Indian immigrants constitute a growing majority over the indigenous Fijians – the Fijian *coup* in 1987 may well have set an ominous precedent there; while developments in 1988 in Vanuatu do not bode well for the future either. Yet the fact remains that the remarkable story of the early decades of political independence in the South-west Pacific[34] puts firmly into question the common Africanist assumption that anything other than the road that so much of Africa took upon independence was at all conceivable.

We therefore need to unearth for Africa those further circumstances that can plausibly be advanced as providing some explanation of why it was that

[34] For an early summary, see G. Fry, 'Succession of Government in the Post-Colonial States of the South Pacific: New Support for Constitutionalism?', *Politics*, 18 no. 1 (May 1983), 48–60, and, for example, J.A. Ballard, *Policy Making in a New State. Papua New Guinea 1972–77*, St Lucia, 1981. On the 1987 Fiji coup see E. Dean and S. Ritova, *Rabuka. No Other Way*, Suva, 1988; D. Scarr, *Fiji. The Politics of Illusion*, Sydney, 1988; B.V. Lal, *Power and Prejudice. The Making of the Fiji Crisis*, Wellington, 1988; R.T. Robertson and A. Taminasau, *Fiji. Shattered Coups*, Canberra, 1988; C. Herder, *The Guns of Lautoka*, Auckland, 1988; K. Bain, *Treason at 10*, London, 1989. On the Vanuatu episodes in 1988 see S. Littlemore, *Mistake of Law? The Vanuatu Sedition Trial, Port Vila, 20 February–7 March 1989*, Sydney, 1989.

so many countries in Africa slid down the spiral of political debacle which do not seem to have been replicated elsewhere. For until further consider-ations can be brought to bear upon this issue than those canvassed above, any convincing explanation for the fashioning of Africa's distinctive political high culture after independence remains out of reach.

In the end, therefore, seven suggestions can be offered.

First, it does seem that the euphoria that accompanied the attainment of independence in Africa was significantly greater than occurred elsewhere. Independence in South Asia was won at the conclusion of a long and wearying struggle, and was immediately marred by appalling massacres, particularly in the Punjab. Decades later when independence came to the South-west Pacific it certainly brought great joy, but it was not the sensational achievement there that it was almost everywhere in Africa. Even in British West Africa 'Self Government Now' arrived a great deal more speedily than anyone had anticipated. Its advent in the French and Belgian colonies was sudden in the extreme; whilst in the light of earlier events, and the alternatives, the attainment of black majority rule in East and Central Africa was all but miraculous. The intoxicating excitement which the precipitant advent of independence stoked in so many parts of Africa does seem to have presented its newly installed political leaders with consider-ably greater demands upon them than were ordinarily advanced elsewhere.

Secondly, there is the intriguing contrast between the overall electoral majorities which very many African nationalist leaders and their then political parties secured in the run up to independence, and the fact that except in Vanuatu no nationalist party or nationalist leader in any of the South-west Pacific countries succeeded in the period prior to independence in winning an overall electoral majority. In the South-west Pacific the consequence was that coalition-making, consensus-building, necessarily became the order of the day, and the key to political power. Once that pattern had been set ('the Pacific Way', as Ratu Mara called it), a readiness to follow it, or so it would seem, persisted – except when, as in the case of Fiji, coalition-making, in which the Fijians remained dominant over the Indian majority, finally failed (after some notable earlier successes) to be satisfactorily effected. By contrast the overall electoral majorities which a number of African leaders won in the pre-independence years (and which thereby, or so it appeared, forced their colonial rulers to grant indepen-dence to them) seem to have led a good many of them, along with their associates, to the conclusion, not just that they were entitled to enjoy the fruits of their achievements, but (in a number of cases) that they were God's own gift to their country. Not merely did this mean that they became exceedingly impatient of political opposition, especially from those who for a range of reasons had recently challenged them unsuccessfully at the polls. All too many of them came to view opposition itself as unwarranted, illegitimate, seditious, even indeed treacherous; and from that it was often a short step to all the draconian measures to curb, imprison, even kill their opponents and rivals that have punctuated the history of so much of post-independence Africa.

Then thirdly, whilst it is certainly true that in a number of other situations there were good grounds for fearing that separatist breakaways could occur, there can be no doubt that until the defeat of Biafra these fears in Africa were both real and profound. The significant point here is that it was not until after the defeat of Biafra that any corresponding concerns arose in the South-west Pacific, and for the reasons canvassed above they could never as a consequence have been nearly so substantial there. The real anxiety upon this score in the minds of many African leaders during the 1960s – when Zaire was riven, the Somalis fought, and Biafra threatened – is not to be gainsaid. It made the arguments for a firm grip upon Africa's fledgling states a great deal more plausible than may have been implied above.

A fourth consideration relates to each of these three collectively. The advent of independence in many tropical African states was marked not only by speed, the political success of a majority party, and inchoate apprehensions of internal disruption. It was rare for any of these to be counterpoised by extensive local participation in the new states' constitution-making. As things transpired there was next to no time for this in either the former French or the former Belgian colonies. In the British African countries there were often several constitutional conferences; but, for East and Central Africa, these were invariably focussed upon inter-racial issues (how many seats for Europeans, how many seats for Africans), and in any event, both there and in West Africa, principally took the form of negotiations between the nationalist leaders and the British, rather than between different indigenous elements within the countries concerned themselves. Even where such negotiations did take place, they were generally conducted in London, under the shadow of the imperial power, and not in the country, and amongst the people, who would have to live with the consequences. The net result, almost invariably, was that in the making of the new independence constitutions in Africa quite inadequate consideration was given to the latent interests of a number of strongly placed elements within its new states – all too often with dire results.

Here again there are notable contrasts with the South-west Pacific. There a very different pattern was set, initially in Western Samoa around 1960, where not only was the constitution principally thrashed out by local leaders amongst themselves (admittedly with the help of European constitutional experts – variously Professors Davidson, Aikman, Ghai or Murray – who were, however, advisers *to them* rather than to their imperial power), but a number of them took quite a long time to do this, and moreover consulted their publics widely whilst they were doing so. This does seem to have meant that many more of the potential strains within the new South-west Pacific states were faced and accommodated than was ordinarily the case in Africa.[35]

A fifth consideration calls for particular emphasis. One-party states of an increasingly despotic kind began to be fashioned in independent Africa at a very early date. These developments occurred most substantially in the francophone states. Here it is necessary to remind ourselves of a very particular situation. In the immediate pre-independence years many of the nationalist leaders of the French West African countries were keenly alert to political developments within France itself, more particularly because a number of them were personally much involved with France's national politics – through direct association with one or other French political party; through membership of the French National Assembly in Paris; occasionally as a minister in a French government (associations that had no counterparts on the British side). It is of singular importance to remember that – during the highly impressionable years preceding independence – this meant that significant numbers of them lived at first hand through the ignominious collapse of the French Fourth Republic and the advent of the strong man to save the French state – General de Gaulle. In contemplating their own impending situation at that time it is hardly surprising, therefore, that they should have drawn some very direct conclusions from these events. For if France, with its longstanding democratic traditions, seemed incapable of making a multi-party system work, and indeed found its democracy driven to its knees and forced to accept an authoritarian leader who would exercise firm authority over it, what hope was there (so they quite reasonably concluded) for their own, new and far more fragile countries? Prime Minister Denise of the Ivory Coast soon said it all: 'therefore, if a country such as France, with a solid administrative base managed with superlative skill, nearly sank because of a deficient parliamentary regime, I believe that the danger is even greater for a young country such as our own, because we have a great deal left to create.' Amongst the francophone African leaders there was at the time much admiration for General de Gaulle. Strong centralised control under a single dominant personality seemed to have a great deal to commend it. As, in a great hurry, they then proceeded to draft their own constitutions, they not only adopted the principles of this doctrine. They very often lifted from the constitution of the new Fifth Republic the wording that embodied it.[36]

[35] The classic account is in J.W. Davidson, *Samoa mo Samoa. The Emergence of the Independent State of Western Samoa*, Melbourne, 1967. See also Ballard, *Papua New Guinea*; P. Sack (ed.), *Pacific Constitutions*, Canberra, 1982; Y. Ghai (ed.), *Law Politics and Government in Pacific Island States*, Suva, 1988.

[36] A.R. Zolberg, *Creating Political Order. The Party-States of West Africa*, Chicago, 1966, canvassed most of this close to the time.

As it happened their example meshed with the personal concerns of Kwame Nkrumah in Ghana next door. There his Convention Peoples' Party preached the slogan: 'the CPP is Ghana and Ghana is the CPP'. During the 1950s the CPP had indeed regularly secured an overall electoral majority based upon its regional base in 'the Colony' (near the coast). But it had then been sharply and even violently challenged by the Ashanti-based National Liberation Movement. In 1956 the CPP won pluralities in only two of Ghana's four regions, and in several subsequent ballots the proportion of the population that voted for it dropped considerably. In these circumstances the doctrine of the one-party state and the case for an authoritarian ruler exerted with Nkrumah and his associates a quite irresistible pull. It was soon to be the same in Zaire (to which we must return); while in countries such as Tanzania, Zambia and Malawi, where monolithic nationalist parties had been crucial to their escape from the maw of European dominated regimes, the doctrine had much to commend it as well.

The circumstances in the South-west Pacific at the formative time – if we may take their case again – was in each of these respects in no way similar. There the prevalent political models were neither the French Fourth nor the French Fifth Republic, but, in the first place, positively, the parliamentary systems (despite their weaknesses) of Britain, Australia and New Zealand, and then negatively, the nearby authoritarian right-wing regimes of Presidents Suharto in Indonesia and Marcos in the Philippines. Since these South-west Pacific countries possessed very few white settler problems, they felt none of that compulsion for unity, moreover, which had exerted so strong a pull in East and Central Africa.

Beyond these there were two further considerations. As to the sixth, Africa arguably shared this with a number of other states such as Pakistan, Burma and Indonesia; but, once again, apart from any conclusions the Fijian Colonel Rabuka may have drawn from his UN peace-keeping service in Lebanon, it did not apply in the South-west Pacific. This was the proximity to tropical Africa of the post-Second World War rash of military *coups* in the Middle East. The first of these had occurred in Syria in 1949. There were eight more there before 1966. There was then the major Neguib–Nasser takeover in Egypt in 1952; and in 1958 the Iraq *coup*, which, as in Egypt, swept aside an entrenched aristocracy.

In the formative years around 1960 when the greater part of Africa became independent it needs to be remembered that there were particularly close associations between the first African independent countries (and especially perhaps the then very influential Ghana) and the Arab countries to the north. President Nasser in particular was extremely active in the more radical Casablanca group of African nations. Cairo Radio played a considerable part in articulating Africa's anti-imperialist feelings; while

Nasser's Egypt presented a striking model for those who were minded to create a radical nationalist, anti-imperialist and internally reformed regime elsewhere.

Earlier in this chapter we noted that the first military *coup* in ex-colonial Africa occurred in Sudan as early as 1958. It there took place on the Middle Eastern–tropical African borderline, and it was from there that a conduit was opened up by which this Middle Eastern phenomenon, that could trace its roots back to Ataturk in Turkey, began to flow into tropical Africa to the south. Its key element lay in the belief that army officers were uniquely well placed to effect a renaissance in the state where civilian politicans had shown themselves incapable of managing it. On independence Africa's first nationalist leaders were generally permitted a honeymoon period of three to five years. But once those were over, the demonstration effect of these Middle Eastern *coups* (reinforced by the second Sudan coup in 1964) became very difficult for many of Africa's younger officers to withstand. By the mid 1960s army officer *coups* were beginning to spread in many parts of the continent in a way that no one had predicted.

So much of all this was then compounded by a seventh phenomenon. This was *la pagaille*, the shambles, in Zaire. This is not the place to rehearse that story in any detail.[37] For present purposes it had four important aspects. First, the mutiny of the Force Publique within a few short days of independence in 1960 provided a precedent for 'other ranks' elsewhere to erupt in their own cause. That precedent was soon followed by 'other ranks' in Dahomey in 1963, in East Africa in 1964, in Nigeria in July 1966, in Sierra Leone in 1967, and periodically in a good many other places thereafter, most notably perhaps by Staff Sergeant Doe in 1980 against the long-entrenched True Whig elite in Liberia. An ominous variant upon the officer *coup* thus became a further feature of Africa's high politics. Secondly, the murder at Katangan hands in 1961 of Patrice Lumumba, the country's first prime minister, set a momentous precedent too. It not only stoked the paranoia of incumbent presidents. It fatefully undermined any inhibition there may have been elsewhere to repeat the performance. Thirdly, the Zairean crisis heavily reinforced the belief already gaining credence that only resolute action by the powers-that-be could preserve the integrity of the African state. In this connection it is worth recalling just how much the Zairean crisis plagued the mind of Britain's then prime minister, Harold Macmillan, who became excessively anxious lest it be replicated in Kenya or in Central Africa. If that was his reaction concerning a matter that was in no way central to the ordinary concerns of his faraway countrymen – however important it was to his own government and his

---

[37] C. Hoskyns, *The Congo since Independence, January 1960–December 1961*, London, 1965; Young, *Politics in the Congo*; Young and Turner, *Zairean State*; Callaghy, *State–Society Struggle*.

party[38] – the impact it had upon others so much closer to it is not to be wondered at. Thereafter their authoritarian propensities were immensely reinforced when out of the Zairean morass there emerged in 1965 – the fourth point – the highly authoritarian, rhetorically-impelled figure of General Mobutu, who to all appearances soon proceeded to bring *la pagaille* to an end (his later achievements were a good deal less commendable). Given this baneful Zairean story unfolding at the heart of the continent during these first impressionable years, it is in no way surprising that it should have immensely influenced developments in neighbouring countries – reinforcing paranoias, justifying dictatorships, encouraging ruthless, ambitious, over-confident unknowns. The malignity of its influence ran well beyond measure.

It may be felt that not enough attention has been paid above to the international dimensions of this whole story. But whilst there can be no doubt that the commitment of the major world powers to the notion of the nation state helped to buttress the juridical existence of Africa's fledgling nations; whilst there can be no doubt too that the western powers were intensely concerned about the possibility that independent Africa could fall into Soviet clutches (and were much concerned about Soviet involvement in such places as Zaire, the Horn, and South Central Africa); and whilst, moreover, there is abundant evidence that external powers intervened in critical political situations in Africa so as to exploit and aggravate its conflicts sorely, it is nevertheless much more difficult than is sometimes suggested to adduce reliable evidence that there was substantial foreign involvement in Africa's fateful slide into one party states and political and military coups in the first place.

As it was, the outcome of the other factors outlined here had led, before the end of the 1960s, to the lifestyle of Africa's high politics taking the forms that were now to be so familiar. One party states developed into one-person dictatorships, were then cut short by coups, sometimes led by officers, sometimes by NCOs. The cures, moreover, were frequently worse than the disease. If one knot of people could seize power, so could another. Over the years many people sought to do so. Not all of them succeeded. Many of them paid with their lives for botching the attempt. But numbers of others pulled it off even so.

One can get a telling glimpse of the situation all this created in the importance attached to a president's praetorian guard, fashioned to provide for his own personal safety. Nkrumah had his Own Guard Regiment; Kenyatta and (during his first presidency in Uganda) Obote had their General Service Units; Mobutu in Zaire and Ahidjo in Cameroons drew theirs from their own particular regions; Senghor in Senegal, Houphouet-

---

[38] H. Macmillan, *At the End of the Day, 1961–1963*, London, 1973, *passim*.

Boigny in the Ivory Coast, each relied upon the French; while Amin at the end relied upon the Libyans, as at one stage did Rawlings in Ghana.

Through it all some presidents survived, notably Senghor, Sekou Touré, Ahidjo and Houphouet-Boigny in the west; Houphouet-Boigny both by judging skilfully when to be adamant and when to be flexible and, as he himself is reported to have stated, by sleeping like a crocodile – with one eye always open. Outside Uganda (which in this respect as in so many others is far from being a typical East African country), all the first East and Central African presidents survived as well, despite occasional threats. It needs to be remembered, however, that they possessed the quite special prestige of having led their countries out of the clutches of potentially apartheid-minded white settler regimes, an advantage that not even Ghana's Nkrumah enjoyed. Nevertheless, they too soon embraced a good deal of the political high culture that so much of the rest of independent Africa had come to espouse. They presided over one-party states; regularly employed preventive detention; outlawed organised opposition, and became as personally authoritarian as many of their contemporaries. Even the ostensibly mild-mannered Julius Nyerere displayed none of the forbearance for political opponents that characterised his long-admiring counterpart in Papua New Guinea, Michael Somare. But then the two men belonged to two very different politico-cultural environments.

We must, of course, allow that a great deal of what obtains in Africa is not always as wracked and tortured as the above discussion may suggest. There are very many peaceful countrysides, much local gossiping, a good deal of busy farming. There is as well much creative endeavour – to frame future policies, to develop new products, to effect public improvements. There are many large problems too beyond those of a regime's political high culture – of health, of drought, of floods, of food, housing, and poverty. There are immense problems as well of economics and international politics – a severe lack of financial resources, adverse world trading patterns, the albatross of debt, and apartheid to the south. On all these matters immense efforts have been expended, strong personal commitments displayed, and much ingenuity deployed.

It was thus inexpressively tragic that in so many places the manacles of a malign political lifestyle should have been welded on. The omens were never perhaps very promising. Too many elements stood in the way of a more fruitful outcome. Civil society is, of course, a far more fragile construct to maintain than is ordinarily allowed. Even in the oldest of western democracies there persists a quite appalling inability to ensure that civil order prevails right across the land. No one is, therefore, throwing stones in someone else's glass house. If there are still long-running conflicts in some parts of Africa, they very rarely match the case of Northern Ireland.

Three conclusions from what has been said above may, none the less, be repeated. Since 1970 Africa has not been torn by violent state separatisms as just a decade earlier looked to be very likely. Second, it is just not the case that in poor, new nations, political authoritarianism and violent *boulever-sements* are quite unavoidable. And third, whilst Africa's high-political debacles post-independence were no doubt always on the cards, their onset derived primarily from a quite fatal concurrence during a critical period of time of half a dozen or so distinct eventualities.

It may then be emphasised what this story confirms: that for all Africa's size, and for all its great disparities, seeming distinctions between circumstances in different parts of the continent often pale before its pervasive commonalities. Thus just as nationalism was a continent-wide phenomenon in the post-Second World War years, so in the years following independence certain common traits came to mark the high politics of Africa's new nations too. Those traits were forged in the hammerings of the late 1950s and early 1960s, and can no longer be accounted the unavoidable concomitants of poverty and previous history only, important as these have been.

One example must suffice to illustrate the case. In January 1966 Prime Minister Obote of Uganda came back from an up-country tour of northern Uganda to find that he had lost the support of the majority of his cabinet colleagues. Such was the culture of Africa's high politics in the years after independence that in such a position an African head of government was already conditioned to treating a situation like this as a form of grave *lésé majesté*. Accordingly when his cabinet next met, Obote had five of his colleagues summarily arrested and imprisoned without trial (as they remained until released by a further *coup* five years on). Then, promptly on his own say so, he had Uganda's independence constitution abrogated and his own position elevated to an authoritarian presidency – fully in accord with the autarchic tenets that were now sweeping right across the continent. Outside Africa one can cite a number of comparable situations where a prime minister, faced with this situation, would simply have resigned; someone else would soon have been installed in his place; and, like as not, a few years later he would have found himself back as prime minister once again; no one would have been arrested, no one imprisoned, let alone killed; and there would have been none of that descent into the abyss of political and personal disaster into which Uganda now fell. As it was, Obote very soon sent his armed forces under Colonel Amin to root out Uganda's lawful president from his palace; and for the next twenty years pre-eminent political power in Uganda passed into the soon-to-be grotesquely besmirched hands of Amin and Obote alike. Historical concurrences helped immensely to bring all this about. Yet there was in no sense a fixed mould which made so dire an outcome certain.

There is one slice of comfort to draw from all of this. If there was nothing ineluctable in the course that Africa's high politics took by the mid-1960s, there is no need to believe that its galling course thereafter is quite inescapable. 1979, we may recall, saw the departure of Nguema, Bokassa, and Amin. As the 1980s end there are still, alas, regimes which if not quite so horrendous offer very little comfort. Yet the sequence of *coups* does seem to have slowed up. The idea does seem to be spreading that one more coup is not very likely to make a great deal of difference. The evidence accumulates that widespread state violence frequently ends by devouring its own perpetrators. Several long-running rulers have now voluntarily handed over power – Senghor in Senegal, Ahidjo in Cameroon, Nyerere in Tanzania – while Rawlings in Ghana, Mwinyi in Tanzania, Mugabe in Zimbabwe, Chiasso in Mozambique, Diouf in Senegal, Momoh in Sierra Leone, Museveni in Uganda, Lansana in Guinea, Babangida in Nigeria, and Masire in Botswana are amongst those heads of government clearly attempting to turn the old tide. Their task is not at all easy. Once patterns of high politics have been set they are extraordinarily difficult to change. Yet a number of valiant attempts are being made. What is more, the initial populist notion that civil society is fuelled by dreams, ideals and visions is giving way to an overdue concern to make states effective, see institutions work, and obviate the disarrays which have hitherto prevailed. Moreover the earlier fixation with the state – the unavoidable concomitant perhaps of its sudden inheritance and very exiguousness – is now being supplemented by a much greater awareness that there are all sorts of other quarters in which people can operate creatively besides those controlled by the state. A far more resilient, multi-faceted political culture is thus beginning to emerge.[39]

If the preceding analysis is anything to go by some comfort can be drawn from the thought that demonstration effects in Africa could be here as powerful as they have been on previous occasions. As this story unfolds it could well be too that a far clearer understanding will develop that there have been not just political situations in Africa after independence but political *histories*. The delineaments of that upon as large a scale as for previous periods may soon, moreover, be a great deal more satisfactorily drawn, as in skilful hands the economic history of these years has already been.[40]

[39] Hyden, *Beyond Ujamaa*; J. MacGaffey, *Entrepreneurs and Parasites. The Struggle for Indigenous Capitalism in Zaire*, Cambridge, 1987.
[40] Fieldhouse, *Black Africa*.

11

Political superstructures in post-colonial states

(1) A REGISTER OF CONSTRUCTS

We are beginning to know something of the political structure of what have been called the new states, many of them post-colonial ones. It is of major importance to understanding the great majority of them to draw a distinction from other, principally western states, whose populations are overwhelmingly urban. In new post-colonial states the population is principally, sometimes overwhelmingly, rural. That has major implications for their polities, since it is a characteristic of rural societies, not just that they are quintessentially committed to agriculture, but that their human settlements are dispersed and not congregated – and therein are often nucleated. As a consequence they have community lives of their own that are ordinarily clearly demarcated from those of surrounding and otherwise like communities; and despite the fact that the political structure superimposed on them may appear, and seek to play, a pervasive role, there are many respects in which so much of rural existence continues entirely, or almost entirely, without any reference to it. That means that at most the political superstructure can only partially, and sometimes no more than marginally, determine the manner in which rural entities actually operate.

It is of some importance that, as in the western world, large landlordism – say of the Egyptian pasha type – has for the most part gone from the new states (it remains more especially in those areas where the Spanish hacienda model held sway, very strikingly, for example, in the Philippines). It has no doubt marginally survived, or wormed its way back, in this or that place; but for the most part it no longer dominates the scene in those places where it used to do (and not so very long since either).

Yet that does not mean, as was all too often implied, that some great levelling of human inequality has consequently taken place. All that has happened is that one particular kind of social domination has been attenuated. The effect has in a sense simply been to place rural regions that lately had large landlords back in that major category of those who never had them anyway (in large parts of Africa, for example). And the principle political (not to say economic or cultural) fact about this category is that there long seems to have been, and certainly abundantly continues to be, many sharp differentiations in power and influence amongst those within a particular rural locality – such as the innumerable villages in which so large a part of humanity still lives. There is now overwhelming evidence indeed that whatever the distinctive particularities of different places, regions, countries or continents, a common phenomenon ordinarily obtains here. There are almost invariably those at the apex of these rural communities who are 'the top of the bottom', 'the big fish in a small pond', village elders, Big Men, dominant peasants, *et hoc genus omne*.[1] In a variety of ways and in a wide manner of respects these men – for they are almost invariably men – 'rule the roost' in their circumscribed rural communities and possess the necessary resources to enable them to do so (economic ones not least); and because of that it is principally with them that agents of the political superstructure have to do their business. Moreover, it is characteristic of these rural leaders that while they are exceedingly jealous of their power and resources, if these are not threatened they are ordinarily very ready to do business with the agents of the superstructure. Political superstructures have, indeed, almost invariably had to come to terms with these leaders. As each of the twentieth century's largest revolutionary figures – Lenin, Stalin, Ho and Mao – all in their different ways fully realised, the power of these 'big fish' in their 'small ponds' can ordinarily only be tampered with at very considerable cost.[2]

The form of the nexus that is then established in the bodies politic of new states between the superstructure and those that command the rural infrastructures entails a study in itself, but it can broadly vary across several different possibilities (large landlordism used often to be one of them). Thus, in some instances (such as India or Malaysia or, to begin with, Sekou Toure's Guinea) political parties have played a considerable part in establishing and maintaining it. Elsewhere it has sometimes been encompassed within a commune structure (as in many of the Communist states of course). In some places – Indonesia provides a striking example – it is

---

[1] I hope to enlarge on these issues elsewhere, but see, for example, J.M. Potter, *Thai Peasant Social Structure*, Chicago, 1976; R.F. Salisbury, *Vunamami. Economic Transformation in a Traditional Society*, Berkeley, 1970; J. Vincent, *African Elite. The Big Men of a Small Town*, Columbia, 1970; M.N. Srinivas, *The Remembered Village*, Berkeley, 1976.

[2] A.B. Ulam, *Lenin and the Bolsheviks*, London, 1969, pp. 279, 350, 374; M. Lewin, *Russian Peasants and Soviet Power. A Study of Collectivization*, London, 1968, p. 516; *Selected Works of Mao Tsetung*, vol. 5, Peking, 1977, pp. 24–5.

effected within a much articulated bureaucratic structure. All in all, however, one has a pervading impression of the similarities which these seemingly different circumstances present. Recalling an Indian *Sarpanch* and his *Panchayat*, the vice-chairman (it was always a vice-chairman) of a Revolutionary Committee of a Chinese Production Brigade, the village headman and village officials of a Javanese village, or the Ggombolola Chief and his Ggombolola Council in Buganda in Uganda, it is hard to resist the conclusion that they represent a widespread political phenomenon. Each of these men and their accomplices were Janus-like persons, representing their localised community to the superstructure, and the superstructure to their community, whilst exercising very considerable power in their community in association with their more powerful fellows there. The prevalence of this situation in quite countless particular terms is one of the best documented features of the Indian body politic. The point to be made here is that such, in the broad terms being outlined here, has also been the case in most other new post-colonial states which are principally rural. Something of such a nexus is found below most of the superstructures of these states, and constitutes a phenomenon of principal importance to the manner in which their bodies politic actually operate. (Some important Africanist writing has shown, for example, how in the 1970s and 1980s 'the top of the bottom', and all which it dominates, has proceeded to opt out of its former associations with the superstructure[3] – which is a measure of the power the 'top' can muster when it wishes.) So in considering how in such widespread places superstructures are maintained it is vitally important always to bear in mind what it is they are superimposed upon.

At the same time it is also important to bear in mind the great differences between those new states that are heirs to a long-standing heritage of overarching political authority and those that are not. The possession of the mantle of traditional authority, as Weber emphasised,[4] is of inestimable value to a regime in securing its political legitimacy; its absence entails a far larger task. It is of great importance, for example, that India's government after independence was the ultimate heir to the major dynasties of India's past, from the Mauryas through the Mughals to the British. It was heir too to the Hindu notion of the Supreme Ruler, the *chakravartin*. Delhi itself, moreover, had been India's major capital for seven centuries past. Communist China, of course, also enjoyed the position of heir to China's long sequence of imperial dynasties. Moreover, its public modes of address are clearly Confucian. What is more, the Peoples' Republic came to be centred from the start in Peking, China's ancient capital; and there has never been any doubt that it there enjoys China's ancient 'mandate of heaven'.

[3] K. Hart, *The Political Economy of West African Agriculture*, Cambridge, 1982; G. Hyden, *Beyond Ujamaa in Tanzania. Underdevelopment and an Uncaptured Peasantry*, London, 1980.
[4] M. Weber, *The Theory of Social and Economic Organization*, New York, 1947, part III.

Interestingly, independent Burma bears even more closely many of the marks of having inherited the mantle of the Burmese kingdoms before it, not least in its commitment to an associated ideology – Burmese Socialism for Theravada Buddhism.[5] To some degree the Indonesian state likewise benefits from its inheritance of Javanese rulership,[6] while the traditional authority of the independent Malaysian state is still represented in its Sultans, and in the head of state elected from amongst them, the Yang di-Pertuan Agung.

Very few tropical African countries have any such advantages, nor Pakistan either (as its building of a new capital, Islamabad, illustrates). Ethiopia is the principal tropical African exception, plus Swaziland, Lesotho and Botswana. Elsewhere, in northern Nigeria for example, some elements of traditional authority in the Weberian sense remain, but, as in Uganda, efforts have frequently been made to sweep this aside. For all that the point is sometimes very well taken, as the naming of Ghana, Mali and Zimbabwe after ancient African polities suggests. Generally, however, post-colonial states, not least in Africa, are largely devoid of this great advantage.

They are generally devoid too of much of a heritage of that further buttress of political legitimacy which Weber signalled, legal-bureaucratic authority. Here again China presents an obvious case to the contrary, with the communist regime standing four-square in the ancient Confucian mandarin tradition of legal-bureaucracy (despite its efforts to disown this). Independent India too is in many important respects heir not only to nearly two centuries of British legal-bureaucratic rule, but to the earlier precedents of the Mughals and others before them. Again there are next to no counterparts of this in many of the other new post-colonial states. Very many of them, especially in Africa, could only look back at independence to something like half a century of even the most exiguous legal-bureaucratic rule. It was in this situation that so many nationalist leaders attempted upon independence to bolster – Weber again – their personal charisma; but that was never easily 'routinised'.

In these circumstances it seems therefore of first importance to discern the political constructs which came to be employed within these new states in their efforts to sustain the operational viability of their superstructures, since the effectiveness of these was frequently vital not only to ensuring a sufficiency of political order but a modicum of personal security within them. When one reviews the range of possibilities here it seems that there have been at least some regularities in the ways in which these have operated. The various possibilities that seem to exist have sometimes coalesced. One can see too that they have on occasion superseded one

5 R.H. Taylor, *The State in Burma*, London, 1987.
6 Cf. C. Geertz, *Negara. The Theatre State in Nineteenth-Century Bali*, Princeton, 1980.

another. The principal purpose of the first part of this chapter is to try to spell out how these might be characterised.[7]

Dominant parties

In the first place a major role in sustaining the superstructural parts of a body politic can be played by a country's largest, or indeed only, political party. India under the Indian National Congress between Independence in 1947 and 1989 was palpably one case; China since the establishment of the Peoples' Republic in 1949 under the Chinese Communist Party a second; Japan with its post-Second World War Liberal Democratic Party a third. There have been a few, partial, approximations to this elsewhere – in, for example, Malaysia, Tanzania, Zambia, Ivory Coast, Guinea, Senegal – but, outside the communist world, this situation is comparatively rare. Not often are overarching authorities commanded and buttressed by dominant political parties, because not all that often do such dominant parties survive.

Competitive electoral systems

It has been emphasised in the preceding chapter that national superstructures have been sustained in a number of post-colonial states where competing political parties have continued to enjoy a real opportuity to win control from time to time of the national government. Elections, as for example in Jamaica, may be scarred by all too many political killings, and a national election may be boycotted by one of the two major parties, as happened there in the mid-1980s. But genuine general elections are nevertheless held; parties compete; there is a real possibility that existing holders of office can lose power following defeat at the polls; and in this situation existing democratic political structures very evidently endure.

Entrenched elites

Yet even where that is the case there can often be other elements which are at least as important as this in maintaining the national body politic, and elsewhere these are often more central. In Asia and Africa there are just a few countries where landlords, or at all events highly prosperous landed elites, along with a commercial and bureaucratic elite compose an interlocked governing oligarchy so as to form the major buttress of (and of course the major beneficiaries from) their country's superstructural authority. The Philippines would be one such case in Asia. In the 1960s it was described as 'a democracy of the rich, by the rich, for the rich'. Of its 24

---

[7] Reference to most of the matters adduced below is ordinarily to be found in standard accounts of the countries mentioned.

senators, 10 were multi-millionaires; of its 120 congressmen, 40 were millionaires. Despite Mrs Aquino's supersession of President Marcos in 1986 little came to be fundamentally changed there. A further case in Asia (though, as we shall see, there have been other factors as well) would be Pakistan, where much power resides with a landed-commercial-bureaucratic elite (there has been no real landlord abolition in Pakistan) which is especially linked there with the army. The Bhuttos – father in the 1970s; daughter in the 1980s – have each become heads of government in Pakistan, but each has lain at the mercy of this dominant ruling coalition. A comparable case in Africa would be the Ivory Coast under President Houphouet-Boigny, where 'by 1965, a wealthy planter class of about 20,000 had emerged and employed approximately two-thirds of agricultural wage labour'. In association with the 'political elite constituted of politicians and bureaucrats who use their positions to move into capitalist farming',[8] these were the people who commanded the state superstructure.

In so many countries, however, and not least a good number of post-colonial new states, it needs to be remembered that the principle forces making up the critical elements underlying their overarching regimes are social entities, often of an ethnic, sometimes of a racial, occasionally of a religious kind. These form what (to adapt Benedict Anderson's language) we may call sub-national 'imagined communities'.[9] Here a principle requirement in constructing and maintaining a new state superstructure has most frequently been to find some means by which these sub-national communities could either be accommodated or, if not accommodated, then effectively marginalised. A *tour d'horizon* suggests that there are not more than perhaps six or seven ways in which this can be done. In listing these one is offering just one register of the alternatives which are available to those seeking to maintain political superstructures in many new states, especially when these are not effectively sustained by a political party, or an acceptable multi-party system, or a strongly entrenched landed-commercial-bureaucratic-militarily-allied elite.

Natural majorities

The first possibility turns on the existence within a number of new states of what one may call a natural majority. For here, so the evidence suggests, it is very often possible to maintain the political superstructure of a state by mobilising the support for it of a core community within it. A conspicuous example would be Indonesia. There the 90 or so millions of Javanese clearly

[8] B. Campbell, 'The Ivory Coast', in J. Dunn (ed.), *West African States: Failure and Promise*, Cambridge, 1978, p. 104; R. Sandbrook, *The Politics of Africa's Economic Stagnation*, Cambridge, 1985, pp. 71–2.

[9] B. Anderson, *Imagined Communities, Reflections on the Origin and Spread of Nationalism*, London, 1983.

form the dominant community in a country of around 150 million all told. It is they who provide the controlling nucleus and the crucial supports of the Indonesian state. Following the separation of Bangladesh in 1971, Pakistan more generally provided another example. There the Punjabis clearly hold the pre-eminent position, more especially as against the Pathans, Sindhis, and Baluchis. Similarly, the Burmese dominate Burma – as the Karens and the other tribal hill communities know only too well. In Africa a like position is held in the Sudan by the Muslim northerners as against the Christian (and 'pagan') southerners. In Nigeria the northern majority is in a similar position vis à vis the southern peoples. The Mossi are numerically and politically dominant in Burkina Fasso, at the expense of the minorities there, the Hausa, Fulani etc.; while in Zimbabwe the Shona came to hold sway in the years after independence in 1980, not least at the expense of the Ndebele minority whose forebears had dominated the region in the past.

Here and elsewhere there are a number of cases where natural majorities that previously had felt themselves disadvantaged set about employing their superior numbers upon independence to assert their primacy over those who had hitherto lorded it over them. Thus, in Sri Lanka the Sinhalese moved against the Tamils; in Burma the Burmese against the Indians; in Sierra Leone the 'Protectorate' peoples against the Creoles. Continuing efforts were made in this direction on behalf of the Malay *bumiputras* – the 'sons of the soil' – against the immigrant Chinese and Indians, who might well together have overborne them. After a hesitant start the Malays resisted British plans for a Malayan Union in 1945–6 that would have given equal citizenship to all Malaya's communities; instead they secured a Malay-dominated Federation of Malaya.[10] Later they were glad to join with Sabah and Sarawak to form a larger Malayan Malaysia in 1963, and were happy to see the Singaporean Chinese leave Malaysia two years later. Elsewhere there were one or two violent revolutions upon independence aimed at securing a hitherto subordinate majority's primacy; in 1961 by the Bairu majority against the Tutsi elite in Rwanda; in 1965 by the Afro–Shirazi majority against the previously ruling Arab minority in Zanzibar.

On securing their dominance the natural majority has generally found its predominant position to be highly advantageous. But it can be very different for the minority – as the Catholics have found in Northern Ireland, and as Ulster would surely have found in Eire. It is not surprising, therefore, that there were Sumatran revolts against Javanese dominance in Indonesia in the 1950s; that there have been long-standing tribal revolts against the Burmese in Burma; that persistent civil war by the southerners against the northerners has prevailed in the Sudan; that the Tamils have revolted against the Sinhalese in Sri Lanka; and that bitter hostility has long

[10] A.J. Stockwell, *British Policy and Malay Politics during the Malayan Union experiment 1942–48*, Kuala Lumpur, 1979.

been displayed by the Baluchi, Sindhi and Pathan minorities against Punjabi dominance in Pakistan. Nor can one be altogether surprised that in order to hold on to their highly privileged position the Tutsi elite in Burundi should on more than one occasion have committed genocide against the subordinate Bairu majority; or that Igbo officers from Eastern Nigeria were much involved in the bloody coup in January 1966 against what they saw as creeping northern–western dominance there. Nor indeed is it surprising that the Chinese in Singapore should so readily have accepted their separation from Malaysia in 1965. For all these occurrences stemmed primarily from the structural position in which these communities found themselves. Given this position it is especially notable that in 1988 President Mugabe of Zimbabwe should have made such strenuous and seemingly successful efforts to bring key representatives of the minority Ndebele people into his Shona-dominated regime. It was an unusually shrewd move by an astute national leader concerned to remove a running sore from his country.

There are in these connections some intriguing examples of what can happen at the margin. There are many indications that upon Nigeria's independence in 1960 northern Nigeria – an 'imagined community' in so many ways – had a much larger population than the two southern Nigerian regions put together. It was this which so greatly irked the *soi-disant* more advanced southerners as to make them dangerously eruptive (and led some of the easterners among them in the late 1960s to attempt to create the separate state of Biafra). It is clearly arguable that one principle reason why Nigeria succumbed to such internecine conflict in the years after independence lay in the (unusual) refusal of northern Nigeria's principal leader before 1966, the Sardauna of Sokoto, to move from his base in the north and assume the role of Nigeria's head of government in Lagos; as he was wont to put it, he sent his 'clerk', Sir Abubaker Tafawa Balewa, to represent him there as Nigeria's original prime minister instead. Admirable as Abubaker personally was, he had none of his master's political authority; very little authority outside Lagos, the Federal capital; and he could provide no substitute for the Sardauna's refusal to bother himself overmuch with Nigeria at large. Here was a clear case of a majority not assuming its political mantle. In 1966 the Sardauna and Abubaker and many others suffered grievously for that omission by being murdered. Since 1966 every Nigerian government has had a northerner at its head, and behind the coups and elections that have occurred much more overt northern dominance has come to characterise Nigeria's overarching regime. But the ethnic balance remains very uncertain, and Nigeria's problems still remain.

There was a contrary example in the case of Pakistan. Eventually in the late 1960s its Bengali majority came together. That threatened the formerly predominant position of Pakistan's Punjabis (to whom we shall return shortly) who would have none of the predominance the Bengalis were now moving to assert. Here, as we know, a complete separation ensued.

Composed majorities

Natural majorities are not, however, all that common. Where they do not exist it is sometimes possible to compose a majority. In Senegal Leopold Senghor developed close associations with the four major Islamic brotherhoods; but 'of more immediate political significance [was the emergence] . . . of an unofficial national language – Wolof'.[11] At the beginning of this century Wolof was the language of only one third of the population of the country. By the 1970s it was spoken by four-fifths. 'Wolofisation' clearly enabled a substantial composed majority to be created on which Senghor's regime and that of his successor, Diouf, could stand. By all accounts President Banda has long based his regime in Malawi on a composed southern majority based upon his own Chewa peoples; while President Kaunda's regime in Zambia has stood upon a fairly constant rejigging of a composed majority there.[12] There was once an especially notable case in Fiji. There, Indians outnumber Fijians, but as immigrants they held their hands, and in any event were soon riven, so that the long-standing Fijian prime minister Ratu Mara, was able to attract to his Fijian-dominated government Fiji's Gujaratis and Muslims, so as to leave its north Indian Hindus, who comprised the Indian majority, in an overall political minority.[13] It was when such expedients finally broke down in 1987 that the first *coup* in the South-west Pacific occurred.

All these instances indicate, however, that where leaders of composed majorities do manage to assert their predominance, they can fairly readily play a commanding role in their countries (even if, as in the case of natural majorities, this can periodically be very uncomfortable for the remaining minorities – the northerners in Malawi; those excluded each time around in Zambia; the north Indian Hindus in Fiji).

'Prussians'

Not infrequently, however, there is not only no natural majority but no one is able to compose a majority either. Yet all is not then lost. To begin with there is the 'Prussian' possibility, where in the absence of an effective majority, a cohesive group can use its muscle to secure its pre-eminence at the centre. This has its model in the role the Emperor Wilhelm, Chancellor

[11] D.B. Cruise O'Brien, 'Senegal', in Dunn (ed.), *West African States*, pp. 183–4.
[12] W. Tordoff, *Government and Politics in Africa*, London, 1984, pp. 83, 85, 115–18.
[13] B.V. Lal, 'The Fijian General Election of 1982', *Journal of Pacific History*, 18 nos. 1–2 (1983), 134–57.

Bismarck and their Prussian associates played so assiduously in late nineteenth century and early twentieth century Germany.

In the post-colonial states perhaps the most vivid example was in pre-Bangladesh Pakistan, where the Punjabis, who even though significantly less numerous than the East Pakistan Bangladeshis, managed very successfully to dominate the whole Pakistani state throughout its first two decades of independence. It was precisely because their 'Prussian' position was so directly threatened by the eventual coherence in the late 1960s of the East Pakistanis – who composed the natural majority in the original Pakistan state – that the reaction of the West Pakistanis (= largely the Punjabis) to the Bangla threat became so brutally hostile.

In Africa the most prominent of such cases has long been found in Ethiopia. There the Christian Abyssinians formed the Prussian-like core that dominated the old imperial state from Menelik's time in the nineteenth century to Haile Selassie's in the twentieth. They continued to dominate Ethiopia following the military takeover in 1974. They were principally made up of the Amhara who have generally constituted no more than a quarter of the country's total population. Even with the associated Tigre they have only constituted around one third; whilst along with the Shoan Galla they still only amount to perhaps two fifths. 'Their coherence, which has evolved over hundreds of years, is the glue which has bound together the different parts of the Ethiopian state'.[14] By contrast the Oromo (Galla-) speaking peoples, who comprise a full 40 per cent of the population, have never been able to assert their numerical dominance successfully, because they have always been greatly scattered.

A further graphic example of the 'Prussian' variant can be found in Kenya. There in the years following independence the Kikuyu – not much more than 20 per cent of the population – dominated the country, especially under the leadership of the long standing Kikuyu first president of Kenya, Jomo Kenyatta. There was another one in Guinea: by the 1970s Sekou Touré felt that his party organisation there needed supplementing if his own position was to be secured. So he elevated his own Malinké, who comprised only one third of the population, into a pre-eminent role – more particularly at the expense of the Foulah.[15] In these two last instances (as in Bismarck's case as well) focussing upon distinct enemies has been part of the workings of the formula (in the case of the Kikuyu, against Kenya's Jaluo).

One can discern several other instances in Africa too. It seems, for example, as if the regime in Chad under President Tombalaye (1960–75) was built principally upon the support of the Sara clans in the south who by no means comprised a majority in the country as a whole. In the Central African Republic, President Bokassa's regime between 1966 and 1979

[14] P. King, *An African Winter*, Harmondsworth. 1986, p. 140.
[15] R.W. Johnson, 'Guinea', in Dunn (ed.), *West African States*, pp. 57–8.

rested a good deal upon the support of his own Ngbaka ethnic group. In Somalia, following an unsuccessful *coup* in 1978, General Said's regime came to stand a good deal more than at the outset in 1969 on his own Marehan clan.[16] For many years President Houphouet-Boigny's already remarkably strong position in the Ivory Coast has, moreover, been supported by calling in aid his own Baoulé people. But perhaps the most notable instance of this situation in Africa has obtained in Zaire, where the long-standing regime of President Mobutu was above all underpinned by a pre-eminent coterie drawn almost entirely from his own North-east Equateur region. Almost all of his own presidential staff, and all his top service, police, intelligence and defence ministry personnel came from this one area.[17] There seems a good deal of evidence indeed that where no one commands a natural majority, and no one seems able to compose one, a Prussian-type construct can frequently provide remarkably strong support for a state's governing superstructure.

The interstitial role

Yet there are some other possibilities too. For example, a leader can grasp the 'interstitial' position. The efficacy of state formation along these lines was most dramatically demonstrated over a millenium ago by the prophet Mohammed at Medina. For Mecca, from which he was summoned, was a city, Medina an oasis, in which the former 'Prussians', some Jewish clans, had lost out, so that the oasis was given over to chronic conflict. Mohammed was summoned to pull it together again. The Hijrah ensued. Fulfilling his role, Mohammed declined to set up his tents with any one of Medina's warring clans and determined to do so on his own. He married, however, into several of them, thus reinforcing the interstitial position which he had adopted. His welding of church and state, as westerners call these, thereupon formed a formidable, religiously dominated construct.[18] The classic statement in the social science literature of this particular variant is to be found in E.E. Evans-Pritchard's *The Sanusi of Cyrenaica*[19] in which he described how a similar religious figure, the Grand Sanusi, came to occupy precisely this interstitial position between the warring tribes of his country, and thus welded them together into a functioning body politic which first resisted and then outlived the Italian imperialists.

In the post-colonial states the most arresting case would seem to be that of Tanzania. There there are several powerful, even ambitious, ethnic groups – the Chagga, the Nyamwezi, the Nyakyusa, and so on. None of them, however, constitutes a majority; there have been no likely majority alliances

[16] Tordoff, *Government and Politics*, p. 213.
[17] C. Young and T. Turner, *The Rise and Decline of the Zairian State*, Madison, 1985.
[18] W.M. Watt, *Muhammad. Prophet and Statesman*, Oxford, 1961, ch. 4.
[19] Oxford, 1949.

amongst them; none of them has moved to assert a Prussian position; all continue to be somewhat wary of each other. Julius Nyerere, Tanzania's first president, had many qualities, personal and otherwise. None in this context was more important than that he came from one of the smallest tribes in the country. Within Tanzania's tribal-ethnic mix it was, that is, of singular importance that in his personal affiliations he never threatened any of the larger ones. Instead he occupied the 'interstitial' position between them. And that was the basis of the primacy he held for so long in his country. It seems to be no coincidence, moreover, that his successor came from Zanzibar. Again, over and beyond his personal capabilities, President Mwinyi had the inestimable advantage in Tanzanian terms of being yet another 'interstitial' figure – from the major island off Tanzania's coast. Tanzania's political system has come to be built upon this construct.

Tanzania, however, is by no means the only example from a post-colonial state where the seizure of the interstitial position has been politically important for underpinning the state superstructure. Nigeria's principal figure following the collapse of the Sardauna–Abubaker regime in 1966 was General Gowon, Nigeria's longest standing head of state (1966–75). He had the particular advantage in a large country, broadly divided between Christian south and Muslim north, or being a Christian from the Middle Belt (*sic*) to the north of the North's southern border. There is no reason to doubt the significance of that in sustaining his position. One of his eventual successors, President Babangida, who came to power following a *coup* in 1985, had somewhat similar attributes; coming from an ethnically mixed part of the (northern) Niger State, and with a not easily attributable name, he had a (southern) Igbo wife. This gave him an important advantage over the former (northern) 'Kaduna mafia' which had come to hold sway through three previous regimes.

But a still better example would be President Ahidjo of Cameroun (1960–82 – a remarkably long innings in late-twentieth-century Africa). He too had considerable personal capabilities – no politician can make a state formation work without these. But these abilities were not only somewhat hidden; they were by no means all that mattered.

Taciturn, withdrawn, quite lacking in personal charisma, Ahidjo initially seemed an unlikely candidate for such a role. Yet these very qualities and canny political sense, proved to be elements of strength. His father was a Fulani of middling status, and his mother was from a non-Islamic northern group. Because he was not tied to the Fulani aristocratic or clerical class, he could be relatively acceptable to the south. Because he had northern antedecents, even if he lacked high customary status, he could quieten Fulani fears of southern domination.[20]

---

[20] C. Young, 'The Northern Republics 1960–1980', in D. Birmingham and P.M. Martin (eds.), *History of Central Africa*, London, 1983, II, p. 317.

Along with this went a sophisticated balancing of representation in the organs of rule of the various regional, linguistic, ethnic and religious elements in his country [21] One can adduce some other examples from Africa too. In Sierra Leone the two leading sub-national ethnic communities have been the Mende and the Tembe. In 1887 President Momoh, a Limba, came to hold the balance between them.

In certain situations where the main basis of the underpinning of a state's superstructure is principally one of the other constructs we have mentioned here, the interstitial role, if carefully played, can be a useful additional support. In Kenya, for example, following Kenyatta's death, President Moi (not a Kikuyu but a Kalenjin, and the former vice-president), succeeded him. The rival Kikuyu factions clearly preferred an interstitial outsider (à la Mohammed) to be president of Kenya rather than one of themselves. He had, moreover, the particular advantage of occupying a rather wider interstitial position in the country at large. For while not a Jaluo, Moi did at least come from western and not central Kenya where the Kikuyu live. This is not to say that he could in any way throw off altogether the Kikuyu's 'Prussian' dominance; but it did give him some additional leverage. These features were well demonstrated when he replaced Kibaki, who was a leading Kikuyu with a substantial political base, as Vice-President in 1988 with Karanja who had no such political following, but was nevertheless a Kikuyu. Elements of the same phenomenon have been displayed in Pakistan. Each of its three military Presidents came from a peripheral area in the Punjab, and not from any of its leading 'connections'. To a significant degree they profitably held the interstitial position between them.

Primus inter pares

There are then a couple of further possibilities too. There is first what may be called the *primus inter pares* option. One important example of this comes from Papua New Guinea. No natural majority exists there; nor has one been composed; nor have any 'Prussians' succeeded (though in the mid 1980s under Okuk and Prime Minister Wingti the 'highlanders' partially tried). As, moreover, in a country of around three million people, in which no less than 500 different languages are spoken, the aggregations which have developed are all largely coterminous with equally structured regions (to one of which by residence everyone automatically belongs), so no interstitial position is easily secured there either. In these circumstances the overarching regime has invariably been made up of *de facto* regional representatives in the central government with the prime minister as no more than *primus inter pares*. When the first prime minister, Michael

[21] P. Duignan and R.H. Jackson, *Politics & Government in African States 1960–1985*, Stanford, 1986, pp. 153–4.

Somare, became by 1981 more *primus* than *inter pares*, he was forced to give way to Chan. He won his way back in a subsequent election. But his new position was very much as it was before, and in 1985 he fell from power for the second time. However, he was back in office in 1988, but this time as foreign, not as prime minister. Yet since he had never been accorded an exceptionally pre-eminent stature in the country (despite having long been dubbed 'The Chief') a lesser position was perfectly acceptable to him. In these circumstances the regime's effective authority over the country's regions has remained far from strong, and in a way that is now very unusual in post-colonial new states regional governments of real significance have persisted. Moreover, as various political upheavals in Papua New Guinea have shown, the regional representatives in the National Parliament (formally belonging to a plethora of parties but individually or collectively quite ready to cross the floor whenever that suits them – thus displaying the basic irrelevance of party alignments) are perfectly capable of looking elsewhere for someone to chair another coalition when this seems to them to be called for. So far, however, the *primus inter pares* mode apparently works reasonably satisfactorily.

There have been one or two other examples of it elsewhere. For example, on establishing military control of Somalia in 1969, General Said sought to put an end to the debilitating rivalries amongst the various Somali clans by very deliberately appointing to his Supreme Revolutionary Council members from each of the major clan communities into which Somali society was divided (only later did he turn towards a Prussian-type regime, as noted above). In Nigeria one can point to two or three intimations of this same expedient too. In support of his not altogether firmly fixed role as an interstitial figure, General Gowon, after assuming office in 1966, appointed to his Federal Executive Council twelve civilians, each drawn from one of the states into which Nigeria was by then divided. He also appointed Awolowo, the principle figure of the former Western Region, as its vice-chairman,[22] and so linked together (particularly in opposition to Biafra, the separatist form of the old Eastern Region) the other two old Regions (he himself coming from the Northern), with himself as *primus inter pares*. Four regimes later General Buhari in 1983 likewise appointed to his eighteen-man Federal Executive Council one representative from each of the states into which Nigeria had by then been divided, with the exception of Bendel which provided the head of the civil service.[23] In similar fashion, Houphouet-Boigny, whose regime has been based, as we have seen, in the first place upon the creation of a landed-commercial-

[22] Tordoff, *Government and Politics*, p. 169.
[23] D. Rothchild, 'Hegemony and State Softness: Some Variations on State Responses', in Z. Ergas (ed.), *The African State in Transition*, London, 1987, p. 124.

bureaucratic elite (with a good deal of French support too), and then upon his own Baoulé people, nevertheless has striven to accommodate the interests of most of the ethnic groups which are to be found in the Ivory Coast also. There are, that is, reinforcing possibilities in a simultaneous multiplication of the constructs outlined here.

50:50 (and 33:33:33)

Beyond this one further possibility remains, with a curious addendum. This is the 50:50 system. It is most notably followed in Belgium, as between the Flemings and the Walloons. For some decades it constituted the basis for the state superstructure in Lebanon; and in a sense formerly, as we have seen, in Fiji as between the commercially dominant Indians and the politically dominant Fijians. As those two examples indicate, however, all may be well so long as the arrangement persists, but when it breaks down the consequences can be highly disruptive.

Africa has seen three or four examples of 50:50 arrangements. There is a sense in which the Mende–Temne balance in Sierra Leone comes close to being one. In Mauretania there have been various awkward attempts since independence to balance its White Moors and its Black Moors. Following Eyadema's *coup* in Togo in 1967 there have been varying efforts to secure a balance in the state superstructure between its predominant northerners and its ambitious southerners (especially the Ewe).[24]

Dahomey (as Benin used to be called) saw in the years before and after independence something of a 33:33:33 situation, during which the Abomey–Fon following of Ahomadégbé, the Nagot–Yoruba following of Apithy, and the northern following of Maga, each attempted to secure some kind of primacy. 'Each leader attempted to create a presidential regime in which he and his group dominated the country's politics, and each failed; each tried an alliance with one of the others against the third and that also failed; the three then tried a somewhat bizarre three-man presidency in which each man was president for a year (1970–2), and that did not work either'. As a result in 1972 the army despatched the three leaders to Paris – though without disposing thereby of the ethnic rivalries which they had chosen to represent.[25]

It seems that when none of these constructs can be put into place, or sustained, a regime is thrown back upon terror as the only remaining means of exerting its authority over a new state.

---

[24] S. Decalo, *Coups and Army Rule in Africa*, New Haven, 1976, pp. 111–21.
[25] Decalo, *Coups and Army Rule*, pp. 48–53; V.T. LeVine in Duignan and Jackson, *Politics & Government*, p. 98.

(II) A DISLOCATED POLITY: UGANDA 1960—86

The usefulness of this analytical register can be well illustrated by considering at greater length the particular case of Uganda. Over a period of fifteen
years, from early 1971 to early 1986, Uganda seemed the worst possible
case. It was for a time closely paralleled by Equatorial Guinea, but its
trauma lasted longer. It was not merely that there were all the grotesque
slaughterings of the years of President Amin (1971–9) and of President
Obote's second term (1980–5). There were the gross structural defects that
lay behind these as well. The tragedy of independent Uganda in the years
between 1960 and 1985 was that none of the structural possibilities
canvassed above, some at least of which have more than half worked
elsewhere, were successfully instituted here. The attempts of both Presidents Obote and Amin to pursue instead a populist course proved entirely
useless, and that led them to the last resort of the politically bankrupt:
terror. That very fortunately destroyed their regimes from within – though
not before there had been terrible loss of life. In 1979–80 there was an inept
attempt to operate the Prussian possibility. It was left to President
Museveni to try once again in 1986 to work one of the more promising
structural alternatives outlined above; but with what success only the future
can tell.

We may remind ourselves that like most African countries Uganda was
an artificial creation comprising the northern interlacustrine Bantu along
with the south central Nilotes; that it encompassed a large assortment of
pre-colonial polities (upwards of thirty or so rulerships for start, in the
southern areas alone); and that at its core it had the large kingdom of
Buganda. It is an old point that from the early 1950s there was scarcely a
doubt that it would have independence as a 'primarily African state'. Since
the issue thereby became, not whether independence would come, but the
distribution of power upon its attainment, the Uganda National Congress
which originally sought to mobilise a unified nationalist campaign, never
had very much chance. From the mid-1950s Uganda saw instead political
parties that approximated more to its old political cleavages between
Protestants and Catholics – the various fragments of the Uganda National
Congress (and such, briefly, as the Progressive Party) culminating in the
Uganda Peoples' Congress on the one side, and the Democratic Party on the
other.[26]

Unlike Zimbabwe (or a number of other countries, as we have seen)
Uganda has no natural majority. The Baganda at its core might well have
become its Prussians. There have certainly been some Baganda politicians
who have always seen its future as lying principally in playing a major role

[26] D.A. Low, *Buganda in Modern History*, London, 1971, ch. 6; and *The Mind of Buganda.
Documents of the Modern History of an African Kingdom*, London, 1971.

in the larger Uganda – from the early nationalist Ignatius Musazi to his long-running former associate Paulo Muwanga (and certain others besides). At independence Buganda held, moreover, an extraordinary plurality of elite positions in the country as a whole; it enjoyed great prestige; it was relatively well-endowed economically; and it straddled the country's heart-land. But in contrast to the Kikuyu in Kenya next door, they had early on been used by the British as 'sub-imperialists' in the wider Uganda, and long before independence had come to be greatly resented and feared in the rest of the country.[27] They made their first run, that is, rather too soon. Knowing this they sought in the run up to independence to protect the remnants of their primacy either by a separated independence for their kingdom or by entrenching special privileges for it in a federal constitution. All this was reinforced by the prominent role in pursuing these ends played by their Cambridge-educated Kabaka Mutesa II. In 1953 he was deported by the British for pressing his case for the separated independence of his kingdom (as in different circumstances was to be achieved by the compara-ble royal dynasty in Swaziland). But he was then returned in triumph in 1955, and thereafter as a hereditary ruler with next to no chance of operating politically outside his kingdom as the principal political leader of the whole country, and fearful of the threat to his own position and to that of his kingdom in the larger Uganda from the free play of the ballot box, he encouraged his people to support the neo-traditionalist Kabaka Yekka (Kabaka only) political movement, and so passed up their principal chance of becoming Uganda's Prussians. These antics compounded the opposition to them in the rest of the country, and that gave Milton Obote, a rising politician from northern Uganda, the chance he seized to compose in his UPC a non-Baganda majority against them.[28]

It is of central importance to understanding the Ugandan story to note that in the years 1961–6, before and after Uganda's independence in October 1962, there were no less than five successive attempts to compose a governing majority in Uganda, none of which succeeded for any length of time. In varying sequence three of these were constructed by Obote himself; one by some of his opponents; one, against him, by some of his colleagues. Obote's first attempt, institutionalised in the principally anti-Baganda, largely Protestant, UPC, seemed headed at first for political control of the whole country via the first full Ugandan national elections of 1961. Precisely because these looked like delivering Uganda to his anti-Baganda UPC, those elections were widely boycotted by the Baganda under Kabaka Mutesa's increasingly evident leadership. But that had the extra-

[27] A.D. Roberts, 'The Sub Imperialism of the Baganda', *Journal of African History*, 3 no. 3 (1962), 435–50.
[28] Low, *Buganda*; D.E. Apter, *The Political Kingdom in Uganda*, Princeton, 1961; Mutesa, Kabaka of Buganda, *Desecration of my Kingdom*, London, 1967.

ordinary effect of handing the victory at the 1961 elections not to the UPC but to the countrywide Democratic Party which had largely Roman Catholic support and which took upon itself to mobilise some of its following in Buganda notwithstanding the more general election boycott there. In the outcome the DP won only a minority of seats outside Buganda, but on an exiguous poll it won almost all of the seats in Buganda itself, and thus secured a majority in the country overall. Under the Muganda Catholic, Benedicto Kiwanuka, it thereupon formed the first African government in Uganda.

This second composed majority was not quite as ephemeral as is sometimes suggested, for in Uganda as a whole there were almost certainly more Catholics than Protestants. But its very success led its opponents to think furiously, and out of that came the second of the attempts Obote made in the early 1960s to compose a governing majority. For against the DP he was persuaded to concoct a quite extraordinary alliance between his own anti-Baganda UPC and their erstwhile foes, Buganda's neo-traditionalist KY. Together they forced a further general election in 1962 in which they trounced the DP, and thereafter constructed the coalition government that before the end of 1962 took Uganda into independence.

That coalition was then shored up during the following year when Obote supported Kabaka Mutesa for the presidency of Uganda whilst holding on to the office of prime minister himself. The alliance rested however, less upon a securely composed majority than upon a 50:50 split, and very soon suffered from all the ills to which such regimes are prone. There was a special crisis over the 'Lost Counties' which at the end of the nineteenth century the British had transferred from Bunyoro to Buganda and which Obote was committed in the rest of the country to restoring to Bunyoro from Buganda by referendum. If this was to be effected something other than the 50:50 regime with Buganda would be required. The difficulty here was that at the 1962 elections Obote's UPC had not won an overall majority, and was critically dependent on KY support. Obote, however, quietly proceeded to put together his third composed majority by wooing some of the disheartened DP to this side. During 1964 several ex-DP followers were given positions in his Cabinet, and before long, following the referendum on the Lost Counties which was won for Bunyoro, its KY members left his government.

But no sooner had that happened than Obote's third composed majority began to fall apart as well. It is often argued that the rift that now opened within his government did not follow precisely north/south lines; but it certainly had that appearance. There are clear indications too that, in the aftermath of the referendum on the Lost Counties, there were moves to oust him from within his own government through a combination of western kingdom leaders and some easterners (including the army leader, Opolot, from Teso) in conjunction with a number of Baganda, or in other words by means of yet one more, again differently composed, majority.[29]

The crisis came early in 1966 when in the course of a tangled dispute concerning the provision of financial and other assistance to a rebel group in the Congo (Zaire to be) in which the Ugandan army's second-in command, Colonel Amin, was involved, and with which Obote himself came to be tarred, the whole of Obote's cabinet during his absence from Kampala unanimously decided to institute a committee of inquiry that among other things was palpably directed against him personally. Such were now the uncertainties, with one composed majority tumbling over another – five indeed in so many years – that, feeling cheated of his rightful inheritance as the man who had finally brought Uganda into independence, now at the end of his tether, moreover, with all this politicking, and wondering where any further majority he might compose could come from, Obote succumbed to the spreading African political disease, arrested five of his ministerial colleagues at a cabinet meeting, and suspended the constitution fashioned at independence. Mutesa and the greater part of the Baganda naturally erupted. Obote was told to remove himself and his government from off Buganda's soil, and popular disturbances in Buganda quickly ensued. Obote's fateful riposte was then to despatch armed forces, principally of northern Ugandan troops under Colonel Amin, against the Kabaka's palace, from which Mutesa was lucky to escape with his life to London.[30]

By these means Obote hamstrung the moves to create a newly composed majority without him. But his own third composed majority had now collapsed as well. By contrast, say, with Senghor's composed majority in Senegal, or Kaunda's successive coalitions in Zambia, he had entirely failed to hold any of his together. Accordingly after 1966 he not only had no majority behind him. He found himself operating in a limbo without any of the structural expedients that have been canvassed here to give him support. Worse, having turned to the army to cut his gordian knot, he was now more at its mercy than he would have cared to admit. For Uganda the bells began to toll.[31]

---

[29] Low, *Buganda*, ch. 7.

[30] Mutesa, *Desecration*, chs. 1 & 11; C. Young, 'The Obote Revolution', *Africa Report*, 11 no. 6, June 1966; I. Hancock, 'The Uganda Crisis 1966', *Australian Outlook*, 20 no. 3 (December, 1966); M. Doornbus, 'Uganda's Coup', *International Spectator*, 20 no. 10 (1966).

[31] Many of the details specified here and below were first publicised in press releases made available over many years by the Government of Uganda's Department of Information. It is scarcely feasible to set out anything more than some strictly selected references from amongst the very large number which are now available. A largely comprehensive bibliography to date can be found in H.B. Hansen and M. Twaddle, *Uganda Now. Between Decay and Development*, London, 1988, pp. 359–66. But see especially, N. Kasfir, *The Shrinking Political Arena*, Berkeley, 1976; A.A. Mazrui, *Soldiers and Kinsmen in Uganda*, London, 1975; H.B. Hansen, *Ethnicity and Military Rule in Uganda*, Uppsala,, 1977; P.M. Gukiina, *Uganda: A Case Study in African Political Development*, London, 1972; J.J.

In these circumstances it is very instructive to see what Obote did next. He first proclaimed himself Uganda's executive president. Throughout his ensuing first term he then made sustained efforts to undermine and cut across existing ethnic entities so as to create a quite new kind of majority for himself based upon populist appeals. His principal efforts were directed at destroying Uganda's kingdoms, the 'feudalism' they represented, and their institutional quasi-replicas in the rest of the country. Then, whereas at the climax of the 1966 crisis he had dictatorially handed down a new constitution, in 1967 he promulgated a revised constitution, and deliberately encouraged its discussion for three months on end. At the same time he embarked on a speech-making tour in outlying parts of the country. In the following year he went further still: in March 1968 he held a large rally in Kampala to which religious leaders and the diplomatic corps were invited. In June he called a meeting of secretaries-general of Districts (key local figures he had decided to retain). Immediately afterwards he held the first UPC Conference since 1964, to which Presidents Nyerere and Kaunda were both invited. In September he summoned a further conference, for senior officers of the army, the police and the prison services, and meanwhile embarked on a series of 'meet-the-people' tours in most of the non-Buganda parts of the country, in the course of which he not only denounced Uganda's elite but proclaimed that he and his ministers had come 'to meet their masters'. It was soon fairly clear, however, that he was making very little progress, particularly at the core of the country in Buganda. When at the end of 1968 he announced that he would address a meeting at Bombo in Buganda, the hour for this was suddenly brought forward; troops and police were much in evidence; and no more than 100 people attended.[32]

Economic and class considerations have been advanced for his next steps, and these are not to be gainsaid.[33] But taken in the round it is evident that they were principally designed to promote still further his continuing efforts to secure popular support for his regime. To this end he launched in 1969 his 'Move to the Left' with his *Common Man's Charter* (Uganda's surrogate for Tanzania's Arusha Declaration, which Nyerere had issued two years before) which was designed to foster a 'new political culture' from which all traces of 'feudalism' would be removed. That objective seemed assisted by the death of Mutesa in London at the end of the year, and in May 1970 Obote followed it up with his Nakivubo Pronouncements in which he announced that his government would take majority holdings in the major commercial enterprises in the country. In July 1970 he capped all this with

Jorgensen, *Uganda: A Modern History*, London, 1981; T.V. Satyamurthy, *The Political Development of Uganda: 1900–1986*, Aldershot, 1986.
[32] Low, *Buganda*, ch. 7.
[33] M. Mamdani, *Politics and Class Formation in Uganda*, London, 1976.

his *Proposals for New Methods of Election of Representatives of the People to Parliament* by which, within the constraints of a one-party state, candidates were to be required to secure votes both in their own 'basic' constituencies, and in three other regions of Uganda as well. This remarkable concoction was explicitly designed to break up the persisting ethnic matrixes which he believed so plagued the country, and thereupon secure a new political legitimacy for his regime.

But by now he was becoming increasingly beleaguered. There had been several attempts on his own life, notably in December 1969 as he was leaving a further UPC conference. That turned out to be a particularly ominous occasion, for not only did elements of the army go on a rampage in Kampala, but Amin, the head of the army, disappeared, and upon his reappearance was accused by his second-in-command, Brigadier Okoya, of deserting his post. Soon afterwards Okoya was found murdered, and there were clear indications that this had been done at Amin's bidding. Violent tendencies were clearly mounting. It was becoming increasingly clear too that Obote did not have the political authority to bring them to a halt. Not only was police morale slipping. As Okoya's murder had shown, there was growing cleavage within the army. This was exacerbated by Obote's increasing alignment with the Sudanese President Nimeri – a move which threatened the Anyanya guerillas operating against the Khartoum regime in the southern Sudan, which had Uganda-based support from Israel. For that fed into a growing rift between Obote, who was giving promotion in the army to his own Lango and their Acholi neighbours, and Amin, whom Obote now promoted out of control of the army, but who nevertheless was enlisting Anyanya and other recruits into the army, especially from his own West Nile district.[34]

The denouement came in January 1971 whilst Obote was away at a Commonwealth Conference in Singapore.[35] Before his departure he had left instructions that Amin was to explain his involvement in yet another financial imbroglio. Having survived his dependence on the army for nearly five years, and no doubt believing that having formally promoted Amin out of direct control of the army he had drawn his teeth, Obote disastrously underestimated Amin's likely reaction. There is some evidence that the chief Israeli representative in the country, perturbed at Obote's rapprochement with Nimeri, bolstered Amin's resolution at the critical moment, and that British firms and the British Government, much concerned about the Nakivubo Pronouncements, were party to what was soon afoot. Warned that a *coup* was planned, Obote's ministers summoned the army's principal

[34] D. Martin, *General Amin*, London, 1974; G.I. Smith, *Ghosts of Kampala*, London, 1980.
[35] M.J. Twaddle, 'The Amin Coup', *Journal of Commonwealth Political Studies*, 10 no. 2 (1972); J.H. Mittelman, 'The Anatomy of a Coup', *Africa Quarterly*, 11 no. 3 (Oct.–Dec. 1971); A. Southall, 'General Amin and the Coup', *Journal of Modern African Studies*, 18 no. 4 (1975).

officers other than Amin, and attempted to prevent it. But the plotters were too quick for them. The coup erupted on 24 January 1971. The Obote regime was quickly toppled. Amin was installed in his place, and, in an almost literal sense, all hell was then let loose.[36]

At the time of the major assassination attempt on Obote in 1969, the army had already shown its fangs. Its ruthless tendencies were now greatly aggravated. Amin's more recent recruits were inherently more hardened and less disciplined than their predecessors. They were not just set loose by a failed assassination attempt, but by a resoundingly victorious military coup. All this entailed sharp confict between the recently recruited West Nilers and Anyanya on the one side, and the lately Obote-favoured Acholi and Lango on the other. It involved as well bitter cleavage between the victorious Amin and a considerable number of senior army officers who had given their support to Obote's ministers' attempt to forestall the *coup*. It happened, moreover, that Amin had a long-standing record of inflicting the utmost personal brutality upon those against whom he proceeded. Any military *coup* is almost bound to be accompanied by violence. On this occasion it entailed not only the extensive slaughter of Lango and Acholi, but the brutal killings of senior officers who had not switched swiftly enough to Amin's side. The homicidal patterns of the Amin years thus became set very early.

It is important to recall, however, that initially these did not engross the scene, and that there are many indications that at the outset Amin set himself to face the same fundamental problem which had confronted Obote – the need to create popular support for his regime. For a start he was careful to call it the 'Second Republic' of Uganda, so that he could draw all the legitimacy from such state authority as had belonged hitherto to it. He made an early bid, moreover, for the support of the Baganda by arranging that Mutesa's body should be returned to be buried near his forebears. By these means he distanced himself from Obote. But in a fascinating way he then went through a whole series of exercises, remarkably comparable to those pursued by Obote himself. During 1971 he too went on much publicised visits to all parts of the country. He did not of course laud 'the common man' – for that had been Obote's gambit. Rather he acclaimed 'the elders', and before very long held meetings of 'representative elders' in several parts of the country. He then tried the notable innovation of donating 'Sh. 100,000 each to the Muslim, Roman Catholic and Protestant Faiths'. In 1972 he followed that up by launching an appeal for the Anglican

---

[36] Martin, *General Amin*; Smith, *Ghosts*; I. Grahame, *Amin and Uganda*, London, 1980; D. Gwynn, *Idi Amin. Death-Light of Africa*; D. Hills, *The White Pumpkin*, London, 1975; S. Kiwanuka, *Amin and the Tragedy of Uganda*, London, 1979; B. Kyemba, *State of Blood*, London, 1977; J. Listowel, *Amin*, Dublin, 1973; J.M. & M. McLady (eds.), *Idi Amin Dada. Hitler in Africa*, Kansas, 1977; D. Woodlings and R. Barnett (eds.), *Uganda Holocaust*, London, 1979; M. Mandani, *Imperialism and Fascism in Uganda*, London, 1983.

church; granting money and land for a new headquarters for the Supreme Muslim Council; and presenting the Catholic Archbishop with a sizeable cheque with which to build a martyrs memorial at Namugongo. The climax here was reached when in his official party to an OAU meeting in Rabat he took one of his wives, one of his ministers, the Anglican archbishop, the Catholic archbishop, and Uganda's Chief Khadi. Clearly he was looking for support from Uganda's extensive religious networks with their close associations at 'grass-roots' level.[37]

Yet as Obote had found before him, such contrivances availed very little. So in August 1972 Amin made his most eye-catching move. Having earlier rescinded Obote's decision to take a majority holding in Uganda's principal private enterprises, he now mounted his own 'economic war' – by expelling Uganda's Asians.[38]

But having gone through his own series of Obote-like efforts to establish his political legitimacy, at roughly twice the pace Obote had done, Amin found himself no better off. Twice over populist contrivances had totally failed to secure the political authority which, in different ways, Nyerere currently enjoyed in Tanzania and Kenyatta in Kenya. That suggests that a populist policy cannot of itself provide an adequate basis for a state's authority. If he had had more nous Amin might perhaps have played the interstitial role, not just because as army chief he could have stood above the political fray, but because as a Kakwa from one of Uganda's numerically smallest peoples away in the distant northwest, he shared in this one particular Nyerere's vital advantage. But he made no attempt either to create a composed majority, nor to take the Prussian road nor the interstitial one. Despite his initial success in securing support in Buganda, he soon squandered this entirely by breaking the kingdom up into separate districts to an even greater extent than Obote had done. At the same time by remorselessly setting loose his own troops against both the Acholi and the Lango, he totally alienated the two most important of the northern peoples (while following the earlier murder of Brigadier Okoya, there was not much support for him in Teso either).

By the latter part of 1972 his situation had indeed become even more parlous than Obote's. The Asian expulsion had given him no more than a passing popularity (as, to his chagrin, he very soon realised). It had gravely aggravated the economic crisis he had inherited. *Kondoism* (armed robbery) was by now out of hand. From the outset the army had been out of control too. In June 1971 he had announced that 'any soldier caught looting property will be treated as a kondo and will be liable to be shot on the spot'. In March 1972 he summoned a large meeting of 'all of the country's top Army, Air Force, Police and Prison Officers' and administered 'a very

[37] D.A. Low, 'Uganda Unhinged', *International Affairs*, 49 no. 3 (April 1973).
[38] M.J. Twaddle (ed.), *Expulsion of a Minority: Essays on Ugandan Asians*, London, 1975.

severe address' to them to 'see that civilians got the full protection of the law of Uganda'; and in July 1972 he issued a dire warning to 'high ranking officers in the Police Force and civil service who are connected with highway robbery and killing of innocent people by assisting kondos, that he is going to deal with them very mercilessly'. All of this availed little. His operational capacity as president was then destroyed by his decision in April 1972 to retire twenty-two senior officials, ten of them permanent heads of government departments. In making his decision to expel Uganda's Asians, he had never consulted his cabinet. At the end of 1972 he sent all of its members on indefinite leave.[39] Meanwhile he had faced an invasion of armed exiles into southern Uganda, who under Obote's guidance had been training in the Sudan and Tanzania. The invaders as it chanced quite incredibly mismanaged their assault. But it was an ominous development. For while Obote's principal opponent, the Kabaka, had remained a focus of opposition in London, at least he had not set about creating a military force to overturn the Obote regime. From the outset Amin always faced a much greater threat from Obote, and the other exiles across Uganda's borders, and that clearly stoked his already well established paranoia. Following the September 1972 invasion, he loosed his troops once again against both the Acholi and the Lango.

Against this background, it is not too difficult to see that under threat from without, with his successive attempts to win popular accord all proving fruitless, with armed robbery now going unchecked, with a governmental regime in collapse, and an evidently restless, often uncontrollable army, Amin by late 1972 was politically at his wit's end. Given his personal and cultural background, it is not at all surprising that he should now have turned to the one expedient which so far had most unerringly put his enemies to flight – terror. We seriously misjudge the Amin years if we fail to recognise that such an outcome represented the final solution of a hamfisted and politically obtuse soldier-dictator now at a loss to know how else to secure his regime in power. That he should so evidently have relished the course to which he now so wholly succumbed made his commitment to it all the more reckless and bestial.

The slaughter which eventuated, to communities at large and to symbolic individuals, such as the chief justice of Uganda, Makerere's vice-chancellor, and the Anglican archibishop, make the killings of Kabaka Mutesa I of Buganda seem very limited. When Amin originally came to power he had appointed the most technically expert cabinet Uganda had seen. In a very short while every one of its members had either fled the country or been killed. More portentously his initially none-too-broad army support soon steadily shrank as well. From an early date amongst his own West Nilers the Alur were squeezed from influence. At the end of 1972

39 Low, 'Uganda Unhinged'.

some Madi began to be killed. By 1974 the Lugbara were being attacked as well, and soon his own position came to rest upon little more than his own numerically tiny Kakwa, upon the Nubian miscellany to which he also belonged, and upon some wandering mercenaries from southern Sudan and Zaire. In due course even these were assaulted, and by 1978 he was at odds too with his principal Kakwa henchman, his brother-in-law, Vice-President Adrisi, whom he unsuccessfully tried to have murdered. Terror thus steadily devoured his regime from within. In a classical manner he desperately sought at the end of 1978 to rally his remnants by launching a diversionary attack upon Tanzania. Nyerere's army, however, riposted, with numbers of Ugandan exiles now in tow, and shortly afterwards found their advance to Kampala little resisted by Amin's now disintegrating forces. By April 1979 Amin's regime simply collapsed.

The aftermath was pregnant with better possibilities, but the offspring was dreadfully stillborn.[40] There had been various refugee groups of Ugandan exiles; Obote had enjoyed Nyerere's patronage and succour; the Acholi officers, Ojok and Okello, headed a number of military recruits; and various elite figures had scattered into jobs, in Africa and elsewhere. As Amin's regime started to crumble so very hesitantly they came together – but without Obote, who was *persona non grata* to most of them – at the Moshi conference late in March 1979, and from that sprang the presidency of Makerere's former vice-chancellor, Yusufu Lule.

The political ingredients here need to be specified. Amin might have been toppled by another military officer. There were some suggestions that his last chief-of-staff, the Sandhurst-trained Brigadier Emilio Mondo, might have mounted a coup against him. It was accordingly of great significance that Amin's army simply disintegrated, as that left the way open for a civilian regime. That possibility was reinforced when Colonels Ojok and Okello accepted Lule, not just as president of Uganda but as minister of defence. It was initially encouraging too that Nyerere did not push the claims of his confidant Obote, and that Obote himself accepted the wisdom of remaining off stage. The significant fact about the post-Amin regime was that Lule was not only a Muganda but a non-royal Muganda at that. Since the Baganda stand at the heart of the country it is difficult to see how any Uganda government that aspires to permanence can operate without them. Mutesa II's personal position as a royal figure had hitherto made this peculiarly difficult to effect. But he was now dead, and that allowed a non-royal Muganda to sit in the principal position in Uganda in a way that Benedicto Kiwanuka, Uganda's DP prime minister back in 1961–2, had never been able to do. That in turn meant that in 1979 the ingredients were in place once again to enable the Baganda the play the role

[40] C. Gertzel, 'Uganda after Amin: The Continuing Search for Leadership and Control', *African Affairs*, 79 no. 317 (1980), 461–89.

of the Prussians in Uganda which the Kikuyu so successfully played in Kenya next door. There were rifts along ideological lines amongst those who attended the Moshi conference, both before and after their grasp of power; but the fact that the leftists soon fell out amongst themselves hardly suggests that they were a major obstacle.[41]

It was clear, however, that a Baganda-topped regime would need to establish a close bond with the Ojok–Okello army, and that in emulating the Kikuyu they would need to do so to the full, viz. by embracing a sufficiency of others in their support. In the past Buganda had thrown up adept politicians – Mutesa I, Apolo Kagwa, Martin Luther Nsibirwa. It totally failed to do so now. At first Lule included in his cabinet a convincing spread of ministers from all significant parts of the country. But he then set out to assert his own primacy as president before either his own or his regime's authority had been effectively established, and then capped this by the crass error of reshuffling his cabinet, introducing four more Baganda and demoting three non-Baganda so as to give the Baganda no less than ten out of nineteen positions all told. He soon realised his mistake, made a further reshuffle, and publicly announced 'that the various regions of the country would be proportionately represented in the cabinet'. But it was too late. In effect he was no more than *primus inter pares* and had no standing of his own. In an overnight *coup* he was swiftly replaced by Godfrey Binaisa. Binaisa was a Muganda too; but a great many Baganda soon took to the streets to protest at Lule's replacement, and that boded ill for Buganda's continued support for Uganda's new government. In particular it meant that Binaisa never secured the political legitimacy he needed to establish his government's authority at the heart of the country. Amin had disappeared, but sporadic, especially nightly, violence appallingly persisted, in Kampala in particular.

Then within a few short months Binaisa threw away even such shreds of authority as he retained. It was clearly crucial that he should maintain his nexus with the Ugandan army. But in November 1979 he sacked Museveni, the minister of defence, and in May 1980 the rising army chief-of-staff, Colonel Ojok, as well. Thereupon the army moved into control. Binaisa was replaced by another Muganda, Obote's old associate – and one time secretary of the long-since-dead Uganda National Congress – Paulo Muwanga. But he had no personal support either, least of all in Buganda. So for lack of any other credible political figure to whom to turn, and following the now total collapse of the further Prussian possibility, the way stood open for Obote's return.

There followed the Uganda national elections of 1980, the first since the pre-independence elections of 1962. Formally these were fought between

---

[41] For some indication of this see D.W. Nabudere, *Imperialism and Revolution in Uganda*, London, 1980, ch. 16.

the same two political parties that had last competed twenty-three years before; the UPC and the DP. But despite the continuing undertones of one being Protestant and the other Catholic, the first now principally represented the old Obote alliance (now supported by the new Uganda army led by Obote's fellow Lango, Oyite Ojok), the second the Baganda and all the other southern opposition to it. The results were highly disputed. Muwanga was evidently determined they should yield a victory for the UPC. The DP initially claimed the victory, but in the event this was secured by the UPC. As a consequence Obote was now installed as Uganda's executive president for the second time.

But it was never a re-run. Obote probably possessed even less legitimacy than during his first presidency. Civil (dis)order was now in a far worse state. The composed majority his election victory should have implied was essentially spurious. Revealingly he made no attempt to mount anything comparable to the gamut of populist measures he had run in his first term. Such expedients were now completely discredited. Within four months he was faced, moreover, not with a remonstrating opponent in London, nor just with an exile movement upon Uganda's borders, but by a National Resistance Army operating right within Uganda itself under the leftist leader, Yoweri Museveni. It was particularly active in Ankole from which Museveni himself came, but in Buganda and Toro as well. It operated, moreover, on Mao's principle of winning popular support by treating peasants with every consideration. There followed as a consequence civil war in Uganda. That in turn triggered anew a reign of terror from Obote's side which was far worse in its slaughter of hapless villagers than even Amin's had been. Yet just as the terror in Amin's regime had gnawed at its heart, so terror during Obote's second term ate at its vitals as well. As under NRA pressure Obote's Lango–Acholi army found itself under increasing strain, so in the end it broke apart, once its Acholi members sensed that Obote's Lango were leaving the brunt of the conflict to them. Ojok had been killed in an aircraft accident. That had left the Acholi leader Tito Okello in command of the army. When he and his fellow Acholi eventually turned on their Lango associates in July 1985, Obote was forced to flee, and Okello took over.

Momentarily the ever resilient Paulo Muwanga daringly tried to seize the interstitial position. But Okello quickly realised how completely *non grata* he was to the Baganda and to all who abhorred the Obote regime. Okello seems to have understood, moreover, that he had now very little choice but to negotiate with Museveni. That became complicated, however, because some of his fellow Acholi, realising that even with the Lango they had not been able to withstand the NRA, turned to the residue of Amin's following to take their place. Museveni thereupon became all the more determined that he would not settle easily. Skilfully, laboriously, and at great cost in lives he had built up the first military organisation of southern Ugandans the country had ever seen. 'The NRA', he now declared, 'will never accept a settlement that could perpetuate the same problems of insecurity, misuse of the army, corruption and murder that have been the order of the day for the past 23 years.' Specifying that time frame was very significant. It looked back over all the years, not just to Obote's (and Amin's) attack upon the Kabaka's palace in 1966, but to the original independence concordat of 1962.

For a while, the principal ethnic groupings in northern and southern Uganda now became quite explicitly represented by two armed forces, Okello's essentially northern, Acholi-led army on the one side, and Museveni's essentially southern-supported NRA on the other. They could either now fight, or Okello could provide the southern elements, not only with a major place in a political settlement, but in a new Ugandan army as well. After several months of negotiation President Moi of Kenya eventually pressured the two sides into the Nairobi Agreement of December 1985. But that essentially comprised a 50:50 arrangement which had as little chance of working as the UPC–KY concordat of twenty-three years before. With his accustomed caution Museveni thereupon inched his way forward. In the new year he finally captured Kampala, and within a bare six weeks of the Nairobi Agreement had himself installed there as Uganda's eighth president. The NRA then pursued the northerners' diminishing forces to the distant borders of the country, whilst he himself set about fashioning a new order for Uganda.[42]

His regime possessed three sets of attributes that gave it more chance than any of its predecessors. Above all it constituted as credible a composed majority as Uganda had ever seen. It came very close to being the kind of coalition Obote's cabinet colleagues had been trying to put together twenty years earlier and which was so abruptly cut short when Obote delivered his fateful blows early in 1966. It included representatives of the country's former political parties and of its non-Amin military factions. But principally – though by no means exclusively – it was built upon an alliance of Uganda's numerically preponderant Bantu southerners. More particularly it included within its ranks the Baganda at the core of the country. But they were not at its head: Museveni from the neighbouring ex-kingdom of Ankole was; and that was probably as satisfactory a structural position for Buganda to hold as both its own interests and those of the rest of the country called for. These ingredients were exemplified by the calculation that within Museveni's first thirty-three man government, there were thirteen Baganda, twelve more southern Bantu, and eight from various other districts in the east and north of the country. Museveni's own position closely accorded, moreover, with that of Kenya's President Moi. Both

[42] Hansen and Twaddle, *Uganda Now*, *passim*.

headed substantial composed majorities. Neither of them came personally, however, from the largest entity in the country. Perhaps that gave each of them something of an interstitial position, with some at least of the advantages which that can provide.

Secondly, Museveni's NRA, for the first time since independence, gave the southerners an army to back them. Hitherto Uganda's armies had all been dominated by northerners of one kind or another. Southerners were unlikely to allow that ever to happen again. Moreover – if only to draw the sharpest contrast between his NRA and the murderous armies of Amin, Obote and Okello alike – Museveni was throughout committed to the Maoist principle of the people's army, under which the most serious offence which any of its soliders could commit, entailing exemplary execution when the occasion warranted, was the abuse or killing of members of the ordinary populace, whom it was there to defend and with whom it must live. This was a far more efficacious populist expedient than either Obote or Amin had ever attempted.

There was a further consideration too. Not only was there a deep-seated desire in so much of the country, the north included (which had suffered so much along with the rest) to see the interminable killings come to an end. Because there was now a southern-based regime holding the levers of power in the capital which lies in the south, it did not have to be as paranoid as its predecessors, all of whom coming from the north invariably felt themselves to be in considerable danger there. The new southern-based regime had, that is, a great deal less need to take to terror to maintain its dominance than any of its predecessors. Correspondingly, in the course of any crisis it had less need to terrorise the north – which could be so much more easily marginalised than the south could ever have been by the northern regimes.

The record nevertheless calls for caution. Too many have misplayed their hand in Uganda to have any clear assurance that its nightmare years are over. Skill, patience, a readiness to make the creative compromise, are all at a premium. But at least in the terms adumbrated here the structures underpinning the state still look in the late 1980s to be much more promising than ever before.[43] The point to watch will be whether these continue intact, or are at any rate modulated into some effective alternative.

---

[43] O.H. Kakole and A.A. Mazrui, 'Uganda: the Dual Polity and the Plural Society', in L. Diamond, J.J. Linz & S.M. Lipset (eds.), *Democracy in Developing Countries. Africa*, Boulder, 1988, ch. 7.

12

Little Britain and large Commonwealth

(1) THE POST-IMPERIAL COMMONWEALTH

As this is written the Commonwealth is about 100 years old. At all events, it was in conjunction with Queen Victoria's Golden Jubilee in 1887 that a conference of representatives of the British colonies was first held in London. It was a relatively large gathering of 121 delegates, by no means confined to heads of government. A second such conference took place in 1894 in Ottawa at the invitation of the Canadian government. A more significant conference for the future was then held in London in 1897 at the time of Victoria's Diamond Jubilee. This was confined to a number of British ministers and the premiers and prime ministers of Dominions and Colonies, and that set the pattern for the further Colonial and then Imperial Conferences (as they came to be called) of 1902, 1907, 1909 and 1911. As during the first decade of the twentieth century the original Dominion of Canada came to be joined by the three new dominions of Australia, New Zealand and South Africa, these meetings began to take on the intimate quality that persisted through to the early 1960s, being presided over by the British prime minister, meeting in 10 Downing Street, and organised by the British cabinet secretary.

What did these conferences discuss? Their records are replete with debates about imperial defence (the contributions of ships and men by the outlying Empire to add to or serve alongside the Royal Navy; commitments to provide colonial troops in British wars; local colonial defence arrangements, and so on). There was much discussion too of economic matters (whether, for example, there should be an imperial customs union, or a free trade zone, or a preferential customs system). In these early years there was periodically more enthusiastic public discussion as well about the possibility of Imperial Federation. That idea, however, was finally scotched in the course of the First World War, largely because of the opposition of the new Dominions.

In the course of that war there was even so an extraordinary, yet abortive, development which is now often forgotten. For two to three months during 1917, and again in 1918, an Imperial war cabinet met in London in which all the Dominion prime ministers sat down in the British cabinet room with the small British war cabinet. There was some thought that this practice might continue in peacetime but, largely because the Dominions did not wish to be too tied in with the United Kingdom, it was never pursued. After the war the Dominions had other concerns. More especially they wanted to assert their position as independent nation states. This was half granted to them in the arrangements made for them to sign the Versailles Peace treaty, and more particularly in their being permitted to become founding members of the League of Nations in their own right. Through the 1920s several of them sought to establish a corresponding autonomy within the Empire itself: Canada because it was anxious to be no less independent than the United States; South Africa because the Afrikaaners were concerned to ensure they were in no way subordinate to the British; and Ireland (which had become a Dominion following the Anglo-Irish treaty of 1921) because it wanted to lessen its British ties too. All this led first to the Balfour Report of 1926, and then to the Statute of Westminster of 1931, wherein was promulgated the new formula governing the 'British Commonwealth of Nations' under which its member states recognised each other as 'autonomous communities . . . in no way subordinate to one another . . . though united by a common allegiance to the Crown'.

During the ensuing years there were a number of further such issues. In 1929 there were problems over the Australian decision to appoint the first Australian-born governor-general. In 1932 amid much controversy an economic conference in Ottawa created an imperial preference system. In 1937 Ireland abolished its governor-generalship and elected a president, and thus came within an ace of repudiating the hitherto essential commitment to 'the common allegiance to the Crown'. Then came the Second World War, during which Ireland remained neutral, and Britain failed to uphold its undertaking to Australia to secure the Singapore base. After the war Burma on securing independence in 1948 abruptly left the Commonwealth, and Ireland finally left it too in April 1949 when it declared itself a Republic.

That very same month saw the climax, however, to the quite remarkable development whereby, by contrast, India, having declared its firm intention to become a Republic, and likewise do away with the hitherto vital commitment to 'the common allegiance to the Crown', was accepted as a continuing member of the now once more renamed 'Commonwealth of Nations'. But there soon followed other problems. There was the major dispute over Kashmir between the two new Asian members, India and Pakistan; then the grievous split over the Suez affair in 1956; while in 1961 there was the considerable contretemps which led to South Africa's departure from the Commonwealth. Thereafter between 1964 and 1979 there was much disputation over Rhodesia, and in 1971, and more substantially through the 1980s, serious disagreements between Britain and the rest of the Commonwealth over sanctions against South Africa.

Since the early 1960s Commonwealth membership had multiplied several times over as the British Empire came steadily to an end. A Commonwealth Secretariat, separate from the British bureaucracy, and now more particularly responsible for administering the biennial Heads of Government meetings (soon ordinarily held outside London) was formed in 1965. It gradually took to itself other functions, such as, for example, the administration of the Commonwealth Fund for Technical Co-operation created in 1971.

This is a familiar recital,[1] but it now warrants extension.

'Little Britain' in the title of this chapter may sound rather too aggressively denigrating. That is not its purpose. Rather the concern is both to argue for a greater degree of realism, and to comment on the 'Little Englandism' that has been displayed in Britain over the Commonwealth since the 1960s.

When we think of the world in which today's younger people will spend their lives, it is only realistic to recognise that – for all the great achievements of the British in creating civil order, parliamentary government, Shakespeare and the English language, and the industrial revolution – Britain cannot hope to be again the great power that it once was. In one not unimportant respect it seems to continue to enjoy its special relationship with the United States. The United States still shares more security secrets with Britain than it does with any other nation. But when Mrs Thatcher sought to stir the embers of the old special relationship, she several times conspicuously failed – over the Grenada affair in 1983; late in 1985 over the sale of Plessey's Ptarmigan system to the American army; in 1986 over President Reagan's talks with General-Secretary Gorbachov in Reykjavik. That does not suggest that there is as much of the old special relationship left as her much vaunted relationship with President Reagan might appear to suggest. More ominously, Britain was made to look very small indeed when, for example in 1985, in the vote in the United Nations over the Falklands issue she was supported by Oman, Belize, and the Solomon Islands only. Britain is not ordinarily quite that small; but she is clearly not as big as she used to be. It has now to be remembered that (as none other

---

[1] N. Mansergh, *The Commonwealth Experience*, 2nd edn, London, 1982; W.D. McIntyre, *The Commonwealth of Nations: Origins and Impact 1869–1971*. Oxford, 1977; P. Gordon Walker, *The Commonwealth*, London, 1962.

than the Australian prime minister, Bob Hawke, with no apologies to the original version, infelicitously put it shortly before the Commonwealth Heads of Government meeting in Nassau in 1985) 'Britain no longer rules the world'.

It is well to recall too Britain's relative position in the world in demographic terms. Taking the World Bank's population figures for the mid-1980s Britain stood there sandwiched between Egypt, Thailand, and Turkey on the lower side, and Bangladesh, Nigeria, Mexico, and Germany on the higher, in the company of France, Italy, Vietnam and the Philippines at around the 55 million mark. This, moreover, was in a world where the largest countries were already Brazil, Japan, Indonesia, the United States, and the Soviet Union, without mentioning the two giants, India and China. No one has to be reminded how very small in their heyday, Athens, Medina or indeed England were. But increasingly size clearly has considerable comparative advantages – as indeed by her tardy adhesion to the EEC Britain also acknowledged. Britain may cut a dash there (though sometimes rather a controversial one), but it does not nowadays always do so elsewhere.

It is an intriguing fact that in the course of the protracted debate over Britain's entry into the EEC a great deal seemed to turn on her having to make a choice between the Commonwealth and Europe. No doubt that notion was fostered by the ardour with which many Commonwealth countries argued at the time – and not least Australia and New Zealand – in defence of their overseas markets in the UK. But there were at least two anomalies in that statement of the case so far as Britain itself was concerned.

First, the depth of Britain's special relationship with the Commonwealth was rarely as profound as was usually suggested. For Australia and New Zealand it turned a good deal between the wars on Britain's commitment to arm and maintain the Singapore base. In 1942 those commitments quickly proved to have been disastrously unfulfilled; and thereafter it was not the Royal Navy which halted the Japanese advance on the Australian mainland but the American Fleet at the Battles of the Coral Sea and Midway. Despite the efforts of the Imperial Federationists, of the Ottawa Conference, or the managers of the Sterling Bloc, the actual nexus between Britain and the Commonwealth was never as strong as rhetorical fervour was apt to proclaim. If since the 1960s British ministers and officials have felt that the actions and rhetoric of some of the Commonwealth's heads of government have been hard to bear, there is nothing at all new about that. Their predecessors had to fend with earlier thorns in the flesh – W.M. Hughes, Mackenzie King and de Valera, for a start – who would have yielded to none of their successors in these respects.

But second, and suffusing so much of the argument over British entry into the EEC, there ran a strain of deep disappointment in the UK with the

Commonwealth for having totally failed to be the central underpinning of Britain's continuing greatness in its post-imperial era which it was supposed to be. The eagerness with which India's membership of the Commonwealth was sought by Britain in the 1940s, and of so much of tropical Africa and the rest of the former dependent empire in the 1950s and early 1960s, bore eloquent testimony to Britain's ardent concern to continue to perform a role on the world's stage analagous to the one it had previously played. It was splendid when India, Pakistan, Ceylon, Ghana, Malaya and Nigeria joined the hitherto white man's club. But far from the Commonwealth proving to be a buttress to Britain in its post-colonial era, as was confidently expected, it turned out to be instead a new, unplanned, and quite major arena in which Britain actually found itself pilloried.

It was bad enough when two of the Commonwealth's major countries, Canada and India, were amongst Britain's sharpest critics at the time of the Suez crisis, or when this was followed in 1961 by the new members and Canada – contrary to the clear desires of Britain's prime minister – forcing an old member, South Africa, to leave. It was altogether more appalling when thereafter successive Commonwealth Conferences remorselessly harried Britain over its Rhodesian policies in the 1960s, over its arms sales to South Africa in 1971 and over its opposition to economic sanctions against South Africa in the 1980s. There were now Commonwealth heads of government, moreover, who broke the long-standing rule that prime ministers' meetings should not discuss the domestic affairs of member countries. There were even Commonwealth heads of government who demanded that the British should use force against their own kith and kin in Rhodesia. In 1966 one British prime minister was loudly denounced at a Commonwealth conference as a racist. Another was pushed into an inescapable corner in 1979 over Rhodesia, and a campaign was mounted thereafter to push her into a further corner over South Africa.[2]

And, so ran the rhetoric, who were these people anyhow? Destroyers of democracy, perpetrators of bloody coups, leaders of authoritarian regimes, upstart soldiers, Nkrumah, Amin and their like. And the whites were not much better either. Menzies, the Australian, had, of course, been staunch, as had Smuts before him. But over the Suez and South African affairs in the 1950s and 1960s, first the Canadian St Laurant, the Liberal, and then Diefenbaker, the Conservative, had taken the Afro-Asian side. Over Britain's entry to the EEC the Australians and New Zealanders had made a good deal of trouble. Over Rhodesia, Fraser, the Australian, came to play fast and loose on the Zimbabwean side, and then Hawke, his successor,

---

[2] On so much of this, see N. Mansergh, *Survey of British Commonwealth Affairs: Problems of Wartime Co-operation and Postwar Change 1939–1952*. London, 1958; and J.D.B. Miller, *Survey of British Commonwealth Affairs: Problems of Expansion and Attrition. 1953–1969*, Oxford, 1974.

Lange the New Zealander, and Mulroney the Canadian, all came out heavily against Britain over South Africa. To Harold Wilson, Edward Heath, Margaret Thatcher and very many British commentators and diplomatic officials throughout these years, the Europeans might some times seem very difficult; but they were rarely quite as bad as that.

The ensuing rift was made all the worse because in the course of these events Britain's former control of the Commonwealth's principal mechanisms slipped from its grasp. Prime ministers' conferences were no longer held automatically in London. Following the Singapore heads of government meeting in 1971 they were now peripatetic around the globe (apart from the meeting in London in the Queen's Silver Jubilee year, 1977). Moreover, the whole operation was managed, from 1965 onwards, no longer by the British cabinet secretary and Britain's Commonwealth Relations Office, but by a quite separate Commonwealth secretary-general. The first of these, Arnold Smith, forcefully resisted any interference in his role by some testy British bureaucrats. He, and particularly his successor Sonny Ramphal, then seemed to go out of their way to see that the Commonwealth represented the interests of the majority of its members, rather than the interests of Britain. Deferential meetings of Dominion prime ministers around the cabinet table in 10 Downing Street were now a thing of the past. They had given way to plenary meetings of heads of government with a good deal of high-blown rhetoric which had somehow to be endured.[3]

There had been little enough to soften these developments. Britain had supported Malaysia through the confrontation with Indonesia in the early 1960s and had assisted federal Nigeria during the Biafran secession in the years that followed, but its aid policies in its ex-colonial territories had never equalled those of the French.

From one point of view the French had been even less successful than the British in shaping their relations with their former colonies. Their plans for a French Union, and the revised plans for a French Community, had both aborted. Yet they ended up with much closer relations with some of their former West African territories than Britain seemed to have even with the old white Dominions. It was the healthier state of the French economy, particularly following its founding participation in the EEC, which made the crucial difference. After its defeat in Indochina in 1954, France was never, of course, going to help Vietnam, so it could concentrate its attention on those francophone West African states who were most prepared to

---

[3] J. Garner, *The Commonwealth Office 1925–1968*, London, 1978; A. Smith (with C. Sanger), *Stitches in Times: The Commonwealth in World Politics*, London, 1981; S.S. Ramphal, *One World to Share: Selected speeches of the Commonwealth Secretary-General*, London, 1979; R. Saunders (ed.), *Inseparable Humanity. An Anthology of Reflections of Shridath Ramphal*, London, 1988; M.M. Ball, *The 'Open' Commonwealth*, Durham, 1971; M. Doxey, *The Commonwealth Secretariat in the Contemporary Commonwealth*, London 1989.

succumb to its blandishments.[4] Britain in these connections continued to
have India to think about. But her mid and late 1940s economic crisis,
culminating in the 1949 devaluation, occurred just at the time when
substantial aid to the new South Asian dominions might have made a
marked difference; while later, the collapse of the sterling bloc in the early
1960s, the mid-1960s economic crisis, and the 1967 devaluation, occurred
just as much increased aid to the ex-British colonies in Africa could have
made a considerable difference to that relationship too. As it was political
estrangement between Britain and so many countries in the Commonwealth was never successfully counterweighed, as in the francophone
states, by the close bonds of cordiality which substantial economic aid
could produce.

In its absence the pervasive disillusion with the Commonwealth in
Britain's establishment circles soon generated a profound antipathy there
towards the Commonwealth and all its works which amounted to a revival
of a degree of 'Little Englandism' of which, Sir William Harcourt, its arch
exponent in the late nineteenth century, might well have been proud. 'The
Commonwealth – a good idea. A pity it failed', Lord Beloff remarked as
early as 1970 (and he remained at least as dismissive thereafter). Enoch
Powell (who apparently hoped he might one day become viceroy of India)
brushed it off as no more than a 'chimera', while in Britain more generally,
it came to be dubbed 'a talking shop', 'a Third World lobby', 'the ghost of
the Empire', even, incongruously, 'cloud-capped towers' 'signifying
nothing'.

Not all of this was entirely wide of the mark. It would have been no less
of a mistake after 1965 to talk up the Commonwealth as it had been to talk it
up inordinately in the past. Its efforts to help with the Biafran crisis availed
very little. Its record over Uganda was on one occasion appalling to behold.
For India it has never been nearly as important as the Non-Aligned
Movement; to Malaysia and Singapore its importance cannot be compared
to that of ASEAN; while for others it ranks at best with the (considerably
smaller but nevertheless near-at-hand) Pacific Forum, Southern African
Development Co-Ordination Conference, or the Organisation of Eastern
Caribbean States. Although for many of its members it holds an important
place upon their political agendas, nowhere does it lie right at the top.

Yet to talk the Commonwealth altogether down and out is to be, quite
simply, myopic. In the first place it is very plain that it is here to stay. It has
grown enormously. Despite a dozen or so withdrawals or non-adherences,
it has steadily enlarged until today it comprises a very large, very widespread and remarkably representative association of nation states – which
considerable numbers of new emerging states have been anxious to join.

[4] D.K. Fieldhouse, *Black Africa 1945–1980*, London, 1986, *passim*.

With the London Agreement in 1949 over India,[5] 'allegiance to the Crown' – that seemingly irremovable requirement over which Ireland left in that year – has no longer stood as the touchstone for its continuing membership. A majority of members have thereafter employed the Indian precedent so as to continue as members when they have become republics; while those (like Australia and New Zealand) for whom 'allegiance to the Crown' was earlier of crucial importance have simply dropped their sights.

By 1990 the Commonwealth had altogether fifty members.[6] They were to be found in North, Central and South America; in the Caribbean, the Mediterranean, and Western Europe; in West, East, Central and Southern Africa; in South and South-east Asia; in both the Indian and Pacific Oceans: and in Australasia. It was represented in all five of the continents; in two of the world's largest inland seas; in two of the three major oceans, while extensively abutting upon the third. Some of its peoples are pigmentally black; some are yellow; some are brown; some are white. They come from small countries and tiny ones; from sizeable ones, and (in some rather different respects) from at least three vast ones too. Some of them are rich; some of them have been becoming rich; many of them are poor, some indeed quite appailingly poor. They are to be found in the north and the south, in the east and the west. Added together they encompass a quarter of the world's population and a third of its nation states. Upon any calculation they now compose a large international aggregation, which has no real counterpart.

The whole association has, moreover, over the years been steadily developing its own style – with the Royal Family (who somewhat unusually for anyone in the United Kingdom actually know where most of it is) well in the van.[7] Journalists have become vexed when Commonwealth Conferences have generated so little news. They continue, however, to be held, and in regular sequence. Prime ministers, moreover, now assiduously attend these, however sceptical they may have been at the outset. For they have learnt of their considerable value: not of the kind that journalists hope for, but of the kind from which heads of government themselves can benefit so greatly. For here they meet considerable numbers of others of their kind, often drawn from far distant places globally, on a scale and in a manner no other arena can match. Especially if one is head of government in a small state, opportunities for meeting face to face with figures of importance in today's much fragmented world are otherwise difficult to come by. Given the nature of such occasions their periodicity is welcomed by many of the larger figures too. Trudeau began by being sceptical of their value; in due

[5] The authoritative account is now R.J. Moore, *Making the New Commonwealth*, Oxford, 1987.

[6] *The Commonwealth Factbook*, published annually by the Commonwealth Secretariat.

[7] T. McDonald, *The Queen and the Commonwealth*, London, 1986.

course he became a committed attender. Mrs Gandhi needed convincing as well; but she certainly was. Bob Hawke, the Australian prime minister, had many another overseas concern; but he was clearly more active at Nassau in 1985 than at his first Commonwealth conference in New Delhi in 1983, and played a leading part thereafter. Dr Mahathir of Malaysia began by ostentatiously denigrating the Commonwealth. He deliberately cut both the Melbourne meeting in 1981 and the New Delhi one two years later. He would, he averred, 'Look East', to Japan and South Korea instead. But after a while that availed him less than he had hoped for. So he clearly made it his business to be at the Commonwealth Heads of Government meeting in Nassau in 1985, at Vancouver in 1987, and then went to the lengths of inviting his fellow Commonwealth heads of government to hold their next meeting in Kuala Lumpur in 1989.[8]

From these meetings wordy statements are apt to be issued that not many people will trouble to read; but amidst the dryness of so much current international discourse it may be that a little rhetoric and ideology should not be taken amiss. In any event as every rugby football fan knows, the Commonwealth's Gleneagles Declaration of 1977 against sporting links with South Africa managed over the years to grow some remarkably strong teeth, whilst the cricket agreement in 1988 to punish those who played cricket in South Africa by excluding them from test selection for four years thereafter was hardly less notable.

Some useful reports have emanated from the Commonwealth heads of governments' initiatives – on the recession in the world economy; on student mobility; on the grievous vulnerability of so many small states; towards a 'commonwealth of learning'. It was appropriate to be sceptical about whether the Commonwealth 'Eminent Persons' Mission to South Africa in 1986 would make a great deal of difference.[9] Its purport seemed principally to lie in placing a delayed fuse under the British government while it thought rather harder about its future policy towards South Africa. One of the Mission's most interesting features in the long run may prove to have been the promise its membership provided – Pierre Trudeau's refusal to participate notwithstanding – that senior politicians with first-hand experience of the Commonwealth could be employed in its service after they had relinquished the bonds of office (rather as Willy Brandt was called on in Germany. Herbert Hoover used to be in America, and so many others are in Britain, in the House of Lords and elsewhere). Arguably the Eminent Persons Group came back empty-handed. But at least it had succeeded in focussing world attention on South Africa once again; it had come remarkably close to instituting a dialogue between the South African government and the African National Congress – which propelled the

---

[8] *The Round Table, passim.*
[9] Commonwealth Eminent Persons Group, *Mission to South Africa*, Harmondsworth, 1986.

South African government into brusquely breaking off discussions with it; it formulated a negotiating framework; and it thereby put the Commonwealth into a prime position from which to take a further initiative sometime in the future.

These developments tell only part of the new Commonwealth story. Finance ministers, health ministers, agriculture ministers, education ministers all meet as well. Universities and their students have benefited greatly from the now long- and well-established Commonwealth Scholarship and Fellowship Scheme. For small states the economic and technical assistance, which upon a modest scale the Commonwealth Fund for Technical Co-operation has provided, has frequently been invaluable; while the Commonwealth Secretariat's assistance to many small countries in organising their participation in larger arenas (such as the UN's Women's Conference in Nairobi in 1985) has clearly been welcomed as well.

It is always important to remember that many a Commonwealth country has regularly employed the Commonwealth membership for its own particular purposes – just as Britain once used it to smooth the trauma of transition to a post-imperial era. Its Third World members have long since used it to try to put together a lobby on the New International Economic Order. Since mid-century Canada has employed its Commonwealth link to facilitate its ongoing connections with the Third World – and to distinguish itself there from the United States. Mrs Gandhi used her Commonwealth involvement to hinder Pakistan's recovery of its international position following the Bangladesh war. Australia in the 1970s, under Prime Minister Malcolm Fraser, began to use it as a principal instrument of foreign policy – because Australia could not become a member of ASEAN to its north, and like so many other medium-sized states found the United Nations to be too large an arena in which to operate significantly. These countries, and the African states in particular,[10] then used the Commonwealth successfully to keep Britain from making the egregious mistake of recognising Ian Smith's 'internal settlement' in Rhodesia when scarcely anyone else would have done so; and in 1985 at Nassau they started to fashion a much more integrated diplomatic front against South Africa. More particularly – to take two further examples – the Commonwealth was of great personal importance to a man like Prime Minister Lee Kwan Yew of Singapore, since it provided the only arena where this singularly able man was listened to – with rapt attention – when he expounded his current views on the state of the world's affairs. It provided too the only arena where the potentially disastrous consequences of the 'greenhouse' effect upon a tiny state like the

---

[10] On their interests see A.A. Mazrui, *The Anglo-American Commonwealth: Political Friction and Cultural Fusion*, London, 1976.

Maldives received any attention at all; the Commonwealth in 1987 set up an expert group to advise upon this.

The critical point which the denigrators of the Commonwealth in Britain do not seem to have grasped is that while for Britain's establishment the 'Commonwealth experience' (to use Nicholas Mansergh's term) has often been very negative, for very many of its other members their 'Commonwealth experience' has often been strikingly positive. It has a record for them of serving a number of very useful, highly pragmatic purposes, and they have no interest in seeking its demise.

It always needs to be remembered, moreover, that the Commonwealth is not just another, but smaller United Nations. The United Nations is an organisation of governments. The Commonwealth is a great deal more than that. The Commonwealth Secretariat is apt to call the largest parts of the Commonwealth connection, invidiously, the 'Unofficial Commonwealth', made up (worse still!) of 'NGOs' ('Non-Governmental Organisations').[11] But it is not oblivious of the fact that the most public parts of the Commonwealth are – along with the Royal Family – the Commonwealth Games, and cricket. (If the Olympics were as closely associated with the United Nations as the Commonwealth Games are with the Commonwealth, the analogue with the United Nations might be rather closer.) Not only has the United Nations none of these adjuncts. It has none of the plethora of voluntary professional and charitable organisations that are so characteristic of the Commonwealth either.

Their range can be illustrated by reference to the group of a dozen Commonwealth Foundation Fellows who went the rounds of a number of British institutions and universities in 1985. Where did they come from? Australia, Canada, Fiji, Kenya, Nigeria, Cyprus, Jamaica, Singapore, Vanuatu, and the Bahamas. And from what organisations? The list included: the Association of Commonwealth Literature and Language Studies; the Commonwealth Agricultural Bureaux; the Commonwealth Association of Planners; the Commonwealth Association of Tax Administrators; the Commonwealth Broadcasting Association; the Commonwealth Forestry Association; the Commonwealth Geographical Bureau; the Commonwealth Institute; the Commonwealth Library Association; the Commonwealth Press Union; the Commonwealth Trades Union Council. Multiply these by at least three, to encompass the other associations of this kind; then multiply again by the number of member countries; then by the members of these associations; add in the Commonwealth's Boys Scouts and Girl Guides Associations, the Duke of Edinburgh's Conferences, the Anglican, Presbyterian and other churches, and a good deal else besides, and then one will begin to get some idea of the multiplicity of personal

[11] J. Chadwick, *The Unofficial Commonwealth: the Story of the Commonwealth Foundation 1965–80*, London, 1982.

linkages that criss-cross this allegedly dead, or at least dying, connection, even before one takes into account all the kinship links it possesses, and the frequently treasured memories so many individuals in it hold of visits to, and residences in, other parts.

The Commonwealth connection is in these terms vastly more intimate and extensive than the passing reporting of heads of government meetings would lead one to suppose, and far larger too than sometimes even the Commonwealth Secretariat has readily allowed. To take a further example. By the late 1980s the Association of Commonwealth Universities, founded in 1912, had 328 member universities in 29 Commonwealth countries; their representatives met every two or three years, and were in touch with each other across the globe on a personal basis far more frequently than would meet the eye. Even in the narrowest political terms, let alone in these far more extensive, largely unseen terms, the Commonwealth had now become a far more elaborate enterprise than even the British had ever bargained for. There is an institution here that is obstinately resistant to being summarily dropped in the dustbin of history.[12]

All this warrants labouring for three particular reasons – one may be called national, one political (or at all events diplomatic), and the third academic.

It is a common complaint by British visitors to India, Australia, and South Africa, not to mention many a smaller country, that there never seems to be very much news there about what is happening in Britain. The fact is that Britain's internal affairs are no longer of very much interest to other peoples with their own concerns to worry about. The British after all are nowadays not a great deal more than the inhabitants of some not very large islands tucked away off the north-west coast of Europe. The outside world is a great deal larger, and in demographic terms is growing steadily bigger yet. (At the beginning of the twentieth century the territories that now comprise Pakistan had a population of 14 millions; by the late 1980s it had grown to 100 millions; given the women already born it will rise to at least 200 millions before there is any chance of it flattening out. Britain remains, meanwhile, at around 55 millions.) In these circumstances it would be extraordinarily foolhardy for the British to cut their remarkably well-established links with large parts of the rest of the world. For all its shortcomings the Commonwealth, it can confidently be said, provides much the most convenient, ready made, connection that any country can possess, if it is to orient itself sensibly to very large parts of its common humanity.

Secondly, the day must surely then come when – to make the politico-diplomatic point – Britain's politicians and diplomats will once again wake

[12] A.J.R. Groom and P. Taylor, *The Commonwealth in the 1980s: Challenges and Opportunities*, London, 1984.

up to the possibilities which the Commonwealth offers to advance Britain's own political and diplomatic interests on a wider stage – just as so many of its other members have very intelligently been doing all along. In these circumstances Mrs Thatcher's visit to Australia in its Bicentennial year 1988 could perhaps prove a turning point. For, on the quiet, there were important Anglo-Australian discussions (that set to one side the still continuing controversy over Mrs Thatcher's refusal to support economic sanctions against South Africa). It began to be appreciated that whilst Britain's expertise on the EEC was useful to Australia, Australia had accumulated an impressive expertise on the now burgeoning Western Pacific region upon which Britain could very helpfully draw as well. As a consequence, for the first time for well over a decade, an Australian prime minister visited London in 1989 (along with several senior ministers) for reasons other than to attend a Commonwealth meeting or pay his respects to Australia's Queen. A more adult relationship seemed in the making.

Then the academic point. This is simply to insist that it is of crucial importance to avoid the serious mistake of treating Commonwealth Studies as if (amidst a plethora of 'area studies') they were simply like the Classics – the study of a past, great, of course, in its day, but otherwise only residually part of our present-day experience. Commonwealth Studies has a rich heritage to draw upon. There should be no need to remind ourselves, however, that there are large matters for study in a Commonwealth context which are continuously being added to all the time.

This is palpably the case in Commonwealth literature. Those who work upon it can point not only to three Nobel Laureates – Rabindranath Tagore, Patrick White, Wole Soyinka – but in the 1980s to four recent winners of the Booker prize – from Trinidad, India, New Zealand, and Australia. Very evidently there continue to be distinguished poets and novelists in Canada, Australia and New Zealand. South Asian writers abound too, some of them of remarkable quality; while Heinemann's African Writers and Caribbean Writers Series (and some of their Malaysian items too)[13] would have to count amongst the most notable publishing achievements of the post-imperial era. There is, moreover, a clear four-cornered framework for comparison here: apart from British writers in Britain itself, there is writing by those of British stock in non-British environments; writing in English by heirs of a different literary high culture; writing in English by those writing on a literary *tabula rasa*.

Beyond the traditional studies of imperial and Commonwealth history, and the study of the Commonwealth as an institution, there continue to be important issues for study in comparative Commonwealth law. The 1980s saw the Canada Act of 1982 (which secured the 'patriation' of the right to amend the Canadian constitution – the British North America Act of 1867 –

[13] A. Hill, *In Pursuit of Publishing*, London, 1988, tells a good deal of this important story.

to Canada itself), and the Australia Act of 1986 (which broke the final legal bonds between Britain and the Australian states).[14] There continue to be issues relating to the ways in which federations operate in the Commonwealth (concerning, for example, their federal financial relations) that are best studied in their Commonwealth context.[15] There are a number of matters relating to the manner in which 'Westminster' systems of government operate in the eighty-five or so instances, at national and 'state' level, where they can be found within the Commonwealth.[16] And there is clearly a great deal more to the notion of the development of science, medicine and environmental concerns in their Commonwealth contexts than has hitherto been appreciated (much of it stemming from Sir Joseph Banks in the late eighteenth century).[17] And so on.

Of course the notion of Commonwealth studies raises all sorts of anomalous boundary questions. How stands, for example, 'American' literature alongside 'Commonwealth' literature? Should not one talk preferably of 'International' English literature? Does not the prevalance of authoritarian regimes in the Commonwealth (though not in truth to the extent that is sometimes suggested) invalidate a good deal of comparative legal and political study on a *Commonwealth* basis? There is nothing unusual, however, about any of this. Are North African studies, for example, African studies or Middle Eastern studies? Do European studies include British studies? Or are they really just EEC or West European studies? Is Russia to be considered as part of Europe? Corresponding anomalies abound elsewhere, and whilst not to be ignored it is rarely necessary to be constricted by them.

By the late 1980s four flourishing academic journals testify to the range and strength of academic Commonwealth Studies: *The Journal of Commonwealth Literature*, the *Journal of Imperial and Commonwealth History*, the *Journal of Commonwealth and Comparative Politics*, and *The Round Table. The Commonwealth Journal of International Affairs*. There are few other such fields that are quite so well served.

(II) COMMONWEALTH STUDIES AND COMMONWEALTH COUNTRIES

Whilst a good deal of Commonwealth studies are fruitfully pursued in a comparative context, Commonwealth studies also imposes upon some of its practitioners an obligation to further the understanding of some of the

---

[14] L. Zines, *Constitutional Change in the Commonwealth*, Cambridge 1991.
[15] See the work of the Federalism Research Centre at the Australian National University.
[16] D. A. Low, ed., *Constitutional Heads and Political Crises*, London 1988; David Butler and D. A. Low, ed., *Sovereigns and Surrogates*, London 1990.
[17] For example, R. MacLoed and M. Lewis, *Disease, Medicine and Empire. Perspectives on Western Medicine and the Experience of European Expansion*, London, 1988 (and not least the

Commonwealth's member countries. That entails detailed study of one or more of them. It calls more particularly for the development of insights into their distinctive characteristics. These are most profitably examined, of course, in depth. But perhaps some illustrative explorations are worth essaying. At all events the remainder of this chapter will be devoted to three brief enquiries along these lines – of, respectively, Uganda, India and Australia.

Uganda

In the preceding chapter an attempt was made to enquire how it was that Uganda, which Winston Churchill once described as 'the pearl of Africa', saw so much disaster in the twenty years and more following its independence in 1962. Underlying that story stood the combination within Uganda's boundaries of two portions of two very different cultural groupings, principally those whom the anthropologists have called the northern Interlacustrine Bantu peoples in the south, who had traditions of rulership, and principally parts of those whom they have variously called the south-central Nilotes in the north, whose political traditions have been generally acephalous. How was it that this eventually disastrous conjunction came about?

In the broadest of terms it was the result of a wide range of contingent events in the late nineteenth century.[18] The area involved extends between the great Lakes Victoria and Albert and the meandering headwaters of the White Nile. Together these stand upwards of 500 miles and more from the East African coast, on and immediately north of the equator. Here there were in the nineteenth century a number of African kingdoms, Rwanda, Bunyoro and Buganda being perhaps the largest. Arab slave traders advanced on this region from Khartoum in the north and Zanzibar in the East. The former became tied up with the ambitions of the Egyptian state under its successive Khedives to extend their dominion deep up the Nile. The latter brought more of their religion Islam to the area, and owned many fewer political ambitions. Rwanda assiduously excluded all intrusions; it was eventually conquered by the Germans, and was not therefore part of this story. Bunyoro first sought to absorb the Khartoumer's intrusion; then expelled it; and thereafter kept itself closed as long as it could to any external involvement.

bibliography in R. Grove, *Conservation and Colonial Expansion, the origins of colonial forest and conservation policy in St Helena, Mauritius and India 1660–1860*, Cambridge 1989.
[18] D.A. Low, 'The Northern Interior, 1840–84', and M. de K. Hemphill, 'The British Sphere, 1884–94', in R. Oliver and G. Mathew (eds.), *History of East Africa*, vol. 1, Oxford, 1965, pp. 297–351, 391–432; M.S.M. Kiwanuka, *A History of Buganda from the foundation of the Kingdom to 1900*, London, 1971, chs. 6–10; D.A. Low, 'Uganda: The Establishment of the Protectorate 1894–1919', in V.T. Harlow and E.M. Chilver (eds.), *History of East Africa*, Oxford, 1965, III, pp. 57–122.

Buganda stood south-east of Bunyoro and was only intermittently approached from the north. It vigorously traded, however, with the Zanzibaris, some of whom were allowed to settle, and soon won converts to their Islamic faith. By the 1870s Christian missionaries had arrived too. They could not enter Rwanda, and an earlier idea that they might go to Bunyoro was never pursued. They were, however, welcomed in Buganda, partly to offset the Zanzibaris; more as an insurance against a more determined Egyptian advance from the north. They too won converts to their religion; actually two versions of it since they included both French Roman Catholics and British Anglicans. The upshot was that in the course of some turmoil at the ruler's court in the late 1880s armed forces of Baganda Muslims, Baganda Catholics and Baganda Protestants began fighting each other for supremacy in the kingdom. By this time Captain Lugard of the Imperial British East Africa Company was advancing from the East African coast to establish British imperial domination over the region.

The particular territorial outcome which led to the creation of Uganda as it has been throughout the twentieth century – after independence with such disastrous results – was in no sense a foregone conclusion. For a start the whole area might have become part of Egyptian territory, or at the very least the Sudan. That first possibility was put paid to by the revolt of the Mahdi, and the collapse of the Egyptian empire up the length of the White Nile. Instead, the old Egyptian-created dominion on the headwaters of the Nile might perhaps just have survived in an entirely residual, but conceivably crucial form, as a territory called Equatoria, since the German traveller, Emin Pasha, who had been the Egyptians' southernmost governor held on there and was variously wooed by more than one European interest. He, however, was 'relieved' and withdrew at the hands of the British/American explorer H.M. Stanley.

Alternatively most of what became Uganda might have become part of what we now call Tanzania, since Lugard was actually beaten into what became Uganda by the German annexationist, Karl Peters. In that case its peoples would have found themselves ruled for much of this century from Dar-es-Salaam, on the central part of the East African coast. But Peters' success was not upheld by Bismarck, who for his own entirely European reasons preferred to accept Lord Salisbury's desire that the headwaters of the White Nile should pass to the British. That outcome was effected by the two governments' decision to accede to the Anglo-German Agreement of 1890 which divided their 'spheres of influence' in East Africa.

But while in view of Bunyoro's persistent resistance to opening its doors to any foreign intrusion, there was never much chance that Bunyoro would become the focal point of any European presence in the far interior of East Africa, it was by no means initially likely that Buganda would either. For a start there was never a presumption that the British sphere in East Africa would ever be divided into two. The German sphere never was, and to this day Tanzania runs from the coast to the lakes (having incorporated Zanzibar as recently as 1965). There was never any initial reason to suppose, that is, that what is now Uganda might not have been part of a single country with its capital in Mombasa, or at any rate somewhere eventually like Nairobi. It hardly needs to be emphasised what a different future that would have entailed! In any event as Lugard advanced, Buganda was deep in the throes of a civil war, and so far as he was concerned was a place to be carefully avoided. He therefore made tracks for Emin Pasha's old headquarters at Wadelai, to the northwest of the interlacustrine kingdoms. If – by contrast with the German sphere – there was to be a focal point for the creation of a separate political entity in the interior of the British sphere in East Africa, it was at the outset far more likely to have been in Emin Pasha's old station at Wadelai in what actually became the far north-west of the Uganda than was in the end actually created.

To a degree that was in no way assured at the time, these many alternatives began to be resolved when in 1890 the agents of the Imperial British East Africa Company received an appeal from the Christian faction in the civil war in Buganda to come to their aid. Lugard momentarily provided this, though he soon thereupon resumed his advance to Wadelai, where he hoped to recruit the remnants of Emin's Egyptian and Sudanese military force in his service. This he successfully did (they were indeed President Amin's direct cultural predecessors – so perhaps Lugard has more to answer for than ordinary justice could allow). He then returned via Buganda to collect the tiny force he had very hesitantly left behind there.

Once back in Buganda he was soon drawn, however, into its still persisting civil war once again, this time specifically on the side of the Protestant faction. Early in 1892 the crucial events ensued. Assisted by his maxim gun, Lugard first established his own predominance over Buganda, and then returned to Britain to argue vehemently and successfully that unless a British force was retained in Buganda the converts whom British missionaries had secured would be massacred. That was too much for even the anti-imperialist Liberal cabinet under Gladstone to stomach; so in a quite extraordinary way a special British Protectorate was established in the far interior of the British sphere before most of the rest had even begun to pass under British rule.[19]

Thus was born the quite separate country of Uganda, composed, because of the Anglo-German Agreement covering the boundary between the British and German spheres west of Lake Victoria, of the northern half of the Interlacustrine Bantu, and, because before very long the British

[19] M. Perham and M. Bull (eds.), *The Diaries of Lord Lugard*, 3 vols., London, 1959; M. Perham, *Lugard. The Years of Adventure 1858–1898*, London, 1956, part 3.

reconquered the Sudan, and reextended its borders well up the Nile, of those south central Nilotes and others who stood closer to Buganda than to the Khartoum-centred British interests in the southern Sudan.

It was based in the kingdom of Baganda – and not, as we have seen might well have been the case (and would have made it so very different a country) – at Wadelai off to the northwest. It centred upon an alliance with Buganda's Christian and more particularly Protestant faction, who were much dependent for the primacy they secured in their country upon British support. Since they were chiefly mission educated they proved to be useful subordinate administrators.[20] So useful indeed did they become that the British used significant numbers of them as what has been termed 'sub-imperialists' in the gradually enlarging Uganda Protectorate round and about, until such areas produced their own mission educated subordinate administrators, whereupon the Baganda withdrew, or at least were not replaced.[21] All this had the important effect of making the Baganda greatly feared and disliked almost everywhere else in the country; and it was that in the eventual upshot that led to the disastrous confrontation around the time of independence between a political party, which held the core of the country and was dedicated to preserving the remnants of Buganda's primacy, and an initially powerful alliance of non-, indeed anti-Baganda, under the later President Obote – a Nilote from the north. It was this confrontation which after independence set off all the quite appalling conflict that so traumatised Uganda in the decades that followed.[22]

In such a way, this is to suggest, can a little investigation of just one Commonwealth country's history begin to provide some understanding of how its destiny has been shaped.

India

A further example can be drawn from India. We have considered in earlier chapters some of the factors that go to explain why India has not seen the authoritarian regimes or internal political collapse that not only Uganda, but in their different ways Pakistan, Ghana, Nigeria, Burma and so many others have seen. It is important, as we have noted, that large parts of India had experienced political domination by a succession of overarching political regimes for the best part of two millenia. It would seem important too that after independence it has been able to employ the device of 'President's Rule' when (more frequently than in Africa at the national level) there have been breakdowns of constitutional government at the state

---

[20] D.A. Low and R.C. Pratt, *Buganda and British Overrule 1900–1955. Two Studies*, Oxford, 1960.
[21] A. Roberts, 'The Sub-Imperialism of the Baganda', *Journal of African History* 3 no. 3 (1962), 435–50.
[22] Ch. 11 above.

level (and in a crude form there has been something of a replication of this at the all-India level too, as Mrs Gandhi's 1975–7 emergency exemplified).[23] We have seen as well how important to the maintenance of India's political order the Indian National Congress has so far been. We have noted how it began in 1885 as the political vehicle for the new 'western educated', 'the teacher and lawyer class', 'the microscopic minority', as the British came to call them. Although it attracted a miscellany of other supporters from the start, it was not until the First World War that it secured the vital support of so many of India's merchant communities. For them Gandhi, as we have seen, was crucial.[24] Thereafter he and his principal lieutenants were no less notable for seeing that the Indian National Congress 'went rural', chiefly in association with India's well-to-do peasant communities.[25] At the end of the First World War Congress enjoyed a good deal of Muslim support, but during the years that followed it lost this disastrously, so that the partition of India followed.

Meanwhile Congress continuously marginalised much poorer peasant and worker activity,[26] not least because as against the British it was hardly necessary to mobilise very deeply (as it was for the Vietnamese nationalists against the French). The Congress which won independence in 1947 was thus composed not so much of the mass of the population but principally of an alliance of India's professional, commercial, and well-to-do peasant classes (as it has generally remained ever since). Whilst it preached socialism, it actually supported a mixed economy. While it abolished the princes and larger landlords, it resolutely resisted every attempt to under-mine the well-to-do peasant regime out in the countryside.

To all these considerations four further ones need to be added.[27]

First, comparisons suggest that it was of great importance to the predominance of the Congress that, throughout its first century, support for it remained extensively countrywide. Jinnah was long plagued in the 1940s precisely because in places this was only fitfully true of the Muslim League. It might not have been true of the Congress. There were several places before independence where potent regional parties – the Justice party in Madras, the Unionist party in the Punjab – to whom some of Congress' otherwise 'natural' supporters adhered, could be found. There have been still more such parties after independence.

In this connection we may note that in another, relatively large, country, Nigeria, political parties have almost invariably been confined to one region, so that national unity has there been peculiarly difficult to forge. Many a smaller country has had several, limited, political parties too.

---

23 Ch. 6 above.   24 Ch. 4 above.   25 Ch. 3 above.
26 R. Guha, *Subaltern Studies*, 5 vols., Delhi 1982–87, *passim*.
27 The best general accounts are S. Sarkar, *Modern India 1885–1947*, 2nd edn, London, 1989; F.R. Frankel, *India's Political Economy 1947–1977*, Princeton, 1978; J.M. Brown, *Modern India. The Origins of an Asian Democracy* Oxford, 1984.

Uganda, for example, just prior to independence, had Kabaka Yekka (in Buganda only), the (Catholic) Democratic Party, and the (largely Protestant, non Buganda) Uganda People's Congress; while from shortly before independence Ghana's Nkrumah-led CPP found itself strongly opposed by the Ashanti-based National Liberation Movement (and their respective legatees disastrously plagued the country for the next twenty years).

In the Indian case it warrants therefore stressing that back in the late nineteenth century the Indian National Congress began its existence as an already extensive countrywide body, drawing its support from all of India's principal cities right across the sub-continent. This characteristic was then reinforced by the annual Congress gatherings which met each year in some different part of the country. Its countrywide connections were then assisted by India's extensive cross-linked railway, telegraphic and postal network (which made interaction amongst its leadership relatively easy to accomplish), while it was immensely assisted too by Gandhi's extensive journeyings. It proved to be of unsurpassed importance that Congress encompassed north and south, east and west, Calcutta and Bombay, and so much else besides, including by the 1940s the Princely States.

Secondly, despite more than one accompanying trauma, Congress successfully managed its leadership successions too. There was a hiatus after Gokhale died, which, among other things, Tilak was unable to fill. So (incredibly) the Englishwoman, Mrs Besant, moved to the centre of the stage, with C.R. Das from Bengal in the wings. Soon of course Gandhi succeeded. Upon his murder in 1948 Jawaharlal Nehru inherited his mantle. Subsequently there was much uncertainty over Jawaharlal's successor, since, unlike Gandhi, he took no steps to name one. But upon his death in 1964 Sastri smoothly succeeded. When two years later Sastri also died there was a bitter encounter following the elevation of Indira Gandhi; in the end, however, that was decisively resolved in her favour; and following her murder in 1984 the political succession to her son, Rajiv Gandhi, was swiftly accomplished.

Behind all this lay a good deal more deliberation than may at first be remembered. For Gokhale identified Gandhi as the coming man much before his time had come; while Gandhi authoritatively designated Jawaharlal Nehru to be his successor from an early date as well. Gandhi was always acutely concerned, however, not just with the leadership succession as such (by the early 1940s he was looking ahead to the post-Jawaharlal generation in thinking of Jayaprakash Narayan), but with the wider generational succession as well (as his interest at that time in Narayan further illustrated). Thus, for example, he was most assiduous in the 1930s in keeping close to the younger generation through Jawaharlal (and probably delayed his departure for the Round Table Conference in London until 1931 in that cause); and he then rebuffed Bose lest the succession he had chosen should be upset. Thereafter, of course, Jawaharlal persistently deflected the question 'After Nehru Who?'. But, by contrast, his daughter Indira became obsessed by the succession after her, and when one of her sons was accidentally killed she quickly sent for the other. In the end her obsession dramatically paid off. The upshot was particularly spectacular because following her assassination Rajiv Gandhi's dramatic accession to the prime ministership seemed to represent the succession of a whole new generation as well.

Thirdly, Congress has survived its many splits too (it is difficult to keep track of those which have occurred since 1969). There was first the major split at Surat in 1907, which was eventually healed at the Lucknow Congress in 1916; then in 1918 the split by the Moderates who became the Liberal party; and later the breakaway by the Socialists in 1948. Earlier Gandhi was much involved in what might perhaps have been much the most serious disjuncture of all. For during the First World War, in emulation of the Irish nationalists, Indian Home Rule Leagues had been formed, and soon became the principal vehicles for a rising Indian radicalism. Gandhi moved into the leadership of the Home Rule Leagues before he took over that of the Congress. Thereupon he might conceivably have done to Congress what Nkrumah later did to the United Gold Coast Convention, when in 1949 he broke away from it and formed the quite separate Convention Peoples Party. Gandhi, however, did not look to the Home Rule Leagues superseding the Congress, and before very long they withered away. That obviated the largest cleavage that might have occurred in Congress' first century's history.

Whilst no doubt many of these matters are well understood, what does not seem to be quite so generally well appreciated has been the immense importance to the Congress of its long succession of 'waves'. They first warrant listing. Congress was originally launched on the crest of the wave in the early 1880s that swept through India's urban elites in support of Lord Ripon and against the Ilbert Bill and the 'White Mutiny'. The 1890s were then slack water. but in the following decade a second Congress wave was propelled into being by the insensitivities of the imperious Viceroy, Lord Curzon, and then spread over the years from 1904 to 1908. That was followed by one of the longest waves of all, being largely supercharged by the primacy within it – and for the only time other than in their own later Pakistan movement – of India's Muslims. It stretched from around 1917, with scarcely a break, through to 1922, when Gandhi's post-Chauri Chaura decision eventually brought it to an end. Ten years later there were the two further Civil Disobedience waves between 1930 and 1934.

The one that tends to be forgotten occurred in 1936–37. In several respects it was very revealing. It arose in connection with the Provincial elections at that time in which the Congress triumphed to a degree it had never dared to hope. There have been several explanations for this. Some have it that the old political congeries mishandled the pork barrel; others that the elite, outraged by Britain's repression of the Civil Disobedience movements, emerged from their foxholes as soon as the hunt was gone, and in the safety of the ballot box enthusiastically gave its votes to the Congress. Nehru had become deeply troubled by this time (as his Presidential speech at the Lucknow Congress in 1939 made very plain) that Congress had quite lost its contacts with 'the masses'. At the end of the election campaign, however, he came back from 130 days on tour, having spoken before perhaps 10 million people (sometimes addressing a *lakh* or more at a time), utterly euphoric at the quite unexpected mass support he had encountered, and the immense reinforcement to Congress' primacy which that had brought. This euphoria was then triumphantly confirmed by Congress' resounding election victory. That had the curious consequence that Nehru never made any real effort again (until the last year of his life) to organise support for the Congress in any systematic way.[28]

Three further waves followed: 'individual satyagraha' in 1940–41; 'Quit India' in 1942; and the 'independence' wave from 1945–52. There was then a hiatus during which Congress' position steadily declined (to the point where Nehru accepted in 1963 the Kamaraj plan to revitalise the Congress by organisational improvement). But then Indira Gandhi generated another wave – by her attack on the Congress 'syndicate' in the late 1960s; her support for Bangladesh's Liberation; and her *garibi hatao* (abolish poverty) election campaign in 1971. Whilst that was followed by the Janata wave against her (following her declaration of an emergency between 1975 and 1977), there then ensued (following the collapse of her opponents' coalition), first the Indira wave of 1980, and then the Rajiv wave of 1984.

Over the years these successive 'waves' vitally recharged Congress' strength. Cumulatively they seem to have been vital to the maintenance of its position in India, and thus to the integrity of the Indian body politic. It is scarcely surprising therefore that it was argued that Mrs Gandhi's handling of the Sikh crisis in 1984 was principally designed to stir yet one more wave into life, since (as latterly for her father before her) strong support for her was not coming to her rescue otherwise – and when, so the specialists would have it, the Congress organisation out in many parts of the country had fallen on its beam ends.

That raises a closely related point, upon which the story of the 1936–7 campaign is once more revealing. The papers of the Congress' abortive 'Mass Contacts Committee' of 1936 show that even in the months immedi-

---

[28] On this and the third following paragraph see D.A. Low, 'Congress and "Mass Contacts", 1936–37: Ideology, Interests and Conflict over the basis of Party Representation", in R. Sisson and S. Wolpert (eds.), *Congress and Indian Nationalism. The Pre-Independence Phase*, Berkeley, 1988, pp. 134–58.

ately preceding the triumphant 1936–7 election, Congress' organisation out
at the 'grass roots' was in most parts of India ramshackle at best, where
indeed it was functioning at all. Congress' momentum in 1936–7 did not,
that is, turn (so this evidence would imply) on the strength or otherwise of
its organisational structure, but upon the personal efforts of those who had
enough commitment and resources to call out mass meetings and processions and/or print and write newspapers on its behalf, and on the ability of
Jawaharlal Nehru particularly to produce the necessary rhetoric to meet
their demands.

As the electorate then quadrupled all this became very much more
difficult to effect. But this evidence does perhaps suggest both a caveat, and
some explanation of how a Congress which was in such dire organisational
straits as we are led to believe it displayed by mid-1984 – and by her actions
in Kashmir, Karnataka, and Punjab, and by her holding of special
Congresses at that time, Mrs Gandhi herself seemed to believe – could at the
end of that year prove so extraordinarily triumphant. Following her murder
the oft-recurring and quite vital occurrence for the Congress of a political
'wave' had come to its rescue yet again.

These characteristics of the Indian body politic need, so this is to suggest,
to be constantly borne in mind.

Australia

More briefly Australia provides a further example of how a little investigation can provide some understanding of how a Commonwealth country's
destiny has been shaped. Curiously, because the documents are so thin,
there continue to be disputes about the reasons why the first convict
settlement was established at Sydney Cove in 1788.[29] An Australian
passport holder resident in Canberra, its twentieth-century capital, would,
however, have to say that there continues to be a divide there, not so much
between classes, as between those (principally on the Australian left) who
continue to express the convicts' spirit of defiance, and those (principally on
the Australian right) who see themselves as being the necessary warders of a
worryingly unruly society.

A good deal of Australian history has long been written around the theme
of Australia's coming of age during the First World War, amidst the
murderous fire of Gallipoli.[30] There has been Geoffrey Blainey's immensely
stimulating thesis about Australia's 'tyranny of distance',[31] and a number of
other insights too.[32] A less noticed interpretation warrants major attention.
In a special number of the American journal *Daedalus* (to which a galaxy of

[29] For example, G. Martin (ed.), *The Founding of Australia*, Sydney, 1978.
[30] For example K.S. Inglis, *The Australian Colonists*, Melbourne, 1974.
[31] G. Blainey, *The Tyranny of Distance*, Melbourne, 1966.
[32] See generally F. Crowley *et al.*, *Australians*, 11 vols., Cambridge, 1988.

Australian talent contributed) Hugh Collins, in a brilliant and largely novel way, captured a large part of the essence of Australia's *persona* when he argued that Australia was best understood as a Benthamite society.[33] Australian society, so Collins aptly put it, is at once deeply utilitarian, legalist, and positivist.

It is pre-eminently utilitarian, being both anti-collectivist and strongly antipathetic to doctrines of social contract. Policies are almost invariably judged in terms of their impact upon the interests of the majority of Australians as individuals.

Legalism is pervasive as well. It is not just that there is a written constitution. It is widely – and, of course, erroneously – assumed that all constitutional issues are essentially legal ones. More strikingly, industrial relations are all but wholly conducted by means of the hugely elaborated mechanisms of the legally supported Conciliation and Arbitration system. Bob Hawke became prime minister of Australia in 1983 principally because for twenty-five years he had been its most accomplished operator.[34] For any academic audience it will suffice to underline the point by saying that in Australia academic salaries are fixed not by negotiations between individual chief executives, the Vice-Chancellors' Committee and the Association of University Teachers or some kind of counterpart, but by a special statutory tribunal, conducted by a judge of the Arbitration Commission, before whom governments, vice-chancellors, and staff associations alike make their formal and public submissions, prior to the commissioner handing down his formal determinations.

Positivitism, too, is no less prevalent. In Australia, fact and value are clearly separated. As Collins remarks, the controversy in Australia over its participation in the Vietnam war in the late 1960s was not about natural rights – as so much of it was in the United States – but about the importance of that participation in that way for securing Australia's longer term defence interests.

Chartism was the crucial conduit that carried Benthamite doctrines to Australia. Upon this point one can be very specific. Henry Parkes had been a 'badge-bearing member of the Birmingham Political Union' at the time of the First Reform Bill in Britain prior to his migration to New South Wales. In the late nineteenth century he became in many ways Australia's principal political figure, deservedly earning the soubriquet of 'the Father of Australian Federalism'.[35] Whereas Chartism had very little success in Britain, in Australia 'within ten years of the discovery of gold' in the 1850s, so Sir Keith Hancock, the doyen of Australia's historians, put it, 'practi-

---

[33] H. Collins, 'Political Ideology in Australia: The Distinctiveness of a Benthamite Society', *Daedalus*, 114 no. 1 (Winter 1985), 147–70.

[34] B. d'Alpuget, *Robert Hawke*, Melbourne, 1982.

[35] A.W. Martin, *Henry Parkes*, Melbourne, 1980.

cally the whole programme of the Chartists was realised in the Australian colonies'.[36] As Collins arrestingly writes, over a century later 'the Benthamite centre holds', impervious alike to 'the Hayek push or . . . the Habermas collective'. Thus in the 1980s the Hawke government successfully pursued consensus politics (at the time when they were fiercely rejected by Mrs Thatcher). They pivoted upon a widely supported statutory economic planning advisory council of government, business and union representatives, and the creation of a national 'accord'. 'In the "wages accord" . . .' so Collins perceptively averred, 'that reconciliation between master and man that is at the heart of Hawke's policies, there is more of Birmingham' than of any of the world's corporatist capitals. 'For these are a people proud in their pragmatism, skeptical of speculative and abstract schemes, wedded to "common sense".'

Armed with these insights, a wide range of Australian circumstances become a great deal more explicable than they would otherwise be. It is for students of Commonwealth studies to pursue such insights vigorously. The following chapter picks up a further Australian theme with a similar purpose in mind.

[36] W.K. Hancock, *Australia*, London, 1930, p. 54.

13

Australia in the eastern hemisphere

By the early 1980s Australia was not only the largest producer and the largest exporter of wool of any country in the world, but also the second largest exporter of sugar, and a significant supplier on the world market of fruits, dairy produce, meat and wheat. Yet it was in the minerals and energy area that the most striking developments were occurring, since it was now as well the world's largest exporter of iron ore, alumina and mineral sands, and the second largest exporter of coal, bauxite, nickel, lead and zinc. It was an important world supplier too of copper, tin, tungsten, silver and gold, the largest producer of bauxite, and the second largest producer of aluminium. Moreover, it was well on the way to being the largest producer of coal, with reserves of 600 billion tonnes. There were estimates indeed that by the year 2000 it would be exporting three times the amount of coking coal it was already doing, between seven and ten times as much steam coal, as well as 50 per cent more iron ore and 50 per cent more aluminium and alumina. By any account it was a resource rich country.

Where did its exports go? Two-thirds of its trade was with the free-market economies of the Pacific Basin area, with the Pacific islands, New Zealand, the ASEAN countries, South Korea, Hong Kong, Japan, Canada and the United States. That proportion thereafter continued to grow. Moreover if one took away the United States and Canada, and added in their place China, India and the other South Asian countries, two-thirds of its trade was still with its own region. This was growing enormously.

In 1981 Australia's real growth rate stood at 5 per cent per annum and was the highest of all the OECD countries. But Malaysia's was 7 per cent, Indonesia's nearly 8 per cent, South Korea's 8 per cent, Singapore's nearly 10 per cent. Singapore's per capita income, moreover, was on the way to overtaking first New Zealand's and then Australia's, with that of the United

States in its sights as well. More generally, during the 1970s the Indo-nesian economy had growth at twice the Australian rate. During that decade the Western Pacific region had shown considerably stronger economic growth than the rest of the world. Its economic growth rates were on average one and a half times that of the world as a whole. Growth, moreover, was here significantly higher in the poorest countries of the region than in other poor countries. Similarly, growth in Japan was much stronger than in other high-income industrial countries; and growth was much higher too in middle income countries in the Western Pacific region than in other middle income countries. It was most rapid in the densely populated countries of the East Asian rim – Japan, South Korea, Taiwan, Singapore and Hong Kong.

Most of this growth was based on rapid industrialisation, and that required resources of the kind that Australia was superbly well equipped to provide. As these countries moved from labour-intensive to capital-intensive industry, moreover, so they left openings for other countries to move into a labour-intensive phase. Malaysia, Thailand, the Philippines, China and even Indonesia took steps to do so. That in turn provided still further markets to which Australian resources exports could go.

These developments were paralleled by some dramatic financial devel-opments. As the 1980s opened London still headed the list of the world's financial centres. US$250 billions worth of capital assets were owned out of London. That was much larger than could be claimed for any other European centre, and was still significantly more than could be said of New York. But if one took the two major centres of financial power in East and Southeast Asia, Hong Kong and Singapore, they together com-manded US$87 billion, or already one-third of London's total – though London had been at this business for over four centuries, whilst they had only been at it for a few short decades. If Japanese overseas investment was at this time curiously smaller than these, it was certainly enlarging, and would shortly be very considerable.

There was here, therefore, a situation where Australia possessed a great many resources which the economically burgeoning countries to its north were very keen to purchase, and to whose development their financial resources could contribute. As a consequence Australia's economic orien-tations were changing rapidly. Its mineral exports were becoming as important as its agricultural exports, and its exports to Asia were now sub-stantially more important than its exports to western Europe. Already its trade with Japan was worth around US$1 billion annually; while Japan and the ASEAN countries were rivalling the United States as the second largest source of foreign investment into Australia.[1] The implications of all

[1] There is a large literature on all of this. Surveys include W. Kaspar and T.G. Parry, *Growth, Trade and Structural Change in an Open Australian Economy*, Canberra, 1978; R.E. Caves

this for Australian society much more generally were potentially profound.

It is well here to review some of the long-run history that preceded this upshot. There is still argument as to what precisely led to the establishment of the original colony of New South Wales. Yet it certainly owed something to a global, strategic concern in London to establish an undisputed British presence somewhere on the rim of the Pacific Ocean.[2] Botany Bay, that is, had affinities with Gibraltar, Malta, and the Cape, and later Suez, Aden, and Singapore, as part of that world-wide network of British controlled staging posts, vital to Britain's strategic and commercial position in the world. Unlike those other staging posts, however, (other than the Cape) Australia developed into a series of white colonies strung around the vast Australian coastline. There they stood very isolated, at the other end of the world, at a great distance from the 'mother country'.

A great deal of effort was consequently expended by Australian governments, both before and after Federation in 1901, in attempting to secure Australia's position against intrusions from the north, first by other European powers, and then more particularly (from the time of the Russo-Japanese war of 1904–5 onwards) by the Japanese.[3] Understandably in these circumstances Australia's direct links with Britain became – and long remained – very much more important to it than for many of the other imperial outposts.[4] There were countless signs – culminating perhaps in the tumultuous welcome for the first visit of a ruling monarch from Britain as late as 1954[5] – that most Australians sought a tight grip upon what they saw as their British lifeline.

During the nineteenth century there were two very important developments: the growth of Australia's wool exports, and the discovery of Australia's gold. The implications of these are sometimes missed. One major consequence was that between 1860 and 1890 Australia almost certainly

and L.B. Krause, *The Australian Economy: A View from the North*, Washington, 1984; R. Maddock and I.W. McClean, *The Australian Economy in the Long Run*, Cambridge, 1987. For a useful review at the time see 'The Raw Economy. Australia: A Survey', *The Economist*, 31 October 1981. For a most helpful account, as of mid-1982, I am much indebted to Sir Laurence Muir, then of Potter Partners.

[2] G. Martin (ed.), *The Founding of Australia: The Argument about Australia's Origins*, Sydney, 1978; A. Frost, 'Towards Australia: The Coming of the Europeans 1400–1788', in D.J. Mulvaney and J.P. White (eds.), *Australians to 1788*, Broadway, NSW, 1988, ch. 19.

[3] N. Meaney, *The Search for Security in the Pacific, 1901–1914*, Sydney, 1976; R.C. Thompson, *Australian Imperialism in the Pacific: The Expansionist Era, 1820–1920*, Melbourne, 1980.

[4] The most important surveys, on these and later matters, are T.B. Millar, *Australia in Peace and War. External Relations 1788–1977*, Canberra, 1978, and P.G. Edwards, *Prime Ministers and Diplomats. The Making of Australian Foreign Policy 1901–1949*, Melbourne, 1983.

[5] P. Spearritt, 'Royal Progress: The Queen and her Australian Subjects', in S.L. Goldberg and F.B. Smith (eds.), *Australian Cultural History*, Cambridge, 1988, pp. 138–57.

came to have the highest standard of living of any country in the world; certainly higher than Britain's, probably higher than that of the United States.[6]

This remarkably high standard of living was jealously guarded by Australia's Britons. In its defence they soon committed themselves to a 'White Australia' policy. That meant, among other things, that whereas the South African mining industry came to be developed by the exploitation of non-white labour, the major mines in Australia came to be worked by white miners only, and that in turn meant that the Chinese, who at one stage made up 10 per cent of the male population of Victoria and had contributed greatly to the opening up of Australia's first alluvial mines, were steadily excluded.[7] By the opening of the twentieth century 'White Australia' had become 'the indispensable condition of every other Australian policy'.[8]

In the first half of the twentieth century there was a consequential development of hardly less significance. This centred upon a widespread determination to maintain the integrity and independence of the White Australian order at almost any cost. With changes in the balance of world power both before and after the First World War, there was increasing concern over the continuing isolation of Australia from its natural allies and protectors. There was great concern too over the vulnerability of Australia's endlessly indefensible beaches, and its even more endlessly empty lands. In particular there was deepening anxiety over Australia's great distance from those important centres of manufacturing industry which were so essential for providing key components for its self-defence. As a consequence – so the economic historians tell us – some of that late nineteenth century pre-eminence by world comparisons in Australia's standard of living was foregone in an effort to make White Australia a little more industrially self-sufficient, and its white population larger.[9]

Now behind all of that there lay, from the later nineteenth century onwards, a great fear of Asia, and the possibility of invasion by some of its culturally very different and poverty-stricken millions. These fears were aggravated by profound worries over the threat of competition from labour-intensive industries in the Asian countries to the north. They were then enormously enhanced by Japan's victories in South-east Asia during the Second World War; by Britain's 'Great Betrayal' in not fulfilling its long-standing promise to defend at all costs the Singapore base; by the

---

[6] A convenient summary is R.V. Jackson, *Australian Economic Development in the Nineteenth Century*, Canberra, 1977.

[7] A.T. Yarwood, *Asian Migration to Australia: The Background to Exclusion, 1896–1923*, Melbourne, 1967; D. Denoon, *Settler Capitalism: The Dynamics of Dependent Development in the Southern Hemisphere*, Oxford, 1983.

[8] W.K. Hancock, *Australia*, London, 1930, p. 59.

[9] N. Butlin, 'Australian Defence: Our Own Worst Enemy?', in R. O'Neill, *Australia Defence Policy for the 1980s*, St Lucia, 1982, p. 104.

advance of the Japanese to as close as the islands immediately to the north and northeast of Australia; and by the fortuitous good fortune of the American successes against the Japanese at the Battles of the Coral Sea and Midway in 1942.[10]

One consequence of all this was that at the end of the Second World War, following upon the eventual defeat of the most serious of all the threats ever made to the existence of Australia as an independent nation, a major national enterprise was undertaken. Its purport was clearly articulated by Arthur Calwell, minister for immigration in the post-war Labor government (and later the leader of the Australian Labor Party), when he declared that: 'We have only the next 25 years in which to make the best possible use of our second chance to survive'. Logically that led on to the great post-Second World War migration programme to Australia, mainly paid for by the Australian taxpayer. Overwhelmingly it came from Europe, often from quite new quarters in Europe, so that Australia not only came to have (for example) a large Yugoslav community, but both Sydney and Melbourne soon came to rank amongst the largest Greek cities in the world.[11]

For a number of clearly identifiable reasons, however, many Australians remained gravely apprehensive about their Asian neighbours to their north. In 1934 Latham had led a goodwill mission to Japan and South-east Asia, but it was not significantly followed up. During the later 1940s Australia gave a good deal of support to the Indonesian revolution;[12] but before long apprehensions about some of the directions which independent Indonesia was taking had rubbed the shine off that. In the 1950s Casey, minister for external affairs in the Menzies' Liberal-Country Party government (who had served not only in London, Washington and the Middle East, but in the mid-1940s as Britain's governor in Bengal), made a number of attempts to persuade his countrymen to take a more positive attitude towards Asia (particularly in respect of the Colombo Plan, in whose making his predecessor, Spender, had played such an important part), but with next to no success.[13] His colleague, the Trade Minister, McEwan, concluded in 1957 a seminal Japan–Australia Trade Agreement, and by the 1960s Australia was selling a great deal of wheat to China,[14] but most Australians remained deeply concerned with the continuing competition, as they saw it, from the use of cheap Asian labour. For several decades, moreover, Asia spelt for them war and rumours of war: following the Japanese invasions of China in the 1930s, and the major crisis of Japanese forces at the gates of Australia in

[10] G. Long, *The Six Years War*, Canberra, 1973; D. Day, *The Great Betrayal*, Sydney, 1988.
[11] C. Price and J.I. Martin (eds.), *Australian Immigration: A Bibliography and Digest*, Canberra, 1976.
[12] M. George, *Australia and the Indonesian Revolution*, Melbourne, 1983.
[13] W.L. Hudson, *Casey*, Melbourne, 1986.
[14] J.G. Crawford, *Australian Trade Policy 1942–1966: A Documentary History*, Canberra, 1968.

the 1940s, there was first the Korean war in the 1950s,[15] then *Konfrontasi* between Indonesia and Malaysia in the early 1960s,[16] and all the while the long succession of wars in Vietnam – through indeed into the mid-1970s (not to mention the Vietnamese invasion of Kampuchea thereafter). Furthermore, throughout these years Australians of a right-wing persuasion were gravely troubled by revolutionary forces to their north; those of a left-wing outlook by the dictatorships that were spreading there.

By the 1970s, however, the economic growth of the countries to Australia's north, and the implications of that for Australia's export trade, and thus for its economic advantage – especially once the former British market was becoming so much more difficult, following Britain's entry into the European Economic Community – called for a substantial reappraisal. As we have seen, much the largest part of Australia's exports were now going, not just to Japan, but to South Korea, Taiwan, the Philippines; and all the signs were that they would probably soon be going in increasing quantities to other countries in the region as well. All that in turn was leading to the establishment of new links, and soon ever closer links, with these countries to the north, and in all kinds of ways that was altering quite substantially Australia's traditional overseas orientations.

When Gough Whitlam came to office at the end of 1972 as Labor prime minister of Australia he finally proceeded to grant Australian recognition to the Peoples' Republic of China (which had always hitherto been withheld). He completed the withdrawal of Australian troops from Vietnam; granted independence to Papua New Guinea; concluded treaties of friendship with Japan; and put a formal end to the White Australia immigration policy. He succeeded, moreover, in instituting a new Australian national anthem. Yet there was no chance of his changing the Australian flag (as the Canadians had done). The Union Jack remained firmly fixed in its top left hand corner,[17] and Britain's Queen remained Australia's Queen as well.

Behind all that lay a considerable dilemma. There could be no denying that Australia's British links were now thinning, not least on the British side; perhaps the decisive event had been the British Labour government's decision in 1968 to 'withdraw the legions' – to pull out all that remained of Britain's active military presence 'east of Suez'.[18] Following the bitter experience of the Second World War, Australia's American alliance (which was institutionalised in the ANZUS Treaty of 1951 between Australia, New Zealand and the United States) now became of great importance.[19] But there was no suggestion that Australia should thereupon join the United

---

[15] R. O'Neill, *Australia in the Korean War 1950–53*, 2 vols., Canberra, 1981–6.

[16] For a major Australian account, see J.A.C. Mackie, *Konfrontasi. The Indonesia–Malaysia Dispute 1963–1966*, Kuala Lumpur, 1974.

[17] E.G. Whitlam, *The Whitlam Government 1972–1975*, Ringwood, Victoria, 1985.

[18] P. Darby, *British Defence Policy East of Suez*, London, 1973.

[19] H.G. Gelber, *The Australian–American Alliance*, Ringwood, Victoria, 1968.

States (as half a dozen Hawaiis). At the same time the notion that was periodically canvassed that Australia should now see itself as an Asian country cut no ice either.

Only slowly did the larger conceptual issues here come to be faced. Australian statesmen – Deakin, Hughes, Menzies, Evatt – had long proclaimed Australia to be a Pacific power. But their concern had been for Australia's position in the balance of power in the Pacific. They had never seen it as being principally and intimately involved in the region's affairs on the inside. Whitlam described Australia and Japan as 'two Pacific powers'; but he did very little to elaborate upon this theme other than to argue elegantly the conventional wisdom of the late 1970s that international co-operation was essential to tackling the issues that faced the Western Pacific countries.[20]

It was not until the early 1980s that the issues here came finally to be faced, and even then in terms which to begin with were often very hesitant. One can see this in a series of academic discussions in this period of Australia's external relations.[21] One can see it more particularly in ministerial statements.[22]

In two speeches in 1982, Tony Street, Australia's minister for foreign affairs in Malcolm Fraser's Liberal-National Party government, set out the fundamental dilemmas as so many Australians still saw these at that time. 'While', he said (speaking to the Foreign Correspondents' Club in Singapore in June 1982), 'a number of factors place us squarely with the western group of nations, the facts of our geography mean that we have special characteristics and interests which differ from those of most other westernised industrialised countries'. 'We are', he declared, 'basically a western nation located among the predominantly Third World countries of the Asia-Pacific region.'[23] In an earlier speech he had set out, moreover, exactly what he meant by calling Australia a western country. One should note, he told the Australian Institute of International Affairs, not only Australia's 'relatively high standard of living, but our defence alliance with the United States; and the importance of our economic relations with Japan, the United States and Western Europe'. 'We have', he went on, 'a very large stake in the preservation of western democratic values and in the continuation of western security and economic stability.'[24] In saying these things he was accurately reflecting the continuing attachment of most Australians to their

[20] E.G. Whitlam *A Pacific Community*, Boston 1981.
[21] For example, C. Bell (ed.), *Agenda for the Eighties*, Canberra 1980; P. Dibb (ed.), *Australia's External Relations in the 1980s. The Interaction of Economic, Political and Strategic Factors*, Canberra 1983. These canvass many of the other issues referred to below.
[22] The text of these speeches are derived from issues of Australian Department of Foreign Affairs (later, Foreign Affairs and Trade), *Backgrounder*, under the dates mentioned.
[23] Singapore, 18 June 1982.   [24] Sydney, 14 May 1982.

European cultural heritage, and by clear implication specified the barriers which still remained to be crossed.

Behind all this lay a fundamental misconception. Variously expressed, this essentially affirmed that Australia's European connections placed it, with New Zealand, in a quite special category in its region – unique, an anomaly, an odd man out.

A number of considerations suggested, however, that the case here was far less well warranted than was ordinarily believed.[25]

For a start there were several other countries in the region who by any tally were anomalies as well: Singapore, for example, a country of two and a half million people, most of whom were Chinese, living on a small island south of a great land mass where there were already at least a billion Chinese – in the Peoples' Republic of China. Then there was Indonesia: a country well beyond what was ordinarily thought of as the Muslim World, containing, however, much the largest Muslim population of any Muslim country in the world – and with hinduised Bali in its midst. Further, there was the Philippines; not merely the one overwhelmingly Roman Catholic country in Asia, but with a great deal of Chinese, Spanish and American admixture in its elite, making it culturally and genetically of an order that really was unique in the region. And so on. There were, that is, not just one, or two, odd men out in the region, but upwards of half a dozen, and Australia was just one of them.

Whilst Australians rightly believed that their prime cultural roots lay not within their own region, but away in western Europe, that too was a great deal less unusual than they generally believed. Singapore (again for a start) did not find its cultural roots within its own island, but away in mainland China to the north. One of the major concerns, indeed, of Lee Kwan Yew, its long-serving prime minister, was precisely to re-emphasise the immense importance to Singapore of the traditional Confucian values of ancient China, whose elaboration had taken place well outside his own country. It was much the same with Dr Mahathir's regime in Malaysia – and for the greater part of Indonesia's population too. For so many of them their key cultural roots lay not in their own countries but in the Middle East – in Saudi Arabia, above all in the holy city of Mecca. If there was, therefore, something anomalous about a crowded Australian airport shortly before an aircraft took off for a culturally oriented trip – for many of its passengers – to Europe, it was paralleled at Jakarta airport shortly before a Garuda 747 took off with a planeload of Indonesian Muslims, embarking on their pilgrimage to Mecca. It was not very different for so many Sri Lankans, Thais and Burmese. For the many Buddhists amongst them, their cultural homelands stood likewise not within their own countries but a long distance off in

[25] I discussed these issues in a Presidential Address to the Asian Studies Association of Australia in Melbourne in May 1982.

faraway north India, where the Buddha had first taught his followers. And as for many Filipinos, especially within its prospering elite, their key associations lay far distant from them too, first in Spain and then in the United States. The fact that Australians' cultural roots lay a long distance away from their own country in no way placed them, that is, in any very unusual situation amongst the other peoples of their region.

There were few things that really were quite so anomalous in the region as the huge differences in population between, on the one side, the billion and more people who made up the nation state of China, and the 700 millions and more that made up the nation state of India, and, on the other, the few hundred thousands that made up the nation state of Fiji, and the few thousands and less that made up the nation states of Vanuatu and the Solomons. In this company Australia belonged firmly in the middle, with the smaller, but by no means the smallest countries of the region. In that respect too Australia was actually much less of an anomaly than most Australians liked to believe.

What was more, whilst many Australians may periodically have felt that Australia's relations with the 150 millions and more who made up its northern neighbour, Indonesia, were really quite unusually difficult, again this was not at all peculiar in the region. Sri Lanka, with its 15 millions or so, was in a much worse position vis à vis India to its north. Vietnam was even more uncomfortably placed as against China; while periodically Thailand, the Philippines, Malaysia and Singapore felt greatly troubled too by the possibility of a link at their expense between the two very much larger states in their vicinity, Indonesia and Vietnam.

If, moreover, Australians continued to feel that, at the end of the day, there were great differences between their own predominant culture and those of their neighbours to the north, the fact was that there were at least as large differences between the Chinese and Indian civilisations to their north, and between the Hindu societies and Islamic societies there, as there were between Australia's European civilisation and any of these others. In half a dozen respects, therefore, Australia was far more like the other countries in its region than most Australians ordinarily allowed.

By the late 1970s and early 1980s these considerations were just beginning to be sensed by many Australians, at all events in their more immediate and more pragmatic terms. Increasingly the major importance of Australia's growing economic links with the Asian countries to its north was becoming understood. In one of several important statements during 1982, Malcolm Fraser as prime minister[26] – a few months before he was defeated in a general election – elaborated on his government's view about 'Pacific development: the Australian involvement'. Clearly this had now become extensive. There were annual talks with the Association of South

[26] P. Ayres, *Malcolm Fraser. A Biography*, Richmond 1987.

East Asian Nations (ASEAN), and with China; 'a highly sophisticated pattern of contacts with Japan', and with South Korea too. Australia, moreover, was an active member of the Asian Development Bank, of the South Pacific Commission, and of the South Pacific Forum. Furthermore, apart from its 'important bilateral relationships with New Zealand', it had 'a special relationship in both aid and trade' with Papua New Guinea also.

The case here was underlined by Fraser's overseas travels in that year. In 1982, he went to Washington; but elsewhere outside Australia he only went to countries to Australia's north and in the South-west Pacific. In June he went to Japan and South Korea; in August to Malaysia and China. On his return journey, he called in briefly in the Philippines; then attended the South Pacific Forum meeting in New Zealand; and in October went to the Commonwealth Regional Heads of Government meeting in Fiji. In the course of these various travels he met a dozen and more heads of government in the region – for personal conversations on a wide range of bilateral, regional and global matters, all in a very short space of time. During 1982 he never once went to Europe, let alone to Britain, and that was now becoming typical.

It was very significant, moreover, that the traffic was by no means only one way. In 1982 there was, for example, one more of the now regular series of ministerial meetings between Japanese ministers and Australian ministers which were now taking place every eighteen months or so. This time the Japanese delegation which came to Australia was composed of no less than five of Japan's most senior ministers – the ministers of foreign affairs, of finance, of international trade and industry, and of agriculture, together with the vice minister for economic planning. That was much the strongest Japanese ministerial delegation to go overseas anywhere in that year, other than to the Versailles 'summit' of major industrial powers.

Parallel with these growing official contacts there were now all sorts of non-official contacts too. A higher proportion of people from Australia was now visiting China each year than from any other country. There was a good deal of talk, moreover, in business and academic circles about the possibility of creating a Pacific Community, a Pacific Economic Community, a Western Pacific Economic Community. In the minds of its progenitors this was to cover Japan, South Korea, Southeast Asia, Australia, New Zealand and perhaps China, and to a degree Canada and the United States as well. An important conference on this matter was held in Canberra in September 1980, and another in Bangkok in June 1982. Out of the latter came the establishment of a steering committee chaired by the then very influential Indonesian minister, Ali Murtopo, and included such significant figures as Sir John Crawford from Australia, Dr Saburo Okita from Japan, and deputy prime ministers from both South Korea and Thailand. No one imagined that any great progress could be made very quickly. What was significant was that men of very considerable substance from right across the region were fully prepared to explore this idea closely.[27]

There were certainly still problems for Australia. It had been denied entrance to ASEAN, and its connections with a number of Southeast Asian countries still tended to be soured by a number of contentious issues, more especially by Australia's residual protectionist policies that worked to the detriment of important parts of their trade. There were special difficulties too with Indonesia. In part these stemmed from differences in the values of the ruling establishments in the two countries – the one generally authoritarian, the other more populist. These differences were aggravated, moreover, by the fact that while Australia had become economically very important to places like Japan and Korea, it was now less economically important to Indonesia than it had been a decade earlier. And so on.

All the same Australia did now hold 'dialogues' with ASEAN at ministerial level. Australia, as Fraser always emphasised, was a full and active member of the South Pacific Forum. It was prominent too in the Commonwealth's then regional group that included India, Malaysia, Singapore, New Zealand, Papua New Guinea and the other Pacific Forum countries. It had a number of close treaty relations, moreover, with Japan; and a variety of connections too with China and South Korea, as we have seen.

In all of this Australia enjoyed, of course, the immense advantage that stemmed from the fact that the international language of the region was not one of the main Asian languages, but its own language, English. As the 1980s opened, moreover, war and rumours of war had finally come to an end in the countries to its north. For Australians of a right-wing cast of mind the evidence now was, moreover, that revolutionary upheavals were a good deal less likely there; while those of a left-wing outlook could note the greater relative equality in the poor countries to their north than in comparable countries elsewhere. Furthermore birth-rates were coming down there too, sometimes dramatically; 47 per cent down in nine years in China; 15 per cent in fifteen years in Thailand; and noticeably in India, Indonesia and Vietnam as well, even if the peak of population growth there had still to be reached. What was more, whereas a decade previously there had still been much anxiety lest there should be severe famines in the countries to the north leading to millions of deaths by starvation (and much fall out from that besides), all the signs now were that – natural disasters aside – the necessary minimum of food supplies was likely to be available there.

---

[27] On all this see, for example, Sir John Crawford and S. Okita, *Australia, Japan and Western Pacific economic relations*, Canberra, 1976; and *Raw Materials and Pacific Economic Integration*, Canberra, 1978; R. Garnaut (ed.), *ASEAN in a Changing Pacific and World Economy*, Canberra 1980.

At the same time a major change had occurred on the Australian side. Australia's post-Second World War migration programme had brought its white population to over sixteen million. There it stood on a par with that of other countries of the region, such as Malaya and Sri Lanka. Whilst, therefore, Australians continued to inhabit a huge, seemingly very empty continent, it was now possible to feel that there was a sufficiency of White Australians in Australia to ensure that they would not be overrun by any external invasion – such as, in the not so distant past, Australia's Aborigines had been.

All of this made the thought of living much more closely with Australia's Asian and Pacific neighbours a great deal easier to contemplate than had ever seemed to be possible for previous generations of white Australians.

The essence of the position which Australia had reached by 1982 seemed to be summed up that year by Tony Street, Fraser's minister of foreign affairs, in that same speech to the Foreign Correspondents' Club in Singapore which has been quoted above. 'We had sought', Street put it, 'to be accepted as part of the region, on an equal basis. Our acceptance on this basis is now reflected in the straightforward and businesslike basis which characterizes our day to day relations through periods of both agreement and disagreement.'[28]

None the less, there still remained bridges to be crossed. These were neatly identified by the Australian political scientist, Dr Peter Polomka, in a paper to a conference in Canberra in September 1982.

Approaching its bicentenary Australia remains something of a misplaced continent, or 'frightened country', which too often succeeds in persuading its neighbours that it would prefer to be elsewhere. Many Australians apparently continue to feel the need to be reassured from time to time by their national leader that, notwithstanding the country's remoteness from 'traditional centres of Western power' and its Asian-Pacific Third World setting, Australia's "Westernness" is assured and immutable'. However Australia need not deny its important stake in the preservation of Western democratic values and in the Western alliance to admit to being a South Pacific state and part of the Western Pacific region rather than some unique, endangered species.[29]

It remained for the succeeding Labor government, elected in March 1983, to go the distance with Polomka's points.

The essential step here was finally to clear the Australian mind of its deep-seated but erroneous notion that Australia was still some kind of extraneous adjunct to its region, and see itself rather, as the facts of

[28] 18 June 1982.
[29] P. Polomka, 'Australia and the Pacific Community Idea', in Dibb (ed.), *Australia's External Relations*, p. 139. The quoted references were to A. Renouf, *The Frightened Country*, St Lucia 1979, and very directly to Street's Singapore speech, 14 May 1982 (see above).

geography and its growing economic linkages proclaimed it to be – as one of the region's constituent members.

There were three requirements here. First, it was necessary to see Australia for what it was, one of the two white countries (with New Zealand) in the region. Australia had to free itself, that is, from the long-standing sense of feeling awkwardly marooned at the other end of the globe, as a distant outpost of the western world, and see itself rather as a fully participant member of the multi-racial, multi-cultural, numerically much larger half of the world, which promised, moreover, to be its economically stronger half.

Then it would help if the region in question could be rather more precisely defined. Australians had long thought in terms of a relationship between Australia and Asia – but in polar rather than all-inclusive terms; and that had left the issue open. The tendency now was to speak of the Asia-Pacific region. There was some danger of a certain ambiguity here, unless the term was used with care. For whereas for some purposes Canada and the United States were deemed to be of the region, that was only partially true, and was never true of the other Americas that bordered the Pacific. Where, moreover, Asia extended to the Middle East that too fell outside the region in which Australia stood as this was ordinarily perceived. The term 'Asia-Pacific region' only sufficed if it meant precisely that region where Asia and the Pacific Ocean directly abutted upon each other. A readier solution, however, lay to hand. That was to call Australia's region by its most appropriate name: the eastern hemisphere; and sometimes this was now done.

There was one further essential step too. Australians had to bring themselves to talk of 'our' region. For their part Street and Fraser never quite seem to have brought themselves to do so.

The new Labor government soon moved, however, in each of these directions. By 1984, Bill Hayden, its foreign minister, could be heard saying:

It is the Labor Government's strong view that our policies must reflect the fact that the South Pacific and Asian areas are part of *our* environment. They are *our* home . . . The basis of such action is to support the interests of our region as a whole . . .[30]

To this he added, in 1985, that the 'timorousness' which had hitherto made Australia a 'reluctant and not always helpful observer of events in our region', had

retarded us in many ways that we have come to appreciate only relatively recently. With the fixed idea that we were an anomaly in our region, we kept it at arms length in our arrangements for defence, our trade, our economic development and our

[30] Perth, 14 November 1984.

external and internal affairs . . . The breadth of range of contact between Australia and its neighbours [was, however, now enormous]. We are involved in all these ways because we are part of the region . . . Australia is not some kind of artificial arm or leg grafted on to the region. Our sharing in regional affairs cannot be turned on and off whenever convenience dictates. It cannot be turned on and off according to the colour of our skin or an interpretation of our history or as punishment for our deeds or omissions. Australia is not going to go away from here. This is our home. Our being here is an inescapable fact . . . we are part of the Eastern Hemisphere.[31]

Before very long that became the new credo. By the time of Australia's Bicentennial year, 1988, Hawke, Labor's prime minister, was emphatically declaring:

This is a time when we must remember that Australia is not a place to put up barriers around itself and pretend that we, a nation of some 16 million people, can become an island or a continent unto ourselves. Never before in our history has there been a greater importance for the people of Australia to understand that we are part of our region, we are part of this vibrant world of over five billion people.[32]

That was now fast becoming conventional wisdom in Australia's Department of Foreign Affairs and Trade. At a press conference in September 1988 upon taking up its secretaryship, Australia's senior diplomat, Richard Woolcott, went out of his way to make it plain that a principal preoccupation of his Department 'lay in our adjustment to our own geopolitical environment':

If I had to identify [he went on] those areas of primary interest apart from, let us say, the relationship with the United States and our vital commercial relationship with Japan, which is also very important politically and the opportunities which China will present to the future, I imagine our principal areas of concern will be the South-west Pacific and South-east Asia because, you know, this is where we are.[33]

There was no mention here of Europe, let alone of Britain. It was all a far cry from the long established view – over most of the preceding two centuries of white settlement in Australia – that Australia was indissolubly linked to its British base.

The rhetoric here was perhaps a little embellished, but in October 1988 Hawke's new minister of foreign affairs (following Hayden's appointment to the governor-generalship of Australia) put the balance right – in accordance with the position Polomka had spelled out, and in line with the position espoused by the other middle powers in the region. 'Our future', Senator Evans told a Washington audience,

lies, inevitably, in Australia becoming more and more closely integrated with the region of which we are geographically so inescapably a part. My point is essentially that we have no choice, and the faster that any lingering nostalgia for the "European

---

[31] Griffith University, 13 April 1985.   [32] Townsville, 15 August 1988.
[33] Canberra, 6 September 1988.

outpost" model is dropped the better. Our cultural, economic and military linkages with Europe and North America will remain of basic importance. But there is no necessary contradiction between this and the growth in and transformation of our relationship to our region, which must be pursued if we are to shape and secure our future.[34]

That summarised the breakthrough beyond the half-formed, half-articulated formulae of the preceding government of Fraser and Street half a decade earlier. No one was suggesting that everything would henceforth be plain sailing. There were contretemps with Papua New Guinea, with Fiji, with Indonesia, with the Philippines, with Malaysia, and with ASEAN much more generally. Nevertheless, the idea was now becoming common-place that Australia's destiny lay where geography had placed it, in a close association with its neighbours, within the Eastern Hemisphere. Australians were now seeing themselves as part of their region on the inside; seeing this, moreover, as being theirs as much as anyone else's; as the habitat to which they belonged; whose future it was for them and their neighbours to enhance together from within. It is 'our own region', Senator Evans now characteristically put it in his Roy Milne Memorial Lecture in April 1989, and Australians should no longer believe, he said, that they are

cultural misfits trapped by geography. Australia and Australians should see the region not as something external which needs to be assuaged, but as a common neighbourhood of extraordinary diversity and significant economic potential. The region is primarily for Australia because it is where we live, and must learn the business of normal neighbourhood civility. It is where we must find a place and a role if we are to develop our full potentiality as a nation.[35]

The new logo which the Australian High Commission in London started to employ in 1988 strikingly expressed the central point. It portrayed in one colour on a single map, India, China, Korea, Japan, South-east Asia, the Southwest Pacific islands, New Zealand and Australia. It made a dramatic contrast with those old school maps where Australia stood large in the bottom right hand corner, in a world-wide British Empire, blocked out in bright red.

How it would all work out, only the future would tell. But there could be very little doubt that by 1988, the bicentennial year of European settlement in Australia, a great change in self-perception was well upon its way.

One striking result, moreover, was immediately noticeable. Australia's relations with its old mother country, Britain, were finally placed upon a fully adult footing. In 1988 Britain's prime minister, Margaret Thatcher, visited Australia to share in its Bicentennial celebrations. The opportunity

---

[34] Washington, 7 October 1988.
[35] Melbourne, 27 April 1889. He said much the same in a speech in Chatham House, London, on 20 June 1989.

was taken to hold Anglo-Australian consultations on a quite new basis. Whilst the Australian government was concerned to draw upon Britain's expertise on the immensely important closer economic association which was in the offing in western Europe in 1992, the British were now concerned as never before to tap Australia's expertise on the Asia–Pacific region. Considering that throughout the Hawke–Thatcher years major differences over sanctions against South Africa had hitherto befogged Australian–British Relations, this was a remarkable development.[36] It was capped in June 1989 when for the first time for twelve years an Australian prime minister paid an official visit to Britain, accompanied by three of his senior ministers – for industry, technology and commerce, for foreign affairs and trade, and for defence.[37]

During the intervening hiatus a great deal had changed. Britain had ceased to be Australia's homeland, and Australia a distant outpost. Australia was now an eastern hemispheric state established within the Asian–Pacific region; Britain, the re-discovered friendly power away in western Europe. Comment accordingly came from quite distinct perspectives; was entirely even-handed; and ranged right across the globe. In all this Australia's re-orientations were nowhere placed in doubt. The long shadow of empire had finally passed from the scene.

[36] The British Government published a pamphlet of Mrs Thatcher's speeches, *Britain and Australia, 'A Closer Relationship'*, 1–6 August 1988.
[37] Speeches by Prime Minister Hawke in London on 21–2 June 1989.

Index